1/14

DISCARDED

D0003808

INSIGHT GUIDES
INDIA

APA PUBLICATIONS L

Part of the Langenscheidt Publishing Group

The first Insight Guide pioneered the use of creative full-colour photography in travel guides in 1970. Since then, we have expanded our range to cater for our readers' need not only for reliable information about their chosen destination but also for a real understanding of the culture and workings of that destination. Now, when the internet can supply inexhaustible (but not always reliable) facts, our books marry text and pictures to provide those much more elusive qualities: knowledge and discernment. To achieve this, they rely heavily on the authority of locally based writers and photographers.

Insight Guide: India is structured to convey an understanding of the country and its people as well as to guide readers through its attractions:

How to use this book

Insight Guide: India is structured to convey an understanding of the country and its people as well as to guide readers through its attractions:

The **Best of India** section at the front of the guide helps you to prioritise what you want to do.

The **Features** section, indicated by a pink bar at the top of each page, covers Indian history, society, geography, culture, art and architecture in a series of informative essays.

The main **Places** section, indicated by a blue bar, is a complete guide to India's sights and areas worth visiting. Places of special interest are coordinated by number with the maps.

The **Travel Tips** listings section, with a yellow bar, provides details on transport, hotels, activities from festivals to shopping, and an A–Z of essential practical information. There is also a handy language section.

The contributors

This tenth edition of *Insight Guide: India* was commissioned by **Sarah Sweeney** and copyedited by **Naomi Peck**. The book was comprehensively updated by frequent Insight contributor **David Abram.** A freelance author and photographer specialising in India, David first visited the country in the early 1980s and has since written more than a dozen guides to the country, and contributed numerous items for radio and magazines. He spends a couple of months researching in the subcontinent each year. His work for previous editions includes the chapters on Rajasthan, Gujarat, Mumbai, Goa, Maharashtra, Madhya Pradesh and

Chattisgarh, Karnataka and Kerala, as well as sections of Tamil Nadu and Offshore Islands.

The current edition builds on the work of **Matt Barrett**, who overhauled the last edition and provided the photo essay on Indian Railways and feature boxes on Conservation, Hill Stations, Spas and Retreats, and Clothing. Other former contributors whose work appears in the book include **Maria Lord**, a one-time Insight staff editor (Delhi, Kolkata, West Bengal, Jharkand and Odisha, the Northeast, Andhra Pradesh, Chennai, part of Tamil Nadu and Offshore Islands, Contemporary India, Peoples and Religions, Performing Arts and Cinema, Adivasis); **Gavin Thomas**, a travel writer and regular visitor to the subcontinent since 1991 (Travel Tips); **Roy Moxham**, author of *The Great Hedge of India* (History); **George Michell** (Art and Architecture); and **Jan McGirk** (politics, society, wildlife and environment).

The principal photographers for this book were **Britta Jaschinski**, who covered much of the country, **David Abram**, who focused on the area around Goa, and **Julian Love**, who photographed Delhi and the northern plains.

The index was compiled by **Penny Phenix**.

Map Legend

— · —	International Boundary
— — —	Disputed Boundary
- - - -	State Boundary
— • —	National Park/Reserve
Ⓜ	Metro
✈ ✈	Airport: International/ Regional
🚌	Bus Station
❶	Tourist Information
✝ ✝ ✝	Church/Ruins
✝	Monastery
∴	Archaeological Site
🏰 🏛	Castle/Ruins
☪	Mosque
✡	Synagogue
∩	Cave
⚊	Statue/Monument
★	Place of Interest
✉	Post Office

The main places of interest in the Places section are coordinated by number with a full-colour map (eg ❶), and a symbol at the top of every right-hand page tells you where to find the map.

Contents

Introduction

The Best of India.....................6
The Allure of India..............17
Land and Climate 19
Wildlife 22
Society and Religion.............29

History

Decisive Dates.....................42
Beginnings............................46
Europeans in India 55
Independent India 65

Features

Contemporary Issues 75
Food and Drink 85
Performing Arts.....................92
Cinema..................................96
Art and Architecture 101

Insights

MINI FEATURES

Conservation 27
The Adivasis...........................32
Hill Stations 180
Gujarati Textiles 234
The Parsis 254
Indian Tea 342
Yoga, Spas and Retreats... 404

PHOTO FEATURES

Festivals.................................90
Hindu Deities 110

The Taj Mahal 172
Indian Railways 228
Ajanta and Ellora 266
Khajuraho 286
Hampi.................................. 378
Cruising Kerala's Green
    Backwaters 428

Places

Introduction 119
The North 123
Delhi.................................... 127
The Northern Plains 145
The Himalayas................... 175
The Desert States 201
Rajasthan 203
Gujarat 231
West-Central India 247
Mumbai (Bombay)............. 249
Maharashtra, Madhya
    Pradesh and
    Chattisgarh 269
Goa...................................... 289
East and Northeast India 301
Kolkata (Calcutta).............. 303
West Bengal, Odisha and
    Jharkhand 319
The Northeast.................... 337
The South.......................... 355
Karnataka and Andhra
    Pradesh.......................... 357
Chennai (Madras).............. 381
Tamil Nadu......................... 391

Kerala............................... 413
Offshore Islands 431

Travel Tips

TRANSPORT
Getting There 440
Getting Around.................... 440

ACCOMMODATION
Choosing a Hotel 446
Delhi................................... 447
Punjab and Haryana.......... 449
Uttar Pradesh..................... 449
Bihar.................................. 451
Uttarakhand....................... 451
Himachal Pradesh............. 453
Ladakh 454
Rajasthan 455
Gujarat 460
Mumbai.............................. 461
Maharashtra....................... 463
Madhya Pradesh 463
Goa..................................... 465
Kolkata............................... 467
West Bengal....................... 467
Odisha (Orissa) 468
Sikkim 468
Assam 469
Karnataka 469
Andhra Pradesh................. 471
Tamil Nadu......................... 471
Kerala................................. 473
Lakshadweep 476

Andaman Islands 476

ACTIVITIES
The Arts.............................. 477
Nightlife.............................. 478
Outdoor Activities 480
Shopping............................ 481
Spas and Retreats............. 484
Wildlife Parks..................... 485

A – Z
Admission Charges 487
Budgeting for Your Trip 487
Children.............................. 487
Climate............................... 487
Crime and Safety............... 487
Disabled Travellers 488
Embassies and
    Consulates.................... 489
Etiquette 489
Health and Medical Care .. 490
Insurance........................... 492
Media 492
Money Matters 493
Postal/Courier Services.... 494
Tipping................................ 495
Tourist Information 495
What to Bring..................... 496
Women Travellers.............. 496

LANGUAGE
Traveller's Hindi 497
Traveller's Tamil 498

FURTHER READING
History................................ 501
Fiction 502
Travel................................. 503
Wildlife 503

Maps
India 120
Delhi................................... 124
The Northern Plains 146
The Himalayas................... 176
Rajasthan 206
Gujarat 232
Mumbai.............................. 252
Maharashtra, Madhya
    Pradesh and Chattisgarh 270
Goa..................................... 290
Old Goa 295
Kolkata............................... 304
West Bengal, Odisha and
    Jharkhand 323
The Northeast.................... 340
Karnataka and Andhra
    Pradesh......................... 358
Bengaluru (Bangalore) 361
Hyderabad 371
Chenai (Madras)............... 384
Tamil Nadu and Kerala...... 392
Lakshadweep 432
Andaman and Nicobar
    Islands............................ 434
Inside front cover India
Inside back cover Delhi

THE BEST OF INDIA: TOP ATTRACTIONS

Discover the very best that India has to offer, from the bright lights of Mumbai and colourful Rajasthani cities to ancient ruins and the cool heights of the Himalayas.

△ **Kerala.** The intense greens of the Kerala backwaters, overhung by innumerable coconut palms, encapsulate tropical India like nowhere else. See page 428.

▽ **Jaisalmer.** The desert citadel of Jaisalmer, with its golden sandstone fort and wonderful havelis, is the oldest Rajput capital. It also has some beautiful and ornate Jain temples, and is the base for excursions into the Thar Desert. See page 224.

◁ **Hampi.** The ruined Vijayanagar capital is perhaps India's most evocative archeological site, set amidst a wonderful boulder landscape in the heart of India. A World Heritage Monument, the Vittala Temple has a wealth of sculptural detail. See page 378.

▽ **The Taj Mahal.** It is India's most recognisable sight. This truly stunning monument in white marble is seductive in its perfect proportions and fine details. See page 172.

▷ **Udaipur.** One of India's most romantic locations, Udaipur is centred on its famous lake and overlooked by one of the most resplendent Rajput forts in Rajasthan. See page 218.

◁ **Kullu Valley.** Set in the beautiful lush green foothills of the Himalayas, the valley is a relaxing and picturesque place to unwind. See page 182.

▽ **Varanasi.** This is the most sacred place on India's most sacred river – the bathing ghats present a spectacle that covers the panoply of human existence. See page 162.

▷ **Darjeeling.** A summertime retreat for the British Raj, the city has extraordinary views over the eastern Himalayas. It is reached by a "Toy Train", itself a World Heritage Monument. See page 325.

▽ **Ajanta.** Dating back to the 2nd century BC, these carved rock temples lie in a beautiful, forested ravine. The stunning frescoes are some of the greatest works of ancient Buddhist art. See page 266.

△ **Mumbai.** It is the heartbeat of modern India, brash and vibrant, sometimes frustrating, always fascinating. See page 249.

THE BEST OF INDIA: EDITOR'S CHOICE

From the essential experiences that make a visit to India live long in the memory, to temples, festivals, food, fascinating cities, beautiful beaches and tiger-spotting in the national parks... here at a glance are our recommendations on what to prioritise to make the most of your trip.

MOST MEMORABLE INDIA EXPERIENCES

Tiger-watching at Corbett, Ranthambore or Kanha National Parks. Ranthambore offers the best chance of seeing a wild tiger in India, although Bandhavgarh and Kanha give a more complete experience. See page 178, 215 and 281.

Riding the rails. There is nothing quite like an overnight journey on an Indian train. See page 228.

Mumbai at night. The vibrant megalopolis is at its best in the evening. Bars, cafés and clubs are here in abundance, with a dash of Bollywood glam. See page 259.

Khajuraho at dawn. These temples, famed for their erotic sculpture, are best seen in the early morning before the tour groups arrive. See page 286.

A Rajasthan fort. To capture the romance of India visit one of Rajasthan's flamboyant forts – the best are at Jodhpur, Amber, Bikaner, Udaipur and Jaisalmer. See page 203.

Hindu festivals. There is no better way to experience India's amazing colour than by seeing a Hindu festival in full swing. See page 90.

Camel safari. Setting out from Jaisalmer for a desert safari is for many people the most long-lasting memory of India. See page 225.

Sleep in a palace. Many of India's old royal palaces have been converted into luxury heritage hotels. See page 205.

Indian food. The cuisine in India is quite different from that found abroad, and varies a great deal from north to south. Street food can be very good, too. See page 85.

Mumbai at night.

URBAN HIGHLIGHTS

Delhi. India's dusty capital is full of interest, from Connaught Place to major sights such as the Red Fort and Qutb Minar. See page 127.

Jaipur. The pink city is an intoxicating introduction to Rajasthan. See page 205.

Kolkata (Calcutta). Centre of British power, this dynamic city lies off the main tourist trail. See page 303.

Bengaluru (Bangalore). At the forefront of India's brave new 21st-century world. See page 360.

Chennai (Madras). This steamy southern metropolis has great food, colonial relics and vibrant culture. See page 381.

Varanasi. Arguably the most intense, atmospheric place anywhere in India. See page 162.

Hyderabad. Historic Muslim hub of the south. See page 369.

Mysore. The old sandal-wood city is one of India's most pleasant urban centres. See page 362.

Kochi-Ernakulum (Cochin). Reached by ferry from Ernakulam, the historic Fort quarter recalls the hey day of the region's colonial trade. See page 423.

Holi festival celebrations.

The shops on Hazratganj in Lucknow.

TEMPLES AND ANCIENT SITES

Well-preserved ruins at Fatehpur Sikri.

Golden Temple, Amritsar. Shimmering in the Punjabi heat, the magnificent Golden Temple is the centre of the Sikh universe. See page 150.

Bodhgaya/Mahabodhi. The founding place of Buddhism is commercial but still fascinating. See page 168.

Orcha. An ancient treasure trove combining Hindu and Mughal architecture to stunning effect. See page 279.

Fatehpur Sikri. This ruined Mughal city is a magnificent ensemble, and very well preserved. See page 156.

Tibetan monasteries in Ladak. Dozens of medieval Buddhist monasteries nestle in the Himalayan valleys around Leh. See page 193.

Ellora Caves. Ellora is remarkable for its scale, notably at the Kailasa Temple. See page 275.

Mamallapuram. The wind-eroded shore temple is a mini masterpiece of Tamil (Dravidian) religious art. See page 393.

Bhubaneshwar. A stunning array of temples featuring some of the finest stonework anywhere in India. See page 329.

The train to Simla.

BEST ACTIVITIES

Ayurveda. India's ancient system of herbal medicine has been adapted to create soothing spa treatments: enjoy oil massages and steam baths with distinctively Indian aromas at any luxury hotel. See page 484.

Houseboat cruises, Kerala. There's no better way to experience the special atmosphere of Kerala's Kuttinad backwater region than from a converted rice barge. See page 428.

Elephant safari, Kaziranga. India's benchmark wildlife park offers tiger- and rhino-spotting safaris on elephant back, allowing you to get closer to the big fauna than you can in Jeeps. See page 343.

Bollywood movie, Mumbai. Catch the latest Hindi blockbuster at one of Mumbai's lavishly restored Art Deco cinemas. See page 477.

Saree shopping. Kanchipuram and Varanasi are the two most illustrious sources of luxury, hand-woven, brocaded silk sarees, but you can admire their output at emporia in towns and cities across the country. See page 481.

BEST HILL STATIONS

Simla. The summer capital of the British Raj, the town retains a handful of evocative British vestiges, among them some delightfully stiff-upper-lipped hotels. See page 179.

Kodaikanal. A cool retreat, high above the Tamil plains on the rim of the Palani hills. See page 408.

Matheran. Perched at a refreshing 800 metres (2,600ft) in the forests of the Western Ghats, this former hill station offers a welcome escape from the heat and fumes of nearby Mumbai. See page 272.

Ootacamund (Udhagamandalam). 'Snooty Ooty' was once a fixture on the British social calendar. The surrounding hills offer opportunities for walkers. See page 406.

Dharamsala. Home to the exiled Dalai Lama and a large Tibetan community in the upper town. The surrounding mountains form an exquisite backdrop. See page 186.

Mount Abu. Rajasthan's only hill station is also a sacred Jain pilgrimage site, renowned for its elaborately carved white-marble temples. See page 221.

Tiger at Ranthambore.

BEST BEACHES

Goa. Mile after mile of palm-fringed sands and tourist facilities well ahead of those elsewhere in the country, plus the enduring Portuguese influence, make Goa unique. The most congenial, low-key resorts are Benaulim, Agonda, Palolem, Aswem and Arambol. See page 289.

Lakshadweep. This remote and rarely visited archipelago in the Arabian Sea has wonderfully pristine beaches and some of the world's best scuba-diving. See page 431.

Puri. A combination of a Hindu pilgrimage centre and one of India's finest beaches – though the currents can be treacherous. See page 331.

Kovalam/Varkala. Kovalam is the best-known beach in India's deep south, and a fully-fledged resort. A little further up the coast, Varkala is much quieter. See page 418.

Goa is famous for its beaches.

Kanheri Caves, Mumbai.

BEST NATIONAL PARKS AND SCENERY

Kanha. In the heart of the Deccan Plateau of central India, the Kanha area provided the inspiration for Rudyard Kipling's *Jungle Book*. The beautiful forests and grasslands of the park are some of the best places in India to see tigers, and a wealth of other wildlife. See page 281.

Kaziranga. Last stronghold on the Indian one-horned rhino, this world-famous park on the floodplains of the Brahmaputra in Assam is one of the few places in the subcontinent where you can track tigers on elephant back. See page 343.

Corbett. Another prime tiger-spotting location, this time in the beautiful Himalayan foothills. Named after Jim Corbett, tiger hunter turned conservationist. See page 178.

Periyar. High in the Western Ghats of Kerala, Periyar has a superb setting and is one of the best places to sight wild elephants. See page 422.

Kullu Valley to Leh. The spectacular road route from the lush Kullu Valley up to the arid heights of Leh is one of India's great journeys. See page 182.

Sikkim. With the gleaming snowfields of Kanchenjunga on the horizon, this remote Himalayan region has some of the most magnificent scenery anywhere in the world. See page 337.

Ranthambore. Aside from its relative high tiger density, this reserve in Rajasthan is dotted with pretty lakeside ruins that make an irresistibly photogenic backdrop for photographing wildlife. See page 215.

OFF THE BEATEN TRACK

Gujarat. Most travellers skip Gujarat en route between Mumbai and Rajasthan. This is a mistake – the state has a great deal to offer from other-wordly salt flats to superb hilltop temples. See page 231.

The Northeast. Almost cut off from the rest of India by Bangladesh, the northeastern hill states are a fascinating mosaic of different ethnic groups and landscapes, ranging from ice peaks to jungles. See page 337.

Andaman Islands. A two-hour flight east of Chennai (Madras), the Andamans are home to a fascinating minority culture, wild forests and pristine, coral-fringed beaches. See page 433.

Madhya Pradesh. The best known sights are Khajuraho and Kanha National Park, but other parts of this large central state are of interest, too, with a significant proportion of India's remaining forest cover surviving in the rural backwaters. Gwalior Fort, Orcha's riverside cenotaphs and ancient Sanchi are other highlights. See page 277.

Andhra Pradesh. Another large, seldom-visited part of India, Andhra has a distinctive culture and some stunningly beautiful rocky landscapes. See page 369.

The hennaed hands of an Indian girl.

BEST FESTIVALS AND EVENTS

Kumbha Mela. These huge Hindu festivals take place every three years, culminating in the Maha Kumbha Mela at Allahabad every 12 years, the world's largest religious gathering. See page 161.

Holi. The North Indian harvest festival, taking place in March, is celebrated with brightly coloured powder – bystanders are not excluded! See page 90.

Divali. A celebration of Rama's return from exile, the festival of lights is a magical spectacle. See page 90.

Pushkar. Over the full moon of November (Karthik Purima), the holy Hindu lakeside town of Pushkar hosts a spectacular festival, with a vibrant camel fair amid the dunes. See page 214.

Navaratri. The 'nine nights' festival takes place in September or October, celebrating Kali and Durga. See page 90.

The festival of Durga Puja in Kolkata.

A beach hut at Palolem, Goa.

TIPS FOR TRAVELLERS

India can be a daunting place for the uninitiated and it is true that chancers seek to take advantage in the major tourist spots, but by following simple rules you can minimise the chances of being ripped off or robbed.

It's best to use a pre-paid **taxi** from airports; pay at dedicated desks. Black city taxis should generally be metered, but get an estimation of the fare before you set off.

When travelling by **rickshaw**, always agree a fare beforehand to avoid arguments later on.

Don't let rickshaw or taxi drivers take you to a hotel you don't want to go to – insist that you have a reservation at your specified hotel.

Beware of **credit card fraud**, and don't let your credit card out of your sight when paying by plastic. Pay with cash where possible.

Carry **valuables** on your person at all times if possible, or leave them in your hotel safe, rather than unsecured in your room. When travelling on overnight trains, padlock your bags to the frame of the bunk to avoid midnight pilferers.

Make sure you have comprehensive **travel insurance**, and that it covers you if you're doing any adventure activities such as trekking, climbing or whitewater rafting.

Birla Mandir, Delhi.

Kanheri Caves, near Mumbai.

Colourful fabric on display in Jaipur.

THE ALLURE OF INDIA

India is like nowhere else on earth – thrilling,
frustrating, inspiring and, most of all, incredibly
diverse. With around 850 different languages in daily
use, the sheer profusion of its peoples and
landscapes is unparalleled.

Auto-rickshaw in Delhi.

India's long history of accepting and absorbing newcomers, and of changing over time to express their ideas, is reflected in its open-minded and welcoming attitude, and fascinating range of cultures and beliefs. With landscapes that vary from the world's highest mountain ranges to tropical beaches, India has an almost endless variety of peoples and places to explore; the sights and sounds of this enormous country have a spellbinding effect, and live long in the memory. Despite the advances brought by 21st-century globalisation, with rising prosperity, high-tech industries and burgeoning car ownership, India largely retains its mesmeric otherness, a kind of old-fashioned handmade, homespun quality that sets it apart from everywhere else.

Roadside shrine in Kerala.

There is evidence, from the earliest times, of great movements of peoples across South Asia, sometimes replacing existing populations, sometimes integrating with them. They came from West and Central Asia in massive sweeps through the lofty passes in the northwest, bringing with them the rudiments of the Hindu faith, later to be developed on Indian soil into a subtle and highly complex religion. Other religions, such as Buddhism, Islam, Christianity and Zoroastrianism, have developed and been absorbed into India's proverbial sponge. With these peoples and religions have come a variety of ethnicities, art, architecture, culture, philosophy, science and technology that have all influenced India's intricate mosaic.

While it is India's variety and complexity that make it so appealing, negotiating the turmoil can be a challenge. But if you are prepared to delve deeper than the first, chaotic impression, the rewards can be substantial. Be ready to take things as they come: for things that shouldn't work at all to work perfectly, and for the simplest things to go wrong. Everyone's perception is different. The prominent, 20th-century British journalist James Cameron summed up its appeal when he wrote: 'I like the evening in India, the one magic moment when the sun balances on the rim of the world, and the hush descends, and 10,000 civil servants drift homeward on a river of bicycles, brooding on the Lord Krishna and the cost of living.'

View of the Western Ghats from Eravikulam National Park.

LAND AND CLIMATE

Few countries encompass as richly varied topography, or as extreme swings in climate, as India. From the world's highest mountains in the north to the tropical south via plains and plateaux, the land is watered by the monsoon and burnished by the sun.

From snow-clad Himalayan peaks to sun-baked plains, deserts and rocky plateaux, lush jungles and mangrove swamps, India is a vast and varied land. Extending through 30 degrees of latitude, it is the world's seventh-largest and second-most populous country – home to more than one sixth of the world's people.

Mountains and plains

The Himalayas form an unbroken chain along India's northern frontier, a forbidding 2,500km (1,600-mile) barrier that emphatically separates the tropical climes of the subcontinent from the cold, arid Tibetan Plateau to the north. One small corner of India – Ladakh – lies beyond this great divide, its camel-coloured high-altitude landscapes in complete contrast with the rest of the Indian far north. The country's highest peak is Kanchenjunga in Sikkim, towering 8,598 metres (28,209ft) over the tea plantations of Darjeeling.

The great Ganges and Brahmaputra rivers surge southwards from the frozen wastes, tumbling down to vast, fertile plains in which cluster some of the world's greatest concentrations of humanity. The Ganges plain is home to almost 40 percent of India's 1.2 billion people, its farmland producing almost four-fifths of the country's food with intensive cultivation of wheat (mainly in the drier west), rice (in the wetter east), maize and sugarcane. Far to the east, the Brahmaputra cuts its way south from Tibet through the Assam-Burma range, running across its wide valley in an immense rocky corridor.

The Brahmaputra and Ganges rivers merge to the east of Kolkata, forming an enormous, and ever-growing, delta. This swampy region is criss-crossed by tributaries and home to some

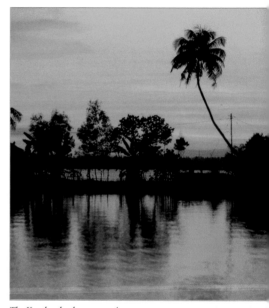

The Keralan backwaters region.

INDIA'S FRUIT BOWL

Due to the extreme variation in elevation, Himachal Pradesh in the western Himalayas offers a wide range of landscapes. Numerous rivers feed the Indus and Ganges basins, and the area is rich in agriculture. In the southern part of the state, forests of Chir pine and deodar (Himalayan cedar) enclose the steeply sloping terraces of the Sutlej River, covered with potato and rice fields. Orchards are plentiful, with apples the most popular crop. Flowers such as lilies and roses are cultivated, while the higher slopes and meadows above the Kullu and Parvati valleys, in the north of the state, are one of the world's main centres of cannabis cultivation.

of the world's most extensive mangrove forests – preserved in the Sunderbans National Park, which is also a refuge for tigers.

The desert states

To the west of the Gangetic plain the land becomes ever drier and dustier. The plains of the Punjab receive moderate amounts of rainfall – although the reliability of the rains is more of an issue than further east. Rajasthan is drier still, and towards the Pakistan border the true desert, the Thar, takes over, extending southwards to the Rann (saline marshlands) of Kutch in Gujarat.

Boulder-strewn hills mark the backdrop to the dramatic ruins at Hampi in the southern Deccan.

Elsewhere, Rajasthan is open scrub country, with rocky hills often capped by the forts of the Rajput kings and populated by wandering herds of sheep, goats and camels. Separating these lands from the Gangetic plain and the Deccan lava tableland are rugged plateaux and badlands, interspersed with fields of mustard and wheat.

Deccan plateau

It was on the "table-tops" hills of the black lava-covered Deccan plateau, India's dry and stony heartland, that the Marathas built a series of impregnable fortresses. For much of its extent the Deccan, which averages 600 metres (3,000ft) in altitude, is separated from the coast by the lush, forested heights of the Western and Eastern ghats, the latter being lower and more broken. The north of the plateau is edged by the relatively low Aravali, Satpura, Sahyadri and Vindhya ranges.

To the east, forming a large part of the states of Odisha, Jharkand and parts of Bihar and Chattisgarh, is the Chota Nagpur plateau, heavily forested and populated by Adivasi tribal peoples. The plateau is also home to extensive mineral and coal deposits, which have been the source of increasing conflict between mining companies eager to exploit these natural resources, and tribal peoples determined to preserve their hereditary land. Significant areas of forest remain in the state of Madhya Pradesh.

In the southern Deccan, the relatively wet Karnataka plateau is home to dense sandal, teak and sissoo forests, where elephants roam wild. The Telengana plateau, largely within the state of Andhra Pradesh further east, has only a thin cover of red lateritic soils, where thorny scrub and wild Indian date palms grow.

The coastlands and the deep south

India's east coast, the Coromandel, is characterised by long, exposed beaches scattered with aloes and palm trees, and swampy alluvial shores, merging northwards into the fertile deltaic lowlands of the Krishna, Godavari and Mahanadi rivers. Fields of sugar cane and tobacco give way to forested areas as the land rises inland to the Eastern Ghats and the Deccan plateau.

Luxuriant rainforests blanket the hills along the southwest coast (the Malabar) in Kerala, where the lowland lagoons are canopied by coconut trees. A narrow coastal strip extends north to the estuarine plains of Goa, where wide sunny beaches are lapped by the gentle waves of the Arabian Sea. The rest of the littoral is mostly rocky, rising to the forest-covered slopes of the Western Ghats, reaching 2,695 metres (8,842ft) in Kerala. North of Mumbai the coastal plain becomes salt-encrusted, with marshy lowlands rich in birdlife.

India's deep south is predominantly Tamil. The Western Ghats reach their highest point in the blue Nilgiri Hills, home to coffee and tea plantations, and wildlife sanctuaries. Just to the east are the cloud-covered Palani Hills, reaching

In contrast to the rest of the country, India's southeast has not one, but two monsoons: the first from June to September, as is usual elsewhere, but then again from October to December; the second is generally less severe.

over 2,500 metres (8,200ft). In the rain shadow of these heights is the Coimbatore plateau, which extends east to the coast near Chennai. The Kaveri River, which rises here, flows east into the Tamil Nadu plains. Its fertile delta is

In November, with the strength of the sun diminishing, the winter season starts in the northern plain. Until February the weather remains cold in the Himalayas and their foothills, and pleasantly warm in the plains. Central and southern India remains warm to hot throughout the year. The Deccan and the northern plains start to warm up from late February, and from March until the end of May and into June the heat steadily builds, the land becomes sunburnt and dusty, a shimmering heat haze under the blue-white sky. The intense heat of the northern plain eventually

Beach and calm waters at Galjibag, near Palolem in south Goa.

the rice bowl of the south.

Strung out across the warm waters of the Indian Ocean, the archipelago of Lakshadweep is comprised of coral atolls, while the Andaman and Nicobar islands in the Bay of Bengal, part of India but actually much closer to Thailand, are protrusions from an undersea mountain range. There are few significant islands immediately offshore from the Indian mainland.

Weather patterns

Indian life has always followed the rhythm of the monsoon, with the life-giving rains dominating the whole country from late June to the end of September, and continuing as late as December in the southeast.

forms an area of low pressure, which draws the monsoon winds across the entire country. Starting from the southwestern coast in early May, the rains extend inexorably eastwards and northwards, typically reaching the Ganges plain in torrential cloudbursts by early or mid-June, although the timing does vary from year to year, and in some years the rains can fail catastrophically.

As these winds retreat in October, the land dries out. Southeastern areas, however, have rainy weather until January. India's Bay of Bengal coastlands are vulnerable to tropical cyclones from September to December and March to May.

For more on India's climate, see page 487.

WILDLIFE

Habitats are diminishing and poachers are flouting the laws, but the astonishing variety of animal, reptile, bird, insect and plant life in India is there for all to see.

Animals are never far away in India. Even common house pests could include such exotic creatures as a red-rumped monkey or a mongoose, besides the geckoes flexing on the wall or a scorpion hiding inside a shoe. Mynah birds and an occasional cobra in the garden come as no surprise. Camels and elephants wander in the street traffic, and humped cattle sometimes outnumber the vehicles on the road. Water buffalo loll beside the dhobi ghats, where laundry is done, while huge birds of prey – vultures or pariah kites – spiral overhead.

Big cats and bears

Lions, tigers and bears – savage and shy – inhabit South Asia from Himalayan cloud forests to desert scrub. Land-clearance has encroached on much of the former hunting grounds, and without the game reserves and sanctuaries many more might disappear. There's no chance of spotting a cheetah now; the last of these died in 1994. The government of India continues to permit the destruction of big cats that are proven man-eaters, and so-called 'cattle-lifters' are often gunned down for revenge as well. These can be leopards or tigers, though snow leopards and the daintier clouded leopard are often spared.

Hundreds of stocky Asiatic lions prowl the Gir Forest Reserve in Gujarat, the only place in the world where they thrive. Unlike African lions, these cats don't have much mane, but carry most of their shaggy hair on the tip of their tails and elbows. In the 1990s some young males strayed outside the park and were neutered by rangers, who were anxious that local cattle-herders shouldn't start shooting the lions if they dared put a paw outside their sanctuary. Striped hyenas feed on the lions' leftovers, and there are more

A one-horned Indian rhinoceros.

leopards visible in the Gir – pronounced 'gear', not 'grrrr' – than in any other Indian park.

Bears are more aloof. Himalayan brown bears are heavy-set and larger than their black cousins, who live below the tree line on Himalayan slopes. Sloth bears, found over much of India, are mostly nocturnal. All three varieties can climb trees and swim if put to the test. The sloth bear grunts with pleasure or anger, and digs for termites and other grubs. It gobbles bees, but prefers honeycomb or sweet fruits and berries. The bears are hunted for their gall bladders, sold for Chinese fertility medicine. Miserable-looking sloth bears used to be a feature in the most touristy cities, shuffling along in chains and a muzzle, and earning a few rupees for their captors, but this loathsome tradition has now largely died out. In the forests of the northeast red pandas, resembling slim, auburn raccoons, are found.

Tigers

Tiger sightings are rare these days. A census conducted in 2011 by the National Tiger Conservation Authority estimated only 1,706 adult tigers in existence in India, down from 3,300 in the 1990s (the figure showed a small increase from the previous count of 2008, but – controversially – included data from the Sunderbans region of the Ganges Delta, hitherto excluded from national tiger statistics, which critics claim many have skewed the overall number).

Whatever the true extent of the country's big cat population, the threat to the Indian tiger remains critical; its habitat has been drastically reduced by a rapidly growing human population, and lack of food makes it virtually impossible for tigers to survive outside protected areas. Poaching is still widespread, fuelled by an international demand for tiger parts used in Chinese medicine. Poorly paid game wardens are no match for the organised poachers working in remote game parks (for more on conservation, see page 27).

A formidable hunter, the tiger usually takes its quarry from behind, laying its chest on the back of the animal, grabbing the neck in its canines, sometimes bracing a forearm on the forelimb of the quarry and trying to pull it down by their combined weight. The tiger's sharp retractile claws also play a significant role in capturing and holding on to its quarry. A swipe of the forearm is sometimes used to stop a fleeing animal or to kill very small prey like monkey or peafowl. Depending on the size of its kill, a tiger may feed on it for four to five days. By the end, it will have eaten all the flesh, small bones, the skin and hair.

The tiger's choice of quarry is not chosen by species. It is, rather, by size; the bigger the better. With very large prey, such as the gaur or the buffalo, a tiger will generally go for the sub-adults. When a tigress is training her cubs, many monkeys and langur are killed, regardless of size: this is the only form of communal hunting seen among tigers.

The best bet for glimpsing a tiger in the wild is to visit an Indian sanctuary. At Kaziranga (Assam), Bandhavgarh or Kanha (Madhya Pradesh), Dudhwa or Corbett (Uttar Pradesh), Ranthambore (Rajasthan) or Bandipur (Karnataka), odds are more favourable than at parks where poachers penetrate. Even during the dry season, when thirsty animals slow down and are visible against the parched leaves, luck is still a key ingredient. Dusk or dawn is a likely hour. Jeeps, elephants, and even dugout canoes carry visitors deep into the bush, and few will be disappointed by the experience, even if they only see the pug marks of big predators.

Rhinos and elephants

The one-horned Indian rhinoceros keeps mainly to the northeastern woods around

The sloth bear is an endangered species.

Kaziranga in Assam, though a number have been reintroduced to Dudhwa park in Uttar Pradesh, nudging India's total of rhinos to around 2,200. They stand about 1.6 metres (5.5ft) at the shoulder and weigh around 1,820kg (4,000lbs). Adult males are larger than females, with horns that are usually thicker at the base and often broken or split at the tip (the horn of the female is usually slender and unbroken). Adult females may also be accompanied by calves. Floodplain grassland interspersed with marsh, swamp and lake, and the adjoining riverine forest, are their favoured habitat. Rhinos prefer to feed on short grasses and seek shelter in thick stands of tall grass, sometimes 6–8 metres (20–5ft) high.

Rhinos are usually viewed from the back of domestic elephants. Wild tuskers found in the jungles are feared, with good reason. Some may roam close to villages, developing a taste for alcohol after drinking the contents of a still. Others stampede through villages, mowing down everything in their path – usually after being provoked by villagers defending their crops. Yet spying a herd of wild elephants tearing calmly through the shrubbery is a definite thrill. Such enormous beasts can move with surprising silence.

There are an estimated 30,000 wild elephants in India, with thousands more working at tem-

Rhesus macaques are comfortable around humans.

ples, logging camps, game parks, or hired out for weddings. Wayanad, in Kerala, is the best place to view elephants in the wild. Parks in West Bengal and Assam are also good bets.

Other creatures

A wide range of animals can be seen inside all of the wildlife parks. Look out for the pangolin, a scaly anteater that resembles an armadillo but lives high in the treetops. This nocturnal creature, found mainly in dense eastern rainforest, hisses and rolls up into an armoured ball when agitated. The rare slow loris curls into a fuzzy ball by day, then moves hand over hand through the trees, hunting in slow motion.

> One of the major nesting sites for Olive Ridley marine turtles, a threatened species, is the Bhitar Kanika National Park in Odisha. More than 200,000 turtles come ashore at Gahirmatha beach over just three or four days in January.

Mugger crocodiles are extremely adaptable and live in any freshwater (sometimes even brackish water) habitats, from large reservoirs to small streams. During extreme dry months or drought they make deep tunnels or even trek miles overland throughout India but, again because of hunting pressure, are now confined to a few protected reservoirs and rivers. Narrow-nosed gharial live well on fish, growing up to 5 metres (16ft) long in Indian rivers. In winter, they emerge to sun themselves and are more easily spotted. The huge saltwater crocodiles (the biggest in the world) are confined to the Andaman Islands, the Sunderbans in West Bengal and Bhitar Kanika in Odisha.

Of the 238 snake species in India, the four most common poisonous snakes are the cobra, krait, Russell's viper and the saw-scaled viper. Together, they cause 10,000 snakebite deaths every year in India alone. There are several species of non-venomous 'garden snakes' common throughout the region. The large rat snake is often mistaken for a cobra but has a more pointed head, large eyes and, of course, does not spread a hood. The biggest snake in India is the reticulated python, which grows up to 10 metres (30ft) in length.

SAVING THE TIGER

Tiger numbers have sunk to catastrophic levels. In 2005 the Sariska Reserve in Rajasthan was found to have been emptied by poachers. This discovery led the Indian government to work with conservation agencies to try to save the tiger from extinction. Two were airlifted from Ranthambore National Park to Sariska in 2010 and appear to be thriving, meaning that more animals will be moved in to re-establish a viable community. Meanwhile, tiger deaths from poaching continue to spiral elsewhere. In 2012, the government of the western state of Maharasthra gave permission for forest guards to shoot on sight any poachers encountered on patrol.

Elsewhere on the plains, groups of blackbuck, recognisable by their elegant antlers, cluster together. Other antelopes, such as the large nilgai (or blue cow), prefer open forest. The widespread sambar deer can be found from the Himalayas to Kanniyakumari; and on the higher slopes of the Himalayas ibex clamber freely. Brow-antlered deer, one of the country's rarest creatures, hide in the dense northeastern forests.

Himalayan flowers seem to hover above the meadows, until closer inspection reveals that

in rural areas keep an eye out for the bright-blue flash of the common kingfisher. Other water birds to be found in India include herons, spoonbills, flamingos, egrets and teal ducks.

The Keoladeo Ghana National Park at Bharatpur, near Agra, is renowned for the number and spectacular variety of its visiting species. However, in most recent years the Siberian cranes that usually spend winter at the park have failed to show up. Scientists blame fighting in Afghanistan, which lies beneath their migratory flight path, for the disruption of their journey,

Tiger stripes are as unique as human fingerprints.

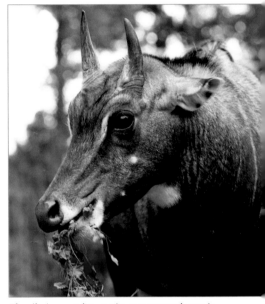

The nilgai, an antelope species most commonly seen in northern India.

they are in reality butterflies evaporating dew from their iridescent wings. Many species take sanctuary in game reserves around the country, including gazelles, wild boar, leatherback turtles, blind river dolphins (often spotted playing in the Ganges), porcupines and flying squirrels.

Bird life

Perhaps the most iconic of India's huge variety of birds is the peacock, found predominantly in Rajasthan but widely used as a national symbol. Many rare birds stop over in India, joining the beauties that reside year-round. Heavy-headed hornbills fly in pairs over northeastern and southern jungles. Apart from the ubiquitous crows and kites, raucous flocks of rose-ringed parakeets wheel over the trees in city parks, while

ELEPHANTS

Elephants have voracious appetites: an adult consumes around 200kg (450lbs) of green fodder a day. The elephant has few natural enemies; calves are jealously guarded by their mothers and tigers seldom get the chance to take them. The elephant, therefore, is an apex species and an excellent indicator of the health of its habitat; where elephants thrive, so do their associate species, such as deer, which in their turn support predators like the tiger or the leopard. Poaching represents the main threat to elephant populations in India, but dozens of deaths each year are also caused by train and road accidents, and by electrocution.

but the drying up of the lake on which the birds depend, a consequence of local water management policy, has doubtless played its part.

Another major problem is the near extinction of the once widespread vulture, whose numbers have declined by 98 percent in the last 10 years or so. At first it was thought that an unknown virus was to blame, but researchers have now discovered a link between the drug diclofenac (widely used as a veterinary painkiller in South Asia) and kidney failure in vultures. Vultures perform the vital function of scavenging rotting carcasses (from which they absorb the

The peacock is the subcontinent's most iconic bird.

diclofenac). This helps prevent the spread of disease and keeps down the population of feral dogs. The Parsis of Mumbai are also facing problems because it is the vultures who dispose of the corpses from their Towers of Silence.

Game tourism

Indian game-viewing began on a grand scale in the 1950s, and even today the arrangements sometimes resemble gentlemen's shooting parties of that era. Creature comforts are not ignored in the wild, and some tents are amazingly luxurious, though many forest houses are rustic, and safari suits are now worn mostly by chauffeurs for the middle class.

Wild animal watching in India takes patience. Many of the most spectacular beasts hide in the shadows, lone predators waiting for their opportunity. Game reserves are not easily accessible (except for Ranthambore in Rajasthan, near a railway connection). A few parks require special permits in advance, usually for a minimum group of four. In the northeast, where shy pandas and macaques hide, militants and Adivasis often do, too. The government limits visits near strategic borders or guerrilla areas. It is always wise to check before setting out, since situations change without warning. At any sanctuary, dress in sensible camouflage and keep quiet; the creatures are easily frightened. Yet with almost 350 species of mammal, a couple of thousand types of bird, and at least 30,000 kinds of insect (more than you want to know personally), India provides an unmatched range that justifies several trips.

For more on India's national parks and sanctuaries, see page 485.

FLORA

You will frequently spot huge versions of familiar houseplants growing wild in India. There are some 15,000 different species, including rare ladyslipper orchids, groves of precious sandalwood or pines interwoven with scarlet rhododendrons. Tangled mangrove swamps compete with casuarina trees. Thickets of bamboo thrive in the northeastern states, where it is used for papermaking. Wild flowers carpet high Himalayan meadows in the summer and salt breezes toss the fronds of several types of palm. Although the mixed deciduous forests have been severely depleted, fire-resistant stands of sal trees or teak are still found. Banyan trees with multiple trunks, sacred pipal figs and Ashoka trees with spear-shaped leaves remain quintessentially Indian. What often fascinate visitors are the flowering trees that shade city parks: jacarandas unfurl blooms like lavender-blue fans, while white magnolia flowers gleam against glossy leaves. Feathery gulmohar trees suddenly blaze bright crimson. The Flame of the Forest's large orange flowers are used to make yellow dye. Blossoms of the frangipani (temple tree) can be cream, pink or deep fuschia. Most fragrant of all are jamun plum trees, the blossoms of which emit a scent to rival tuberose or jasmine. Tamarind is another beautiful flowering tree commonly seen in Indian towns and cities. Its leaves have many uses in traditional medicine.

Conservation

Despite some honest endeavours, conservation in India has been dogged by corruption and poaching, although there are recent signs that things are improving.

Animal conservation in India has had something of a chequered history. Many of the country's game reserves were created from hunting grounds established by the British, and the transition from shooting for sport to protecting from poachers has not always been easy. One of the most renowned practitioners was Jim Corbett, an avid hunter who vowed to kill only big cats that had turned man-eaters, and later kick-started the conservation movement in India; a national park was named after him in 1957. With so much of the human population living in poverty, attempts to prioritise the welfare of India's wildlife have sometimes been ignored. India's old nemesis, corruption, has also seen several well-meaning projects end in scandal.

Project Tiger

The best-known animal conservation project in India is the government-run Project Tiger. Established in 1973 in response to the alarming demise of national tiger populations, the project has overseen a period of further decline in tiger numbers, as well as a number of unfortunate controversies. Directors have been accused of manipulating tiger census numbers in order to encourage more funding from international agencies such as the World Wildlife Fund. In 2008 the Indian government set up the Tiger Protection Force to combat poachers, and has relocated more than 200,000 villages to minimise human–tiger interaction. More controversially, in 2012 the Indian government announced blanket ban on all tourism in core areas of the country's national parks. Opponents of the new laws were quick to point out that banning visitors would do little to protect the tigers. However, following an outcry from businesses and communities dependent on wildlife tourism in and around the sanctuaries, the government capitulated.

Elephants and crocs

While tigers tend to grab the headlines, there are numerous other species under threat in India; Project Elephant, for example, was established in 1992 both to protect the wild tusker and to ensure humane treatment of captive animals, many of which are employed in the logging or tourism trades. One example of an animal-conservation project gone right is the Madras Crocodile Bank, 40km (25 miles) south of Chennai in Tamil Nadu. Founded in 1976 to protect the mugger, gharial and saltwater crocodiles from extinction, the park has since bred over 6,000 crocodiles, which are now supplied to zoos and wildlife parks around the world. While the initial aim was to re-stock natural populations, the dwindling habitat in India has stopped this after significant early success.

Efforts are now being made to protect Indian elephants from ill-treatment.

Rhinos at risk

Another success story has been the one-horned rhino. The majority of the world's population of these formidable beasts now live in Assam's Khaziranga National Park. From 10 to 20 rhinos at the park's creation in 1905, the population during its centenary year was at least 2,050, a remarkable turnaround given the high value of rhino horns to Chinese medical practitioners. But concerns have been raised over the fact that this success has not been replicated elsewhere in India despite many attempts to do so, and that the concentration of such a large proportion of the world's rhinos in one place leaves them vulnerable to medical or natural calamities.

A Hindu temple in Mumbai.

SOCIETY AND RELIGION

India's greatest resource is the number and variety
of its people, but the social order is hugely intricate,
with myriad religious traditions and institutions
such as the caste system spinning a formidable web
for the outsider to untangle.

With over 1.2 billion people – around
17 percent of the world's total – and
a hugely diverse range of cultures, languages and belief systems, it's impossible to
identify just one representative "Indian" society, let alone a representative 'Indian'. For every
example of what is typical there will be another
group of people whose ideas and social practices operate in an entirely different way.

The caste system

Traditionally the overarching form of social
organisation in South Asia is the caste system.
While this is now complicated by the emerging issue of class, caste is still the primary way
in which people identify and group themselves.
The concept has proved so enduring that even
religious communities that are theoretically
outside the system have retained caste structures. In the case of Muslim, Sikh and Christian
groups this is often a hangover from their families' pre-conversion days.

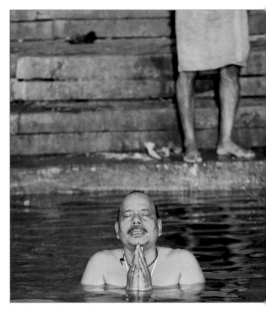

Bathing in the sacred Ganges river.

DALITS AND DISCRIMINATION

Although banned by the Indian constitution for 50
years, discrimination against the lowest castes is still
a daily occurrence. In the early 20th century, Mahatma
Gandhi took some of the first steps in combating this
prejudice and insisted that everyone must take turns
cleaning the toilet. He renamed outcastes (then known
as 'Untouchables') the Harijans ('Children of God'). The
low castes now prefer the less patronising term Dalit
(literally 'the oppressed'), which is more forthright
than the bureaucratic acronyms SC and ST (Scheduled
Castes and Scheduled Tribes). This terminology comes
from the Indian constitution, written by B.K. Ambedkar,
an early Dalit campaigner and brilliant lawyer, who

converted to Buddhism in protest at what he saw as
the Hindu veneration of caste.

A verse in the *Upanishads* (800–400 BC) illustrates
the despicable religious discrimination faced by Dalits.
Only through a life of virtue could they seek to improve
their lot in their next life. In no way, however, could they
aspire to boosting their current status in this world:

'*Those whose conduct on earth has given pleasure
can hope to enter a pleasant womb, that is the womb
of a Brahmin, or a woman of the princely class.*

*But those whose conduct on earth has been foul can
expect to enter a foul and stinking womb, that is, the
womb of a bitch, or a pig, or an outcaste.*'

There are a vast number of castes, most relating to a traditional profession, although the structure is more flexible than it might at first appear. New castes can sometimes be created to accommodate new arrivals, and castes can reposition themselves within the overall structure, usually by adopting names associated with higher castes or achieving hegemony in certain economic activities, thereby gaining more power and status. Such adjustments take time, however, and it is far more difficult for those at the bottom, or the Dalits who are positioned below the lowest

Sadhus (holy men) are dedicated to achieving moksa (liberation) through meditation and contemplation.

stratum of the system, to improve their lot, even if they convert away from Hinduism.

India's caste system is based on the twin concepts of *dharma* and *karma* – the duties one must fulfil in this life and the effects one's actions will have on any future lives. These, coupled with the principle of hereditary occupation and strong concepts of 'pollution', have produced a highly stratified society, which, due to its flexibility, is one that can absorb new peoples without much difficultly.

The Laws of Manu (*c.*AD 150) spell out codes for life in a multiracial society. Each individual is born into a particular *jati* or caste that predetermines both profession and status,

regardless of the wealth of the parents. These castes are said to fall into four basic divisions, or *varna*.

The Brahmins are intellectuals and priests – the link between mortals and millions of Hindu deities. Kshatriyas are rulers and warriors, in charge of justice and administration. Both Brahmins and Kshatriyas are considered "twice-born" and display their status with a sacred thread worn over the shoulder. Below them are the Vaishyas, merchants or traders, and the Shudras, agriculturalists. However, the most menial tasks are reserved for the outcastes, in practice the peoples conquered by higher castes and considered unworthy to be part of the system. Their jobs include cleaning latrines, sweeping the streets, scavenging, burning corpses and gathering dead animals (which extends to working with leather, making shoes and playing drums at funerals or weddings).

In the social division imposed by the Laws of Manu there was an implicit racism based on skin colour (*varna* derives from the Sanskrit for 'colour'). Within the new hierarchy the lighter-skinned arrivals from the northwest were at the top of the heap, with the darker Dravidian and indigenous peoples pushed to the bottom and into menial positions, a distinction that exists to this day.

Rites of passage and family life

The concept of caste has a great impact on the life-cycle rituals of birth, coming of age, marriage and death. Midwives have traditionally been from the low castes, as blood and afterbirth are seen as polluting. In the past, and even now among some very strict adherents to the caste system, if a high-caste person was to come into physical contact with an item or person who was considered polluting then they would have to go through elaborate rituals of cleansing and purification.

On coming of age (essentially reaching puberty), high-caste males go through a ritual whereby they receive their 'sacred thread' – a string worn across the body over one shoulder that is a marker of their high-caste status. This practice has now been adopted by some lower castes in an attempt to raise their status and profile.

Marriage is traditionally the most important event in anyone's life in India. Fraught with

Two concepts govern many aspects of South Asian society; they are 'auspiciousness' and 'pollution'. Not necessarily mutually exclusive, they lie at the heart of the workings of the caste system.

complications, from caste and the negotiation of a dowry, the vast majority of marriages in India are still arranged by the couple's parents. In the past a marriage broker would have been employed to find a suitable match for a son or daughter, but now newspapers are full of 'matrimonials', and the internet has greatly expanded the family's potential for finding a spouse. For high-caste matches the demands are often very specific, demanding and tinged with an underlying racism; women are advertised as having 'wheatish complexions', and there are requests for Green Cards, higher degrees and high potential earning power. Nowadays, these kinds of ruthless demand are not only restricted to the upper castes as a pan-Indian 'Sanskritisation' encourages the low castes to ape the behaviour of those more rich and powerful.

Extended family life in a densely populated country can be fraught with problems of privacy. Most societies in India are patriarchal, and a daughter must leave her parents to set up a household with the groom's family. There are a bewildering number of terms for family relationships. It can sometimes seem that everyone in a room is distantly related in some fashion. '*Bahu*', the daughter-in-law, and '*Sas*', the mother-in-law, are notorious adversaries in the Indian family and a focus for conflicts over duty, obedience and respect.

Brother, '*Bhai*', and older sister, '*Didi*', are affectionate and respectful terms of address, even for people outside the nuclear family. It is common to call a visitor 'Aunty' or 'Uncle', and older people may call you son, '*Beta*', or daughter, '*Beti*.' '*Mata*' and '*Pita*' are terms for mother and father (often with the respectful tag, *ji*, added), and there are many other names for relatives that indicate the birth order and branch of the family.

A deeply religious country

In many ways India's multiplicity of peoples and forms of social organisation are best seen through the prism of its numerous religions. These are not only the repository of many of its subtle philosophical traditions, but have also proved flexible enough to absorb influences from newly arrived traditions, such as Islam and Christianity, as well as influencing the new arrivals in turn. While, in general, the interaction between different religious groups has been positive, at times there has also been considerable friction.

Hinduism

There is no one set of beliefs that might sum

Hindu temple offerings.

up India's dominant belief system, Hinduism. No other religious tradition, or group of devotees, is so eclectic; it is not traced to a specific founder and does not have a single holy book as its scriptural authority. There are a plethora of deities, some only local, that can be worshipped through a tradition of direct devotion *(bhakti)* or by elaborate temple rituals. The land and landscape of India is intimately entwined with Hindu beliefs, from holy rivers such as the Ganges, to Mount Kailash in Tibet – the holy mountain of Shiva – and sacred groves of trees.

Hinduism thrives on contrasts. At one end is the most abstruse metaphysical speculation about Ultimate Reality; at the other there are

The Adivasis

Adivasis, literally 'original inhabitants', comprise a substantial indigenous minority of the Indian population, though their way of life is under threat.

Also known as 'tribals', the Adivasis are found from the Nilgiris to the Himalayas, and from Rajasthan to Arunachal Pradesh. This blanket term refers to a hugely diverse selection of societies and cultures, and is used as a catch-all for peoples who are not easily categorised in terms of India's dominant groups or ideologies.

Many Adivasi groups, particularly those living in Odisha, Bihar, and Madhya Pradesh, may be descendants of the first inhabitants of South Asia. Linguistically and culturally distinct, it's thought

A Lamani woman in Goa.

that their presence in the region predates the two waves of immigration from the north and west that brought the now dominant groups of the north and south.

As these new peoples moved in, they displaced the existing inhabitants, forcing them into the hills and forests where there was less pressure for land. Over time there was interaction between these groups, but due to their relative isolation, many Adivasis have retained highly individual identities.

The northeastern states have, after Madhya Pradesh, Chattisgarh, Jharkand and Odisha, the highest concentration of Adivasis. The groups who live here have more in common culturally and linguistically with peoples living in Burma (Myanmar) to the east than they do with, say, the Todas or Kotas of Kerala and Tamil Nadu.

What does unite these peoples, however, is the degree of discrimination they have suffered. Where Adivasis have had close contact with Hindus, their place within the caste system has been considered extremely low, working as agricultural labourers or undertaking menial tasks (often those believed to be "polluting" by high-caste Hindus).

Adivasi land

Traditionally, landownership patterns among Adivasi groups are not governed by individual ownership laws, making it easy for unscrupulous politicians and landowners to appropriate Adivasi lands.

Some of the worst offences have been committed by the state. Many large dams have flooded areas populated by Adivasis, providing power and drinking water to urban areas while handing out pitiful, or no, compensation to the people they displace. Land-reform programmes in states such as Kerala have redistributed land that had traditionally supported Adivasi groups. Logging has decimated many of the forests previously inhabited by Adivasi groups, and areas such as Jharkand, which are rich in mineral wealth, have seen the displacement of many people, as well as widespread pollution of their lands. However, a potential breakthrough in this otherwise downward trend came in August 2010, when the Union Environment Ministry withdrew permission that had earlier been granted to the Vedanta mining company to extract bauxite, the main ore of aluminium, from the Niyamgiri Hills in Odisha, traditional home and hunting ground of the 8,000-strong Dongria Kondh tribal community.

popular practices based on the worship of local deities.

Absolute monism goes hand in hand with extreme pluralism. On the one side, Hinduism accepts the validity of many paths leading to the same goal, and is willing to recognise the divinity of the prophets of other religions. But along with this tolerance, at present under threat, go a continuing rigid adherence to caste distinctions and custom-ridden practices. Defying attempts to define it, this multiplicity is perhaps Hinduism's most defining characteristic.

The Vedas and early texts

It is thought that peoples arriving from Central Asia in around 1500 BC brought the prototypes for the body of Sanskrit hymns and prayers recorded in the four *Vedas* (from the Sanskrit root *vid*, to know). These form, in essence, the founding texts of Hinduism, of which the most important is the *Rig Veda*. The hymns and rituals were transmitted orally for centuries, but were not written down until the beginning of the first millennium AD.

Composed between 1600 and 1000 BC, the Vedic hymns were addressed to gods and

Riverside ghats are used for bathing, laundry and performing rituals.

CANONICAL HINDUISM

In the ancient Sanskrit texts such as the Upanishads, it is asserted that Brahman, the Creator, is the sole reality and everything else is a mere 'appearance'. However, the reality of the world and the values and distinctions of human life must be accepted. The fundamentals of canonical Hinduism might be summarised as:

Goal and paths: the ultimate goal is *moksa*, liberation from the cycle of existence.

Karma and rebirth: until *moksa* is attained, all human beings are subject to rebirth. The conditions of life in each birth are determined by the cumulative results of the *karma* (deeds) that were performed in previous lifetimes.

Four objectives: in addition to attaining *moksa*, three proximate ends are recognised as legitimate: *kama* (pleasure, including sex), *artha* (prosperity and fame) and *dharma* (truth or correct behaviour).

Four stages in life: these are the stage of the learner, demanding self-control and abstinence; the stage of the householder, when *kama* and *artha* are valid ends; the stage of detachment; and the stage of renunciation with a wholly spiritual life, preparing for *moksa*.

Four *varnas*: differences in aptitudes are reflected in four social divisions: Brahmins (priests and teachers); Kshatriyas (warriors and rulers); Vaishyas (traders and merchants); and Sudras (agriculturalists).

goddesses who were regarded as personifica-
tions of the powers of nature: Indra, god of
rain and thunder; Prajapati, lord of the creatures; Agni, god of the sacred fire; the Maruts,
gods of winds and storms; Savitr, the sun god;
Ushas, goddess of dawn; and Varuna, god of the
sea and upholder of the moral law. The hymns
are believed to have been composed by *rishis*
(sages) who were divinely inspired.

The *Vedas* contain ideas and suggestions that
have shaped the entire Hindu tradition and
show a tendency to move from pluralism to
monism. Although different gods were, and

*A scene from the Bhagavad Gita, a section of the
Mahabharata.*

continue to be, worshipped, they were increasingly seen as manifestations of a single divine
principle. The Vedic concept of *rita* (cosmic
law) points to a single rhythmic force animat-
ing the entire universe.

Vedic religion consisted mainly of sacrificial
rituals. A sacred flame was kindled in the centre of a raised platform, and the sacrificer gave
offerings to the flame while the priest chanted
hymns and invocations. In the centuries that
followed, the mystical and symbolic meaning
of the *yajna* (sacrifice) receded into the background as the ritual became all-important.
Every detail had to be meticulously followed:
the kindling of the fuel, the shape of the vessel

containing the holy water, the intonation of
the words. The Brahmins, who performed this
ritual, became the dominant class of society.

> By combining religion with philosophy and poetry,
> the Vedas initiated a typical Hindu concept of
> perfection – that wisdom must combine the
> intellectual clarity of the philosopher with the faith
> of the sage and the aesthetic of the artist.

The *Upanishads*, written between 800 and
400 BC, represent a reaction against a perceived
decline in values and seek to impose a more systematic form of the religion. They are dialogues
between teachers and disciples and are regarded
as a continuation of the *Vedas*. The Hindu epics
(the *Mahabharata* and the *Ramayana*) were
probably composed in the 1st century AD.
Stories from these epics were later elaborated in
a literature known as the *Puranas*, which were
completed by AD 500.

The basic principles of Hinduism received
fresh support from the *Vedanta* philosophy. Based on the *Upanishads*, *Vedanta* was
brilliantly put together by the Hindu pandit Shankaracharya in the 8th century. This
Sanskritised orthodoxy has attained the status
of what might be described as a 'Hindu canon'.

The Hindu epics

Perhaps the most popular philosophical Hindu
text is the *Bhagavad Gita*, the final section of
the *Mahabharata*. Krishna's discourse, with
occasional questions from Arjuna, covers

THE MAHABHARATA

The *Mahabharata* revolves around the conflict
between the five Pandava brothers, their joint wife
Draupadi, and the Pandavas' cousins, the Kauravas,
who have wrongly laid claim to the kingdom.
Krishna becomes the charioteer of Arjuna, the commander of the Pandava army. But on the eve of
battle, Arjuna refuses to fight against his relatives
whereupon Krishna gives him a discourse on the
immortality of the soul and his obligation to fulfil his
dharma (sacred duty). Roughly ten times the length
of Homer's Odyssey and the Iliad combined, the
Mahabharata is often likened in terms of its cultural
significance to the Bible and Qu'ran.

almost every aspect of human life. The *Gita*'s tremendous appeal derives from its earnestness, optimism and tolerance. As with many popular religious texts, there is something in it for everyone. The *Gita* accepts the validity of three different paths leading to the common goal of self-realisation: the path of *jnana* (knowledge), the path of *bhakti* (devotion and love) and the path of *karma* (work). These are said to equate with the intellectual, emotional and practical sides of human nature. In addition, the special path, the path of *yoga*, is also recognised. The central message of the *Gita* is sometimes said to be: work without attachment, dedicating the fruit of your work to the divine.

The *Ramayana*, whose author, Valmiki, is a legendary figure, has exerted a deep influence on the religious and cultural life of India. A different message comes from this text. The hero Rama, an incarnation of Vishnu, emerges from the narrative as Purushottama (Perfect Man). He is the ideal king, the ideal brother and the ideal son. Stories of Rama's devotion to his parents and teachers and his courage and compassion are woven into the poem, and there are vivid descriptions of the regions through which he passes.

Mythology and local deities

In India, mythology has always been close to the actual life of the people. There are hundreds of stories about gods, goddesses, heroes, sages, demons, and natural phenomena like the sun and the moon, lakes, rivers, mountains, trees, flowers and animals. They are kept alive through fairs and festivals, in traditional songs, dramas and dances, and provide the main motifs in court and stage performances, as well as hugely popular TV 'dramas, or 'mytholgoicals'.

As the Vedic deities (such as Brahma and Surya) lost some of their importance, other gods, particularly Rama and Krishna, probably local hero-gods that were absorbed into Hindu mythology, became popular. Vishnu and Shiva, who were minor deities in the *Vedas*, became predominant in the later Hindu pantheon.

The *Mahabharata* and the *Ramayana* are a treasure house of mythology, as are the *Puranas*. Of these, the *Shiva Purana*, the *Vishnu Purana* and the *Bhagavata* are especially important since they contain myths of Shiva, Vishnu and Krishna respectively.

However, it is not necessarily these canonical deities that are closest to the lives of many, particularly rural, Indians. It is their pantheon of local village gods and, more often, goddesses that claim the greatest attention. These local deities perform vital functions in delineating and protecting the village. Goddesses, in particular, are associated with disease – most commonly smallpox, as with the powerful South Indian goddess Yellama – and their appeasement is an essential yearly ritual.

The shrines of the more powerful, and hence most dangerous, deities are often to be found

A Hindu shrine in Mumbai.

THE RAMAYANA

The story of the *Ramayana* is known by almost all Indians. Rama, the eldest son of King Dasharatha of Ayodhya, is banished for 14 years following a plot by the mother of one of Rama's brothers (the king has three queens). He goes into the forest, accompanied by his wife, Sita, and his younger brother, Laksmana. Sita is then kidnapped and taken to Sri Lanka on the orders of the demon-king, Ravana. Rama is helped in his mission to rescue his wife by an army of monkeys led by Hanuman, who assumes a giant form to strike across the straits to Lanka, where they defeats Ravana before returning triumphantly to Ayodhya.

outside the village boundaries, where they are not only at a safe distance, but form a protective ring around the dwellings, warding off disaster such as famine or disease. The *pujaris*, or priests, of these local deities are generally not the Brahmins of the village temple, but are drawn from the lower castes.

Not only does this caste division emphasise the divergence of the Sanskritised pan-Indian Hindu tradition from local religion, but also points out differences in ritual. The local goddesses often demand blood sacrifices, of a buffalo, goat or chicken, thought

The mosque at Kodungallur, Kerala, is believed to be the oldest in India, dating back to the 7th century.

of as "polluting" by the higher castes, and the rituals are often accompanied by drumming, an activity also associated with the lower castes as animal skins also carry the stigma of "pollution".

Hinduism and Islam

The coming of Islam to India in the 12th century was a turning point in the evolution of Hinduism. The Sikh religion, founded by Guru Nanak in the 15th century, played an important part in bringing the two faiths (Islam and Hinduism) together. In orthodox terms, no two religions in the world appear on the surface to be as dissimilar as Hinduism and Islam. Islam was founded by a historical

person and has a specific scripture, the *Qur'an*; Hinduism's origins lie in a speculative distant past. Hinduism is eclectic and pluralistic; Islam is homogeneous and has a definite concept of God. The Hindu temple is enclosed on three sides, and there is mystery in the dark inner sanctum; the Muslim mosque is open on all sides, exposed to light and air. Hindus worship sculptured images of deities; to the Muslim, worship of images is a sin. Hinduism has traditionally shunned proselytising; Islam welcomes converts.

Yet these two faiths met in India, influenced each other and, after initial conflict, enriched each other. Within a few decades of their arrival in India, Muslims began to consider the Subcontinent as their home. Between the 13th and 18th centuries, northern India witnessed a synthesis of Hindu and Islamic elements in almost every sphere of life. This unique Indo-Islamic culture gave rise to a huge flowering of cultural endeavour in poetry, painting, architecture and music. Indeed, India is unimaginable without Islam; its influence is everywhere, from music and architecture to food.

Islam in India

Arab traders came to India as early as the 7th century, and the first Muslim invaders came as far as Daibul, close to present-day Karachi, and Multan (both now in Pakistan), in 712. Islam gradually spread north through missionary activity, and in 977 Mahmud of Ghazni, a Turkish ruler from Central Asia, invaded India as far as the Ganges. His descendants consolidated their hold over the Punjab and, when the Ghaznivad dynasty was replaced by Muhammad Ghauri at the end of the 12th century, Islamic influence reached Delhi and Ajmer. By the beginning of the 13th century the Delhi Sultanate was established and Muslim rule gradually extended eastwards and southwards.

When the Sultanate's power declined, the Mughal Empire, founded by Babur in 1506, replaced it as the ruler of North India. One of the greatest Mughal emperors was Akbar (1556–1605), whose policy of religious tolerance brought Hindus and Muslims together. Subsequently, Emperor Aurangzeb (1658–1707) gained notoriety for destroying many temples and thereby alienating his Hindu population.

In its first phase, Islamic rule in India was aggressive, but it was not through the temporal power of the Islamic armies that the vast majority of converts were made; the mystics of Islam, known as Sufis, played an important part in spreading the message of universal love. The Sufi saints, or *pirs*, taught their disciples through *zikr*, or the repetition of religious formulas. The message of Islamic mysticism was also conveyed effectively by the classical Persian poets, particularly by Rumi, who expressed the spirit of Sufism through beautiful symbols and images. Persian,

Sikhism

This process of bringing the religions of Hinduism and Islam close to each other was continued by Kabir and Nanak. Born into a Brahmin family, Kabir was brought up by Muslim foster parents. He was a disciple of Ramananda, a famous Hindu saint, but he was also deeply influenced by Sufism.

Nanak came from the Punjab, a region where Hindus and Muslims had come into close contact. A Hindu by birth and training, Nanak was attracted from his childhood towards both Hindu and Muslim saints and poets. He visited

Buddhist monks in a monastery near Darjeeling.

not Arabic, was the court language during Muslim rule.

Among the *pirs* who settled in India, Mu'inuddin Chishti of Ajmer and Nizamuddin Aulia of Delhi were the most influential. Annual festivals held in their honour are celebrated to this day. Amir Khusrau was a disciple of Nizamuddin and was famous as a poet in the classical Persian tradition, but he also wrote religious poetry in Urdu. The prevalent spirit of Hindu-Muslim integration was reflected admirably in Khusrau's work. The tombs of these poet-saints are still places of pilgrimage for both Muslims and Hindus, particularly at the time of the saints' *urs* (anniversary of their death).

the sacred places of Hinduism and also made the pilgrimage to Mecca. He saw the essential teachings of both religions as being the same and began to preach a message of unity. He attracted many followers and soon came to be known as Guru Nanak. His disciples came together, and a new religious tradition was born. The term Sikh is derived from the Sanskrit *shishya* (disciple).

Angad succeeded Nanak as the Guru of the Sikhs, and started compiling Nanak's writings. He also used a script that was used by some Punjabis, called *Gurmukhi*, and it became the official script of the Sikhs. Guru Arjun, the fifth in succession, started building the temple at Amritsar, which later became the holiest Sikh shrine. Arjun also systematised the collection of sacred hymns and poems by Nanak, Kabir and other saints. This collection became the holy scripture of the Sikhs, known as Adi *Granth Sahib* (Book of the Lord).

The spread of Sikhism alarmed orthodox Muslims, which led to the persecution of the faith. Guru Arjun was put to death on a charge of sedition in 1606. Arjun's martyrdom convinced his successors that Sikhs must have military training to defend themselves. The 10th Guru, Govind Singh, transformed the pacifist Sikh sect into a martial community and intro-

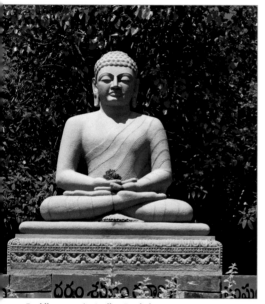

Buddha statue in Andhra Pradesh.

duced rites of initiation into a well-organised Sikh army known as the *Khalsa*. Govind Singh also decided to terminate the succession of gurus. He asked his followers to look upon the Adi *Granth Sahib* as the sole object of veneration. The holy book became the symbol of God.

Buddhism

The teachings and stories of the life of the Buddha have influenced the lives and thoughts of millions of people in Asia. The Buddha was born in India in *c.*563 BC, and until his death in *c.*483 BC he travelled extensively, disseminating his teaching to disciples. His life forms the backdrop to many Buddhist teachings, from his disillusionment with the material world,

to the sermons he preached as he travelled, to his meditations through which he gained enlightenment.

While Hindu thought was preoccupied with the essential nature of absolute reality, the Buddha avoided metaphysical controversies. 'The arising of sorrow, the termination of sorrow, that is all I teach,' he said. Two philosophical principles are implicit in the Buddha's teaching. First, there is the Law of Impermanence. Everything in the phenomenal world is subject to change. The second assumption is the Law of Causation; nothing happens

> Guru Nanak (1469–1539) founded the Sikh religion with the avowed purpose of synthesising Hinduism and Islam. Islam's spirit of brotherhood helped in loosening the rigidity of the caste system.

by chance. Apart from natural causes, we are subject to the operation of our *karma*. It follows that the popular notion of a soul that somehow survives the body is illusory. The Buddha urges us to discard this illusion.

The Buddha's first sermon is called the Sermon of the Middle Way and steers between two sets of extremes: on the ethical plane, the extremes of self-indulgence and asceticism; on the philosophical plane, the extremes of naive acceptance of everything as real and the total rejection of everything as unreal. He described the Eightfold Path of the good life, consisting of right conduct, right motive, right resolve, right speech, right livelihood, right attention, right effort and right meditation. By following this path of restraint and self-perfection, Buddha claimed one could conquer craving. Having achieved that, one is within sight of *nirvana*, the transcendental state of complete emancipation.

Shortly after the Buddha's death, his oldest disciple, Kashyapa, convened a council at Rajagriha. The Buddhas's teachings were classified into three sections, known as *Tripitaka* ('three baskets'). These, along with later commentaries, became the scriptures of Buddhism.

In the 3rd century BC the Mauryan emperor Ashoka, shocked by the destruction wrought by a battle at Kalinga (modern-day Odisha), became a Buddhist. Ashoka's conversion marked the beginning of a period of Buddhist expansion. Ashoka set up inscriptions throughout South Asia exhorting his subjects to follow the Buddha's message of compassion and tolerance.

In modern India, there has been a revival of interest in Buddhism, particularly among outcaste Dalits following Dr Ambedkar's public conversion. Buddhists constitute a very small proportion of the Indian population, but refugee communities of Tibetan Buddhists and Dalit converts have significantly boosted their numbers since the 1960s.

Jainism

About the same time as the Buddha was preaching his *dharma*, and in the same region, another religious tradition was being established. Vardhamana, better known by his title Mahavira ('great hero'), was an elder contemporary of the Buddha. The two teachers had much in common: both were Kshatriyas of royal descent but renounced the worldly life; both rejected caste barriers and questioned

> The theme of self-conquest is supremely important to the Jains. The word Jain is derived from jina ('conqueror'). Carrying the idea to its extreme, Jainism has become the world's most rigorously ascetic faith.

the sacredness of the *Vedas*. Unlike the teachings of the Buddha, Jainism, the religion preached by Mahavira, did not travel beyond South Asia, but it established a significant presence within India.

The concept of a deity has little or no place in Jain doctrine. The popular deities of Hinduism are accepted, but they are given less significance than the *jinas*, who are regarded as the true focus of devotion. Mahavira, though usually accepted as the founder of the faith in the context of history, is said to be the last of a line of 24 *jinas*. All of them are said to have attained perfect wisdom *(kaivalya)* through different penances, to vanquish desire and break their bonds with the material world. The *jinas* are also known as *Tirthankaras* ('crossing-makers'), referring to the passage from the material world to the realm of enlightenment.

Jainism not only rejects the notion of a personal deity, but also the idea of a single impersonal absolute reality. It regards each living being as an independent *jiva* (soul). In its mundane condition, the soul is permeated by material particles through the working of *karma*. To attain liberation, a double process is necessary: the incursion of new *karma*-particles must be stopped; and those that have already tainted the soul must be expelled. This is possible only through right faith, right knowledge and right conduct: the *tri-ratna* ('three jewels') of Jainism.

Right conduct is seen as the rejection of falsehood, theft, lust, greed and violence. Of

A Jain monk and disciple.

these five sins violence is the most heinous. The highest virtue is the total abjuration of any thought or action that can hurt a living being. Sometimes the Jains carry their non-violence, like their asceticism, to extreme limits. For instance, Jain monks and nuns can be seen with their nose and mouth covered by a fine cloth mask to ensure that they do not involuntarily kill insects while breathing, and may use a broom to sweep their path clear.

Jains have made valuable contributions in many areas of Indian culture, including philosophy, literature, painting, sculpture and commerce. However, the greatest glory of Jain religious art lies in its temple architecture, particularly at Girnar, Palitana and Mount Abu.

Holy cow on the Vishram Ghat at Mathura.

DECISIVE DATES

Early history

c.2500–1600 BC

Urban settlements of Harappa and Mohenjodaro established in the Indus Valley.

A statue at the Indian Museum in Kolkata.

c.1500 BC

Peoples from Central Asia invade northern India. Sacred Sanskrit texts of the *Vedas* are composed.

521–486 BC

The Persian king, Darius, occupies Punjab and Sind. Buddhism and Jainism develop.

321–184 BC

Northern India is ruled by the Mauryan emperors; the most notable ruler is Ashoka (269–232 BC).

AD 319–606

Gupta Empire is established in the north. Science (especially astronomy and maths), literature and the arts flourish. Brahmanical Hinduism reasserts itself.

550–1190

The Chalukya and Rashtraka dynasties rule central India from Karnataka. The Pallava and Chola dynasties rule the South and establish trading links with Indonesia.

The Rajput Period: 900–1200

c.850

Anangpal builds Lal Kot, Delhi's first city.

1000–1300

Hoysala Empire rules the South.

1192

Muhammed of Ghor invades the north and makes Qutb-ud-Din Aibak Delhi's first ruler.

The Delhi Sultanate

1206

Qutb-ud-Din becomes sultan of Delhi. His dynasty is overthrown in 1296 by Feroz Shah, a Turk, who builds Delhi's second city east of Lal Kot.

1321

Ghias-ud-Din Tughlaq is proclaimed sultan. He starts building Tughlaqabad, the third city of Delhi.

1325

Muhammad-bin Tughlaq becomes sultan and builds Jahanpanah, the fourth city of Delhi. In 1351 Feroz Shah Tughlaq builds Ferozabad, the fifth city.

1414

Power passes to the Sayyids.

1451

Buhlbal Lodi, an Afghan noble, captures the throne and founds the Lodhi dynasty.

14th–16th century

Islam is established throughout the North. The South remains independent under the Hindu Vijayanagar dynasty.

Hampi (Vijayanagar Dynasty).

1498

Vasco da Gama completes the first ever sea voyage from Europe and India via the Cape of Good Hope. Portugal quickly establishes trade links with kingdoms on the Malabar Coast (Kerala), importing spices and cotton for vast profits. Rival powers Holland, France and England follow suit.

The Mughal Dynasty: 1526–1857

1526

Babur, from Samarkand, defeats the Sultan of Delhi at the Battle of Panipat, and proclaims himself the first Mughal emperor.

Purana Qila, Delhi.

1540
Humayan succeeds his father, Babur, and starts to build Purana Qila, Delhi's sixth city.

1556
Akbar is enthroned, aged 13. Considered the greatest of the Mughal emperors, he pushes the borders of the empire three-quarters of the way across South Asia.

1565
Akbar starts to build the Red Fort in his capital city, Agra. Meanwhile, a coalition of forces led by the Muslim Bahmani dynasty bring down the Vijayanagars in the South.

1569–74
Akbar moves his capital to Fatehpur Sikri, near Agra, but the court returns to Agra ten years later. Akbar then starts to build his tomb at Sikandra.

1600
Queen Elizabeth I grants a trading charter to the British East India Company; English merchants set up a trading base at Surat (Gujarat) in 1608.

1605
Akbar is succeeded by his son, Jahangir.

1627
Shah Jahan, Akbar's grandson, becomes emperor. In 1632 he starts to build the Taj Mahal in memory of his wife. In 1638 he moves the capital from Agra to Delhi and lays the foundations for Shahjahanabad, the seventh city. He begins work on Lal Qila (the Red Fort) in 1639.

1659–1707
Aurangzeb becomes emperor by imprisoning his father, Shah Jahan, in the Red Fort, Agra, and killing his brothers. Following his death the Mughal empire declines. Calcutta begins to expand as a trading post of the East India Company.

1739
Persian king Nadir Shah invades Delhi and slaughters 30,000 residents of Shahjahanabad before returning to Persia with the Peacock Throne and the Koh-i-noor Diamond.

1756–63
In the Seven Years War the British East India Company ousts the French from Bengal.

1857
Uprising against British rule breaks out in Meerut. The campaign spreads across India, causing much bloodshed. The British defeat the insurgents. Bahaudur Shah, last of the Mughal emperors, is exiled to Burma. The reign of the East India Company comes to an end.

The British Raj: 1858–1947

1858
The British Crown imposes direct rule and appoints a viceroy as the sovereign's representative.

1877
Queen Victoria is proclaimed Empress of India.

1885
The first political party, the Indian National Congress, is founded.

Procession of the last Mughal Shah, exiled to Rangoon tafter the Uprising.

Prince of Wales and Maharajah, 1922.

1911

George V, king and emperor, announces that the capital will be transferred from Calcutta to Delhi.

1908

The Muslim League is set up.

1915

Mohandas Gandhi, dubbed "Mahatma" (great soul) by Rabindranath Tagore, returns from South Africa and starts to campaign against British rule.

1919

General Dyer orders his Gurkha troops to open fire on a peaceful anti-British protest meeting in Amritsar, killing at least 379 and wounding 1,200.

1930

Gandhi's non-cooperation movement gains momentum with his Dandi Salt March from Ahmedabad to protest against taxes on Indian-produced salt.

1931

New Delhi inaugurated as the capital of India.

1935

Mohammed Ali Jinnah, head of the Muslim League, calls for a new Muslim nation of Pakistan.

Independence (1947–present)

1947

India gains independence at midnight on 15 August. Jawaharlal Nehru becomes first prime minister. India is divided in two: the mainly Hindu nation of India and the Muslim nation of Pakistan. Pakistan is divided into West and East Pakistan. During Partition more than 10 million migrate in each direction across the divided Punjab. Communal violence between Hindus, Sikhs and Muslims claims between 200,000 and 1 million lives.

1948

Mahatma Gandhi is assassinated on 30 January, shot at point-blank range by a Hindu nationalist.

1950

The constitution of India comes into force.

1964

Nehru dies. In 1965 his successor, Lal Bahadur Shastri, defeats Pakistan in a war over Kashmir.

1966

Indira Gandhi, Nehru's daughter (no relation to Mahatma Gandhi) becomes prime minister.

1971

War with East Pakistan leads to the creation of the new independent nation of Bangladesh.

1975–77

Indira Gandhi imposes a state of emergency, suspends civil liberties and imprisons her political opponents. She is defeated in the 1977 elections.

1977–79

Janata Party in power under Morarji Desai.

1980

Indira Gandhi returns as prime minister.

1984

Sikhs demand independence for Punjab; 1,000 people die when the army storms the Golden Temple in Amritsar. Indira Gandhi is assassinated on 31 October by Sikh militants. Her son, Rajiv Gandhi, becomes prime minister, and immediately sets about liberalising the Indian economy, opening it to foreign investment.

Rajiv Gandhi.

1990

Communal and civil disturbances in Jammu and Kashmir and Assam. Religious violence in Punjab.

1991
Rajiv Gandhi is assassinated. Congress forms a minority government led by Narasimha Rao, who continues Rajiv's programme of economic reform.

1992–93
Destruction of Babri mosque in Ayodhya by Hindu militants provokes riots nationwide.

1996
A leftist coalition under Deve Gowda, later succeeded by I.K. Gujral, takes office.

1998
BJP-led coalition; Atal Bihari Vajpayee becomes prime minister. India carries out nuclear tests in the Thar Desert.

1999
A BJP-led coalition (the NDA) under Atal Bihari Vajpayee wins a general election. Fighting breaks out in the Kargil Valley between India and Pakistan.

2000
India's population surpasses 1 billion.

The aftermath of the tsunami in the Andaman Islands.

2001
Huge earthquake hits western Gujarat.

2002
Communal violence between Hindus and Muslims kills over 1,000 in Gujarat.

2004
India and Pakistan begin talks to resolve "all outstanding issues". Congress-led coalition wins general election, Manmohan Singh is prime minister. A tsunami devastates the Andaman and Nicobar Islands and parts of the Tamil coast.

2005
The first bus service starts between Indian-administered and Pakistan-occupied Kashmir.

2006
More than 200 people die and over 700 are injured from bombs placed in Mumbai's transport network.

2008
Islamist terrorist attacks in Mumbai kill 173 and bring the city centre to a standstill for 3 days.

2009
Tata launch the Nano, the world's cheapest car. The Congress Party unexpectedly records a sweeping victory in the national elections.

2010
India hosts the Commonwealth Games amid allegations that $4bn (£2.7bn) were embezzled by officials. September saw the long anticipated court verdict in the Ayodhya temple dispute, with a third of the site going to each of the three parties involved.

2011
Anti-corruption campaigner, Ana Hazare, begins a series of high-profile hunger strikes which form the focus of a mass movement against India's culture of corrupt officialdom.

2012
A report stating that despite GDP growth rates of between 5–9 percent, child malnutrition in India reaches levels of 40 percent – a statistic prime minister Manmohan Singh describes as 'a national shame'. Meanwhile, hundreds of thousands of landless poor march on New Delhi, and a massive electricity black out leaves 700 million people without power.

2013
The year begins with mass demonstrations in Delhi after the victim of a violent rape on a city bus dies from her injuries. Five men are charged with the murder.

BEGINNINGS

India's history is epic, going back to the first traces of
human culture and punctuated by invasions, the birth
of religions and the rise and fall of great civilisations.

The Indian Subcontinent has many rivers, fertile soils and a benevolent climate.
Cultivation and settlement have a long
history here: there is a Neolithic site, with the
remains of mud-brick buildings, at Mehrgarh,
now in western Pakistan, that dates back to
around 6500 BC.

A much more highly developed Harappan civilisation was well established by 2500 BC, with
settlements in the Indus Valley of Pakistan, and
over a wide area of northern and western India.
Among the Indian sites are the ones at Ropar in
Punjab, and Lothal and Kalibangan in Gujarat
and Rajasthan, whose towns housed tens of
thousands. They were built of baked bricks
and well laid out on a grid system. Pottery was
made on the wheel, furnaces were used to produce bronze, copper, lead and tin, and wheeled
wagons were drawn by oxen. Thousands of seals
have been found with elaborate depictions of
humans and animals, some with the symbols
of a script. Unfortunately, this has yet to be
deciphered. In the second millennium BC the
Harappan civilisation went into decline and
eventually expired. The reasons are not known,
but they were possibly flooding, salination and
desertification.

The court of Akbar.

Aryan invasion

Much controversy surrounds the origin of the
successors to the people of Harappa, the Aryans.
At one time it was suggested that the Aryans
were a race rather than a linguistic group. This
view was vigorously propagated by the Nazis
and also by some Indians. It is now agreed by
most experts that there is no genetic evidence for
this theory. The language of the Aryans in India
was Sanskrit, and this is closely related to a large
number of languages in Europe, including Latin,
Greek, English, French, German, Russian, Polish
and Spanish.

In about 1500 BC, Aryan tribes from Central
Asia invaded Northwest India. Their horses
and chariots, and the fact that they were semi-
nomadic, gave them considerable advantage in
warfare. Although there is virtually no archaeological evidence from this early period, the
Aryans composed a series of orally transmitted Sanskrit religious and secular verses, the
Rig Veda, which have been dated to around
1400 BC, and give some idea of their life. They
originally invaded the Punjab and then spread
east to the plain of the Ganges river, bringing
with them a new set of gods and a new social
structure.

The Vedic age

The Vedic gods included Indra, the god of war, Agni, the god of fire, and Varuna, the god of the cosmic order. A hereditary priestly caste, the Brahmins, supervised the placation of these gods with prayers and sacrifices, while the Aryan tribes each had an elected chief from among the warriors. Society was divided into three groups – the priests, the warriors and the common people. When the indigenous people where subjugated, they became a fourth class of low labourers, the Shudra. Later, another class was added who, because of their occupation or strange habits, even the Shudra despised; these were the "untouchables". Within the Aryan family there was a strict hierarchy too. The father was all-powerful over his wife and children, boys were prized over girls, and property was inherited only by men. The Aryans were fond of singing and dancing, gambling with dice and drinking. Apart from alcohol they also drank *soma* at religious ceremonies, the composition of which is disputed, but it seems to have been a herbal concoction that was both narcotic and psychedelic.

As the Aryans became more settled and more powerful they began to set up kingdoms based on territory rather than on roving bands of warriors. Agriculture flourished on the rich lands under the plough; the population grew rapidly and sizeable towns were established. Chiefs who previously had been elected were replaced by hereditary kings. Religious sacrifices became more elaborate, with hundreds of bulls being killed as well as horses. The most important kingdoms in North India were those of Kosal on the plain north of the Ganges, and Magadha, south of the river and further east. Deposits of iron ore were found at Magadha, which the people learnt to smelt. The religion of the Vedas was supplemented by the sophisticated ideas of *karma* and rebirth in the 8th century BC.

In 326 BC, Alexander the Great invaded India. His army, consisting of 25,000 or more cavalry, crossed the Indus river, took Taxila without opposition and defeated some Aryan armies. Moving east across the Punjab, Alexander learnt of the wealth of Magadha and contemplated an assault. His army, however, was exhausted and forced him to return home.

This enabled Magadha to expand into the areas Alexander had conquered.

Mauryan India

Chandragupta Maurya became king of Magadha around 324 BC. His armies moved west and defeated the garrisons left by Alexander. Even further west they took control of Gujarat, in the east they took Bengal, and in the north, Chandragupta acquired the Greek conquests. He established an empire that reached the ocean to both the east and west, stretching from Afghanistan southwards all the

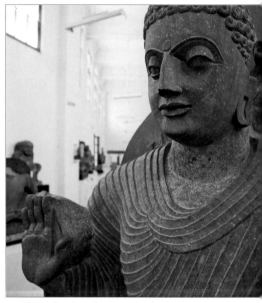

Buddha, Archaeological Museum, Mathura.

way to Karnataka, where it is said he passed his final days as a Jain monk.

The Mauryan Empire under Chandragupta and his successors was vastly different to anything that had gone before. The capital at Pataliputra (now Patna, the capital of Bihar) on the banks of the Ganges was 13km (8 miles) long, and surrounded by a wall with 570 towers. During this period, weights and measures were standardised, coins were minted, wages were fixed – from the highest officials to the lowest labourers – and remissions were given to those who opened up new land. The empire established and managed mines, shipbuilding yards and factories for arms. Visitors reported that it had an army of 600,000, with 30,000 cavalry and 9,000 elephants.

Emperor Ashoka

Chandragupta abdicated in 301 BC and was succeeded by his son, who in turn was followed by his son, Ashoka, the most famous ruler of ancient India. He inherited an empire that covered most of northern India, with the exception of Kalinga (modern-day Odisha), and ruled from 269 to 232 BC. This Ashoka conquered, but the sight of battlefields littered with dead bodies so shocked him that

At the Indian Museum, Kolkata.

he renounced worldly ambition and became a convert to Buddhism. He had edicts, written in Brahmi, the first Indian script, carved on pillars throughout the empire, calling for wise government and a moral lifestyle, in accordance with the Buddha's teachings. However, Ashoka did sometimes resort to force to impose order, and his empire expanded; eventually he ruled from Kashmir to southern Karnataka, from what is now Bangladesh to Afghanistan. Pataliputra became what was probably the biggest city in the world at the time.

Ashoka travelled widely across his empire, ensuring that roads were lined with shady trees, wells dug, and that rest-houses for travellers were established. He forged contacts with

Around the time of Stonehenge, complex urban settlements existed in India, with fortifications, public buildings, granaries, baths, and separate areas for housing the better-off and the artisans.

many foreign countries, exchanging diplomatic missions with Syria, Egypt and the Greek kings. This period also saw the development of Buddhism, with missionaries despatched across the Subcontinent, and a flourishing of the arts, especially sculpture. Ashoka's mark on the country is best represented by his standard, surmounting one of his pillars at Sarnath – the four lions and the Wheel of Law that are now the symbols of India.

Such were Ashoka's powers of leadership that on his death in 232 BC, the Mauryan Empire went into a rapid decline. It was confined to Magadha, which it managed to rule until about 184 BC, when the last ruler was assassinated. However, the idea of an India united under enlightened rule would echo down to modern times.

The Gupta Empire

The second vast empire in Indian history emerged in the 4th century AD. It too covered a large part of South Asia, though not as large as the Mauryan Empire. This was the Gupta Empire, which ruled northern India from about AD 320 to AD 700. Orthodox Hinduism reasserted itself against the heretical sects that had sprung up, but Buddhists and Brahmins lived in peaceful coexistence. This was a time of considerable achievements in literature, science and the arts, during which exquisite sculptures, particularly of the Buddha, were carved. The playwright Kalidasa produced his great Sanskrit plays, including the masterpiece *Shakuntala*.

The Guptas opened up commerce with China and Southeast Asia, with ships sailing through the Straits of Malacca to Indonesia. It was not only Indian goods which were exported at this time; Hinduism and Buddhism spread east to places where they can be found today, like in Bali, and the large number of Buddhists who went to China were so successful that in 397 Buddhism became the state religion.

Feudal society

The Gupta era was a period of high cultural achievement, but there were also defects. The Guptas had a much less centralised administration than the Mauryans, and many decisions were taken locally. It became common to assign land, and the tax revenue from it, to Hindu priests, the Brahmins, or to provincial officials, which tended to put them outside central control; the owners had the right to as much as one-third or even half of the crop produced by the cultivators. These changes marked the beginnings of a feudal society. The position of women deteriorated, early and child marriages were advocated, while widows were urged to remain celibate. It was during this time that the religious self-immolation of widows, known as *sati*, began. The position of those at the bottom of society also deteriorated as laws were increasingly biased against the Shudras. The "untouchables" had to announce their arrival at the market in advance so that others could avoid them.

In the 5th century the now weakened Gupta Empire was attacked from the northwest by nomadic tribes from Central Asia, the Huns.

The South

The people of South India were Dravidians, speaking languages that bore no relationship to those of the north. It is presumed that they predate the arrival of the Aryans; little is known of their early history, but they were helped by the opening up of trade routes, by land and sea, to distant markets. They were fortunate in having produce, such as pearls and pepper, which was in great demand, bringing Romans to their ports, as well as traders from Southeast Asia and China. Although the region lacked the great flood plains of the north, the Dravidians developed sophisticated irrigation systems that boosted agricultural productivity, and with their wealth they developed advanced kingdoms.

The early trade links of southern India brought Christianity in to the 1st century. It is believed that St Thomas the Apostle arrived on the Kerala coast in AD 52 and on a second visit died in Tamil Nadu. In the 6th century, Christian missionaries from the Middle East made further conversions. The mechanism of how Vedic traditions and later Hindu rituals reached the south is disputed, but one theory is that they came on the trade routes. It is known that both Buddhism and Jainism had many adherents until the 7th century, but when the Pallava king transferred his patronage to Shavism, the worship of the Hindu god Shiva, the Hindus gained ground. The priestly caste of Brahmins became politically and culturally dominant, and the position of the lower castes, who were excluded from the temples, deteriorated further. In opposition, a separate Tamil cult of the Hindu gods arose that was followed by large numbers of the lower castes.

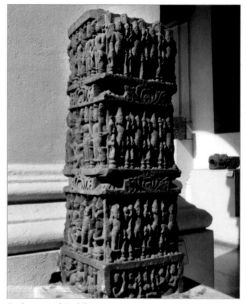

Sculpture and Buddhist stupa.

BUDDHISM AND JAINISM

As society grew, the division between rich and poor became more and more marked. In the 6th century BC, the stark contrast between the abject poverty of the masses and luxurious decadence of the few led two men, Buddha and Mahavira, the founder of Jainism, to seek answers to the question of why people suffer. Both men came upon the same ideas as answers; a moderate, balanced life would free one of greed and suffering. The philosophies of the Buddhists and Jains, preached in commonly spoken languages, won popular acceptance owing to their immediacy and practicality, and would profoundly affect the future history of India.

Arab traders brought Islam to what is now Kerala, and the first of many mosques were built in the 7th century. There was no conflict with the Hindus or Christians – a pattern of peaceful coexistence that was to continue.

The Sultanates

In the north the arrival of Islam was extremely violent. A Turkish Islamic dynasty had established itself at Ghazni in Afghanistan in the 10th century, and in 997, Mahmud of Ghazni started making annual raids into India. His own kingdom was a centre of culture, but his

The Iron Pillar, erected in Delhi in the 4th century, still stands today, upright and without trace of rust, evidence of the Gupta's considerable knowledge of metallurgy.

seen. A new state was established in 1206 which came to be known as the Delhi Sultanate; it would pass down through five dynasties and last for 320 years.

During the Sultanate the main tax was on the cultivators of the land, who usually had to give

The caves at Ajanta (2nd century BC).

armies looted, killed and raped without mercy. They made a point of attacking Hindu temples, taking their treasures and smashing their idols. Mahmud took possession of the Punjab, and further raids by other Muslim rulers followed. In the 12th century, Muhammad of Ghur took Lahore and Delhi, although the Rajput dynasties of north India never completely surrendered. Buddhist monasteries were attacked by the Muslims with such fervour that Buddhism was almost extinguished in India, the land of its birth. The first mosque in North India, the "Might of Islam" at the Qutb Minar in Delhi, was completed in 1198 and still stands. It was constructed from the remains of 27 Hindu and Jain temples, whose decorations can still be

THE GOLDEN AGE

The time of the Gupta Empire (from around AD 320 to 700) is referred to by some scholars as the Golden Age of India, akin to the Han and Tang dynasties and the Roman Empire, It was during the Gupta's reign that the classical Hindu temple emerged. Some of the finest examples still survive at Deogarh and Aihole. Temples were dedicated to the increasingly popular deities of Shiva and Vishnu; the goddesses Durga, Parvati and Lakshmi became generally worshipped. Animal sacrifice was largely discontinued, and meat-eating gave way to vegetarianism. It was at this time that the Buddhist caves at Ajanta were painted.

up half their crop. There was also a poll tax, the *jizya*, levied on non-Muslims, which meant that many people converted to Islam. In addition, thousands of those who were captured in the wars were enslaved and forcibly converted.

A series of rebellions led to the break-up of the Delhi Sultanate during the rule of Muhammad bin Tughlaq (from 1325–51). Bengal declared independence, and two new kingdoms were established in the south. A Muslim official set up an independent Bahmani kingdom, with its capital at Gulbarga, and the other kingdom was Vija yanagar.

(Tamburlaine) crossed the Indus river. Having already taken Baghdad and plundered much of Russia, he marched towards Delhi, destroying towns and taking 50,000 prisoners as slaves. At the battle for Delhi, Timur stampeded the enemy's elephants with burning bundles of grass tied to the backs of camels and buffaloes, and a rout ensued. Delhi was looted and burnt, while neighbouring rulers bought off invasion by sending tributes. Craftsmen were rounded up and packed off to embellish Timur's capital at Samarkand. A few days later, laden with booty, Timur began the journey home, leaving behind him devas-

The Qutb Minar, Delhi, built in the 13th century and still the tallest free-standing minaret in the world.

The founder of Vijayanagar was Harihara I, who ruled from 1336–57. He had converted to Islam so as to serve as a governor for the Delhi Sultanate. Sensing its weakness, he reconverted to Hinduism and set up a new empire with the help of Hindu warriors who had been forced south by the Sultanate. The empire expanded and was to last for 200 years. Proceeds from spices and cotton financed the construction of a spectacular capital at Hampi, whose ruins can still be seen today.

The arrival of the Mughals

The collapse of the Delhi Sultanate opened the way for a new force from the north. In 1398 a Mongol army under the command of Timur

tation and famine. It would be more than 100 years before the Mongols, or the Mughals as they became known, would return to Delhi.

Babur, the first of the Mughal emperors of India, was born in 1483. On his father's side he was descended from Timur, on his mother's from Jenghiz Khan. He was a petty prince in the empire assembled by Timur. Based in Kabul in Afghanistan, he acquired artillery and Turkish gunners and then marched into India with 12,000 men. They defeated the Sultan of Delhi's army at Panipat in 1526, and within a few days he occupied Delhi and Agra. The following year he defeated an army of Hindu princes from Rajasthan. He died at Agra in 1530 and was eventually buried at Kabul.

Akbar

It was during the reign of Babur's grand-son Akbar (1556–1605) that the basic institutions and policies of the empire were framed. A series of campaigns against the Hindu rulers of Rajasthan brought most of that province under Akbar's control, and despite all the bitter fighting, Akbar proved pragmatic in victory. He allowed the Hindu rulers to continue in power provided that they recognised his supremacy. To cement these ties he took several of their daughters as wives, and, unlike previous Muslim rul-

Vijayanagar ruins at Hampi.

ers, he allowed them to continue to practise Hinduism.

There were two categories of land in Akbar's empire. Some land was under the crown, which collected the tax on the peasants, while the rest was assigned to the empire's military and civil officials, for them to take the revenue in lieu of salary. The cultivator normally had to give one-third of his harvest, which was collected in cash at local prices. This system had been much abused in the past, but Akbar ensured that the official assessment was rarely exceeded. He also gave tax concessions to those who opened up new land, which considerably expanded production and the amount of revenue collected.

Despite having 300 wives, Akbar had produced no children. He visited a Sufi mystic at Fatehpur Sikri, 32km (20 miles) southwest of Agra, who predicted he would have three sons. When this was fulfilled, Akbar moved his capital there, building a magnificent palace.

Akbar used religion to consolidate his position, realising that any dynasty that wanted to rule India needed support from both Hindus and Muslims. In his numerous buildings at Fatehpur Sikri and Agra, there is an exquisite assimilation of Islamic and Hindu architectural styles. He abolished the *jizya*, the tax on non-Muslims, and he introduced Hindu festivals, such as Divali, to his court. In order to liberate himself from the Muslim clerics, Akbar made himself the arbiter of their disputes, and he began to move away from orthodox Islam. Searching for enlightenment, he discussed religion with Hindus, Jains, Zoroastrians and Jews, and even with Portuguese priests.

Although only semi-literate, Akbar was fascinated by books. He commissioned a comprehensive history of his reign, and everything that occurred in his court was recorded in minute detail. He had works in Sanskrit and Latin translated, and many books were finely illustrated. A synthesis of Persian and Hindu painting produced exquisite illuminated manuscripts.

A keen interest in the arts was characteristic of the Mughal Empire. Akbar's son and grand-son, Jahangir and Shah Jahan, are notable for their extensive patronage of the arts and architecture. Shah Jahan's fame rests on the creation of the Taj Mahal, built in memory of his queen

MUGHAL EMPIRE

The time of the great Mughals was a time of great art, poetry and architecture. Akbar managed to establish religious tolerance, although other Mughals were not so benign. The central fault of the empire was in its administration of the land. Many officials took everything they could from the peasants, and when they died their wealth reverted to the emperor. While technology was transforming the outside world, the Indian economy stagnated, drained by Aurangzeb's endless military campaigns in the Deccan, and by the inexorable rise of the British East India Company in the eighteenth century.

> The Sultanates introduced new styles of architecture: minarets, as at Qutb Minar; the perfect round dome on a square or rectangular base; and the true arch.

who had died giving birth to their 14th child. Other monuments left by Shah Jahan include the Red Fort and Jama Masjid in Delhi, which became his capital.

Shah Jahan did not share his grandfather Akbar's liberal religious policies. Although by

restrictions on the building of new Hindu temples. He reversed the policy of Akbar and reimposed the *jizya*. The last 26 years of Aurangzeb's long reign were largely spent on the battlefield. He invaded Rajasthan and destroyed the alliance with its Hindu rulers, and then fought a series of wars further south, trying to put down the Marathas led by Shivaji.

Aurangzeb died in 1707. His long absence from the bulk of his empire in the north led to serious administrative failure, and the Mughal Empire collapsed. The emperors that succeeded Aurangzeb became little more than ciphers.

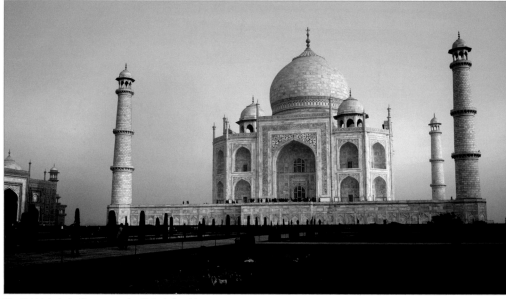

The Taj Mahal, the finest example of Mughal architecture.

birth he was three-quarters Hindu, he took no Hindu wives, he ordered the destruction of all new Hindu temples, and demolished Christian churches at Lahore and Agra.

Aurangzeb

Aurangzeb, an ultra-orthodox Muslim and the third of Shah Jahan's four surviving sons, came to the throne after imprisoning his father and killing his brothers. The deposed Shah Jahan remained confined until his death eight years later, and was buried next to his wife in the Taj Mahal.

Aurangzeb ruled India for 48 years, imposing an austere regime. He banned music, took no interest in literature, and imposed orthodox

MUGHAL EMPEROR AKBAR

The greatest Mughal is said to have been Akbar, who inherited the throne in 1556 when barely in his teens and went on to rule for 49 years and build an empire that lasted two centuries more. He controlled virtually all of North and Central India and most of Afghanistan. Akbar became a patron of literature and the arts, even though he was illiterate. He had 300 wives and 5,000 concubines. Rajputs were permitted to keep their kingdoms and in turn they happily supplied soldiers to this Mughal overlord. Akbar received ambassadors from Elizabethan England and Jesuit priests from Portugal, and synthesised a new religion with himself as God King.

Engraving from 1842 depicting the pampered life of Anglo-Indians.

EUROPEANS IN INDIA

Of all the Europeans who came to trade in India, it was the British who ruled, making the Subcontinent the 'jewel in the crown' of their empire. Successive campaigns finally led to Indian independence in 1947.

By the time the last great Mughal leader Aurangzeb died in 1707, the Europeans were well established in India. It was the Portuguese who were the first to begin trading when, in 1498, the explorer Vasco da Gama landed at Calicut, having sailed via the Cape of Good Hope. He arrived in Malabar (Kerala) looking for a mythical Christian empire and for spices, particularly pepper, which were in great demand in Europe.

Knowing that the island of Goa had an excellent harbour, the Portuguese set about conquering it, the first annexation of Indian territory by a European power since that of Alexander the Great. Throughout the 16th century the Portuguese managed to send valuable cargoes back to Europe and to construct impressive buildings in India. There were at least 50 major Portuguese forts in India and many minor fortifications.

It wasn't long before other European countries followed Portugal's lead and took advantage of India's commerce; in the 17th century, England, France, the Netherlands and Denmark floated East India Companies. Chartered as trading companies by their respective governments, they sought chiefly Indian textiles – silk, cotton and indigo.

The Dutch and English soon emerged as the dominant European powers, however, as both countries had developed navies

Vasco de Gama.

which could outfight the clumsy Portuguese galleons.

English merchants

The East India Company established by English merchants in 1600 was to be strictly for peaceful trade; having obtained a royal charter to pursue their ambitions in the East, the merchants had guns on their ships only for defence against European and other rivals. A major reason for the company's success was its policy of religious tolerance, attracting skilled artisans and merchants from all communities. Slowly but surely the English company expanded, and many Indian rulers allowed it to establish trading posts, including those at Chennai and

> *The Portuguese introduced many plants to India from the New World, including pineapples, papaya, prickly pears, passion fruit, cashew nuts, cassava, maize and even chillies. The first known reference to them in India is in 1604.*

Kolkata. In 1662 the English king Charles II married a Portuguese princess and, as part of her dowry, received the islands of Mumbai, which were transferred to the company. Indian textiles became the fashion in England, and by the end of the century they had far overtaken spices as the company's main source of income.

The Portuguese were defeated in the Far East by the Dutch and constantly attacked by them on the high seas. This pushed the Portuguese into a decline in India, which was accelerated by their attempts to maintain too many forts and garrisons. The Dutch then returned to

Viewing an elephant fight.

India and captured the Portuguese bases in the south, including that at Kochi. The Portuguese holed up in Goa, which fell into decay. The Dutch themselves became involved in wars with Indian rulers, and the expense of these forced them to scale down their operations. With the Portuguese and Dutch both being eclipsed it seemed that, at the dawn of the 18th century, England (or Britain as it would become after the Union with Scotland of 1707) was in the ascendant.

British conquest

The Dutch soon shifted their focus to Indonesia, and the Portuguese were no longer a significant threat; the real contest was between

The beginning of the 19th century saw a huge increase in British control over India. The East India Company gradually became an organisation that governed much of India for Britain.

the English and the French. It was in Bengal that the English made the first successful bid for rule in India. In 1757 and again in 1765 they defeated the Bengal ruler. This was made easier by the vacuum left after the disintegration of the Mughal Empire that followed the death of Aurangzeb.

There were successful wars against the Marathas and the Sikhs, and the Punjab and a number of other states were annexed. In other places, particularly in Rajasthan and Hyderabad, treaties with local rulers took away many of their powers. A huge army, comprised mostly of Indians, facilitated this expansion, and by 1850 most of India was either directly or indirectly under British rule.

A new system of administration was put into place, which has remained largely unaltered to this day. Each district was put under the charge of a 'collector' (of taxes), who was answerable to the governor of the province. There was a separate police service and an independent judicial system was created.

The British made fundamental changes to the ownership of land. Previously, although the right to part of the revenue from crops had been asserted by the state or its assignees, the owner of the land had been the peasant cultivator. The British, seeing similarities between those who took the tax revenue and large landlords in Britain, changed the system. The person who had collected the tax became the legal owner of the land, and was responsible for paying the tax to the government. The peasant became a tenant who paid part of his crop to the landlord. This new system left the peasant at the mercy of the landlord, and resulted in many of the new landlords defaulting on their tax, and being forced to sell. Much land passed from the control of local families to merchants and bankers in the cities, who were only interested in extracting the maximum return from their investment. The new landlords became enthusiastic supporters of British rule. Slavery was abolished in India in 1843, but many of the peasants were little more than serfs, bought and sold with the land. Unscrupulous moneylenders also reduced many to debt-bondage.

Anglo-Indian culture

Kolkata (Calcutta) was the British capital in India. It also became the centre of what came to be known as the Hindu Renaissance, where an Anglo-Indian synthesis of culture grew up. Hindu College, where the Kolkata intelligentsia sent their sons, was founded in 1816, and two

and higher courts. Ambitious Indians, who wanted jobs in the civil service or in the British companies that were coming to India, realised that English was the key to advancement. In 1857 the universities of Delhi, Chennai and Kolkata were founded.

The economy

Under British rule there was considerable development of the Indian economy. Large-scale irrigation was used to great effect, particularly in the Punjab, and raw cotton and jute became major exports. But the most profitable crop

Depiction of hunting tigers around 1800.

years later the city boasted India's first public library. There was a keen desire among many of India's elite, in the south as well as the north, to learn more about Western science and culture, and to learn English. In 1835 the Company decided to make English the medium for the education it financed; English replaced Persian as the official language of the administration

> Many blamed the East India Company for the Uprising, and the administration of India passed directly to the British crown. The Governor-General became the British Queen's Viceroy.

was opium. The East India Company needed something to export to China to pay for the tea it was exporting from there to Britain, and opium, although illegal, was much in demand. The Company encouraged the planting of the poppy in India, and the crop was bought by the East India Company for auction in Calcutta and onward transmission to China. By 1838 India was exporting 4 million pounds of opium a year; it had become the world's most valuable trade commodity.

The Uprising

In the 1850s a series of events in North India came together to cause an uprising against the British. A new rifle was issued to the army which required the soldiers to bite off the end of the cartridges before loading. A rumour spread that the cartridges had been coated with fat from cows and pigs, which alienated both the Hindu and the Muslim soldiers. When they refused to load their rifles with the new cartridges they were expelled from the army, without pay or pension, and left to walk back to their faraway villages. On 10 May 1857 soldiers at Meerut, near Delhi, mutinied; they freed their comrades who had been shackled for disobedience, and killed several British officers. Then they headed for Delhi.

Queen Victoria, "Empress of India".

At Delhi, the Indian soldiers threw open the gates for their comrades and then joined the revolt, which spread quickly through northern and central India. It was a bitter fight, with bloodshed and violence on both sides, and the outcome did not favour India. The mutiny failed, and peace was declared on 8 July 1858.

In victory the British showed no mercy. The roads were lined with gallows, from which hung some mutineers but many innocents, and whole villages were destroyed. In some respects the Uprising was not too serious; it had been confined to a relatively small area of North India, and southern India was completely unaffected. Many rulers in the north, who had no love for the Mughals, had stayed loyal to the

British, and some had even fought for them. Nevertheless, it had profound and long-lasting repercussions. Parliament in Britain was appalled at the events.

The psychological legacy of the Uprising was lasting. The mutiny produced a sense of unity between the Hindus and the Muslims, and the British never really trusted the Indians again. They made sure that, in future, large numbers of troops from Britain were always on hand. Many Indians, too, were scarred by the events; defeat and retribution had stirred resentment.

The British Raj

The British policy of gradually absorbing the independent states came to a halt. The rajas and nawabs had their treaties confirmed, and became, in most cases, fervent supporters of British rule. In 1876 Queen Victoria was proclaimed Empress of India, and the following year an Imperial Assemblage was staged at Delhi, where India's hereditary rulers came to pay homage to the British viceroy. In all, 84,000 Indians guests came to pay their respects.

This pageant coincided with a famine that claimed at least 5 million lives. There had been famines in India before the British arrived, but the supposedly superior British rule did nothing to check them, and there had never been a shortage of food across the whole country. The problem was that those whose crops had been ruined by drought no longer had money to purchase anything to eat. Camps were set up for some victims, who received food in exchange for work on public projects, but huge numbers died. Well-meaning British officials at local

INDIA'S RAILWAYS

In order to capture the vast Indian market, the British recognised that transport had to be developed. Steamships started navigating Indian rivers and roads were improved, but it was the railways that really boosted the economy. The first few miles of railway line were laid before the Uprising, and by the end of the 19th century there were 40,000km (25,000 miles) of track. Industries like coal mining could take advantage of cheap and efficient transport to expand. What really spurred expansion of the rail network, however, was the cotton crisis in America after the Civil War, which fuelled a boom in Indian exports.

level often did their best to alleviate hardship, but they were powerless against the ruthless indifference of the hierarchy.

Improved communications

Better roads, river steamers, railways, the telegraph and the post produced great changes, and the opening of the Suez Canal in 1869 put India closer to the markets of the West. Mumbai became one of the world's busiest ports. The first telegraph line and postal service opened in 1854, and prices were kept low. Those who had gone off to the expanding cities could now

Political activity

In 1883 a bill was introduced that would have made it possible for a European to be tried by one of the few Indian magistrates or judges. This provoked uproar among the British community, who held meetings and ran newspaper advertisements proclaiming that 'niger nativeswere' not the equal of Britons. As a result of this, they managed to have the bill watered down. Educated Indians, and some supporters among the British, had united in the battle to save the bill. One of these, Allan Octavian Hume, a retired mem-

East India Company cavalry at Queen Victoria's Golden Jubilee, 1887.

afford to keep in touch with their families. The villages, where the vast majority of Indians resided, became significantly less isolated.

From the great Uprising to the end of the 19th century the British tightened their hold on India. Revenue that came from agricultural and commercial expansion was used to expand the army and civil service. One hugely successful crop planted around this time was tea. When the East India Company's monopoly of trade between Britain and China came to an end it planted up experimental tea plantations in India. The success of these led to British companies planting up vast acreages, mostly in Assam and Bengal. By the 1890s India was exporting more tea than China.

ber of the Indian Civil Service, wrote to Kolkata University graduates proposing that an umbrella organisation be set up to protect Indian interests, and the Indian National Congress had its first meeting in Mumbai in 1885. This organisation became the vehicle for the new middle class to make their grievances felt. Congress urged that 'the basis of the Government should be widened and that the people should have the proper and legitimate share in it.'

A quarter of India's revenue was used to cover the 'home charges' – the money that was sent back to Britain to pay for recruitment costs, pensions and the interest on loans. A sharp rise in home charges coincided with

At the beginning of the 20th century, 90 percent of India's cloth came from Britain. Cheap imports from Lancashire, boosted when the Indian government removed import duty, had largely destroyed the livelihood of India's weavers.

a series of poor monsoons and famine. Grain had been exported to meet the cost of the home charges, which left insufficient for famine relief. Millions died.

Gandhi with Nehru in 1946.

The Independence movement

In 1905 the government implemented a measure that galvanised Indian public opinion. Without any consultation, it decided to partition Bengal. Supposedly this was to improve the administration, but Indians did not believe this. The division of Bengal would create an eastern half, merged with Assam, where Muslims would be in a majority. The western half of Bengal would be Hindu but would have a majority of non-Bengali-speakers. The Bengali-speakers from Kolkata, who were proponents of Indian nationalism, would lose their power. It was seen as a part of a deliberate British policy of divide and rule.

There were mass protests all over Bengal, and Congress took up the cause across India.

Petitions attracted innumerable signatures, but the government refused to give way. In demonstrations in Kolkata, bonfires were made of imported British cloth. The government broke up demonstrations using excessive force, but the movement spread across the country, and Congress became a major political force.

The division of Bengal had other political consequences. The Muslims in eastern Bengal were happy to be running their affairs free from the politicians of Kolkata, and a new capital was established at Dacca. A university for Muslims had already been established in 1875 at Aligarh, between Agra and Delhi. The Muslims of eastern Bengal combined with those at Aligarh and others from further south to ask the viceroy for Muslim representation on any official council. The viceroy was sympathetic to this, and in 1906, only a year after the partition of Bengal, Muslim delegates from across India met in Dacca to found the All-India Muslim League. Initially, the League was largely composed of nobility and landowners, and was generally pro-British. Many other Muslims still supported Congress.

To appease Bengalis for Kolkata's loss of status, Bengal was reunited, and the success in reversing government policy on Bengal boosted Congress. The Muslim League became less conservative. Both organisations were now calling for self-government within the British Empire.

World War I

When war broke out in 1914, the viceroy told India that it, too, was at war. Somewhat surprisingly, all factions in India offered their loyalty. Congress imagined that their support, followed by victory for the British, would bring self-government. The Indian contribution to Britain's war effort was very substantial, with 1 million going overseas and Indian troops fighting in many battles. The British exported large quantities of wheat out of India, which inflated the price within the country and caused much hardship.

The end of World War I did not bring the benefits hoped for by Congress. There was a small increase in democratic representation,

No Indian was allowed to rise to an officer's position in the army until after 1910. Indians could compete for high civil service jobs, but few were successful.

but this was more than counterbalanced by the extension of the wartime state of emergency and press censorship. A flu epidemic that claimed 12 million lives strengthened disillusionment with British rule.

The Gandhi era

During the war two Indian lawyers had come to prominence in Indian politics, Jinnah and Gandhi. Muhammad Ali Jinnah (known officially as Quaid-e-Azam in Pakistan) was born into a wealthy Gujarati family in 1875. He went to London to study law and, aged only 19, qualified as a barrister. Returning to India, he became a successful lawyer, joined Congress and was a member of the government's legislative council, expounding ideas of Muslim-Hindu unity. He joined the Muslim League, was elected its president in 1916 and masterminded a pact to act jointly with Congress. Jinnah believed in a constitutional approach to achieving self-rule, putting him at odds with Gandhi.

Mohandas Karamchand Gandhi was born in Gujarat in 1869. He had travelled to Britain, been called to the Bar, and then gone to South

Many Indian soldiers fought in World War I; this is a training exercise in southern England.

M.K. GANDHI

Mohandas Karamchand Gandhi (1869–1948) was a British-trained lawyer and a radical proponent of non-violence, pioneering mass civil disobedience as a form of protest. He was the spiritual leader of the Indian Independence movement,

Born in Porbander, Gujarat, 1869, he left Mumbai in 1893 for South Africa to work as a lawyer, where he became involved in the struggle for workers' rights. In 1915 he returned to his homeland and became involved in the movement for Indian self-rule, assuming leadership of the Indian Congress Party in 1921. Gandhi revived the hunger strike as a potent political protest, and his passive resistance tactics inspired freedom movements worldwide. While arch enemy Winston Churchill dubbed him 'that half-naked fakir', his followers called him 'Mahatma' (Great Soul), though many preferred 'Bapu' (Little Father). An ascetic, he preferred village to urban life and adopted the villagers' dress of dhoti and shawl. Gandhi led a Salt March in 1930 in defiance of British tax demands. In 1947 he negotiated an end to 190 years of British colonial rule. The following year he was assassinated at the age of 78 by a Hindu nationalist who objected to his continued religious tolerance, following the savage communal violence that accompanied Partition. Gandhi's birthday, 2 October, is a national holiday in India.

Africa, where he championed equality. When he returned to live in India in 1915 he was given an enthusiastic reception, and in 1917 won his first victory when he defended the peasants of Bihar against their oppression by European indigo-planters. The following year he led a successful campaign for higher wages in the cotton mills at Ahmadabad. Gandhi believed that non-violent protest would achieve self-government.

In 1919 Gandhi urged Indians to protest against the post-war restrictions on political action. Defying laws frequently led him into

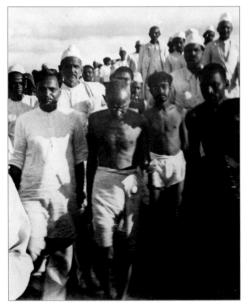

Gandhi's salt protest.

prison, but Gandhi always imposed one inviolable condition – that civil disobedience must be completely peaceful. In a march in 1919 in the Punjab, British troops opened fire and killed several marchers, after which General Dyer banned all public gatherings. When 100,000 people gathered to celebrate a Hindu holiday in Jallianwala Bagh, General Dyer marched his troops in, closed off the exit, and without giving a warning ordered them to open fire. Four hundred Indians were killed and 1,200 wounded.

The government of India eventually decided that there had been "an error of judgment". Dyer was sent back to Britain, where he received a hero's welcome. The repercussions in India were enormous; millions of Indians who had

backed British rule now became committed nationalists, and Congress abandoned cooperation with the government to adopt Gandhi's policy of non-violent protest. Jinnah opposed Gandhi and resigned from Congress.

Salt protest

The Prince of Wales's visit to India in 1921 was met with protests and black flags, and subsequently, 20,000 activists were imprisoned. In 1930 Gandhi embarked on a new crusade that captured the imagination of the country and the world. The British had enforced a monopoly on the manufacture of salt, which they taxed. Gandhi led his followers from his ashram in Ahmedabad to Dandi on the coast in order symbolically to make salt from the sea. The government took no action. However, similar defiance of the salt laws across India brought thousands of arrests. Gandhi himself was arrested and imprisoned, as was the entire working committee of Congress.

In 1931 Gandhi was released from jail and invited to talks with the viceroy. Gandhi suspended non-cooperation, and was invited to a conference in London to discuss India's future. Immediately after his return to India, however, he was rearrested. Under a new viceroy, the government had decided to toughen its stance, and 80,000 Indians were jailed. Boycotts, protests and terrorism spread across India.

Success for Congress

In 1937 the government granted some provincial autonomy. All members of the legislative assemblies were to be elected, a property qualification gave 35 million men and women

> Gandhi put much effort into trying to abolish untouchability. An Act in 1933 to support this was only partly successful, and great prejudice against the Untouchables continues to the present day.

the vote, and there would be special representation for Muslims, Sikhs, Anglo-Indians, Europeans and the lowest castes. In the election Congress was victorious and formed ministries in most provinces. Jinnah proposed that the Muslim League and Congress should join forces. However, he stipulated that Congress must accept the League as the only voice of the Muslim community. As Congress had many Muslim members, his proposal was rejected. Some of the new Congress ministers seemed to favour their own Hindu community and this caused resentment among Muslims, who started to look towards the League for protection. There were voices calling for a separate Muslim province in northeastern India.

India at war

When World War II broke out in 1939, the viceroy declared that India was at war with arrests. Many Indians, however, supported the British in the war, and the Indian army grew ten-fold to around 2 million.

One of the worst episodes of British rule occurred during the war when, in 1943, there was a famine in Bengal. The war had cut off rice supplies from Burma and the military were stockpiling in case of invasion. These events caused a rumour that there was a shortage of food, which led to hoarding and price rises. The government was very slow to act, allowing the export of food from Bengal for some time and not providing sufficient food aid. At least 2 million died.

Quit India movement march, Mumbai, 1947.

Germany. Congress was appalled at the absence of any consultation and its provincial ministers all resigned. The Muslim League offered up thanks for deliverance from Congress 'oppression'. This marked the end of the dream of a united independent India.

Congress decided to oppose the war effort with non-violent protest, and Gandhi and 14,000 others were jailed. When Japan entered the war and captured Malaya and Singapore, the threat of India being invaded led the British to release Congress dissidents for talks. These came to nothing. In 1942, Gandhi launched the Quit India campaign in which he urged the British to leave India immediately. Demonstrations and violence led to 60,000

INDIAN NATIONAL ARMY

Subhas Chandra Bose had originally been in Congress but, as he believed in violent resistance to the British, broke away to lead his own party in Bengal. Bose escaped arrest in 1941 and managed to reach Berlin, where he received help from Hitler to beam anti-British broadcasts to India. He then went to Singapore by submarine. The Japanese helped him form an Indian National Army from the prisoners of war in order to liberate India; they reached northeast India but were repulsed. Most surrendered in Burma. Bose escaped and was probably killed in a plane crash in Taipei on 18 August 1945.

The Mountbattens on their way to the Constituent Assembly, August 1947.

INDEPENDENT INDIA

From independence to a burgeoning economy now competing on the world stage, India's democracy is a triumph in a land of multiple ethnic, religious and secessionist interests.

At the end of the war a Labour government came into power in Britain that was sympathetic to Indian Independence. New elections were held, and although Congress did well, the Muslim League took all the reserved Muslim seats. A trial of the captured Indian National Army officers, who had fought alongside Japan in the war, made them heroes and they received suspended sentences. Further anti-British sentiment was expressed in mutinies carried out by the Indian Navy and Air Force.

In 1946 more talks to devise a constitution ended in stalemate. Jinnah felt the Muslims were being marginalised by the British and Congress. He decided to abandon constitutional methods and resort to direct action. Muslim demonstrations in Kolkata degenerated into attacks on Hindus, and the Hindus retaliated. In three days 5,000 died, and the violence spread to other cities. The viceroy asked the Congress leader, Jawaharlal Nehru, to form an interim government. Nehru was born to a wealthy family in Allahabad and, after graduating from Cambridge University, he qualified as a barrister and rose to be president of Congress. Despite being a protégé of Gandhi, he was an atheist, and a pragmatic, capable administrator.

The new state of Pakistan

In February 1947 the British government announced that it would hand over power no later than June 1948. Lord Mountbatten, a man of great charm who was related to the British royal family, became Viceroy of India.

Mountbatten formed a close friendship with Nehru, but did not see eye to eye with Jinnah. The date of Independence was brought forward,

Lord Mountbatten announces Independence.

and the end of empire was accelerated with disastrous consequences. On 15 July 1947 it was announced that one month later Partition would create two independent countries, India and Pakistan. There was a frantic scramble to divide up all of the government's assets in proportion to the populations of the new countries – 82.5 percent to India, 17.5 percent to Pakistan. It was already clear that Pakistan would be itself divided into two provinces, West Pakistan and East Pakistan, separated by a thousand miles of Indian territory.

A British lawyer, Sir Cyril Radcliffe, who had never been to India, was charged with dividing the country – those areas with a Hindu majority to India, those with a Muslim majority to

Pakistan. On the borders of these zones there was terrible bloodshed as those of the majority religion tried to remove any possible ambiguity. Following Independence, a massive migration across the new border – of Muslims to Pakistan, Hindus and Sikhs to India created terrible violence on both sides, resulting in about half a million deaths. At least 10 million people changed countries.

Independent India

At midnight on 14 August 1947, Jawaharlal Nehru, India's first prime minister, had pro-

Indira Gandhi and her father, Nehru.

claimed independence. One of the first tasks for the new government was to force accession on a number of undecided Princely States. Most acceded peacefully. Hyderabad and Junagadh had Muslim rulers, but their populations were mostly Hindu. Both were eventually taken over by force. Kashmir was a largely Muslim state ruled by a Hindu. Hoping that he might retain an independent status, the maharaja prevaricated. Some Muslim peasants revolted against their Hindu landlords, and Muslims from Pakistan crossed into Kashmir to give them help. The maharaja then acceded to India and asked for assistance. Mountbatten stipulated that once order was re-established there should be a plebiscite to establish what the people

of Kashmir wanted. Fighting continued until Kashmir was split in two. A ceasefire in 1949 left Kashmir divided, as it still is.

Gandhi assassinated

Gandhi was appalled by the Hindu attacks on Muslims and the callous treatment by Congress of the refugees. To force a change of policy, he went on hunger strike. Hindu nationalists opposed Gandhi for his liberal views, and as Gandhi walked to his prayer platform, one of them opened fire and killed him. The shock brought the nation to its senses. Nehru was able to act against the extremists and impose order.

The new India was broadly Socialist during Nehru's many years as prime minister. The economy was directed from the centre through a series of five-year plans. Nehru managed to negotiate a non-aligned foreign policy, which enabled India to profit from the Cold War rivalry; both Western and Russian finance and technical assistance enabled India to industrialise. Major facilities were installed to manufacture steel, fertilisers and cement, and to build the power stations India needed. The increases in food production, however, were largely offset by large increases in the population. Although malnutrition was (and still is) common, there were none of the famines of the British period or its predecessors.

Jawaharlal Nehru died, while still prime minister, in 1964. Millions attended his funeral and mourned the loss of probably the most powerful and most loved ruler India had ever had. After his death there was a more collective

THE NEW CONSTITUTION

India became a republic on 26 January 1950, with a new constitution that stressed the secular nature of India and the equality of all its citizens. Although untouchability had been outlawed in the constitution, the position of the Dalit community was, after many centuries of discrimination, still notably inferior. Penalties were introduced to stop oppression, and a quota was established to give the Dalits representation in the legislatures and government service. Measures were also introduced to emancipate women. Child marriage was banned and Hindu women received the right to initiate divorce proceedings and inherit property.

rule by Congress, but this new leadership was almost immediately challenged by Pakistan.

Un-neighbourly relations

The civilian government here had been toppled in a military coup in 1958, and General Ayub Khan had become president. America saw him as a bulwark against Communism and gave Pakistan much military hardware. Pakistan had tried to reopen negotiations on Kashmir with India, but India had insisted that Pakistan vacate Kashmir first. Ill feeling between the two countries was exacerbated by Pakistan allying itself with China after India's defeat in the Indo-Chinese War.

Following Pakistan's foray into Gujarat in early 1965, a ceasefire brokered by the UN forced Pakistan's withdrawal. When Pakistani-trained guerrillas crossed into Indian Kashmir, India sent its troops across the demarcation line and so did Pakistan. The Indians, who had been receiving help from America since the war with China, were stronger, and their army almost reached Lahore. The Soviets arranged a summit meeting and a ceasefire, and both countries withdrew their armies.

Indira Gandhi

Nehru's daughter, Indira Gandhi (not related to Mahatma Gandhi), was a close companion and confidante of her father. She travelled widely with him, and her international connections were to prove useful later in her political career. After his death, she became Minister for Information and Broadcasting, which would prove to be beneficial experience. When she became prime minister in 1966, the monsoon had failed and the country was facing starvation. She flew to Washington and was able to secure from a sympathetic American government millions of tons of wheat and financial assistance.

Mrs Gandhi devalued the rupee to help exports. This, however, was interpreted as a manifestation of Congress's economic mismanagement. Faced with militant demands by Sikhs for a separate state, she split the old Punjab into a smaller Sikh-dominated Punjab and a Hindi-speaking Haryana. Many saw this as weakness and to add to these difficulties, there were strikes and food riots.

Indira Gandhi fought the old guard of the party to move to increasingly socialist policies.

She nationalised the banks and started the redistribution of agricultural land. She took away the privileges of the former rulers of the Princely States. In the election of 1971, with the slogan 'Eliminate Poverty', she won a sweeping victory.

India opposed American policy in Vietnam. The Americans resumed arms shipments to Pakistan and backed the new military ruler, Yahya Khan. India had refused to sign the Treaty on Nuclear Non-Proliferation and was producing plutonium. Meanwhile, the relationship between West and East Pakistan

Muslim refugees cram onto a train bound for Pakistan from New Delhi in 1947 following Partition.

was deteriorating. The Bengali-speaking East was ruled by the army and bureaucrats of the Urdu-speaking West. A clampdown on politicians and dissent in the East was supported by the Americans. In March 1971, the people in the East took to the streets to demand freedom. The West Pakistan army then killed thousands of East Pakistanis as it restored control. By the end of the year 10 million refugees had fled to India.

New challenges for Mrs Gandhi

The centralised economy was hugely bureaucratic and corrupt. Rampant inflation, which destroyed people's savings, also fuelled discontent. In Bihar, J.P. Narayan led a coalition against the government; in Gujarat, Morarji Desai led the attack on the corrupt state government of Congress. Mrs Gandhi was dealt a severe blow when the High Court ruled that she had been guilty of electoral malpractice. Next day it was announced that Morarji Desai had defeated Congress in the Gujarat elections. He and J.P. Narayan joined forces to urge anti-government protests and disobedience. Mrs Gandhi then declared a state of emergency. Desai, Narayan and many thousands of politicians, student activists, lawyers and journalists were arrested and jailed.

Mrs Gandhi initiated a drive against corruption and inefficiency. A good monsoon helped bring down the price of food. The banning of strikes raised industrial production. Business leaders were sympathetic to the authoritarian regime and boosted investment. In 1977 Mrs Gandhi felt confident enough to release her opponents and call an election. But Morarji Desai and J.P. Narayan revived their Janata Party and won a resounding victory. Desai became prime minister.

The Janata government was plagued with dissent and was ineffectual. Inflation rose again. Indira Gandhi fought a by-election and won. In January 1980, Mrs Gandhi became prime minister again, with a large majority.

Problems in Punjab

Indira Gandhi's administration was plagued by separatist insurrections. In the northeast seven tribally dominated states were engaged in violent protests against an influx of Bengalis. After many of the migrants were killed, Mrs Gandhi imposed martial law. The biggest threat to the central government, however, came from the Punjab, India's most affluent state. Jarnail Singh Bhindranwale, a fundamentalist who wanted a Sikh nation, became the Punjab's leader. In 1984, he and his armed followers took over the tower of the Golden Temple at Amritsar and resolved to stay until the state was given autonomy. Mrs Gandhi ordered in the army. In a two-day battle, Bhindranwale and thousands of Sikhs were killed. The Sikhs' holiest temple was badly damaged. Eighteen months later two of Indira Gandhi's Sikh bodyguards gunned her down. As news of Mrs Gandhi's death spread, Hindus took to the streets of Delhi, and thousands of Sikhs were killed.

Gandhi's successor

Mrs Gandhi had groomed her son, Sanjay, to follow her, but he had died four years earlier. The other son, Rajiv, had originally chosen to avoid politics, but he became politically active on his brother's demise. He was only 40 when he became prime minister. He called an immediate election, which he won by a huge majority. Rajiv Gandhi was a champion of new technology and modern management. He moved away from the Socialist policies of his mother. He removed many of the restrictions on business and relaxed the controls on

Harvest, Punjab, 1970. India benefited from the so-called "Green Revolution", bringing new, high-yield crops.

CREATION OF BANGLADESH

Hostilities between India and Pakistan began in December 1971. To counteract pressure from the Americans, who supported West Pakistan, India entered into a mutual defence treaty with the Soviet Union. India trained East Pakistani guerrillas and then invaded. The Pakistan air force attacked Indian airfields, after which India attacked West Pakistan as well as East Pakistan. Within a few days the Indians crushed the Pakistan army in the East and forced their surrender. East Pakistan then became independent Bangladesh. The new, smaller Pakistan was no longer a serious threat to India.

imports. Rajiv Gandhi also became involved in the efforts to stabilise the conflict in Sri Lanka.

Rajiv Gandhi came in on a promise to curb corruption. This was taken seriously by his Finance Minister, V.P. Singh, who was moved to defence when he began to probe too deeply. Singh uncovered signs of corruption at the highest level of Congress in the award of a massive contract to the Swedish company Bofors. He resigned to form the National Front party.

The election of 1989 brought the National Front to power in a coalition with a small majority, with V.P. Singh as prime minister. This administration had a short but important tenure. Singh went to the Golden Temple and apologised for the attack in 1984, which led to an easing of the confrontation with the Sikhs, and also withdrew the peacekeeping force in Sri Lanka. In Kashmir, however, heavy-handed interventions escalated the conflict. Singh also introduced legislation to reserve a proportion of government jobs for the lower-caste Hindus who had been historically disadvantaged, and this had a considerable long-term effect on social mobility.

Rajiv Gandhi was assassinated by a Tamil woman suicide bomber in 1991. Elections then brought Congress back to power under Prime Minister P.V. Narasimha Rao. The Indian stock exchange was opened to foreigners and foreign capital poured in; industrial production and exports grew rapidly, although the benefits did not percolate down to the poor. Meanwhile, Rao's government was perceived to be engaged in widespread corruption.

Ayodhya and the rise of the BJP

In 1992 a group of Hindu zealots destroyed a 16th-century mosque at Ayodhya, which they claimed had been built on the site of an important Hindu temple. Riots and curfews spread across India. Next year a series of bombs were set off in Mumbai that killed 250 people. This attack was widely seen as a reprisal for Ayodhya. Reprisals were, in turn, made against Muslims.

The BJP (Bharatiya Janata Party), was able to take advantage of the sectarian unrest. Founded in 1980, the party was the political arm of a group of Hindu right-wing organisations that championed the idea of Hindutva, a Hindu homeland. In the 1996 elections, no party had

an overall majority, but the BJP secured the most seats. The BJP leader Atal Bihari Vajpayee put together a coalition, but it lasted barely two weeks, and was replaced by a Socialist-led coalition under H.D. Deve Gowda and, later, Inder Kumar Gujural. Gujural was able and honest, but the warring factions in his coalition made decisive government impossible.

In 1998 the BJP did well in the elections and Vajpayee became prime minister again. The opening up of the economy to foreign companies proceeded apace, but the BJP's rather extreme form of Hindu nationalism meant

Indira Gandhi, election campaign, 1971.

that national scientific and cultural institutions were purged of those who did not follow the Hindutva line, and school textbooks were rewritten to promote their interpretation of history. Meanwhile, violence against Hindus led to anti-Muslim riots across Gujarat. About 2,000 Muslims were killed and 150,000 fled to refugee camps.

Relations with Pakistan were growing more strained. After the Indian government authorised nuclear tests in the Thar Desert, Pakistan detonated its own bomb. Pakistan had managed to infiltrate remote areas of Kashmir for several months before India noticed, and it required the loss of 1,000 Indian soldiers to eject them. In 2001 an attack by terrorists on the Indian parliament, thought to have been backed by Pakistan, brought the two countries close to nuclear war.

The return of Congress

The press assumed that the election of 2004 would return the BJP to power. The party campaigned on the slogan 'India Shining.' It was true that the upper segments of society had never had it so good, but the poor had seen very little improvement in their lives, and voted accordingly. A Congress-led alliance won power. The leader of the

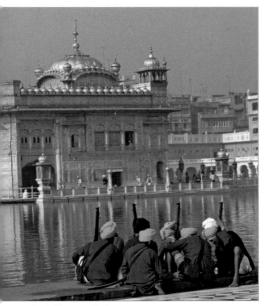

The Golden Temple siege, 1984.

Congress was the widow of Rajiv Gandhi, Sonia Gandhi. Italian-born and Catholic, she would have been unacceptable to many. She therefore decided to exercise her influence from behind the scenes and nominated the ex-Finance Minister, Manmohan Singh, to lead the country – India's first Sikh prime minister. There was a swift improvement in relations with Pakistan.

The economy continued to grow strongly. By 2007 India had the fourth-largest number of dollar billionaires in the world, although the global economic slowdown of 2007–10, while affecting India less than other countries, took its toll, with GDP down 1 percent at the lowest point. The economy has since recovered and is predicted to maintain its meteoric growth rate of at least 7 percent for some time; it's now ranked as the 11th-biggest economy in the world. Crucially, and almost uniquely in Asia, this growth is largely fuelled by domestic consumption, whereas Japan, China and the 'Asian tigers' have all largely relied on export-based growth. India is expected to overtake China as the world's most populous country within two decades.

The Left parties in the ruling coalition were able to modify the neo-liberal economic policies of Congress, and more money was allocated for the poor, although economic inequality is still a major cause for concern. In 2008, around 300 million of the population of 1.2 billion was living in abject poverty, although this represents a decline in percentage terms, and the figure has remained at 25 percent since then. As the largely urban middle class continues to expand, the rural poor are being left ever further behind. A champion of this cause is Rahul Gandhi, son of Congress premier Sonia Gandhi and a scion of this famous political family. His prime minister-elect status, although refuted by the man himself, was recently acknowledged by current prime minister, Manmohan Singh.

Terrorist attacks

The relative calm that had prevailed since the attacks on the parliament building in Delhi was shattered at the end of 2008 when a series of bombings by Islamist militants, took place across northern India, including several at Delhi markets.

STATE OF THE PARTIES

The political kaleidoscope of India is forever changing, creating unlikely patterns and alliances. Parties include the Congress (Indira), which still plays on the Nehru legacy; the Bharatiya Janata Party (BJP), Hindu nationalists; the Left Front, a coalition of parties, including the Communist Party of India and the Communist Party of India (Marxist); and the Samajwadi Party, representing the low castes and Muslims. Regional parties include the Sikh activists, Akali Dal; two Dravidian parties in Tamil Nadu, the AIADMK and their rivals, the DMK; the Telugu Desam Party from Andhra Pradesh; and the Hindu and Maratha extremist Shiv Sena, based in Mumbai.

This new wave of violence was to break even more dramatically into the news across the world when a group of ten Islamic suicide attackers arrived by hijacked trawler in Mumbai and started randomly shooting people in the streets, railway stations and hospitals. Two luxury hotels, including the famous Taj Mahal Palace, were besieged and set on fire. 'Black Cat' commandos eventually liberated the buildings and killed the Islamists, but not before the eventual death toll had reached 173. India was left reeling from these attacks on such high-profile targets, and security was stepped up across the country.

In April 2009, over 400 million people cast their votes in the country's general election, resulting in an unexpected triumph for the Congress Party.

Meanwhile, in the wake of 104 civilian deaths in a period of two months in Kashmir, concerted attempts were made to calm a population on the brink of full-scale uprising. The much-loathed shoot-to-kill powers granted the Indian army were repealed, and since then the political situation has been calmer than it has for decades. Even the British Foreign Office finally agreed to modify its advice not to travel to the region, spurring a tourist boom. August 2010 saw the long-awaited verdict in the Ayodhya dispute, which had been ongoing since 1992. In the end, the three parties involved were each given a third of the disputed site, a resolution which seemed at least to pacify the situation.

Earlier in the year, Delhi had hosted the Commonwealth Games – an event marred by the failure of the Indian government to complete the sporting facilities on schedule. The red faces got even redder when it emerged the reason for the debacle was that an estimated $4billion of public money had been embezzled during the run up to the games – a revelation that surprised no one in a country whose population has grown increasingly frustrated and angry at the ineptitude and dishonesty of its politicians.

The following year, a 74-year-old anti-corruption activist named Ana Hazare became a rallying point for the nation's fury when he staged a series of hunger strikes in New Delhi to protest at the abuses of power perpetrated by India's elected representatives. Numerous high-profile scandals only fuelled the flames, and the protests quickly coalesced into a mass movement.

In 2012, the anti-corruption lobby was momentarily upstaged by a march involving hundreds of thousands of landless poor aimed at drawing attention to rural poverty. A report published shortly after highlighted the scale of the problem: despite boasting 5–9 percent growth in annual GDP, an estimated 40 percent of Indian children suffer from malnutrition. The country may be on the rise economically, but it holds a gradually increasing number of the world's poor – a situation

Pakistan's ex-president Musharraf and M. Singh.

Prime Minister Manmohan Singh described as 'a national shame'.

Another source of shame in modern India is the generally poor status of women, and in particularly the country's poor record with sexual crime – a fact highlighted in December 2012 when a young medical student was gang raped on a night bus in Delhi. She subsequently died of injuries sustained in the attack, which prompted a national outcry against the lack of seriousness and vigour with which rape cases are prosecuted by the Indian police. Mass demonstrations were organized in the capital as the country once again found itself in the international spotlight – for all the wrong reasons.

A devotee at a Hindu temple in the
Kalbadevi neighbourhood of
Mumbai.

A young Indian family.

CONTEMPORARY ISSUES

Although India has seen record rates of growth in the past few years, it still faces huge problems of illiteracy, poverty and vast disparities in wealth.

Contemporary India can be bewildering, a place of extremes shot through with contradictions and seemingly changing from week to week. Visitors seeking to negotiate this phenomenally complex country may well find much of what they see makes them uneasy. The juxtapositions of extreme wealth and appalling poverty alongside a liberated young middle class and levels of social repression rarely encountered in the West make a visit to India at once fascinating, challenging, frustrating and disturbing.

Money and power

Full-blown capitalism is a recent arrival in India. While the country has always had strong mercantile instincts – the Gujaratis in particular are famed for their trading prowess – for many years after Independence the economy followed a nominally state-controlled pattern of development. This was put in place by the socially minded Nehru, whose dream was to see state ownership, industrialisation and an 'India first' policy – indigenous production and consumption coupled with protectionist import policies. He also pushed for universal literacy and education, as well as land reform and a redistribution of wealth. In these he was far less successful, and subsequent governments have done little to improve India's record on human development and sanitation.

Recent commentators have tended to denigrate the industrial legacy of Nehru, but they often fail to take into account that at the time of Independence India was in a less than flourishing state; there was hardly any indigenous industry, and literacy rates were exceptionally low. As part of a move towards an increasingly service-based economy, much effort has

Dehusking rice, a labour-intensive process.

GOING FOR GROWTH

One of the reasons that India has fared better than most during the recent global economic meltdown was that as businesses in the West looked to tighten their belts, India's highly qualified, but low-salaried workforce became difficult to ignore. Initially seen as a call-centre-based industry, today, from medical reports to pharmaceutical research to IT, India has emerged as a leading player for back office work/outsourcing. Even so, falls in agricultural and manufacturing output, and a widening of the fiscal deficit in 2011–12, have seen India's seemingly unstoppable growth in GDP plummet from 10 percent in 2010 to 5 percent in 2012.

> *It was Nehru who was largely responsible for pushing through the post-Independence programme of industrialisation, famously claiming that large dams were the 'temples of modern India'.*

been expended since the 1990s undoing the structures put in place by post-Independence Congress governments.

Nonetheless, Nehru's radical solutions to the economic difficulties and fragmented nature

A commuter in Chennai.

of India's post-colonial society created the very industrial base that many are now so keen to see privatised. The literate workforce from India's universities that is supposed to take over more service-industry jobs from the West (examples are software industries, some legal positions and call centre work) is, in part, the product of Nehru's progressive education policies.

At a governmental level, a huge programme of 'disinvestment' (privatisation) has recently been put in place, and inward investment has greatly increased, largely to the benefit of the much-lauded Indian middle class. At the same time, attitudes to social welfare have hardened among policy-makers, with large tax breaks given to the well-off, while the nation's poor

become increasingly marginalised in both the political and economic debate. So far the 'trickle down' of wealth has not materialised, and the disparity in income between rich and poor has widened.

One of the most significant problems that stand in the way of Indian development goals is corruption, which is well entrenched at all levels of society. Despite the high profile of campaigns led by hunger striker Ana Hazare in 2011–12, it is hard to see this disappearing in a country where so much depends on favours and connections, and where members of parliament can continue to hold their seat even if they are convicted of a crime and sent to prison.

The middle class and the poor

While caste has traditionally been the dominant organising principle of Indian society, as the country begins to go through what appears to be a period of considerable change, other structures of social organisation are emerging that run both in parallel with and across caste boundaries. At the heart of this change lies the much-vaunted Indian middle class.

This hard-to-quantify group continues to receive a huge amount of attention in the Western press, blamed for, amongst other things – due to its increasing consumption of material goods – world food shortages and the increase in the demand for oil. Untangling the myth from the reality can be difficult. While there is no absolute measure of who exactly comprise the Indian middle class (a very broad category that covers a wide range of people, including larger rural landowners, civil servants, managers

LITERACY

One in three of the world's illiterate people live in India; a staggering number, and a trend that looks set to continue. Only around 48 percent of girls are enrolled in primary education, and for these there is a 10 percent drop-out rate. According to the government, overall literacy is at about 74 percent. However, the government measure is set very low, with many people being functionally illiterate. Kerala, has the highest literacy rate at around 94 percent, Bihar, the lowest, at 63. Investment in education and campaigns to promote literacy by the Keralan government, as against widespread corruption in Bihar, account for the disparity.

and the super-rich), the best guesses seem to be around 250 million people, or just over 20 percent of the population. From this is it possible to calculate a breakdown by class for the rest of the India's many people.

> While India's super-rich indulge themselves in buying teams in the flashy new Indian Premier League cricket competition, many of their compatriots are still sleeping on the streets or dying of malnutrition.

in recent years, economic liberalisation and the expansion of a consuming class.

Many of those living below the World Bank definition of a poverty line might be classed as 'employed', but underemployment remains a serious issue. These include railway workers, factory workers, small landowners and tenant farmers amongst others; while their lives are not as desperate as those who can barely survive, they too have yet to see any real improvement in their lives from India's recent economic progress. Indeed, in rural areas many small-scale famers have been facing ruin through crop failures and debt.

The new India: Hyderabad's 'Cyber City'.

Around one third of India's 1.2 billion people live below the country's official poverty line. This equates to more impoverished people in absolute terms than exist in all of sub-Saharan Africa.

It is not surprising, then, that many – especially children – still suffer from malnutrition, while the country as a whole is a net exporter of food. In addition, India has a comparable infant mortality rate to neighbouring – and much poorer – Bangladesh. Sanitation is an ongoing concern, with much of the rural population still not having access to potable water supplies. Little has been done for this desperate group, as economic policies have tended to concentrate on either large-scale state-owned enterprises or,

Other indicators of public well-being do nothing to brighten the gloomy picture. According to the UN, less than 50 percent of the population have access to essential drugs and there is a chronic shortage of health facilities (in rural India there are only 50 hospital beds per 100,000 people; in the UK there are around 390).

Only 30 percent of people have access to adequate sanitation, and according to the UN, as many as 2.1 million children die before the age of 5 every year – that's one every four minutes – because of malnutrition.

Child labour also continues. While the government figures asserts that there are around 20 million child labourers in India,

All statistics relating to India should be seen as rough estimates; the concept of a national census in a country of this size and complexity is mind-boggling at best.

NGOs, including the International Labor Organization, insist the true figure is probably closer 60 million (with some estimates ranging upwards of 100 million. A huge amount of these are 'bonded', effectively a form of slavery.

(Marxist) sent in the police and cadres from the party to break up the demonstration, resulting in the deaths of up to 50 villagers. There were reports of rape and torture to break the resistance, and at least 3,500 people were forcibly displaced. In this case the state government came under intense scrutiny and pressure and the project was moved to another area. However, people continue to lose their lands and homes as the policy is followed across the country.

As elsewhere, cars are a sign of wealth and status in India, but although it might not seem so from the polluted and congested roads, only

Pupils at a prestigious school.

A sign of India's recent advance into the ranks of technologically advanced nations can be seen in its space program. An unmanned moon mission launched in 2008.

The government has embarked on creating a series of 'special economic zones' (SEZs) as an incentive for investment. This has entailed a huge land grab, with millions being displaced with little or no compensation. In 2007, in supposedly communist-run West Bengal, villagers in Nandigram protested against the allocation of their lands to form a SEZ for a chemical company. The ruling Communist Party of India

15 per thousand people actually own one (as opposed to 526 in the UK, or 809 in the US). This is projected to rise sharply over the next few years, especially following the launch of the world's cheapest new car, the Nano, in 2008.

The 'creamy layer'

Those who are left at the top of the pile are the middle class, known in India as the 'creamy layer'. By no means a homogeneous grouping, they are best identified by their ability to consume, and this increasingly means desirable Western consumer goods. The bulk of the Indian middle class is made up of those who have traditionally occupied the role. These include lower-level civil servants, shop owners and larger farmers. They might have a small car, or almost certainly a 'two-wheeler' (motorbike or scooter), and basic consumer items such as a fridge and a TV. This group has tended to retain traditional ways of thinking and dressing but has seen its capacity to consume increase.

Those most visible on the streets of the large cities are the aspiring young. It is these educated 20- and 30-year-olds who present the glamorous face of contemporary India. They work in service industries such as IT, PR or in call centres, earning around 10,000 rupees upwards per month. They dress fashionably, shopping in new air-conditioned malls, own cars and two-wheelers and drink and smoke in chic bars.

However, not all is what it seems: for all their apparent modern worldliness, the vast majority of this group follow traditional paths: they are likely to live at home with their parents, and follow their wishes in whom they will marry, and much of their consumption is based on credit (now easily available in India). Most people in this income bracket who own a car or other expensive items calculate their monthly salary as a system of units, a certain number of which are already spent (through paying off loans on items or for cash) before they actually get the cash in their hands. This represents a large social shift, with the middle class traditionally having been wary of debt and now, to a certain extent, selling off the family silver to finance their new lifestyles.

At the very top of the heap are the policy-makers: top managers, politicians and civil servants, who can comfortably afford their large houses and cars. These are eclipsed by an even more select few, the super-rich. These industrialists and film stars are some of the wealthiest people on the planet, such as the chairman of Reliance Industries, Mukesh Ambani, the nineteenth-richest man in the world, the controversial steel magnate Lakshmi Mittal (the twenty-first richest), and Azim Premiji, chairman of software giant Wipro.

The political challenge

The greatest challenge facing India's politicians is to reduce the gap between rich and poor, and in so doing, stave off social unrest (already rife in some parts of the country, particularly the 'Naxalite belt' of Central India) in the face of such startling inequalities.

On current showing, this is not something with which they are having much success. The UPA government's rural job-guarantee scheme (promising 100 days' paid work to all workers in rural areas) was lauded as a huge step forward when launched in 2006, but has been beset with problems – not the least of which is corruption.

The major parties, however, may be facing the results of their decades of inaction as regional low-caste parties continue to gather support. Currently the most prominent of these is the Bahujan Samaj Party (BSP), whose

At the Taj Hotel Club in Hyderabad.

former leader, the charismatic Dalit spokeswoman, Mayawati, served as chief minister of India's most populous state, Uttar Pradesh until 2012. Her coalition of the low castes, Muslims and impoverished Brahman families remains a potent force in Indian politics, with a power base spreading across neighbouring states. Currently sitting in the Upper House of the Indian parliament, the Rajya Sabha, Mayawati is hotly tipped to be India's first Dalit prime minister.

The temple and the bomb

Alongside the socialist policies put forward after Independence by leaders such as Nehru, secularisation and, to borrow a government slogan of the time, 'unity through diversity' were also encouraged. These liberal ideas, however, have been under attack since the inception of modern India. While a disturbing political phenomenon of recent years has been the rise of the chauvinistic religious right, the movement's roots lie much further back in the country's political history.

This rise of the religious right has been dubbed 'saffronisation' after the colour associated with high-caste Hinduism, and its moment of arrival, and defining point in modern Indian history, was seen by many as the destruction of

Worshippers at a Kolkata mosque.

the Babri Masjid (mosque) in Ayodhya in 1992. This was the culmination of a process leading back to the Independence struggle.

Anti-Muslim riots at Partition saw the prominent Congressmen Sardar Vallabhai Patel, India's first Home Minister, and Rajendra Prasad call for the withdrawal of protection for Muslim citizens and the sacking of Muslim civil servants. However, the cause of Hindu nationalism suffered a severe setback when Gandhi, who preached tolerance, was assassinated by Nathuram Ghose, a Marathi Brahman with links to the RSS (Rashtriya Swayamsevak Sangh, a hard-line Hindu nationalist organisation). This gave Nehru the chance to outlaw communalist organisations,

thus burying the ambitions of the Hindu right for the next two decades.

It was Nehru's daughter, Indira Gandhi, who next indulged in communal politics. Although she declared allegiance to the secular ideals of her father, she actively courted Hindu support by surrounding herself with Hindu holy men and being seen to participate in Hindu rituals, particularly after her defeat in 1977 by a coalition government, which included a fledgling BJP (Bharatiya Janata Party).

The flirtation of Congress with communal politics (not only Hindu but also, with more immediately disastrous consequences, Sikh separatism in the Punjab) broke the taboo that had existed since Mahatma Gandhi's assassination, and the 1980s saw a steady rise in support for overtly communal parties, aided by disillusionment with the corruption-ridden Congress.

The main challenger was the BJP, led by veteran politician L.K. Advani (currently leader of the right-wing opposition in the Lok Sabha), formed out of the Janata Party of the late 1970s and with close links to the RSS and Sangh Parivar (a collection of right-wing Hindu groups). They campaigned on a high-caste, right-wing agenda, espousing the ideal of Hindutva, a Hindu homeland.

The BJP got its first taste of power in 1989 as part of the coalition government of V.P. Singh. This did not last for long. Advani started to campaign for the destruction of the Babri Masjid, which Hindus were claiming was built on the site of Rama's birthplace and of an earlier temple. He embarked on a countrywide *yatra* (pilgrimage) to raise support for the building of a new temple, culminating in a visit to the site at Ayodhya itself. Advani was arrested and the government fell. However, the campaign continued to gather support, and in 1992 hundreds of *kar sevaks* (Hindu volunteers) tore down the mosque. This led to some of the worst communal rioting India has ever seen, in which many Muslims and Hindus were killed, particularly in Mumbai. In 2002, Hindu extremist mobs in Gujarat killed and displaced thousands of Muslims in a frenzy of violence that erupted after a lethal fire started on a train of Hindu pilgrims. Numerous mosques and shrines have also been destroyed, allegedly with the connivance of the BJP-led state government. The BJP Chief Minister, Narendra Modi, was himself implicated in the carnage, after accusations that he expressly held back police so that rioters could kill and loot (accusations which were rebuffed in a subsequent government report). The darling of Gujarat's business community, Modi, however, continues to enjoy great popularity in his home state, where he has been Chief Minister since 2001. Having won convincingly the state elections of 2012, he is set to be catapulted to the leadership of the BJP, which will pose the main opposition to a fractured and unpopular Congress-led coalition in national elections of 2013–14. The man much reviled by Indian liberals for his auto-

Christians, too, have been set upon by Hindu militants – as in Odisha (Orissa) in 2008. The unholy alliance between reactionary, right-wing Hinduism as espoused by the BJP and economic liberalisation remained in opposition after the elections of 2009, which were a triumph for Congress, but at the time of writing, in late 2012, looks poised to dominate the national government again.

Although at first neo-liberalism and a fantastical reworking of the religious past seem strange bedfellows, given the disruption neo-liberal policies cause to people's lives, religion

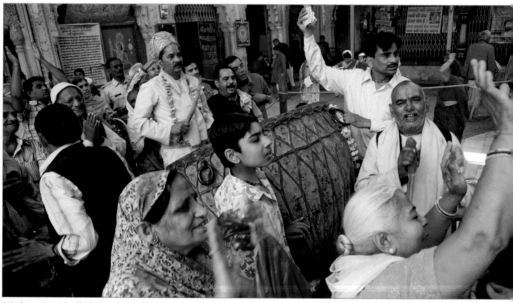

Hindus at Dwarkadhish Temple, Mathura.

cratic tendencies and connections with far-right Hindu organizations may thus be India's next prime minister, which explains the readiness in October 2012 of Britain's foreign office to break ranks with all other EU countries and the US and end a decade-old boycott on Modi and his political allies.

During its period in power between 1999 and 2004, BJP-led national government gave 'saffronisation' momentum. Religious minorities came under attack, and schoolbooks were rewritten glorifying India's mythological 'Aryan' past, describing *kar sevaks* as heroes and vilifying Islamic contributions to society. Long after the fall of the BJP-led government, attacks against Dalits and Muslims have continued, and

and an aggressive promotion of the national myth are useful tools for keeping the populace onside while state and national governments push through unpopular measures.

In an Indian context this saw an individualisation of Hindu identity, while at the same time there was an attempt to homogenise a highly disparate and eclectic group of beliefs and practices. Modern Hinduism, at least as promoted by the Sangh Parivar, is increasingly coming to resemble evangelical Christianity. An individual's relationship with a deity and personal observance of ritual, rather than action for the social good, are seen as the key to salvation. Thus, limiting consumption and displays of wealth in the face of deprivation is of less spiritual importance than, say, taking part in the building of a new temple to Ram at Ayodhya.

This move away from Gandhian ideals has been accompanied by a more canonical approach to the religious texts. Writings such as the *Vedas*, *Bhagavad Gita* and *Ramayana* have acquired the status of historical document rather than spiritual tract; they are statements of absolute fact, rather than guides towards universal truths that are open to interpretation. Modern right-wing Hinduism is far more interested in having a rigid rule book of rights and wrongs than in the traditional subtleties of reli-

from rival Pakistan that it too had successfully tested long range nuclear missiles. India, never a signatory of the Nuclear Test Ban Treaty, became a nuclear rogue state watched nervously each time tensions rose on the Line of Control separating Indian and Pakistan-controlled Kashmir.

Gaining a nuclear arsenal was integral to India's desire to become a major player on the world stage. It has ambitions to have a permanent seat at the UN Security Council and wields considerable clout in climate-change talks. Geopolitically, India is now being

Keralan school.

gious debate, which in the past made the Hindu world relatively inclusive and tolerant.

As with any insistence on the observance of a series of rules, minority viewpoints have suffered. In India this has had the most noticeable effect on the country's 100 million-plus Muslims. The national myth promoted by the BJP is fiercely anti-Islamic. For all the recent peace talks between the two countries, the external bogeyman has been largely identified as Pakistan, something reinforced by the murderous terrorist attacks in Mumbai in 2008.

All this was brought into sharp relief in 1998, when India tested a series of nuclear devices at Pokhran in the Thar Desert, followed only 15 days later by an announcement

courted by the US, which sees it as a strategic bulwark against the rising power of China. To this end, the US has proposed a nuclear cooperation deal that would unilaterally bring India in from the cold. Highly controversial, it is seen by many nations as fatally undermining the Nuclear Test Ban Treaty and has even been problematic on the domestic front. In 2008 the UPA government faced (and won) a vote of no-confidence when the Left parties, in this case supported by the opposition BJP, withdrew their support, fearing undue US interference in India's internal affairs. The deal was finally approved by the US Congress in October 2008, but continues to be contentious; in July 2009 India identified two sites on which US nuclear reactors could be built, but an August 2010 nuclear liability law passed by the Indian government has further stymied progress.

Gender issues

Womens' rights have crept up the political agenda in India, at least among the urban middle class. A huge outpouring of anger accompanied the news in December 2012 that a young female medical student had been gang raped on a moving bus in the city. Her subsequent death from injuries sustained in the attack, and mass demonstrations across the country at India's seeming inability to transform traditional attitudes to gender, have prompted a fervent national debate that, at the very least, look likely to improve the seriousness with which rape is regarded by the country's law enforcers.

But there is, of course, a long way to go. The dowry system is still thriving, and payments can reach into many hundreds of thousands of rupees. Inheritance and property rights are another area in which women are heavily discriminated against, and, as the country remains in thrall to traditional social roles, women face discrimination in the workplace, not least in terms of the salary they can expect to earn.

Greater wealth for the middle class has not necessarily led to positive social changes for women. The problem of female infanticide is on the increase, with some areas of the country now showing figures of fewer than 850 girls to every 1,000 boys. Some of the worst districts are in wealthy regions such as the Punjab, Haryana and Gujarat. Ironically, rising standards of living have increased the availability of foetal ultrasound screening and abortion to families. With an ongoing social and economic prejudice against having daughters, the gap in the male-female population ratio has increased. Overall in India there are about 40 million fewer women than men, and the overall female-to-male birth ratio has fallen to around 914

> The rate of female infanticide increases in proportion with wealth. Haryana, one of richest regions in the country, has only 846 girls per thousand boys – the worst child sex ratio in India.

girls to every 1,000 boys, with the trend getting worse, especially in the north.

As the lower castes begin to adopt the social mores of the rich and wealthy, aping their aspirational lifestyles, they are beginning to embrace the dowry system on a scale never seen before. So far from dying out (it is technically illegal), the system is becoming more widespread, and the demands on the bride's family are increasing to a ridiculous extent (asking for cars, foreign holidays and houses). This in turn puts even greater pressure on couples to produce a son, and as the practice of giving

Walking home from school in Chettinad, Tamil Nadu.

dowries spreads across the social spectrum, the fear is that there will be an even greater increase in the abortion of female foetuses and female infanticide.

On the other hand, it is true that in New Delhi, Mumbai and Bengaluru amongst other cities, young women are leading relatively free and independent lives, and wearing clothes that would not long ago have been considered 'immodest'. As with many things, middle-class women, with their access to education and health care, have seen their prospects and freedoms open up, while poorer women concern themselves with the struggle for survival. The vast majority of women all over India are still restricted to the domestic sphere.

FOOD AND DRINK

With its increasingly discerning restaurant clientele pushing the quality of what is on offer ever higher, India is now, more than ever, a genuinely world-class culinary destination.

The cuisines of India are as diverse as the country's culture. From the tandoori cooking of the north to the spicy curries of the south, every region has its own distinct flavours. North India tends to rely on a variety of breads, predominantly *rotis*, chappatis, *parathas* and naan, as a staple, whereas a southern meal is incomplete without rice. The sauces of the North tend to be pungently spiced, and feature either butter or ghee, clarified butter, in almost every dish, whereas southern dishes are lighter and tend to include coconut. A further defining feature of the northern kitchen, and unheard of in the South, is the *tandoor* oven, used to produce a range of *tandoori* dishes. History has also had a strong influence on Indian cuisine. The Mughal rulers left an enduring legacy; Mughlai cuisine, twinned with the flavours of the Punjab, has long dominated the dishes of the North. The Portuguese occupation of Goa also left its mark, with *vindaloo* perhaps the most famous Portuguese-Indian collaboration.

Nuts for sale at the Zaveri Bazaar in Mumbai.

Essential ingredients

Despite the regional variation, there are significant similarities, the most obvious being the use of spices, an integral part of Indian cuisine appreciated not only for flavour but also as appetite stimulators and digestives. Care is taken to ensure that the spices enhance rather than dominate the basic flavour. Traditionally, the ingredients in each meal were governed by the time of the year and classifications of heating or cooling foods, age, and even personality. Once there were also injunctions on the six *rasas* or flavours to be included in every meal: sweet, salty, bitter, astringent, sour and pungent. Each was believed to have its particular physical benefit and was prescribed in specific ratio to the others.

ANGLO-INDIAN CUISINE

Visitors coming to India having had Indian cuisine in restaurants at home may be surprised to discover just how different the real thing is. A simple explanation for this is that the majority of what pass for 'Indian' restaurants abroad are, in fact, Bangladeshi, meaning they serve a cuisine similar in style to that found in the Indian state of West Bengal but markedly different to that found elsewhere in the country. An added surprise is that many of the staples of 'Anglo-Indian' cuisine, *phal* and *balti* for example, simply don't exist in India, and even if they do, generally bear no resemblance to their namesakes elsewhere.

Other than spices, the important ingredients in Indian cuisine include milk and milk products, particularly ghee and *dahi* (curd or yoghurt). Served to mitigate the chilli 'hotness' of some dishes, *dahi* is often mixed with vegetables or fruit and is lightly spiced to create the *raitas* of the north and the *pachadis* of the south. It's also churned and served in summer as lassi, a cooling drink.

Dals (split lentils) are common to most parts of the country. Regional preferences and availability have resulted in a bewildering variety, from the thick tamarind-flavoured *sambars* of

Samosa with lime.

the south and the sweetish dals of Gujarat to the delicious *makhani dal* of North India.

Vegetarian variety

The style of vegetable cooking is determined by the cereal or main dish with which they are served. Deep-fried vegetable crisps are perfect accessories to the *sambar* and rice of Tamil Nadu. The thick *avial* stew of Kerala cooked in coconut oil, or the *kaottu* in a coconut and gram sauce, are perfect for rice-based meals. *Sarson ka sag*, mustard greens, eaten with *maki ki roti* (maize bread), are a particular favourite in the Punjab, while the delicately flavoured *chorchori* of Bengal complements Bengal's rice and fish.

> To the orthodox Indian, a meal is 'pure' only if cooked in ghee (clarified butter), an emphasis that derives not just from its distinctive fullness and unique flavour but from its preservative qualities.

India presents a vast range of vegetarian cooking. The roasted and steamed food of the south is lighter than northern cooking. Rice is the basis of every meal. It is served with *sambar*, *rasam* (a thin peppery soup), vegetables, both dry and in a sauce, and *pachadi*. Coconut is used in cooked foods as well as chutneys. Made of fermented rice and *dal* batter, the *dosa*, *vada* and *idli* are South Indian snacks popular all over the country.

The semolina-based *upma*, cooked with curry leaves and garnished with nuts and copra, is another favourite. Other in-between bites found everywhere are the *samosa*, a three-cornered deep-fried pastry parcel with potatoes, and *pakoras* or *bhajiyas* – vegetables coated in a gram batter and deep-fried. In Gujarat, another region famous for its vegetarian food, gram flour is used in bread-making and as a component of various dishes.

Kadi, made from *dahi* and gram with spices, is popular. *Gur* or *jaggery* (unrefined sugar) adds a hint of sweetness to piquant sauces, as does *am rasa*, the puréed pulp of mangoes eaten with *puris*.

Although Bengali food is never sweetened, it is customary to serve a sweet along with the other food as a foil to the hot chillies, or for

SOUTHERN MEALS

Meals in the south revolve around rice, which comes in two forms: 'white' and 'red' (the latter being par-boiled before it's dried so that the grain absorbs the goodness of the husk. Rice is eaten with *dal*-based soups, thin, sour rasams and the thicker *sambars*, which are often flavoured with tamarind. To these are added 'sambar powder', made up of spices such as coriander and *methi* (fenugreek) seeds. Often they are finished by 'tempering'; chillies and whole spices are heated in oil until the important black mustard seeds 'pop', then poured on the top of the dish. Dry vegetable dishes are also served with rice, with curd (yoghurt) and fiery pickles.

a change in flavour. Possibly the 'purest' form of North Indian vegetarian food is the Banarsi. Lightly spiced, many specialities are based on *panir* (soft cheese). A good source of protein, it is cooked in innumerable ways, with spinach (*palak panir*), in a gravy with peas (*matter panir*) or lotus seeds (*panir phulmakhana*).

Then there are the deep-fried or stuffed breads, made of combinations of refined and wholemeal flour; the golden puffs called *puris*, the *parathas*, *baturas* and so on. Most widely eaten is the simple chapatti, baked on a griddle.

Meat and fish delicacies

Muslim influence is most evident in the cooking of meats. The major contribution was the *tandoor*, the conical earthen oven from which emerged a delectable array of *kababs* and *rotis*. This was the origin of the famous *tandoori* cooking including *tandoori* chicken and fish, *seekh*, *boti* and *barra kababs*. Among the *rotis* are the *naan*, the *tandoori roti*, and its richer equivalent, the *tandoori paratha*.

The fastidious Mughals transformed local recipes, developing what has become known as Mughlai cuisine, with its luscious sauces of *dahi*, cream and crushed nuts. An amazing variety is on offer, including: the rich *kormas* and *nargisi koftas* (meatballs shaped around a hard-boiled egg) of Lucknow; the *pasandas* or mutton steaks cooked in an almond sauce; the biryani, a layered rice and meat concoction famous in Hyderabad; and a variety of *kababs* that literally melt in the mouth.

Laden with nuts, dried fruits and saffron, Kashmiri Muslim food is a gourmet's joy and has much in common with Persian food. *Haleem*, mutton pounded with wheat; *gaustaba*, incredibly light meatballs; and *rogan josh* are well-known Kashmiri specialities.

Vinegar lends a different taste to the meat dishes of Goa. Pork *sorpotel*, *vindaloo*, Goan sausages and chicken *shakuti* or *cafreal* are inimitable.

> *Ahimsa, or non-violence, is one of the central tenets of the Hindu faith, and by extension includes the practice of vegetarianism. The variety of vegetarian dishes readily available in India is perhaps unrivalled.*

> *In keeping with religious mandates, Gujarati (especially Jain) and Bengali vegetarian food is often cooked without the 'heating' or stimulating spices.*

Fish, too, is prepared in many ways: the mustard-flavoured *macher jhol* and *malai* or cream prawns of Bengal, the chilli-hot curries of Andhra, the coconut and curry-leaf flavoured specialities of the south and the memorable fish and shellfish curries of Goa. *Hilsa*, a

Indian sweets.

Bengali speciality, has spiky bones that support meltingly delicate flesh and requires careful chewing. Dried fish, misleadingly known as Bombay Duck, is cooked with vegetables or *dals* and adds interest to the simpler fare of Maharashtra.

The Parsis also contributed interesting dishes, like *dhansak*, meat cooked with five different *dals* and an unusual blend of spices, and *patrani machi*, lightly spiced fish steamed in banana leaves.

Chutneys and pickles, sweet, sour, hot, or all three, stimulate the appetite and add relish to a meal. Many ingredients can be used: mint, coriander, mango, ginger, lime and vegetables with extravagant spices or just salt.

Sweets

Often too sweet for the non-Indian palate, the huge array of Indian confections and desserts are largely milk-based. Bengal is particularly well known for its confections. These include the *rasagulla*, *sandesh*, *rasamalai* and the steaming hot *gulab-jamuns*. Typical of the north are the *barfis* (milk cakes), some of pure milk, others of coconut or various types of nuts. Crisp golden *jelabis*, dripping with syrup, made even in the tiniest bazaars all over the country, are breakfast and teatime favourites.

It is a combination of betel leaf, areca nut, catechu, cardamom, cloves and other fragrant ingredients.

Where to eat

Choosing where to eat can be a tricky business, with such a wide range of eateries, from street stalls to the swankiest restaurants, on offer. One solution is simply to follow the crowd; the most popular places tend to serve the tastiest and most hygienically prepared fare, although people's perceptions of 'tasty' may vary. The cheapest places – street stalls

Fish curry is ubiquitous in South India.

Common northern desserts include *kheer*, the Indian equivalent of rice pudding, usually flavoured with cardamom, saffron, pistachios, almonds, cashews or dried fruit; *shahi tukra*, a variation on bread pudding; *phirni*, made of powdered rice and served in earthenware bowls; and *kulfi*, a rich nutty ice cream. Sweets from the south include Mysore *pak* and the creamy *payasam*, while the Gujaratis are partial to *srikhand*, made of drained, sweetened and spiced *dahi*. *Halvas* are created from ingredients as diverse as carrots, semolina, *dals*, eggs or even wholemeal flour.

Finally, there is the satisfying ritual of the after-dinner *masala pan*, which is praised for its digestive and medicinal, if addictive, properties.

and the most basic restaurants – will typically have only a limited choice of dishes on offer: as often as not you get what you're given. Owners and staff are unlikely to speak English, or have menus, so be prepared either to point out what you want or to take it as it comes. *Thalis* in the North or *meals* in the South will generally include a variety of dishes, and are often replenished free of charge.

Next up would be the *dhaba*, or roadside restaurant. The most basic and traditional of these will double as truck stops, and often have only *charpois*, a wooden framed bed with a latticed cloth top, to sit on. They'll generally have a limited range of dishes, and while quality can vary, the food is often much better than the surroundings would suggest. More sophisticated examples of the *dhaba* now feature tables and chairs, menu cards in English, a wide range of dishes and overall can represent not only great value but a great eating experience as well.

Plush restaurants are becoming more and more common in the bigger cities, and often pride themselves on being 'multi-cuisine'. This typically means that Indian, Chinese and some Continental dishes will be on the menu, although all are likely to have at least an Indian twist to them. Five-star hotels tend to offer the finest dining experiences, with the whole range of international cuisines, from Thai to Mongolian to Italian and Lebanese, usually available in one or other of the best hotels in the biggest cities.

Water is about the only thing that most Indians would drink with a meal. Here again there are various categories; the cheapest restaurants are likely to serve only tap or well water, which should be strictly avoided. Next up is 'filter water', which is generally fine but quality will depend on the sophistication of the filter and regularity with which it has been maintained. The vast majority of bottled water in India is in fact 'filter water', but can generally be regarded as safe to drink, particularly if it comes from one of the nationwide brands. Top of the heap are the handful of genuine mineral waters on offer, distinguishable by their higher price and superior taste. The other drink which is taken with food is *lassi*, a yoghurt-based concoction famed for its cooling properties, useful in mitigating the effects of a hot, spicy meal. *Chai*, sweet, spicy, milky tea, is often served after a meal in the North, whereas coffee is the hot beverage of choice down South.

Cafés are becoming increasingly widespread, with several local, as well as one or two international, chains now operating in most major cities and towns. They have become very popular meeting places for both students and businesspeople, who often use them for activities as diverse as board meetings, interviews and matchmaking.

Soft drinks are available in all but the most remote locations and are generally safe; most of the popular local brands have now been either bought or eradicated by the major global companies.

India's relationship with alcohol is nothing if not complicated. Gujarat and Mizoram are the only officially dry states, with alcohol available to varying degrees everywhere else. Government-run 'English Wine & Beer Shops' are widespread, but vary significantly in what they offer. The 'English' has nothing to do with being from England, but instead denotes company-made alcohol, rather than local hooch. In smaller towns and villages, these shops will often serve hooch as well – locally made home brew that is responsible for hundreds of deaths every year and should be avoided at all costs,

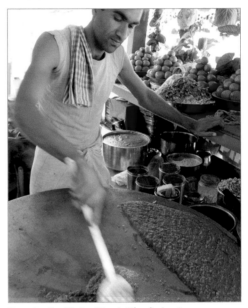

Preparing Pao Bhaji, a Mumbai fast food option.

despite the temptingly low cost. In all but the major cities these shops will offer a selection of Indian-made beers and liquors, often in quarter- or half-bottles intended for immediate consumption, making for something of a rowdy atmosphere come night-time. An increasingly wide range of well-priced international spirits is available in the big cities, although wine is still hard to come by despite some decent local produce. All restaurants technically require a liquor licence in order to serve alcohol. However, these are often expensive and/or difficult to obtain, meaning that many places will serve beer on the sly, often in mugs or teapots to disguise the contents in the event of a surprise police inspection.

FESTIVALS

India has a huge number of festivals throughout the year, from pan-Hindu celebrations to the appeasement of local deities and political parades.

Festivals are a part of daily life in India, perhaps an inevitability given the thousands of deities, saints, prophets and gurus who must be honoured. Myriad practices and an enormous body of legend and history bring an extensive range of significance to most Hindu religious occasions.

There are numerous local and regional festivals but the most important are celebrated nationwide. The first of the significant pan-Hindu festivals to occur after the monsoon is **Navaratri**, or 'nine nights' (September to October). This is a major celebration of the goddess Devi or Shakti in her more fearsome aspects. At the end of Navaratri comes the day of **Dussehra**, the celebration of Durga's victory over Mahisasura, the buffalo-demon.

Divali, also known as 'festival of light' (usually October to November), is both a celebration of Rama's return from exile and of the goddess Lakshmi. Following the spring festival of **Vasant** (when the goddess Sarasvati is worshipped in January to February) the next major celebration, aside from **Pongal** (the southern harvest festival also known as Sankranti), is Sivaratri, the Shiva festival in February or March. This is followed in North India by **Holi**, the North Indian harvest festival. The festival year comes full circle with **Janmastami**, the birthday of Krishna, and **Ganesh Chaturthi** in August/September.

The Maha Kumbha Mela at Allahabad, on the confluence of the Yamuna and Ganges rivers, is the largest religious gathering in the world. Kumbha Melas take place every three years, moving between Allahabad, the most important, and other sites at Haridwar, Ujjain and Nasik: each site hosts the festival every 12 years.

The North Indian springtime festival of Holi is a time of abandon and is celebrated by the throwing of coloured powders.

Brightly coloured powders can be found for sale during the Holi festival. The throwing of these powders symbolises the festival as a game that breaks down social conventions.

A statue of the Hindu god Lord Krishna.

NON-HINDU FESTIVALS

Islamic festivals occur throughout the year and range from major events to localised *urs* (the anniversary of a saint's death) held in *dargahs* (tombs) across the country. The most important of the pan-Islamic festivals are 'Eid-al-Fitr and 'Eid al-Adha, both dependent on the lunar calendar and so are moveable. The first celebrates the end of the fast of Ramadan and the second the end of the period of the Haj, or pilgrimage to Makkah (Mecca). The most important festival of Shia Muslims is Muharram, which mourns the matrydom of Hussain, the grandson of the Prophet.

The major festival of the Buddhist year is Buddha Jayanti, which takes place in April to May. It celebrates the birth of the Buddha and also his reaching of enlightenment. Jains commemorate a similar event at Dip Divali. This occurs 10 days after the Hindu festival of Divali and celebrates the liberation of the tirthankara Mahavira from the wheel of life.

Divali, the festival of lights, sees families set 'diyas', small oil lamps or candles, outside their doors to guide Rama back to Ayodhya and also to welcome Lakshmi into their homes, hopefully ensuring a prosperous year ahead.

Shivaratri, a festival held to honour the god Shiva's dance of creation that brought the world into being, and also his joining with his consort Parvati.

Each Hindu temple has a festival in honour of the deity it enshrines, often accompanied by processions, music and important pujas (acts of worship).

PERFORMING ARTS

From classical performances on the concert stage to brass bands playing at weddings, India's musical and dance traditions are many and varied.

India's performing arts permeate every aspect of society and culture, forming one of the richest complexes of music, dance and drama anywhere in the world. Perhaps most famous in the West for the classical music of northern India (also known as Hindustani music), there is also a separate, though related, classical tradition in the south (known as Karnatak music) and a myriad of separate local dance and theatre genres.

Hindustani and Karnatak music

The two classical music traditions of South Asia share certain common ideas and techniques, but in presentation, repertory and even instruments they are radically different. Broadly, the classical music culture of the north may be seen as a Muslim tradition, emerging from the Mughal courts. Indeed, many lineages of musicians (family and teaching pedigrees known as *gharanas*) trace their origins back to the famous performer Tansen who was employed at the court of Akbar (1556–1605).

In contrast, classical musicians in the south are overwhelmingly Hindu and trace their musical roots back to singer-saints of the 17th and 18th centuries. The three most famous of these (known as the 'musical trinity') are Tyagaraja (1767–1847), Syama Sastri (1772–1827) and Muttusvami Diksitar (1775–1835), whose compositions still form the backbone of the Karnatak repertoire.

Raga and tala

The works of these singer-saints also highlight a further difference between the two traditions. In general Hindustani music is improvised while Karnatak music is dependent on compositions (either written or passed

Musicians playing centa drums and ilatalam (cymbals) at a festival in Kerala.

POPULAR MUSIC

Until recently, popular music in India was dominated by film songs from Bollywood and South Indian movies. While this still forms the bulk of the popular music heard in the country, there is a small but steadily growing indigenous pop, rock and dance music scene, prompted in part by the arrival of MTV on Indian televisions. Largely based in the major cities, it has its greatest following among the newly wealthy young middle class. There are now several dozen indigenous rock bands, while on the dance scene *bhangra* is still popular, with many of the artists coming from NRI (non-Resident Indian) communities.

down orally). There are, however, two concepts that they share – *raga* and *tala*, the first dealing with the organisation of pitch, the second with the organisation of rhythm and musical time.

Ragas are collections of notes (like a Western scale) that have a particular musical 'flavour' (the word *raga* comes from the Sanskrit for 'colour') and which must be performed in a certain way. The names of *ragas*, particularly in the north, often refer to the 'piece' being performed. So, you might hear musicians say they are going to play *Yaman*, *Bhairav* or *Desh* (all popular Hindustani *ragas*). In the south the piece will take its name from the text of the music being performed, although that too will be composed in a specific *raga*.

Tala is used to describe the repeating rhythmic cells (measured by the number of beats) that give the performance a rhythmic form. In the West we are used to hearing music with four-beat units (most popular music) or three beats (like a waltz), but in India these can be much more complex, especially in the south, with repeating *talas* of five, seven and eight beats being common. This complexity increases as musicians employ techniques of doubling or tripling the speed of the music within the *tala*.

Genres and instruments

Indian classical music is dominated by two different vocal genres, *khayal* in the north and *kriti* in the south. While there are numerous other musical forms, these are the two you are most likely to hear performed in concerts. *Khayal* is said to have been invented by Sultan Husain Sharqi in the 15th century, and it comprises two short, contrasting compositions (known as a *bandish* or *ciz*) that are used as a vehicle for improvisation. There is also a short, unaccompanied introduction that presents the notes of the *raga* about to be played.

In the instrumental adaption of *khayal* now familiar to many in the West, the performer (usually on either the sitar or *sarod*, both plucked lutes) gives a longer introduction, an *alap*, adopted from the more austere

Vina player, Trivandrum, Kerala

DEVOTIONAL MUSIC

While all music in India is, at least theoretically, considered to be auspicious and so in some way devotional, there are certain types of performance that are used explicitly in praise of deities or in temples. Not restricted to Hindusim, there are songs from the Sikh holy book – the *Granth Sahib* – known as *kirtan*, and Muslim devotional songs known as *qawwali*.

The most widespread devotional form, however, that you are likely to encounter is the Hindu *bhajan*. This is a collective song form usually performed in temples. Often the text is limited to a repetition of the name of the deity being praised and the performance is usually of call-and-response singing. The standard accompaniment is a *dholak* (a small barrel drum), small pairs of cymbals (usually called *tal*) and a harmonium. While bhajan performances are generally given by groups of non-professional devotees, there are professional *bhajan* groups who have made numerous recordings and even a sub-genre of pop *bhajans* with a strong rhythmic beat.

Other music-making you may encounter in South Indian temples is the processional music of the *periyar melam*, an ensemble consisting of long oboes called *nagasvarams* and *tavils* (very loud barrel drums). In Kerala temple festivals often include performances by large ensembles of drummers.

– and highly valued – vocal genre *dhrupad*. This presents a highly worked-out presentation of the *raga*, introducing each note in turn. The instrumental version of the *bandish* or *ciz* that follows is known as a *gat*, and this too gives the basic material for further improvisation.

Both the vocal and instrumental performances are accompanied by a number of other performers. The most prominent of these is the tabla player, who keeps the tempo and marks the *tala* on a pair of small kettledrums. Also on stage will be a *tambura*, a

Local traditions

As well as its impressive classical musical heritage, India is also home to numerous local performance genres, many of which are intimately tied in with the wider functioning of South Asian society. Due to its inherently auspicious nature, music is used to mark calendrical festivals and rituals, such as the Ganapati *puja* or Holi, as well as being used in the worship of local deities. Weddings are one of the occasions that demand music, and there is a complex set of songs and processional music – usually performed by brass bands playing film songs – that

Young dancers of Mohiniattam, a classical dance from Kerala.

long lute a little like a four-string sitar that keeps a drone throughout the performance. At vocal performances you may also see either a *sarangi* (a short lute played with a bow) or a harmonium, that imitate the line of the soloist.

In the south the dominant form is the *kriti*. This is a devotional song form that grew out of the three-part *kirtana*. The composers of the 'musical trinity' developed the *kirtana* by adding a series of composed variations known as *sangati* to the form. *Kritis* are performed not only by singers but also on the *vina* (a large plucked lute) and sometimes the violin, now the most popular accompanying melodic instrument in South India.

forms part of the celebrations. These can make for quite a spectacle; visitors to the North during the auspicious winter months are likely to see a horse-mounted groom riding slowly down the road, followed by a quaintly uniformed, and singularly loud, brass band. Next in line will be the male wedding guests, all dancing to the beat blaring from speakers trundling along on home-made chariots towards the back of the procession, with a truck struggling along under the weight of a smoke-belching diesel generator bringing up the rear.

Classical dance

As with music, there are a huge number of dance forms in South Asia, some of them

The earliest textual source for South Asian performance traditions is the Natyasastra, thought to have been written by the sage Bharata around AD 150. In it he describes the practice of music, dance and theatre.

still undocumented. From these a select few have been identified as 'classical' dances – those with long and identifiable histories and with a body of laws *(sastras)* that govern their performance.

The style now known as *bharatanatyam* grew out of Tamil temple dance. The female dancers, called *devadasis*, would perform for the deity as part of temple rituals. Although the dancers were considered to be married to the deity, they were also taken as sexual partners by the temple priests or local king (the patron of the temple). This outraged Victorian sensibilities, and an 'anti-nautch campaign' (from the Sanskrit *naca* for dance) eventually led to the dancers being banned from temples in 1947.

At the same time a Brahman dancer and teacher, Rukmini Devi, sought to put elements of the dance on stage to promote an indigenous cultural identity in the run-up to Independence. It is this solo dance, accompanied by an ensemble of Karnatak music, that is now seen on the concert stage.

Another form of dance with a similar history is Odissi. This dance derives from the temple dancers at the Jagannath temple in Puri, Odisha (Orissa). In 1950, following the ban on temple dance, a group of scholars met to reinvent the tradition for performance on the stage, taking their ideas from temple sculpture and paintings.

The most popular classical dance in the north is *kathak*. Closely linked to the rise of Hindustani music at the North Indian courts – particularly the 'light' forms of *khayal*, *thumri* and *dadra* – it was traditionally danced by courtesans. The dance itself is characterised by fast pirouettes and rhythmic patterns created by the sound of the pellet bells worn around the dancers' ankles.

Dance-dramas and theatre

A slightly different form of performance is found in India's many dance-dramas. These use music and dance to tell a story, often one derived from the Hindu epics. One of the

most spectacular performances you are likely to encounter is of *kathakali*. In this male Keralan dance form the characters – from the *Ramayana* or *Mahabharata* – wear dramatic costumes and make-up. The different colours used in the make-up give the audience a clue as to the role of the character; green is good, red is evil and white is for deities.

Andhra Pradesh also has a traditionally male-only dance-drama, *kuchipudi*, which is named after the village in the Krishna-Godvari delta where it originated. The stories portrayed by the dancer are taken from the life of Krishna

A colourful Theyyam dancer in Bekal, Kerala.

and his consort Bhama.

As well as these classical dramas, there are many local theatre forms across India. In the north one of the more racy is the secular *nautanki*, unusual in that it only uses religious themes to denote concepts of good or evil and often draws on Muslim romance stories. In *nautanki* the actors use the drama to comment on current affairs, as they also do in the Tamil street theatre *terukkuttu*. More religiously-minded dramas performed at festivals are the *Ras* and *Ram lilas* of Braj and Varanasi that depict the lives of Krishna and Rama respectively, while both Kerala and Andhra Pradesh have shadow puppet theatres akin to those found in Indonesia.

CINEMA

In 1896, the Lumière Brothers' films were first shown in Mumbai; now India's film industry is even bigger than Hollywood, producing around 900 feature films a year.

Think of entertainment in India and you are bound to imagine the cinema. The biggest film industry in the world is character-ised by big blockbusters that incorporate love stories, action, violence and song-and-dance routines. Gaudy sets and set pieces inhabit an imaginary world of glamour with an at times eye-wateringly tasteless array of costumes. That, at least, is the popular perception.

While there is some truth in this characterisa-tion, the films are perhaps best seen as moral-ity plays – good versus evil plays a prominent part – that draw on some of the conventions of traditional Indian theatre. Also, in recent years, more nuanced films have explored tradition-ally grey areas of morality (such as affairs and divorce in *Kabhi Alvida Naa Kehna*) or idealistic notions of unity and difference, in *Amar, Akbar, Anthony, Chak De India* and *3 Idiots*.

Huge amounts of money are made and invested in the cinema, and there have long been accusations of Bollywood's connections with the Mumbai underworld, perhaps adding an extra frisson of glamour for its vast number of adoring fans.

Bollywood, Kollywood, Tollywood

India's mainstream blockbusters are made by the three main regional films industries, Hindi cinema (Bollywood) made in Mumbai, Tamil films (Kollywood) from Chennai, and Telugu movies (Tollywood) made in Hyderabad. While Bollywood is generally held to be the biggest film industry in the world, at times Telugu output has beaten the Hindi industry and, overall, South Indian cinema is more productive than that in the north. South Indian cinema has even given Bollywood some of its biggest stars, including

Poster advertising a Konkani movie in Goa.

FILM CITY

One of Asia's biggest studio complexes is just beyond the jaws of a fake shark that guards MGR Film City. This vast site on the outskirts of Chennai is funded by the state government. Here, 36 sets stand ready. Films are shot in Tamil and also dubbed into Malayalam, Telugu, Kannada and Hindi. Tourists are sometimes asked to be extras, especially on Raj-era films. Notable crossover successes into Bollywood include Sri Devi and Rekha. But the most powerful figure is Jayalalitha Jayaram, one-time starlet turned politician, who built the studio in memory of her lover M.G. Ramachandran, former chief minister and megastar.

Sri Devi, Aishwarya Rai and A.R. Rahman, who have all made the transition to Hindi movies. The South Indian industry has also given birth to a number of highly influential politicians: M.G. Ramachandran, M. Karunanidhi and Jayalitha in Tamil Nadu, N.T. Rao in Andhra.

The first silent film made in India was *Raja Harishchandra* (1913) filmed in Mumbai, followed in the south by Tamil Nadu's *Kicaka Vadam* in 1917. While these were popular and the industry grew considerably during the 1920s, it was not until the advent of the 'talkies' in 1931 that India's close and passionate affair with the movies began in earnest. These early films were quite racy, featuring plenty of flesh and kissing, and it was not until Independence in 1947 that a form of 'moral censorship' came into play. The banning of the on-screen kiss and physical contact between a film's lovers led to inventive ways around the problem, and a whole host of wet-sari scenes, suggestive dances around trees and just-in-time fades.

Until the 1970s most films were romances, and the on-screen loves of stars such as Nargis and Sunil Dutt (who became real-life lovers after starring in *Mother India*, 1957), and Madhubala and Raj Kapoor were all-consuming topics of discussion among their many fans. This changed in the 1970s with the arrival of a new generation of actors, including Amitabh Bachchan. His appearance in the 1975 mega-hit *Sholay* ushered in an era of action movies, dubbed 'Curry Westerns' in homage to the Italian movies that inspired them.

While Sholay played on an appetite for violence, the 1990s saw the rebirth of the family drama and romance. Films such as *Hum Aapke Hain Hum*, *Raja Hindustani* and *Maine Pyar Kiya* managed the difficult task of promoting traditional family values while chaste but scantily clad actresses and muscle-bound heros flirted and revelled in material excess. In Bollywood the superstars of the period included Karisma Kapoor and Madhuri Dixit as well as Salman, Shah Rukh and Amir Khan. In the south, Rajnikant and Simran Bagga shot to fame. Today, Shah Rukh Khan is the King of Bollywood and Rajnikant has near-godlike status in the South.

Film music

The popular music of India par excellence is film song *(filmi git)*. It is heard almost everywhere, from shops and the backs of rickshaws to temples

playing songs from devotional films (known as 'mythologicals'), as well as in the cinema itself. The first Indian 'talkie' was *Alam Ara*, made in Mumbai in 1931. Based in some respects on traditional Indian theatre, the plot was broken up by songs and dances that pushed the action forward and represented the passing of time. Not only were these early films extremely popular, but so were the songs associated with them, and the first pan-Indian form of popular music was born.

In the early films the actors and actresses sang themselves, but when recording technology allowed the songs to be dubbed in

Anil Kapoor is well known internationally for his roles in '24' and 'Slumdog Millionaire'.

the late 1930s most film music became prerecorded. It was at this point that specialist 'playback singers' began their rise to superstardom. The biggest of these was, and continues to be, Lata Mangeshkar. Along with her sister Asha Bhosle and Geeta Dutt, her high-pitched voice has come to represent the ideal female vocal style. Of course the heroine had to have a hero, and the male singers Muhammad Rafi and Mukesh became as idolised as Lata and Asha.

The composers who write the songs, known as 'music directors', command huge payments and are almost as famous as the singers. While early music directors based their songs on traditional Muslim genres such as *ghazal* and *thumri*, soon composers such as the duo Shanker-Jaikishan, S.D. Burman and the brothers Kalyanji Anandji were bringing ever more eclectic influences to bear on the music. These ranged from *bhajans* to jazz and Latin music to Western pop and rock.

Particularly influential were Western film scores like that for the Blaxploitation movie *Shaft* or the TV series *Mission Impossible*. Contemporary music directors, such as A.R. Rahman, are now global names, their music having spread through extensive NRI (non-resident Indian) communities or, in the case of Rahman, making it onto London's West End stage via his musical *Bollywood Dreams* and into Western cinemas via his soundtrack for *Slumdog Millionaire*, for which he won an Oscar.

The New Wave

After Independence some film-makers were not drawn by the glamour and excess (or vulgarity, depending on your point of view) of Bollywood and turned instead to the French *Nouvelle Vague*. In India the initial inspiration came from the Bengali director Satyajit Ray (see page 307), who brought India into the international film scene with *Pather Panchali* (*The Song of the Road*, 1955).

The actress Nagma.

Bollywood star Shah Rukh Khan.

THE TELEVISION REVOLUTION

For decades, until the early 1980s, television was controlled by government and concentrated on a heavy-handed mix of education and propaganda. It reached only 13 percent of the country. Then the focus shifted from social development to entertainment; the government liberalised the import of colour TVs and VCRs, and television proliferated, along with pirated videos.

The launch of Star TV in 1991 brought an entertainment channel, Star Plus, Prime Sports, MTV and the BBC World Service to Indian screens. In 1992, a Hindi channel was added to Star. Zee, with its talk shows, games, sitcoms and soaps, turned out to be a huge hit with the young and burgeoning middle classes. Stung by this competition, Doordarshan, the Indian state-owned television network, launched an entertainment channel, Metro. Independent entrepreneurs also jumped into the fray by hiring transponders on various satellites and floating channels in Hindi and other Indian languages.

A substantial segment of this new programming was film-based, but social issues were tackled; one channel even took to telecasting a late-night 'adult' film on Saturdays. Now there are more than 500 channels and the major cities have access to over 100 cable and satellite channels, more than half of which are free. This has made India the world's third-largest TV market; 130 million households are tuned in daily.

Later, aided by the government-funded Film Finance Corporation (FFC), other directors began to emulate his example. Mrinal Sen, also from Kolkata, was both critically and commercially successful with *Bhuvan Shome*, and soon directors were making films in other regional languages, especially Malayalam through the work of P. Bhaskaran and Ramu Kariyat (who made the critically acclaimed *Nilakkuyil* in 1957), M.T. Vasudevan Nair and Aravindan.

Despite a flowering of Hindi realist cinema during the 1980s (including films by Satyajit Ray), by the 1990s the New Wave had

markets often outstrip those in India itself, and have spurred a dramatic increase in production values, as well as innovations to the standard Bollywood format. Over the past few years, nearly all the highest grossing Indian films have been genre flicks: 3 Idiots (2009), starring Amir Khan, broke all box office records, despite being a feel-good comedy drama. Ghajini (2008), the previous chart-topper, was a dark psychological thriller; while Don 2 (an action thriller; 2011) and Ra I (a sci-fi superhero blockbuster; 2011) were both radical departures from the Bollywood mainstream.

A Bollywood film dance scene.

lost its way. Aside from one or two films by indigenous directors, the headlines have been grabbed by expatriate film-makers, especially the controversial Deepa Mehta. Her films have tackled taboo subjects in India, such as lesbianism in *Fire* (1998) and the treatment of widows in *Water* (2005).

The future

While more 'art house' films from India have achieved audiences beyond the Subcontinent, such as Meera Nair's *Monsoon Wedding* (2001), Bollywood has gained a substantial following outside India, principally with expatriate South Asians resident in the US and UK. Because of the higher ticket prices, receipts from overseas

Bollywood actors and actresses have found other ways to gain fame abroad. Shilpa Shetty's headline-grabbing encounter with the UK version of the reality TV show *Big Brother* in 2007 raised the profile of the industry (even if she subsequently found herself in trouble back home after being kissed in public by Richard Gere). The trade goes both ways, however, with the 'Big B' (as Amitabh Bachchan is known) revitalising his career by hosting *Kaun Banega Crorepati* (India's *Who Wants to be a Millionaire?*). In a final twist, Kaun Bangega Crorepati became the starting point for the massive international hit, *Slumdog Millionaire*, the 2008 Anglo-Indian rags-to-riches film which scooped eight Oscars.

The giant statue of Gomateshwara at Sravanabelagola.

ART AND ARCHITECTURE

A highlight of any visit to India is the wealth of artistic treasures, from exquisite temple architecture to ancient murals and sculptures and beautiful book illustrations.

For more than 2,000 years India has been witness to a succession of amazingly diverse artistic traditions. While Buddhist architecture and painting are now only found in the Himalayan valleys in the far north of India, temple construction and the fashioning of bronze and stone images for worship continue to be funded by wealthy Hindu and Jain patrons throughout the country. Indeed, Akshardham, reputedly the largest Hindu temple in India, was inaugurated in Delhi as recently as 2005.

Public mosques and tombs of saints are continuously refurbished and extended so as to serve the needs of India's substantial Muslim population. The descendants of India's royal families may have stopped building massive forts and sumptuous palaces, but many are successfully converting their ancestral residences into luxury hotels. Meanwhile, a new wealthy class of industrialists and IT specialists have begun to erect high-rise offices and ostentatious residences – the latest of which is 27 storeys high and includes three helipads, parking for 100 cars and employs 300 staff – and to collect the works of contemporary lauded Indian painters and sculptors.

In spite of this enthusiastic patronage, India is dotted with abandoned monasteries, temples, forts and tombs. Unesco has now inscribed some 23 Indian properties on its prestigious World Heritage List, but India's historical legacy is still at risk from unprecedented urban development.

Buddhist shrines and monasteries

The earliest surviving architecture in India is Buddhist. From the 5th century BC onwards hemispherical earthen mounds known as

Ancient sculpture of a Hindu deity, State Government Museum, Chennai.

stupas were raised to enshrine the relics of the Buddha and his followers, and to symbolise the precepts of the new religion. Stupas built by the emperor Ashoka in the 3rd century BC at the various holy sites of Buddhism in North India, as well as in neighbouring Nepal and Sri Lanka, are faced with stone, and topped by umbrella-like stone finials that represented the ascending heavens.

The best-preserved stupa of this era is at Sanchi in Madhya Pradesh. Its hemispherical solid mound is surrounded by a pathway defined by a railing with monumental portals. Though built of limestone, the posts and lintels at Sanchi clearly imitate the details of timber construction. The portals are enlivened with relief carvings that illustrate episodes from the life of Buddha, though without any representation of the Master, since this was forbidden in early Buddhism.

Other reliefs at Sanchi depict popular tales, known as Jatakas, describing events from the Buddha's previous lives. Similar panels adorn the railings and portals of other stupas, such as those at Bharhut in Madhya Pradesh and Amaravati in Andhra Pradesh. These carvings are now on view in the Indian Museum, Kolkata, the Government Museum, Chennai, and the British Museum, London.

The Ajanta murals date back to the 2nd century BC.

Buddhist sites were also provided with monasteries, known as *viharas*, to accommodate the growing community of followers. Here, small residential chambers are arranged on four sides of a courtyard, often with a shrine in the middle of one side. Kitchens, wells and stores are generally located a short distance away. Constructed of brick, *viharas* survive today only in a dilapidated condition, as at Sarnath, on the outskirts of Varanasi in Uttar Pradesh. Among the carved sandstone images found here is a masterpiece portraying Buddha preaching the "First Sermon" in the deer park at Sarnath, dating from the 5th-century Gupta period, now displayed in the local archaeological museum. Here, too, is a magnificent polished sandstone lion capital that once topped a column erected by Ashoka.

Buddhist sculptures have also been found at numerous other sites in India, notably at Mathura in Uttar Pradesh. The finest is a Gupta-period Buddha dressed in a toga-like robe, with a full halo, now in the Government Museum, Mathura, Uttar Pradesh. Commemorative shrines, too, were erected at Buddhist holy sites, the most famous being that at Bodhgaya in Bihar, the site where Buddha attained enlightenment beneath the bodhi tree. The steeply pyramidal brick tower of the shrine dates back to the 7th century, but has been much altered in recent times.

A more complete idea of ancient Buddhist architecture and art may be had from the cave-temples of Maharashtra. Excavated into basalt cliffs, these monuments were intended as retreats for religious communities supported

BOOK ILLUSTRATION

In the Sultanate courts of the 13th–15th centuries book production was encouraged. The Mughals who followed were also a literary dynasty, with Babur, their 16th-century founder, having written his memoirs in the first guidebook to Hindustan. His son, Humayan, brought over the great painters Mir Sayyid Ali and Abd us-Samad from Persia. Almost 100 years later his grandson, Jahangir, wrote his memoirs and in a move to outdo Babur he employed the master painter of animals, Mansur, to illustrate his descriptions of the natural world.

The Emperor Akbar, who is reputed to have been illiterate, became a great patron of the arts,

particularly painting. Illustrated histories of the Mughals were commissioned as official chronicles – the *Babur Nama*, *Timur Nama* and *Akbar Nama* – and artists recruited from all over India. One of the greatest works of the period, a vast illustrated version of the epic Hamza Nama comprising 1400 canvas folios, was produced by Akbar's atelier between 1562 and 1577. The style was bold and dynamic, fusing Islamic and Hindu elements, and heavily influenced the other Indian courts, where versions of the popular epics the *Ramayana* and *Mahabharata* were soon commissioned in the new style. Mughal painting introduced a quality of portraiture still unsurpassed today.

> The depiction of the Buddha, the 'Enlightened One', in painting or sculpture, represented one of the highest aspirations of human art and thought.

by local merchants. Shrines known as chaitya halls at Ajanta date back to the 2nd century BC, though examples from the 5th–7th centuries AD are also found at Ajanta and Ellora. Chaitya halls have nave-like interiors divided into triple aisles by lines of columns. The central aisles are roofed with barrel-vaulted ceilings that recall bamboo construction; these vaulted ceilings are expressed on the outside of the hall as horseshoe-shaped windows. The principal object of devotion inside chaitya halls is a monolithic stupa, embellished in later examples with sculpted images of the teaching Buddha. The halls have part-circular ends that define a pathway proceeding around the stupa.

Like brick-built *viharas*, rock-cut monasteries at Ajanta also have cells arranged around a square hall, with a shrine on one side accommodating a seated Buddha figure. The walls are covered with murals portraying Jataka stories, as well as scenes showing Buddha as a prince, ascetic and teacher, there being no prohibition on the representation of the Master by the 5th century. The Ajanta murals are the earliest Buddhist paintings to be found anywhere in Asia; but they are also vivid records of contemporary life in Indian palaces, cities, gardens and forests. Later examples of Buddhist paintings are found in the remote sub-Himalayan valleys of Ladakh in Kashmir. The shrines of the monastic complex at Alchi, for instance, have their interiors cloaked in brightly coloured murals showing diverse Mahayana divinities. Dating from the 12th century and later, they reflect artistic and religious influences from neighbouring Tibet.

Hindu and Jain temples

Stone temples enshrining votive images of Hindu divinities as well as of Jain saints date back to the Gupta period. As in Buddhist architecture, the earliest examples are cut out of solid rock. The cave-temple on Elephanta Island in Mumbai harbour, excavated in the 6th century, consists of a spacious columned hall, or *mandapa*, with a central shrine housing a *lingam*, the cosmic phallic emblem of Shiva. Scenes deeply sculpted into the surrounding walls represent Shiva as the dancer or the ascetic; seated in meditation or spearing demons; marrying his consort, the goddess Parvati; and playing dice with her on Kailash, their mountain home. At the end of the central aisle is a colossal bust of the god with three heads, those on the side representing Shiva's contrasting feminine and demonic aspects. Smaller Hindu cave temples of the same period are found at Mamallapuram in Tamil Nadu. These too are embellished with

Carvings in the Elephanta caves, Mumbai. Both complexes are Unesco World Heritage Sites.

mythological wall-carvings, especially of Vishnu asleep on the cosmic serpent, and the fierce goddess Durga.

Temples in North India

From the 7th century onwards, structural temples were constructed in two contrasting styles. The nagara temples of northern India have square sanctuaries topped by towers with curving profiles, known as *shikharas*. In later times these *shikhara* towers were multiplied and combined to create complex clustered forms. One of the best-preserved groups of fully evolved *nagara* temples is that at Khajuraho in Madhya Pradesh, dating from the 10th to the 11th centuries. Dominated by clustered *shikhara* towers that soar dramatically above their sanctuaries, the Khajuraho temples are approached through a line of porches and *mandapas* with projecting balconies. The outer faces of their golden sandstone walls are covered with carvings of gods and their consorts, as well as magically protective prancing beasts, and human couples in provocative sexual postures. Temple interiors feature ornate columns with angled brackets sculpted as alluring maidens.

That the *nagara* style spread to eastern India is evident from temples in Bhubaneshwar in

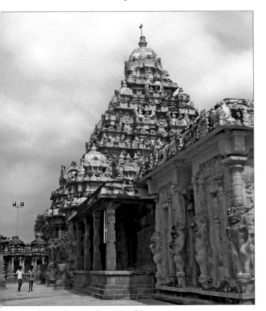

Kailasanatha temple in Kanchipuram.

Odisha (Orissa). Temple sanctuaries here are topped by vertical *shikhara* towers, which curve only at the very top to support heavy, disc-like ribbed finials. These towered sanctuaries are preceded by *mandapas* with pyramidal roofs. The climax of the Orissa style is represented by the 12th-century Jagannatha temple at Puri, celebrated for its chariot festival (hence the English word 'juggernaut'). The 13th-century temple at Konark, now reduced to a grandiose ruin, stands a few kilometres away. Its sculpted basement is covered with friezes of human figures, horses and elephants. Twenty-four gigantic wheels, carved in full relief, suggest that the temple was conceived as an allegorical chariot that

> *Larger dravida temples with steeply pyramidal towers divided into multiple storeys are associated with the Chola rulers of Tamil Nadu in the 10th–11th centuries.*

conveyed Surya, the Hindu sun god, across the heavens.

Nagara-style temples in Rajasthan are often dedicated to Jain saints, such as those in the 11th–13th-century complex at Mount Abu. Here, temple sanctuaries are preceded by columned *mandapas* roofed with domical ceilings, with angled bracket figures and pendant lotus flowers, all in exquisitely worked, white marble. The temple at Ranakpur, dedicated to Adinatha, the first of the 24 Jain saviours, dates from the 15th century. Its central sanctuary is topped by a clustered *shikhara* tower. This is reached through elaborate but identical *mandapas* on four sides.

Temples of the South

Temples in southern India and the Deccan are built in the contrasting *dravida* style, with multi-storeyed towers of granite or sandstone. Hindu shrines in this style dating from the 8th century are found at Kanchipuram in Tamil Nadu and at Pattadakal in Karnataka. Their outer walls are divided into niches framed by pilasters and filled with carvings of gods and goddesses. This same scheme is imitated in solid basalt in the colossal, monolithic Kailasanatha temple at Ellora in Maharashtra. The great Shiva temple at Tanjavur (Tanjore) has a tower that rises more than 65 metres (215ft) high. The walls beneath have double tiers of niches filled with magnificently carved images of Shiva. In later times temple towers tended to be built of brick and covered with brightly painted plaster sculptures. Such towers rise over the *gopuras*, or gateways, that lead into to the sacred compound. Among the largest *dravida*-styled monuments in Tamil Nadu are those at Srirangam and Madurai dating from the 16th–17th centuries. Here the religious monument is transformed into a vast walled complex, entered through *gopuras* on four sides. The interior is divided into courtyards, some with bathing pools, as well as extensive *mandapas*, columned corridors, and shrines dedicated to different gods and goddesses.

Dravida temples in southern India are also the settings for impressive works of Hindu art. Other than carvings on sanctuary walls, interior columns are often sculpted in almost three dimensions as lifelike leaping horses or fantastic beasts known as *yalis* ridden by armed warriors, as at Srirangam. Images of gods, goddesses and Hindu saints displayed in temple sanctuaries are cast in bronze with amazing elegance. The finest such bronzes are those dating from the Chola period, now displayed in the Government Museum, Chennai, and the Art Museum, Tanjavur.

Murals represent another aspect of *dravida* temple art. Ceiling paintings at Lepakshi in Andhra Pradesh, for example, illustrate Hindu legends, including the story of Shiva disguised as a forest hunter fighting the hero Arjuna. Here, too, are portraits of the governors who built the temple in the 16th century, accompanied by their elegantly dressed retinues.

A variant version of the *dravida* style is seen in the 12th-century Hoysala temples of Belur and Halebid. Built out of chlorite, these Hindu monuments are celebrated for their sharply carved figures of Hindu gods and goddesses, as well as minute friezes of animals and episodes from popular legends. Temple interiors at both sites are enhanced by polished, lathe-turned stone columns; angled brackets

> Prior to the introduction of paper in the 14th century, writings and illustrations were inscribed on palm leaves or parchment and 'bound' in wooden covers wrapped in cloth.

are fashioned as three-dimensional maidens posing beneath trees.

Mosques, tombs and palaces

With the establishment of Muslim power in Delhi at the end of the 12th century, the architecture and art of India came under the sway of well-established Islamic traditions imported from Iran and Central Asia. This is first seen in the mosques and tombs with pointed arches and lofty domes built for successive sultans in the 14th–15th centuries, a tendency that was to continue under the Mughals in the 16th and 17th centuries. Yet these Islamic buildings were

essentially Indian since they were constructed out of local materials by local workmen. This is already evident from the Quwwat-ul-Islam mosque and adjacent minaret, known as the Qutb Minar, in Delhi, which are the first monuments to proclaim Muslim supremacy in India. Its prayer hall has a facade of pointed arches built of sandstone without any mortar, in the typical Indian dry masonry technique. Arabic inscriptions bordering the arches are enlivened by sculpted lotus embellishment similar to that found on temples. The same motifs decorate the tapering flanged shaft of

Halebid temple detail.

the nearby minaret that rises more than 72 metres (240ft) high.

Muslim religious architecture outside Delhi assumes a range of styles, reflecting the impact of regional building practices. Mosques and tombs in Ahmedabad in Gujarat, for example, have temple-like columns and corbelled domes, as well as perforated screens, known as *jalis*. The finest *jalis* in Ahmedabad are those in Sidi Sayyid's mosque of 1572; they are carved with astonishing skill to portray palm trees and creepers. Basalt is the medium of religious architecture in Bijapur in Karnataka. The Ibrahim Rauza, built in 1626, is roofed with an exaggeratedly bulbous dome framed by ornamental turrets and finials. The walls of the tomb chamber beneath are covered with superbly carved inscriptions and geometric patterns. The nearby Gol Gumbaz, the mausoleum of Sultan Muhammad Adil Shah, who died in 1656, has a colossal dome, some 44 metres (144ft) in diameter, making it one of the largest in the world. This is supported on an ingenious structural system of intersecting pointed arches. In the middle of Hyderabad in Andhra Pradesh stands the Char Minar of 1591, named after its quartet of circular minarets, rising 56 metres (183ft) high. These frame the mosque elevated over the intersection of the two main streets of the city.

Fatehpur Sikri, the work of the 16th-century emperor Akbar.

The Mughal Era

Mughal architecture begins with the tomb of Emperor Humayun in Delhi, completed in 1571. This stands in the middle of a vast *charbagh*, or four-square walled garden with axial waterways, of obvious Persian inspiration. The tomb itself, raised on a lofty podium, has red sandstone arched portals facing in four directions; above rises a white marble dome with a slightly bulbous profile, revealing Central Asian influence. The next three Mughal emperors were also responsible for building grandiose garden tombs. The most famous of these is the Taj Mahal in Agra, Uttar Pradesh, built in 1632–53 by Shah Jahan for his beloved wife Mumtaz Mahal.

The Mughals also undertook ambitious military constructions. The Red Fort overlooking the Yamuna River in Agra is protected by massive ramparts and a deep moat, mainly the work of Akbar. The same emperor was also responsible for founding the nearby palace city of Fatehpur Sikri in 1571. Its audience halls, residential suites and pleasure pavilions of different designs are all built out of red sandstone, and have survived amazingly well. The great mosque nearby is entered through a lofty arched portal. In the middle of its courtyard stands the white marble tomb of Salim Chishti, the saint who predicted the birth of Akbar's son. Its veranda is lit by superb *jalis* with geometric designs.

In 1639 Shah Jahan founded his own new city, Shahjahanabad, in Delhi. Its Red Fort is entered through a great gateway facing the main street of the city. This leads via a covered bazaar to the audience hall that once housed the celebrated, gem-studded Peacock Throne. Beyond lie the private gardens and white marble residential pavilions, linked by waterways and scented fountains.

In spite of their grand planning and sumptuous ornamentation, Mughal palaces are now empty and forlorn. Nothing now remains of the woven carpets, embroidered textiles, silvered vessels and jade *huqqa* bowls that were produced in the imperial workshops. However, an idea of the Persian manner of these luxurious objects may be had from collections of Mughal art displayed in the National Museum, New Delhi, and Prince of Wales Museum (renamed

THE PEACOCK THRONE

Shah Jahan's legendary throne is said to have been made from 230kg (508lbs) of precious jewels, including rubies, emeralds, pearls and diamonds, among them the 105-carat Koh-i-noor, as well as 1,150kg (2,535lbs) of gold. When Nader Shah invaded India in 1738 he took the throne home with him to Persia as the world's most expensive souvenir. What happened next is something of a mystery: Nader Shah was assassinated, and nobody seems quite sure what became of the throne, with various theories attributing its fate to the Kurds, the British or the Iranians themselves. In any case, it was never seen again, although imitations have been made.

The Taj Mahal's perfect proportions and immaculate white marble cladding, enhanced by delicate pietra dura inlays of semi-precious stones, mark the high point of Mughal artistic achievement.

the Chhatrapati Shivaji Maharaj Vastu Sangrahalaya), Mumbai. Here, too, are miniatures that portray the Mughal emperors and their nobles, as well as episodes from Persian epics and Hindu legends.

Rajput families. The interior of the palace at Amber, capital of the Kachhwaha maharajas before their move to nearby Jaipur, even has a Mughal-styled *shish mahal*, or mirrored hall. Here, countless tiny pieces of reflecting glass are set into the plastered ceiling to create a glittering interior. Palaces at Kota and Bundi are enlivened with murals that depict contemporary life, with Rajput rulers receiving visitors, riding in procession, hunting deer, enjoying performances of music and dance, and going on pilgrimage to Hindu shrines. Some Rajput palaces still preserve their royal

Agra Fort.

Realistic paintings of animals, birds and flowers prove that Indian artists took genuine delight in the world of nature. Evidence of this could be seen from the earliest miniatures, painted on palm leaves from the 11th century onwards, but really brought to prominence as an art form in their own right under Mughal rule.

Throughout the 17th and 18th centuries the Rajput princes of neighbouring Rajasthan were closely allied with the Mughals, with the result that their forts, palaces and arts were much affected by Mughal taste. Mughal-styled audience halls and residential apartments crowd the interiors of the citadels that mark the headquarters of the different

art collections, as can be seen in the spectacular costumes, carpets, weapons and miniature paintings on display in the City Palace Museum, Jaipur.

Here, too, mention must be made of the Sikh shrines of the Punjab, known as *gurudwaras*. Topped by Mughal-styled gilded domes, they commemorate the lives of successive Sikh teachers. The most famous Sikh monument is the Golden Temple in Amritsar, built by the fourth Sikh guru, Guru Ram Das, in the 16th century. A large tank was excavated, and the gold-covered temple built in its centre; the tank was then filled with water, the shimmering gold of the temple reflected on all sides to mesmerising effect.

Impact of Europe

The arrival of the Portuguese on the Arabian Sea coast in the early 16th century signalled the beginning of European influence. Italianate traditions were imported by the Portuguese for their cathedrals and monasteries in India, as is evident from the Baroque style of Sé Cathedral and Bom Jesus in Old Goa. The interiors of these churches are further enhanced with European-styled altarpieces created from gilded wood. Bom Jesus even incorporates the ornate marble tomb of Francis Xavier, the celebrated Jesuit saint. Ecclesiastical items produced in

Basilica of Bom Jesus, Old Goa.

workshops in Goa under the Portuguese in the 17th and 18th centuries are displayed in the Museum of Christian Art in the Convent of St Monica, Old Goa. Churches in Puducherry show that Catholic architecture and art also flourished in India under the French.

It was, however, the British who had the most widespread impact on Indian architecture. The star-shaped forts that they constructed in the 17th century to protect their trading 'factories' at Chennai, Kolkata and Mumbai survive, though their ramparts and moats are now much dilapidated and overgrown. Churches within these forts display pedimented facades and pointed steeples typical of Classical Revival architecture. A similar mode was also adopted

for the civic monuments that represented English supremacy on Indian soil, notably Government House in Kolkata, begun in 1758, and the British Residency in Hyderabad of 1809. Neoclassical facades even graced the mansions of wealthy English merchants in Kolkata.

In the 19th century Gothic Revival became the preferred mode, not only for churches but also for urban projects. This is best seen in Mumbai, in the High Court (still called the Bombay High Court), Victoria Terminus railway station (now the Chhatrapati Shivaji Terminus, known as CST) and University Library, all built in the 1870s and 1880s. The turn of the 20th century was marked by the invention of the novel Indo-Saracenic style, in which European Gothic features mingled freely with domes and turrets derived from Mughal and Rajput architecture. This somewhat eccentric idiom was also sometimes chosen by Indian princes for their public buildings, as in the High Court and Osmania General Hospital in Hyderabad. Indo-Saracenic royal residences also sprung up, like the exotic palace of the Wodeyar rulers in Mysore, which even employs cast iron and stained glass imported from Glasgow.

For their own monuments the British preferred a more restrained version of Classicism, such as that practised by Sir Edwin Lutyens and Herbert Baker, principal architects of New Delhi. Completed in 1931, with broad boulevards, imposing civic monuments and garden bungalows, the new British capital was dominated by a central axis, at the end of which stood the Viceroy's House, now Rashtrapati Bhavan, residence of India's president. This domed building is an eclectic blend of Buddhist, Mughal and Rajput features, organised according to Classical proportions. In the course of the 20th century, European Modernism took widespread root in India, mostly at the hands of English and German architects employed by local princes. The masterpiece of Indian Modernism is Umaid Bhavan, now a heritage hotel, commissioned by the Jodhpur maharajas. Its lofty domed rotunda and splendidly appointed Art Deco apartments were completed in 1944.

Post Independence

Indian architecture after Independence displays a similar dependence on European models, especially once Le Corbusier and Louis Khan were invited to work in India in the 1950s. The layout and civic monuments of Chandigarh, new capital of Indian Punjab, reflect French urban ideals not necessarily suited to India. That the modernisation of Indian architecture is now an accomplished fact is obvious from the high-rise concrete and glass buildings that crowd most cities today. Some architects now seek an authentic Indian aesthetic by reverting to traditional materials, such as sandstone and marble, and geometric patterns borrowed from earlier Indian Islamic buildings.

The same quest is taking place in the fine arts, with a new generation of Indian painters and sculptors drawing on indigenous themes. Some of these artists are concerned to reconcile the latest Western trends with a genuine Indian aesthetic. Although quality varies substantially, the discerning eye may pick out very accomplished and expressive works from the mediocre. Today, Kolkata and Delhi are the best cities in which to find interesting art. Meanwhile, there is a vigorous revival of textile arts and village crafts throughout the country.

An evocative modern sculpture at the National Gallery of Modern Art in Delhi.

CONTEMPORARY INDIAN ART

In the years following Independence, Indian art was dominated by the Progressive Artists of Mumbai, including Ara, Souza, M.F. Husain, Raza, Ram Kumar and Kishen Khanna, most of whom are now at the top of the contemporary art ladder. Unlike the masters of the earlier Modern Movement, the Progressives styled their Indian themes in the modern European mould, and their followers have become increasingly influenced by the avant-garde movements of the West. This is one of the reasons why so much contemporary work appears derivative. But it must be remembered that many artists are genuinely inspired by the modern urban environment with its Western influences. It is also important to

note, when touring the galleries (the National Gallery of Modern Art in Delhi is a good place to start), that the hallmark of contemporary Indian art is diversity. Artists work in a wide range of media and styles and with an immense variety of themes. It is possible to see everything from installations to narrative paintings, portraits to abstracts and works with Adivasi and local motifs.

A great place to gets to grips with what's hot on the contemporary scene is the December art biennale held in the southern city of Kochi (Cochin), whose faded Raj-era warehouses provide perfect backdrops for cutting-edge installations and video films, as well as painting and sculpture.

HINDU DEITIES

Hinduism recognises a bewildering number of deities, from powerful Sanskritic gods, sometimes thought of as manifestations of one single divine entity, to local goddesses.

Hinduism has been called the 'religion of 330 million deities,' a deliberate exaggeration merely intended to refer to the divine present in all beings. However, this claim does point to the vast number of gods and goddesses that this extremely heterogeneous religion embraces.

Some Hindus believe that the various incarnations of these deities (known as avatars) all descend from one central divine being known as Brahman, others that the Brahman manifests as three centrally powerful gods – Brahma, Vishnu and Shiva – known as the Trimurti, and others still that each deity is a distinct and separate entity to be worshipped in its own right. Of course, these are not necessarily mutually distinct positions and there are almost as many variations and gradations of belief as gods and goddesses.

The first deities that appear in the Hindu canon are those of the Vedas, powerful gods that personify elements of the temporal world. These include Agni, the god of fire, Indra, the god of thunder and war, Brahma and Surya, the sun god. These Vedic deities were supplanted by gods perhaps more familiar such as Vishnu (and his avatars, or incarnations, Rama and Krishna) and Shiva. The exploits of these gods are contained in a body of scriptures known as the Puranas.

Of great importance, although less canonical perhaps than Vishnu and Shiva, are the various aspects of the goddess (Devi or Shakti), from Sarasvati, the goddess of learning and music, to Durga, slayer of the buffalo demon Mahisasura. This manifestation of female power is considered vital for the balance of the universe and Devi is often seen paired with a male god as a consort, for instance Vishnu and Lakshmi.

Shiva is the oldest of all Hindu gods; origins are thought to date back to the Harappan civilisation.

The three gods that form the Trimurti – from left to right Brahma, Vishnu and Shiva – are generally considered the most powerful and important of the gods (the Mahadevas) representing the creator, preserver and destroyer respectively.

This goddess, usually depicted with many arms and a garland of skulls, represents the most fierce and destructive aspect of Devi. She is one of the consorts of Shiva and is sometimes thought of as the most powerful avatar of Durga.

Two sadhus.

SADHUS

A feature of Indian religious life is the presence of numbers of sadhus (wandering hermits). They can be seen in cities and villages, in forests, on the banks of rivers and in the Himalaya. Usually dressed in saffron or ochre robes, their bodies smeared with ash and foreheads anointed with sandal-paste, the sadhus carry all their possessions with them: a bowl, a staff, a blanket. Some travel alone, others in small groups. Some have taken vows of silence, others preach or chant hymns. They are broadly divided into followers of Vishnu, Vaishnavas, and those of Shiva, Saivas. Those who worship Vishnu can be identified by three vertical lines painted on their foreheads (a *tilak*, usually in white and red), those for whom Siva is the object of devotion have a *tilak* of three horizontal lines.

he monkey god, Hanuman, was Rama's helper during his battle against the demon Ravana. He is considered to be strong and loyal and is among the most popular Hindu deities.

The son of Shiva and Parvati, Ganesh is the god of wisdom and auspicious beginnings, and he is invoked before setting out on a journey or a new venture.

Often the focus of devotional religion, bhakti, Vishnu is considered to have 11 avatars, or manifestations: Matsya, a fish; Kurma, a turtle; Varaha, a boar; Narasimha, a lion; Vamana, a dwarf; Parasurama, a man wielding an axe; Rama, the hero of the Ramayana; Balarama, an earlier incarnation of Krishna; Krishna, a well-loved god who appears in many stories; the Buddha; and Kalki, the horseman who will usher in the Kali Yuga, the age of destruction.

Taking in the view in Mumbai.

The ghats at Varanasi.

Harvesting red chillies.

Keralan paddy field.

INTRODUCTION

The following chapters offer a detailed guide to the entire country, with principal sights clearly cross-referenced by number to the maps.

Elephant and mahout.

No one feels neutral about India. It slams you in the face with heat, spice and dirt, then seduces you with colour and sensual pleasure. Time distorts and assumes surreal yogic contortions: distances take longer to travel, minutes crawl during interminable waits, then vanish into a blur of hours, even days. The constant chaos can charm or repulse.

There are so many different facets of India: the 28 states, six Union Territories and the National Capital Territory of Delhi offer a bewildering number of travel options. Trekking to Adivasi villages in the Western Ghats is a physical challenge. Chugging across the Deccan Plateau in a three-tiered sleeper car while the other passengers snore is a mental one. The pride of an artisan working at a potter's wheel or loom is obvious; the appeal of rural villages trimmed with intricate murals is unforgettable.

Bengaluru.

Visit an old Portuguese fort or an ancient Jewish synagogue. Take refuge in a remote pleasure palace a full day's camel ride away from the rest of the world. Barter in a bazaar for old silver, new rugs, inlaid daggers, or go for the miniature paintings brushed with a squirrel's whisker, the antique opium boxes, or new jewellery made with crushed gemstones: it's all spread out before your eyes in a former caravanserai.

Other visitors come to India seeking something within themselves, some spiritual calm beyond the cacophony. Some enrol in meditation centres, others opt for social or environmental work, either can teach you something more about yourself.

India's travel experiences can be similarly uplifting, from boating down a river where elephants bathe, to the colour and spectacle of an esoteric religious festival. White-water rafting down the Ganges, practising yoga on a sunrise beach, tracking wildlife in game sanctuaries, climbing a Himalayan peak, sketching wildflowers in a hill station meadow, or examining erotic sculpture at Tantric temples: it would need immense stamina to undertake all the travel possibilities in India.

Some run away from India; others keep returning.

India

C H I N A
Yushu

A
M
I

T i b e t
Bangda

H I M A L A Y A

anda Devi
81f0
nora

Lhasa

inkhand

Arunachal

bad
arelly

Dibrugarh
Pradesh

tla
Shahjahanpur
Tansen
Sikkim
Thimphu
Gangtok

BHUTAN
Barpeta
Assam
Nagaland
Guwahati
Kohima

Pradesh
Lucknow
Gorakhpur
Kathmandu
Darjiling

N E P A L

Kanpur
Faizabad
Muzaffarpur
Goalpara
Rangsat

h
Varanasi
Bihar
Patna
Bhagalpur
Shillong
Meghalaya
Manipur
Allahabad
Sasaram
Ganga
Malda
Mymensingh
Imphal
Mirzapur
Gaya

BANGLA
Rewa
Hazaribagh
Biharampur
Agartala
Aizawl

Murwara
Jharkhand
Dhanbad
Durgapur
DESH
Tripura

Jabalpur
Ranchi
Jessore
Mizoram
MYANMAR

D
Jamshedpur
West
Khulna
Chittagong
Mandalay

Bilaspur
Rourkela
Bengal
Haora
(BURMA)

Durg
Rajpur
Sambalpur
Kharagpur
Kolkata
Pakokku
Meiktila

Chattisgarh
(Calcutta)

jpur
Cuttack
Ganga Delta
Minbu
Naypyidaw

ja
Odisha
Bhubaneshwar
Sittwe (Akyab)
Chiang

andhra
Puri
Pye
Mai

Brahmapur
Irrawaddy
THAILAND

a a n
Jeypore
Thandwe

dhra
Vizianagaram
B a y   o f

Rajahmundry
Vishakhapatnam
Hinthada

gonda
Eluru
Yanam
B e n g a l
Thaton

wada
Machilipatnam
Yangon
(Rangoon)

Moktama Kwe
(Gulf of Martaban)
Erawadi Myitwana

Nellore
I N D I A N
Narcondam
(India)

upati
Andaman
(India)
A n d a m a n

Chennai
(Madras)
O C E A N
Barren
(India)

anchipuram
Islands
Port Blair

Puduchery
Duncan Passage

apalli
Ten Degree
Channel

u
Strait
Jaffna
S e a

anushkodi
Nicobar
Trincomalee
Sombrero Channel

SRI LANKA
Islands

Coromandel Coast

Eastern Ghats

Andaman and Nicobar Islands (India)

Tropic of Cancer

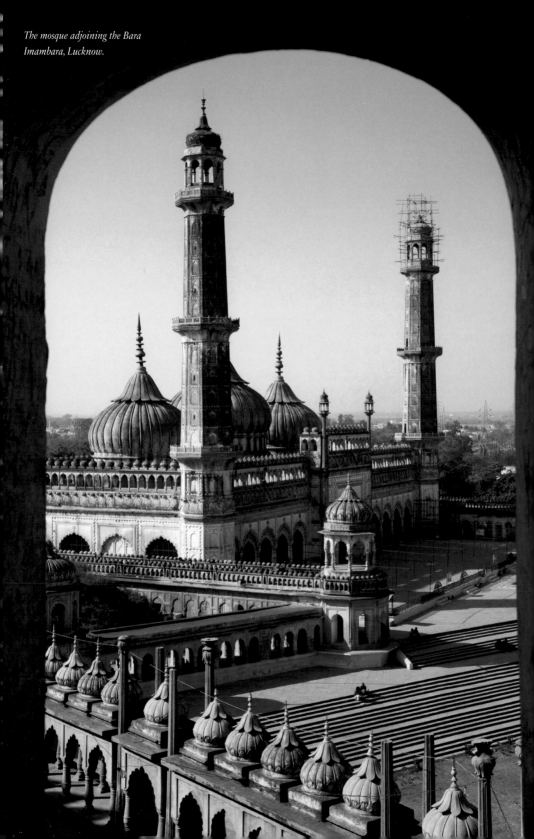

The mosque adjoining the Bara Imambara, Lucknow.

THE NORTH

Northern India covers a vast swathe of constrasting country, the dusty flatlands of the Punjab and the Gangetic plain giving way to the mighty Himalayas. The great Mughal cities of Delhi and Agra lie to the south.

Sarees for sale in a Delhi market.

Hot, dusty, crowded, loud and proud, this is the India of the popular imagination; but it can also be cold, calm, pristine and clean. Plains and mountains, chalk and cheese. The fertile flatlands are India's breadbasket, worked to good effect by the prosperous Punjabis. But move east and the good times fade; as the population increases, prosperity takes a nose dive, corruption cripples and industry blackens the horizon. Uttar Pradesh is the centre of much of India's politics, industry and divinity. Lucknow has witnessed the rise and fall of many of India's most influential political parties, as well as being the stage for the Uprising of 1857; its impressive array of architectural treasures bear witness to this turbulent past. Varanasi, on the Ganges and famed for its cremation ghats, is one of India's most intense experiences and not to be missed.

The mountains are another world entirely – of shining glaciers, flower-filled meadows and inaccessible ice peaks. Head north from the plains and it's all change, although the influence of the cities, and their increasingly well-travelled citizens, can still be felt, particularly in the 'hill stations'. Established by the British as places to escape the summer heat of the plains, these days they tend to be popular with Indian tourists and honeymooners, leading to an intriguing blend of

Cycle rickshaw on the streets of Delhi.

anachronistic charm and Indian kitsch. Keep heading north, though, and the green – and everyone – is gone. This is nowhere truer than in Ladakh, and particularly on the epic road that leads there from Manali, home to massive moonscapes and roads so high you can barely breathe.

A journey through this part of the country will do much to help unravel the complexities of its capital, Delhi, a compelling fusion of all things North Indian. From there it's a short hop to India's most iconic site, the Taj Mahal, a building so familiar and yet so achingly exquisite.

Delhi

0 ————— 1000 m
0 ————— 1000 yds

N

→ Indira Gandhi Airport

DELHI

The capital of India presents an arresting combination of ancient and modern. And as a major cultural centre, Delhi offers a glimpse of the diversity of the country's many states.

India's capital is one of the world's largest cities, both in terms of population and extent – and among its most vibrant and dynamic metropolises. The urban sprawl long ago erupted from the confines of the walled city built by Shah Jahan, these days known as Old Delhi, whose crowded lanes and markets are as densely populated, intense and bewildering to the outsider as any in Asia. A short distance to the south but a world away in terms of style and atmosphere, New Delhi was the elegant British riposte to the clutter of the old, designed with trademark Raj era bravado as a demonstration of colonial might. Ironically, independence was ushered in only a few years after New Delhi was completed and, from a population of fewer than 2 million at that time, has mushroomed into a vast megalopolis of over 22 million people.

Visitors to Delhi are likely to divide their time between the central and southern areas of the city, where most of the major sights can be seen and where most of the action is. It can be a tough place to fathom at times, but try not to focus exclusively on the sights and aim to do what you would do in a big city at home – enjoy the experience of seeing it all done so differently.

Devotions at the shrine of Sheikh Nizamuddin Aulia.

Expansion and reinvention

During the 1990s and early years of this century the city struggled to cope with the effects of rapid expansion – pollution, traffic congestion, shortages of water and power, continual construction – and an extreme climate. And while there is still a long way to go, more recently, as befits the capital of this rapidly developing country, Delhi has reinvented itself as the most forward-thinking and one of the best-run cities in India. Pollution was greatly curbed by a 2003 Supreme

Main Attractions

Connaught Place
Lakshmi Narayan Temple
Lal Qila
Purana Qila
National Gallery of Modern Art
National Museum
Lodi Gardens
Shrine of Sheikh Nizamuddin Aulia
Qutb Minar Complex
Garden of the Five Senses

Court order that forced all public transport to convert from running on diesel to compressed natural gas (CNG), although levels are now back to what they were prior to the ruling due to the increased number of cars on the roads. Delhi's popular Chief Minister Shiela Dixit must also take much of the credit – her administration has clamped down on illegal building, attempted to clean up the city's streets and pushed through major infrastructure projects. The most prominent of these is the construction of a new metro system, which has garnered country-wide praise for its swift progress and lack of corruption.

A further boost to the city came when it was awarded the 2010 Commonwealth Games. Although the games have been used to justify much-needed improvements to the city's infrastructure, including a new international airport, some of this development was made at the expense of the poor. Large areas of slums were cleared and people dispossessed of what little they had in the name of beautifying the city. The Games themselves were not without controversy, with the athletes' village pronounced uninhabitable by the first groups of competitors to arrive, as well as minor building collapses and technical issues with the running of the events themselves. Less satisfactory still were the reports of wide-scale corruption in the build-up to the Games, the consequences of which are still being calculated.

Delhi is now the most expensive place to live in India, and has overtaken Mumbai as the most desirable, attracting a greater influx of people than its great rival. While Mumbai remains the indisputable financial hub, Delhi is not only the political centre but increasingly the focus of much of India's cultural life. It is home to many of the country's leading fashion designers, as well as numerous writers, artists and musicians. It also has a booming retail sector, with glossy new malls springing up all the time and numerous chic boutiques in its colony markets. All these developments are epitomised by the vast new DLF Mall of India (www.dlfmallofindia.

TRANSPORT TO AND FROM DELHI

Buses: Long-distance buses arrive and depart from the Inter-State Bus Terminal (ISBT) at Kashmir Gate. Private bus companies offer more comfortable facilities than trains, but their services invariably travel through the night and have a notoriously bad safety record.

Flights: As befits the capital, Delhi is the major hub for all international and domestic flights, with daily arrivals from all over the world. Indira Gandhi International Airport was renovated for the Commonwealth Games in 2010. Domestic flights, on Indian and many other airlines, regularly depart to all areas of the country. The best source of up-to-date timetable information, and most convenient way to book flights on all airlines, is the website www. ClearTrip.com.

Trains: As with air travel, Delhi is the major rail hub for India, with regular departures to almost everywhere in the country from the three main stations, New Delhi, Delhi and Nizamuddin. For foreign travellers, the tourist reservation facility on the first floor of New Delhi railway station offers an invaluable service, giving anyone in possession of an overseas passport access to special quotas. Without this booking facility, you'd be unlikely to be able to procure seats or berths on any trains departing from New Delhi – tickets sell out with days, or hours, of the reservation release time. Be warned, however, that touts hang around the entrance to the station attempting to divert tourists by claiming the office on the first floor is closed, or not the correct one, then taking them to private travel agents nearby where they'll be sold wait list or fake tickets. To book in the bona fide office you'll need your passport and receipts for any currency exchanges or withdrawls by ATM you've made in Delhi. Travelling by train will usually be a quicker and far more pleasant journey than by bus.

There are trains to Agra (many daily; 2–3hrs); Amritsar (many daily; 6–7hrs); Bengaluru (4 daily; 33–40hrs); Bhopal (many daily 8–11hrs); Chennai (3–4 daily; 28–36hrs); Goa (2–3 daily; 25–30hrs); Jaipur (10 daily; 5–6hrs); Kolkata (8–9 daily; 18–26hrs); Lucknow (frequent service daily; 6–9hrs); Mumbai (many daily; 16–23hrs); Secunderabad (2–4 daily; 22–25hrs); Varanasi (7–8 daily; 12hrs).

in), just over the state boundary in Gurgaon, planned to be the largest in the country when it opens in August 2013.

The ancient cities of Delhi

Strategically located between the Aravalli hills and the Yamuna River, Delhi has been the site of more than a dozen cities. It is named after an earlier settlement, 'Dillika'. The first of the cities was Indraprastha, legendary capital of the Pandavas, epic heroes of the *Mahabharata*. Recent excavations at Purana Qila (Old Fort) date the settlement to between the 1st century BC and the 4th century AD.

The next documented city was Lal Kot, founded in the 8th century AD by Tomar Rajputs. It was captured and renamed Qila Rai Pithora by the Chauhan Rajputs in the 12th century. Later it was occupied by Qutb-ud-din, who founded the Delhi Sultanate and began construction of the Qutb Minar. The monuments and ruins from this era stand in and around the Qutb Minar complex in South Delhi.

The ruins of Siri, a capital established by the Turkish Ala-ud-Din Khilji, can be seen around Hauz Khas colony. In 1320 Ghias-ud-Din Tughlaq moved to his fortress city of Tughlaqabad, east of Qutb Minar. His tomb, overrun by monkeys, stands across the road from the ruins.

Ferozabad, once the richest city in the world, was founded in 1351 by his successor, Feroz Shah Tughlaq, on the banks of the Yamuna River. The ruins of his palace and other monuments are situated in Feroz Shah Kotla, south of the memorials on the Ring Road.

They were followed by the Sayyids and the Lodis, whose tombs stand in Lodi Gardens, south of India Gate. Their defeat by the Central Asian invader Babur, in the 16th century, marked the end of the Delhi Sultanate and the dawn of the Mughal Empire. Din-Panah Fort (Purana Qila) was built above the Yamuna by Babur's son, the studious Humayun, who was forced to flee by Sher Shah, an Afghan invader. Sher Shah began constructing his new

Tomb of Bara Gumbad, Lodi Gardens.

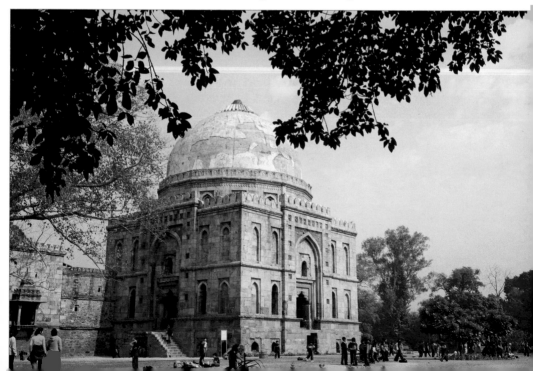

capital of Shergarh, but Humayun won back Delhi in 1555 only to die a few months later when he fell down his library stairs. Akbar, Humayun's son, moved his capital to Agra. His grandson, Shah Jahan, who built the Taj Mahal, returned to Delhi in 1638 to build the glorious Shahjahanabad. This walled capital, bound by 14 gates, included most of Old Delhi, Jama Masjid (Friday Mosque), the bazaars around Chandni Chowk and Lal Qila (Red Fort) from where he ruled his empire. Successive invasions from Persia reduced the power of the Mughals until the British took over Delhi in the 19th century.

In 1911, during the visit of King George V, Delhi was declared the capital of the British Empire in India. The present city of New Delhi, designed by Edwin Lutyens and Herbert Baker, was completed by 1931. Considered one of the great examples of colonial town planning, the architecture draws on European classical designs as well as Indian decoration, even though Lutyens famously declared his dislike of Indian buildings.

The Lakshmi Narayan Temple, aka Birla Mandir, is an imposing example of Hindu architecture.

Around Connaught Place

The circular shopping arcade of **Connaught Place ❶** (properly Rajiv Chowk) forms the heart of modern Delhi. The colonnaded corridors were built for the British to be able to shop in style. Concentric roads create an Inner, Middle and Outer Circle lined with shops, restaurants, street stalls and cinemas. The underground **Palika Bazaar** on the Outer Circle has tiny shops overflowing with tourist tat and touts. The tourist theme continues to the north, with the backpackers' ghetto of **Paharganj Bazaar**, opposite New Delhi railway station. With a huge concentration of cheap doss houses and eating places, it has been responsible for generations of cases of Delhi belly and the city authorities have recently moved in to close some of the worst fleapits and to try to improve the area.

To the southwest, Baba Kharak Singh Marg has a row of State Government emporia where regional handicrafts are sold at regulated prices. Opposite is **Hanuman Mandir** a temple dedicated to the monkey

LUTYENS

Sir Edwin Lutyens (1869–1944), principal architect of New Delhi, was as versatile as he was prolific. Having initially honed his skills on a series of English country homes and gardens, and in doing so created a style almost entirely his own, he went on to design an array of public buildings and monuments around the world, including Westminster's cenotaph. But Delhi was his most ambitious project, an unprecedented opportunity to design a whole section of a city, and is perhaps his masterpiece. It is a unique blend of Classical British and Indian styles that continues to house much of the Indian government, as well as its president, and lends the city a character and elegance that would be unimaginable without Lutyens's grand vision and meticulous execution.

god Hanuman, helper of Rama and Lakshmana in the *Ramayana*, much revered by wrestlers. At the end of this road, to the left, rises the golden dome of **Bangla Sahib Gurudwara**, the city's principal Sikh temple and well worth a visit, particularly for those not planning to make the trip to the Golden Temple in Amritsar.

Going southwest along Sansad Marg (Parliament Street) is the red sandstone **Jantar Mantar** ❷, an open-air observatory built by Maharaja Jai Singh I of Jaipur (sunrise to sunset; charge), a popular focal point for political protests. Constructed in 1724, it was the first of several observatories the ruler had built; others were later constructed in Jaipur, Ujjain, Varanasi and Mathura.

To the south, **Janpath** is the location of the huge **Central Cottage Industries Emporium** (CCIE), which offers a glimpse of the wide range of handicrafts available in India. Also here is the large, elegant Imperial Hotel, the only one to be included in Lutyens' designs for the new capital.

To the west of Connaught Place, on the aptly named Mandir (Temple) Marg is the **Lakshmi Narayan Temple**, otherwise known as the Birla Mandir. It was built in 1938 and financed by the industrialist B.D. Birla. M.K. Gandhi opened the temple but only on the condition that it should also be open to Dalits (then known as 'Untouchables'). The main celebrations take place here on Janmashtami (Krishna's birthday).

Old Delhi

The peaceful 18th-century **Qudsia Bagh** (gardens), near the Interstate Bus Terminal (ISBT) and Kashmir Gate, marks the northern boundary of the Mughal **Shahjahanabad** (often referred to as 'Old Delhi'), Delhi's seventh city.

The spectacular **Lal Qila** ❸ (Red Fort; open Tue–Sun sunrise to sunset; charge) faces Chandni Chowk (meaning moonlit or silver crossroads), once

the central avenue of a bazaar that is still an important commercial centre. A Persian couplet by Shah Jahan's court poet Amir Khusrau ('If there be paradise on the face of earth, it is this! Oh it is this! Oh it is this!') is inscribed on the walls of the Diwan-e-Khas (private audience hall), which once housed the legendary Peacock Throne and the Koh-i-noor diamond (later looted by Persian forces; see page 106). Shah Jahan, the Mughal emperor whose paradise this was, built the immense red sandstone fort with its palaces and halls in 1648.

The entry point is Lahore Gate. Inside, passing through the Chatta Chowk covered market, one enters Shah Jahan's elaborate gardens. To the far right is the Mumtaz Mahal, possibly a former harem but now a museum with a collection of Mughal artefacts including miniatures, porcelain and costumes. Next to it are the Rang Mahal and Khas Mahal, the emperor's private apartments. The octagonal tower was used for royal public appearances (including that of Britain's George V and Queen Mary

TIP

There are a number of useful websites for visitors to the city. A good all-round site is www.delhievents.com. Official government sites include: the Archaeological Survey of India (www.asi.nic.in), Delhi Government (www.delhigovt.nic.in) and Delhi Tourism, (www.delhitourism.nic.in). For information on nightlife, see www.explocity.com.

TRANSPORT WITHIN DELHI

Delhi's ever-expanding metro network is generally the best way to get around town (see www.delhimetrorail.com for the latest information). Easy to use, single fares operate by means of a token that you hold by the reader at the start of your journey and feed into the machine at the automatic barrier when you exit the station. Fares are cheap, and services run from 6am to 11pm. A rail link to Indira Gandhi airport departs from New Delhi Station (express journey 20mins).

While autorickshaws can be the most convenient way to get around the city centre, it is often hard for visitors to negotiate a fair price for their journey. The Delhi government is wise to the problem and has put an extremely useful fare calculator online (www.delhitrafficpolice.nic.in/auto-taxi-fare.htm) which will give a good idea of what to pay.

Stick to government-run buses, safer and more reliable than other operators', though still cheap. The city authority recently inaugurated an entirely new fleet of modern vehicles.

Delhi's yellow-and-black **taxis** are difficult to flag down on the street and are best picked up at their transport company's kiosks, which can be found close to all the main markets or commercial areas. Two companies that are reliable, honest and can be booked by phone are: Mega Cabs, tel: 011-4141 4141, www.megacabs.com; Meru Cab, tel: 011-4422 4422, www.merucabs.com

during their visit to India in 1931). Other buildings include the Diwan-e-Am (public audience hall), the royal baths, and the tiny white marble Moti Masjid (Pearl Mosque). Ugly concrete army barracks, a British addition to the fort, can also be seen dotted inside the massive walls. Now that the Yamuna has retreated, the fort, originally built on its banks, overlooks a large open ground, previously the site of Chor Bazaar (the thieves' market, now held near the Jama Masjid).

Chandni Chowk

Chandni Chowk ❹ is the main road leading from the Red Fort into the heart of Shahjahanabad, or Old Delhi. This now busy, crowded and noisy road was once an elegant boulevard with a canal running along its centre. Each street leading off the main road has its own speciality: silver and gold at Dariba Kalan, wedding paraphernalia and theatrical props at Kinari Bazaar, silk saris, copper and brassware and a fascinating wholesale spice market (with dried fruit and nuts from Kabul) at Naya Bazaar. On Chandni Chowk itself is the **Digambara Temple**, the oldest Jain temple in Delhi, and the **Bird Hospital**, where injured birds are nursed back to health.

The **Sispganj Gurudwara** (Sikh temple), **Sunehri Masjid** (Golden Mosque), and **Fatehpuri Masjid** (1650) are some of the sites crowded between stalls selling a jumble of wares, and the hawkers and touts. The Sisganj Gurudwara is one of the most important in the city, and is dedicated to the guru Tegh Bahadur – killed by Aurangzeb in the 17th century for refusing to renounce his faith. The famous sweetmeat shop of **Ghantewala**, established in 1790, is worth a visit. Specialities include *sohn halva* and *sohn papri* (caramelised sweets made with ghee, clarified butter).

Jama Masjid

South of Central Road, follow Dariba Kalan to the massive red sandstone and white marble **Jama Masjid** ❺ (Friday Mosque; open daily; charge; you must cover up to enter – robes are available for hire at the north gate), the focal point for Delhi's Muslims. Commissioned by Shah Jahan in 1644, the mosque can hold 20,000 people in its huge courtyard, in the centre of which is a tank used for ritual ablutions. The mosque and fort, opposite each other, were integral to the complex plan of the walled city. Outside of Friday prayers, it is sometimes possible to climb the southern minaret, although women are only admitted with a male companion.

Raj Ghat

Eastward, behind the Red Fort, the Ring Road along the Yamuna river is connected by three bridges to the Trans-Yamuna residential areas. On the river bank from Red Fort south to ITO Bridge are the cremation grounds, now mostly used as memorial parks dedicated to national leaders such as Nehru, Lal Bahadur Shastri, and Indira and Rajiv Gandhi.

Colonial architecture at the Jawarhalal Memorial Museum.

The biggest complex here is **Raj Ghat**, where M.K. Gandhi was cremated, and there are two museums dedicated to him. **Gandhi Darshan** (www.gandhismriti.nic.in; Tue–Sun 10am–5pm; free) has a good collection of paintings and photos, and charts the history of the *Satyagraha* (non-violence) movement. Close by is **Gandhi Smarak Sangrahalaya** (Fri–Wed 9.30am–5.30pm; free), which houses a display of Gandhi's personal belongings and has a library of recordings of his speeches.

North Delhi and The Ridge

British Delhi (which was strung out to the east of the Northern Ridge), with its cantonment bungalows and administrative buildings, begins to the north of Kashmere Gate. This area was known as the **Civil Lines ❻**, and a number of mementoes of British rule can be found here. One of the more beautiful is **St James's Church** (find the caretaker to ask for access). This was built in 1836 at the behest of James Skinner, a famous soldier of mixed race who, in the 19th century, formed an irregular cavalry brigade known as 'Skinner's Horse.' He initially fought on the side of the Marathas in their wars against other Indian rulers, but eventually joined the East India Company armies when the Marathas turned their attention to the British. With a large central dome and a cruciform plan, the church has a classical elegance not seen again in Delhi until the architecture of Lutyens and Baker.

Other remains of the era can be seen in the administrative buildings of the **University** campus and Delhi's most prestigious private school, **St Stephen's College**; many of India's upper crust have been educated either here or at 'Doon' School in Dehra Dun in the Himalayan foothills.

A more sombre reminder of the rule of the British can be found up on **The Ridge**. This wooded line of hills runs roughly northeast–southwest across the top of Delhi and acts in part as the city's 'lung' as well as being the refuge of much of Delhi's remaining wildlife. Here is the **Mutiny Memorial**, a neo-Gothic monument to the British and (loyal) Indian soldiers who died in the 1857 Uprising. Close by, to the north, is one of Delhi's **Ashokan Pillars**, placed here in 1867 after it had been reassembled from pieces returned from Kolkata.

At the highest point of The Ridge is the **Flagstaff Tower**, one of the earliest British buildings in Delhi. This spot was where the British civilians and wounded gathered during the 1857 Uprising while waiting for relief to arrive.

The British were not exactly modest when it came to celebrating their imperial ambitions in India. Delhi was used as the site of a number of *durbars* (processional celebrations), of which the most elaborate was that of George V in 1911 when he announced the relocation of the capital from what was then Calcutta to Delhi. The former *durbar* ground, just off K.B. Hedgewar Marg in the north of the city, is now known as Coronation

Shopping at Baba Kharak Singh Marg.

TIP

Fans of oddball
museums will want to
visit the idiosyncratic
Sulabh International
Museum of Toilets. As
well as cataloguing the
evolution of the WC, the
museum traces the
history of sanitation in
India.

Park and has been put to good use as
a dumping ground for British monuments. The most impressive of these is
a huge statue of George V that used to
stand near India Gate.

West of the city centre, out in
Mahavir Enclave, is one of Delhi's
more unusual sites, the **Sulabh
International Museum of Toilets**
(www.sulabhtoiletmuseum.org; Mon–Sat
10.30am–5.30pm; free). Set up by the
social campaigner Dr Bindeshwar
Pathak, the museum traces the evolution of sanitation from its earliest
beginnings to the most modern flush
systems (the mock-up of Louis XIV's
'throne' is quite something). The more
serious side of the museum and the
attached organisation is Dr Pathak's
work in campaigning for better sanitation across India and for better treatment of India's sanitation workers,
who come from the very lowest strata
of the caste system and face considerable discrimination.

Rajpath and India Gate

Barakhamba (Twelve Pillar) Road
leads southeast from Connaught Place

to Mandi House Chowk, which is
home to the **Rabindra Kala Sangam**
(Triveni Theatre) and café, and various auditoria hosting regular performances of dance, music and theatre.
The Rabindra Kala Sangam also contains the contemporary art gallery of
the **Lalit Kala Akademi** (Mon–Sat
11am–6pm; free) and the **Sangeet
Natak Akademi** museum, showcasing
traditional musical instruments.

The next main thoroughfare leading off the Connaught Place hub is
Kasturba Gandhi Marg, which runs
to India Gate in the heart of Lutyens'
New Delhi. The road is the location of
the cultural centres of Germany and
the UK, which have good libraries and
reading rooms in addition to regular
cultural events.

The area around **India Gate ❼**
formed the British administrative centre of Delhi with the local 'Champs
Elysées' of **Rajpath** surrounded by
lawns and shady trees, water channels
and fountains. India Gate, a 42-metre
(138ft) high archway, was built by
Lutyens at the eastern end in 1931 to
honour Indian soldiers who died during World War I and on the Northwest
Frontier. There is an 'eternal flame' to
commemorate those killed in the 1971
war with Pakistan. The area comes
alive at sunset, when many locals
gather with their families to enjoy the
wide open spaces, fly kites, play cricket
or eat an ice cream.

Rashtrapati Bhavan ❽, the presi-
dential residence (former Viceregal
Lodge), can be seen at the western end
of Rajpath with the circular **Sansad
Bhavan ❾** (Parliament House) nearby.
The huge formal Mughal-style gardens
of Rashtrapati Bhavan are among the
finest in Delhi but are only open to
the public from February to March
(see www.presidentofindia.nic.in for
more details). Flanking the approach
to Rashtrapati Bhavan are the North
and South Block Secretariats, housing
the Ministries of Finance and Home
Affairs, and Ministries of Foreign
Affairs respectively (usually referred

Kashmir Gate.

to in news reports simply as North or South Block).

To the west of Rajpath, behind Rashtrapati Bhavan, is Buddha Jayanti Smarak Park, part of the Central Ridge Reserved Forest. On the corner of Willingdon Crescent that runs alongside the park and Sardar Patel Marg stands the **Dandi Statue**. This impressive bronze shows Gandhi leading the demonstrators on his march to Dandi on the Gujarat coast to protest against the British imposing a salt tax.

Southwest of Rajpath is **Chanakyapuri**, the diplomatic enclave where the majority of foreign missions and embassies are located. Nearby is the **Santushti Complex** (opposite the Ashoka Hotel), with shops of Indian designers.

At the eastern end of Rajpath (by India Gate) are two magnificent residences, **Hyderabad House** and **Baroda House**, built for the two most powerful rulers of the so-called Princely States of British India. Along Rajpath is the headquarters of the **Indira Gandhi National Centre for the Arts** (www.ignca.nic.

in), with an auditorium and a library. Beyond India Gate lies the National Stadium, used for hockey tournaments and a key venue for the 2010 Commonwealth Games.

Further east is **Pragati Maidan**, a huge exhibition complex. Facing its entrance stand the ramparts of the **Purana Qila** ❿ (entrance by the zoo; daily sunrise to sunset; charge also covers Archaeological Museum). The fort was built by Afghan ruler Sher Shah Suri (1540–5) and was taken over by Mughal emperor Humayun when he regained the throne in 1555–6. Its Qila-e-Kunha-Masjid is the best-preserved Lodi mosque in Delhi.

Just to the right inside the main gate is the fort's **Archaeological Museum** containing artefacts that date back to the first human settlement here in around 1000 BC. The well-proportioned **Sher Mandal** pavilion, set in beautifully maintained gardens, was used as a library by the Mughal emperor Humayun and was where he fell to his death in 1555. Outside the main entrance is an attractive park and

A backstreet near Chandni Chowk..

lake (once part of the moat) surrounding the fort.

Delhi Zoo ⑪ is nearby. With its relatively large, open enclosures, it is said to be one of the better examples in the country, but Indian zoos are on the whole depressing places, resembling concentration camps rather than, at best, places to breed endangered species (for further information visit www.petaindia.com, www.aapn.org and www.zoocheck.com). The zoo shares a border with the wealthy **Sundar Nagar colony**, with some interesting shops specialising in jewellery and antique artefacts.

New Delhi museums

The area around Rajpath contains a wealth of museums. The national historical, archaeological and modern art collections are all here, as are some interesting sites relating to India's political history.

South of Rashtrapati Bhavan is Teen Murti Bhavan (Tue–Sun 10am–3pm; free), which houses the **Jawaharlal Nehru Memorial Museum** in the prime minister's former residence.

Faces of the new India at the Pragati Maidan conference centre.

Nehru's study, sitting room and bedroom have been preserved, and there is a very detailed exhibition of the history of the Independence struggle. The modesty of the interiors reflects well on one of India's greatest leaders. The research library here is one of the most important for studying modern Indian political history.

The story of the Nehru/Gandhi dynasty is continued at the **Indira Gandhi Memorial Museum** (Tue–Sun 9.30am–5pm; free) at 1 Safdarjang Road. This bungalow was her residence and the place where she was killed by her bodyguards. Bloodstains are still visible at the spot in the gardens. Inside you can see her study and her wedding sari, woven by Nehru. The path of her last moments is marked by a glass walkway in the garden.

Close by, on Tees January Marg, is the site of another political assassination, the **Gandhi Smriti** (also known as Birla House: www.gandhismriti.nic.in; Tue–Sun 9.30am–5.30pm; free), museum and memorial, in the house of the industrialist G.D. Birla. In the garden, the place where Mahatma Gandhi was shot in 1948 is marked by a simple memorial. Again the route taken by the assassinated leader is marked out, this time by a series of concrete 'footsteps'.

Southeast of India Gate is the **National Gallery of Modern Art ⑫** (www.ngmaindia.gov.in; Tue–Sun 10am–5pm; charge), in the former Delhi home of Jaipur's royal family. Its impressive permanent collection includes 1930s paintings by Jamini Roy and Nandalal Bose and 18th-century Indian landscapes by Thomas and William Daniell. The ground floor is devoted to exhibitions of work by contemporary Indian artists and photographers.

The **National Museum ⑬** (www.nationalmuseumindia.gov.in; Tue–Sun 10am–5pm; charge), south of Rajpath on Janpath, is noted for its Indian sculpture and jewellery collections, Chola bronzes and a Buddhist gallery, including a carved Buddhist gateway from Sanchi. Among the most important artefacts here are those from the Harappan excavations at Mohenjadaro (including the famous small bronze statue of a dancing girl) and the holdings of Mughal manuscripts and miniatures. Especially good, on the second floor, is the Verrier Elwin collection of Adivasi art, from northeastern, central and southern Indian states.

The **National Rail Museum** ⑭ (Tue–Sun Oct–Mar 9.30am–1pm, 1.30–5.30pm, Apr–Sept 9.30am–1pm, 1.30–7.30pm; charge), lies just off Shanti Path in Chanakyapuri, and is well worth a visit. There are some interesting period coaches and a large array of steam engines, including the huge Garratt, built in 1930 in Manchester. As well as the informative indoor displays outlining the functioning of the modern Indian rail network, there is also an unusual working steam monorail that takes visitors around the site.

The **Crafts Museum** ⑮ (www.nationalcraftsmuseum.nic.in; Tue–Sun July–Sept 9.30am–5pm, Oct–June 9.30am–6pm; charge) on Bhairon Marg by Pragati Maidan has demonstrations by regional craftsmen, huts built in regional styles and a good crafts shop. The fascinating exhibition galleries have displays of Adivasi art, woodcarving and textiles. There are *bhuta* figures from Karnataka, brightly decorated Naga objects from the northeast and some wonderful bronzes from Odisha (Orissa). The textile galleries are superb – the collections run to over 22,000 objects – as well as some astounding embroidery, especially the Kashmiri examples. There are also weaving demonstrations.

Lodi Gardens

South of India Gate lie most of the sites of the former cities of Delhi. There are also many good shopping areas, such as **Khan Market** ⑯, which has a wide range of bookshops, cafés

The Nehru Museum.

and restaurants, as well as upmarket stores selling everything for the house, including fresh flowers.

A short walk southwest along Subramaniam Road brings you to the beautiful **Lodi Gardens** ⑰ (sunrise–sunset), with fascinating tombs set in well-maintained lawns lined with rows of flower beds, immense trees, a bridge and walkways. At the Lodi Road end is the octagonal tomb of the Sayyid ruler **Muhammad Shah** (1434–44), and by the lake near Subramania Road is another octagonal tomb, of Sikandar

SHOPPING IN DELHI

Delhi has everything from bookshops and crafts to high-end fashion from India's top designers. If you are after gifts and souvenirs the first place to head for is the enormous Central Cottage Industries Emporium (CCIE) on Janpath, an excellent, fixed price, one-stop shop for Indian crafts and fabrics (available by the metre). The second is Baba Kharak Singh Marg, where you will find many of the state government emporia. The most interesting market for general shopping is Khan Market. Here you will find branches of the clothing and interior design chains Fab India and Anokhi, the booksellers Bahri & Sons and more interior design from Good Earth and Oma.

Not far away in Lodi Colony Market (Jor Bagh) are the shops of some of India's finest fashion designers, including Manish Arora and Abraham & Thakore. Manish Arora, and many more Indian designers, can also be found at the swish Crescent at the Qutb mall in South Delhi. Other good places to explore for interesting boutiques include Defence Colony and the Santushti Complex.

For antiques, curios and pieces of traditional Indian art, you can't beat Haus Khas village, in Central Delhi, where numerous boutiques and hip galleries crowd the winding medieval alleyways. Perfect for reviving pitstops, rooftop cafés afford views of the surrounding ruins and tomb gardens.

Lodi (1489–1517). In the centre of the gardens is the large Shish Gumbad, another tomb from the Lodi period. The gardens are a favourite spot for families to picnic and for young couples to grab a few moments away from the watchful eyes of their parents.

Go immediately across Lodi Road to the entrance to **Lodi Colony Market** in the colony of Jor Bagh. This has a number of upmarket boutiques and one of Delhi's best fish restaurants, Ploof (see page 142).

East along Lodi Road is the **India Habitat Centre** (www.indiahabitat. org), a cultural and conference centre which hosts regular exhibitions and film festivals. Just a few hundred metres along from the centre, in the Institutional Area, is the **Tibet House Museum** (www.tibethouse.org; Mon–Sat, July–Sept 9.30am–1pm, 2.30–6pm, Oct–June 9am–1pm, 2–5pm; charge). It has some fine exhibits, including *thankas*, sculptures and a range of Tibetan musical instruments.

There are two other cultural institutes in the area: the tiled facade of the **India Islamic Cultural Centre** (Lodi Road; www.iiccentre.org), which holds conferences and temporary exhibitions, and the **India International Centre** (Max Mueller Marg; www. iicdelhi.nic.in), haunt of Delhi's intellectuals and academics. It is notoriously hard to get access to the IIC (you must be invited by a member), but if you can it has a superb library and a pleasant café.

Mughal tombs

Safdarjang's Tomb ⑱ (daily sunrise to sunset; charge) and its adjoining rose garden are at the western end of Lodi Road just across Aurobindo Marg. This huge monument, dating from 1753, is the last significant piece of Mughal architecture to be built in Delhi. The gardens have been renovated and are now beautifully maintained.

At the eastern end of Lodi Road is **Humayun's Tomb** ⑲ (daily sunrise to sunset; charge). Set in beautiful gardens, the red sandstone monument is the finest Mughal building in Delhi (listed as a Unesco World Heritage Site in 1993) and was the prototype for the Taj Mahal. It was commissioned by Humayun's senior widow, Bega Begum, and completed in 1565. Also in the grounds are the remains of the octagonal tomb of Isa Khan. To the north, easily visible from the gardens, is the modern Damdama Sahib Gurudwara. Not far from the tomb complex is the **Nila Gumbad**, a blue-tiled late-Mughal tomb.

To the west of Humayun's Tomb is the shrine, or *dargah*, of the Sufi saint of the Chisti order, **Sheikh Nizamuddin Aulia** ⑳ (1236–1325), after whom the surrounding colonies are named. The *dargah* is a haven of peace in this busy Muslim area; the tomb of the saint is in a pavilion with beautiful marble screens (note that women are not allowed in the tomb itself). Also buried here are the Mughal emperor Muhammad Shah (1719–48) and the saint's disciple and

Indira Gandhi Memorial Museum.

poet Amir Khusrau. Qawwali singing sessions often happen after the evening *namaz*, making it a good time to visit, particularly on a Friday.

Heading south down Aurobindo Marg, past Safdarjung airport, brings you to the popular INA fruit and vegetable market consisting of warrens of covered shacks selling meat, fish, poultry and every imaginable household good. Across the road is the **Dilli Haat Food and Crafts Bazaar**, which provides a pavilion for regional craftspeople from all the Indian states and an opportunity to taste their varied cuisine (10.30am–10pm; charge) from the very hygienic stalls.

South Delhi

Just to the south of Dilli Haat is Delhi's Inner Ring Road. Crossing underneath the flyover, past the well-maintained gardens planted in memory of Rajiv Gandhi, brings you to South Delhi.

Lying to the west of Aurobindo Marg is one of the most attractive enclaves in South Delhi, **Hauz Khas Village** ㉑. Poised at the edge of a 14th-century water reservoir and madrasa, and the tomb of Firoz Shah Tughlaq, the narrow streets and calm air seem far away from the hectic traffic along the main road. Although the village has been transformed into a colony of expensive boutiques and art galleries (particularly good is the Village Art Gallery, which has a wide selection of modern and contemporary Indian art), it still retains much of its greenery and charm.

Monuments dot the area: the ruins of **Siri Fort** ㉒, now very overgrown and difficult to see, stand near the Asian Games Village complex to the east. Much of the area is open only to members of the sports facilities built for the 1982 games, but the residential village is worth a look for students of architecture. Designed by Raj Rewal, the well-conceived housing project takes its cue from the tightly packed

cubist construction of traditional Indian urban architecture.

To the north of Siri Fort, at Hudco Place, Khel Gaon, is one of the first air-conditioned malls in Delhi, Ansal Plaza. Much loved by the middle classes who come here to eat and shop, it seems to have maintained its place alongside the super malls springing up further south.

Directly south of Nizamuddin in Nehru Place is the modern white marble, lotus-shaped **Baha'i Lotus Temple** ㉓ (daily 9am–5pm; free). Visitors must take off their footwear before entering the gardens around the temple itself. Standing on Kalkaji Hill, this iconic piece of Delhi architecture, designed by Fariburz Shah, was completed in 1986 as a pilgrimage site for the Baha'i faith. Nearby, the colony markets (M and N Blocks) of Greater Kailash offer some of the best shopping and finest restaurants in Delhi.

The Qutb Complex

At the southern end of Aurobindo Marg, past the Outer Ring Road and

WHERE

In addition to the Dilli Haat at the INA Market on Aurobindo Marg, there is another Dilli Haat in Pitampura, northern Delhi on Netaji Subash Place. There is a nominal entrance fee.

Exhibits at the National Gallery of Modern Art.

FACT

The Delhi Metro became India's second underground rail network (after Kolkata's) when it opened in 2002. It is set to expand and by 2020 will contain a greater mileage of track than the London Underground.

the Aurobindo Ashram, lies the district of Mehrauli. Here stands one of the most important sites in Delhi, the **Qutb Minar Complex** ㉔ (daily sunrise to sunset; charge), a Unesco World Heritage Site. The Qutb Minar itself is a remarkable 72-metre (278ft) -high tower, engraved with verses from the Qur'an. It was built in the 13th century by Qutb-ud-Din-Aibak, the first Muslim sultan of Delhi, to celebrate his victory over the Hindu kings. The first storey was finished by Qutb-ud-Din and the final two by his son-in-law Iltutmish (whose tomb lies nearby). The cupola that once sat on the very top was destroyed in an earthquake in the 19th century, and unfortunately visitors are no longer allowed up to the balcony that encircles the top of the first storey.

In the grounds, Aibak's **Quwwat-ul-Islam Mosque** is believed to be the oldest in India, built using parts of the demolished Hindu and Jain temples of Qila Rai Pithora. In the mosque courtyard is a 4th-century iron pillar, remarkable for having never shown any sign of corrosion.

Mehrauli

The ruins of **Lal Kot**, Delhi's first city, are spread across the surrounding district of **Mehrauli** ㉕. The village of the same name lies just to the south amid a labyrinth of old Indian bazaars. Among the most important monuments here is the octagonal tomb of Adham Khan, who was killed by the emperor Akbar. The building is known as the **Bhulbhulaiyan**. As well as the lovely *baoli* (step well), also worth searching out are the *dargah* of **Qutbuddin Bakhtiyar Kaki** (access for males only) and the nearby marble **Moti Masjid**.

In the south of Mehrauli are the colourful tombs of **Jamali Kamali**, and the **Hauz-i-Shamsi** reservoir commissioned by Iltutmish in 1230. On the northeastern corner of Hauz-i-Shamsi lies the **Jahaz Mahal**, a ruined Lodi pavilion.

Chattarpur

Beyond Mehrauli, towards the Haryana border and Gurgaon, are three more interesting sights. The first you come to is the **Garden of**

The resplendent shrine of Sufi saint Sheikh Nizamuddin Aulia.

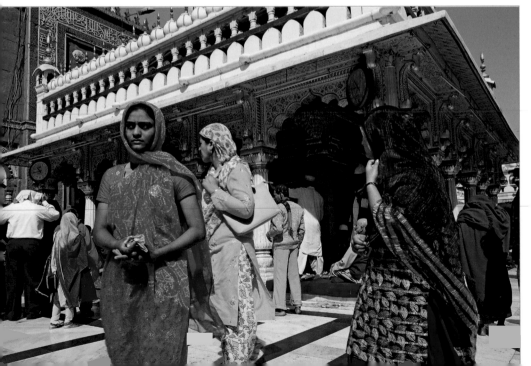

the **Five Senses** (daily 8am–9pm; charge). Laid out by Delhi Tourism and opened in 2003, the extensive formal gardens are quite beautiful and full of running water and sculptures. The higher parts of the hill against which they are laid out have been left to the natural scrub of the area, and there are great views over the city.

Turn south again to see the spectacular modern temples and ashram complexes of **Chattarpur**. This is one of the largest temples in India, all carved white marble and huge statues, some of it in slightly dubious taste.

That is not a charge that can be laid against the nearby **Sanskriti Museums** (www.sanskritifoundation.org; Tue–Sat 10am–5pm; free). The beautifully laid-out displays in the three museums of Indian terracotta, everyday art and textiles make this one of the best museums in the city.

On the Mehrauli–Badarpur road, the 14th-century ruins of **Tughlaqabad Fort** ㉖ (daily sunrise to sunset; free) and **Adilabad**, Delhi's third city, dominate the landscape.

Remains of ramparts, water-storage tanks and subterranean passages can be explored, but this area can be rather dangerous to visit alone. Beyond Tughlaqabad is the large tank at **Suraj Kund**. Excavations here have revealed some of the area's earliest settlements.

Gurgaon and NOIDA

To the far south through the expanding urban sprawl is Delhi's satellite city of **Gurgaon**, which is mostly comprised of middle-class housing and shopping malls, including the vast new DLF Mall of India, which when it opens in August 2013 will be the largest in the country, with parking space for 10,000 cars.

More huge malls are to be found in **NOIDA** (the New Okhala Development Area) across the river. Of most interest to visitors here is the enormous **Akshardham Temple** (www.akshardham.com). Built by the Swaminarayan Foundation and opened in 2005, this confection in sandstone and marble is impressive, if brash, and set in lovely gardens.

TIP

The following venues host dance and music performances: India Habitat Centre (Lodi Road, tel: 011-2468 2001, www.indiahabitat.org); India International Centre (40 Max Müller Marg, tel: 011-2461 9431, www.iicdelhi.nic.in); Kamani Auditorium (1 Copernicus Marg, tel: 011-4350 3351, www.kamaniauditorium.org); Sangeet Natak Akademi (Rabindra Bhavan, Firoz Shah Road, tel: 011-2338 7246, www.sangeetnatak.com).

The spectacular tomb of Sikandar Lodi in the Lodi Gardens.

RESTAURANT AND BARS

PRICE CATEGORIES

Average price for dinner, up to three courses for one person, excluding alcoholic drinks:

£ = up to Rs200
££ = Rs200–500
£££ = Rs500–1,000
££££ = over Rs1,000

Delhi is a good place to try food from all over India, with a range of South Indian, Punjabi, Bengali and Lucknavi restaurants, among others. The food of Delhi itself is partly that of the Punjabi immigrants – meat-based curries and rich *dal* and vegetable dishes – and that derived from the cooking of the Mughal courts, referred to generally as *Mughlai*. The latter makes great use of the *tandoor* oven and marinades in yoghurt with spices. The finished curries are often delicate with dairy products added during the cooking.

Restaurants

Connaught Place

Cibo
Hotel Janpath
Janpath.
Tel: 011-4302 9291, www.cibodelhi.com.
£££–££££
Baroque extravagance is the hallmark of this remarkable Mediterranean restaurant, by the same designer as Veda Lounge, below. The indoor seating is pleasant enough but the outdoor area is exceptional, with a walled garden, flowing water on three sides and a huge bunch of grapes as the centrepiece. The food is equally impressive, with all the Italian favourites done well, plus some interesting new twists.

Saravana Bhavan
46 Janpath.
Tel: 011-2331 7755. **£**
One of a chain of excellent South Indian vegetarian restaurants, with good *dosas* and *thalis*. Very clean and good value.

Veda Lounge
H26–7, Connaught Place.
Tel: 011-4151 3535, www.vedarestaurants.com. **£££–££££**
Decorated with help from one of Delhi's leading fashion designers and so very chic. The inventive modern Indian food is also a break from the

norm, though the North Indian dishes are better than those from the south. The wine list is impressive, and the cocktails well put together.

Yamu's Panchayat
92 NDMC Market, Connaught Place. **££**
The only 100 percent hygienic place in the capital where you can sample the full range of authentic paan, (a 'digestif' made of betel leaf wrapped around various spices and betel nut) prepared and – a first for the city – served by women. Come in a group and you can order the house speciality – paan aadab – seven individual paans wrapped in one big leaf. Everything's beautifully presented and fresh, and they use honey rather than sugar as a sweetener. Beloved of MPs and celebs (Madhuri Dixit is a regular).

Old Delhi

Chor Bizarre
Hotel Broadway, 4/15A Asaf Ali Road.
Tel: 011-2327 3821, www.chorbizarrerestaurant.com. **£££**
Reliably delicious Mughlai and Kashmiri fare in interestingly quirky surroundings. The salad buffet is housed in a classic car, while the tables are made from all manner of oddments, including a four-poster bed. Reservations highly recommended.

Karim's Hotel
Gali Kababiyan, Matia Mahal, near the Jama Masjid.
Tel: 011-2326 9880, www.karimhoteldelhi.com. **£**
Probably the best Muslim food in the city. Mouthwatering non-vegetarian tandoori dishes and excellent breads. There are several other, less atmospheric, branches of this legendary restaurant in other parts of the city.

Around Rajpath

Bukhara
ITC Maurya, Sardar Patel Marg, Diplomatic Enclave.
Tel: 011-2611 2233, www.itchotels.in. **££££**
Often picked out as serving the best tandoori food in the city, this Delhi institution serves up beautifully prepared food from the North West Frontier Province. The kebabs and *makhni dal* are delicious.

Have More
11–12 Pandara Road Market.
Tel: 011-2338 7070. **££–£££**

There are a handful of upmarket *dhabas* here, all of which are reasonable, but this is the best of the bunch. The location of these late-closing Punjabi restaurants close to India Gate makes them a good place to have lunch while taking in the sights, or handy for a late dinner.

Orient Express
Taj Palace, 2 Sardar Patel Marg.
Tel: 011-2611 0202, www.tajhotels.com
££££
The best, and most expensive, modern European food that the city has to offer, and certainly the only place where your meal will be served in a stationary railway carriage. First-class ingredients are worked into classic dishes and the set menus are a very good (and cheaper) place to start. Reserve in advance.

Ploof
13 Main Market, Lodi Colony.
Tel: 011-2463 4666, www.ploofdeli.com.
£££–££££
One of the city's only seafood specialists, and easily the best. Fish is flown in daily, so you need not fret about freshness. Although there is a lot on the menu, the best preparations are those from South India and Southeast Asia.

Around Lodi Gardens

Dilli Haat
Opposite INA Market, Aurobindo Marg.
Tel: 011-2467 8812. **£**
The 'Foods of India' complex here has very cheap and clean stalls, run by different state tourist-development corporations. An easy way to conduct a culinary tour of India and a good place to try unusual dishes, such as Minicoy fish curry.

Flavors
51–4C Moolchand Flyover Complex, Defence Colony.
Tel: 011-2464 5644. **£££**
Italian-owned and run, Flavors dishes up some of the most authentic Italian cuisine in India. The portions are huge, and the desserts excellent. The garden terrace is still the place to sit, making this a great place for lunch, and the space means it is also a good place to bring children.

Lodi – The Garden Restaurant
By Gate 1, Lodi Gardens, Lodi Road.
Tel: 011-2465 5054. **£££–££££**
This restaurant has a beautiful

location in Lodi Gardens. The terrace overlooking the gardens and the outside seating under trees is the biggest draw, although the Mediterranean food comes a close second. Sunday brunch makes for a particularly pleasant experience, though reservations are essential.

Mamagoto
1st Floor, 53 Middle Lane, Khan Market.
Tel: 011-4516 6060, www.mamagoto.in. **£££**
The minimalist interior belies the adventurous menu at this Southeast Asian eatery, where the emphasis is on fun and discovery. It's certainly one of the most varied menus of its kind in Delhi, and the quality of the food and excellent service have made it deservedly popular since its recent opening.

Threesixty Degrees
The Oberoi, Dr Zakir Hussain Marg.
Tel: 011-2436 3030, www.oberoihotels.com.
££££
One of the city's hippest restaurants, with a pleasant, modern interior. The glass-fronted kitchens produce an amazing variety of Japanese, Continental and Indian delicacies. Although not cheap, it's quite an experience, and the buffet lunch and Sunday brunch are good value.

South Delhi

Café Turtle
Full Circle Bookshop, 5B Khan Market.
Tel: 011-2465 5641, www.cafeturtle.com. **££**
Cosy little bookshop café-diner, decorated in sunny Mediterranean colours, with a menu to match: they're big on pasta, Moroccan light bites, pittas, falafels and sandwiches, though to a full range of more filling World dishes too – and the cakes are legendary.

Gunpowder
3rd Floor, 22 Haus Khas Village.
Tel: 011-2653 5700, www.
gundpowderhauzkhas.in. **£££**
Can be tricky to find, but worth the effort for the great views from the terrace. The South Indian cuisine takes its cue from the restaurant's name – this is genuinely hot stuff, so stay away if spices are not your thing. The curries and breads get great reviews, as does the friendly, refreshingly casual service.

Oh! Calcutta
E Block, International Trade Towers, Nehru Place.
Tel: 011-2646 4180. **£££**
This West Bengal place has been a great success. This is first and foremost a seafood restaurant, and particularly recommended are the *kakra chingri bhapa*, steamed crab-

and-prawn cakes flavoured with lime and mustard, along with that Bengali staple *hilsa* and the wonderful dhal and vegetable dishes.

Punjabi by Nature
11 PVR Priya Complex, Basant Lok, Vasant Vihar.
Tel: 011-4151 6666, www.punjabibynature.in.
£££
Perhaps the best Punjabi cuisine in Delhi. The food at this lively place gets consistently rave reviews, and is hugely popular with local diners.

Sagar
18 Defence Colony Market.
Tel: 011-2433 3440. **£**
Delhi's most acclaimed South Indian eatery is famous above all for serving the city's largest, crispest dosas: order a 'family dosa', and you'll be brought a 4ft-long monster which has to be carried by two waiters. The rest of the menu relies more on fabulous southern flavours than visual impact to impress; everything's tasty, the service supreme, and prices more than fair – a winning combination that's been keeping Delhiites coming back for years.

Mehrauli

Olive Bar & Kitchen
Haveli No. 6–8, One Style Mile, Kalka Dass Marg.
Tel: 011-2664 5500, www.olivebarandkitchen.com. **£££££**
One of the city's best Mediterranean eateries; the menu is varied and consistently of a high standard, the service is discreet but polished and the decor superb. Set in a whitewashed old haveli, with a choice of dining inside or out, this could almost be a villa on the Med. Has been a favoured with Delhi's smart set since day one – don't dream of going without a reservation.

Bars

Connaught Place

1911
Imperial Hotel, 1 Janpath.
Tel: 011-2334 1234, www.theimperialindia.com.
The bar at the Imperial is sheer class (in the 'upper' sense). Quiet and refined with a huge selection of drinks, the outside seating overlooking the lawns might well be the best place in the city to have a sundowner. Make sure you are suitably dressed for the occasion.

Q'BA
E42–3, Connaught Place.
Tel: 011-4151 2888, www.bba.co.in
One of the trendier places in town,

this large and super-stylish place is arranged over two floors, with a spectacular terrace overlooking Connaught Place. The food is adequate, but Q'BA is best used for a drink and for spotting Delhi A-listers.

South Delhi

Ai
2nd Floor, MGF Metropoltian Mall, Saket.
Tel: 011-4065 4567.
The Japanese food here is excellent, if expensive, but it's become better known as a bar to hang out at with the young and the glamorous of Delhi's jet set. Could be anywhere in the world, with a fun, energetic vibe.

The Tapas Lounge
Aman Hotel, Lodhi Road.
Tel: 011-4363 3333, www.amanrsorts.in.
Authentic tapas in uber-chic, minimal surroundings. It's certainly not cheap but nor does it feel it, with a sophistication and quality unsurpassed by the competing five stars in the city.

NOIDA

Fluid
Hotel Mosaic, C-1 Sector 18.
Tel: 0120-402 5000.
A bit far-flung but one of the best and most popular DJ bars in the city. Very chic, with a dance floor and spaces to lounge around. The cocktail and wines lists are impressive.

Chor Bizarre.

The Taj Mahal.

THE NORTHERN PLAINS

The flat, sunburnt plains of the Ganges and Yamuna
rivers are India's breadbasket, home to almost 40
percent of the country's population and many of its
greatest sights.

Between the soothing serenity of the Golden Temple to the west and the equally becalming Mahabodhi Temple to the east lies one of the most intense, tumultuous and unmissable parts of this extraordinary country. The further east you travel, the more like the wild west it becomes, from the almost military bearing and discipline of the Punjab's proud Sikhs to the apparent lawlessness of large swathes of Bihar. Between the two, Uttar Pradesh is considered by many to be the heartland of India – its soul enshrined in the incomparable Taj Mahal, its turbulent political life played out on the teeming streets of Lucknow, and religious sentiments laid bare on the burning ghats of Varanasi.

Through it all runs India's most sacred river, the Ganges, known locally as the Ganga. From its source in the high mountains of western Uttarakhand, it combines with an increasing number of tributaries as it heads eastwards, most famously at Allahabad where it merges with the Yamuna; by the time it discharges into the Bay of Bengal, the Ganges has drained an area of 1 million sq km (386,000 sq miles). The plains that the Ganges irrigates support one of the most densely populated areas in the world, all dependent on this great river for their very survival, a

One of the region's 320 million inhabitants.

fact which only serves further to elevate the Ganges's place in the Indian psyche.

PUNJAB AND HARYANA

The Punjab at one time extended northwest to the Indus River and was known to the Greeks as Pentopotamia, because of the five rivers that ran through it. The Persians named it *Panj* (five) *ab* (waters) – a name which has stuck. In 1947 its character, identity and soul were irrevocably torn apart by the atrocities of Partition.

Main Attractions

Golden Temple, Amritsar
Agra Fort
Itimad-ud-Daula
Taj Mahal
Fatehpur Sikri
Vrindavan
Bara Imambara
Varanasi
Sarnath
Bodhgaya

Pakistan was created in response to escalating Hindu-Muslim communal violence and unrest, but the abruptness of its birth left millions of non-Muslims on the Pakistan side of the border, and millions of Muslims on the Indian side. As each community attempted to realign itself via the only border crossing just west of Amritsar, the inevitable clashes developed into wholesale and horrific carnage. Of the 13 million people who attempted to traverse the frontier, over half a million lost their lives.

Although the larger part of the Punjab went to Pakistan, both Pakistan and India retained the name 'Punjab' for their respective states since Punjabi is spoken on both sides of the border. It was this linguistic distinction that eventually led to the further division of the Indian Punjab in 1966 when the new states of Punjab (92 percent Punjabi-speaking), Haryana and Himachal Pradesh (predominantly Hindi-speaking) were born.

The wide-open plains of the Punjab have always been the main route into the country for invaders from the northwest, and have thus witnessed some of India's most momentous battles. Key to securing control of the Subcontinent, these northwestern

The Northern Plains

flatlands were also a major prize in themselves: the region is one of the most fertile in the world, its productive soil watered by the numerous rivers flowing down from the massive mountains to the north. Indian Punjab alone accounts for around 2 percent of the global wheat and cotton harvest.

Their impressive contribution to India's agricultural output notwithstanding, it is the gregarious, assiduous people of the Punjab who exert the largest influence on the country's character. The wide-ranging influence of Punjabi music, culture and cuisine on North India, and particularly Delhi, far belies the relative paucity of the Punjabi population – just 2 percent of the Indian total.

Haryana, also a major agricultural contributor, has more recently come to prominence as India's industrial powerhouse. Half of the millions of cars and motorbikes made in India are manufactured here, while Gurgaon, a Singapore-styled satellite city to the south of Delhi, has emerged as a major player in the IT sector.

Despite the linguistic division that separated the states in the 1960s, the people of the Punjab and Haryana have much in common.

Both Punjab and Haryana have more history than historical monuments, more facilities for tourists than places of tourist interest, and are generally seen as interesting places to stop off on the way elsewhere rather than destinations in themselves. Having said that, Amritsar's Golden Temple is without doubt one of India's star attractions, rated by many visitors as more impressive even than the Taj Mahal.

Historical sites

There are several Mughal monuments in Haryana, of which the most popular is **Pinjore Gardens** at the base of the Sivalik Hills, 20km (12 miles) north of Chandigarh on the road to Simla. Inside the Mughal battlements is a beautifully laid-out garden with fountains and cascades, designed in the 17th century by Nawab Fadai Khan, foster brother of Aurangzeb, one of the great Mughal emperors.

FACT

The Hero Honda plant in Haryana is the world's largest manufacturer of motorcycles, producing 1.7 million units a year.

Worshippers in the Dwarkadhish Temple, Mathura

TRANSPORT

Amritsar now has an international airport, with flights to Asia, the Middle East, Europe and North America, as well as internal connections to Delhi, also available from Chandigarh airport. Both the Punjab and Haryana are very well connected by train, meaning buses only need be used for the most local or far-flung destinations.

Amritsar: Shatabdi (express) train service to Delhi and beyond (2 daily; 6hrs) plus regular services to Pathankot (4 daily; 2hrs 30min).

Chandigarh: Shatabdi train service to Delhi (2 daily; 3hrs30min plus 5 slower trains) and Kalka (7 daily; 30–40min). For services to Amritsar and other destinations, go to Ambala and change. Buses are the best choice for points north: Shimla (4hrs), Manali (11hrs) and Dharamsala (8hrs).

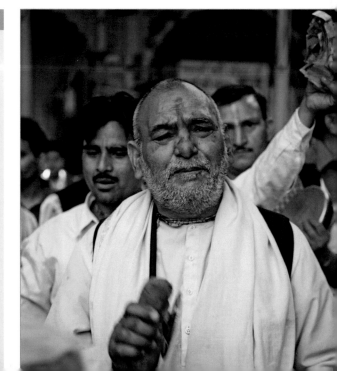

The gardens also offer panoramic views of the Himalayas.

Close to Delhi is **Suraj Kund**, an 8th-century Hindu sun temple, and home to a huge handicrafts *mela* (fair) every February, while beyond lies **Badkhal Lake**, with a resthouse overlooking its stretch of water.

Punjab and Haryana contain some of the earliest evidence of Indian societies. Archaeologists have found implements made of quartzite fashioned over 300,000 years ago. Agricultural tools made of copper and bronze prove the existence of rural communities around 2500 BC. Later excavations have unearthed whole cities built around that period.

It was through these two states that invaders from the northwest – Greeks, Turks, Mongols, Persians and Afghans – entered India, and where many battles were fought. Their sites are marked with commemorative stones and mausoleums of kings and commanders, with the most famous at **Panipat** (also the site of the shrine of the Muslim saint Abu Ali Kalandar) and Kurukshetra in Haryana. There

are innumerable forts scattered all over the countryside, including those of **Bathinda**, **Faridkot** and **Anandpur Sahib** (see page 153). Both states have developed wildlife sanctuaries along lakes, swamps and rivers, equipped with attractive tourist bungalows, while Haryana Tourism has now started to offer 'farm holidays' in an attempt to remind Delhiites of the joys of the country.

Le Corbusier's city

Of the many things that Punjab and Haryana have in common, the most important is their shared capital, **Chandigarh ❶**. Prior to partition the Punjab was governed from Lahore, but once that city had been ceded to Pakistan, the Indian side of the newly bisected state was left without a capital city. The idea of building a brand-new, planned city, rather than expanding an existing one, appealed to Jawaharlal Nehru, India's first prime minister. He saw it as the perfect project to reflect the character and ambition of a brave, newly independent India. Since both states have

Le Corbusier architecture at Chandigarh.

laid claims to the city, it is administered by the Central Government as a Union Territory until a final decision regarding its future is made. However, in the same city reside governors of the two states; in the same office buildings but on different floors are their separate secretariats and their respective High Courts.

Beautifully located below the Sivalik Hills, Chandigarh presented a fascinating challenge for ambitious mid-20th-century architects. The concept was initiated by Albert Mayer, an American, and Matthew Nowicki, from Poland, but the project was then taken over by the famous Swiss-born French architect Le Corbusier, assisted by his cousin Jeanneret and an English husband-and-wife team, Maxwell Fry and Jane Drew. They settled on a grid design for the new city's streets, giving Chandigarh a different feel from anywhere else in India; with all those straight roads and roundabouts it is not unlike an eastern version of the British 'new town', Milton Keynes.

Le Corbusier himself designed most of its important public buildings, including the **Secretariat**, the **Legislative Assembly** and the **High Court**. For those who are interested in the city's design there is an **Architecture Museum** with displays of the original plans and models inside the Government Museum complex. Many of these buildings are on stilts, an architectural style copied by many private institutions and homes.

The city has for some years been generating headlines for the way its architectural heritage – from old chairs out of the Legislative Assembly building, to prints, pictures, tapestries, carvings and even door handles – are being removed and sold piecemeal by officials, who have no idea of their actual worth. Bought at auction by local junk dealers, many of the items – originally designed by Le Corbusier and his team and regarded as collectors' items in the West – find their way to international art houses where they are sold for huge sums; one manhole cover recently fetched an amazing £15,000 in a sale in London. While some are fixtures formerly condemned by beaurocrats as 'unfit for

Nek Chand's Rock Garden.

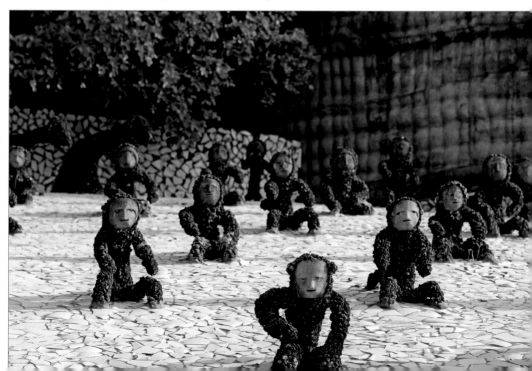

TIP

Tourists are welcome to visit the Golden Temple, but must respect Sikh cultural traditions. Shoes and socks must be left at the entrance cloakroom (no charge), and visitors are expected to wash their feet by walking through the shallow bath at the entrance. It is also necessary to cover one's head with a scarf – these are provided at the entrance. There is an information office (usually open 7am–8pm) near the entrance.

The holy site at the confluence of the Yamuna and Ganges, Allahabad.

use' by the local administration, many are thought to have been illegally removed.

Chandigarh is a very green city, with a large variety of flowering trees. It has an extensive **Rose Garden** with over 1,000 varieties. The **Government Museum and Art Gallery** (Tue–Sun 10am–4.30pm; charge) was also designed by Le Corbusier and features a good collection of Gandharan sculpture and miniature painting. **Sukhna Lake**, a 15-minute walk east from the centre, is a pleasant place for a stroll, its wide boulevard a popular evening hangout.

Chandigarh's quirkiest and most charming attraction is without doubt Nek Chand's compellingly unique **Rock Garden** (Oct–Mar 9am–6pm, Apr–Sept 9am-7pm; charge), just to the north of Sukhna Lake. The idiosyncratic Chand, after starting work in Chandigarh as a roads inspector in 1951, noticed on his travels large amounts of unclaimed, recyclable building material on the city's many construction sites. Ever enterprising, he decided to build a small garden

in which these materials could be fashioned into attractive sculptures. He chose as his site a gorge within a demarcated green zone, the illegality of his endeavour obliging him to work at night for fear of discovery. And so it continued for 18 years until, in 1975, the authorities – presumably to their considerable surprise – discovered Chand's garden. By this time it had grown to cover an area of 5 hectares (12 acres), and consisted of a series of painstakingly crafted courtyards, each containing hundreds of sculpted animals, musicians and dancers.

At this point the authorities should by rights have demolished the garden, but to their eternal credit decided instead to give Chand a workforce of 50, an annual salary and instructions to finish what he started. Today the garden covers 16 hectares (40 acres), attracts 5,000 visitors daily and has received substantial recognition worldwide.

Temples of the Punjab

The Punjab's largest city is **Amritsar** ❷ with its **Golden Temple** (open 24

MAHARAJA RANJIT SINGH

Maharaja Ranjit Singh took over control of a small area of the Punjab from his father at the age of 11. After a series of successful campaigns, he persuaded the various Sikh factions to unite as one state under his leadership, taking the title of Maharaja in 1801. He soon waged the first of many battles, defeating an army in Gujarat before vanquishing the Afghans and taking control of Lahore. For the next 40 years he extended the boundary of his kingdom, eventually to bring Pashtun, Amritsar, Kashmir and all of present-day Punjab under his control. He was famed as a just leader whose court was composed of people of all religions and from every corner of the earth. His army was trained by French, German, British and American officers, and became the most efficient fighting force for miles around.

hours), the holiest of holy Sikh shrines, and, in the past, a flashpoint for religious and political conflict. These days it's a bustling but perfectly safe destination, the urban sprawl outside the old city walls much like elsewhere in India, which only accentuates the tranquillity of the temple within.

The site was stormed by government troops in 1984 in an operation known as 'Blue Star', now seen by some observers as the most embarrassing in the history of the Indian Army. In response to escalating Sikh-Hindu violence, Sikh militants had established the Golden Temple as their military base, turning it in to a formidably fortified stronghold. By mid-1984 the militants had effectively taken the law in to their own hands and Indira Gandhi, prime minister at the time, decided that enough was enough and ordered military intervention.

The Indian Army envisaged a swift, one-sided assault, but had grossly underestimated the firepower of the Sikhs, who were equipped with machine guns and rockets. In the event it took the army three days of heavy fighting and the deployment of 20 tanks to take control of the temple; the official death toll stands at 493, but most eyewitness accounts put it in the thousands, the majority innocent pilgrims. Recriminations were wide-ranging, and the bloody episode led to the assassination of Indira Gandhi by her Sikh bodyguards later the same year.

Amritsar was founded over 400 years ago by Guru Ram Das, the fourth of the 10 Sikh Gurus. His son and successor, Arjun, raised a temple in the middle of a pool, sanctified its waters and installed the Sikhs' holy scripture, the *Granth Sahib*, in its inner sanctum. The sacred pool – *amrit* (nectar) *sar* (pool) – gives the city its name. In 1803, the Sikh ruler Maharaja Ranjit Singh (1780–1839; see panel, page 150) rebuilt the temple in marble and gold, since when it has been known as the Golden Temple. The Sikhs refer to it as the *Harimandir* (the temple of God) or *Darbar Sahib* (the court of the Lord).

Today the temple is a soothing, peaceful place to be, even if (or

The Golden Temple.

Street food in Lucknow.

perhaps because) it is run with an almost military efficiency. It is worthwhile spending an hour or two in the temple complex (be sure to have your head covered and feet bare), listening to the hymn-singing and watching the thousands of pilgrims at worship.

There are a number of shrines of historical importance, notably the **Akal Takht** (throne of the timeless God) facing the temple where arms of the warrior gurus, their dresses and emblems can be seen, and the eight-storey **Baba-Atal Tower**. The temple kitchen, which provides food free of charge to all visitors, is well worth seeking out; in return for the free meal, diners are expected to help with either the preparation of the food or the washing-up afterwards. The 'chapatti factory' should not be missed. There's also a museum above the temple's main entrance, although it's decidedly not for the faint-hearted. It depicts Sikh conflicts over the years, with a number of interesting paintings leading up to more recent times, when photographs take over; some of the before-and-after shots of Sikh martyrs are especially gory.

Besides the Golden Temple, there is its Hindu counterpart, the 16th-century **Durgiana Temple**; and **Jallianwala Bagh** where on 13 April 1919, in one of the worst atrocities of British rule, General Dyer notoriously fired on a peaceful, unarmed crowd and killed at least 300 people, shocking the nation – and boosting the emerging independence movement. The garden has a monument commemorating the event. Amritsar is also an important industrial and commercial centre and, away from the peace of the Golden Temple complex, is a busy and congested city.

TURBANS

Varieties of the distinctive turban – known in India as a pagri or dastar – are worn by Hindus, Muslims and Sikhs, but it is the last group with which they are most associated. Uncut hair is one of the five 'articles of faith' which all baptised Sikhs are expected to wear, and turbans were thus adopted as a practical way of containing such untrimmed tresses. Typically, Sikhs use at least 4.5 metres (15ft) of cloth, sometimes stitched into a double width. You will see all shapes, sizes and colours. Often the hair is first wrapped into a bun and placed into a handkerchief. (On casual occasions, the outer turban may be left off.) Punjabi turbans tend to be neat and tidy, especially compared to the enormous desert turbans seen in Rajasthan, which are up to 7 metres (23ft) long. Turbans are a male preserve: women, also required to keep their hair uncut, usually drape a large scarf over their heads.

In traditional times, Sikhs wore a special protective turban known as dumalla into battle. It featured a chand tora, or crescent sword symbol held in place at the front with a chord of woven chainmail. Tied into various patterns, the chand tora helped protect the wearer against slashing blades. You'll still see it worn by devout Sikh pilgrims at special ceremonial processions and festivals today, usually over in navy blue and saffron dumalla frequently reaching two or three feet in height.

Motorcycle helmets will not accommodate a turban. While helmets are compulsory for non-turban wearers, the law has been amended to allow Sikhs to ride motorbikes without them, although they must legally be at least 5 metres (16ft) in length – anything shorter having been deemed to offer inadequate protection. Protective goggles are strapped on, and fastidious city Sikhs use a dust cover, akin to a tea cosy, for two-wheeler rides around town (beard nets are also commonly seen).

It is considered a humiliating offence to knock someone's turban from his head. Abject apology is shown by removing one's own turban and placing it at another man's feet. In hot lands across the Muslim world, turbans protect men from the heat and blows to the head. Persian invaders brought a refined aesthetic to the Mughal courts, with turban gems and feather adornments to indicate status.

Further afield

There are many other Sikh temples dotted around the Indian Punjab. In the foothills of the Himalaya by the Sutlej river in the northeastern corner of the state is **Anandpur Sahib** where, in 1699, the last of the Sikh gurus, Govind Singh, baptised the first five Sikhs into the militant fraternity he called the *Khalsa* ('the pure'). Here are several temples and a fortress, **Kesgarh**. In the plains west of Chandigarh, a large complex of temples, palaces and forts can be seen at **Sirhind**, while nearby **Patiala** was once the capital of one of the richest 'princely states', in British India: the Shish Mahal palace of the ruling family is worth a visit.

The industrial city of **Ludhiana**, some 125km (78 miles) west of Chandigarh, is known as the 'Manchester of India', but aside from being a good place to buy textiles there is little to see.

Indo-Pakistan border

Thirty kilometres (18 miles) to the west of Amritsar (and midway between Amritsar and Lahore) lies the Indo-Pakistan border, at a village called Wagah, although authorities in Amritsar are now keen for the crossing to be known as Attari, having recently decided that Wagah itself actually lies in Pakistan. There is a highly ritualised border closing ceremony here at sundown every day which is well worth seeing. The tallest soldiers from each country's respective armies perform a series of Monty Pythonesque walks which culminate in the lowering of the national flags and the banging shut of the border gates, while the crowds on both sides shout patriotic slogans in an almost pantomime atmosphere, aptly described by Michael Palin as 'chauvinism at its most camp'. The recent thaw in relations between the two countries, however, has seen a corresponding toning down of the ritual, at least on the Indian side, with the addition of a cursory handshake between the guards before the slamming shut of their respective gates

Kurukshetra

Haryana has very few famous sights of tourist interest; even so, it can rightfully claim to be the birthplace of the most sacred religious scripture of Hinduism. At **Kurukshetra** ❸, situated on the main Delhi–Chandigarh railway line, a legendary battle was fought between two sets of cousins, the Kuruvas and the Pandavas. On the eve of the battle, Sri Krishna, an incarnation of Vishnu, persuaded Arjuna, the reluctant commander of the Pandava army, to wage war on his relatives. This sermon, known as the *Bhagavad Gita*, discusses *dharma*, the moral principle of doing one's duty without consideration of reward, victory or defeat. Kurukshetra is full of temples and tanks where pilgrims come to bathe on auspicious days.

Also in Haryana, in Gurgaon district southwest of Delhi, is the **Sultanpur Bird Sanctuary**. Set up in 1971, the sanctuary is based around a *jhil*, or seasonal lake. A large number of species

Soldiers perform at the Indo-Pakistan border at Wagah/Attari.

Detail from the Itimad-ud-Daula tomb in Agra. The white marble is inlaid with coloured stone to subtle and beautiful effect.

can be seen here in the winter months, including common hoopoe, white ibis and painted stork, as well as nilgai and blackbuck antelopes.

UTTAR PRADESH

Uttar Pradesh (UP), with close to 200 million inhabitants, would be the world's fifth-most populous country if it were independent. As it is, the state is the heartland of the world's largest democracy, and politics here are lively. UP has a broad industrial base but is still predominantly agricultural, with wheat, maize, rice and sugar cane among the main crops. Its name means 'northern state' and it is made up of two regions. The larger part comprises the rich, alluvial, pancake-flat plain of the Ganges and its tributaries, while to the south, the Vindhya Hills rise to the edges of the Deccan Plateau. Although UP is famous worldwide for the Taj Mahal at Agra, it attracts devout Hindus to the many pilgrimage places along the River Ganges, which flows through the holy cities of Allahabad and Varanasi. Buddhists are drawn to the deer park at Sarnath where the Buddha preached his first sermon.

Fifteen percent of the population is Muslim, and in addition to its mosques and Sufi shrines, UP has some of the most prestigious Muslim theological colleges. For the visitor, the state's political, historical and religious importance can be witnessed in a heady mix of destinations, from the sensual intensity of Varanasi, to the architectural wonders of Lucknow and the breathtaking beauty of the Taj Mahal, so familiar and yet so striking.

Agra: city of the emperors

Synonymous with the Taj Mahal, **Agra** ❹ is the prime destination on most tourist itineraries of India. Be warned that a visit can be a crowded, noisy and rather exhausting experience. It is often very smoggy, too, particularly in the winter months. If you can cope with the crowds and the endless hustle, though, Agra has more to offer than its famous mausoleum: the fort and royal tombs are suitably grand reminders of the Mughals' wealth and power, while the old part of town still feels like a medieval city, with narrow lanes and colourful shops selling local handicrafts.

The city achieved greatness under the Mughals, and particularly the emperors Akbar (1556–1605), Jahangir (1605–27) and Shah Jahan (1628–58). The Agra of today is, however, considerably less illustrious than its past glories might suggest. For obvious reasons it has never struggled to attract visitors, but as a result has felt little need to add to its attractiveness. This has also coloured the attitudes of the local residents who most frequently come into contact with tourists; rickshaw

---

THE DIAMOND DALIT

Although she is no longer the Chief Minister of Uttar Pradesh, Mayawati Kumari has dominated politics in the state for the past decade, courting as much controversy as she has praise for her rags to riches rise to power. Born into a scheduled caste family, Mayawati was the first Dalit, or member of an 'Untouchable' caste, to become the head of any Indian state. She was also the youngest Chief Minister ever, when, at just 39, she first came to the position in 1995.

The turbulent nature of UP politics ensured Mayawati has enjoyed four spells in the top job to date. Her political career has been nothing if not colourful. One of her early slogans exhorted fellow Dalits to beat members of the upper castes with their shoe, and while her rhetoric has since mellowed, she's seldom been out of the headlines. Charges of corruption have continued to dog her, fuelled by her expansive property portfolio and diamond-laden public appearances, particularly on her own birthday. Modesty has never been her strong suit; she remains the only chief minister to have ordered a statue of themselves.

In a recent court case, Mayawati revealed that her personal fortunes ran to Rs111.26 crore ($20.3 million). Her lawyers claimed the wealth derived from donations from supporters, rather than backhanders from contractors in the Taj Heritage Corridor (see page 156), as has been alleged by the Indian CBI.

drivers, shopkeepers and hotel touts all seem to work on the premise that however indifferently they treat their clientele, more will turn up tomorrow.

Perhaps wary of its reputation, many visitors choose to see Agra in a day and then sleep elsewhere – even a return day trip from Delhi is feasible, with the express train making the journey in just two hours. While the main attractions can be seen in this way, it's worth remembering that the translucent marble of the Taj Mahal is at its most impressive in the early light of dawn.

Agra Fort and the Taj Mahal

Agra Fort (daily 6am–6.30pm; charge), on the banks of the Yamuna River, is the city's other major sight, and offers great views of the Taj (unfortunately the entrance fee is no longer included with that of the Taj). The structure began to take shape from 1564. Akbar constructed the massive 2.4km (1.5-mile), 20-metre (65ft) -high surrounding walls of local sandstone. It was said of Agra Fort that 'from top to bottom the fire-red stones, linked by iron rings, are joined so closely that even a hair cannot find a way into their joints.'

Of the former '500 edifices of red stones in the fine styles of Bengal and Gujarat', only the Jahangiri Mahal still stands. This was the main part of the women's quarters, constructed in a local Indian style to suit the needs of the emperor's Hindu wives. Akbar's other buildings were demolished to make way for the imperial quarters of Shah Jahan, combining Hindu and Islamic styles of architecture. The Mussaman Burj (Octagonal Tower) is said to be the place where Shah Jahan was imprisoned by his son, spending his last years lying on his deathbed gazing out wistfully at the Taj Mahal. Today this view is still one of the fort's main attractions, giving a perspective of the Taj difficult to obtain elsewhere, the river in the foreground reflecting the impeccable symmetry of this most iconic of buildings.

The tomb of **Itimad-ud-Daula** (daily sunrise–sunset; charge), across the river from the fort, is the most

The King's Gate, one of the entrances to the Jama Masjid at Fatehpur Sikri. As with most buildings in the complex it is built of a distinctive, pink sandstone.

U.P. TRANSPORT

Agra, Lucknow, Kanpur, Allahabad and Varanasi all have regular flights to Delhi. Timetables can be erratic during the winter months, when fog frequently disrupts services. Travelling between Delhi and Agra, you're always better off going by train – it is faster as well as cheaper.

Agra: Regular train service to Delhi; quickest is Shatabdi express (1 daily; 2hrs). Other destinations include Jaipur (5 daily; 5hrs), Varanasi (2 daily; 11hrs) and Kolkata (2 daily; 25–31hrs).

Lucknow: Trains run to Delhi (12 daily; 9–10hrs), Agra (3 daily; 6hrs), Varanasi (14 daily; 5–10hrs) and Kolkata (6 daily; 30hrs).

Varanasi: Trains run to Delhi (6 daily; 12–16hrs), Agra (2 daily; 11hrs), Lucknow (14 daily; 5–10hrs) and Kolkata (6 daily; 21–26hrs).

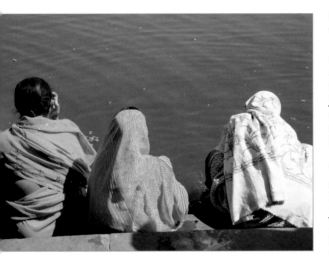

The Vishram Ghat on the Yamuna river at Mathura, Lord Krishna's birthplace.

the minister's penchant for alcohol, of which his daughter disapproved.

Also on the east side of the river, hidden behind the lovely nurseries along Aligarh Road, are the **Chini ka Rauza**, the tomb of Afzal Khan, a courtier to Jahangir and Shah Jahan, and, further on, the **Rambagh** gardens, believed to have been laid out by the Emperor Babur (both sites sunrise–sunset).

Within sight of Agra Fort is the **Taj Mahal** (Sat–Thur 6am–7.30pm; charge). The world-famous tomb of Mumtaz Mahal, wife of Emperor Shah Jahan, this iconic building stands in a Mughal garden on a terrace beside a bend in the Yamuna. Mumtaz Mahal was married to the emperor for 19 years, during which she accompanied him on his military campaigns and shared his confidence on all matters of state. She bore 13 children, including the next emperor, Aurangzeb. In 1631 she died in childbirth. Shah Jahan was desolate and built the Taj Mahal in her honour. He was later deposed by Aurangzeb and imprisoned in Agra Fort. For more on the Taj Mahal, see page 172.

intimate of the three great monuments in Agra, but far less epic in scale than the other two. Itimad-ud-Daula was father-in-law and *wazir* (principal minister) to Emperor Jahangir. Nur Jahan, Jahangir's queen, undertook the construction of her father's tomb (1622–8) in white marble. Included in the design are some interesting details – the wine bottles, for example, are thought to have been a comment on

CONTROVERSIAL CORRIDOR

An example of Uttar Pradesh government-level apathy came in the form of the 'Taj Heritage Corridor', a commercially driven attempt to create a cordoned-off corridor running from the Taj Mahal to Agra Fort, lined with shopping centres, amusement parks and restaurants. The initial phase of the project required 2km (1.25-mile) of the Yamuna riverbed to be filled in, dramatically altering the river's flow and potentially undermining the Taj Mahal's foundations.

Both this work and the construction of a 1.5km (1-mile) -long boundary wall were allowed to go ahead before sense prevailed. Unesco threatened to reconsider their World Heritage status should the project continue, at which point the Minister for Culture stepped in. He had also discovered that the scheme, which cost Rs175 crore ($44 million), had not been approved by any relevant government agency. Attempts were made to prosecute Uttar Pradesh's Chief Minister for her role in the project (and the disappearance of funds earmarked for the development). The legal case against her fizzled out in 2011, after the Supreme Court quashed allegations that her assets of approximately Rs111.26 crore ($20.3 million) were disproportionate to her income, though unfinished construction works remain dotted along the Yamuna, awaiting demolition.

Akbar's capital

Early morning is the best time to visit **Fatehpur Sikri** ❺ (daily sunrise–sunset; charge), Akbar's imperial capital, 35km (20 miles) southwest of Agra. The remarkably well-preserved remains include the palace and the royal Jama Masjid (mosque) where the Sufi saint Shaikh Salim Chisti is buried. Akbar is said to have visited the saint on this site when he was anxious for an heir. He was told that he would have three sons, and when his words came true Akbar chose Sikri for his capital.

Fatehpur, 'town of victory', was built of sandstone quarried from the hill on which it stood. It was, however, only occupied for 14 years before Akbar shifted his capital to Lahore. The usual explanation is that this happened because the water ran out, but it may also have been for strategic reasons. The palace buildings draw on the style of Persian, Mughal and local Indian architecture, skilfully blended by Akbar to create a style all of its own.

The finest monuments include **Diwan-e-Khas**, where Akbar debated religious matters from a platform supported by an ornate octagonal pillar, and connected to each corner of the square building by suspended walkways, **Mariam's House**, home of Akbar's wife and intricately private in design, and the Jama Masjid. Already an imposing structure, the mosque was given further stature by the addition of the **Buland Darwaza**, a massive entrance gate built five years later to celebrate Akbar's victories in Gujarat.

While the buildings are all uninhabited today, the complex gives a uniquely well-preserved insight into how life in the royal Mughal courts was lived, and the extent of the luxury that the Mughal emperors enjoyed.

Sikandra

Akbar also designed his own resting place. The tomb, completed in 1613, is at **Sikandra** (daily sunrise–sunset; charge), 12km (7 miles) northwest of Agra. The mausoleum is four storeys high; the first three are of red sandstone, the fourth of white marble containing the false tomb of the emperor. The real tomb, as in all such mausoleums, is in a crypt below. Outside, blackbuck wander the gardens.

Braj

The area around **Mathura** ❻, on the banks of the Yamuna river 30km (19 miles) north of Agra on the Delhi road, is known as Braj and is popularly believed to have been the birthplace and home of Lord Krishna. According to legend, the young Krishna was brought up in a family of cowherds, where he performed miracles for the good of the villagers, and played tricks on them, and where all the *gopis* (milkmaids) fell helplessly in love with him. He was, Hindus believe, an incarnation of the god Vishnu. In one of the greatest Hindu texts, the *Bhagavad Gita*, Krishna explains the world and how best to live in it.

Mathura today is an industrial town notable for its oil refinery, but it has

Mughal-style colonnades, Agra Fort.

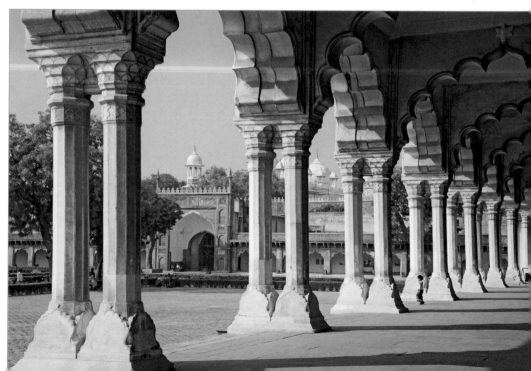

FACT

Following the death of the local rajah of Jhansi in 1853, his widow, Rani assumed power. She was removed by the British, who reserved the right to assume control of any Indian state where there was no male heir. Rani returned during the Uprising of 1857, and the British force was routed. Having later fled to Gwalior, Lakshmibai was killed in battle. She is revered as a hero of independence.

Vishnu temple at Vrindavan.

retained its religious pre-eminence. Highlights include the **Kesava Deo Mandir**, built on the spot where Krishna was born; the stepped tank, **Potara Kund**, where his clothes were washed; and the numerous riverside ghats, of which **Vishram Ghat** is best known. Pilgrims gather to bathe at the ghats on the Yamuna and to visit temples such as the **Dvarkadhish shrine** in the crowded marketplace.

Disciples of the Hare Krishna movement descend on Mathura from all over the world; it was also once a thriving centre of Buddhism and Jainism. Sculptures made by local artists between the 2nd century BC and the 6th century AD are on display at the **museum** (Tue–Sun, July–Apr 10.30am–4.30pm, May–June 7.30am–12.30pm; charge).

There are numerous sites associated with Vishnu around Mathura, although the most impressive is at **Vrindavan**, 10km (6 miles) to the north, home to many Hindu widows who earn a tiny sum each day singing hymns to the Lord. Among the fine temples are those to **Govind-dev** (1590); **Jugal Kishor**, **Radha-Vallabh** and **Madan-Mohan** (17th century); **Ranganathji** and **Shahji** (19th century); the **Vankebehari shrine**; and **Pagal Baba**.

Southern Uttar Pradesh

The area bordering Madhya Pradesh can be explored from **Jhansi** ❼, 188km (117 miles) south of Agra. Jhansi is dominated by its impressive hill **fort** (dawn–dusk), from where the Rani of Jhansi, one of the heroines of the Uprising against the British in 1857, directed her operations. There is a **museum** here (Tue–Sun, July–Mar 10.30am–4.30pm, Apr–June 7.30am–12.30pm; charge) detailing the (mostly pre-British) history of the area.

From Jhansi it's a three-hour drive east to the village of **Khajuraho** (in Madhya Pradesh), renowned for its 1,000-year-old temples and erotic carvings (see page 287). The pilgrimage centre of **Chitrakut**, 235km (146 miles) east of Jhansi, looks like a mini-Varanasi, with ghats on the banks of the narrow Mandakani river.

Central and Eastern UP

The route from Delhi, 446km (277 miles) east to the state capital of Lucknow, passes through **Aligarh**, site of the Aligarh Muslim University founded by Sir Syed Ahmad Khan in 1875 to provide the Muslim community of India with a modern, scientific education.

Kanpur ❽, on the Ganges 70km (44 miles) southwest of Lucknow, is the state's leading industrial city, and as such holds little interest for visitors. In the Uprising of 1857 the British garrison at Kanpur (Cawnpore), home to some 400 British men, women and children, was besieged by Indian forces, and in the face of starvation after 18 days agreed to an offer of safe passage. As they crossed the riverbank they were massacred. **All Souls' Memorial Church** (1875) contains the names of those who died.

Lucknow

Uttar Pradesh's state capital, **Lucknow ❾**, a two-hour journey from Kanpur, stands on the Gomati River, a tributary of the Ganges. It was once a city of gardens, but many have disappeared under the onslaught of offices, shopping centres and residential colonies. The city's skyline is now a heady mix of modern design and some of the most elegant examples of Indo-Saracenic architecture in the country, often used these days as municipal offices for some banal-sounding government departments, the kind of places that would be housed in grey concrete elsewhere.

If you enter the city via the airport at Amausi, you will pass **Dilkusha**, a former royal hunting lodge designed like a Ruritanian castle and a key site in the 1857 Uprising. Several British officers died here, including General Havelock, who is buried in the **Alambagh**.

La Martinière College, one of the city's most extravagant estates, lies on its eastern outskirts. It was built as a home for the French businessman adventurer Claude Martin, who bequeathed his huge fortune to the running of educational institutions for Anglo-Indians. In front of Constantia, the college's main building, is the Lord Cornwallis, a cannon cast by Claude Martin and used in the Battle of Seringapatam against Tipu Sultan. Major Hodson, who killed the sons of the last Mughal emperor Bahadur Shah in Delhi, is buried in the park, as is Martin's Indian wife. Martin himself is buried in the basement of Constantia. Visitors are welcomed, but permission must be granted by the principal's office at the college's east end.

Further west is Claude Martin's former armoury, now the state governor's residence, and beyond it the Anglican church, post office and state legislature, built in 1932 when the capital of Oudh was shifted from Allahabad to Lucknow. Nearby is

Hussainabad Imambara, built during the 19th century by Nawabs of the Oudh Dynasty, shortly before the British took control of the city. No expense was spared in its elaborate construction.

Vishram Ghats, Mathura.

Anand Bhavan, the former family home of Jawaharlal Nehru, Allahabad.

Muktabandhana stupa is said to have been built to preserve the relics of the Buddha by the Mallas who ruled at the time he died. A smaller shrine nearby contains a reclining statue of the Buddha.

Other pilgrimage sites within reach of Gorakhpur are **Piprahva**, 90km (56 miles) away, where the Buddha spent his early years, and **Lumbini**, 8km (5 miles) across the border with Nepal, where he is believed to have been born. To the west, near the Nepal border, is **Sravasti**, where the Buddha spent the rainy season for 25 years. The founder of the Jain religion, Lord Mahavira, a contemporary of Buddha, was also a frequent visitor to Sravasti. Two Ashokan pillars stand at the gate of the **Jetavana monastery**.

Allahabad

Despite its Muslim-sounding name (it was originally called Prayag, but was renamed by Akbar), **Allahabad** ⓭ is one of the most sacred places of Hinduism – in fact it is known as 'Tirth Raj', the king of pilgrimage sites. The holiness is geographical: the

Street barber in Varanasi.

town is located at the point where the Yamuna and the mythical Sarasvati rivers flow into the Ganges, some 188km (117 miles) southeast of Kanpur. At the sacred confluence a religious fair, the Magh Mela, is held each January and February, and once every 12 years the greatest religious festival of northern India, the Purna Kumbha Mela, takes place. To bathe at the confluence at the most sacred times is said to wash away the sins of many births; in 2001 an estimated 66 million people bathed here. Rowing boats will take you to the spot where the milky waters of the Ganges meet the blue waters of the Yamuna.

The city itself is crowded and somewhat dilapidated: **Anand Bhavan** (Tue–Sun 9.30am–5pm; charge) the former home of the Nehru family and a nerve centre of the independence movement is the main sight.

At **Kausambi**, 45km (28 miles) away, are the ruins of one of the great metropolitan forts built during the first millennium BC. Courtyard houses were protected by massive walls of burnt brick. Kausambi was occupied from the 8th century BC to the 6th century AD. Its main Buddhist stupa measured 25 metres (80ft) across.

Varanasi

The most sacred stretch of the Ganges is at **Varanasi** ⓮ (Benares), one of the oldest living cities in the world and arguably the most intense, atmospheric place in the whole of India. For more than 2,500 years it has attracted seekers and pilgrims. Its heart lies between the streams of the Varuna and the Assi, which flow into the Ganges and give the city its name. Another name, 'Kashi', probably derives from the Sanskrit 'to shine or look brilliant'. That light is the god Shiva's, Varanasi is his home. Shiva literally means auspiciousness or happiness and, according to a local saying, every single pebble and stone in Kashi is Shiva. To his devotees, Shiva is the one great God. To die here in his

Dudhwa National Park

The only place in India apart from Assam where you can see rhinos in the wild, **Dudhwa National Park ⑩**, was inaugurated in 1977. Its location, that bit further from Delhi than Corbett National Park (see page 178), has meant that its infrastructure has developed at a steadier rate, but is now more than adequate, and offers an exceptional wildlife experience. The best time to visit is between February and April; the park closes between 15 June and 15 November. The best way to get around once there is by elephant, available for hire in Dudhwa itself.

The east of the Northern Plains

Faizabad ⑪, 150km (93 miles) east of Lucknow, was for a time the capital of the province of Avadh. This busy town has fine monuments, including Bahu Begum's tomb and Gulab Bari, the mausoleum of one of the first rulers of Avadh, Shuja-ud-Daula.

Six kilometres (4 miles) east is the temple town of **Ayodhya**, standing on the banks of the Ghaghara River. This is believed by Hindus to be the capital and birthplace of Lord Rama, another incarnation of Vishnu and hero of the *Ramayana*. Popular devotion to Rama increased in the 16th century after Tulsi Das wrote his great version of the *Ramayana* in Avadhi – the language of the people. The nawabs of Avadh gave donations to various temples, and the oldest and most beautiful buildings of Ayodhya date from this period.

One of the most notable buildings is **Hanumangarhi**, the fort of Hanuman, the monkey god, greatest devotee of Rama, and Sita. Steep steps lead up to the main temple (dawn–dusk), where monkeys are ready to snatch offerings from pilgrims' hands. The peace of the town was broken in 1992 when Hindu extremists demolished a mosque that they believed stood on the birthplace of Rama, 'Ram Janambhoomi'. In July 2005 five Islamic militants attacked the makeshift Hindu temple that

had been built on the site, and were gunned down by security forces. After a protracted delay, a September 2010 court ruling decreed that the site be equally divided between the three feuding parties.

Gorakhpur ⑫, 130km (80 miles) east of Faizabad, is named after Guru Gorakhnath, a pre-medieval saint, whose temple and *matha* (monastery) stand here. During the Khichri Mela festival, culminating on 14 January each year, villagers offer rice and lentils, which are thrown onto a pile in front of an image of the saint. **Jaunpur**, on the road towards Varanasi, was one of India's foremost centres of cultural development in the 14th and 15th centuries, and today, while a shadow of its former self, is home to some partially ruined, but unique, Islamic architecture.

Buddhist sites

Khushinagar, 53km (33 miles) east of Gorakhpur, is identified as the spot where the Buddha left this world and attained *parinirvana* in the 5th or 6th century BC. Here the

FACT

The Maha Kumbh Mela, held at Allahabad every 144 years, is by some margin the largest pilgrimage in the world. The 2001 event saw over 60 million visitors, including over 1 million from outside India, making it the largest gathering in recorded history. However, the 2013 Ardh Kumbh Mela is expected to top 100 million visitors.

Hazratganj, Lucknow's main shopping area.

Anand Bhavan, the former family home of Jawaharlal Nehru, Allahabad.

Street barber in Varanasi.

Muktabandhana stupa is said to have been built to preserve the relics of the Buddha by the Mallas who ruled at the time he died. A smaller shrine nearby contains a reclining statue of the Buddha.

Other pilgrimage sites within reach of Gorakhpur are **Piprahva**, 90km (56 miles) away, where the Buddha spent his early years, and **Lumbini**, 8km (5 miles) across the border with Nepal, where he is believed to have been born. To the west, near the Nepal border, is **Sravasti**, where the Buddha spent the rainy season for 25 years. The founder of the Jain religion, Lord Mahavira, a contemporary of Buddha, was also a frequent visitor to Sravasti. Two Ashokan pillars stand at the gate of the **Jetavana monastery**.

Allahabad

Despite its Muslim-sounding name (it was originally called Prayag, but was renamed by Akbar), **Allahabad** ⓭ is one of the most sacred places of Hinduism – in fact it is known as 'Tirth Raj', the king of pilgrimage sites. The holiness is geographical: the

town is located at the point where the Yamuna and the mythical Sarasvati rivers flow into the Ganges, some 188km (117 miles) southeast of Kanpur. At the sacred confluence a religious fair, the Magh Mela, is held each January and February, and once every 12 years the greatest religious festival of northern India, the Purna Kumbha Mela, takes place. To bathe at the confluence at the most sacred times is said to wash away the sins of many births; in 2001 an estimated 66 million people bathed here. Rowing boats will take you to the spot where the milky waters of the Ganges meet the blue waters of the Yamuna.

The city itself is crowded and somewhat dilapidated: **Anand Bhavan** (Tue–Sun 9.30am–5pm; charge) the former home of the Nehru family and a nerve centre of the independence movement is the main sight.

At **Kausambi**, 45km (28 miles) away, are the ruins of one of the great metropolitan forts built during the first millennium BC. Courtyard houses were protected by massive walls of burnt brick. Kausambi was occupied from the 8th century BC to the 6th century AD. Its main Buddhist stupa measured 25 metres (80ft) across.

Varanasi

The most sacred stretch of the Ganges is at **Varanasi** ⓮ (Benares), one of the oldest living cities in the world and arguably the most intense, atmospheric place in the whole of India. For more than 2,500 years it has attracted seekers and pilgrims. Its heart lies between the streams of the Varuna and the Assi, which flow into the Ganges and give the city its name. Another name, 'Kashi', probably derives from the Sanskrit 'to shine or look brilliant'. That light is the god Shiva's, Varanasi is his home. Shiva literally means auspiciousness or happiness and, according to a local saying, every single pebble and stone in Kashi is Shiva. To his devotees, Shiva is the one great God. To die here in his

Central and Eastern UP

The route from Delhi, 446km (277 miles) east to the state capital of Lucknow, passes through **Aligarh**, site of the Aligarh Muslim University founded by Sir Syed Ahmad Khan in 1875 to provide the Muslim community of India with a modern, scientific education.

Kanpur ❽, on the Ganges 70km (44 miles) southwest of Lucknow, is the state's leading industrial city, and as such holds little interest for visitors. In the Uprising of 1857 the British garrison at Kanpur (Cawnpore), home to some 400 British men, women and children, was besieged by Indian forces, and in the face of starvation after 18 days agreed to an offer of safe passage. As they crossed the riverbank they were massacred. **All Souls' Memorial Church** (1875) contains the names of those who died.

Lucknow

Uttar Pradesh's state capital, **Lucknow** ❾, a two-hour journey from Kanpur, stands on the Gomati River, a tributary of the Ganges. It was once a city of gardens, but many have disappeared under the onslaught of offices, shopping centres and residential colonies. The city's skyline is now a heady mix of modern design and some of the most elegant examples of Indo-Saracenic architecture in the country, often used these days as municipal offices for some banal-sounding government departments, the kind of places that would be housed in grey concrete elsewhere.

If you enter the city via the airport at Amausi, you will pass **Dilkusha**, a former royal hunting lodge designed like a Ruritanian castle and a key site in the 1857 Uprising. Several British officers died here, including General Havelock, who is buried in the **Alambagh**.

La Martinière College, one of the city's most extravagant estates, lies on its eastern outskirts. It was built as a home for the French businessman adventurer

Claude Martin, who bequeathed his huge fortune to the running of educational institutions for Anglo-Indians. In front of Constantia, the college's main building, is the Lord Cornwallis, a cannon cast by Claude Martin and used in the Battle of Seringapatam against Tipu Sultan. Major Hodson, who killed the sons of the last Mughal emperor Bahadur Shah in Delhi, is buried in the park, as is Martin's Indian wife. Martin himself is buried in the basement of Constantia. Visitors are welcomed, but permission must be granted by the principal's office at the college's east end.

Further west is Claude Martin's former armoury, now the state governor's residence, and beyond it the Anglican church, post office and state legislature, built in 1932 when the capital of Oudh was shifted from Allahabad to Lucknow. Nearby is

Hussainabad Imambara, built during the 19th century by Nawabs of the Oudh Dynasty, shortly before the British took control of the city. No expense was spared in its elaborate construction.

Vishram Ghats, Mathura.

TIP

It is possible to travel from Gorakhpur in Uttar Pradesh to the border with Nepal at Sonauli (3hrs) from where there are buses to Kathmandu; minibuses run directly to Chitwan National Park from Gorakhpur. Nepali visas are purchased at the border.

Lucknow's main shopping area, **Hazratganj**, the Gentleman's Market. On Hazratganj itself is the **Imambara Sibtainabad**, built by the last nawab, Wajid Ali Shah, as a mausoleum for his father.

On Shah Najaf Marg, heading north from Hazratganj, is the **Shah Najaf Imambara** and **Sikandarbargh**, a 24-hectare (60-acre) botanical garden named after the nawab's wife. West, along Rana Pratap Marg, is **Kurshid Manzil**, shaped like a moated English castle, now the La Martinière Girls School. Adjoining it is the **Taron Wali Kothi**, the nawab's observatory, now the State Bank of India.

En route towards the Residency further west, you pass Farhat Baksh, Claude Martin's principal residence, now the Central Drug Research Institute (no entry permitted). All of this area, as it leads to the Residency, was the scene of ferocious fighting during the Uprising.

A monument of more recent origin dominates the riverfront to the east of the city centre. Erected by the controversial former Chief Minister of Uttar Pradesh, Mayawati (see page 154), the extravagant Dr Ambedkar Memorial – a vast complex of sandstone ramparts, gardens, canals, walkways and statues sprawling over 21 hectares (53 acres) – was opened in 2009, at vast expense to the Indian tax payer. Quite why one of the poorest regions in the country saw fit to spend a sum estimated at around $127.7 million when tens of millions of inhabitants remain malnourished and without access to clean drinking water, remains a subject of considerable debate.

The Residency

The **Residency Compound** (Tue–Sun 10am–5pm; charge) is a complex that housed about 3,000 mostly European residents prior to the Siege of Lucknow in 1857. Only 1,000 survived the five-month conflict. There is a **museum** (8am–5pm; charge) in the basement of the Residency itself, which gives a good idea of conditions at the time of the Uprising, and of the wretched struggle that the residents had to endure.

Bara Imambara

About 2km (1.25 miles) west beyond the Residency is the **Bara Imambara** (8.30am–6pm, closed during Muharrum; charge). Built in the time of famine in 1784 as a food-for-work programme, it is an architectural marvel built without pillars, and contains a hall 50 metres (163ft) long with acoustics so good you can hear a paper tear at the other end. There is an entertaining maze on the upper floor. The entrance ticket also gives access to the **Hussainabad Imambara** next door, with its fabulous chandeliers and silver pulpit, the Picture Gallery housing portraits of the nawabs, the Hussainabad Clock Tower and the Jama Masjid. Also in this area, south of Victoria Park, is the **Chowk**, or the street of the silversmiths, that now sells items featuring the local style of embroidery (*chikan*) and other local handicrafts.

A busy street in Mathura.

city on the banks of the holy river is to achieve *moksha*, liberation from the cycle of life and death. Death is not hidden in India. It is part of life, and one reason why you find cremation grounds in the very centre of Varanasi, and cremation ghats lining the river.

It is not uncommon to see muslin-wrapped bodies being carried through town and down to the river, placed on a funeral pyre and cremated in full public view. This unlimited access to the practical applications of the Hindu faith, the raw intimacy with death and the stifling intensity of the narrow lanes that lead down to the holy river often combine to leave visitors literally breathless, emotionally overcome but never unmoved, or unimpressed. Perhaps nowhere else in India can offer the visitor such an explicit crash course in the tenets of Hinduism; a visit to Varanasi goes a long way in helping to explain sights and sounds you might encounter elsewhere in India.

Dawn on the Ganges is a fabulous sight. The river flows south to north, with the city on the west bank, and fields and trees to the east. As the sun rises, the golden rays fall on the innumerable temples and 70 bathing ghats, on the priests under their tilted umbrellas, and devout Hindus taking a purifying dip. The one notable mosque on the skyline was built by the Mughal emperor Aurangzeb.

Rowing boats take visitors along the ghats from Assi in the north to Raj Ghat, a highly recommended experience. These trips have become so commonplace that the boats are entirely ignored by the local population, which ensures that the sights on offer remain fascinatingly authentic, and far from the micro-managed stage show that they could so easily have become.

Within the city, the **Vishvanath Temple**, built in the late 18th century, is the main Shiva sanctuary. It is closed to non-Hindus, but visitors can climb surrounding buildings to see the gilded dome. If Shiva is king of Varanasi, the goddess Annapurna is queen. Her temple is close to Vishvanath's. She is the perfect mother, a gentle goddess who provides food (*anna*) and life. Another of the

FACT

Mark Twain could have been writing about Varanasi when he wrote, 'This is India! The one sole country under the sun that is endowed with an imperishable interest for alien persons'.

The famous ghats at Varanasi.

city's busiest temples is in the south and dedicated to Durga, one of its fierce goddess guardians. The temple is often called the **monkey temple** because of the hordes of red macaques which have made it their home.

Nearby is the most popular shrine to the monkey god Hanuman, the **Sankat Mochan**. One of Hanuman's main strengths is the ability to turn away difficulties, and on Tuesdays and Saturdays devotees gather to ask for his help. The chief priest lives in a house overlooking the Ganges on Tulsi Ghat where Gosvami Tulsi Das is said to have written his *Ramayana* epic.

Across the river is **Ramnagar**, home of the Raja of Benares, whose fort houses a private museum (Apr–Sept 9am–noon, 2–5pm, Oct–Mar 10am–1pm, 2–5pm; charge). He is the patron of the Ramnagar Ram Lila, a traditional month-long enactment of the *Ramayana* (Oct and Nov).

About 6km (4 miles) to the north of Varanasi is **Sarnath**, the deer park where the Buddha preached his first sermon after attaining enlightenment, and returned to spend the rainy season several times during his life. It is one of the most important Buddhist pilgrimage sites. The most impressive of the ruins is the **Dhamekh Stupa**, which is said to mark the exact spot where the Buddha preached, and an Ashokan pillar from the 3rd century BC. The lion capital of the pillar, now the emblem of the Government of India, is one of several outstanding exhibits in the nearby **museum** (Sat–Thur 10am–5pm; charge).

BIHAR

The state of Bihar lies in the eastern Gangetic plain, occupying the area that was the seat of several of the most famous ancient Indian dynasties, as well as being the cradle of Jainism and Buddhism. The name Bihar is itself derived from *vihara* (Buddhist monastery). Although the state is situated on the fertile alluvial soils of the floodplain of the Ganges, this is one of the very poorest parts of India, all but untouched by the economic boom taking place in other parts of the country. Bihar is notorious for its rampant corruption, lawlessness, decrepit infrastructure and extreme divisions of caste, manifested in sporadic outbreaks of caste-based violence, adding to the state's lawless reputation. On one side are the brutal private armies of the landlords, and ranged against them, Naxalite insurgents with close links to the Maoist Communist Party of Nepal. Travellers visiting Patna and the major Buddhist sites should face few problems, but visitors travelling off the beaten track should be alert to the possiblity of trouble.

The current Chief Minister of Bihar, Nitish Kumar, has made significant reforms in the time he has been in power. His efforts to improve the state's appeal to both public and private investors have met with the approval of the World Bank, who loaned the impoverished region US$225 million. This type of investment, particularly if private companies

Flooded sugar cane fields near Mothiari, Bihar.

can be tempted to get involved, represents Bihar's best chance of rising out of its current predicament, and the recent signs are good, with the Bihari economy now one of the fastest growing in the country. Rajesh Singh, a Bihari with an MBA from Mumbai University, decided to go back to Bihar to start a business, motivated as he admits by both 'good potential and good intentions'. He typifies exactly the kind of outlook and attitude that the state so badly needs, but several turbulent years later he's still battling against Bihar's traditional woes; asked if there was a harder place in the world to do business he replied, 'Maybe Somalia, they are shooting at you there!'

Patna

Patna ⓫, the capital of Bihar, is a city of more than 1 million people lying beside the Ganges, but feels more like a rural town run wild. Under the name of Pataliputra it was the capital of the Magadha Empire. Patna is divided in two by a large square, the Maidan. To the west lies **Bankipur**, a cantonment and administrative area with colonial buildings, including **Raj Bhavan**, the governor's residence; the **Maharaja's Palace**, now the Bihar State Transport Corporation; **Patna Women's College**, an early 20th-century neo-Mughal complex; and 1920s bungalows for government officers.

The **Patna Museum** (Tue–Sun 10.30am–4.30pm; charge) near the **High Court** houses a collection of Hindu and Buddhist statues and sculptures, 18 of which were stolen in 2006. Among the exhibits is a 15-metre (49ft) fossil tree said to be 200 million years old and the longest of its kind in the world. At the entrance of the hall, on the left, is the **Didarganji Yakshi**, a buff-coloured Mauryan sandstone statue of a woman, remarkable for her brilliant polish, her rounded breasts, her navel, and her aggressive belly and hips. It is considered to be one of the greatest examples of Indian art from any era. Between the Maidan and the Ganges stands the **Golghar**, a beehive-shaped structure, built in 1786 as a granary. It is 27 metres (88ft) high and can hold 150,000 tonnes of wheat.

FACT

The Ganges river dolphin, also known as the susu or shushuk, still survives in the Ganges and its major tributaries in Uttar Pradesh and Bihar, as well as downstream in West Bengal. An endangered species, it is threatened by pollution and reduced water levels caused by irrigation schemes; adults measure over 2 metres (7ft) in length.

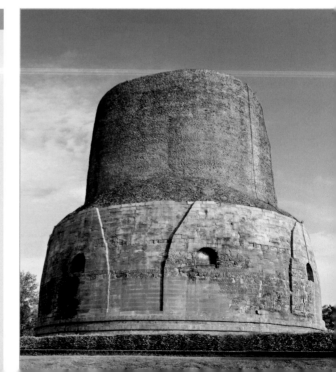

Dhamekh Stupa at Sarnath.

BIHAR TRANSPORT

Patna's Lok Nayak Jayaprakash Airport, 5km east of the city, has regular services to Delhi, Mumbai, Bengaluru, Lucknow, Hyderabad, Ahmedabad and Kolkata, while Gaya also hosts international flights from Thailand and Sri Lanka. The state is well linked by rail with the rest of India. Patna Junction is the most important station, with a foreigners' reservation window on the top floor of the main booking office.

Patna: Trains run to Kolkata (9 daily; 8–12hrs); Delhi (12 daily; 12–23hrs); Gaya (7 daily; 2–3hrs) and Varanasi (11 daily; 4–8hrs).

Gaya: Trains run to Patna (9 daily; 2–3hrs); Delhi (7 daily; 11–17hrs) and Kolkata (11 daily; 6–15hrs).

For much of the state, notably the more remote southern areas, buses form the main mode of transport.

The faithful come to wash and pray on the ghats beside the Ganges at Varanasi.

A market in Patna.

From the top there are fine view across the city.

Old Patna lies to the east of the Maidan. In this district of bazaars, a few buildings stand out: the **Khuda Baksh Oriental Library**, which contains rare Islamic manuscripts, including some from the Moorish University of Córdoba in Spain; **Padri-ki-Haveli** (St Mary's Church), built in 1775; **Sher Shah Masjid** and **Patther-ki-Masjid**, mosques erected respectively around 1540 by Sher Shah, and in 1621 by Parvez Shah, son of Jahangir and Governor of India.

Haramandirji, a *gurdwara* in old Patna, is one of the holiest places in India for Sikhs. Guru Govind Singh, the 10th and last Sikh guru, was born and died here. The *gurdwara*, built in the 19th century around the room where the guru was born, is a white marble building housing a museum

of the Sikh religion. On top is a terrace with marble kiosks from where one can watch the sun going down over the city while loudspeakers broadcast the recitation from the Holy Granth.

Near the *gurdwara*, and visited only by appointment with the owner, is **Qila House**, a private residence built on the ruins of Sher Shah's fortress, which houses a collection of jade, Chinese paintings, silver filigree work of the Mughal period, and a bed that once belonged to Napoleon.

At **Gulzaribagh**, further east near the Mahabir Ghat, is a former East India Company factory, now a government printing press. Visitors can see the opium godowns (warehouses), the former ballroom and the hall where Shah Alam II was crowned Emperor of Delhi (under the protection and patronage of the East India Company) on 12 March 1761. In the same area, to the south at **Kumhrar**, a park has been created around the remains of **Pataliputra**. Here are the foundations of Emperor Ashoka's palace, wooden beams from structures in the former city, ramparts, and the pond where Ashoka is said to have thrown the bodies of his 99 brothers – this was before his conversion to Buddhism.

The **Mahatma Gandhi Bridge** crosses the Ganges east of the city. On the north bank, at **Sonepur** near the confluence of the Ganges and Gandak, an animal fair is held in October/November. Some 40km (25 miles) further north, **Vaishali** is the former capital of the Vajian Confederacy (6th century BC), probably the first republic in Asia. The Second Buddhist Council was held here in 383 BC. All that remains is an Ashoka pillar and ruins of Buddhist stupas.

About 30km (20 miles) from the Nepalese border is the town of **Motihari**, where Eric Arthur Blair, the future George Orwell, was born in 1903. Plans are afoot to make his old two-room house a heritage site. The road reaches the India–Nepal border at Raxaul, the main crossing point between the two countries.

Mughal monuments

Some of Bihar's finest monuments lie to the west of Patna. At **Maner**, 30km (18 miles) away, are two mausoleums. **Choti Dargah**, in a small Muslim cemetery, is the grave of Maneri, a 17th-century ascetic. **Bari Dargah**, on the high bank of an artificial pond, was built in 1620 by Ibrahim Khan, Governor of Bihar under Jahangir, as a mausoleum for Shah Daula, his religious preceptor. At **Sasaram** ⑯, on the Grand Trunk Road southwest of Patna, are monuments from the time of Suri (Afghan) rule, including 16th century Emperor **Sher Shah's Mausoleum**.

Further north on the Ganges, **Buxar** is the place where Rama is said to have fought the demon Taraka and received higher knowledge from the sage Vishvamitra. Rama is said to have left a footprint here at Ram Rekha Ghat. Nearby, in 1764, the British defeated the last independent nawab of Murshidabad, thereby adding Bengal and Bihar to their Indian possessions.

The cradle of Buddhism

Nalanda ⑰, 'the place that confers the lotus' (*nalam* means spiritual knowledge), lies 90km (56 miles) south of Patna. This is the site of **Sri Mahavihara Arya Bhikshu Sanghasya**, a monastic university that flourished from the 5th century until 1199, when it was ransacked by the Afghan invader Bakhtiar Khilji. Lord Mahavira, the last Jain Tirthankara, and Lord Buddha taught here. Nalanda developed as a centre of Buddhist learning.

Leaving Nalanda for Rajgir, the road passes the Nava Nalanda Mahavira Research Centre on Buddhism and Pali Literature and **Wat Thai Nalanda**, a small Thai temple.

Rajgir, or Rajgriha, the 'royal palace', 12km (7 miles) to the south, was the capital of the Magadha Empire in the 6th century BC. It is a holy place for both Jains and Buddhists. Lord Mahavira taught here for 14 rainy seasons. The Buddha, too, spent five rainy seasons at Rajgir. He had so impressed King Bimbisara on his first visit that, when he returned from Bodhgaya

TIP

Most tourists travelling into Nepal take the bus from Patna to the border town of Raxaul/Birganj (5–6hrs), from where an overnight bus runs to Kathmandu, a further 11 hours away. Buses are slow and crowded.

CENTRE OF LEARNING

At its height, the University of Sri Mahavihara Arya Bhikshu Sanghasya at Nalanda had a vast library, 2,000 teachers and more than 10,000 students from as far away as Japan, Sumatra, Java and Korea. It reputedly contained a total of 9 million volumes. Legend has it that following the sack of Nalanda in 1199 it burnt for six months.

Excavations have yielded nine levels of occupation, six temples (*chaityas*) and 11 monasteries (*viharas*), all built in red brick. The monasteries are on the eastern side. The main ones are Vihara 1, founded in the 9th century by King Balaputradeva of Sumatra, and Viharas 4 and 5, built by King Kumar Gupta in the 1st century AD. The viharas show remains of student cells, lecture halls, bathrooms, kitchens, libraries, storage rooms and wells. To the west are the temples. The most imposing is the Sariputra Stupa, built by Emperor Ashoka in honour of Ananda, the Buddha's first disciple. It is a three-level structure, partly covered with stucco figures of Lord Buddha teaching, and surrounded by stupas erected to the memory of students who died during their studies. Nearby are Chaityas 12, 13 and 14, largely in ruins.

A new site, Sarai Mound, has been excavated to reveal faded frescoes of horses and elephants. East of the ruins is a museum containing stone and terracotta sculptures.

The giant 20-metre (65ft) Buddha statue at Bodhgaya is a modern addition to the site – it dates from 1989.

having attained enlightenment, accompanied by 1,000 disciples, the king built a monastery set in a bamboo park for this new order *(sangha)* of monks.

Contemporary Rajgir, a small town, is located north of the ancient site that spreads over seven barren hills surrounding a valley. A 50km (30-mile) wall with watchtowers built of huge stone blocks used to run round the city. Its remains stand on the hills and at the north and south gates.

Passing by the remains of the **Ajatasatru Fort**, built in the 5th century BC, the road reaches a small square lined with shops. On the right is **Venuvana**, the bamboo park where the Buddha and his disciples lived. A small mound, now covered with Muslim graves, marks the site of the stupa and *vihara* built by Ajatasatru. In the park is **Karanda Tank**, where the Buddha is said to have bathed.

Also in the neighbourhood is a large temple built by the **Nipponzan Myohoji** – a Japanese movement whose aim is to spread peace by promoting Buddhism. The Centaur Hokke Club caters to the needs of Japanese pilgrims, offering traditional Japanese meals and accommodation. Burmese Buddhists have also built a temple to the east of the fort, at the foot of Vipula Hill.

Further up the hill, past the **Pippla Cave** and the **Jarasandha-ki-Baithak** – a monastery built out of large blocks of stone – is the **Saptaparni cave**, site of the First Buddhist Council. To the south, a cylindrical stone structure, **Manyar Math**, is a former temple to Maninaga, a serpent demi-god referred to in the *Mahabharata*. Turning left, the road passes **Jivakamhavana**, the site of the mango grove presented to the Buddha, and reaches **Maddakuchchi**. From here one has to walk to **Gridhrakuta Hill**, considered the holiest place in Rajgir, where the Buddha delivered the majority of his sermons. From Maddakuchchi, an aerial chairlift leads to the top of **Ratna Giri** where Japanese Buddhists have built the **Vishva Shanti** (World Peace) **Stupa**, a huge white structure visible from miles around. Four golden statues, one on each side, recall the Buddha's birth, enlightenment, teachings and death.

Places of pilgrimage

Gaya, 90km (56 miles) southwest of Rajgir, is an important Hindu site. Lord Vishnu is said to have conferred upon Gaya the power to cleanse one's sins. Devotees flock here to perform ceremonies to clear their dead of the burden of sin they might have carried over to the next world. They take a holy dip in the Phalgu River and lay offerings of *pindas* (sweets) and ritual rice cakes on the ghats along its banks, before entering the **Visnupada Temple** (closed to non-Hindus), built by the Maharani of Indore in 1787 over the footprint of Lord Vishnu. Within the grounds of the temple stands a banyan tree that is said to be the one under which the Buddha spent six years meditating.

The Buddha attained enlightenment in **Bodhgaya** ⓱, on the Phalgu River 12km (7 miles) to the south. The story

BODHGAYA: HOLY CASH COW

Over 100,000 pilgrims and tourists visit Bodhgaya every year, making it easily Bihar's biggest attraction. The money these visitors spend should be bringing much-needed relief to this desperately impoverished area, however, it would appear that even the administration of this most holy site is not immune to the ills that beset the state as a whole.

Most serious amongst the accusations is that a branch of the ancient bodhi tree that sits on the temple grounds, said to be a direct descendant of the one under which the Buddha sat before attaining enlightenment in the 6th century BC, was severed in 2006 and sold in Thailand for a staggering 60 million rupees – US$1.5million.

Although the current administration has made significant improvements to the site, quite where the income generated under previous tenures ended up is still under investigation. Empty niches around the temple underscore the fact that numerous Buddha statues have disappeared, along with – allegedly – huge sums in donations, both from wealthy foreigners and Indian pilgrims. Priests are demanding that control of the temple's finances should revert to Buddhists and not be maintained by Hindus with no religious connection to the site.

relates how he first meditated in nearby Dungesvari, eating one grain of rice a day for two years, then nothing for four years. Realising that mortification did not bring enlightenment, he moved to a cave where voices told him this was not the place. He then found a *ficus* – now known as the *bodhi* tree – and sat under it to meditate, vowing not to rise until he attained enlightenment.

Emperor Ashoka erected a shrine near the *bodhi* tree, replaced in the 2nd century by the present **Mahabodhi Temple**. In the 17th century, Hindus took over the temple as the Buddha is considered an avatar of Vishnu, and it is now managed by a joint Buddhist-Hindu committee.

Inside is a gilded statue of the Buddha, sitting cross-legged, with his right hand touching the ground in acceptance of enlightenment. Around the temple are votive stupas.

Along the western wall is the *bodhi* tree, or rather its latest successor. The original is believed to have been destroyed by Emperor Ashoka before his conversion to Buddhism. The replacement was cut down by Ashoka's jealous wife. The next in the line was destroyed by Shasanka, a Hindu king of Bengal. The immediate predecessor of the present tree withered in the 19th century. Under the tree is the **Vajrasana**, the **Diamond Throne**, a stone slab marking where the Buddha was sitting when he attained enlightenment.

Along the north side of the Mahabodhi Temple, the **Chanka Ramana**, a platform built in the 1st century BC, marks the place where the Buddha walked in meditation. Carved stone lotuses indicate the spots where the lotuses sprang from his feet. South of the temple a statue of the Buddha protected by a cobra stands in the middle of a large lotus pond.

There are many non-Indian Buddhist monasteries in Bodhgaya, and most accept foreign students. More controversial are plans to build a huge bronze Buddha statue that will dominate the site (see www.maitreyaproject.org). The **archaeological museum** (Sat–Thur 10am–5pm; charge) displays various sculptures, some defaced during the 12th-century Muslim invasion.

FACT

The multi-faith demographic of modern India can be seen by the fact that in 2004 an Italian-born Catholic (Sonia Gandhi) stepped aside so a Sikh (Manmohan Singh) could be sworn in by a Muslim president (Abdul Kalam) to lead a country that's 82 percent Hindu.

The Mahabodhi Temple at Bodhgaya marks the site where the Buddha attained enlightenment around 500 BC.

RESTAURANTS

PRICE CATEGORIES

Average price for dinner, up to three courses for one person, excluding alcoholic drinks:

£ = up to Rs200
££ = Rs200–500
£££ = Rs500–1,000
££££ = over Rs1,000

The food changes as you travel along the Ganges from west to east. Starting in the Punjab, the meat dishes of the Sikhs are spicy and rich, exemplified in concoctions such as butter chicken. There is, however, a vegetarian tradition, too, and these dishes – like those of Haryana and UP – are very tasty, such as *aloo gobi* (potatoes and cauliflower curry) and some wonderful dals. The food of UP is very similar but generally a bit lighter; the lightly spiced vegetarian food of strict UP Brahmans, with its avoidance of onions and garlic, is worth seeking out. The Muslim food of Lucknow is another speciality, with delicious grilled kebabs and meat stews.

Punjab and Haryana

Amritsar
Bhiranwan-da-dhaba
Near the Town Hall. **£**
Excellent vegetarian food. Small menu, but very good *thalis and incredibly good value.* The *chana masala* is particularly tasty; if you go to the Golden Temple at dawn this is a great place to stop off for breakfast on your way back into town.
Crystal Restaurant
Crystal Chowk, Lawrence Road. **££**
One of Amritsar's more upmarket options, with plush seating, attentive service, air conditioning and beer. There's some excellent Indian, Chinese and Continental cuisine, but as usual it's best to stick to the local dishes – the tandoori fare is particularly good.
Kesar-ka-Dhaba
Passian Chowk. **£**
Exceptional vegetarian Punjabi dishes and snacks; all very rich, but this is classic Punjabi fare, renowned all over India and the type of food that is reason enough for many people to make the trip to Amritsar.

Chandigarh
Barbequeue Nation
SCO-39, Sector 26, Madhya Marg
Tel: 0172-606 0000, www.barbequeuenation.com. **££**
Busy live grill restaurant, where you cook your own food – unlimited skewers of tasty marinated chicken, prawns and veg – in a little charcoal grill set in your table. There's also a vegetarian buffet and great selection of Indian desserts.
Bhoj
1090–1, Sector 22B. **£**
Recommended for Indian vegetarian food, including good *thalis*; great value.
Mehfil Hotel and Restaurant
S.C.O. 183–5, Sector 17C.
Tel: 0172-270 3539. **££**
Quality North Indian and other dishes in traditional upmarket surroundings. Overall the food tends to be less spicy than elsewhere, so let the waiter know if you'd like yours pepped up a little. Very popular, so book ahead if possible.

Uttar Pradesh

Agra
Dasaprakash
Meher Theatre Complex, 1 Gwalior Road, Cantonment. **££**
Very good South Indian food from this nationwide chain, especially the *dosas* and desserts. Clean and well run.
Esphehan
Oberoi Amarvilas
Taj East Gate
Tel: 0562-223 1515, www.oberoihotels.com. **££££**
Sumptuous five-star dining in one of India's top hotels. The decor's like something from the Arabian Nights, and they lay on unobtrusive Indian ghazals and sarod recitals most evenings, but the real icing on the cake are the sublime views of the Taj. Reservation essential as it's popular with large tour groups.
Joney's Place
Taj Ganj. **£**
The original and best of the area's cheap eateries; international menu and a warm welcome; Joney himself is one of Agra's enduring characters, and bends over backwards to accommodate all comers – his Korean repertoire is outstanding.

Kwality
Sadar Bazaar. **££**
Like all Kwality restaurants, this is reliable, pleasant and serves good North Indian vegetarian and non-vegetarian food; it's slightly away from most of the hotels, but worth tracking down for a relaxed dining experience.
Maya
18/18 Purani Mandi Circle, Fatehabad Road, near Taj West Gate.. **£–££**
The first-floor, Moroccan-style roof terrace here is a real oasis, with tasty, hygienically prepared food and a most un-Agra-like tranquillity. Also a downstairs A/C option if it's warm out – try the Gujarati *thali* for an excellent introduction to this outstanding cuisine.
Zorba the Buddha
E13 Shopping Arcade, Gopi Chand Shivhare Road, Sadar Bazaar. **££–£££**
A very clean and popular vegetarian restaurant serving tasty and imaginative dishes in an almost doll's house-like interior. The portions, although well priced, tend to be on the small size, so you may need more than one. Wacky but worth experiencing.

Allahabad
Allahbad Regency
Tashkent Road. **£££**
Dinner is served on the lawn of this heritage hotel, with live music and friendly waiters adding to the excellent ambience – the quality of the food is an added bonus, and makes for Allahbad's most entertaining evening.
Coffee House
M.G. Marg, Civil Lines. **£**
Popular café with good South Indian vegetarian snacks and great coffee.
El Chico
24 M.G. Marg, Civil Lines. **££**
Comfortable restaurant with a choice of Indian, Western and Chinese dishes and an adjacent snack shop and bakery (the Espresso Snack Bar). Everyone comes for the sizzlers and steaks.

Kanpur
Chung Fa
94b Canal Road, The Mall. **££**
An old-established restaurant serving decent Chinese food, both veg and non-veg, as well as some Thai dishes.
Pandit
Opposite Green Park, Civil Lines; Katahari

Bagh, Cantonment. £
Tasty vegetarian food, especially the *pakoras*, as well as a good variety of Indian-style sweets. Excellent place if you're in a hurry and in the mood for a tasty snack.

Lucknow

The basic 'meals' places by the M.G. Marg/University Road roundabout, close to the Clark's Avadh, serve safe and decent North Indian food, including tandoori dishes.

Dasaprakash
Jopling Road. ££
South Indian vegetarian food from a dependable nationwide chain. The interiors are bright and clean, the service is no-nonsense and the food is consistently good, with the *dosas* in particular highly recommended.

Falaknuma
Rooftop of Clark's Hotel. £££
Traditional nawabi cuisine, prepared with an intricacy unmatched elsewhere, served by candlelight to the accompaniment of superb live *ghazals*, with great views over the city. Perhaps Lucknow's most sophisticated dining experience, highly recommended.

Indian Coffee House
Ashok Marg, near the Post Office. £
Decent South Indian snacks in this traditional throwback. Popular with the older generation, this is a great place just to hang out and listen to the affairs of the day being discussed over a filter coffee.

Nirula's
Shahnajaf Road. £
A branch of a chain of fast food restaurants – India's McDonald's, although with a more wide-ranging menu, including reasonable *thalis*, sandwiches and own-brand, hygienically prepared ice creams.

Royal Café
9–7 Shahnajaf Road, Hazarat Gunj. £
This famous chaat place in the bazaar whips up some of the tastiest hot and cold snacks in the city, made from potato pieces, crispy fried yoghurt dumplings, sour Indian chilli, fresh green coriander leaves and a panoply of tangy, tamarind and spice-rich condiments.

Shanghai Surprise
Sapru Marg. £
Tastefully furnished, decent portions and good service. The lamb and seafood dishes are particularly popular.

Tunde Kabab
In the Chowk. £
A Lucknow institution, renowned for its buffalo steak kebabs served with tasty

breads and creamy yoghurt, but be warned that this is the real thing – if you like things less spicy this may be one to avoid.

Varanasi

Bread of Life
B3-322 Shivala, off Sonarpur Road. £
A bakery selling great bread and cakes. The attached, pleasantly minimal restaurant serves safe and tasty Western food – including amazing pasta, pizza, lasagna and chocolate brownies – making it a good choice for breakfast or a daytime snack, if a little pricier than the local competition. Live music most evenings complements the dreamy Ganges views.

Shree Café
D 15/2 Man Mandir, Dashashwamedh. £
This great little vegetarian joint, only a stone's throw from the ghats, is a big hit with budget travellers for its filling, freshly cooked thalis – and they do deliciously creamy lassis for dessert. Quality photos of the city hang on the walls, and there's an art gallery next door run by the same family.

Sindhi
Bhelupura, by the Lalita Theatre. ££
Varanasi's traditional pure vegetarian food; tasty and good value.

Bihar

Bodhgaya

Several hotels in the town are good, safe options: try the Sujata on Buddha Road, the Tathagat or

Royal Residency hotels, both on Bodhgaya Road.

Siam Thai
Next to the China Temple, Godhgaya Rd. ££
Dependably hygienic Thai restaurant serving authentic, delicious pad thai, red and chicken curry under the watchful eye of a tubby Buddha.

Patna

17 Degrees
Above Cineopolis, 6th Floor, P&M Mall. ££
With its modern decor and lighting, and great location on the rooftop of a tower block mall, this is the most popular option with Patna's middle classes. Opened in 2011, it offers a huge variety of dishes, attentive service and a superb backdrop. Try their Chadni Chowk paratha, and a mocktail from the non-alcoholic bar.

Abhiruchi
Marwari Awas Griha Compound, Fraser Road. ££
Tasty Marwari and generic North Indian vegetarian food, including *thalis*, in comfortable surroundings – a well-established favourite.

Darpan
Patliputra Ashok Hotel
B.C. Patel Path. £££
The service is not as good as the Indian/Continental food, but this is a pleasant enough place. The poolside barbecue is an added attraction, plus there is a coffee shop which stays open all day, making this a welcome respite from the bustle of Patna.

Street food in Lucknow.

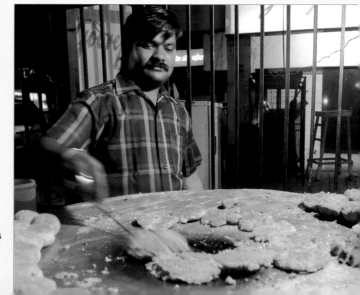

THE TAJ MAHAL

India's most famous sight is every bit as magnificent as it is hyped up to be. Visit in the early morning to avoid the crowds and the heat, or at night during the full moon.

In terms of design the Taj Mahal is the crowning glory of Mughal architecture. Its proportions are stunningly simple. Its height is equal to the width of the plinth on which it stands, while the height of its facade is equal to the height of the bulbous double dome above. It was built between 1631 and 1648 by Emperor Shah Jahan to house the tomb of his beloved wife Mumtaz Mahal, who died in childbirth. The design owes much to Humayun's tomb in Delhi and is believed to have been the work of Ustad Ahmad Lahori, a master architect. White marble, brought by elephant from Makrana 300km (188 miles) away in Rajasthan, adds to its ethereal beauty, as do the floral decorations, bands of black marble Arabic calligraphy, and carved marble screens. To the west of the enclosure is a mosque and, to the east, its replica – known as the *javab* (reply). The latter cannot be used for prayer as its central arch does not face Mekkah (Mecca).

According to legend, Shah Jahan planned to build a similar tomb for himself on the other side of the river out of black marble, linked to the original by a black and white marble bridge, but it remained a dream. He is buried in the Taj Mahal beside his wife.

Visiting for the first time is magical, particularly if you avoid the worst of the crowds (tour groups start to arrive from 9am). The colour of the white marble varies with the light: try to see it at different times. For an even more memorable experience, the site is open for two nights either side of the full moon.

The Taj Mahal is approached through formal gardens, far less impressive than they once were. For the traditionally desert-dwelling Muslims, watered gardens symbolise paradise.

The main entrance to the tomb features a corbelled arch – an Islamic innovation – with a so-called jali screen behind. The construction of the Taj Mahal was said to have involved some 20,000 workers

Shah Jahan (1592–1666) and his wife, Arjumand Banu Begum Mumtaz Mahal (d.1631). The Taj Mahal, Mumtaz Mahal's tomb, was built within sight of Shah Jahan's palace at Agra Fort.

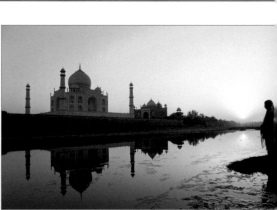

Sunset view from across the Yamuna river.

BUILDING THE TAJ

Twenty thousand labourers were involved in the construction of the Taj Mahal, including sculptors, calligraphers and artists from as far afield as Syria, Iran and Baluchistan. One thousand elephants were involved in transporting building materials to the site, and precious stones were brought from China, Tibet, Sri Lanka and Afghanistan to be used in the inlay. An elaborate brick scaffold was built to mirror the shape of the tomb; when foremen voiced their concern at the length of time this would take to dismantle, Shah Jahan decreed that whoever took the bricks could keep them, and the scaffold disappeared overnight. The green lawns that dominate the garden are a British addition; having defaced the Taj during the Uprising, and reputedly even having planned to dismantle it and sell off the marble, Lord Curzon decided to right the wrongs of his predecessors and ordered a wholesale restoration project, completed in 1908.

No expense was spared in construction, with Italian craftsmen reputedly employed to work on the marble inlay.

Photographing India's most visited sight.

An example of the attention to detail displayed in the construction of the Taj is that the four minarets surrounding the main structure slant outwards, in order to prevent them collapsing onto the tomb in an earthquake.

Scenery reflected in an ice-cold lake near Joshimath.

THE HIMALAYAS

From the lush Kullu Valley to the arid heights of
Ladakh, the Indian Himalayas are much loved by
walkers, climbers and those in search of tranquillity.

Main Attractions
Nanda Devi National Park
Mussoorie
Haridwar
Corbett National Park
Simla
Kullu Valley
Dharamsala
Srinagar
Leh

No matter where you are in the Indian Himalayas, you're never far from a stunning view of a snow-capped peak, rushing waterfall or lush, cedar-lined valley. These can be seen in the company of thousands – Manali is still top of every Indian honeymooner's and snow-seeker's wish list – or entirely alone. The high-altitude deserts of Ladakh are guaranteed to make you feel supremely small, yet sustain a unique culture whose Tibetan-style monasteries and traditional farming practises have altered little since medieval times. Just as Islam dominates Kashmir, so Buddhism is the predominant religion across large swathes of both Ladakh and Himachal Pradesh, while the area is also home to some of Hinduism's holiest sites.

UTTARAKHAND

The mountain districts to the north of Uttar Pradesh form the new state of Uttarakhand (known formerly as Uttaranchal), cleaved off from Uttar Pradesh in 2001. Hinduism regards mountains as the dwelling places of gods, and this stretch of the Himalayas is considered especially sacred as the source of the streams that join to form the Ganges and Yamuna rivers.

Less commercially developed than neighbouring Himachal Pradesh, Uttarkhand, and particularly its western Garwal region, offer some of the most unspoilt and beautiful destinations in the Himalayas. Although not particularly well served by either the air or rail networks, the state's roads are well maintained and make access to some of the highest peaks relatively straightforward.

The highest of those peaks is **Nanda Devi**, rising 7,816 metres (25,646ft) above the eponymous National Park, a World Heritage Site owing to its exceptional natural beauty and populations of rare and threatened

Kashmiri men smoking a shisha pipe in Srinagar.

mammals (although one that is closed to all but a select quota of accredited mountaineers each season).

Dehra Dun ❶ at the foot of the hills is a fast-expanding town and capital of the new state. It is notable for its prestigious institutions, including the Wildlife Institute of India, the Forest Research Institute and the Indian Military Academy. On a ridge 30km (18 miles) beyond Dehra Dun – an hour by taxi – is the hill station of **Mussoorie**, a popular weekend break for Delhi-ites offering impressive views to both the south and north as well as an almost carnival atmosphere in the high season. It's also home to the Lal

Bahadur Shastri National Academy of Administration, which trains entrants to the elite Indian Administrative Service, successor to the British colonial Indian Civil Service, and the Landour Language School, renowned as one of the best places in India to learn the Hindi language.

At **Haridwar** ❷, 50km (30 miles) southeast of Dehra Dun, the Ganges flows out of the mountains into the plains, making it one of the seven most sacred cities for Hindus. This is one of the four places in India that hosts a Kumbha Mela religious festival once every 12 years (the others are Allahabad, Ujjain and Nasik). The evening *arati* (worship) of the River Ganges is held every day at **Har-ki-Pauri**, the main ghat, and the area along the riverbank to the south, dominated by the aptly named Bada (big) Bazaar, is well worth a wander for its many minor ghats and charming period *havelis*.

Rishikesh, a town of temples and ashrams surrounded by forest, is 25km (15 miles) upstream. The northern part of the town, **Muni-ki-Reti**, is very attractive, and the best views can be seen from either of the two footbridges suspended across the river, the Ram Jhula and the Laksman Jhula. Whereas Haridwar has a reserved, sanctimonious feel, Rishikesh seems somehow more on show, the sadhus and ashrams vying for the attention of the legions of foreign visitors who have been coming here since The Beatles' well-publicised stay with Maharishi Mahesh Yogi in 1968.

Sacred mountain sites

Haridwar, Rishikesh and Dehra Dun are the starting points for pilgrimages to the four most sacred places in the Indian Himalayas: Yamunotri, source of the Yamuna; Gangotri, source of the Ganges; and the Kedarnath and Badrinath temples, collectively known as the **Char Dham**.

Yamunotri can be reached from Dehra Dun or Rishikesh. The road stops 13km (8 miles) short of the temple at **Hanuman Chatti**. From here there is a trek along the riverbank. Pilgrims cook rice and potatoes in the water of a hot spring near the temple and offer it to the goddess Yamunotri.

The road to **Gangotri** ❸ runs steeply from Rishikesh to Narendra Nagar, Tehri (where a controversial dam has been built) and Uttarkashi before reaching Gangotri at 3,140 metres (10,300ft). From here it's a day's trek to **Gaumukh** ('cow's mouth'), where the Ganges springs from the base of a glacier. A further day's hiking gets you to Tapovan, a grassy meadow used as the base camp for expeditions

A terraced hillside in the Garwhal mountains.

to Shivling, often referred to as the most beautiful mountain in the entire Himalayan range.

Further to the east, the road to **Badrinath**, home of Lord Vishnu, rises slowly from the steep valley of Deoprayag to the old Garhwal capital of **Srinagar**. From here the route climbs more steeply to **Joshimath**. The **Narsingh Bhagwan temple** here is the main centre of worship to

UTTARAKHAND TRANSPORT

Dehra Dun is the only city with a public airport; it operates regular flights to Delhi. Otherwise, by train is by far the most comfortable way to arrive in Uttarakhand.

Corbett National Park: Trains run from Ramnagar (1.5km/1 mile south of the main gate) to Delhi (2 daily; 5hrs 30min–6hrs). Buses go to Delhi and Dehra Dun (7hrs).

Dehra Dun: Trains run to Delhi (6 daily; 6–11hrs 30mins), Lucknow (3–5 daily; 10hrs 30mins–13hrs 30mins), Varanasi (3 daily; 15–21hrs 30mins) and Kolkata (2 daily; 29–34 hrs). There are 12 trains daily to Haridwar (1–2hrs).

Haridwar: There are trains to Delhi (10 daily; 4hrs 30mins–9hrs), Lucknow (4 daily; 9–11hrs), Varanasi (3 daily; 13hrs 30mins–19hrs) and Kolkata (2 daily; 27–35hrs), plus 11 daily to Dehra Dun (1–2hrs).

Nainital: The nearest rail is at Kathgodam, 35km (20 miles) away, with trains to Delhi (2 daily; 6hrs 30mins–7hrs 15mins), Lucknow (1 daily; 8hrs), Gorakhpur (1 daily; 14hrs 30mins) and Kolkata (5 daily; 15hrs).

Rishikesh: The daily train to Haridwar takes an hour, slower than by bus. There is also a train to Jammu city (1 daily; 12hrs). During pilgrim season from May to October, buses run to Badrinath (12hrs), Gangotri (12hrs), Kedarnath (12hrs), and also go to Joshimath (10hrs), Uttarkashi (7hrs) and Nainital via Ramnagar (18hrs).

TIP

The Indian ski scene offers a low-cost and very different experience from that in the West. There's a good range of equipment available in Auli (above Joshimath), and enough slopes, lifts and instructors to keep all but the most experienced skiers entertained. Kufri, 16km (10 miles) from Simla, is a centre for winter sports. The ice-skating rink is the only one in this part of the world. Skiing is also available at Narkanda, 64km (40 miles) from Simla, Solang, 10km (6 miles) from Manali, where a lift is under construction, and Gulmarg in Kashmir.

Tigers at Corbett National Park.

Vishnu when his shrine at Badrinath is closed during winter. Joshimath is connected by India's longest cable-car ride (4km/2.5 miles), to **Auli**, one of the country's best-known ski resorts.

Beyond Joshimath, Govindghat is the starting point for treks to the majestic **Valley of Flowers National Park** ❹ (best seen June–Aug when it is carpeted with over 300 varieties of flowers thanks to the monsoon), and to the modern Sikh temple at **Hemkund**. The road continues up to Badrinath, with the **Kedarnath** route branching off. The shrine at Kedarnath is dedicated to Shiva and contains one of the 12 *jyotirlingas*, or *lingas* of light. The temple stands at the head of the Mandakani river, in a stunning valley surrounded by snow-covered mountains.

Hill stations

In the Kumaon district to the east are the popular hill stations of Nainital, Ranikhet and Almora. **Nainital**, built around a lake surrounded by for-ested hills, was originally the summer capital of the government of United Provinces – as Uttar Pradesh and Uttaranchal were known under the British. It is by far the most developed of the three resorts, its proximity to Delhi guaranteeing floods of tourists in the peak season.

Naukuchiyatal, 25km (15 miles) from Nainital, is the most secluded and peaceful of the nearby lake resorts, while **Ranikhet**, home of the Kumaon Regiment of the Indian Army, is one of the least spoilt of the hill stations, very well maintained and devoid of the rampant over development found elsewhere. **Almora** itself has nothing as such to recommend it, but is an ideal starting point for exploring the majestic oak forests of **Binsar**, or for visiting the 150 magnificent temples at **Jagesvar**.

Corbett National Park

Corbett National Park ❺ (mid-Nov–mid-June), 300km (186 miles) north of Delhi, is considered by many to be India's premier national park. Its pristine forests and meadows shelter a population of tigers (around 135), elephants and deer, and a variety of birds, including the maroon oriole, fairy bluebird, green magpie and red-breasted falconet. The Ramganga River provides a habitat for crocodiles and gharial, as well as the impressive mahseer fish. It was named after the hunter-turned-conservationist Jim Corbett, whose gung-ho adventures *The Man-Eaters of Kumaon* and *The Man-Eating Leopard of Rudraprayag*, are perennial best-sellers.

All individuals and vehicles require a permit to enter, which can be obtained from the reception centre in Ramnagar. There is a choice of five different areas of the park to be visited, with Dhikala offering the widest range of accommodation as well as the greatest variety of wildlife.

HIMACHAL PRADESH

The picturesque state of Himachal Pradesh straddles the Himalaya from the foothills to the high, remote valleys of Lahaul and Spiti, with a swathe of snowy peaks in between. Its capital, Simla, had the distinction of serving as the summer capital of India in the days of the British viceroys, a refuge for the sahibs from the heat of the plains.

In summer, the fragrance of fresh flowers pervades these enchanting hills and the coolness of the melting snow tempers the heat. The monsoon brings a spectacle of lush greenery and cascading waterfalls. Autumn is marked by pleasant sunny days, clear views and gorgeous sunsets. Winter brings snow.

The majority of Himachalis are Hindus, but Buddhism is also a major influence, particularly with the presence of the exiled Dalai Lama at Dharamsala and the large settlements of Tibetan refugees.

The state is predominantly rural and its towns are small. The traditional village house is of special interest: the lowest storey is occupied by the household cattle; the middle provides space for storing grain and other things, but also for sleeping in winter;

the top floor *(dafi)* provides living space. These days, however, traditional lifestyles are becoming increasingly marginalised as tourists encroach in ever greater numbers. In this regard Himachal feels significantly more developed than neighbouring Uttarakhand.

Simla to Kinnaur

Simla ❻ (Shimla) lies on a ridge at a height of 2,100 metres (6,900ft). It was previously the official summer location for the government of British India, and much British influence survives in the upper town. It is linked to the plains by the Kalka–Simla narrow-gauge railway, with four departures a day in each direction: the train slowly winds its way up the picturesque mountainside in about six hours. The level ground of Simla's ridge is a favourite evening rendezvous, particularly Scandal Point, and the main street, the Mall (from which Indians were infamously banned), is the place for shopping.

In spite of its considerable growth since Independence, Simla, perhaps

HIMACHAL PRADESH TRANSPORT

At the time of writing (2013), neither of the two domestic airports in Himachal Pradesh – at Simla and Kullu – were up and running. Train services remain limited within the state, with the result that most visitors either travel by bus or taxi.

Dharamsala: The closest mainline train station is at Pathankot, but this can be reached via the narrow-gauge Kangra Valley Railway. The closest station to Dharamsala is at Kangra Mandir, 20km (12 miles) away. Buses run from here to Pathankot (4hrs), Delhi (12hrs), Manali (10hrs) and Dehra Dun (13hrs).

Simla: The best and most scenic way to reach Simla is via the 'toy train'. From Delhi take a train to Kalka (6hrs), from where the narrow-guage locomotive winds it way up to Simla in a leisurely 5 hours. Onward journeys are by bus or taxi; buses leave regularly for Manali (10hrs), Dharamsala (10hrs) and Chandigarh (4hrs).

Manali: Pending the resumption of flights connecting Delhi and Bhuntar, the only way in or out of the Kullu Valley is by road. In the summer buses run to Simla (10hrs) and Dharamsala (10hrs), as well as over Rohtang Pass to Kaza (11hrs), Keylong (9hrs) and Leh (2 days including overnight stop in Sarchu). The alternative option is to investigate joining a share taxi or jeep, which are also available for the journey to Leh.

Hill Stations

The architecture and ambience of the Raj has been largely sidelined elsewhere, but high in the hills of India it still takes centre stage

Perhaps nowhere in India gives as evocative an impression of life during the Raj as one of its many hill stations. Initially designed as summer retreats from the heat of the plains, these quaint throwbacks often include many of the components of the classic British summer holiday: donkey rides, pedalos, golf courses, rain, promenades, tea rooms, ice creams, gymkhana clubs and character-building walks through the woods. The clubs are especially antiquated, often requiring temporary membership to be arranged before entry, and enforcing strict dress codes of an evening, typically including a tie and jacket for men, who often have their own menonly bars on the premises.

There are hill stations dotted all over India, from the Nilgiri Hills to the Western Ghats, to Rajasthan and the Himalayas, but they all retain a remarkable similarity. Whatever the extent of

Viceregal Lodge, Simla.

modern additions, a certain proportion of the buildings will always date back to the Raj, as will the interior decor and furniture. British-style churches are often a centrepiece. Menus are likely to include at least some British staples – bread and butter pudding, scones and apple pie are not unheard of.

Modern resorts

Hill stations have long been the favoured by Indian honeymooners, and are nowadays among the most popular short-break holiday destinations for the Metropolitan middle classes, which has spawned a rash of glitzy-looking hotels – round beds and mirrored ceilings are a regular feature, along with plate-glass exteriors and all mod cons.

Newlyweds aside, the number of Indian tourists hitting the hill stations in the summer is growing rapidly, meaning congestion has become a real problem in the typically narrow streets. Local businesses have developed to reflect this trend, with many of them now offering the latest electronic gadgets, trendiest fashions and designer shades – a glaring contrast with the old-fashioned provisions stores that often sit next door. Nationwide coffee-shop chains are also moving in, again often in close proximity to their traditional counterparts, as are international sportswear brands.

Adding to the mix are several other demographic groups: hill stations tend to have a fairly large military presence – they were originally used by the British as sanatoriums for their troops, and the tradition has lived on. Buddhist monks have established monasteries in many of the Himalayan hill stations and boarding schools are often located nearby, some attracting students from the world over.

The areas surrounding these towns are often the main attraction, typically thickly wooded and offering stunning views of the plains below and mountains above. Trekking and camping trips can be arranged in most places, and adventure sports such as paragliding, mountain biking and rock climbing are becoming increasingly widely available, a far cry from the traditional evening stroll down the promenade.

The other defining feature of India's British-era hill stations are the narrow-gauge trains which served as their principal link with the plains. These days, they've been superseded by roads but still survive as popular tourist attractions, and in the case of Darjeeling, Ooty and Shimla have been declared world heritage sites.

more than any other spot in India, is reminiscent of an attempt to recreate England in India. Its colonial domestic architecture and Christchurch (the second church to be built in North India) give it the air of a neglected Edwardian town. It was the setting of many of Rudyard Kipling's stories in his book *Plain Tales from the Hills*, and the bazaar below the ridge was famously described in his novel *Kim*.

Simla is a pleasant place to relax, although the centre of town gets very overcrowded during the peak summer season, at which time it makes sense to stay in the outskirts, where there are excellent walks through the woods. The green slopes are covered with fir, rhododendron, pine and Himalayan oak.

One of the most popular walks is up to Jakhu Temple, 2km (1.25 miles) from Christchurch, dedicated to Hanuman, the monkey god, and appropriately enough surrounded by monkeys. Care should be taken with these extremely brazen animals – keep all food items firmly out of sight. The views from the top more than compensate for the obstacles en route, however.

Chail, 63km (39 miles) south of Simla, was once the summer capital of the Maharaja of Patiala and is now a lovely tourist resort. Its cricket pitch is reputed to be the highest in the world and certainly one of the most scenic. The town and its environs provide excellent facilities for fishing, tennis, squash, bird and wildlife enthusiasts.

Narkanda ❼, at a height of 2,700 metres (8,850ft), and 64km (40 miles) from Simla on the Hindustan–Tibet road, is famous for its apple orchards and scenery. It is one of the state's ski resorts, albeit one without any real skiing infrastructure, and is a convenient starting point for visiting the heart of Himachal Pradesh. Naldera, famous as a golf destination, and Mashobra, both a short detour from the main highway from Simla, make very peaceful places to relax, and both offer wonderful

views of the higher peaks. Travelling east from Narkanda along the valley of the Sutlej River brings you to the border region of **Kinnaur**.

On the bank of the Sutlej, **Rampur ❽**, 140km (90 miles) from Simla, is one of the largest towns in the state and is a good place to pick up a permit to visit Kinnaur. It is noted for its three-day market fair, *Lavi*, which is

A grey langur with baby.

The Kalka-Simla Railway was completed in 1903.

FACT

The 1st-century AD Greek traveller and philosopher, Apollonius Tyaneus, could have been describing much of modern-day Himachal Pradesh when he said: 'In India I found a race of mortals living on the Earth, but not adhering to it. Inhabiting cities, but not being fixed to them, possessing everything but possessed by nothing.'

held in November. While the days are spent in making bargains, the evenings are given over to song and dance.

Kinnaur is one of the most unspoilt and least visited regions of Himachal Pradesh. Its proximity to the Tibetan border makes it a restricted zone, but permits are now easy to obtain. **Rekong Peo** is the main town, but a better place to head for is **Kalpa**, a little way along the main road, which has stunning views of the Kinner-Kailash Mountains and a wider choice of accommodation. Buses run from Rekong Peo and Kalpa to **Sangla** in the beautiful valley of the Baspa River.

There are some lovely treks in the region. The old Hindustan–Tibet road is recommended: starting in Sarahan, passing through Kalpa and continuing into Upper Kinnaur (for which an Inner Line permit is needed) and the Rupa Valley. Another spectacular trek is the pilgrims' circuit of the Kinner-Kailash range.

The Valley of the Gods

The **Kullu Valley** ❾ on the Beas river, at an altitude of 1,200 metres (3,900ft),

is renowned for apple orchards, beautiful scenery, wooden temples and its music and dance. Its mountain surroundings offer scope for all manner of outdoor pursuits, including trekking, climbing, mountain biking, paragliding, skiing, rafting and angling.

The regional hub, **Kullu**, has fewer attractions to detain travellers than places further up the valley, although there are two Hindu shrines in the town that are worth seeing: the Raghunathji temple and the cave-temple of Vaisno Devi. Kullu really comes to life during the *Dussera* festival (usually in October), when tourists and locals flood into the town to see the spectacular procession of village deities. Carried on the shoulders of bearers in specially decorated palanquins, between 100 and 200 gold-faced devtas and devis (gods and goddesses) converge on Kullu's maidan, where they pay homage to the royal family's tutelary deity, Raghunathji. Accommodation should be booked well in advance at this time.

The most remarkable temple of the valley is **Bijli Mahadeva**, 8km (5

TREKKING ROUTES

There is no end to the trekking possibilities in Himachal Pradesh and routes are generally far less crowded than in Nepal. It's always a good idea to hook up with a guide, best booked through an agency in Manali or Chamba. Apart from ensuring you don't lose your way, a guide will also help shop for the necessary provisions for the trek, arrange accommodation in villages and act as a translator.

Chamba District

Dharamsala–Chamba via Bleni Pass, 5 days: Kareri, 1,980m (14km); Gaddikhot via Bleni Pass, 3,560m (16km); Drakund via Lam Dal Lake, 1,800m (20km); Donali, 1,525m (18km); Chamba by road.

Chamba–Manali via Sach Pass, 10 days: Bairagarh by car, then Satrundi, 3,500m (16km); Bindravani via Sach Pass, 4,367m (18km); Killar, 2,245m (13km); Sach Khas, 2,200m (15km); Purthi, 2,255m (15km); Raoli, 2,591m (19km); Tindi, 2,250m (16km); Udaipur (25km); Manali by car via Rohtang Pass.

Manali District

Manali–Chandratal 11 days: Chikka, 2,956m (13km); Chatru, 3,360m (16km); Chota Dara (16km); Batal (16km);

Chandratal (18km); Topko Yongma (11km); Topko Gongma, 4,730m (10km); Baralacha, 4,870m (10km); Patseo, 3,820m (19km); Jispa (14km); Keylong, 3,340m (21km). Manali–Solang Valley 7 days: Solang, 2,480m (11km); Dhundi; Beas Kund, 3,540m and back (10km); Dhundhi–Shigara Dugh (8km); Marrhi, 3,380m (10km).

Manali–Chandrakhani–Malana 7 days: Ramsu, 2,060m (24km); Chandrakhani, 3,650m (6km); Malana (6km); Kasol (8km); Jari (14km); Bhuntar, 1,900m (11km).

Simla District

Simla–Manali via Jalori Pass, 9 days: Narkanda by car, 2,708m, then Hatu Peak, 3,136m (16km); Luhri, 792m (19km); Ani,1,240m (18km); Khanag, 2,530m (15km); Shoja, 2,683m (14km); Banjar, 1,524m (15km); Larji, 975m (17km); Manali, 2,050m by car.

Simla–Sangla via Rohru, 8 days: Rohru, 1,550m, by car then Chirgaon, 1,800m (15km); Larot, 2,440m (15km); Dodra, 2,800m (18km); Kuwar, 2,300m (17km); Jakka, 3,100m (19km); Ruknal, 4,400m (16km); Sangla, 2,800m (17km).

Simla–Mussoorie via Tuini and Simla–Churdhar via Fagu.

miles) southeast of Kullu and accessible only by a long flight of steep steps (with tremendous views from the top). It is built of large blocks of stone without the use of cement, and its 20-metre (65ft) flagstaff is reputed to attract lightning – considered an expression of divine blessing. Every time the flagstaff is struck by lightning, the Shiva *lingum* (phallic symbol) inside the temple is shattered. It is put back together each time by the priest and stands until another flash repeats 'the miracle'.

Kullu's airport is at Bhuntar, 10km (6 miles) south of the town. At the time of writing in 2013, flights from Delhi had been suspended following the demise of Kingfisher Airlines, although it is hoped the national carrier, Indian Airlines, will cover the route in future. Bhuntar also marks the turning-off point for the **Parvati Valley**, which runs to the northeast. Along the valley are the hot springs at **Manikaran**, a Sikh and Hindu pilgrimage town. Although this dramatically beautiful area is best explored on foot, dozens of foreigners have disappeared here over the past decade. Bodies washed downstream by the Beas River have confirmed that at least a dozen of these disappearances were the result of violent murders, but many more – perhaps as many as sixty – remain a mystery. Local police and journalists connect them with the local trade in charas, or marijuana resin. Another theory is that a large proportion of the disappeared are simply travellers who have settled in remote villages, and now live off hashish cultivation, having long outstayed their visas and passports. Either way, if you wish to trek here, take the precaution of hiring an experienced guide and travel in a group. Further towards Mandi, just south of the road tunnel, lies the turn-off to **Jalori Pass**, a protracted but picturesque route that leads to Narkanda and ultimately Simla. The road becomes particularly steep as it approaches the pass at 3,000 metres (10,000ft), and is best attempted in a four-wheel-drive. There is good accommodation available at **Shoja**, a great place to unwind far from the madding crowd.

EAT

For inexpensive but well-prepared North Indian food in Simla, try the vegetarian restaurants below Himani's on the Mall.

Christ Church, Simla.

FACT

Himachal Pradesh is noted for its wide range of traditional songs and dances. Nati is the most widely performed dance, in which the masked dancers link hands and form a chain. In Kinnaur and Lahaul-Spiti, some dances depict the perpetual strife between gods and demons.

The road from Kullu to Manali runs along the rushing torrents of the Beas. It is flanked by lofty mountains and spreading forests. Near Katrain is the small town of **Naggar**, where the Castle Hotel is said to be haunted. The town has been made famous by the late Russian painter Nicholas Roerich, whose **gallery** can be seen here (Tue–Sun 9am–1pm, 2–5pm; charge). It is also increasingly popular as a less hectic alternative to Manali as a place to stay, with more and more hotels springing up in the area.

Manali

Manali ❿ is encircled by beautiful glades of deodars and flowering horse chestnuts. Traditionally an important trading centre, in recent years it has become a popular resort for Indian honeymooners and holidaymakers, as well as Western tourists, and can get overcrowded in the summer months.

The town is split into two parts: the New Town is where the bus-stand and most of the hotels are, while along The Mall (the main street) and over

the Manalsu River is the more atmospheric old village, where it is possible to find accommodation in traditional houses. The Hindu **Dhungri Temple**, dedicated to the goddess Hadimba, is believed to be more than 1,000 years old, while Manali's large Tibetan population has built two new *gompas* (monasteries).

Three kilometres (2 miles) up the valley are the hot springs of **Vashisht**. The temple complex here has separate outdoor baths for men and women. The Kullu Valley ends as the road passes the ski resort of **Solang** – the best place to learn to paraglide in northern India – and winds up through rocky ranges to the Rohtang Pass, gateway to the enchanting Lahaul and Spiti valleys and onwards to Ladakh.

Lahaul and Spiti

In the northeastern corner of Himachal Pradesh, across the 3,978-metre (13,050ft) **Rohtang Pass**, lie the two valleys of **Lahaul** and **Spiti** at a height of 3,000–4,800 metres (9,800–15,700ft). Both valleys are cut off

Men woodworking in Himachal Pradesh's Kulu Valley.

from the rest of the world for much of the year, though this state of isolation is set to end as a new road tunnel beneath the pass nears completion. While the road is only open from May through October, the 8.8km (5.5-mile) tunnel will provide a year round link to the two valleys beyond.

Rohtang, for the time being the only gateway to this spectacularly beautiful trans-Himalayan region, marks a stark climatic divide. In the summer monsoon, the climb from Manali is often misty or rainy, but on crossing the pass you tend to find a much brighter, sunnier day. Once on the far side, the culture of the valleys' inhabitants also contrasts with those of Kullu. Lahaulis are half-Buddhist, half-Hindu, while people from Spiti are of Tibetan origin and almost entirely Buddhist.

At the town of **Gramphu**, on the far side of the Rohtang Pass, the road from Manali splits: one route runs eastwards into the Lahaul Valley and then on to the Kunzum Pass and Spiti. The other, far better, surfaced route heads north to Ladakh via the district capital, **Keylong** (the only market between Manali and Leh).

Continue east to cross the **Kunzam Pass** at an altitude of 4,550 metres (15,000ft) and then descend into the Spiti Valley. As well as cultural distinctions, there are pronounced climatic and topographical differences from one side of the pass to the other. While Lahaul is relatively fertile, with an almost Mediterranean look and feel, Spiti has a far more barren, almost lunar landscape. The Lahaul Valley is an important route to Ladakh, particularly for the army, but Spiti feels utterly remote, seeing far less traffic and giving the impression of having existed more or less in its current form for hundreds of years.

In Spiti, the town of **Kaza** is the place to plan treks and arrange permits for Inner Line areas, and is a good base from which to visit the spectacular *gompa* at **Kyi**, 12km (7 miles) away. Some of the world's greatest examples of Buddhist painting and sculpture can be seen 46km (28 miles) further up the valley in the Chos Khor Gompa at **Tabo**, founded in 996.

Hindu pilgrim in the Himalayas.

The Tibetan flag. There are are an estimated 100,000 Tibetan refugees in India, and the region is naturally a focus for the Free Tibet campaign.

The Kangra District

Kangra is one of the most beautiful valleys in the Himalayas. **Dharamsala** ⓫, the headquarters of the district at the foot of the Dhauladhar Range, consists of a lower and an upper town, its altitude varying from around 1,000 to 2,000 metres (around 3,300–6,600ft). Upper Dharamsala, better-known as **McLeod Ganj**, has since 1959 been the home of His Holiness the Dalai Lama and the Tibetan Government in Exile, and is the main tourist destination. While much of the accommodation is here, the smaller villages in the surrounding area are much quieter and can make excellent bases from which to explore the area; **Naddi** has particularly impressive views.

The large Tibetan population supports many organisations, including TIPA (Tibetan Institute of Performing Arts), which preserves and arranges performances of traditional Tibetan music and dance, particularly the drama *lhamo*. **Namgyal Monastery**, just below the bazaar in McLeod Ganj, makes a fascinating visit and

an excellent first introduction to the Buddhist faith. Assuming he's in town, audiences with His Holiness can be arranged through the security office by Hotel Tibet. Also well worth a visit is the **Norbulingka Institute**, 5km (3 miles) below the lower town. The institute was established with the aim of preserving the cultural heritage of Tibetan Buddhism, and has become a major seat of learning, offering classes in Tibetan language, crafts, Buddhism and meditation. There's also a small museum and a well-stocked library. In the lower town is the **Museum of Kangra Art** (Tue–Sun 10am–1.30pm, 2–5pm; free), housing a collection of miniature paintings and other local artefacts.

The ancient town of **Kangra** ⓬, 48km (30 miles) south, is well known for its temples, the most popular being the one dedicated to the goddess Vajresvari. Also worth visiting is the fort, once the palace of the local Katoch kings, with an outstanding view over the valley below.

Continuing south from Kangra, **Jawalamukhi** is one of the most

View of Chamba, and the surrounding scenery of the Ravi river valley.

popular pilgrimage sites in Himachal, notable for its 'eternal flame', where a fissure in the rock face emits a constant stream of flammable gas. Off the road to Hoshiapur, **Pragpur** is India's first 'Heritage Village', painstakingly restored to depict life in the region hundreds of years ago, with the added benefit of a hugely atmospheric hotel. Some 34km (22 miles) southwest of Dharamsala are the 10th-century rock-cut temples of **Masrur**, similar in style to those at Ellora in Maharashtra (see page 266), though not as well preserved.

Chamba Valley

Further north, the romantic valley of **Chamba**, a former princely state, has few rivals for scenic beauty. Its valleys, meadows, rivers, lakes, springs and streams have a unique charm. The town of **Chamba** ⑬ is situated on the right bank of the Ravi river at an altitude of 900 metres (2,950ft). It is noted for its ancient Shiva and Vishnu temples, some of which date back to the 10th century. The **Bhuri Singh Museum** (Tue–Sun 10am–5pm; free)

is a treasure trove of exquisite paintings from the famous Kangra and Basohli schools and has a mass of material relating to the history of the region.

Among the innumerable fairs and festivals celebrated in Himachal Pradesh, the most important is the *Minjar* fair, held at Chamba around August to celebrate the coming of the rains and the flowering of maize. A procession of decorated horses and

A protector deity in a Tibetan Buddhist fresco, Dharamsala.

The Himalayan foothills around the Kullu Valley are crisscrossed with hiking trails offering stupendous scenery.

TRANSPORT

During the summer months, both Air India and Jet operate daily flights to and from Srinagar and Leh. AI also fly to Jammu. However, in the winter, schedules may be disrupted for days by adverse weather conditions. Travellers on flights to Leh or Srinagar should also note that due to the increased security, no hand baggage is allowed in the cabins; you also have to check in at least three hours prior to departure. Jammu is the only railhead in the state. If you're flying direct to Leh, see page 490 for advice on altitude acclimatisation.

Leh: In summer only, buses go to Manali (2 days, overnight in Sarchu) and Srinagar (2 days, overnight in Kargil).

Srinagar: Buses go to Jammu, the closest train station (10hrs), Delhi (24hrs) and Leh (2 days, with overnight stop in Kargil).

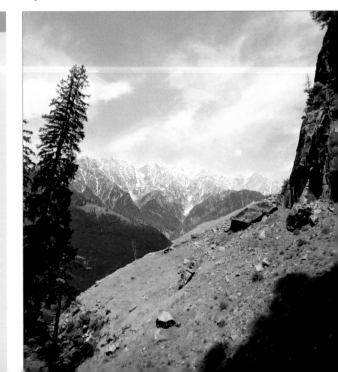

banners marks the beginning of the week-long fair.

Some 56km (35 miles) from Chamba town is **Dalhousie**, a quiet hill station located on five hills, which offer pleasant walking and superb mountain views. At the eastern end of the valley, **Brahmaur**, the ancient capital of Chamba, is famous for the Pahari architecture of its ancient temples and its lovely location, while **Nurpur** is known for its textiles.

In the Himalayan foothills

En route from the plains to the Kullu Valley, **Mandi** ⓮, on the left bank of the Beas river at an altitude of 750 metres (2,460ft), has several stone temples with beautiful carvings, but is otherwise of little appeal to the visitor. For the *Shivratri* Fair (February/March) devotees put the *rathas* (carriages) of their village family gods and goddesses on their shoulders and process to Mandi town. They present themselves at the **Raj Madhan Temple** and pay homage to Lord Shiva at **Bhutnath Temple**. On this day, a week-long fair of selling, music and dance begins.

Bilaspur lies 40km (25 miles) south of Mandi in the Siwalik Hills. Among the town's major attractions are **Vyas Gufa** (cave) and the **Lakshmi Narayan** and **Radheshyam temples**. The **Shri Naina Devi Temple**, which attracts thousands of pilgrims during its many fairs, is situated at the top of a triangular hillock just 57km (35 miles) from Bilaspur. This sacred place provides an unparalleled view of the holy **Anandpur Sahib**, the birthplace of a Sikh guru, on one side, and Govind Sagar (named after the guru) on the other.

Paonta Sahib, on the road between Dehra Dun and the small holiday resort of **Nahan**, is a pilgrimage centre for the Sikhs. Its impressive *gurdwara* (temple) on the bank of the Yamuna River is thronged by pilgrims during the *Hola* festival in March. **Renuka** is a picturesque lake town 45km (30 miles) northeast of Nahan. Kasauli, just above Chandigarh off the main Simla Highway, is the closest hill station to

Kashmir scenery.

Delhi, but sees relatively few visitors, and offers attractive walks through the nearby pine forests.

JAMMU AND KASHMIR

Although famed as one of the world's most beautiful mountain regions, Kashmir found itself isolated from India's tourist circuit in the mid-1990s, after six Western travellers were killed by a militant Islamist group. The tragedy brought to the world's attention a long-running insurgency that over the course of the following fifteen years would result in the deaths of thousands of Kashmiris and see the valley swamped by Indian military personnel. The situation, however, has improved greatly in recent years. Although there was a brief escalation in tensions in 2010, the conflict in no way targeted at tourists, and in 2012 the slow rehabilitation of Kashmir as a destination took a major step forward when the British Foreign Office finally revised its travel warning for the region. Visitor numbers have been increasing rapidly ever since.

Throughout the troubles, neighbouring Ladakh, the eastern part of the state, remained peaceful, and can has reaped the rewards in terms of tourism receipts, although it remains a sensitive border area.

Geography

The area is divided into three regions. Jammu occupies the plains, and is populated by Dogras and Punjabis, who are primarily Hindu and Sikh. Further north, Kashmir includes the Kashmir Valley and surrounding mountains that stretch from Banihal north into Pakistan. The third region is Ladakh (see page 192).

The present border between India and Pakistan (known as the Line of Control) is the ceasefire line from the 1948–9 war. At Independence it was still undecided which country Kashmir was to enter. The Hindu ruler took his majority Muslim population into the Indian Union in 1948, under circumstances that are still heavily disputed. The referendum on the issue of accession, promised by Nehru, has never been allowed to take place.

WHERE

A resort that opened in 2009 has made the Srinagar–Leh drive even more enticing. Situated on the banks of the Sindh River, and with a backdrop of pine forest, Rah Villas is 12km (7½ miles) before Sonamarg, and has 15 luxurious tents in peaceful surroundings. For more details, visit the website at www.sonamargnature resort.com.

Nain Singh, one of the first men to explore the Himalayas for the British.

KASHMIRI PANDITS

The Kashmiri Pandits are something of an anomaly – Hindus in today's predominantly Muslim Kashmir. They are followers of a branch of Hinduism which was established long before Islam became the region's dominant religion. Following the start of Muslim rule, and the destruction of many Hindu temples at the start of the 1400s, large numbers of Pandits left the Kashmir Valley for other parts of India. Their numbers have continued to decline; from 15 percent in 1941, they now form just 1 percent of the Kashmiri population. Their influence, however, far outweighs their numbers, with many influential positions in Indian political life having been held by Kashmiri Pandits, including independent India's first and third prime ministers, Jawaharlal Nehru and Indira Gandhi.

Dal Lake in Srinagar, one of the most romantic spots in Asia. The picturesque houseboats and surroundings remain, but the lake itself is increasingly polluted.

A skier in Gulmarg, Kashmir.

Jammu

Jammu ⓯ is the only railhead in the state of Jammu and Kashmir. Situated amid the Siwalik Hills, its low elevation (300 metres/ 984ft) makes it hot and humid in summer. Traditionally it is a stopover on the way to the Kashmir Valley or for pilgrims visiting the Vaishnodevi cave temple, although as the scene of some of the most notorious and bloody terror attacks in the Kashmir insurgency, the town saw comparatively few foreign tourists until the recent lull in the dispute.

There are two temples of note in Jammu town; the **Ranbireshwar Temple**, dedicated to Shiva, and the **Raghunath Temple**, dedicated to Rama. Both temples were constructed in the 19th century under Dogra *rajas*. These kings were patrons of the arts, and there is a collection of miniatures from the Basholi, Jammu and Kangra schools on show in the **Dogra Art Gallery** (daily 10am– 4pm; charge).

Out of the town centre is **Bahu Fort**, which is perched on a hill across the Tawi River. Within the fort is a temple dedicated to Kali, the Hindu goddess of time and change. At the northern edge of town sits **Amar Mahal Palace** (Tue–Sun, Oct–Mar 10am–12pm and 3–5pm, Apr–Sept 5–7pm; charge) now a museum with some fine Pahari miniatures, which provides an excellent view of the surrounding countryside and city.

Kashmir

Srinagar ⓰, around 10 hours by bus from Jammu, is situated on the shores of Dal Lake in the heart of the beautiful Kashmir Valley. People still live on the houseboats on the lake, also the location of a daily floating vegetable market, and ringed by high mountains. A stay in one of the many houseboat hotels has traditionally been one of the main attractions of the city.

Several Mughal gardens are located on the boulevard that skirts Dal Lake: **Chasma Shahi**, built by Shah Jahan; **Nishat** and **Shalimar**, both with fountains, marble terraces and latticed marble pavilions; and the smaller garden of **Harwan**. Near Harwan are the ruins of a Buddhist college. There are several important mosques and *dargahs* in Srinagar. The huge **Jama Masjid** dates from the late 17th century. The **Shah Hamadan Mosque** is famous for the papier-mâché work on its walls and ceiling, and for its construction without nails or screws. Across the river is the stone **Pather Masjid** (1623). In Nagin the modern, lakeside **Hazratbal shrine** is said to preserve a hair of the Prophet Muhammad.

Elsewhere in the valley, **Pahalgam** (east of Srinagar) is from where pilgrims make a four-day trek to a Hindu shrine held sacred to the god Shiva, the **Amarnath Cave**. The high profile of the Indian military during the festival is a consequence of the terror attack of 2000, when Kashmiri separatists massacred thirty pilgrims and horsemen.

Off the road from Pahalgam to Anantnag to the south of Srinagar, at Mattan, are the ruins of the **Martand Temple** complex and a sacred spring. South of Anantnag are **Achabal**, site of elaborate Mughal gardens, and more gardens at **Verinag**, while towards Srinagar there are temple ruins at **Avantipur**.

Gulmarg and Sonamarg

An hour by road from Srinagar is the ski resort of **Gulmarg** ⑰, used as a backdrop for old Hindi films, a major attraction in the 1970s and now experiencing something of a renaissance following the completion of an 8km (5-mile) ski lift, the highest gondola in the northern hemisphere. Experienced skiers rave about the abundant snow and lack of other skiers – like skiing in the Alps but with none of the queues. There is, however, a serious avalanche risk; extreme care should be taken, particularly if attempting unpatrolled slopes. A good standard of ski equipment is available for hire, and there are

TIP

Dzomsa in Leh is a one-stop shop for ecologically sensitive laundry, water bottle refills and a range of healthy drinks and snacks, including seabuckthorn juice, an amazing concoction possessing remarkable medicinal qualities, not to be missed. In general, the shopping – dominated by refugee Tibetans – is nothing great, and most items are expensive.

"Stakna", meaning "Tiger's Nose", is built on the summit of a high rock in the middle of the Indus Valley.

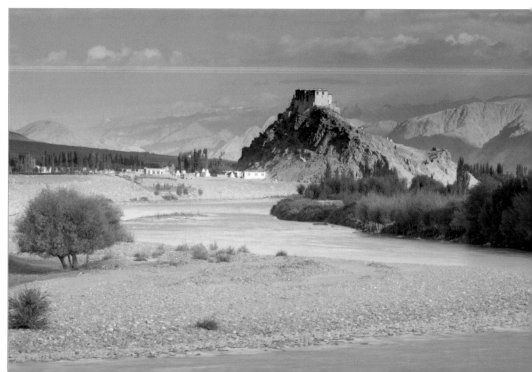

TIP

It is quite difficult to change or obtain money in Leh, although there are now several ATMs (and a few places accept credit cards), so make sure you have plenty of cash. Internet connectivity is now fast, efficient and available all over town.

plenty of English-speaking instructors on hand to guide beginners on the two nursery slopes, each of which has its own drag lift.

The alpine meadows at **Sonamarg** , once a popular stopping place for Ladakh-bound travellers, are also seeing an increase in visitor numbers, as the Srinigar–Leh route has once again become a viable alternative to Manali–Leh. If anything it's more picturesque and carries fewer health risks, as its highest passes are significantly lower than those encountered when coming via Manali.

Ladakh

The far-northern region of Ladakh was formerly a kingdom of western Tibet, but following invasions by the Dogras in the 19th century it was annexed by India. Geographically and culturally it has more in common with Tibet than with India and provides travellers with an insight into that fascinating region. The Ladakhi language is closely allied to Tibetan, and Buddhism is the predominant religion, although there are many Muslim Ladakhis. This identity,

Alchi Monastery (Gompa).

very different to the rest of the state, has led to calls for either separate statehood or for separate administration from Delhi as a Union Territory, in part to disassociate Ladakh from the troubles elsewhere in Jammu and Kashmir.

Ladakh was only opened to tourists in 1974; a measure of the region's limited exposure to the outside world up until that point came when the first commercial flight landed. Ever hospitable and considerate, the local population carried grass to the runway in order that the metal beast may have enough energy for its return flight. While things have of course moved on since then, the region retains a character and charm all of its own, and for many visitors is a magical, incomparable place.

The best time to visit Ladakh is June to September, when you can travel by road. Travellers either fly into Leh from Delhi or Srinagar, or cross the 5,328-metre (17,476ft) Tanglang Pass from Manali in Himachal Pradesh, although increasing numbers are now entering via Srinagar and Kargil.

The landscape changes from lush to stark as you emerge on to the Tibetan Plateau, the mineral-streaked mountains set against a brilliant blue sky. It is a tough 475km (295 miles) from Manali to Leh, the Ladakhi capital, but the two-day journey is certainly one of the most spectacular drives in the world. Flights to Delhi, Chandigarh and Srinagar operate all year at Leh, although winter flights can be suspended for days on end without warning owing to bad weather conditions, and summer flights are often heavily overbooked.

Whether you fly or travel to the region by road, expect to experience mild altitude sickness – either at the midpoint camp on the Manali–Leh Highway, or else on arrival at Leh.

Allow yourself a day or two to acclimatise by doing absolutely nothing. Drink plenty of water – 3 litres (6 pints) a day is not excessive – and not only when you are acclimatising, since the dry air and altitude mean you still have to take in a lot of fluid. Ladakh is a very sensitive environment and bottled water should be avoided at all costs. Take your own water bottle and fill it for a nominal fee with pressure-boiled water from one of the eco-projects such as Dzomsa, or else invest in a portable water filter, available from any good outdoor equipment shop.

The traditional staples of the Ladakhi diet are *tsampa* (roasted barley flour), yoghurt, salt tea and butter. Tibetan dishes are widely available, particularly *momos* (dumplings) and *thukpa* (noodle soup). The most useful word of Ladakhi for travellers is '*Jullay!*', which can mean 'hello', 'good-bye', 'please' or 'thank you'.

Leh

Arriving in **Leh** ⓲, particularly if coming by road, can be quite a revelation. The arduousness of the journey is more than compensated for by the comforts on offer. The peak tourist season is the exact opposite of that in Goa, meaning that many of Goa's chefs and hotel staff move up to Leh in the summer. The resulting range of cuisine is especially impressive given the severity of the surrounding landscape; perhaps nowhere else on Earth can you enjoy a calzone pizza in the middle of a high-altitude desert.

Leh's bazaar was once a trading post on the route between India, China and Central Asia. When the Chinese border closed in the 1950s its importance soon declined, but it is still a pleasant place to wander, with numerous shops selling Kashmiri and Himalayan handicrafts.

The most ambitious walk in town is up to the imposing and partially ruined 16th-century **Leh Palace** (May–Sept daily 7–9.30am; charge), home to the kings of Ladakh until the early 1940s, when the royal family moved out to Stok. If you are fit and energetic, you can visit the **Tsemo**

Gompa (May–Sept daily 7–9am; charge), perched on Namgyal hill, above the palace. The narrow streets of **Old Leh** below the palace evoke the medieval town it once was; close by, on Main Street, is the new **Soma Gompa**. An interesting place to visit is the **Ecology Centre**, run by the Ladakh Ecological Development Group (LEDEG). The group aims to promote ecological awareness and sustainability through traditional methods. The centre has a library and craft shop. **Dzomsa**, at the end of Main Street, has an ecological laundry, recycling bins and pressure-boiled water, as well as local produce such as dried apricots and apples for sale.

The village of **Changspa** (a continuation of Leh to the west), with its small vegetable gardens and peaceful guesthouses, is a pleasant place for a stroll. At the end of Changspa Lane is the new **Shanti Stupa**. A steep line of steps leads up to this Japanese-built peace shrine, and the views from the top are wonderful; there is also a small café in which you can recover your breath.

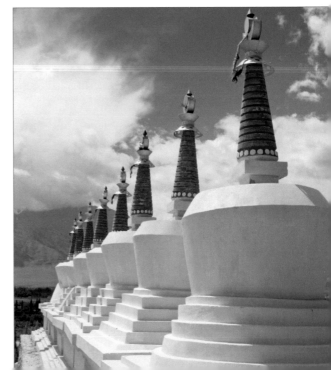

A row of stupas topped with gold crowns at Shey Buddhist monastery, Leh, Ladakh, India.

Ladakh's gompas

Within a day's journey of Leh are some spectacular *gompas*. It is easy to arrange a driver and guide from either a travel agency or the Taxi Operators' Union. Prayer halls in monasteries are decorated with silk hangings in auspicious colours and sacred paintings, called *thankas*, and the walls are lined with stacks of Buddhist texts swathed in silk. Shrines dedicated to the Buddha and Bodhisattvas were traditionally lit with smoky, pungent butter lamps (now largely replaced by oil lamps), and are heaped with offerings of incense, water, tea, food or money. Most monasteries charge entrance fees towards their upkeep and are administered by the Archaeological Survey of India.

Ladakh is also known for its 'oracles'. According to Tibetan Buddhist belief, an oracle is a person who goes into a trance to heal people or animals, or predict the future. Oracles are possessed by benevolent spirits, serving as their channels, for the good of all beings. Several monasteries and villages have a resident oracle;

ALCHI MONASTERY

Perhaps the most exquisite of Ladakh's monasteries is that at Alchi, some 60km (40 miles) from Leh, west along the Indus. Unique in being built on the flat valley floor, Alchi was established in the 11th century by the Tibetan Kal-dan Shes-rab. Much of the monastery, now no longer in use but maintained by the monks of nearby Likir, is made of locally grown willow. However, it seems to have been constructed by artisans from Kashmir; their work is seen in the intricate woodcarving and painted ceilings. The paintings are some of the oldest and most extensive surviving examples of Kashmiri Buddhist art.

The earliest temple is that of Du-Khang, with its ornately carved doorway and walls decorated with mandalas. The walls of the three-storey Sum-tsek Temple are also covered with mandalas; the carving of the wooden structure is very fine. The square shrines of Lotsava Lha-Khang and Manjusri Lha-Khang are side by side; the walls of the latter are covered with representations of the 1,000 Buddhas. The figures in the temples are of Bodhisattvas, including Avalokitesvara and Manjusri.

Alchi is currently being restored, and there is a nominal charge to help with its upkeep; if you are with a local guide they will help you gain access to the locked shrines.

Mulbekh, on the Srinagar–Leh road, has one, as does Stok, the royal residence near Leh.

There are two basic routes around the monasteries, one up and one down the Indus Valley. The road leading south from Leh up the **Indus river** to Hemis Gompa passes a number of monasteries of importance, including the small but interesting **Sankar** monastery on the way out of town. Along this road is **Shey**, the 17th-century summer palace of Ladakhi kings, which houses the largest Buddha in Ladakh. The 600-year-old **Shey Gompa** is here, too. Hundreds of *chortens* – whitewashed reliquaries – can be seen scattered around the barren plains. **Tikse** is a large hilltop monastery noted for its monumental statue of the Maitreya Buddha.

Hemis ⓴ (45km/28 miles from Leh) lies across the Indus at the end of a winding road. Founded in the 1630s, it is the largest monastery in Ladakh, known for its festival in June which features a traditional dance-drama. The greatest treasure of the *gompa* is its enormous embroidered *thanka*, only shown every 12 years – the next display is in 2016.

The road back to Leh on the southern side of the Indus travels past **Stagna**, noted for its images of Bodhisattvas, and **Matho.** Just before the bridge that crosses the Indus is a turn-off to the 18th-century **Stok Palace** (May–Sept daily 7am–7pm; charge), the more recent home of the kings of Ladakh and of the present Gyalmo. The palace houses a well-labelled display of some of the royal family's most precious ritual and ceremonial objects.

Heading west from Leh, down the Indus, brings you to one of the most beautiful monasteries at **Alchi** ㉑.

Spituk and **Phyang** monasteries also lie along this route. Beyond Spituk, as the road emerges from a steep gorge, is the confluence of the Indus and Zanskar rivers. The view here is spectacular, and the different colours of the two waters can be clearly seen. Beyond, up a newly paved road, is the monastery of **Likir**, a Gelugpa *gompa* with a small museum and beautiful prayer hall. A right turn after **Saspul**, noted for its apricots, and the bridge which takes you over the Indus and to Alchi, brings you via an impressive gorge to **Rizong** *gompa*, perched high up at the end of a valley and regarded as the most staunchly traditional of the region's monasteries.

Nubra Valley and beyond

Many areas previously out of bounds to travellers have now opened up. Chief among these is the **Nubra Valley** ㉒, which lies over the Khardung La (5,602 metres/18,370ft), one of the highest roads in the world. The valley itself is surprisingly green after the heights of the pass. Panamik, at the far end of the valley, has hot springs, while the most important local *gompa* is at Deskit. Somewhat improbably, there are also sand dunes close to Nubra itself, where descendants of the two-humped camels that once transported goods from China to India and back can sometimes be seen, although they are now quite rare.

The lakes of **Tso Moriri** ㉓ and **Pangong Tso** ㉔ lie to the southeast, each a three-day return trip from Leh – assuming a day's drive each way and two nights' stay at the water's edge. Tso Moriri is an important nesting site for the barheaded goose and brahminy duck. Some 130km (80 miles) long and wonderfully clear, Pangong Tso crosses over into Tibet proper. The small kingdom of **Zanskar** lies to the southwest, over a fearsome range of peaks. This remote area is cut off by snow for seven months of the year, and this limited access has helped to preserve its strong Buddhist identity. The capital, **Padum** ㉕, lies over the Pensi La (4,450 metres/14,600ft); the only other access to the city is to walk in along the Zanskar River.

Padum can presently only be reached by road from Kargil, but plans are under way to build a road north from Padum to the Leh–Srinagar highway. The completion of this road is expected to change the nature of Zanskar for ever, and so visitors are advised to get there sooner rather than later.

Trekking can be one of the most rewarding ways of exploring the region. Popular treks include the Markha Valley, which takes in the Nimaling Plain and the 5,200-metre (17,056ft) Kongmaru Pass; and the trek from Lamayuru to Alchi or Chiling, which has some stunning views. One of the best, but more arduous, routes is over to the beautiful Zanskar Valley, while Stok Kangri is the most easily accessed of the surrounding high peaks. Short treks may also be taken to the monasteries near Leh, and along the Indus. It is strongly recommended that you hire an experienced guide and ponies, that you have the necessary permits and are well equipped and provisioned. Ladakh has a delicate ecosystem, with little

Temple door decorated with tassels at Tikse monastery.

RESTAURANTS

PRICE CATEGORIES

Average price for dinner, up to three
courses for one person, excluding
alcoholic drinks:
£ = up to Rs200
££ = Rs200–500
£££ = Rs500–1,000
££££ = over Rs1,000

The cuisine of India's Himalayan
regions is often similar to those of
the nearby plains. Kashmiri Muslim
food is a delicate mix of Mughlai and
Persian-influenced dishes with lightly
spiced meat curries that use cream,
nuts and dried fruits. The often-found
mix of dal and rice, with perhaps
a vegetable dish, reflects the food
brought by Nepalis, while the large
Tibetan population has introduced
items such as momos, steamed
meat or vegetable dumplings, and
thukpa, noodle soup.

Thukpa; noodle soup.

Uttarakhand

Dehra Dun
Dosa King
76 Rajpur Road. £
If you like *dosas* you'll love this place,
with a bewildering variety on offer, but
the *masala* classic is hard to beat.

Haridwar
Big Ben
Ganga Azure Hotel, opposite the railway
station. £–££
Diner-style decor, with good service
and a wide-ranging menu, this place
definitely stands out and is well
worth a visit if you're pining for some
Western-style, spice-free fare. Close
to the ghats and railway station,
it's also a good place to kill time
crowd watching between transport
connections.
Chotiwala
Lalta Rao Bridge, Upper Road. £
Well known for its pure vegetarian
food and *thalis*, this is a no-frills option
where you may not even get to sit
down, but the food and outstanding
value make it all worthwhile.

Joshimath
Almora
Shikar Hotel, High Street. £
Long-established, no-frills restaurant
serving the usual staples – but does
everything well and is a better choice
than the similar-looking places around it.

Mussoorie
Emily's
Rokeby Manor, Landour Cantonement. £££
With its yellow-painted farmhouse
dresser, wood floors and deck
overlooking the valley, this cute little
dining hall in a heritage boutique
hotel preserves a quaint British feel.
A perfect place for afternoon tea or
main meal, whether shepherd's pie or
chicken curry.
Prakash
Landour, above Woodstock School. £££
Best sandwiches in town but at a
steep price; popular with students
from the nearby international school.
The Tavern
The Mall, Kulri. ££
Popular restaurant and bar,
specialising in non-veg Mughlai
and tandoori cuisine. Live music at
weekends adds to the atmosphere.

Nainital
Ashok
The Mall. £–££
Deservedly popular snack joint serving
particularly good juices and shakes at
down-to-earth prices.
Embassy
The Mall. ££
Quirkily different, the log cabin-
inspired interior is a cosy place to
enjoy a good range of Indian staples
in this long-established favourite. The
prices are on the high side, but worth it
if you're in the mood for a splurge.
Kumaon Restaurant
Grassmere Estate, Mallital. ££
Excellent, long-established and
comfortable restaurant serving tasty
Pahari food, as well as Chinese and
Continental dishes in upmarket
surroundings.

Himachal Pradesh

Dalhousie
Dalhousie Heights
Lovers' Lane.
www.dalhousieheights.com. ££
Whether you're dropping by for a plate
of hot pakora and chai, or a blow-out
Punjabi feast of butter chicken, sabji
and nan, this hotel restaurant, on a
steep hillside close to the bus stand,
is a commendable option. The food is
terrific, the black-tie service efficient
and prices reasonable.
Friend's Dhaba
Subhash Chowk. £
Perhaps the best of Dalhousie's
dhabas, this serves many of the
Punjabi staples – the *paneer bhurji* in
particular comes highly recommended.

Dharamsala
Chocolate Log
Jogibara Road, McLeod Ganj. £
Cakes, brownies, pies, quiches and
other Western treats – all baked to
a high standard, and they do great
coffee too, which you can enjoy on a
pleasant roof-terrace café, a little away
from the main bazaar but still with
some spectacular mountain views on
a clear day.
Jimmy's Italian Kitchen
Jogibara Road, McLeod Ganj. ££
Italian dishes and great desserts in a
lively dining hall with lots of Hollywood
film posters and terrific views. Long
established and much loved, this is

a great place temporarily to escape the bustle of India and feast on some Western-style treats.

Malabar
Near Chorten, Jogibara Road. **££**
Small, cosy interior makes this a comfortable place to spend an evening, enjoying the above-average north Indian and Chinese cuisine and relaxing music.

Shambala
Jogibara Road, McLeod Ganj. **£**
Good-value Tibetan and Chinese food, great breakfasts and delicious cakes plus friendly service make this one a winner.

Snow Lion Restaurant
Snow Lion Guesthouse, Jogibara Road. **££**
Great place to sample Tibetan dishes – the spinach *momos* and *thukpa* are particularly good, plus it's well situated for crowd watching opposite the Namgyalma temple prayer wheels.

Manali

Chopsticks
The Mall. **££**
Excellent Chinese and Tibetan food, including great *momos*, as well as being good for breakfast. This also serves as one of Manali's main meeting places, popular with locals and visitors alike.

Johnson's Café
The Mall. **£££**
This beautifully designed garden restaurant on the way to Old Manali (before Johnson's Lodge) serves top notch Continental food, including exceptional trout; be sure to consult the daily specials board. This is Manali's best kitchen by miles.

Kwality Sher-e-Punjab
The Mall. **££**
Dependable Punjabi cuisine in clean and efficient surroundings, slightly superior to nearby imitations of similar names.

Mayur
Mission Road, just off the Mall. **££**
Linen tablecloths, candles and classical Indian music combine to give this place an exceptional ambience, with the international cuisine just as satisfying.

La Plage
Club House Road, Old Manali. **£££**
Off-shoot of the famous beachside French restaurant in north Goa (see page 297). Though pricy by Manali standards, the food – from the mutton caillettes to the trout carpaccio and chicken in fresh mushrooms – is an exquisite blend of local ingredients and Gallic savoir faire, beautifully presented and served against a

fabulous backdrop. Look out for the complimentary (blue-painted) rickshaw from town.

Simla

Devico's
5 The Mall. **£–££**
Popular Indian, Chinese and Western fast food, milkshakes and bar, choice of three different restaurants – front one does South Indian dishes as well, but they are all dependable and have been popular for years.

Himani's
The Mall. **££**
Head upstairs for tasty Mughlai cuisine, attentive service and a relaxed atmosphere. One of the few places that will serve a beer with a meal – a real bolt hole.

Indian Coffee House
The Mall. **£**
Worth experiencing for the old-world charm alone. Just the place for a cup of tea and a slice of cake. An institution not to be missed.

Wake & Bake
34/2 The Mall **££**
This tiny café on Shimla's main drag is the perfect place for a quick bite, serving crepes, pizza, chapatti wraps, panneer rolls and wonderful plates of hummus and falafels. Grab a window seat to watch the world go by, or at sunset time a table on the rooftop,

Momos, Tibetan dumplings.

where superb views of the bazaar can be savoured over a hookah pipe.

Ladakh

Leh

Pumpernickel German Bakery
Main Street. **£–££**
A large range of delicious Western dishes, including breads, pasta, muesli, cakes and pastries, and wonderful apple pie. A travellers' favourite, this cosy café has become something of a Leh institution.

La Terrasse
Main Square. **££**
The best pizza in town, plus a good range of tasty pasta dishes and a dependable supply of beer. Always busy, but well run and deservedly popular; try to get here early to be sure of a table.

Wonderland
Changspa Lane. **££**
Great budget restaurant with a rooftop terrace and chill-out area – the perfect place to gaze at the snow peaks over a storming cup of freshly ground coffee. They service a Western traveller-oriented menu of Tibetan, Chinese and Continental dishes, including delicious vegetarian lasagne, wood-baked pizzas and a divine lemon cake – one of many treats prepared fresh each day in the bakery downstairs.

THE DESERT STATES

Easily accessed from either Delhi or Mumbai, the largely arid northwestern states of Rajasthan and Gujarat are India at its colourful best.

Amber Fort.

Rajasthan and Gujarat, with their predominantly desert climates, are unlike anywhere else in India. The tough geography has bred a culture of resilience, the monochrome landscape a famously fluorescent dress sense.

In Rajasthan in particular this has been twinned with a tradition of strong Maharaja rule, and while the Maharajas' power has waned over the last century, the legacy of their remarkable reign can be seen in the incredible forts and palaces that dominate the state. Many of these have now been turned into unique heritage hotels offering a fascinating taste of how royal life was lived. A-list destinations include the pink city of Jaipur, and the gorgeous lake and palaces of Udaipur, Jodhpur, Pushkar, the Shekhavati region and Mount Abu are all fascinating, and – as if that wasn't enough – Ranthambore is probably the best place in India to see tigers in the wild. Camel treks from the romantic citadel town of Jaisalmer offer another un-missable experience: the chance to step off the road and into the flat, arid scrubland of the Thar Desert, where a unique way of life survives despite the perennial shortage of water.

Water carriers in the Thar Desert.

The desert conditions of both states have led to traditions of music and dance, and arts and crafts, that are carried on to this day and are an added attraction of the region, both in terms of performances to be enjoyed and shopping to savour. Gujarat, although much less visited than its northern neighbour, is as a result much less touristy, and offers an altogether more authentic experience. While the cities are of no special appeal, it is the wide open spaces and vibrantly dressed residents of the Rann of Kutch that are the real draw, with traditions and wildlife all of their own. This is also the only place in India, and one of the few remaining places in the world, where Asiatic lions can be seen in the wild.

RAJASTHAN

A desert state it might be, but India's 'Land of Kings' is bursting with colour and exuberance. Ornamental palaces, impregnable forts and painted towns all vie for attention.

F rom the salmon-pink facades of Jaipur to the indigo blues of Jodhpur, the ochre ramparts rising from Jaisalmer's sandflats to the red *havelis* of Bikaner, each city in Rajasthan has its own hallmark hue. Out in the countryside, the drabness of the landscape only serves to highlight the vibrancy of Rajasthani costumes: brightly dyed turbans, voluminous pleated skirts spangled with mirrorwork and intricately embroidered veils set against a backdrop of scrub and spindly *khejri* trees.

Always central to the region's identity, Rajasthan's flamboyance reaches its most arresting heights in the palaces and forts erected by the local Rajput maharajas. Bountiful trade and expedient military alliances with the Mughals paid for a building boom of lavish proportions in the medieval era, which lasted well into British rule. As a consequence, nowhere else in India can boast such exotic skylines. Royal abodes, combining the graceful lines of Islamic architecture with the desert kings' love of ornamentation, enclose beautifully preserved pleasure halls whose surfaces sparkle with mosaics of semi-precious stones and glass. From the courtyard gardens, exquisite cusped arched windows overlook cubic expanses of flat rooftops far below to the arid landscapes beyond.

Rajasthani woman.

Desert tourism

Drought has always haunted this dry northwestern corner of India, and continues to undermine the lives of Rajasthan's 60 million inhabitants, 70 percent of whom depend on small-scale agriculture for survival. Per capita income and levels of female literacy lag well behind the national averages, and access to health care, education and clean water remain the preserve of the region's affluent minority.

Yet in spite of such challenges, Rajasthan's distinctive culture

Main Attractions

Jaipur
Shekhavati
Pushkar
Ranthambore National Park
Udaipur
Ranakpur
Jodhpur
Jaisalmer

TIP

Arriving in Jaipur by train
or bus can be an
intimidating experience
for independent
travellers, due to the
gangs of pushy
autorickshaw-wallahs
that pounce on visitors
at the stations. The best
way to avoid the hassle
is to ask your hotel or
guesthouse owner to
send a driver to meet
you when you book your
room.

continues to flourish: this is where the romantic vision of India comes to life like nowhere else. Tourism has boosted traditional arts and crafts, and everywhere you travel in the state you will come across wonderful hand-woven textiles, wooden puppets and silver jewellery, as well as captivating performances of local dance and music. The tourist influx of the past few decades has also proved a boon for the landowning Rajputs, many of whose properties have been converted into wonderful heritage hotels, where you can experience life inside a maharaja's palace at close quarters, taking elephant rides to tumbledown forts and exploring the desert on camel back.

Geographically speaking, Rajasthan is divided between a semi-arid zone in the southeast, where the densely populated plains are intersected by perennial rivers and broken sandstone escarpments, and the flat, parched Thar Desert to the west and north. Between the two, the Aravalli Hills ripple diagonally from northeast to southwest. Peaking at 1,722 metres (5,646ft) near the hill station of Mount Abu, the range is draped in forest and remote valleys, where communities of subsistence farmers and hunter-gatherer Bhils and other minority Adivasi people still scrape a living from the land.

The first dwellers

It is now thought that the ancient cities of the Indus Valley had their precursors in northern Rajasthan. It seems that the area was inhabited by the Bhils and Minas people, who dispersed following the arrival of horse-riding nomads from the northwest some time around 1400 BC. These newcomers were here to stay, just like the Afghans, Turks, Persians and Mughals who followed, first in war then in peace, giving the Rajputs a martial ancestry.

From the reign of Harsha (7th century AD) to the time when the Delhi Sultanate was founded by the Muslims (AD 1206), Rajasthan fragmented into competing kingdoms. In the 16th century the Mughals made northern India their home. Winning over Rajasthan was the achievement of

RAJASTHAN TRANSPORT

Jaipur, Jodhpur and Udaipur are connected with regular flights to Delhi and Mumbai, and a few cities in Gujarat and South India. A new civil airport is also under construction near Jaisalmer which will provide a fast link to this remote desert area near the Pakistani border, rendering the overnight train from Jodhpur all but defunct when it is completed sometime in 2014–2015. New Delhi is the nearest international airport.

With the main Delhi–Mumbai line slicing through the centre of the state, rail connections with India's metropolitan cities are fast and frequent. Train travel is generally safer and more comfortable than bus travel, although high demand for seats and sleeper berths means you have to book well in advance and for shorter trips between towns, buses are more convenient. Private firms operate comfortable "video coaches" on inter-city routes (book through travel agents), while the state transport company, RSTC, runs to all but the smallest villages.

Jaipur: Trains run to Agra (14 daily; 4–6hrs 30min); Ajmer (19 daily; 2–3hrs); Bikaner (5 daily; 8–10hrs); Delhi (17 daily; 4hrs 30min–6hr 30min); Mumbai (4 daily; 17–22hrs); Udaipur(2 daily; 12hrs). Buses go to Agra (hourly; 5hrs); Ajmer (hourly; 2hrs 30min); Bikaner (11 daily; 7hrs); Delhi (every 15min; 6hrs); Jodhpur (every 30min; 8hrs); Udaipur (hourly; 10hrs).

Jodhpur: Trains run to Bikaner (7 daily; 5–7hrs); Delhi (4 daily; 10hrs 30min–12hrs); Jaisalmer (2 daily; 6hrs). There are buses to Agra (1 daily; 10hrs); Ajmer (hourly; 5hrs); Bharatpur/Keoladeo (3 daily; 10hrs); Bikaner (hourly; 6hrs); Delhi (3 daily; 12hrs); Jaipur (every 30min; 8hrs); Jaislamer (hourly; 5hrs 30min); Mount Abu (1 daily; 9hrs 30min); Udaipur (2 daily; 12hrs).

Udaipur: There are trains to Ajmer (4 daily; 5hrs); Chittaurgarh (6 daily; 2hrs); Delhi(2 daily; 12hrs); Jaipur (2 daily; 12hrs); Jodhpur (3 daily; 7–8hrs), Ahmedabad (2 daily; 10hrs 40min–13hrs) and Mumbai (1 daily; 16hrs). Buses go to Agra (1 daily; 14hrs); Ajmer (hourly; 7hrs); Bundi (10 daily; 7hrs); Chittaurgarh (hourly; 3hrs 30min); Kota (10 daily; 6hr); Mount Abu (10 daily; 7hrs); Ranakpur (6 daily; 3hrs).

Akbar, who mixed military might with the soft touch of religious tolerance. His trump card was matrimonial alliances with the Hindu Rajputs, which turned them from dangerous enemies into faithful allies.

Many princesses from Jaipur and Jodhpur married into the Mughal royal line, but when the Mughals weakened, the Rajputs were quick to reassert their sovereignty. After the British captured Bengal in 1757, Rajasthan resisted, although by the beginning of the 19th century the British were in control. Rajputana was Rajasthan's old name under the British, 'land of the Rajputs', and the Maharaja of Mewar (Udaipur) was the acknowledged head of their 36 states. When India became independent, 23 princely states were consolidated to form the State of Rajasthan, 'home of rajas'.

The pink city

Jaipur ❶ (the city of *jai*, or victory), the capital of Rajasthan, was not always pink. The original city was light grey, edged with white borders and motifs. In honour of the visit in 1883 of Prince Albert, it was ordered to be painted the traditional colour of welcome, and it is this which has been retained in the picturesque Old City.

The city was laid out in 1728 in a simple grid pattern by a young Bengali, Vidyadhar Bhattacharya, architect to Maharaja Sawai Jai Singh II (of the royal lineage that had ruled from Amber, 11km/7 miles to the north, since the early 10th century). Seven blocks of buildings are divided by wide, tree-lined avenues; at the heart of the city is the palace, which covers a further two blocks. These rectangular divisions represent the nine divisions of the universe. The whole is surrounded by a crenellated wall with seven imposing gates (*pols*), still in use today. Each of the blocks houses *mohallas*, districts given over to the practice of various crafts or trades, from bangle-making to fabric dyeing

to *minakari* (enamel work), for which Jaipur is famous.

Lying within easy reach of Delhi and Agra, the Rajasthani capital forms a prominent port of call on northern India's popular 'Golden Triangle' of sights, attracting streams of visitors through the winter. Other than its flamboyant Rajput architecture, Jaipur holds one of the country's biggest bazaars, renowned above all for its handicrafts – particularly textiles

Participating in Jaipur's Elephant Festival.

HERITAGE HOTELS

There's no better way to gain a sense of what life must have been like for residents of Rajasthan's historic properties than to spend a night or two in one. Small palaces and forts across the state have been converted by their owners to accommodate visitors. Some offer simple budget rooms in rambling, run-down wings, occupied by less affluent branches of old aristocratic families. Others have been restored to exceed their original splendour, augmented with swimming pools, ayurvedic health spas and other five-star trimmings. You may get to see traditional musicians, sleep in historic, mirror-encrusted bedrooms and lounge around on the terraces gazing across the desert. The decor is often spectacular, featuring antique furniture and traditionally decorated walls.

At the top of the range are the über-luxurious heritage hotels run by the maharajas of Udaipur, Jaipur and Jodhpur – the gargantuan Umaid Bhavan Palace on the southern outskirts of Jodhpur being the most astonishingly grand example. However, you can also stay in comparably sumptuous accommodation on remote country estates. Many offer nights in specially erected luxury camps, where guests can ride through the desert on camel or horse back, dine under the stars and sleep in traditional Rajasthani hunting tents.

and gemstones. Be aware, however, that a number of unscrupulous gem dealers are at work here – try to deal only with reputable companies that have been recommended to you by a trusted source.

Jaipur's palaces

The **City Palace** (palace and museum, daily 9.30am–5pm; charge), occupying the most auspicious central portion of Jaipur's grid plan, formed the political hub of the maharaja's ambitious design, and remains the residence of Jaipur's royal family. Although its innermost enclosures date from the 18th century, other wings were added

in subsequent eras, fusing Mughal and Rajput architectural motifs.

A series of ornamental gateways, large enough to admit processions of elephants, lead to the interlocking courtyards at the heart of the palace, many of whose pavilions, or *mahals*, are given over to the **Sawai Man Singh II Museum**. Armour, weapons, priceless carpets, state regalia, jewellery, miniature paintings, manuscripts and precious ritual paraphernalia make up the bulk of the collection, all lavishly decorated by craftsmen whom the Jaipur maharajas recruited from the courts of the Mughals as the empire lapsed into decline. Turbaned retainers with luxurious handlebar moustaches stand guard over the exhibits, the most famous of which is a pair of huge silver urns, 1.5 metres (5ft) tall and featured in *Guinness World Records* as the world's largest hand-made silver object. They were commissioned by Maharaja Man Singh II to transport Ganges water to London during a state visit in 1907, and allegedly held 8,181 litres (1,800 gallons).

Four exquisitely decorated doors lead to the innermost enclosure of the palace open to the public, the **Pitam Niwas Chowk** (Peacock Courtyard), from where you can admire the delicate exterior of the seven-storey **Chandra Mahal**, home to the present-day maharaja (Bhavani Singh) and his family.

The most photographed sight in Jaipur, however, is the **Hawa Mahal** (Palace of Winds; daily 9am–4.30pm; charge), dating from 1799, which stands at the eastern perimeter of the palace, overlooking the bazaar. A five-floored confection of domed balconies, delicate cupolas and pierced stone *jali* screens, all painted Jaipur's trademark salmon pink, it is not in fact, a palace, but an extraordinary facade of 953 airy niches and windows, used by the royal women in *purdah* (secluded from the public) to watch the outside world of the streets below.

Immediately behind the Hawa Mahal, the **Jantar Mantar** (daily 9am–4.30pm; charge) stands in surreal counterpoint to the traditional Rajput splendour surrounding it. Made up of 16 colossal geometric structures which Maharaja Jai Singh – a keen astronomer – used to calculate celestial latitudes and planetary movements, it is one of five such complexes built at Hindu cities across India (the others are at Delhi, Mathura, Ujjain and Varanasi). Pride of place goes to the giant Bihat Samrat Yantra, an enormous sundial whose shadow moves 4 metres (13ft) each hour, enabling calculations of time down to intervals of five seconds. In times past, drummers stationed on the high gnomon arm (the part of the sundial that casts the shadow) used to sound the hours.

Jaipur Palace.

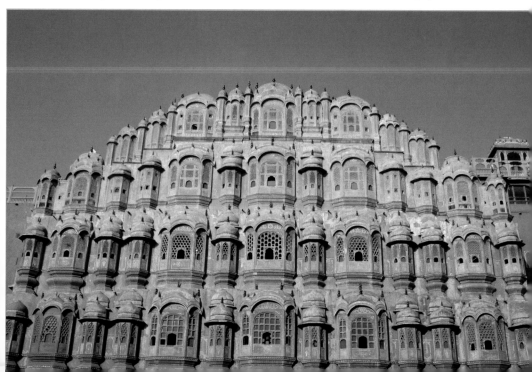

FACT

Amber's painted
elephants often suffer
chronic dehydration and
sunstroke, as well as
foot problems and
malnutrition, after hours
of trudging to and from
the palace. To alleviate
their plight, the NGO
Elephant Family provides
water troughs,
sunshades, a mobile
veterinary clinic and
training for their
mahoots. Find out more
at www.elephantfamily.org.

Bikaner Fort.

Around Jaipur

Immediately south of the old city, in the centre of the Ram Niwas gardens, stands the Albert Hall containing the **Central Museum** (Sat–Thur 10am–4.30pm; charge). The ornate Indo-Saracenic building houses a rather disorderly collection of costumes, ivory, brasswork and jewellery, as well as some unintentionally amusing models of Rajasthani festivals, occupations and trades.

The stark desert hills encircling Jaipur are crowned by some impressive Rajput fortresses, whose ramparts reveal magnificent views over the city. **Nahargarh Fort** (daily 10am–5pm; charge) is the best one to head for at sunset to enjoy a drink on the café terrace, with perfect views of the pink city fading to grey. Built in 1734 by Maharaja Jai Singh II to house his various concubines, it can be reached by road, or on foot (in just under an hour) via a footpath starting at the northwest corner of the palace.

Other popular escapes from the city include the **Royal Cenotaphs** (daily 9am–4.30pm; free) at **Gaitor**, just north of the palace complex, where elaborately carved white marble *chhatris* (cenotaphs) stand as memorials to Jaipur's former rulers, and the **Monkey Temple** at **Galta**. Hidden in a fold on the ridge overlooking the city's eastern limits, this Rama shrine plays host to troupes of splashing, squabbling macaques.

Amber and Samode

Amber (daily 9am–4.30pm; charge; 11km (7 miles) from Jaipur, was once the capital of the Minas – believed to be the original inhabitants of this area. Painted elephants take visitors up the hill to admire the massive gateways, pillared pavilions and palaces that recall the glory and wealth of Amber's association with the Mughals: Raja Man Singh was the commander-in-chief of Akbar's army, while Mirza Raja Jai Singh was a powerful ally of Jahangir. Of special interest are the **Diwan i Am**, Jai Singh's audience hall, and the **Shish Mahal**, the Hall of Mirrors, where the walls are inlaid with exquisite mirrored motifs that dance to the flame of even a single candle.

A 20-minute uphill walk from Amber palace is **Jaigarh Fort** (daily 9am–4.30pm; charge), opened to the public in the late 1980s after being sealed for decades following a rumour that an enormous quantity of gold was buried in vaults under deep reservoirs. This forced isolation ensured the complex's many palaces and temples remained better preserved than those further down the hill. Jaigarh was renowned for its arsenal, and one of the highlights of any visit to the fort, apart from the views back over Amber, is the **Jaya Vana**, the largest antique cannon in India, said to have been able to fire over a distance of 35km (22 miles), a feat requiring some 100kg (220lbs) of gunpowder.

Before leaving Amber, it's worth paying a visit to the splendid new **Anokhi Museum of Hand Printing**

(www.anokhimuseum.com; Tue–Sat 10.30am–5pm, Sun 11am–4.30pm; charge), housed in a grand old *haveli* at Kheri Gate, 10 minutes on foot from the fort. The collection charts the evolution of this quintessentially Rajasthani textile form, which uses carved woodblocks to pattern fabrics, with antique pieces displayed alongside examples of more recent, export-oriented garments.

Proceeds from the Anokhi Museum are used to support block-printers working in the Jaipur area, the largest community of whom live in the village of **Sanganer**, 16km (10 miles) south of the city. This is the best place to see traditional dyers and printers in action, squeezed into rows of small shops lining the bazaar. Along the riverbanks, lengths of vibrant cotton are hung out to dry – a great photo opportunity. Since the 16th century, Sanganer has also been a major centre for paper-making: cotton scraps are used as raw material for manufacturing sheets of paper distinctively textured with flower petals, and bound into books.

Continuing north from Amber on the main Jaipur–Delhi road brings you to the turning for **Samode**, 42km (26 miles) from the capital, and the site of a spectacular palace hotel set among the Aravalli Hills. The building and its adjacent village served as the setting for the 1980s hit movie *The Far Pavilions*, based on the Raj-era romantic novel by M.M. Kaye. Its beautifully preserved Durbar Hall and Shish Mahal (Hall of Mirrors) are among the most delicate in Rajasthan. Non-residents are welcome to visit, but are required to pay a small charge.

Alwar and Sariska

National Highway No. 8 runs north from Jaipur to Delhi. About 60km (35 miles) from Jaipur a turning leads northeast to Alwar, picturesque and dotted with historical sites. En route, at **Bairath**, are ancient Buddhist rock edicts of Emperor Ashoka, a 3rd-century BC Buddhist *chaitya* (temple) and a painted garden pavilion built around AD 1600.

Founded in 1771, **Alwar ❷** is one of the newest of the princely states

Common langurs (Hanuman monkeys) at Amber.

TIP

The Sariska Tiger
Reserve is most easily
approached from Alwar.
Any of the buses heading
to Jaipur pass the park
gates. For safaris, Jeeps
offer the best way of
spotting wildlife; booking
should be made through
the Forest Reception
Office opposite the
Sariska Palace, near the
main entrance.

of Rajasthan. Starting out as distant cousins of Jaipur, the Alwar Rajputs manoeuvred their way through the chaos of the 18th century, skilfully changing sides as necessary, until the British finally acknowledged and rewarded them for their help against the Marathas (even so, the affairs of Alwar remained troubled, with only a few scattered years of peace). Some handsome palaces survive, chief among them Raja Bakhtawar Singh's resplendent **City Palace** (1793), built from half the state exchequer – a high proportion even by feudal standards. An exuberant mix of Mughal symmetry and Rajput extravagance, the building holds a small **museum** (Sat–Thur 10am–-4.30pm; charge), whose collection of miniature paintings, manuscripts, arms and furniture evoke the opulence of the Alwari court, which saw its heyday in the early 20th century, when the state was legendary for the pomp of its processions and tiger hunts.

Next to the palace stands a reservoir featuring delicate temples, kiosks and symmetrical flights of stairs.

Considered a masterpiece of Indo-Islamic architecture, the highlight is the double-storeyed *chhatri* (cenotaph) commemorating the self-immolation *(sati)* of a favourite royal concubine, Moosi Maharani.

A second royal palace, 37km (23 miles) south of Alwar, once served as a hunting lodge, but is now a hotel on the outskirts of the **Sariska Tiger Reserve**. The sanctuary made international headlines in 2005 when it admitted that its tiger population (estimated at 28 in 2003) had been completely wiped out by poachers working in cahoots with park rangers. However, a total of five tigers were reintroduced to the park in 2005–2009, with initial signs looking positive for their future survival. With or without the big cats, the reserve is still worth visiting for its abundant bird life and delightful scenery, dominated by the rippling, forested hills of the Aravalli range.

Deeg Palace

Another little-visited town on the fringes of Rajasthan that holds some

The cenotaph at Alwar's City Palace.

unexpectedly fine architecture is **Deeg**, on the road between Alwar and Bharatpur, 34km (21 miles) southeast. The town became the second capital of a dynasty of Jat warrior-farmers who wrested control of the region from the Mughals through the 18th century. Hemmed in by a dry moat and 28-metre (92ft) walls, the fort they erected here saw some particularly fierce battles, but the **palace** – comprising a collection of finely proportioned pavilions overlooking an Indo-Islamic-style *charbagh* garden (daily 8am–4pm; charge) – is what most visitors come to see. Built in 1767, the **Gopal Bhawan** is the largest of the buildings, and preserves much original furniture, including a swing said to have once belonged to the empress Nur Jahan, and which was brought to Deeg as booty after Maharaha Suraj Mal's daring raid on Mughal Delhi in 1762. It stands in front of the structure regarded as the finest of its kind anywhere in Rajasthan, the **Keshar Bhawan**, or 'Monsoon Palace', an ornately carved pavilion to which the royals used to repair in hot weather.

Shekhavati: decorated towns

The second northern road (National Highway No. 11) from Jaipur leads to the painted towns of **Shekhavati ❸** and on to Bikaner. Once subordinate to the maharajas of Amber, the region asserted its independence in 1471 under Rao Shekhav – after whom it is named.

Being located on the caravan route connecting the Gujarat ports and Central India with Delhi, trade in opium, silk, cotton and spices flourished, attracting wealthy Marwari traders in the 18th and 19th centuries. Elaborate cenotaphs and reservoirs, temples and caravanserais stand as a testimony to the wealth produced by this commerce, but it was the tall houses (*havelis*) which the merchant families built to combat the heat and glare that best expressed the confidence and prosperity of the era. Dynasties competed with each other to erect the grandest, most elaborately decorated homes.

FACT

In Deeg's Keshar Bhawan, a network of pipes fed 500 sprinklers designed to recreate the cooling atmosphere of the rainy season, while cannon balls rolled and rumbled around outside in specially constructed channels, replicating the sound of thunder – a major extravagance considering the reservoir that fed the fountains took a week to fill and only a couple of hours to empty.

Sambar deer.

FACT

The Rani Sati Temple in the town of Jhunjhunu, in northern Shekhavati, is the centre of an immensely popular cult revolving around a merchant's wife who committed ritual self-immolation on her husband's funeral pyre in 1595. Although banned since the time of the British, the custom of sati is still occasionally practised. An 18-year-old Rajput girl, Roop Kanwar, burnt herself to death near Jaipur in 1987, sparking national outrage.

A typical painted wall in the Shekhavati region.

The walled courtyards where the women spent most of their lives, screened from the outside word in the seclusion of *purdah*, were enlivened with extravagant murals depicting mythological scenes of gods and goddesses in vibrant colours. The men, meanwhile, conducted their business on the white cotton mattresses of their sitting rooms, which were also richly embellished with scenes from the wider world, many showing modern contraptions – such as trains, hot air balloons and motor cars – which had not yet arrived in this corner of Rajasthan. Erotic motifs were also camouflaged in discreet niches.

Time has certainly taken its toll on this rich storehouse of traditional art, but enough survives to make a journey through the region worthwhile. Some of Shekhavati's most richly painted *havelis* line the sandy backstreets of **Nawalgarh**, 120km (74 miles) north of Jaipur, where a better-than-average crop of hotels provide congenial accommodation for trips deeper into the area. On the east side of town,

the **Dr Ramnath A Podder Haveli Museum** (daily 8.30am–5.30pm; charge) ranks among the few mansions to have been restored to their former glory. Nearby, the Moraka Haveli and Bhagton ki Choti Haveli hold the usual quirky mix of Hindu mythological scenes and images of British Victoriana.

Dundlod, 7km (4 miles) north, is the site of an old Rajput fort, converted into a small heritage hotel. But the most imposing of the region's former forts towers over the tightly packed lanes of **Mandawa**. Several large hotels scattered around the edges of town serve through traffic on the tour-group trail, but these impinge little on the old-world feel of the bazaar and its disintegrating, charismatic *havelis*. **Fatehpur**, in the far west of the Shekhavati region on the road to Bikaner, sees far fewer visitors, in spite of the presence of the **Nadine Le Prince Haveli** (daily 10am–7pm; charge), restored by the French artists whose name it bears. Some of the overpainting carried out has been criticised for being heavy-handed, but it conjures better than anywhere else the splendour in which the region's merchants must once have lived.

Bikaner: city of the desert

Bikaner ❹ 190km (118 miles) west of Fatehpur, was founded in 1488 – 29 years after Jodhpur. A younger but more intelligent son of Jodhpur's founder Rao Jodha, Rao Bika, was given an army and asked to seek his own fortune to avoid a war of succession. Thus Bikaner was founded in the heart of the wilderness called Jangaldesh. Perhaps the very bareness of the landscape spurred the human hand to create beauty.

Erected towards the end of the 16th century, unconquered **Junagarh Fort** (daily 10am–4.30pm; charge) harbours palaces, temples and pavilions of unrivalled refinement. None, however, are more sumptuous than the **Anup Mahal**, which is encrusted with red and gold filigree (*usta*). Lavish frescoes, gilded stucco mouldings, floral patterns and enormous carpets (woven by former inmates of Bikaner jail) adorn the suitably grand **Durbar Hall**, where examples of Bikaner's renowned school of miniature painting are displayed.

By comparison, the home of the present-day royal, **Lalgarh Palace**, 3km (2 miles) to the north, is more restrained. Designed by Sir Swinton Jacob (architect of Jaipur's Albert Hall), it's less alluring than its predecessor, with some wings serving as a luxury heritage hotel. Dusty old photographs and royal memorabilia are showcased in the **Shri Sadul Museum** (Thur–Tue 10am–5pm; charge).

Encircled by 6km (4 miles) of dark red sandstone ramparts, Bikaner's **Old City** is a warren of twisting, sandy streets, many of them lined by crumbling Jain temples and some of Rajasthan's most eccentric *havelis*. The latter date from the textile boom of the early 20th century and present an unlikely mix of styles, fusing Art Nouveau with Victorian Municipal brickwork. Call at the tourist office, in the RTDC Dholamaru Hotel on Pooran Singh Circle, for their leaflet outlining a 'heritage route' that

TIP

Bikaner may be less well known as a camel-trekking destination than Jaisalmer, but several companies operate out of the town, taking visitors into infrequently visited desert areas where wildlife is abundant and traditional villages numerous. One commendable outfit is run by Vijay Singh Rathore (www.camelman. com).

Ajmer.

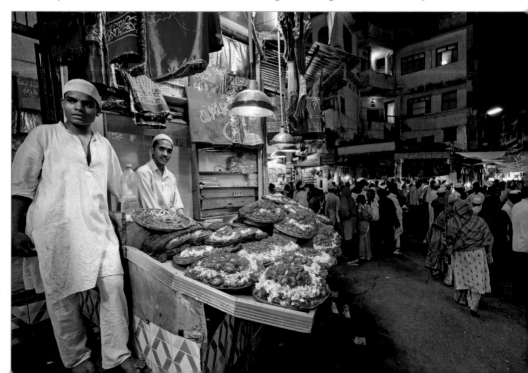

TIP

During the annual Urs Mela festival, held in October to November, auspicious kheer pudding is cooked in the huge degs (metal vats) that stand inside the Dargah's main gates. Over-zealous devotees literally dive into the pans when it's ready, getting plastered from head to toe in the sweet rice porridge – an unmissable photo opportunity.

Pushkar Lake.

strings together the old city's architectural highlights.

Around Bikaner

Outside Bikaner, the countryside is arid desert, dotted with mud villages still heavily dependent on camels for transport and agricultural work. Around 10km (6 miles) south of town, the **National Camel Research Centre** (daily 2.30–6pm; charge) makes an interesting visit, particularly at sunset when the herds return from the dunes. In addition to a breeding programme, investigations are being carried out here into the health-giving properties of camel milk, which appears to reduce the incidence of diseases such as tuberculosis and diabetes.

The village of **Deshnok**, 30km (19 miles) south of Bikaner, is an important Hindu pilgrimage site for local desert-dwelling people. Its presiding deity, Karni Mata, was a real historical figure, a miracle-working bard, or *charani*, who rose to become an influential cult leader in the 14th century, and who, after her death, was elevated to the position of the royal family's patron goddess. The shrine is famous above all for the fact that thousands of holy rats, or *kaba*, scamper across its marble floors after food that is brought for them by devout visitors. The rodents are believed to be reincarnations of Karni Mata's relatives; it is considered highly auspicious if one runs across your foot or, better still, nibbles your toe during a visit.

Ajmer and Pushkar

About 135km (80 miles) southwest of Jaipur lies **Ajmer** ❺, the most sacred of all Sufi pilgrimage places in India. Its Muslim history began in 1193, when Sultan Muhammad of Ghori captured the town. The Persian saint, Khwaja Mu'inuddin Chisti, who had come with Ghori, settled and preached here. The **Dargah Sharif**, where the saint is buried, lies at the foot of Taragarh Hill. When Akbar took Ajmer in 1556 he made it his military headquarters and visited the tomb on foot to pray for a son. The request was granted and Ajmer's reputation soared. Large cauldrons (*degs*) were presented by Akbar to

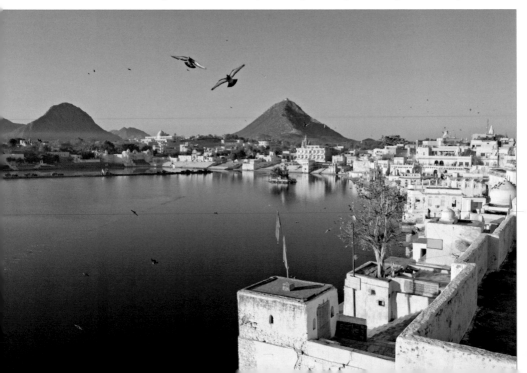

be filled with food for distribution among the pilgrims at the shrine; this continues today, but the original *degs* were replaced in the 19th century. Important monuments within the *dargah* include the delicate white marble mosque of Shah Jahan (*c.* 1650).

The **Arhai din ka Jhonpra** mosque is just west of the *dargah*. This Sanskrit college was converted to a mosque in 1210 by Qutb-ud-Din-Aibak. It is one of the finest monuments of medieval India, with beautiful decorations and ornate calligraphic inscriptions.

Just off Station Road is Akbar's red sandstone palace, the **Daulat Khana**, where in 1610 the emperor Jahangir met the first envoy sent to India from the court of a British monarch. Sir Thomas Roe had been despatched to extract trading rights from the Great Mughal – he was only partially successful in this, but his efforts paved the way for what would, over the coming decades, snowball into the East India Company. Nearby is the **Nasiyan Jain Temple**, a depiction in gold of the Jain interpretation of the universe and well worth a visit.

Divided from Ajmer by the corrugated slopes of Nag Pahar (Snake Mountain), **Pushkar** ❻, 14km (9 miles) northwest, is considered high up in the hierarchy of Hindu places of pilgrimage.

Pushkar has one of the few temples in India dedicated to Brahma, the Creator. Here every year, on the full moon of Kartika month (Oct–Nov), hundreds of thousands of pilgrims gather to bathe in a sacred lake, believed to have been created when Lord Brahma dropped a lotus flower to earth. This is the occasion for one of the largest cattle and camel markets in Rajasthan, Kartik Purnima, where the abundance of colour, jewellery, turbans and moustaches is unmatched. Aside from the livestock market, traditional funfairs and races draw huge crowds. However, the exotic swirl of blue- and whitewashed temples, onion-domed pavilions and ghats

enfolding the northern shores of the lake remain busy throughout the year, and have become a second home for the backpacker crowd in particular. Every morning and evening, drums and ringing bells accompany worshippers as they bathe in the sacred water, which Hindus maintain holds the power to cleanse the soul of all sin.

Flanking the town and lake are a pair of beautiful, low desert hills crowned by small temples. Dedicated to Lord Brahma's wives, Savitri and Gayatri, can both be reached via paved paths that make great walks, with tremendous views across the slopes of Nag Pahar to the south and the sand flats of the Thar spreading north and west.

Ranthambore

From Tonk, 95km (58 miles) south of Jaipur on the main road to Bundi and Kota, a road leads east to **Sawai Madhopur** where the royal Jaipur household used to come for tiger hunts accompanied by their VIP guests. Overlooking the wildlife sanctuary of Ranthambore, 13km (8 miles)

THE CAMEL FAIR

Over the fortnight leading up to the full moon of Kartika month (late Oct/early Nov), villagers from the desert regions of western India congregate around Pushkar Lake for the famous Kartik Purnima festival and camel-trading fair. Decked out in their finest traditional dress, they come to buy and sell livestock, strike marriage deals, meet with relatives and generally enjoy themselves after the annual harvest. The spectacle, set against a sea of 50,000 dusty camels and rolling dunes, ranks among the most compelling in India, though don't expect to be the only foreign visitor in attendance.

Next to the trading grounds, a funfair also takes place, complete with races, camel 'fancy fur' contests and other events. With all the camel-related entertainment, however, it's easy to forget that the festival is primarily a religious one, commemorating Brahma's marriage to Savitri and Gayatri. Hindus believe the waters of the lake can cleanse all sins and congregate in huge numbers around the sacred ghats, or steps, encircling the lake to bathe at dawn – an unforgettable sight.

Accommodation can be scarce over the festival period, the local tourism department and several upscale hotels erect temporary tent compounds on the sand flats around the town. The tents are fitted with fans, electric light, bathrooms and other mod cons. Book in advance through www.rajasthantourism.gov.in.

FACT

It's easy to see why Rudyard Kipling, who stayed in Bundi as a guest of the local Rao in 1892, thought the extraordinary palace 'such a place as men build for themselves in uneasy dreams... the work of goblins'.

from the town, is the fortress of Rao Hamir, which was conquered by Ala-ud-Din Khilji in the 14th century and then again by Akbar in 1569. Despite being in ruins, its palaces, temples and cenotaphs are well worth a visit.

Ranthambore 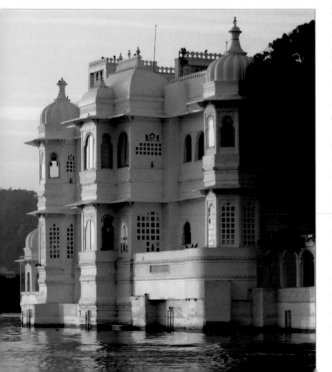 is famous for its tigers, which can often be sighted prowling among the medieval ruins or in the shallows of the lake. The lure of such exotic wildlife has ensured that Ranthambore has become India's most visited national park – in spite of the fact its fragile tiger population is in perilous decline, with only an estimated 40 animals surviving. Tickets for safaris, which happen either early morning or late evening, are strictly limited, although you should be able to get hold of one through your hotel. Visiting the park is either in a jeep or in a larger 'canter' (a kind of open-top bus). In addition to the big cats (there are also leopards), the park supports blackbuck, hyena and several species of antelope. Ranthambore is also something of a hotspot for birding, with around 300 species on record. One of the park's defining sights is

Udaipur.

that of its resplendent wild peacocks perched on the crenellations of the old fort.

Jat states

The Jaipur–Agra road leads east to **Bharatpur** and **Dholpur** – unusually, both Jat states in the predominantly Rajput stronghold of Rajasthan.

Bharatpur Fort houses a museum with exhibits of mixed antiquity, but what makes Bharatpur famous is its 29-sq-km (11-sq-mile) **Keoladeo Ghana National Park** ❽ (daily dawn–dusk; charge), with the largest concentration and variety of bird life in Asia. Prior to 1940, this was the favourite shooting ground of the British viceroys, with a record kill of 4,273 birds in a single day. Sunrise or sunset from October to February is the best time to see the birds.

A total of 375 species have been recorded here, of which around 150 are migrants from as far afield as Siberia and Europe. Among the numerous aquatic residents of the Keoladeo wetlands are giant Sarus cranes, which grow to the height of a human and sport striking scarlet hoods. Until 2002, the sanctuary also hosted a few nesting pairs of rare Siberian cranes, but sadly, none have been sighted since then. No one has been able to account for their disappearance, though it is known that the cranes are hunted during their epic high-altitude traverse of the Himalayas. Repeated droughts have also impacted on Keoladeo's bird life, drying up the wetlands entirely in 2007, when drastic measures to divert rainwater from surrounding fields into the lake were met with stiff resistance from farmers. A compromise has since been reached, meaning that the park now has at least some water during the winter months.

Southeast Rajasthan

Founded in 1342, the ancient kingdom of **Bundi** ❾ (from *bando nal*, 'narrow passage') in southeast Rajasthan lies well protected in the ranges of the rugged Aravalli Hills that drop into rocky ravines traversed by four narrow passes.

The secluded position of its capital screened it from the hybridisation that held sway elsewhere in the 19th century, even though the British virtually controlled its affairs from 1818. 'Bundi is deliciously behind the times,' wrote the maharaja of Baroda – a remark that, in many ways, still holds true today. No other town of comparable size in Rajasthan feels as untouched by modern trends.

Bundi's undisputed highlight is its **palace** (daily 7am–5pm; charge), whose faded serpentine, ochre and red sandstone walls are reflected to magical effect in the **Naval Sagar** lake below. Incredible ramps and stairs zigzag between the ramparts, overhanging balconies and forest of domes and cusped arches.

Unlike most of its counterparts elsewhere in the state, the palace shows little influence from Islamic architecture and is regarded as the purest example of Rajput style. Large areas of it are open to the public. Visits begin at the splendid Hathi Pol, flanked by statues of rearing elephants, and progress through a disorienting series of halls, *zenanas* (women's quarters), antechambers and enclosed courtyard gardens. Some of the finest murals surviving in all of India are to be found in the exquisite Badal Mahal, most of them depicting scenes from the life of Krishna in subtle turquoise, blues, greens and terracotta tones.

The **Chitra Shala** (daily sunrise–sunset; free), just above the main palace, holds more refined frescoes painted in the 17th and 18th centuries. Immediately behind it a path leads steeply up the hillside to the ruins of the medieval **Taragarh Fort**, and

Udaipur textiles.

A bridal procession in Udaipur.

massive television booster mast, from where you get an unrivalled view over the rooftops.

Crammed with traditional shops and buildings, Bundi town itself is fascinating to explore on foot. Local guides will show you the way to hidden step wells – such as the **Raniji-ki-Baori**, embellished with carved panels showing the 10 avatars of Vishnu – and walled *havelis* on the lakeside.

The territory hereabouts was first claimed by Udaipur and later by Jaipur. Part of it was given in 1579 as patrimony for a favoured younger son, and this tract, set in the open plains, grew to be **Kota** ❿ – larger than its parent state and bustling with the youth of a commercial city. In contrast to secluded Bundi, Kota had to be on constant alert because its strategic location on the plains along the Chambal River drew the envy of Udaipur, Jaipur, the Marathas and also the British – to whom it was the first state to accede, due to the foresight of Zalim Singh, the regent. Spasmodic interludes of peace led to spurts of architecture and a mélange of pillared halls, kiosks,

The Lake Palace at Jaipur.

commemorative gateways, carving and painting. Some of the finest frescoes and miniature paintings of India belong to the Bundi-Kota school. The **City Palace** at Kota abounds in ornamentation, and the first-rate **Maharao Madho Singh Museum** (Sat–Thur 10am–5pm; charge) shows treasures from the ruler's private collection. The most exquisite room is the **Raj Mahal**, hung with paintings from the Mughal to British periods.

Udaipur

The royal house of Mewar, now better-known as **Udaipur** ⓫, is one of India's most rewarding cities to visit. It has two reasons for pride. The first is that its rulers, the Sisodia Rajputs, can trace their recorded history back 16 generations to Bapa Rawal (AD 728), whereas Jaipur and Jodhpur lag behind by 200 and 483 years respectively. The second is pride in being Hindu and not losing honour to Muslim invaders. Mewar resisted such alliances for at least 50 years longer than the other Rajput states. This sense of history and pride

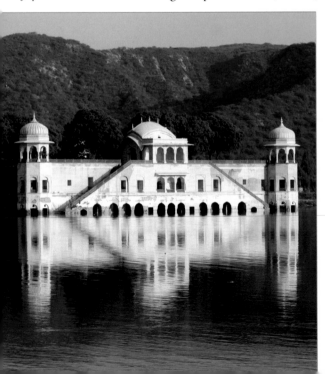

PEACOCKS

The national bird of India, Blue peacocks are particularly common in the state of Rajasthan. They have long held a cherished place in Indian culture, with the peacock feather a much-used motif in Indian temple art, and associated with many of the more popular gods, particularly Kartikeya, who rides on a peacock's back. Their sudden appearance in full fan mode can be both startling and alluring, and their haunting cry is believed to foretell rain. Although they tend not to fly long distances, the sight of a peacock in flight is compelling, the abundant tail feathers trailing behind making this one of the longest flying birds in the world. Such is the beauty of the omnivorous Blue peacock, it is even said to be able to charm snakes and steal their eggs.

persisted during the British period, earning them the highest gun salute in Rajasthan: 19 guns as against the 17 each of Jaipur, Jodhpur, Bundi, Bikaner, Kota and Karauli. Maharana Fateh Singh of Udaipur had the distinction of not attending the Delhi Durbar for King George V in 1911 (obligatory attendance being, essentially, a ritual of submission to a higher rank).

The Sisodias moved to Udaipur after their former seat, Chittor (Chittaurgarh), fell for the third time to the Mughals in 1567. More easily defensible, the new site soon acquired a profusion of magnificent palaces, lakes, temples and cenotaphs, grouped around the shimmering waters of Pichola Lake, which the family's chief annalist and historian, the East India Company Resident Colonel James Tod, famously applauded as 'the most diversified and... romantic spot on the continent of India'. In these drought-prone times, the waters of the lake come and go, but Udaipur's wondrous architecture retains its former splendour, floating with regal disregard above the guesthouses and hotels that have mushroomed on the slopes below it.

City palace of the Sisodias

First stop on an visitor's itinerary has to be the Sisodias' splendid **City Palace**, which surges vertically from the lakeside – an imposing wall of plain yellow plaster topped by a crowning layer of domes, golden finials, fluted pillars and whimsical arches, all facing east towards the rising sun (the Sisodias' royal symbol). Much of the complex is still occupied by the maharaja of Udaipur, but the most historic, and vibrantly decorated, portions have been allocated to the **City Palace Museum** (daily 9.30am–5.30pm; charge).

An array of ostentatious mirror-work, mosaics, murals, porcelain tiles, glass inlay and semi-precious stones encrust every surface of the palace's interior. Wandering between the various halls you can trace the shift in emphasis from the glorious cusp-arched, onion-domed extravagance of Mughal times to the Bohemian-crystal,

Rajasthani children on their way to school.

TIP

Guided walks into the forested valleys and hills surrounding Mount Abu town are organised daily from the Shri Ganesh Hotel *(see page 458)*. The routes cover some of the area's lesser-known, least accessible panorama and wildlife-viewing points, where bears, jungle cats and other rare species may be spotted.

Ranakpur.

gilded stucco pomp of the Raj era. The most elaborate decor appears in the famous Mor Chowk ('Peacock Courtyard'), in which 5,000 pieces of tinted glass were deployed to create the four peacocks adorning the walls.

Lake palaces

Other palaces were built on the lake itself, to which Udaipur's rulers used to escape the heat of high summer. The largest, **Jag Niwas**, dates from 1746 and today houses the unashamedly luxurious and romantic Lake Palace Hotel (note the hotel is no longer open to non-guests). To its south, the older **Jag Mandir** is where Prince Khurram, who was later to become Emperor Shah Jahan, took refuge in 1624; British refugees also sheltered here from the horrors of the 1857 Uprising.

In the Old Town, the tangle of narrow lanes winding from the stepped banks of the lake are lined by historic buildings in various stages of collapse. Among the few that have been restored is the **Bagore-ki-Haveli** (daily 10am–7pm; charge), a 138-roomed

mansion that once belonged to the prime minister of Udaipur state. It now holds a small museum and concert hall where recitals of traditional Mewari music and dance are staged for tourists. Just up the hill, the **Jagdish Temple**, built in the mid-17th century, has a remarkable bronze statue of Garuda (a mythical bird) facing his revered Lord Vishnu. The fascinating shops and craftsmen's studios in the narrow streets of the bazaar justify lengthy exploration.

On the outskirts, **Shilpgram** (daily 11am–7pm; charge) is a lively folk museum where reconstructed village houses from across western India showcase traditional arts and crafts of the region, while music and dance performances are held throughout the day on open-air stages in front of them. A visit to Shilpgram can be easily slotted into a trip to the **Sajjangarh** hill palace, 5km (3 miles) west of the city. Built in 1883 by the royal family as a monsoon retreat, the now poorly maintained structure is of less interest in itself than the wonderful views that extend across the lake and hills surrounding Udaipur – especially serene at sunset time.

Forts and temples of Mewar

In the erstwhile princely state of Mewar there were three almost impregnable forts: **Chittaurgarh** (112km/70 miles east of Udaipur), **Kumbalgarh** (84km/52 miles north) and Mandalgarh (near Kota).

Set deep in the Aravalli Hills, **Kumbalgarh** ⓬ remains difficult to reach, even today, but more than repays the effort. The journey leads through delightfully unspoilt countryside – much of it farmed by minority Bhil tribespeople. The citadel itself, approached via seven fortified gates, occupies an eagle's-nest summit ringed by enormous ramparts that fall away dramatically to the hazy plains below. It takes two days, with a night under the stars halfway, to hike around them – an adventurous trek that takes you past forgotten ancient shrines infested with jungle and monkeys, affording superb panoramas throughout.

The Jain temple complex of **Ranakpur** ⓭, 160km (100 miles) northwest from Udaipur, can be reached in a scenic hour's drive from Kumbalgarh, dropping through old-growth forest to the floor of a shaded, thickly wooded valley, Built in the mid-15th century of milk-white Makrana marble, the temples – important way-stages on the region's Jain pilgrimage circuit, but rarely visited by foreigners – are renowned above all for their intricately carved columns, no two of which are identical.

Chittaurgarh ⓮, also known as Chittor, became the first capital of Mewar in the early 13th century under the reign of Jaitra Singh (1213–53). The siege of Chittaurgarh in 1303 by the sultan of Delhi, Ala-ud-Din Khilji, is notorious. The sultan had heard of the beauty of Princess Padmini, wife of Maharana Rawal Ratan Singh, and determined to bring her back to his harem. Despite a courageous Rajput defence, the citadel was captured by the sultan's force. Rather than face dishonour, the women committed *johar*, mass suicide. Chanting verses from the *Gita*, they threw themselves on the funeral pyre.

Chittor was later recaptured by the Rajputs. Two centuries later, in 1535, it was attacked by the sultan of Gujarat, Bahadur Shah; a total of 13,000 Rajput women are said to have sacrificed themselves in the flames. But by far the bloodiest siege here was the one laid by the Mughal emperor Akbar 32 years later, in which the entire female population of the fort committed *johar* on a mass pyre, while their husbands and male relatives rode to an honourable death in battle outside the walls.

Spread over a huge, sheer-sided plateau, Chittaurgarh Fort holds monuments spanning nine centuries of Rajput history, from grandiose gateways to temples, palaces and stepped tanks. Its defining landmark, however, is the 37-metre (121ft), nine-storey **Jaya Stambha**, or 'Victory Tower'. Ornately carved from top to bottom, it can be scaled via 157 internal steps for superb views over the town and fortress.

Mount Abu

Mount Abu ⓯, 100km (62 miles) west of Udaipur, is one of the most sacred places of Jain pilgrimage. According to the Jain tradition, Mahavira, the last of the 24 *Tirthankara* (saints), spent a year there. At an altitude of 1,220 metres (4,000ft), it is the only bona fide hill resort in Rajasthan. Many princes built summer bungalows and small palaces around Nakki Lake, and visitors flock there during the summer to take advantage of the cooler temperatures. The surrounding countryside attracts less attention, but its woods and boulder-studded hillsides are criss-crossed by woodcutters' trails offering some wonderful walks to viewpoints with panoramas extending

FACT

The famous riding breaches named after the Marwari capital are said to have been invented by Regent Pratap Singh, who disliked the cloth wrappings worn around soldiers' shins and devised an all-in-one trouser alternative, based on traditional Rajput garb. The fashion spread to London after Singh's visit to Queen Victoria's Diamond Jubilee in 1887.

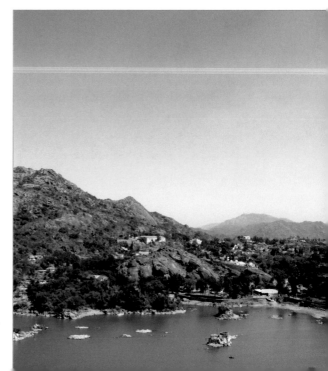

Mount Abu.

FACT

Much of what we know about the history of Rajasthan is due to 23-year-old Lieutenant James Tod, who arrived in 1805 as the East India Company's representative. Over the next decade, he roamed across 'Rajpootana', compiling the royal genealogies, folklore, poetry and history he acquired along the way into the Annals and Antiquities of Rajasthan – the most authoritative account of the region ever written.

The blue city of Jodhpur viewed from the Fort.

westwards across the plains, far below, into Gujarat.

The main attractions in Mount Abu, and one of the great sights of Rajasthan, are the **Dilwara Jain temples** (daily noon–3pm; free). Of the five main shrines here, **Adinath** and **Neminath** display the finest carving in white marble. Adinath, the most celebrated, was built in 1031 and is dedicated to the first Tirthankar. The lotus ceiling in the main shrine is carved from a single block of stone. Neminath was erected in 1230 to celebrate the 22nd Tirthankar, and the **Hall of Donors** is particularly fine. Of the other three, the Chaumukha Temple is later and built of sandstone, the Risah Deo Temple is unfinished, while the Dagambar Temple is much less highly decorated. The 24 elite Chauhan clans of Rajasthan claim descent from the holy fire that springs from the central peak of the Abu, **Guru Shikhar** (1,772 metres/5,813ft), the highest point in Rajasthan and site of the much venerated Atri Rishi Temple. Mount Abu is particularly popular with

Gujarati tourists, who come here to take advantage not only of the cooler climes but also the ready availability of alcohol – Gujarat is a dry state.

Jodhpur

The Rathores of Kanauj (in modern Uttar Pradesh) moved in ad 1211 to Marusthal – literally 'Land of Death' – the arid desert spreading westwards from heart of Rajasthan. Their territory, crossed by the major trade artery connecting northern India with the ports on the Gujarati coast, came to be called Marwar, and furnished them with untold riches.

In 1459, Rao Jodha ploughed much of the wealth gleaned from taxing this commerce in sandalwood, spices, copper and silk into the construction of a new stronghold at **Jodhpur** ⑯ after the Rathores old seat at nearby Mandore had proved too vulnerable. Thereafter, allegiances with the Mughals, whom the Rathores' helped in their conquest of Gujarat, saw the family's fortunes rise still further, but after the demise of Shah Jahan, Rao Jaswant Singh backed the wrong brother in the ensuing war of succession and was attacked by Aurangzeb, his subjects forcibly converted to Islam. Two centuries of fratricidal disputes and famines ensued before the city experienced a resurgence during the British colonial period.

The Raj era saw the construction of one of India's most decadent palaces, Umaid Bhavan, on Jodhpur's outskirts, but it is still the stupendous profile of the glittering **Meherangarh Fort** (daily 9am–5pm, museum closed 1–2.30pm; charge) that entirely dominates the city. Floating 125 metres (410ft) above the rooftops of the old town, the citadel sprawls over a flat sandstone plateau, protected on all sides by sheer cliffs and a crust of crenellated ramparts. The approach to it winds through seven fortified gateways. Emerging from the last of these, **Loha Pol**, or 'Iron Gate', you'll see a series of *sati* stones showing the hand prints of royal widows burnt on the maharajas' pyres. The palaces within, sculpted from hard sandstone and marble, were designed to catch the breeze to keep them cool. An extensive museum displays howdahs, paintings, thrones, banners, doors, weapons, and a spectacular 17th-century tent made for Shah Jahan. The fort also boasts an excellent audio guide, available for hire at the ticket office.

The old city of Jodhpur below the fort is an intriguing place to explore. Its maze of narrow streets, where you'll find dozens of shops selling traditional *kathputli* puppets and mirror-inlaid textiles, is painted a striking shade of blue. Tourist guides will tell you the distinctive colour denotes the homes of Brahman families, but the truth is more prosaic: it derives from copper sulphate, traditionally added to limewash to deter termites and other insects.

Umaid Bhavan palace

Across town, the scrubby southern outskirts of Jodhpur are overshadowed by the monolithic bulk of

Mehrangarh Fort.

Umaid Bhavan palace, built from red sandstone by famine victims in the 1920s and 1930s. It took 3,000 labourers more than a decade and a half to construct the 347-roomed behemoth, which centres on a gigantic domed hall. No expense was spared on the interiors. When the original fittings and furniture, ordered from Maples of London, were lost in a U-boat attack during World War II, Maharaja Umaid Singh ordered a new Art Deco look, embellished with oodles of Rajasthani gilt flourishes. It was among the most extravagant designs ever created, and stands as a fitting monument to the iniquities of Rajasthan's age-old feudal system.

One closed wing of the building remains occupied by the royal family, but the rest has been dedicated to a luxury heritage hotel; non-residents are, however, welcome to take tea and watch the peacocks patrol the vast lawns, and there's a small **museum** (daily 9am–5pm; charge) displaying the usual array of royal treasures, regalia, hunting trophies and old photographs, alongside a video on the making of the palace. Unless you're staying there, you'll have to shell out Rs1,500 for a ticket to look around the rest of the building.

SHOP

Jaisalmer is a great place to shop for souvenirs, especially crazy-patchwork quilts, sold in boutiques across town, and traditional Rajasthani puppets, or *katputli*. The latter are still made by a local caste of puppeteers at their desert village on the northwestern outskirts; ask for '*katputli bastee*'.

North of Jodhpur

The Rathores' old capital of **Mandore**, 8km (5 miles) north of Jodhpur, boasts landscaped gardens surrounding temples and the *chatris* of the Marwar rulers. Sights include the **Hall of Heroes**, with larger-than-life figures painted in gaudy colours, and the temple of the black Bhairav and the white Bhairav (manifestations of Lord Shiva), where the idols are pasted over with layers of foil paper.

The **Osian Temple** complex (daily 6am–8pm; free), 65km (40 miles) north of Jodhpur, has 16 very fine Hindu and Jain temples, dating from the 8th–12th centuries. The first group, of 11, represents the earliest phase of temple-building in Rajasthan. The largest temple, **Mahavira**, has a sanctum dating from 783–93. As well as rich decoration, the halls are open, with balustrades rather than walls, to provide more light. This group also contains one of the few temples to Surya (the sun god). The second group is later and contains the fine 12th-century **Sachiya Mata Temple**.

Jaisalmer

Jaisalmer ⓱, land of the Bhatti princes, born of the moon, is by far the oldest Rajput capital, dating from AD 1156. The vision of its crumbling sandstone ramparts rising seamlessly from the desert sands, capped by carved temple towers and the domed kiosks of medieval palaces, is one of the most compelling in India, drawing tens of thousands of tourists each winter across the Thar from Jodhpur, a six-hour train ride to the west. The resulting commercialism has proven a mixed blessing for the town, but Jaisalmer remains – for all the signboards, touts and gimcrackery crammed into its narrow streets – undeniably beautiful. It's also the region's main springboard for camel safaris, offered by every hotel and guesthouse, and easily the most memorable way to engage with the unique landscape unfolding from the citadel walls.

Jaisalmer's fort, built in 1156 of soft yellow Jurassic sandstone, is like a city in miniature, enclosing a tightly packed warren of *havelis*, shops and hotels divided by narrow alleyways. A

Gadi Sagar Tank.

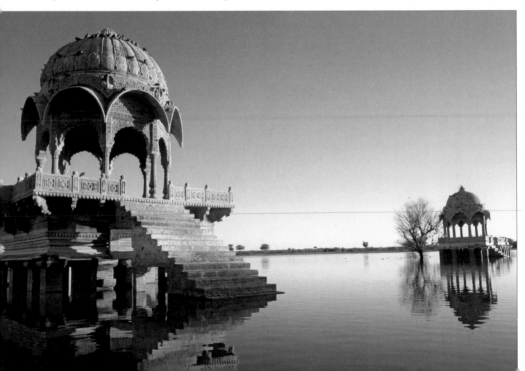

paved road winds to the square standing in its centre, **Main Chowk**, which is overlooked by the five-storey facade of the **Palace of the Maharawal** (daily 9am–6pm Oct–Mar, 8am–6pm Apr–Sept; charge). Royal heirlooms and medieval sculpture make up most of its interesting collection, but the architecture itself is the main attraction.

Tours wind up at the **Rani ki Mahal** (Queen's Palace), an ornately filigreed chamber that was recently rebuilt using funds donated by the NGO Jaisalmer in Jeopardy (www.jaisalmer-in-jeopardy.org). JIJ was set up to help forestall the fort's buildings from literally falling apart: the erosion of its foundations caused by a dramatic increase in water consumption over the past couple of decades has resulted in the collapse of several major landmarks, including parts of the palaces and two whole bastions.

Jaisalmer's havelis

In the town, wrapped around the base of the fort, stand many beautiful *havelis*, dating from the era when Jaisalmer formed an important outpost on the trans-Thar caravan route. Before the creation of the Indo-Pakistan border in 1947 brought overland trade with neighbouring Sind to an abrupt end, the bazaars here were stacked with exotic produce carried by camel across the sandy wastes to the west. The trade peaked in the 18th and 19th centuries, when vast sums were spent on building and decorating houses out of the malleable local stone. Jailsamer's *silavats* (stone carvers) were famous all over western India, and their work continues to look as fresh as it did 100 or more years ago: projecting balconies, door surrounds, eaves, pillars, domes and window frames were all exquisitely sculpted into elaborate forms.

One of the finest examples is **Patwa Haveli** (also known as Patwon-ki-Haveli; daily 8am–6.30pm; charge), constructed in the first half of the 19th century by a family of Jain traders. Further southwest on Gadi Sagar Road, **Salim Singh Haveli** (daily 8am–7pm; charge) once belonged to a former prime minister and ranks among the town's top three period properties in the town, along with **Nathmali-ki-Haveli**, off Court Road, immediately north of the fort.

Flanked by ghats and little domed shrines, the **Gadi Sagar Tank**, on the south side of town, dates from 1367 and affords a lovely view of Jaislamer's amber-coloured ramparts. The triple-arched gateway leading to it, the Tilon-ki-Pol, was commisioned in 1909 by a wealthy courtesan named Tilon, much to the displeasure of local worthies, who tried to get the structure pulled down on the grounds that it was built using ill-gotten gains. The maharaja eventually bowed to public pressure and ordered its removal, but Tilon outwitted everyone by having a shrine to Vishnu installed on the gate's upper parapet, thereby making any attempt to destroy it an act of desecration. The gateway stands to this day, forming the perfect frame for what must rank among the most perfect views anywhere in India.

TRIPS INTO THE THAR

There's no better way to explore the Thar Desert than on camel back, and in Jaisalmer, camel safaris are big business. Trips range from half-day tours of the outskirts to week-long expeditions, complete with luxury hunting tents, gourmet meals and performances by music and dance troupes. Two or three nights tends to be long enough for most people. Accompanied by a cook, English-speaking guide and camel man, you can plod around a constellation of mud-and-thatch villages, taking in some of the less accessible highlights in the desert around the town en route.

Topping most itineraries are the ruins of ancient Loduvra, capital of the Bhatti rulers before the foundation of Jaisalmer, and the Akal Fossil Park, where the fragments of huge Jurassic trees are scattered over a patch of remote desert. Some safari operators also start their tours at the photogenic village of Khuri, beautifully decorated with geometric white murals and mirror-encrusted mudwork. The honeypot of the safari scene, however, is Sam, 40km (25 miles) west of Jaisalmer, where a wedge of soft sand dunes attracts swarms of hawkers, guides, itinerant musicians and busloads of day trippers, which can make the whole experience of watching the fabled sunsets an anticlimax if you've spent days riding there.

RESTAURANTS

PRICE CATEGORIES

Average price for dinner, up to three
courses for one person, excluding
alcoholic drinks:
£ = up to Rs200
££ = Rs200–500
£££ = Rs500–1,000
££££ = over Rs1,000

Combining ingredients from across the
subcontinent with centuries of Hindu,
Islamic and Jain culinary know-how,
Rajasthan's cooking traditions are
every bit as sophisticated and refined
as the interior decor of Rajput palaces.
Wherever you eat – whether in desert
villages or royal palaces – you'll be
amazed at the variety and complexity
of the dishes served.

Jaipur

Chokhi Dhani
22km (13 miles) south of Jaipur on the
Tonk Road.
Tel: 0141-277 0555. £££
Middle-class Jaipuris pour south
down the main highway at weekends
to eat at this open-air 'special
village' restaurant, where you can
enjoy sumptuous traditional thalis
and live music, dance and puppet
shows. Camel and elephant rides
will amuse the kids. Worth the trip,
and food, prepared in wood fires and
clay ovens and served in rustic style
on long, low tables, is scrupulously
authentic.
Copper Chimney
Maya Mansions, M.I. Road. £££
Quality North Indian food served
in plush surroundings. Specialities
include traditional Rajasthani mutton
mince, prepared desert-style with
proper gatta (gram flour balls steeped
in yoghurt).
Four Seasons
Bhagat Singh Marg. ££
Enduringly popular vegetarian
restaurant and café, where you can
tuck into the crunchiest masala dosas
in town, along with the full gamut
of other South Indian snacks, and
noodle-based 'Chindian' dishes.
Lassiwala
M.I. Road. £
A series of street-side stalls serving
snacks and renowned clay cups of
thick, creamy lassi to long queues of
customers.

LMB
Johari Bazaar. ££–£££
Zealously pure-vegetarian place in
the Old City. In contrast to its snazzy
modern decor, it has served pretty
much the same menu of traditional,
high-caste satvik cooking since the
1950s. The Rajasthani deluxe thalis
are especially popular on Sundays.
Niro's
M.I. Road. £££
Clean, air-conditioned restaurant
offering tasty food and prompt service
from an extensive menu of Indian,
Chinese and Continental dishes. A
little more expensive than other places
in town, but worth the extra.
Om
Best Western Om Tower, Church Road, off
M.I. Road.
Tel: 0141-236 6683. ££££
Revolving restaurant atop Jaipur's
glitziest skyscraper, from which
you can survey the entire city over
delicious Rajasthani and other North
Indian specialities. Each revolution
takes 45 minutes. A popular night
out for more well-heeled locals and
business types. Advance reservation
recommended.
Peacock Roof Top Restaurant
Hari Kishan Somani Marg, Hathroi Fort,
Ajmer Road.
Tel: 0141-237 3700. £££
The nicest rooftop joint in the city,
especially attractive in the evenings,
when fairy lights adorn its trademark
peacock canopy. The multi-cuisine
menu offers something to please every
palette, and they serve chilled beers.

Ajmer

Ambrosia
Ambassador Hotel, Nagina Bagh, Ashok
Marg
www.ambassadorajmer.com. £££–££££
This swish hotel restaurant near the
shore of Ana Sagar Lake offers fine
dining in a choice of three settings:
a chic, modern air-con restaurant,
Mughal-inspired water garden or
Arabic-style cabanas. Very romantic,
and the neo-Indian cuisine is top notch.
Honeydew
Station Road, next to King Edward
Memorial. ££
Dependable multi-cuisine option with
a relaxing garden terrace where you
can order the standard range of North
Indian vegetarian and non-vegetarian

dishes, as well as passable pizzas. The
only smartish restaurant in the centre
of Ajmer, it's very popular, especially at
weekends, when parents and pupils
from the nearby Mayo College (one
of India's foremost private schools)
descend en masse.
Mango Masala
Sardar Patel Road. ££
The Ajmeri middle classes pour into
this smart little eatery, located just off
the main Jaipur road in the northeast
of town, for Indian and Continental
fast food, fruit 'mocktails' and shakes.
You can also order filling Rajasthani
thalis, Punjabi mains and fragrant
Hyderabadi-style biryanis.

Pushkar

Raju Garden
Near Ram Ghat, Main Bazaar. £
Simple, traveller-oriented place on a
rooftop terrace festooned with fairy
lights and plants. The food consistently
outstrips the competition in this popular
end of town (try their tasty vegetarian
shepherd's pie or wood-baked pizza), as
do the wonderful lake views.
The Sixth Sense
Inn of Seventh Heaven, Mishroo ka Mohalla,
next to Malika temple, Chooti Basti.
Tel: 0145-510 5455. ££–£££
Currently the most hip, and pricy, of
the many tourist restos in the town,
popular above all for its chilled lounge
ambiance – if you're looking for
somewhere to update your Facebook
page, this is the place. Sink into a sofa
for a perfect cappuccino, or order a
copious fresh fruit, muesli and yoghurt
breakfast from their extensive menu
of light bites and multi-cuisine mains,
which feature lots of particularly good
pizza and pasta options.

Bundi

Tom & Jerry's
Nahara Ka Chotta, Palace Road. ££
Popular rooftop restaurant in the Old
Town, with superb views over the
surrounding roofscape and a short but
dependable menu of dishes pitched
at travellers – the curries are mild
and pizza passable. The friendly twin
brothers who run the place also offer
free wi-fi.

Udaipur

Ambrai
Amet Havli, Hanuman Ghat.

Tel: 0294-243 1085, www.amethaveliudaipur.com. £££
Occupying a spit of land that juts into Lake Pichola from Hanuman Ghat, this ranks among Udaipur's best-situated restaurants. The cuisine – mostly rich Mughlai and Rajput specialities prepared by the maharaja's former head chef – rates as highly as the views.

Natraj
New Bapu Bazaar, behind Ashok Cinema. £
Filling, unlimited North Indian *thalis* served in a grubby dining hall in the north of the city. Hard to find and invariably jam-packed, but worth hunting out for the delicious food, cooked fresh each day. Udaipur's best budget eating option.

Queen Café
Chand Pol. £
Proper Udaipuri home cooking, featuring spicy, fruit- and gourd-filled vegetable curries and scrumptious pakora, freshly prepared by a couple of friendly pensioners.

Savage Garden
East side of Chand Pol.
Tel: 0294-2425440. £££
Trendy fusion cuisine (mainly pasta and gnocchi with spinach, mushroom, mozzarella and aubergine sauces) served in a stylishly converted 250-year-old *haveli*. Prices reflect its strong reputation, based on the blue-walled, designer boho-chic decor as much as the food.

Jodhpur Bhojnalaya
Near the Taxi Stand. ££
Traditional Rajasthani *thali* joint, renowned above all for its *churma*: crumbly, slightly sweet dumplings spiced with cardamom.

Kanak
Near the Bus Stand. ££
Gujarati *thalis* differ from their Rajasthani counterparts (lighter on oil and chillies, and often a touch sweeter, with unique combinations of flavours) and this place serves the best one in town. Servings are unlimited.

Veena
Nakki Lake Road. £
Great pan-Indian fast food, from southern-style *dosas* to Bombay *pao bhaji* (spicy lentil-and-tomato stew served with griddle-fried butter rolls). You can eat outside on a convivial roadside terrace around an open fire in the evenings.

Jhankar Choti Haveli
Makarana Mohalla, Behind Clock tower.

Tel: 0982-803 1291, www.jhankarchotihaveli.com. ££
The 'jumbo thalis' served in this prettily situated, Jain-owned restaurant in the Old City are the most popular option here, but the main attractions are the intricately carved courtyard of the 600-year-old haveli itself, and fabulous views over the cubic rooftops to the fort from its rooftop terrace.

Marwar
Vivanta by Taj Hari Mahal.
Tel: 0291-243 9700. ££££
Top-drawer local Marwari cuisine, served by black-tie waiters in smart surroundings. Try the spicy, mutton-based Jodhpuri *mas*, or its vegetarian counterpart, *gatta ki sabzi*.

Midtown
Station Road, opposite Railway Station.
Tel: 0291-263 7001. ££
Reliable local vegetarian restaurant, with a cosy and sedate atmosphere and a well prepared range of dishes including local specialities and superb Gujarati thalis, as well as more mainstream offerings.

The Pillars
Hotel Umaid Bhawan.
Tel: 0291-251 0101. ££
Umaid Bhawan has four restaurants, but its tea-garden terrace is the most affordable and atmospheric, with peacocks strutting picturesquely over the grass and grand views of the distant city and desert. Come here for a gourmet sandwich at lunchtime, afternoon tea or a sundowner.

Shri Mishri Lal
Gateway south of the Clock Tower. £
A Jodhpuri institution, serving mega-rich *makhania* lassis to a steady flow of silently appreciative, sweet-toothed local aficionados. The old-world atmosphere is an attraction in itself.

Little Italy
Inside the Fort's main gates. £
Wonderfully authentic homemade pasta dishes (and somewhat less enthralling pizzas) served alfresco on a terrace on the fort walls – a great location after dark when the ramparts are floodlit.

Natraj
Opp.Salim Singh ki Haveli. £
A pleasant rooftop restaurant renowned above all for its Mughlai-style chicken curry and *malai kofta* – spicy vegetable dumplings in a rich, creamy sauce.

Trio
Gandhi Chowk. ££
A very popular and friendly restaurant, partly set under tents. Good food and drinks, and live traditional music. Get here early for a table with the best fort and palace views.

Vyas Meals Service
Near the Jain temples, inside the Fort. £
Home-cooked paratha-curd and *masala chai* breakfasts, lunchtime thalis and filling traditional *dal batti* suppers served by an endearing elderly couple. Don't come if you are in a hurry for your food.

A street vendor in Jaipur.

INDIAN RAILWAYS

For a true taste of India, its people and landscape, nothing beats travelling by train on one of the most comprehensive networks in the world.

Indian Railways is a huge state-run conglomerate, the world's largest employer, with over a million staff. It moves 10 million passengers a day, yet still remains remarkably efficient – and uniquely poetic. There is no better way to get the pulse of the country than to view the changing scene from a carriage window.

The British laid most of the 62,000km (38,500 miles) of track in the 19th century, but it has been remarkably well maintained and modernised, while reservations are now computerised at most stations.

The stations themselves are hives of human activity, with passengers going one way, red-clad porters the other, and amongst them all a succession of hawkers selling everything from tea to snacks to peanuts to magazines, each belting out their sales pitch more exuberantly than the other. Things calm down a notch once you are inside the train, although silence is definitely rare: those same hawkers often find their way on board, families roam around, doors and windows open and close in a refreshingly un-automated manner.

The scenery can be breathtaking, particularly along the coasts, with the Mumbai–Goa stretch an all-time favourite. The hill railways of India are famous for their character and quaintness, often served by 'toy trains' – narrow carriages ride narrow rails at impossible inclines as forests and occasional panoramic views pass by on either side.

Riding on the roof of a train is less common than it was, but there are certainly exceptions, as these devotees returning from a Hindu festival in Mathura prove.

A porter carries a passenger's luggage on the platform of a railway station.

Waiting for the Darjeeling Himalayan Railway, nicknamed the 'Toy Train'.

The Royal Rajasthan on Wheels; the last word in luxury train travel.

RAIL TOURISM

There are a number of seasonal, super-luxury trains aimed at foreign tourists in India that are the last word in elegance on rails, faithful replicas of the private carriages of the former maharajas. Each runs on a unique route, taking in a selection of outstanding sites on the way, with the journey typically lasting up to a week. Whilst the rolling stock may be old-fashioned, the carriages have been refurbished to a high standard, with each typically featuring private cabins, wall-to-wall carpeting, a mini-bar and a kitchenette.

Best known of them all is the Palace on Wheels, which runs through Rajasthan and features two turbaned valets for each air-conditioned carriage, two dining cars and a luxuriously appointed bar. However, another service, Royal Rajasthan on Wheels (www.royalrajasthanonwheels.com), is even more luxurious, offering contemporary designs with all mod cons. Rajasthan is the most popular area for these trains, although there are a couple of services in the South as well, one plying the Mumbai Goa stretch mentioned above and the other taking a tour of the hills of Karnataka (see Travel Tips, page 444).

hawker sells fruit on a train in Kolkata.

Indian Railways network train passes through the hill ation of Araku Valley on the Kothavalasa-Kirandul railway ae on the East Coast Railway (Odisha and Andhra Pradesh).

A train driver prepares his engine for a daily journey on the Darjeeling 'toy train'.

A Lambada woman wearing traditional jewellery in Gujarat.

GUJARAT

A compelling mix of tradition and modernity,
Gujarat lies off the main tourist trail, making it a
rewarding destination for those keen to discover the
'real' India.

Through the blaring cacophony of bicycles, autorickshaws, cars and bullock carts, a motorcycle with large milk cans tied astride darts through the streets of Ahmedabad with its rider bedecked in a brilliant red turban, flashing golden earrings and a fierce moustache. He is a Rabari from the milk-vending community, who has adopted modern transportation while continuing to wear his traditional dress. He is the essence of Gujarat, where tradition and modernity combine in a vibrant, dynamic fashion.

Past and present

Archaeological finds at Lothal near Dhandhuka in Ahmedabad district and Rozadi in Saurashtra carry the history of this western corner of India back 3,500 years to the age of Harappa and Mohenjodaro. In legend, the epics and *Puranas* tell of how Krishna and his brother Balarama left Mathura and settled at Kusathali (Dwarka) on Gujarat's western coast.

The name 'Gujarat' derives from the Gurjaras, an immigrant people of obscure origin who entered India

Main Attractions

Jama Masjid, Ahmedabad
Sun Temple, Modhera
Kutch
Somnath
Mount Girnar
Sasan Gir Lion Sanctuary
Diu Island
Palitana

*Orantaely carved
palace, Ahmedabad*

GUJARAT TRANSPORT

Gujarat has several airports, the busiest being Ahmedabad. Bhuj is served by daily connections to Mumbai, as are Diu, Porbandar, Rajkot, Vadodara, Jamnagar and Bhavnagar.

Ahmedabad: Trains run to Mount Abu (15 daily; 3hrs 30mins–5hrs); Bengaluru (6 weekly; 36–38hrs); Chennai (1 daily; 33hrs); Delhi (9 daily; 16hrs 30min–19hrs); Dwarka (2 daily; 9–10hrs); Jaipur (7 daily; 9–13hrs); Jodhpur (7 daily; 9–10hrs); Junagadh (4 daily; 6hrs 30mins–9hrs); Udaipur (2 daily; 10hrs 20min–12hrs); Vadodara (18 daily; 1hr 30min–2hrs 30mins).

Vadodara: Trains run to Ahmedabad (43 daily; 1hr 30mins–4hrs); Delhi (10 daily; 11–14hrs); Jaipur (2 daily; 11–15hrs); Mumbai (41 daily; 5–9hrs 30mins); Porbandar (1 daily; 13hrs); Surat (every 30mins; 2hrs).

Fishermen on the Rann of Kutch, a remote marshy area.

through the northern passes, made their way through the Punjab and settled in lands that came to be known as Gujarat from around the 10th century.

Gradually, a flair for maritime and mercantile pursuits developed a spirit of enterprise and produced a prosperous Gujarati middle class that wielded considerable influence, with traders and artisans forming powerful guilds.

The state divides into three principal regions. In the northwest is semi-arid Kutch, while Saurashtra makes up the western Kathiawar Peninsula, between the gulfs of Kutch (Kachchh) and Khambhat (Cambay). The eastern parts of the state, including the capital Ahmedabad, make up the third region – mostly fertile lands of wheat, cotton, peanut and banana plantations. The southern border area is hilly.

A less attractive side of Gujarat is manifest in the popularity of the Hindu chauvinist BJP, which runs the state government. This strain of militant Hinduism was seen at its worst during communal riots in 2002. After a terrorist attack on a train carrying *kar sevaks* (Hindu volunteers) to the disputed religious site at Ayodhya (see page 69), gangs of Hindus roamed the streets of Ahmedabad and other major centres, looting, killing and driving out Muslims. Eyewitnesses report the police standing by, or even helping, while the gangs did their worst, prompting speculation that members of the ruling BJP, marshalled by Chief Minister Narendra Modi, were complicit in the violence (a charge of which he was officially cleared a decade later). By the time the troubles subsided, between 1,000 and 2,000 people had been massacred and 150,000 displaced, the majority of them Muslims. Modi was criticised both in his home state and abroad for the government's failure to halt the carnage (the US revoked his visa), but this didn't stop him from winning a fourth successive term in 2012.

Ahmedabad

The reign of Sultan Ala-ud-Din Khilji of Delhi witnessed the creation of the first Muslim empire in India,

Gujarat

(map)

0	100 km
0	100 miles

and one of his earliest conquests was the wealthy kingdom of Gujarat in 1300. But it didn't last long: following Timur's attack on northern India, Gujarat broke off from the weakened Delhi Sultanate to form its own state. Before long, in 1411, Ahmad Shah I founded **Ahmedabad** ❶ as his capital, on the site of the ancient city of Karnavati.

Today, Ahmedabad's belligerent, swerving autorickshaws, modern Ashram Road with its hotels, shops and cinemas, and the heavily populated industrial sections of town, are all manifestations of its character as a great textile and commercial city of western India. Omnipresent is the Sabarmati River, over which six bridges connect the new city with the old.

The city is famous for its Gandhi connections: India's future leader was born in Porbander, on Gujarat's south coast, but based himself in Ahmedabad during the run up to Independence in the 1940s – partly because of its textile industry (which he sought to revitalise as part of his Home Rule campaign against foreign imports) and partly because the city was a communal flashpoint whose rioting threatened to derail negotiations on the country's future.

Numerous examples of medieval architecture survive amid the hectic streets of the old quarter, sprawling from the river's east bank. In the city's 15th- and 16th-century heyday, the ruling sultans recruited local Hindu craftsmen to decorate the impressive mosques, forts and palaces they erected in the capital, and the result was a hybrid Indo-Muslim style of architecture quite distinct from that of their Mughal rivals. A particularly well-preserved example is the **Teen Darwaza**, a chunky, triple-arched gateway carved with a mixture of Islamic calligraphy and typically Hindu ornamentation. Around its base, a lively fruit and vegetable market spills across the surrounding streets on weekdays.

From the *darwaza*, walk east up Mahatma Gandhi Road – the Old City's principal thoroughfare – to the splendid **Jama Masjid** (1424),

TIP

Ahmedabad plays host to the International Kite Festival (www.facebook.com/InternationalKiteFestival 2013), held annually from 6 to 13 January. A highlight of the event is the battles between kites whose lines have been rolled in glue and crushed glass: standing on the flat rooftops, participants compete to cut each other's strings. After dark, illuminated box kites light up the skyline.

Gujarat is one of the best places in India to buy fabrics and handicrafts.

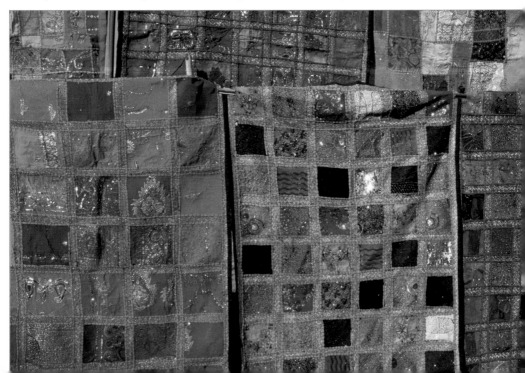

Gujarati Textiles

Perhaps in reaction to the desert surroundings in which they are created, Gujarati textiles are spellbindingly vibrant, colourful and distinctive

Gujarat is synonymous with textiles both within India and the world over. A vast array of different types of cloth is still produced here, using traditional techniques unique to this region, and the results are dazzling.

Patterns and prints

Perhaps the best known of all Gujarati textiles is that made using the tie dye, or *bandhani*, technique. Small portions of muslin cloth, or *mulmul*, are bundled together using fine threads; when the cloth is subsequently dyed, the knotted portions of the cloth do not absorb the colour, leaving a pattern of clear sections of cloth. This process is then repeated several times to produce a multi-coloured, intricately patterned design. The main centres for this type of production are Jamnagar, Anjar and Bhuj.

High-end fashion in a Delhi boutique featuring Gujarati fabrics.

Block-printed cotton fabrics are equally popular. In this process a pattern is chiselled onto the surface of a small wooden block, and the block is then dipped in dye and pressed repeatedly against a cloth to produce a design. The results vary greatly from region to region, from the very fine detailing typical of the *Dhamadka* fabrics to the more free-wheeling, geometric designs of the tribal *Deesa* prints. This type of textile is most commonly made along the Gondali River, whose waters are said to impart a particularly vibrant hue.

Mashru, a fabric produced from a blend of cotton and silk, was originally made all over India but is now found only in Gujarat. It was first made by Muslims as a way of getting round their prohibition on the wearing of pure silk, and is still popular all over the Muslim world. Patan is where most of this lustrous fabric is produced, with *ikkat* designs the most in demand.

Embroidery

The *patola* pure silk fabrics produced in Patan are prized for being completely reversible. They typically feature animal- or flower-based designs, as intricate on the front as on the back. Embroidery is another skill still widely practised in Gujarat, although its popularity has waned since its 17th-century heyday, when it was probably the foremost centre for commercial embroidery in the world. Marriage costumes, quilts, wall hangings and cradle cloths are all embroidered and often form an important part of the wedding dowry amongst the tribes of the Kutch, with all the women on the bride's side of the family working on the textiles to be hung or used in the bride's new home. Embroidery in the region forms part of a hidden language of caste and social status. You can tell where a woman comes from, what her husband does for a living, and even whether she has children or not from the style of mirror work adorning her clothes. Many of the age-old skills are being lost as families move away to the city and women have less time to devote to stitching and sewing.

Kutchi 'bling'

Of all the clothes made from these materials, it is the *abhas* worn by the tribal ladies of the Kutch region that have become the most celebrated, with the best examples being sold at auction in London and New York. These traditional costumes typically use bright colours, gold thread, sequins, mirrored glass and tie-dyed patterns to stunning effect: contemporary versions have now become popular amongst the fashion-conscious Indian elite.

whose domed prayer hall is supported by 120 pillars, all ornately sculpted with patterns that wouldn't look out of place in a temple of the same period.

Opposite the mosque, the incense-filled **Tomb of Ahmed Shah I** (1442) is enclosed by arcaded verandahs, nowadays occupied by cloth merchants rather than the Sufi mystics and pilgrims who would once have gathered here. The tomb stands as an oasis of calm amid the chaos of appropriately named **Manek Chowk** nearby, where rows of traders dealing in silver jewellery lean against spotless white bolster-pillows, waiting for customers. On the upper floors of the buildings on this street are the carved wooden balconies, windows and doorways of old *havelis* (town houses); the most beautiful stand in **Doshivada-ni-Pol**.

Other famous Islamic monuments in the city worth seeking out include **Sidi Saiyad's Mosque** on Dr Tankaria Road, renowned above all for its twin windows of pierced stone, forming a lyrical design of a tree with palm leaves and curving tendrils. The 'shaking' minarets of **Sidi Bashir's Mosque** at Kalipur, just south of the railway station, are among only a few surviving examples of a kind of tower that used to be common throughout Ahmedabad, but which has all but disappeared. Founded on soft sandstone, the minarets sway when their inner walls are shaken – believed to be an anti-earthquake measure.

The **Calico Museum of Textiles** (Thur–Tue, secular textiles 10.30am–12.30pm, religious textiles 2.45–4.45pm; free) in Shahibag is located in an old *haveli* which houses the Sarabhai Foundation, a public charitable trust. The exceptionally fine collections, which attract enthusiasts from all over the world, include rich brocades and fine embroideries from Kashmir, Gujarat and the southern states, all beautifully displayed. The museum

is divided into two wings: the first, given over to its core (secular) gallery, can only be visited in the mornings; the other portion exhibits religious or iconographic material, and is open only in the afternoon. Photography is strictly forbidden in both.

Hridey Kunj (daily 8.30am–6.30pm; free), Mahatma Gandhi's ashram at Sabarmati, is a set of austere yet beautiful buildings nestling amid mango trees. It was from here that Gandhi experimented in non-violent methods of political struggle. The simple museum, added later, is a fitting tribute. Designed by Charles Correa, a well-known Indian architect, it displays Gandhi's spectacles, sandals, photographs, a spinning wheel and some cloth spun by the great man.

Gujarat Vidyapith, a university established by Gandhi, has a vast collection of books, a museum, research centre and the Navjivan Press, which holds the copyright of Gandhi's works. It is located on the busy Ashram Road and visitors can shop for *khadi* (hand-spun) fabrics

Ritual ablutions before worship, Jama Masjid.

and other handmade village industry products at the nearby **Khadi Gramudyog Bhandar**.

Central Gujarat

The central region of Gujarat around Ahmedabad boasts numerous large, highly decorated step wells – *baoli* or *vav*. One of the finest specimens, the **Dad Hari-ni Vav**, stands in the northeast of the city. It was excavated in AD 1500 and decorated with typically Hindu motifs, despite having been paid for by a prominent member of the sultan's harem. Between 10am and noon, when the sun's rays penetrate its interior, is the best time to visit.

An even more spectacular example is the **Adalaj Vav**, located 19km (11 miles) north of the city, which Sanskrit inscriptions record was built by the wife of a local chief in 1498. Carved images of dancing girls, musicians, birds, animals and some erotic scenes adorn the walls, niches and pillars of the rectangular well.

The **Sun Temple** at **Modhera**, a three-hour journey by road north of Ahmedabad, is one of the finest examples of Indian temple architecture. Built in 1026, during the reign of King Bhima of the Solanki dynasty, the shrine is dedicated to the sun god, Surya. It stands on a plinth oriented towards to the east: during the spring and autumn equinoxes the main deity – which for the rest of the year is hidden in half-light – is illuminated by the rays of the rising sun. Elaborately carved figures of gods, goddesses, flowers, dancers, animals and mythical beasts adorn the red sandstone surfaces.

Lothal, 85km (52 miles) southwest of Ahmedabad, is of immense archaeological importance. Only discovered in 1954, and with excavation work still ongoing, a 4,500-year-old city has been unearthed, clearly discernible if only three bricks high. It has been linked to the contemporary remains at Mohenjodaro and Harappa in Pakistan. On the way it's well worth stopping off at **Nal Sarovar Bird Sanctuary**, particularly between November and February when a large number of migratory birds, including

Crowds gather for a Muslim festival at the Jama Masjid Mosque, Ahmedabad.

THE LAST SHIPYARD

An hour's drive south of Bhuj, Mandvi is a small seaside town that used to be one of the major ports in the region. Few vestiges of its bygone prosperity survive, but the riverbanks on the edge of town are the site of an extraordinary shipyard where ocean-going ships are still hand-made entirely out of wood, just as they have been for centuries. It takes teams of Muslim shipwrights an average of two years to construct each vessel, the largest of which fetch up to $500,000 from wealthy Gulf Arabs, who use them as pleasure craft. No written plans, and very few power tools, are used in the process. Visitors are welcome to look around any half-finished ships looming on the riverbanks; just turn up in working hours (any day except Friday) and seek permission from the foreman.

flamingos, make this their temporary home. It is best to get there before sunrise, hire a boat and be in a position to see the birds before they see you as the sun comes up.

Kutch: isolation and refuge

Sandwiched between Indian Saurashtra and Pakistani Sind, Kutch (or Kachchh), in the far northwest of Gujarat, has always been a land apart. Until the recent construction of permanent road and rail links, the region used to be cut off for months on end by monsoon floodwaters flowing off the Aravalli range to its northeast. When these recede, they leave in their wake vast flats of cracked mud and salt, broken by opal-blue pools of brine and distant flocks of flamingo: in the north, the Great Rann, and in the south, its smaller sibling, the Little Rann. In the past, local Rabari camel herders knew the safe routes to the mainland, but nowadays the only footprints you're likely to find on the Ranns are those of arms smugglers, desperate salt miners and herds of wild asses.

This extreme physical isolation explains why Kutch has traditionally been a place of refuge for tribes, castes and clans fleeing persecution elsewhere. Over the centuries, a mosaic of cultures evolved under the umbrella of the region's tolerant Hindu rulers, the Maharaos. In spite of depopulation, each has managed to preserve its distinct traditions, especially when it comes to costume, architecture, art and crafts, making this one of India's most colourful regions.

The survival of so many minority cultures in Kutch is all the more extraordinary given the fact that on the morning of 26 January 2001 (India's Independence Day) the region was devastated by a massive earthquake in which an estimated 25,000 people were killed, and many more made homeless.

One of the worst-hit areas was the medieval walled town of **Bhuj** ❷, regional capital and site of the Maharaos' medieval **palace**. Centrepiece of the complex is an opulent pleasure hall, the Aina Mahal, to which the king would repair to listen

TIP

The best source of information on Kutch, and how to explore the craft villages lying to the north of Bhuj, is the caretaker of the Aina Mahal museum, Mr Pramod Jethi, who runs his informal tourist desk (Sat–Thur 9am–1pm, 3–6pm) from the palace's ticket counter.

Kite festival, Ahmedabad.

WHERE

A rock inscribed with one of the Mauryan emperor Ashoka's famous edicts stands at the roadside 2km (1.25 miles) east of Junagadh. Carved in the 3rd century BC, it proclaims in ancient Brahmi script the ruler's conversion to Buddhism, imploring his subjects to follow the non-violent ethics of the Buddha's teachings. Identical edicts were placed all over the empire. They were first translated by scholar and East India merchant, James Prinsep in 1838.

A Lambani gypsy forest dweller.

to poetry and compose music, soothed by dozens of delicate indoor fountains. Many of its ceilings collapsed in the earthquake, but the famous **Hall of Mirrors** (Sat–Thur 9am–1pm, 3–6pm; charge) came through intact, as did most of its precious contents, which now form the basis of an engaging museum.

Kutch is renowned all over India for its handicrafts, especially embroidery and block printing. Each of the region's minority groups maintains its own styles and techniques, and the best way to experience them is to visit the villages where the work is carried out. The semi-desert area north of Bhuj harbours a major concentration of these, easily explored by renting a car, driver and guide for the day. As a primer, start your tour at the excellent **Kala Raksha Trust** (www.kala-raksha.org; daily 10am–2pm, 3–6pm; free) in Sumrasar, 25km (15 miles) north of Bhuj, an NGO that is working to help preserve the region's crafts; there's a small museum and shop on site, and workshops where you can watch Rabari and Garasia Jat women at work.

With more time, it's possible to travel out to the fringes of Kutch for a taste of life on the **Ranns**. In the far southeast, the Little Rann is the site of the isolated **Wild Ass Sanctuary**, part of the Little Rann Sanctuary – a 4,850-sq-km (1,870-sq-mile) reserve set up to protect the rare Indian wild ass. Distinguished by their buff-brown coat and ridge of dark fur, these beautiful, shy animals survive on the mud and salt flats, retreating to grassy islets called *bets* when the monsoon floodwaters inundate the rest of the Ranns. The best way to see them is on a jeep safari, arranged through either of the two hotel resorts situated just outside the sanctuary (a 30km/18-mile drive from the nearest railhead at Viramgam).

Exploring Saurashtra

Saurashtra, or **Kathiawar** as it's also known, is the large, spatula-shaped peninsula forming the central heartland of Gujarat, flanked by the Gulf of Kutch to the east and Gulf of Khambhat (Cambay) to the west. Its district headquarters is **Jamnagar ❸**, a walled city with several gateways. The older parts are bursting at the seams, but many areas were planned as recently as 1914 and have a systematic layout of facades, squares, circles and broad streets.

The fort-like **Lakhota Palace** is located in a lake and approached over a stone bridge. It could accommodate 1,000 soldiers, and now houses a fine museum (Thur–Tue 10.30am–1pm, 3–6.30pm; charge).

Dwarka ❹, 140km (86 miles) west of Jamnagar, was a flourishing port in ancient times, and a pilgrimage site – believed to have been established by Krishna 5,000 years ago. The **Temple of Dvarkadish** on the northern bank of Gomti Creek is typical of the architecture of old Hindu temples. It has a shrine, a large hall, a roof supported by 60 columns of granite and sandstone, and a conical spire 50 metres (160ft) high.

The shrine is elaborately ornamented and has a sculpted figure of Ganesh over the entrance.

Gandhi's birthplace

For those who have a special interest in the life of Mahatma Gandhi, a visit to **Porbandar ❺**, his birthplace (90km/56 miles along the coast from Dwarka), is a pilgrimage worth planning. Gandhi was born in this quiet town in 1869, in his ancestral home. The house has been preserved as a museum (daily 7.30am–7.30pm; free). With its small rooms, trellised windows and carved balconies, it exudes an air of peace and tranquillity.

Driving along quiet coastal roads through Chorwad and Veraval you will reach **Somnath ❻**, 115km (70 miles) from Porbandar. Standing majestically on the shores of the Arabian Sea is one of the 12 most sacred Shiva shrines in India. Ransacked repeatedly by northern invaders and rebuilt successively in gold, silver, wood and finally in stone, it is said to have been built by Soma, the moon god, in penance and worship of the wrathful Lord Shiva,

who had laid a curse on him. Nearby a temple marks the spot where Lord Krishna is said to have been accidentally killed by a hunter's arrow. Cymbals are played at dusk to mark the time for prayers.

Junagadh and Amba Mata

Junagadh ❼, in interior southern Saurashtra, ranks among the most ancient towns in India. Buddhist caves chiselled between 200 BC and AD 200 into the rocky hills surrounding it testify to the area's importance as an administrative and religious centre during Mauryan times, while the squat Maqbara tombs clustered in the centre of town recall the heyday of its 19th-century Muslim rulers.

Most visitors who pass through these days do so en route to **Mount Girnar**, an extinct volcano rising out of the plains 4km (2.5 miles) to the east. The massif, which reaches 945 metres (3,100ft), has five distinct peaks, joined by 8,000 or more stone steps that thread their way between a constellation of small Jain and Hindu shrines.

Somnath.

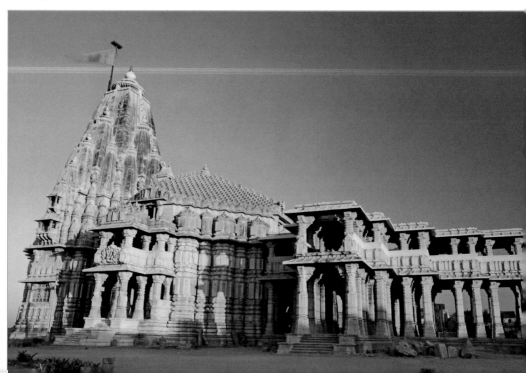

FACT

Gujarat is India's most industrialised state, accounting for 20 percent of the country's GDP (including 50 percent of its petrochemical production and 45 percent of its pharmaceuticals). The pollution resulting from rapid economic growth has made its cities among the filthiest on the planet. To fuel the boom, a series of superdams have been built along the Narmada Valley, displacing millions and provoking outrage among civil-rights organisations.

The lions of Gir Forest are the sole remnant of a once extensive population of Asiatic lions.

By far the most revered of the shrines is the temple dedicated to **Amba Mata**, also known as 'Ambaji', the mother goddess, which attracts young couples from all over northwestern India petitioning for happy and fruitful marriage. The fifth peak, the one furthest from town, is associated with Kalika, the eternal aspect of Durga, and hosts a community of Aghora *sadhus* – hard-core Shiva-worshipping ascetics who demonstrate their renunciation of the temporal world by drinking out of human skulls, smearing themselves in ashes from funeral pyres and eating excrement.

Lions of the Gir Forest

Sasan Gir Lion Sanctuary ❽, 40km (25 miles) north of Somnath (mid-Oct–mid-June, daily 7–11am, 3–5.30pm; charge), is one of the last places in the world where Asiatic lions can be seen in their natural habitat. Efforts at conservation began in the **Gir Forest**. In 1900 the nawab of Junagadh, in whose territory most of the forest lay, had invited the viceroy, Lord Curzon, for a lion *shikar* (hunt). When the viceroy accepted, a newspaper published a letter that questioned the propriety of an important person doing further damage to an endangered species. Lord Curzon not only cancelled his *shikar*, but also advised the nawab to protect the remaining lions, which he duly did. These days the Gir Forest is one of the most important game preserves in India, and a successful conservation project: early in the 20th century there were only 100 lions left here; now they number more than 250.

The Portuguese legacy

The Saurashtran coast always played an important role in the maritime trade between northern India and the Persian Gulf, and the first Portuguese navigators to explore the region were quick to see the strategic potential of a small island called **Diu**, on the peninsula's southernmost tip. In return for military assistance against the Mughals, Sultan Bahadur of Gujarat reluctantly handed over control of the port in 1535, which the Portuguese managed to retain until Nehru expelled them by force in 1961.

Diu town, clustered on a promontory on the island's eastern tip, has retained plenty of Lusitanian character, with a crop of elegant Indo-Portuguese mansions and churches, and more liberal liquor laws than those prevailing on the mainland. A string of quiet beaches lying within easy reach of the town provide further incentive to stop by here for a few days, while birdwatchers are drawn by the migratory flamingos that stop on the mudflats lining the north of the island in early spring.

Bhavanagar district

Palitana ❾ in Bhavanagar district almost completes the full circle of Saurashtra. Just to the south is the **Shatrunjaya Hill**, the most important centre of Jain pilgrimage, with an incredible 863 Jain temples atop its twin peaks.

It is worth heading back in the direction of Ahmedabad via **Surendranagar**

and **Wadhwan**. The ancestors of the stone-carvers of Wadhwan built Dwarka and Somnath. Skilled stone-carvers live and practise their craft near **Hawa Mahal**, a finely conceived but unfinished palace at the edge of the town. Traders in Surendranagar town have a vast collection of old embroideries and artefacts from all over Saurashtra.

Eastern Gujarat

The 'industrial corridor' of Gujarat lies due south of Ahmedabad. In its hinterland is the exclusively Adivasi belt, whose rural societies lead very different lives to those in the mercantile centres elsewhere in the state (see page 32).

The industrial city of **Vadodara** ❿ (formerly Baroda), 115km (70 miles) southeast of Ahmedabad, was capital of one of the richest 'princely states' in pre-Independence India. The Old Town has a number of attractions associated with the ruling maharajas, including the once opulent **Lakshmi Vilas Palace**.

Vadodara serves as a springboard for trips to the deserted Muslim city

A Champaner mosque.

of **Champaner**, 45km (28 miles) northeast. A wealth of intricately carved mosques, tombs and gateways bearing exquisite Islamic calligraphy survive from the late 14th century, when the town, then known as Muhammabad, served as the sultan of Gujarat's capital. Despite being classed as a Unesco World Heritage Site, it sees few visitors and has an almost forlorn feel.

Surat , on the east coast of the Gulf of Khambhat, was the first outpost established (in 1608) by the British East India Company and was on one of the old trade routes for silks, embroideries and spices. Today the city is the epicentre of one of India's fastest growing industrial areas, and a major diamond market accounting for 90 percent of India's diamond trade.

Despite its historic pedigree, however, the city holds few monuments of note. Pollution and appalling traffic rather than heritage architecture are likely to be your most lasting memories. That said, one colonial-era vestige warrants a detour. A fifteen-minute rickshaw ride from the centre off Kataragama Road, a weed-infested British cemetery holds the splendidly hybrid, domed mausoleums of the East India Company officials who died here between the seventeenth and nineteenth centuries, the grandest of them belonging to Sir George Oxenden (1620–69), the first governor of Bombay.

In the far south, the one location worth breaking a journey down the coast to visit is the former Portuguese outpost of **Daman**, where a 16th--century fort encloses a collection of grand Lusitanian churches and *palácios* overlooking the mouth of the Damanganga River. Only at Old Goa will you find Baroque facades so beautifully preserved.

Daman's other claim to fame is its Union Territory Status (shared with Diu), which means its liquor licensing laws are more lenient than those of Gujarat – and why the town gets inundated most weekends by jeep loads of heavy-drinking Gujarati men.

Preparing the catch on Diu Island.

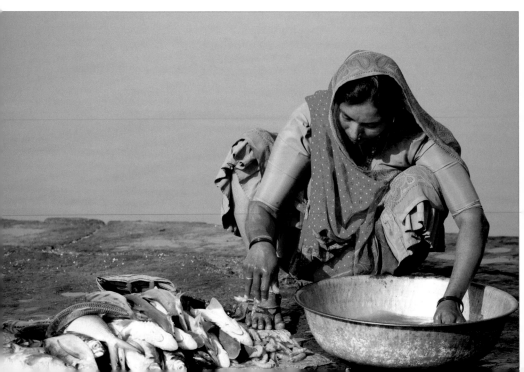

RESTAURANTS

PRICE CATEGORIES

Average price for dinner, up to three
courses for one person, excluding
alcoholic drinks:
£ = up to Rs200
££ = Rs200–500
£££ = Rs500–1,000
££££ = over Rs1,000

Gujarati cuisine is justly renowned
as one of the most sophisticated
and healthy in the subcontinent. The
influence of the Jain community lies
behind the predominance of vegetarian
dishes. The high esteem in which
Gujarat's most famous son, Mohandas
K. Gandhi is still held, accounts for the
continuing prohibition on alcohol.

The quintessential regional meal
is the Gujarati *thali*, comprising a
selection of lightly steamed seasonal
vegetables, tempered with a *vaghaar*
of hot oil, mustard seeds and spices.
They are served with *khichdi* (a
blend of rice and lentils), *kachumber*
salad, *toovar dal* (a runny yellow
lentil stew), sweet and sour pickles,
yoghurt and *bakhri rotal* flatbreads.

Ahmedabad

Agashiye
House of Mangaldas Girdhardas, opposite
the Sidi Sayid Mosque.
Tel: 079-2550 6946. **£££–££££**
Two terraces on the roof of
Ahmedabad's famous heritage
hotel have been fitted with candlelit
tables and tented canopies. Served
in traditional bell-metal *kansa thali*
utensils, the food is freshly prepared
in an open kitchen. The dishes are
subtle, contemporary takes on Gujarati
standards. To round off, *paan* is served
on ice garnished with rose petals.
Advance booking recommended.

Green House
House of Mangaldas Girdhardas, opposite
the Sidi Sayid Mosque. **£££**
Stylish courtyard café on the ground
floor of the Hotel MG serving
traditional Indian snacks, such as
dhoklas (rice cakes rolled in sesame
seeds), *panaki* (rice-flour pancakes
steamed in banana leaves) and
scrumptious corn *handos* (crusty
gram-flour vegetable patties).

Gopi Dining Hall
Opposite Town Hall, Ellis Bridge, Ashram
Road. **£**

An extremely popular, non-smoking
Gujarati restaurant with tasty
vegetarian food at rock-bottom
rates. They are renowned for their
Kathiawadi *thalis* – hotter and spicier,
and less sweet, than standard, with
more ghee. Expect to wait for a table.

Vishalla
On the southern edge of the city, opposite
Vasana Tol Naka.
Tel: 079-660 2422, www.vishalla.com. **£££**
This is the place to sample authentic,
village-style Gujarati cooking. You
eat sitting cross-legged on the floor
on long, rustic timber tables under
terracotta canopies. Waiters in
traditional dress heap fresh, delicious
and healthy delicacies onto leaf
plates while troupes of folk dancers,
puppeteers, magicians and musicians
perform on open-air stages.

Bhuj

Gangaram
Behind the Aina Mahal. **£**
Mr Jethi cooks up a mean, Bengali-
style chicken curry, as well as simple
non-vegetarian dishes. You can eat on
the upstairs verandahs or down in the
sociable basement area.

Green Rock
Opposite STC Bus Stand. **££**
This is the most popular vegetarian
place to eat in town, especially on
Saturdays and Sundays when they
serve a gargantuan 'Special Gujarati
Thali', complete with *farsan*, *chaat*
and mounds of sticky milk sweets.
On weekdays, the usual North Indian
menu returns.

Porbandar

Swagat
M.G. Road. **££**
In addition to local dishes, it also
serves plenty of Punjabi and Chinese
alternatives. Popular with families.

Junagadh

Santoor
MG Road. **£–££**
Popular vegetarian restaurant in the
town centre serving mainly Punjabi
and South Indian dishes. The decor is
a bit downbeat, but the food is fresh
and tasty.

Diu

Herança Goesa
Behind Diu Museum. **££**

A favourite spot among travellers for
breakfast, but also the venue for a
lively buffet dinner featuring Indo-
Portuguese dishes such as fresh tiger
prawns and calamari in sour-chilli
sauce. Try the Israeli-inspired 'Hello
to the Queen': ice cream mixed with
crushed biscuits, banana and warm
chocolate sauce.

O'Coqueiro
Firangi Wadda Road, behind Cidade de Diu
church.
Tel: 0982-468 1565. **££**
Currently the first choice among
budget travellers in Diu, this simple
garden restaurant, run by an amiable
local family, serves the usual traveller-
oriented menu of fresh-fruit-muesli-
yoghurt breakfasts, seafood suppers
and a handful of so-so Portuguese
dishes – all under rustling palms and
a pretty tiled gazebo.

Vadodara

Mandap
R.C Dutt Road. **££**
Indisputably the town's best traditional
Gujarati thali, served in the cool,
clean and modern confines of a smart
hotel against a backdrop of mock
village tents. The sweet selection is
particularly impressive – bring a tiffin
tin and they'll even do doggybags for
you. Pricy by local standards, but worth
the splurge.

Daman

Daman Delite
Hotel Gurukripa, Seaface Road.
Tel: www.hotelgurukripa.com. **£££**
The town's smartest restaurant, and
with a marginally more sober and
polite clientele than is usual. Local
seafood features prominently.

A traditional thali meal.

Tourist headgear for sale at Anjuna flea market.

At the Bhaja Caves, Maharashtra.

WEST-CENTRAL INDIA

From the bright lights of Mumbai to golden Goan beaches, the breathtaking ancient sites and remote jungles of the interior, India's west-central heartlands are full of interest.

Garlanded bus.

Washed by the Arabian Sea, the metropolis of Mumbai, formerly Bombay, is the country's most cosmopolitan city, and sets the pace for all western India. The commerce and cinema of Mumbai draw visitors from all walks of life, and increasingly from all over the world; this is perhaps the only truly international city on the Subcontinent. The hub of the new India, Mumbai is the centre of business and industry that is defining the rise of the country's increasingly global ambitions.

To the south, the lush Konkan coast extends hundreds of miles to the formerly Portuguese Goa, one of the first European toeholds in Asia. A short flight from Mumbai, this is the watering hole for the city's rich and has become a hedonistic beach centre for clubbers, hippies, backpackers, expats and artists – increasing numbers of them from Russian and the former Soviet states. During the winter season it's a busy, bustling, vibey mix; the rest of the year is warmer but more relaxed, and monsoon is a time of thundering waves and spectacular skyscapes above the forts and churches, with the winter tourists long gone.

Sacred bull at Benaulim.

Inland from Mumbai, the forested hills of the Western Ghats form a divide between the coastal plains and the harsher environment of the Deccan plateau. The state of Maharashtra is most famous for the magnificence of the cave art at Ajanta and Ellora, but is also home to the interesting city of Pune, hill stations in the cool heights of the Ghats, and several noteworthy Hindu temples.

Further to the north and east, the sprawling state of Madhya Pradesh in the heart of India is best known for the erotic art at Khajuraho, impressive forts such as Gwalior and Mandu, and magnificent wildlife parks where tigers and leopards prowl by night. Cleaved off from the eastern part of the state in 2000, Chattisgarh is a largely rural backwater seldom visited by tourists; it has a large Adivasi population and some of India's largest surviving forests.

Shoemakers in Mumbai.

MUMBAI (BOMBAY)

Surrounded on three sides by the Arabian Sea, India's most populous city is also the country's glamorous commercial hub – a magnet for rich and poor.

The story of Mumbai is fascinating. From obscure, humble beginnings as a set of seven small islands separated by tidal creeks and marshes, the city has risen to become India's most important commercial and industrial centre. The seven islands have been merged into one and thus survive only as names of localities like Colaba, Mahim, Mazgaon, Parel, Worli, Girgaum and Dongri.

Modern Mumbai is booming. Home to the wealthy and the glamorous, it has long been India's Hollywood (its former name, Bombay, leading to the genre-defining 'Bollywood'), producing more films each year than any other city in the world. Nowadays, it is also the home of India's own fast-growing satellite and television industries, as well as a rapidly expanding call-centre and back-office support sector.

Mumbai has a vibrancy not found anywhere else in India, and which only exists in the world's biggest cities. Like all big cities – albeit in greater measure than most – Mumbai has its seamy side, its slums and its overcrowding, the foothills of poverty on which are built towering skyscrapers. And like all success stories, there have been chapters of intrigue, violence, happiness and calm, and the struggles of the pre-Independence years, when

Mumba Devi Temple, Kalbadevi.

Mumbai became the political capital of nationalist India.

There is a sad history of violence in the recent past, although after each atrocity, the city has bounced back with impressive resilience. In the 1990s, communal riots between Hindus and Muslims were encouraged by the ultra-right-wing Shiv Sena, and its founder, Bal Thackeray. A series of anonymous bombing campaigns were widely interpreted as the Muslim backlash. In 1993, 10 huge blasts ripped apart key landmarks, among

Main Attractions

Gateway of India
Cricket maidans
Victoria Terminus
Jyotiba Phule (aka 'Crawford') Market
Mangaldas Lane
Malabar Hill
Dr Bhau Daji Lad Museum
Elephanta Caves

FACT

Outside India, perhaps the most famous Parsi of all time was the singer and former Queen front man, Freddie Mercury. Born Farok Bulsara in Zanzibar to Zoroastrian parents, Freddie attended a boarding school just outside Mumbai until the age of 17, when his parents fled Zanzibar for London.

them the Air India building and Stock Exchange, while a car bomb killed 107 outside the Gateway of India in 2003. A series of explosions on packed suburban commuter trains resulted in considerable loss of life in 2006, and in November 2008, parts of the city centre were targeted by terrorists in a three-day siege which left 173 dead.

Harbour city

Mumbai is ranged around a natural harbour at the northern end of India's tropical western shore, the Konkan Coast. With its port already developed by the British, the city grew rapidly following the opening of the Suez Canal in 1869. Today it handles more than 40 percent of India's maritime trade.

India's largest city now stretches 22km (14 miles) into the Arabian Sea. The maximum width of the composite island that constitutes metropolitan Mumbai is no more than 5km (3 miles). Into this narrow strip are squeezed the majority of the city's 16 million people, its major business and commercial establishments, its

docks and warehouses, and much of its industry – including most of its textile industry, which employs thousands of workers.

Tourists focus on the older, southern parts of Mumbai, in districts such as Colaba, Kala Ghoda and Fort. This is where you'll find the greatest concentration of Raj-era buildings and monuments, including the iconic Gateway of India, along with the city's most important galleries and museums. Most of the best accommodation and eating options are also in this area; the majority of visitors will find they'll stick to the southern tip of this city, with no need to head north until they're moving out of town. The Gateway also serves as an embarkation point for launches heading across Mumbai harbour to Elephanta Island, site of an ancient rock-cut cave complex where one of India's greatest archaeological treasures – a giant, triple-headed Shiva sculpture – peers out of the gloom.

The best time to visit Mumbai is during the relatively cool, dry winter period, between November and February. From March onwards, the humidity builds as temperatures rise inland on the Deccan plateau, sucking in moist air from the sea. After weeks of suffocating weather, the monsoon finally erupts in June, bringing curtains of heavy rain that obscure the view and flood the roads. The downpours peter out in October, but the humidity can last until well into November.

Mumbai's population

The Mumbai Municipal Corporation provides primary and secondary education in at least 10 languages, including English, and the city has developed its own patter, 'Bombay speak', which regular Hindi/Urdu speakers find rather comical. It is often caricatured in Indian films.

The Hindu population is largely Marathi, though most non-Marathi locals are also Hindus. The city's

TRANSPORT TO AND FROM MUMBAI

Mumbai's international airport – CST – is connected by direct flights to destinations worldwide. Its domestic neighbour serves as the region's principal gateway. Getting to the airports from downtown can take literally hours at peak times, so plan your trip accordingly. Or if you're only passing through between flights, consider booking a room in a hotel close to the airport (see page 461).

Trains run to Ahmedabad (28 daily; 6hrs 30min–9hrs 30min); Aurangabad (4 daily; 7hrs); Bengaluru (6 daily; 23–26hrs 30mins); Chennai (3 daily; 23hrs 15mins–26hrs 30mins); Delhi (15 daily; 16–29hrs); Hyderabad (6 daily; 12–17hrs); Kolkata (5 daily; 30–38hrs); Pune (33 daily; 2hrs 40min–5hrs 15mins).

Private and inter-state buses run to destinations across central and southern India, often more frequently than trains. Although far less comfortable for long overnight journeys, it is usually easier to obtain tickets at short notice for bus travel than rail.

The government bus depot in Dadar handles express buses to destinations in Maharashtra, including Kolhapur (4–6 daily; 9–11hrs); Nasik (17 daily; 4hrs); Pune (half-hourly; 3hrs 30min–4hrs). For cities further afield, such as Goa, Ahmedabad and Bengaluru, you depart from Mumbai Central bus station.

Gujarati population includes a large number of Jains.

When the Portuguese arrived, local Muslim nawabs ruled this corner of India, but they handed it over to the newcomers in 1534 in exchange for support against the Mughals. This was the beginning of Mumbai's large Christian (mainly Roman Catholic) population and its many churches, which led to two separate areas in the city becoming known as 'Portuguese Church'. A few churches retain their Portuguese facades: **St Andrew's** in the suburb of Bandra is a fine example. There are also minor remains of Portuguese fortifications both on the main island and the much larger island of **Salsette** north of the city. At **Vasai** (Bassein), 50km (30 miles) from Mumbai, sprawl ruins of a Portuguese walled settlement.

In 1662 Charles II of England married Catherine of Braganza, a Portuguese princess. As part of the dowry, the British crown received the islands of Mumbai. They were leased to the British East India Company in 1668 at the princely rent of £10 per annum. This company of merchant-adventurers had for some time felt the need for an additional west-coast port, to supplement and ultimately to supplant Surat in Gujarat. Far-sighted governors, such as Gerald Augnier, began the construction of the city and harbour, inviting the settlement of Gujarati merchants and Parsi, Muslim and Hindu manufacturers and traders to help develop the city. This led to the settlement of all these communities in Mumbai.

Cotton boom town

The slow transformation of the swampy islands during the 17th and 18th centuries gave way in the 19th century to rapid change. In 1858, the Honourable East India Company returned them to the British crown. In the 1850s came the steam engine,

Using the older-style Mumbai taxis should work out around 40 percent cheaper than the newer air-conditioned models.

Portuguese ruins at Vasai, north of Mumbai.

Mumbai (Bombay)

Dharavi, Bandra

Haji Ali Tomb **R**

Mahalkshmi Temple

Mahalarxmi Racecourse

Mahalaxmi

Jacob Circle

CHINCHPOKLI

BYCULLA

Byculla

Dr Bhau Daji Lad Museum (Victoria & Albert Museum) **S**

JIJAMATA UDYAN

Reay Road

Breach Candy Club

Sophiya Bhaba Auditorium

Willingdon Golf Club

Dockyard

Mumbai Central

MSRTC Depot

CUMBALA HILL

KHETWADI

MANDVI

Towers of Silence

P Mani Bhavan

Babulnath Mandir

KAMALA NEHRU PARK

Malabar Hill

O Hanging Gardens

Grant Road

GIRGAUM

Chor Bazaar

Round Temple

Sandhurst Road

Chowpatti Beach

Sahitya Sang Mandir

Charni Road

Taraporevala Aquarium

BHULESHWAR

Madhavbaug Temple

Mumba Devi Temple

Minara Masjid

Masjid

KALBADEVI

Jama Masjid **L**

Jyotiba Phule Market (Crawford Market)

K

Marine Lines

Municipal Corporation Building

Back Bay

Wankhede Stadium

AZAD MAIDAN

Chathrapathi Shivaji Terminus (CST)

I

General Post Office

J

BALLARD ESTATE

Patel Stadium

Mahalarxmi Racecourse

Jaihind

JIJAMATA UDYAN

M

Chor Bazaar

Jyotiba Phule Market (Crawford Market)

Jain Temple

Walkeshwar Temple

Chowpatti Beach

Back Bay

Banganga Tank

Raj Bhavan

ARABIAN

SEA

CST

Mumbai University

National Centre for the Performing Arts

Maharaja Chatrapati Sivaji Museum

Gateway of India

CROSS MAIDAN

Churchgate

FORT

India Government Tourist Office

H Flora Fountain

Hutatma Chowk

Brabourne Stadium

OVAL MAIDAN

Mumbai University

Royal Asiatic Society Library

Horniman Circle

G

St Thomas' Cathedral

KALA GHODA

Rajabai Tower **F**

Secretariat

Jehangir Art Gallery

D

E

Maharaja Chatrapati Sivaji Museum (Prince of Wales Museum)

C

Cottage Industries Emporium

World Trade Centre

Afghan Memorial Church

B St Johns

Oyster Rock

Nariman Point

N

National Centre for the Performing Arts (NCPA)

National Gallery of Modern Art

APOLLO BUNDER

Taj Mahal Palace & Tower Hotel

A Gateway of India

Maker Towers

COLABA

Sassoon Docks

0   1 km
0   1 mile

0   1000 m
0   1000 yds

Afghan Memorial Church

T Elephanta Island

and by the end of the century Mumbai was linked with central and northern India by the Great Indian Peninsular Railway and, some time later, with eastern India, too.

During this period, Mumbai became an important cotton town. In an early precursor of globalisation, albeit one that operated in reverse order to the typical 21st-century model, raw cotton from Gujarat was shipped to Lancashire, spun and woven into cloth and brought back to Mumbai for sale all over India. Despite the competition, Mumbai's own cotton textile industry was established in the same period, thanks to the persistence of Mumbai's entrepreneurs. The outbreak of the American Civil War in 1861 and the opening of the Suez Canal gave further impetus to cotton exports, and the city's newfound wealth led to the construction of many impressive buildings.

Gateway of India

The district at the far southern tip of the peninsula, **Colaba**, takes its name from the Koli fisherman who originally inhabited the area when it was an island, prior to British rule. Koli shanty settlements still cower beneath the skyscrapers of **Nariman Point**. After reclamation work in the late 19th century connected it to the rest of the city, the main quayside (Apollo Bunder) served as the landing stage for the massive P&O steamers that brought the burra sahibs and memsahibs of the Raj to India.

Today, Colaba's defining landmark is the grandiloquent **Gateway of India** Ⓐ on the waterfront, a triumphant arch built to commemorate the visit of Britain's George V and Queen Mary for the Delhi Durbar in 1911. Its honey-coloured basalt, decorated with motifs inspired by the Indo-Muslim monuments of medieval Gujarat, catches the light of the rising and setting sun, changing from shades of gold to orange and pink. The King and Queen Empress never passed under the structure, and the monument is – somewhat ironically – better remembered nowadays as the place where the last detachment of British troops slow-marched to their waiting

FACT

Mumbai holds the record for the highest rainfall of any city in a single day. On 26 July, 2005, a drain-defying 942mm (37ins) deluged the Maharashtran capital, causing landslides and extensive flooding estimated to have killed 100 people. It also provoked a storm of criticism for the Shiv Sena municipality, who failed miserably to cope with the emergency and its aftermath.

The fabric bazaar at Mangaldas Lane.

THE KOLIS

The earliest known inhabitants of Mumbai were a caste of fisherfolk called the Kolis, who are thought to have migrated here from the coast of Gujarat in prehistoric times. Their descendants still occupy patches of beach in the south of the city, hemmed in by skyscrapers. In spite of industrial pollution and real-estate pressure, the Kolis continue to maintain their traditional way of life. They're also something of a thorn in the side of the municipality and its land-shark backers, organising marches to protest against over-fishing by trawlers and other factors threatening to squeeze them out. It was the Kolis who first worshipped the goddess Mumba Devi, whose name Maharashtran nationalists insist lies at the root of the word 'Bombay' – hence the Marathi 'Mumbai'.

The Parsis

Although not as influential as they once were, the Parsis are an example of India's cultural diversity, at once completely distinct and yet undeniably Indian

Parsis form a fascinating part of Mumbai's diverse ethnicity. Originally from Iran, these followers of the Zoroastrian faith left their homeland following the emergence of Islam in the 8th century. Mumbai has the greatest concentration of Parsis in India, and while their overall numbers may be small, their influence on the city is far greater than the numbers would suggest.

Migration

The earliest Zoroastrian migrants settled in Gujarat, and it was not until the 17th century, when the British East India Company began to establish Bombay as a trading post, that the Parsis moved south to take advantage of the new job opportunities on offer. They brought with them from Iran an indigenous caste system that they initially tried to maintain, but soon

A Parsi woman.

realised that their limited numbers made such a system impractical, and so abolished all castes apart from that of high priest. This in turn endeared them to the British, who had little patience for the vagaries of the Indian system, with one employee refusing to work with another purely for reasons of caste.

British schools were soon established and enthusiastically attended by the Parsi community, who in turn saw their literacy rates rise high above those of the Indian population (today they're at 97 percent, compared with a national average of 74 percent), and led to even closer ties with the British, who soon had Parsis installed in their most senior positions. From a community largely comprising weavers and small-time merchants, Parsis now rose to prominence as bankers and industrialists, and began to play an increasingly important role in the life of Mumbai as a whole.

Decline

By the end of the 19th century there were 48,000 Parsis living in Mumbai, accounting for 6 percent of the city's population, but since then their relative numbers have gone into decline; they now represent just 0.006 percent of the Indian population. One explanation for this is their extreme longevity: 31 percent of Parsis are over 60 years old, against a national average of only 7 percent. Another statistical quirk is that for every 1,050 female Parsis there are only 1,000 males, against national average of 933 females to every 1,000 males. Out-migration, particularly to the US and Canada, has also taken its toll.

The dwindling numbers are sharply reflected in the declining congregations at Zoroastrian fire temples, or agiaries, throughout the city. Fewer Parsis are also opting for the traditional way of disposing of deceased family members: by placing corpses on top of so-called Towers of Silence on Malabar Hill for vultures to devour their flesh.

Visitors to Mumbai are most likely to encounter Parsis at the long-established eateries around Colaba in south Mumbai. The most famous of these is Leopold Café, which achieved international notoriety after featuring in David Gregory Roberts' hit novel Shantaram, and, during the 2008 terrorist attacks, when gunmen opened fire on its crowded interior, killing 12 people.

For an insider's perspective on life in the Parsi community of post-Independence Mumbai, it's worth seeking out the novels of acclaimed expatriate writer Rohinton Mistry, which include A Fine Balance (1995) and the Man Booker Prize-winning Family Matters (2002).

ships in 1947, marking the official end of imperial rule.

Day-trippers congregate en masse on the paved esplanade fronting of the Gateway, taking rides in silver-plated horse-drawn carriages (*gaddis*), having their pictures taken by itinerant photographers and running the gauntlet of balloon sellers and peanut vendors.

Surveying the scene imperiously from the background is the **Taj Mahal Palace and Tower**. After the Parsi industrialist J.N. Tata was refused entry to the 'European' hotel Watson's, he exacted revenge by constructing a far more opulent competitor nearby. It opened in 1903, and heads of state and celebrities have been passing through its doors ever since (Watson's, by contrast, closed decades ago). Legend has it that the architects who designed the building placed its entrance on the wrong side by mistake (the old main gate used to be on the landward-facing flank, behind a courtyard now occupied by the hotel pool). In fact the choice was intentional: it maximised the number of rooms with sea views.

The huge terracotta dome, Swiss gables and elaborate corner towers of the Taj have become almost as iconic of the city as the nearby Gateway of India. During the 2008 terror attack, TV reports and newspaper front pages the world over featured surreal images of the familiar grey-and-white edifice engulfed in flames and smoke. The building, however, has since seen a complete refit and continues to serve as Mumbai's premier five-star, hosting visiting dignitaries and cricket teams.

Colaba

Head down Colaba's main street, SBS. Marg (still better known by its pre-independence name, 'Colaba Causeway') for 10 minutes and you'll reach the gates of **Sassoon Docks**, where the city's trawler fleet lands its catch each morning. If you can cope with the overpowering stench, it's worth wandering around the quays to watch the fish being flung into

crates of ice balancing on the heads of waiting porters, who carry them at top speed to the adjacent auction halls for sale. Hundreds of boats tie up here during the day, their flags, masts and rigs forming one of Mumbai's more arresting spectacles. This is also where you will see the city's signature dish, 'Bombay Duck', being dried in the salty breezes.

You'll need to jump on a bus, or catch a cab, to reach Colaba's other notable Raj-era monument. Now dwarfed by the tower blocks of Nariman Point to the north, in its mid-19th-century heyday the **Afghan Memorial Church** ⓑ of St John the Evangelist dominated the city's skyline. Consecrated in 1858 as a memorial to those who fell in the First Afghan War, it is a lovely piece of architecture, with Gothic arches and stained-glass windows. Plaques on the walls recall the names of officers who perished in the ill-conceived Northwest Frontier campaign, along with the battle-scarred colours of the Bombay Army, annihilated in the infamous 1842 Retreat from Kabul.

SHOP

The pavement stalls lining the east side of Colaba Causeway (SBS Marg) are good places to pick up inexpensive souvenirs such as soapstone carvings, leather ware, incense and postcards. The best source of quality handicrafts is the Central Cottage Industries Emporium, on Shivaji Marg, where items from all over southern and western India are sold at a discount.

Laundry at the dhobi ghats.

WHERE

Mumbai's former name, Bombay, was almost certainly derived from the Portuguese 'Bom Bahia', meaning 'Good Bay'. In 1995 it was changed to reflect the area's pre-colonial roots. Mumbai is derived from 'Mumba Devi', a popular local Hindu goddess whose shrine was originally on the site of CST (VT) station. To make room, the deity was shifted uptown in the 1880s, where she still presides over a temple in the bazaar district (see page 259).

Kala Ghoda

Immediately north of Colaba is the district known as **Kala Ghoda**, or 'Black Statue', referring to the equestrian figure of Edward VII that once presided over its main intersection. The statue has been removed, but the huge colonial buildings erected around it at the height of the cotton boom still stand as evocative reminders of the Raj at its peak. The most distinctive of them all is the domed **Prince of Wales Museum**, now renamed the **Maharaja Chatrapati Sivaji Museum** **C** (Wed–Mon 10.15am–6pm; charge), on Mahatma Gandhi Road (M.G. Road). A whimsical fusion of Gujarati, Bijapuri and British municipal architecture, the building is of as much interest as the fine collection of antiquities it houses. Treasures showcased in the Key Gallery, just inside the entrance on the ground floor, include inlaid Mughal daggers, Lucknowi *bidri* hookah pipes, and a handful of remarkable 5th-century terracotta bas-reliefs and busts, unearthed in the ancient Buddhist ruins of Mirapur Khas in 1909. On the first floor is the museum's famous collection of Indian paintings, among which are miniatures and illuminated manuscripts from Akbar's own library. Tibetan Buddhist artefacts, coins, Chola bronzes and some wonderfully ornate Gujarati woodcarvings occupy side rooms off the staircase leading to the top floor, where among an array of grizzly weapons hangs a suit of armour recently discovered to have belonged to Akbar.

The **Jehangir Art Gallery** **D**, next to the museum, stages regular exhibitions of contemporary art and crafts. On the opposite side of M.G. Road, completing the cultural triumvirate, is the **National Gallery of Modern Art** **E** (Tue–Sun 11am–5pm; charge), where contemporary paintings and installations occupy an intriguing space converted from a former concert hall.

Bounding the west side of Kala Ghoda are the great **maidans** – open parks that once formed clear fields of fire for East India Company troops, and which now host cricket matches throughout the day. A phalanx of architectural behemoths dating from the late 19th century form a suitably imperious backdrop to the matches. 'A massive pile whose main features have been brought from Venice, but whose beauty vanished in the transhipment', was how G.W. Forrest described the former **Secretariat** in 1903, which today serves as the City Civil and Sessions Court. Next door, **Mumbai University** was designed by the Gothic Revival genius Gilbert Scott, of St Pancras fame. Its centrepiece, paid for by the wealthy Parsi philanthropist, the aptly named Cowasjee Readymoney, is a highroofed **Convocation Hall** whose church-like profile wouldn't have looked out of place beside the Thames. Jan Morris once categorised the library next door as 'Oxbridge Absolute'. In a similarly lofty Victorian style, the **Rajabai Clock Tower** **F**, which overshadows both, once chimed the hours

Tiffin wallah.

with 'Rule Britannia' and 'God Save the King.'

Fort

The name of Mumbai's financial hub, the **Fort** area is a throwback to the all-but-forgotten citadel the East India Company erected after it took possession of Mumbai's seven islands from the Portuguese in 1668. Once British military supremacy had been firmly established in the 19th century, the old ramparts and their three gateways were pulled down and the moat filled in to make way for a much grander downtown area that better expressed the achievements of the Raj. Now, only a few small fragments of the Georgian stronghold remain, but the Victorian streets that supplanted it are still impressive, accommodating the city's biggest banks, financial institutions and newspapers. It's a compelling district to wander around, especially after working hours, when legions of crisp-shirted employees congregate at the *pao bhaji* and tea stalls, girding themselves for the long slog home by train.

The main artery slicing from east to west through this part of town bisects **Horniman Circle** ⑥, an incongruously serene, shady oasis in the heart of the old city, ringed by wrought-iron railings and curved ranks of grand sandstone facades. Formerly known as 'Elphinstone Circle', after a former governor, the garden, which occupies the site of the old cotton auction and parade ground, is overlooked on its east side by the Doric columns and neoclassical pediments of the former **Town Hall**, home to the **Royal Asiatic Society Library** (Mon–Sat 10.30am–5.30pm). Along with copies of every book printed in India, the archives stored on its dusty shelves include more than 10,000 rare antique manuscripts, among them a copy of Dante's *Divine Comedy* rumoured to be worth US$3 million – Mussolini once tried to buy it but was turned down. With its statues of old worthies, dark teak bookcases and paddle fans spinning listlessly overhead, the reading room feels lost in a delightful time warp.

The national pastime played out on the Maidan.

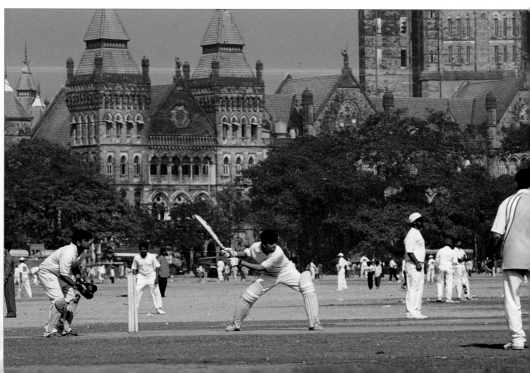

FACT

The very mention of 'Bombay Duck' may conjure up visions of fowl curry, but is in fact the 'marine lizard fish', harpalon nehereus (bummalo in Marathi). Thousands of bummalo fish can be seen drying on the rigging of trawlers moored on the quayside at Sassoon Docks – though be careful if you try to photograph them: the fish market stands next to an important naval base.

On the opposite (west) side of the circle, **St Thomas' Cathedral** ranks among the oldest surviving buildings in the city. It opened on Christmas Day 1718, complete with cannon-proof roof, and is worth a visit for a browse of the memorial plaques to Company servants and soldiers, many of whom met with untimely, and often violent, deaths in the service of the nascent empire.

A five-minute walk west along V.N. Road brings you to **Hutatma Chowk** (Martyrs' Square), a busy intersection formerly known as **Flora Fountain** ⒣. The fountain in question, depicting a scantily clad Roman goddess of spring hewn from handsome Portland stone (nowadays covered with prosaic white paint), was erected in honour of the governor, Sir Henry Bartle Edward Frere, who built the new Mumbai in the 1860s. The rather less elegant memorial that has given the square its new name – Hutatma – commemorates those who lost their lives in the cause of setting up a separate Maharashtra state in the Indian Union.

MUMBAI TRANSPORT

To travel downtown from the airport, it's easiest to take a prepaid taxi from the booth outside the main terminal. (Autorickshaws aren't allowed into central Mumbai.) Mumbai's fleet of ageing, iconic Padmini taxis has been radically overhauled. The new cars come in two categories: standard non-air conditioned, which are yellow-and-black; and blue air-conditioned 'Cool Cabs'. The latter charge 40 percent more. Drivers are generally happy to use their meters, but the actual fare is calculated using a 'conversion chart', which you're entitled to consult, though you usually end up haggling.

The cheapest way to get around town is by bus. The Brihanmumbai Electric Supply and Transport (BEST), operates a network that extends to every corner of the metropolis and its outlying suburbs. For journey planning, consult the website, www.bestundertaking.com, which has a user-friendly 'point to point' facility.

Visitors should probably avoid Mumbai's over-burdened suburban rail network. More than 6 million commuters travel on its decrepit trains each day – during peak periods, carriages carry three times their maximum capacities, resulting in what the rail company refers to as a 'Super Dense Crush Load'. A massive metro system is currently under construction. The first sections are scheduled to complete in 2013, but the full network is not expected to be rolled out until 2021.

Victoria Terminus

Continuing west from Hutatma Chowk, follow the route covered by a tidal wave of commuters each day as they pass between the Oval and Cross maidans to reach **Churchgate station**, a mass of blue-grey basalt and white Indo-Saracenic domes built in the 1890s, and now the headquarters of the Western Railway.

Churchgate and the other Victorian buildings lined up along the maidans may be imposing, but they're small fry compared with the mighty bulk of **Victoria Terminus**, to the northeast. Now renamed **Chathrapathi Shivaji Terminus** ⒤ (CST for short), the headquarters of the **Central Railway** was by far the biggest station in the world when it was built in 1887 – a fitting monument to the Raj at the height of its powers. A British lion and recumbent Indian tiger flank the main gateway, as 'Progress', with arm raised prophetically above the massive central dome, looks down on the traffic swirling past. Inside, polychrome marble, polished Aberdeen granite and richly carved woodwork combine with friezes of carved stone animals and birds to stunning effect – not that the streams of commuters who pour past them have much time to admire the decor. CST remains India's busiest railway station.

A short walk southeast across hectic Nagar Chowk brings you to the **General Post Office** ⒥, another splendid Raj-era vestige, considered as the pinnacle of Indo-Saracenic architecture, which sought to blend Indian elements with civic building. Wander into the cavernous central hall, with its circular stamp counter, for an inside view of the magnificent dome crowning the structure.

Kalbadevi and Bhuleshwar

Kalbadevi, immediately north of CST and the maidans, is the city's main bazaar district: a jam-packed tangle of lanes lined with wood-galleried tenements and pistachio-hued mosques. Before venturing in, browse through the aisles of the British-era covered market on the corner of D.N. Marg and Lokmanya Tilak Marg. The arched entrances to **Jyotiba Phule Market** ⓚ (still widely known as Crawford Market are spanned by bas-reliefs of toiling, well-fed peasants designed by Rudyard Kipling's father, Lockwood. Inside are rows of brightly lit stalls where you can buy anything from wigs to parakeets – though be prepared to haggle hard. The market's future is under threat from developers.

Opposite the market, **Mangaldas Lane** is Mumbai's main fabric bazaar, leading to the heart of the Muslim district centred on the **Jama Masjid Mosque** ⓛ, with its green-washed domes and stucco-covered minarets. In the surrounding streets are many tiny shops selling perfume – a traditional Muslim trade. Keep heading north and you'll eventually arrive at the cream-and-turquoise-coloured tower of the **Mumba Devi Temple**, after whose deity the local municipality renamed the city.

Further north still, **Bhuleshwar** is one of the most charismatic corners of central Mumbai, its bazaars specialising in fresh flowers: lotus blooms, hibiscus and vibrant orange marigolds strung into garlands as offerings for one of the 85 Shiva temples in the neighbourhood. During the 18th and 19th centuries, communities from across western India settled here, and the cosmopolitan feel is clearly discernible in the architecture, which shows Gujarati, Rajasthani and Konkani influences. In a backstreet off the main market, near a couple of white marble temples, immigrant Jains founded the **Panjarapool animal sanctuary**, where 400 or more sleek brown *ghir* cows are cared for, along with countless stray pigeons, chickens and rabbits. Visitors can buy balls of fat and grain to feed to the fortunate foundlings.

Marine Drive

Surrounded on three sides by the sea, life in Mumbai draws much of its character from its beaches, seaside promenades and coastline. The long, gracefully curving **Marine Drive** ⓜ

FACT

The travel writer and critic Robert Byron was less than enthusiastic about British Bombay, which he described as an 'architectural Sodom'. Aldous Huxley was no more impressed: 'Architecturally', insisted the author of Brave New World, 'Bombay is one of the most appalling cities in either hemisphere'.

Bazaar at Mohammad Ali and Crawford roads.

TIFFIN WALLAHS

In the rising heat of late morning, the streets around Churchgate Station are thronged with people pushing hand carts or bicycles laden with little aluminium tins. These porters, distinguished by their traditional Maharashtran 'Nehru caps' and baggy pyjamas, offer a delivery service unique to Mumbai, ferrying some 160,000 home-cooked lunches for local workers from the suburbs each day. They do it using a colour code painted on the lids of the tiffin tins – a system of staggering efficiency (only one box in 6 million goes astray, allegedly). Bill Clinton and Sir Richard Branson are among those who have come to see how they achieve such a success rate. Curious visitors can accompany the tiffin wallahs on their rounds, via a scheme run by the Nutan Mumbai Tiffin Box Suppliers Charity Trust.

EAT

The best place for a quick pit stop while visiting the Mahraja Chatrapati Sivaji Museum is the Samovar Café. Accessed via the adjacent Jehangir Art Gallery, it serves tasty snacks and cold drinks throughout the day on a terrace that opens onto the museum's leafy gardens. Try its delicious stuffed parathas, washed down with a cooling fresh guava juice.

The coast by Walukeshwar Temple, Mumbai's westernmost point.

(Netaji Subhash Chandra Bose Road) links Malabar Hill to Fort and Colaba. It is flanked by a wide promenade, ideal for the early-morning jogger, evening walker and late-night stroller. During the monsoons the turbulent waves splash over the parapets.

Marine Drive ends at **Nariman Point**, and at the very tip of the promontory is the **National Centre for the Performing Arts** , set up by the Tata Trust in 1966. One of India's premier cultural centres, it hosts exhibitions and puts on music, dance and drama performances. **Chowpatti** , at the northern end of Marine Drive, is a stretch of sandy beach. In the evenings, it is crowded with people enjoying the cooling sea breeze and stalls selling delicious Mumbai *bhelpuri* and other snacks. Chowpatti is famous also for its *kulfi* and ice creams. During the Ganesh Chathurthi festival, processions from the city meet here with images of Ganesh, which are then thrown in the sea.

Tucked away in a suburban backstreet 10 minutes' walk north of the Chowpatti seafront, the former house of a wealthy diamond merchant is where Gandhi used to stay on his frequent visits to Mumbai. Gandhi organised strikes among the city's textile workers and addressed rallies as part of his Satyagraha campaign against British import policies. He also launched the 'Quit India' movement from here in 1942. **Mani Bhavan** , at 19 Laburnum Road (Mon–Fri, 9.30am–6pm; charge for non-citizens) has since become a museum to the Mahatma, where exhibits include one of Gandhi's famous spinning wheels, his library and a collection of letters, among them one written to Hitler in the 1930s imploring him to embrace peace.

To the north of Chowpatti Beach, a long promontory bristling with skyscrapers tapers into the Arabian Sea. Fanned by the breezes of the bay, **Malabar Hill** was from the time of the city's birth favoured as a retreat from the heat and frenzy of the Fort, and to this day it holds some of the most desirable, and expensive, real estate in Mumbai.

The thick forest spilling down the south-facing slopes of the hill were chosen by Zoroastrian Parsi immigrants as the site of their mortuary towers – the infamous 'Towers of Silence', or *dhokmas*, where the bodies of the devout are traditionally devoured by vultures so as not to pollute the sacred elements of fire or earth. Hindu cremation rituals, meanwhile, are conducted, as they have been for centuries, around the **Banganga Tank**, an ancient reservoir surrounded by shrines at the far tip of Malabar Hill.

Banganga and its clutch of crumbling temples have become relative backwater these days, but the same cannot be said of the more modern **Mahalakshmi Temple** on the northern side of Malabar Hill, dedicated (appropriately enough for a city obsessed by the pursuit of wealth) to the goddess of prosperity. For non-Hindus, the chief incentive to come here is the dazzlingly colourful flower market leading to the main gates.

A short walk north of Mahalakshmi, on an islet joined to the mainland by the narrowest of tidal causeways, stands the mausoleum of **Haji Ali** ®, whose coffin local Sufi Muslims believe was washed up here after it was thrown into the sea in Sind, Pakistan. Beggars line the whole length of the slender walkway leading to the tomb, which attracts crowds on Thursday and Friday nights, when performances of devotional Qawwali music are staged in the courtyard.

Byculla, Dharavi and Bandra

In the heart of central Mumbai, **Byculla** district was once the powerhouse of the city's textile industry. Partly collapsed chimney stacks, derelict warehouses and the burnt-out shells of cloth mills recall the long-gone cotton boom.

Plans are always being put forward to transform this blot on the urban landscape, but so far only one renovation project of note has been carried out. In Byculla-East, the former **Victoria & Albert Museum**, now the

Dr Bhau Daji Lad Museum ⑤ (Thur–Tue 10.30am–5.30pm; charge), was once applauded as 'one of the greatest boons the British have conferred on India' when it was constructed in 1872. A Palladian-style mansion set in a classical botanical garden, the building has been beautifully restored and merits a visit as much for its architecture as the collection of maps, prints, paintings and scale models relating the Mumbai's colonial history displayed inside. In a plot to its rear, a lone, carved-stone elephant was removed from Elephanta's cave temples by their Portuguese discoverers.

Two wildly contrasting aspects of the city face each other from opposite banks of filthy Mahim Creek, north of Byculla. On one side, **Dharavi** is a vast slum where over one million people live and work in dire conditions, without access to clean water and health care. Amazingly, some 15,000 small factories are crammed into the shanty town, turning over an

School outing to the Victoria & Albert garden, Byculla.

GANESH CHATHURTHI FESTIVAL

One of Mumbai's greatest spectacles is the Ganesh Chathurthi festival, a Hindu celebration held at the height of the monsoon in July and August. Under leaden skies, huge effigies of the god of good beginnings, Ganesh (also known as Ganapati) are paraded through the streets before being immersed in the sea. Crowds of hundreds of thousands gather to watch the event, dancing to the bands that accompany the brightly painted statues as they're carried towards the waves.

The largest mass immersion of Ganesh idols takes place on Chowpatti Beach, at the northern end of Marine Drive. See the Maharashtra Tourism website (www.maharashtratourism.gov.in) for precise dates and other information.

The formerly light-hearted festival has, over the past decades, attracted some controversy. Right-wing Maharashtran nationalists nowadays use the event as a kind of rallying point, sponsoring processions which are marshalled by its cadres of aggressive, saffron-clad senaks – a symptom of the wider communalisation of Mumbai by the pro-Hindu Shiv Sena Party. Environmentalists also have reservations about the festival, claiming the plaster of Paris and paints used to create the idols pollute the sand and sea water around Mumbai when they are immersed on its final day (in former times, *shadu maati*, a natural compound of clay, was used to make the statues).

EAT

During the month of Ramadan, the streets next to the Minara Masjid, just off Mohammad Ali Road, are given over to a lively night market, where Muslims from across the city come to break their fasts. A mouth-watering array of grilled kebabs, pungent curries and piping hot rotis are on offer, as well as racks of traditional milk sweets. The market gets into its stride around 9pm and lasts through the night.

The coast at Carter Road, Bandra.

estimated $1.4 billion annually. Most of these micro-businesses specialise in some kind of recycling: aluminium cans, soap scraps, leather cast-offs, oil drums and other unwanted materials are scavanged by Dharavi residents across the city and brought back here to be remade. The clock, however, may well be ticking on the slum. A $40-million redevelopment project is being pushed through by Mumbai municipality and private backers eager to get their hands on what is among India's most valuable real estate. As with all such projects in India, however, progress is slow. Since the original redevelopment was proposed in 2004, nothing has actually happened on the ground – a fact in part attributable to the raised profile of Dharavi since Danny Boyle's hit 2008 movie, Slumdog Millionaire, which was partly filmed in the area.

A vision of what Dharavi could well turn into if the developers have their way rises from the opposite shore of Mahim Creek, in the form of **Bandra** – north Mumbai's swankiest suburb. This is where the city's affluent elite aspire to live, shop and party. The enclave, bounded on its seaward side by trendy Carter Road where the beau monde promenade on weekends, epitomises the self-assured, go-ahead side of modern India. Hip young things in imported shades and designer jeans hangout in the air-conditioned malls and bars, rubbing shoulders with the many foreign expats who've also made Mumbai their home in recent years.

In the far south of Bandra, the Catholic **Basilica of Mount Mary** attracts worshippers from the low-caste Hindu and Muslim communities on festival days: the church, founded by the Portuguese in the 17th century (but substantially rebuilt in the 20th century after a fire), holds a Madonna believed to possess miraculous powers. Wax models of body parts are piled with candles below the statue.

Elephanta (Gharapuri)

While the city of Mumbai has no ancient monuments, an hour's ride away by motor launch from the Gateway of India (Tue–Sun) is the island of **Elephanta** ❶, site of a magnificent series of rock-cut cave temples (Oct–May Tue–Sun 9.30am–5pm (but boats leave Gateway only until 2.30pm); charge) with large, sculptured interiors, excavated in the 7th and 8th centuries.

'Elephanta' was the name given to the island by its Portuguese discoverers, after the stone elephant they found on the shoreline (this now resides in the Dr Bhau Daji Lad Museum). The same Portuguese mariners inflicted terrible damage on the devotional sculpture they encountered, using some of the deities for target practice. But these depredations have, miraculously, done little to diminish the splendour of the carvings, which continue to exert a powerful spell.

Reached via a flight of 100 stone steps, the pillared cave at the top of the island was dedicated to Shiva. Its centrepiece is the famous Trimurti (or 'Maheshmurti' figure as it's also known), a 6-metre (20ft) tall, triple-headed deity set in an alcove at the back of the cave. Although some debate surrounds the exact date the figure was carved, scholars are united in regarding it as the zenith of ancient Hindu art: no other statue in India emanates such a vivid sense of serenity.

Kanheri Caves

Some 40km (25 miles) north of central Mumbai, near Borivali station on the Western Railway suburban line, is the Sanjay Gandhi National Park. Encompassing tracts of teak forest that are rich in wildlife considering their proximity to the city, the reserve is a popular retreat from the urban sprawl below. It also protects the **Kanheri Caves** complex, one of Maharashtra's most important archaeological sites.

A total of 109 caves were excavated by Buddhist monks over a 700-year period between the 2nd and 9th centuries AD. They range from simple square cells to elaborately decorated monastery halls, connected by a network of steep, stepped pathways. The caves, and indeed the Sanjay Gandhi National Park as a whole, are best visited on weekdays; come here on Saturday or Sunday and you'll find the peace and quiet shattered by parties of noisy picnickers.

TIP

For great views across Marine Drive and the bay, head for the trendy Dome Bar, on the rooftop of the Hotel Intercontinental (see page 461). This is the perfect place from which to enjoy the sunset, lounging on white leather sofas against a background of piped chill-out music.

Kanheri Caves.

RESTAURANTS

PRICE CATEGORIES

Average price for dinner, up to three courses for one person, excluding alcoholic drinks:
£ = up to Rs200
££ = Rs200–500
£££ = Rs500–1,000
££££ = over Rs1,000

Mumbai is a foodie's paradise. Ranging from vegetarian south Indian to rich, meat-based Mughlai cooking from the north of the country, diverse cuisines have been brought here by immigrant communities from all over India.

Churchgate

Pizza By the Bay
Soona Mahal, 143 Marine Drive.
Tel: 022-2284 3646, www.pizzabythebay.in
£££
This popular upscale Italian on the corner of Marine Drive and VN Road does a roaring trade in authentic Neapolitan pasta, pizza and freshly baked pastries. The location's its main selling point, though: grab one of the tables next to the window for a breezy view of Back Bay, and expect a long wait on weekends.

The Tea Centre
Resham Bhavan, 78 VN Road. ££
A cup of top-quality tea can be surprisingly hard to come by in Mumbai, but even aficionados should be impressed by some of the single-estate Assams, Darjeelings and Nilgiris on offer at this charming Raj-era establishment. A perfect place to catch your breath, only five minutes' walk from the seafront and tourist office.

Colaba

Bade Miya
Tullock Road, behind the Taj Mahal Hotel.
£
This kebab-wallah, who's been working from the same sidewalk behind the Taj for three decades, is a Mumbai institution. Try the famous chicken tikka or shish kebab, rolled in hot *rotis*. Evenings only.

Basilico
Arthur Bunder Road.
Tel: 022-6634 5670. £££
This swanky bistro and deli serves very tasty Mediterranean snacks, risottos,

pastas, grills and pastries, as well as good coffee, in a classically styled sidewalk café.

Busaba
4 Mandlik Marg.
Tel: 022-2204 3769, www.busaba.net.
£££
One of the city's hippest restaurants, serving sumptuous dishes from across Asia: Tibetan *momos*, Vietnamese fish sizzlers or Korean glass noodle salad – as well as their justly famous banoffee pie. DJs play on Friday and Saturday.

Cafe Churchill
Ground Floor, East West Court Building, Shaheed Bhagat Singh Road.
Tel: 022-2204 2604. ££
This Colaba throwback serves a fantastic range of wholesome, filling Continental cuisine like no other restaurant in town. The ambience is decidedly cosy, but this is a singularly satisfying experience, and worth the wait if you have to queue for a table.

Harbour View
Aollo Bunder, above Strand Hotel. ££
Sweeping panoramic views over the harbour are the USP of this rooftop joint. It's basically a beer bar, but they offer a tempting range of tandoori mains, as well as Mumbai-style snacks. The perfect spot for an inexpensive sundowner, though not recommended if you're a woman travelling alone.

Indigo
4 Mandlik Marg.
Tel: 022-6636 8999. ££££
South Mumbai's most fashionable place to eat, with A-list celebs swanning in and out. For all that, a laid-back atmosphere prevails, and both the refined fusion food and sophisticated decor warrant the hype.

Kamat
Sahid Bhagat Singh Marg. £
Popular little South Indian snack place on Colaba's main drag – a particularly good spot for fresh *idli-wada* breakfasts; and they do crunchy *masala dosas* throughout the day.

Konkan Café
Taj President Hotel, Cuffe Parade.
Tel: 022-6665 0808. ££££
Haute cuisine from the Konkan coast at surprisingly restrained prices. Signature dishes include tiger prawns in sour *kokum* sauce, snappers

steamed in banana leaves and divine pepper-garlic crab. The flavours are all painstakingly authentic and the service five-star.

Leopold Café
Sahid Bhagat Singh Marg. ££
A legendary travellers' haunt that hit the headlines in the 2008 terrorist attacks. Good if pricey Western food and a bar.

Olympia Coffee House and Stores
Rahim Mansion 1, Sahid Bhagat Singh Marg. £
For a taste of Old Bombay, try this wonderful old Muslim place, with its textbook 'Irani' decor. Settle down at one of the marble tables, and waiters in flowing salwar kameez will bring you the famous house biriyani or shish kebabs with spicy yoghurt dips. There's a special mezzanine floor 'for ladies'. No alcohol.

The Sea Lounge
Taj Mahal Hotel, Apollo Bunder.
Tel: 022-6665 3366. £££
Afternoon tea and cakes at a window seat overlooking the Gateway of India is de rigueur for Raj-ophiles.

Dhobi Talao

Kyani's 'House of Cakes' Bakery
Opposite Metro cinema. £
The definitive old-school Irani café, verging on decrepit but still going strong on a diet of *bun maska* (essentially buttered white rolls) and biscuits dunked in fierce orange chai. Worth at least a pit stop en route to or from the nearby movie houses.

Fort

Apoorva
Vasta House (Noble Chambers), S.A. Brelvi Road.
Tel: 022-2287 0335. ££
Sublime Konkan seafood – including possibly the world's tastiest prawn *gassi* – served in a typically cramped 'Mangalorean' with low ceilings and tacky decor, just off Horniman Circle (look for the fairy lights wrapped around the tree). It also does a definitive Bombay Duck, best enjoyed with steaming hot *appams* and cold beer.

Ideal Corner
12/G Gunbow St ££
Another city institution, where students and local office workers squeeze on to tiny tables for plates

of delicious, reasonably priced Parsi specialities. The menu changes daily but usually features their signature veg or chicken dhansak , aromatic pulao and wonderfully fragrant bread pudding – a Zoroastrian take on the classic British pud, flavoured with rose water and cardamom.

Vithal Bhelwala
5 A.K. Naik Marg (Baston Road), close to CST Station. **£**
Credited with inventing Mumbai's best-loved snack, *bhel puri*, this is a safe, hygienic place to try it. There are 25 or more varieties on offer, along with tasty nibbles such as samosas and *aloo tikki* (fried potato patties).

Kala Ghoda

Brittania & Co., opposite the GPO, Sprott Road, Ballard Estate. **£**
This dowdy old 'Irani' restaurant has a devoted following for its legendary 'berry pulao', made with chicken, mutton or vegetables sprinkled with piquant red berries specially imported from Tehran. But be warned: the portions are gargantuan. Lunchtimes only.

Café Samovar
Jehangir Art Gallery, 161B M.G. Road. **£**
Artists, students and refugees from the stifling heat of the museum form the mainstay of this homely little café, crammed into a long, narrow garden veranda. Stuffed *parathas*, washed down with chilled guava juice or a cold Kingfisher beer, are the regulars' favourite combination, but they also offer main meals such as prawn curry and vegetable *dhansak*.

Khyber
154 M.G. Road.
Tel: 022-2267 3227. **££££**
Classic Mughlai cuisine – from creamy *paneer shaslik* to tender chicken *makhanwalla* – served in opulent surroundings. Waiters in black bowties and paintings by some of India's best-known artists add to the sense of occasion. If you're pushing the boat out, go for the mixed kebab platter (vegetarian or meat).

Trishna
7 Rope Walk Lane.
Tel: 022-2270 3213. **£££**
Mumbai's most famous Mangalorean restaurant was the first to make 'coastal' (ie Konkan) cuisine famous in the city; Bollywood stars, cricket heroes and billionaires have all eaten here over the years – hence the over-the-top kitsch decor and higher-than-average prices. Pepper-garlic crab is the signature dish, and it really is fantastic.

Kalbadevi

Badshah Juice and Snack Bar
Opposite Crawford Market, Lokmanya Tilak Road. **£**
Tall glasses of brightly coloured rose syrup and milk swimming with maize-flour vermicelli, *falooda* is the quintessential Mumbai soft drink, brought here by Irani Zoroastrians from Persia in the 1920s. This cramped little café is its undisputed spiritual home. They also do juices, milkshakes, melba and *kulfi* (India's own sweet version of ice cream).

Khar

Olive Bar and Kitchen
14 Union Park.
Tel: 022-2665 8228. **££££**
Tucked away down a side street and

Tea at the Taj.

serving sophisticated Mediterranean food, this bar and kitchen is very trendy.

Zenzi
Wakefield Road, Bandra.
Tel: 022-5643 0670. **£££**
Elegant Asian interiors and an excellent pan-Asian menu combine to make this restaurant a world-class establishment.

Marine Drive

Haji Ali Juice Centre
Lala Lajpat Rai Road, Haji Ali Circle. **£**
Famous across the city for its fresh pomegranate, *chickoo* (sapodilla), mango, orange and lychee juices, though they also offer *faloodas*, lassis and various milkshakes loaded with ice cream.

266

AJANTA AND
ELLORA

The Buddhist, Hindu and Jain cave
temples of these two magnificent sites
are among the most important
monuments in India.

'The finest gallery of pictures to survive from any
ancient civilisation' is how historian John Keay
described the Buddhist cave murals at Ajanta,
105km (65 miles) northeast of Aurangabad.
Forgotten for nearly 1,000 years, the jungle site was
only rediscovered by a party of British tiger-hunt-
ers in 1819. Today it is classified as one of Unesco's
World Heritage monuments. The frescoes and
sculptures date from around 200 BC to 650 AD, a
period when Buddhism was acquiring some of the
sensuousness of Hinduism. People used to the idea
of Buddhist thought being essentially a negation
of the senses will be startled by the voluptuousness
of much of the imagery. Highlights include Cave
1 with its superb murals, and the painted ceiling
of Cave 2, although for many people the dramatic
cave setting is reason enough to visit.

Ellora, 25km (15 miles) northwest of Aurangabad,
has 34 rock-cut temples representing the Buddhists
(caves 1–12), Brahmanic Hindus (caves 13–29) and
Jains (caves 30–34). The term 'cave temple' cannot
convey the magnitude of the Ellora achievement.
These caves were scooped out of the rocks 10 centuries ago, a feat comparable to carving an entire
cathedral out of solid rock. The work usually began
from the top of the temple and moved downwards
to eliminate the need for scaffolding.

The centrepiece at Ellora is the Kailasa Temple.
Its architects were not modest in their ambitions;
Kailasa is, after all, the mythical mountain where
the gods dwell. In its galleries are recreate scenes
from Shiva myths. One of them repre-
sents the eternal struggle between the
forces of evil represented by Ravana,
the demon king of Sri Lanka, and
the forces of good represented
by Shiva and Parvati.

*Varaha, incarnation of Vishnu as a boar, at
Ellora.*

*Kailasa Temple at Ellora, representation of Shiva's mountain,
was carved out of 85,000 cubic metres of rock.*

*Buddha flanked by apsaras (celestial nymphs) at Ellora. The
Ellora carvings come from three religions, and while the
structures are often similar, differences are discernible: the Jain
caves are ascetic; the Buddhist caves, inspired by Buddhism's
2nd-century attempt at populism, show an austere richness.*

Ceilings at Ajanta are adorned by carved friezes.

THE AJANTA CURSE

Early efforts by 19th-century artists to document Ajanta's art treasures were bedevilled with disasters, leading to speculation that the site was gripped by a malevolent curse. English painter Robert Gill spent 27 years copying the murals, but lost his entire collection in the fire at London's Crystal Palace in 1866. Exactly the same thing happened to another folio of facsimiles when they were destroyed by fire at the Victoria & Albert Museum. A team of Japanese Buddhist artists also lost their copies, crafted on rice paper, after they were buried in an earthquake.

Subsequent attempts to preserve the world-famous wall paintings met with little more success. Restoration work commissioned by the Nizam of Hyderabad in the 1920s nearly destroyed the murals altogether, when the varnish applied began to crack and flake away, taking fragments of paint with it.

Attempts to record and preserve the artwork of Ajanta has proved extremely challenging. The Archaeological Survey of India now oversees all restoration work.

...aintings represent the life of the Buddha at Ajanta.

...eclining Buddha in an Ajanta chaitya (chapel).

The spectacular Ellora caves.

MAHARASHTRA, MADHYA PRADESH AND CHATTISGARH

These central provinces are rich in history, with breathtaking rock temples, forts and atmospheric ruins. The Western Ghats and swathes of the interior are home to some of India's largest forests.

The contiguous states of Maharashtra, Madhya Pradesh and Chattisgarh encompass a vast area of central India. Between them, they hold enough ancient monuments, wildlife reserves, sacred pilgrimage towns and remote forests and mountain ranges to occupy even the most intrepid of travellers for several lifetimes. Yet, compared with other parts of the country, the interior of the Subcontinent sees comparatively few visitors.

Five major river systems flow through the region: the Naramada and Tapti in Madhya Pradesh, which rise in the far east of the peninsula and flow into the Gulf of Khambhat (Cambay); and the Godavari, Bhima and Krishna in Maharashtra, whose sources lie in the Western Ghats (here known as the Sahayadris) and run eastwards. By trapping the lion's share of monsoon rains blowing off the Arabian Sea to the west, the mountains form a precise divide between the lush, densely populated coastal lowlands of the Konkan, and the more arid uplands of the Deccan plateau, or '*desh*'.

A journey through India's core takes in the full spectrum of the country's history: from the earliest Buddhist caves and stupas of the Mauryan era, through the splendours of medieval Hinduism at Khajuraho and Orcha, to the Afghan-influenced palaces and tombs of Mandu, and Maratha forts of the Maharashtran coastline. Along the way, forays into the central Indian *sal* forests for a glimpse of wild tigers will bring you into contract with descendants of aboriginal tribespeople whose presence – most prominent today in rural Chattisgarh – predates even the oldest stone monuments in the Subcontinent.

MAHARASHTRA
The Konkan coast

The narrow, well-watered coastal strip extending south from **Mumbai ❶**

Main Attractions

Matheran
Lonavala Caves
Ellora Caves
Ajanta Caves
Gwalior Fort
Khajuraho
Sanchi
Kanha National Park

Taking in the view at Matheran.

ranks among the least explored corners of India. Known as the Konkan, few of the many tourists heading between Mumbai and Goa consider crossing it overland, but the 500km (310-mile) shoreline sandwiched between the Arabian Sea and the Western Ghats has some beautiful beaches and scenery, as well as a series of wonderful fortresses dating from the era when control of the region's maritime trade was a continual source of conflict. The Portuguese, Siddis, British and Marathas all established strongholds here at one time, some of them on offshore islands from which they traded in rice, precious stones, cotton and silk. In addition to these derelict citadels, the Konkan's settlements possess a distinctive atmosphere, as well as a uniquely fiery brand of coastal cooking.

Travel in the Konkan has always been a stop-start affair, thanks to the innumerable tidal rivers that flow across it, although the recent appearance of a high-speed rail link has made access far easier. That said, as the Konkan Railway (www.konkanrailway.com) runs 10–25km (6–15 miles) inland for most of its course, you'll need to catch a combination of local ferries and buses to reach **Chaul**, on the banks of the Roha River, where

Maharashtra, Madhya Pradesh and Chattisgarh

overgrown basalt ramparts enclose all that's left of a once thriving Portuguese town. **Murud**, 33km (20 miles) further south (and 165km/102 miles from Mumbai), is the springboard for boat trips out to the spectacular island fort of **Janjira**, founded in 1511 by the Siddis, a dynasty descended from freed Abyssinian slaves who made their fortune providing armed naval escorts for Haj pilgrims travelling to and from Mecca. Rising sheer from the waves, the crumbling ramparts of Janjira afford sweeping views of the coast and surrounding countryside.

The next worthwhile stopover, **Ganpathipule**, lies over 200km (124 miles) south of Murud. A popular pilgrimage destination, it's most easily reached via the town of Ratnagiri on the Konkan Railway. Tens of thousands of Hindus pour through each year to pay their respects to a naturally formed image of the elephant-headed god Ganapati (Ganesh). Moreover, a magnificent white-sand beach extends in both directions of the seafront, backed by a string of pleasant hotels.

Coastal citadels

Accommodation and transport options thin out as you head further south, but it's worth venturing into this undeveloped area for the chance to visit **Sindhudurg Fort**, another spectacular island stronghold, located off the coast near the town of **Malvan**. It was built in 1664 by the Marathas and never conquered. The nearest train access is at Kudal station, 38km (24 miles) to the west.

The last, and most splendid, of the Konkan's chain of coastal citadels occupies a lonely promontory at **Vijaydurg**, where the old Bombay–Goa ferry used to dock. Facilities in the sleepy fishing village south of its main gateway are limited to a couple of local chai shops, but you'll have no difficulty in finding someone to show you the dirt tracks winding west across a treeless laterite plateau to a hidden series of exquisite shell-sand coves.

Matheran and Lonavala caves

A busy six-lane highway scythes inland from Mumbai, climbing through

TIP

Local *hodka* boats run throughout the day to Janjira Fort from Rajpuri jetty, reachable by autorickshaw from Murud town, 5km (3 miles) to the north. However, they will only depart once full – not a problem at weekends, when there are plenty of day trippers, but the cause of long waits on weekdays.

Karla Temple at the entrance to the caves.

THE MARATHAS

This whole region was once part of the Maratha Empire, which at its height stretched from Tamil Nadu to modern-day Pakistan and Bengal, a dynasty formed by the enigmatic Shivaji Maharaj. Pre-17th century, the Marathas were known as fierce warriors but lacked cohesion. This all changed once Shivaji assumed leadership of the clan around 1650, and began to extend Maratha rule in all directions. For the next century or so, the Marathas took on all comers, until their defeat at the third battle of Panipat in 1761. The influence of this empire was substantial, representing as it did the re-assertion of Hindu rule in North India after a long period of Mughal dominance, and even today one of Maharasthra's most powerful political parties, the Shiv Sena, is named after Shivaji.

Tea, samosas and other snacks brought to your train window.

Deccan landscape near Karla.

the verdant Western Ghats to Pune, and winding in tandem through the Sahayadri Hills with the rail line built by the British in the late 19th century. The cotton transported seawards along this route from the dark, volcanic-soiled fields of the Deccan fuelled the rapid rise of Bombay. In fact the niche in the range where the hills tumble to the coastal plains must have served as an important corridor for thousands of years, judging by the scale and magnificence of a crop of ancient rock-cut monuments overlooking it.

On a clear day, after rain has dampened the dust, you can see the outlying skyscrapers of Mumbai from **Matheran ❷**, a genteel British-era hill station situated 108km (67 miles) southeast of Mumbai. Yet a more stark contrast between two places it is hard to imagine. Spread over a flat-topped, sheer-sided mountain at an altitude of 800 metres (2,600ft), Matheran is swathed in verdant forest and – thanks to the total absence of motorised traffic (it lies some distance off the main highway) – blissfully insulated from the ravages of the internal combustion

engine. Aside from some delightful Raj bungalows, the main reason to visit the resort is the journey to it from the valley floor via a rattling old narrow-gauge railway. Once installed, there's little to do beyond enjoy the cool air, chew blocks of sticky, nut-encrusted local *tikki* toffee, and savour the panoramas from the various viewpoints that ring the ridge top.

Scattered around the town of **Lonavala**, back on the main highway further to the south, are three main clusters of Buddhist cave temples dating from the Satavahana period (2nd century BC–1st century AD) – collectively the finest crop of ancient monuments in the region after Ajanta and Ellora.

The closest cave to the town is **Bhaja**, 9km (6 miles) east, where a delicately carved facade in the basalt cliff opens to an apsidal-ended hall containing a bulbous votive stupa. **Karla**, 11km (7 miles) east, boasts a spectacular prayer hall writhing with wonderfully well-preserved sculpture depicting dancers, musicians, court scenes and elephants. Next to it, a shrine dedicated to the Hindu goddess-oracle Ekrivi is still a popular pilgrimage destination for members of the aboriginal Koli fishing community from Mumbai. By contrast, the cave temple at **Bedsa**, 12km (8 miles) east from the turning to Bhaja, is nearly always deserted, which allows you to savour the essential serenity that must have attracted Buddhist monks to this region in the first place.

Pune

Pune ❸, (170km/105 miles from Mumbai), was once the capital of the Maratha Empire. The British captured the city at the Battle of Koregaon in 1818 and developed it along the lines of an archetypal army garrison with the usual uncluttered cantonment areas in distinct contrast to the busy, crowded old quarter. Industrialisation has inevitably changed Pune's character to a large extent. A metropolis of over 5 million inhabitants, it's now one of India's boom centres, with a rapidly expanding IT sector. Shiny new shopping malls, car showrooms, gold emporia and high-end, gated residential 'villages' on the outskirts are just some of outward signs of this recent prosperity; appalling traffic congestion and air pollution are others.

Well worth a visit is the **Raja Kelkar Museum** (daily 8.30am–6pm; charge), a wonderful showcase for the traditional Indian arts. It has 36 sections, which include carved palace and temple doors, 2,000-year-old excavated pottery, traditional Indian lamps and 17th-century miniature paintings. Of special interest are a collection of brass nutcrackers (some of them explicitly erotic) and padlocks (including a scorpion-shaped padlock whose 'pincers' lock together). The **Agha Khan Palace** (Mon–Fri 9am–5.45pm; charge), with its Italianate arches and spacious, well-tended lawns, was an unlikely place for a prison, but at one time the British interned Mahatma Gandhi and his wife Kasturba here along with other leaders of the Congress Party. Kasturba died in the palace and a memorial has been erected in the grounds.

Mahadji Scindia, one of the Maratha ruling princes, constructed the small black-stone Shiva temple **Shinde Chatri** in the 18th century. His descendant, Madhavrao II, built an annexe in Mahadji's memory, although his architectural inspiration was not Indian, like Mahadji's, but southern European. The contrast in the two styles is a monument to the assimilative powers of Indian culture. Mahadji's *samadhi* (mausoleum) stands across a courtyard. There is a likeness of him in silver, topped by a flame-coloured turban. **Shanivarvada** (daily 8am–6.30pm; charge), in the Old City, was the palace of the Peshwa rulers who succeeded Shivaji's empire. It was built in 1736. All that remains from a massive fire in 1827 are its

fortified walls, brass-studded gates, 18th-century lotus pools and the elaborate palace foundations.

The 8th-century rock-cut **Temple of Patalesvar** stands in the middle of Pune. Carved from a single boulder of awe-inspiring size, it is still used by worshippers. Other fine temples include the **Parvati Temple** on a hilltop on the city outskirts. A Muslim shrine, the **Qamarali Darvesh**, contains a celebrated 'levitating' stone.

Unrivalled views over the city and the table-topped mountains surrounding it are to be had from **Sinhagad Fort** (literally 'fortress of the lion') 24km (15 miles) to the southwest, where Shivaji notched up a landmark victory against the Sultan of Bijapur's army in 1670. Local legend has it that his right-hand man, General Tanaji Malsure, scaled its sheer precipice with a group of trusted lieutenants using ropes and giant monitor lizards especially trained for the purpose.

Pune is also famous for being home to the Osho Ashram, now known as the **Osho International Meditation Resort,** which is centrally

TIP

The easiest way to get around the three cave sites near Lonavala is to hire an autorickshaw or car for a half-day tour; count on around 4 hours for the whole trip. Soft drinks and bottled water are available at Karla. It's always a good idea to avoid weekends, when raucous crowds can spoil the atmosphere at the archaeological sites.

Votive stupa at the Bhaja caves.

Stupas carved out of the rock at the Bhaja Caves. The complex dates back to the 2nd century BC.

located a kilometre or so from the main train station, next to Koregaon Park. Established by the late and uniquely colourful Osho, this is still an immensely popular destination for spiritual travellers from the world over (see www.osho.com). On 13 February 2010 a bomb ripped apart a German bakery close to the Ashram, killing 17, including a number of international visitors.

Southern Maharashtra

In the heart of the hills south of Pune, **Mahabalesvar ❹** and **Panchgani** are cool hill stations that lend themselves to quiet walks with panoramic views. Horseriding is popular, and horses and ponies can be hired.

One of the most important pilgrimage centres in Maharashtra is **Kolhapur ❺**, 225km (140 miles) south of Pune, close to the border with Karnataka. In fact, it's often called **Dakshina Kasi** (the Varanasi of the south), due to its many temples and the ghats that run down to the Panchganga River. The temple held in highest esteem is the **Mahalaksmi**

An alternative mode of transport in Pune.

Temple (Ambabai Temple), built in the 9th century. To the east of the city is **Kotiteerth**, a temple of Mahadev in the centre of a wide expanse of water.

Kolhapur was the capital of a former princely state and has some splendid palaces. These include the 18th-century **Raj Wada** (Old Palace; daily 10am–6pm; free) near the Mahalakshmir Temple, and a **New Palace** from the 19th century (Tue–Sun 9.30am–1pm, 2.30–6pm; charge), 2km (1.25 miles) north of the city. Kolhapur is also known for its leather *chappals* (sandals). One of India's biggest annual pilgrimages, the **Pandhapur Yatra**, happens in June to July, and attracts over a million pilgrims. They walk from Pandhapur to Alandi, close to Pune, in 21 days, and numbers are rising every year; this is becoming one of *the* religious spectacles of India.

The Northeast

Nasik ❻, 150km (93 miles) northeast of Mumbai, is a holy city. It stands on the banks of the Godavari River, venerated by Hindus, and around 2,000 temples and numerous bathing ghats testify to its sanctity. It is also featured in an episode from the *Ramayana*: when Lakshana, Rama's younger brother, tiring of the efforts of the demon Surpanakha to persuade him to marry her, chopped off her nose, it fell where Nasik now stands. The *Kumbha Mela* (known in Nasik as the *Sinhastha Mela*), held once every 12 years, is the high point of a pilgrimage here, although the focus of the celebrations is at nearby Trimbakesvar. This is safest seen from a distance (at the 2003 *Kumbha Mela* several people were trampled to death).

According to legend, **Trimbakesvar**, 30km (18 miles) west of Nasik, was the site of a dispute which arose between the gods and the demons over the possession of a pot of nectar. In the mêlée, the nectar spilled, and some of the drops fell on Trimbakesvar. The **Trimbakesvar Temple** has an important Shiva lingam and is an imposing monument with splendid carvings. An auspicious site in the neighbourhood is the nearby hill of **Brahmagiri**, source of the sacred Godavari River. As its name suggests, **Aurangabad** ⑦, 370km (230 miles) from Mumbai, has a strong Muslim flavour. The city contains the mausoleum of Mughal emperor Aurangzeb's wife, the **Bibi ka Maqbara** (daily 8am–sunset; charge), a poor copy of the Taj Mahal. There is also an interesting medieval watermill, the **Panchakki**, by a Muslim shrine. Three kilometres (2 miles) from the Bibi ka Maqbara, there are 12 Buddhist caves excavated between the 3rd and 11th centuries AD. The most interesting are Nos 3, 6 and 7; carry a torch.

Daulatabad, 15km (9 miles) west of Aurangabad, has a massive hilltop fort, often described as 'totally impregnable' (daily 6am–6pm; charge). The site dates from the 12th century, and the seven rings of fortifications are from the 15th–16th centuries. To deter invaders further there is a deep moat, once filled with crocodiles and crossed by a single bridge, after which is a dark labyrinth. The views from the top are spectacular. Close by are two sacred sites. At **Khuldabad** is the simple tomb of Aurangzeb (1707), surrounded by the graves of Muslim saints. The Hindu **Ghrusnesvar Temple** near Ellora was founded in the 8th century and houses one of the 12 *syambu jyotirlingas* ('self-born lingams of light'), and is an important pilgrimage centre.

Ellora and Ajanta

Among the most important monuments in India are the magnificent caves at Ajanta and Ellora, both featuring some of the world's most exquisite rock carvings.

Ellora ⑧ (Wed–Mon 9am–5.30pm; charge) is easily accessed from Aurangabad, lying just 25km

(15 miles) northwest of town. The caves here are richly adorned with Hindu, Buddhist and Jain carvings, with the highlight being the eighth-century Hindu Kailasa rock temple. They are best visited in the late afternoon, when their westerly aspect catches the light to mesmerising effect (see page 266).

The Buddhist caves at **Ajanta** ⑨ (Tue–Sun 9am–5.30pm; charge), 105km (65 miles) to the northeast of Aurangabad, not only contain sculptures, but remarkably preserved frescoes as well. Secluded deep in the Deccan backwoods, they were only discovered in the 19th century, which explains why the monuments escaped the depredations of invading armies. To protect the caves from the ravages of pollution, a fleet of environmentally friendly buses takes visitors up to the site.

As much as the caves themselves, Ajanta's position on a forested river gorge – with a spectacular waterfall during the monsoon – makes the place very special. Numbered from the entrance, caves 1, 2, 10, 16 and 17 are

TIP

City buses run from Pune's Swargate stand to Sinhagad village throughout the day. Note that in recent years, heavy monsoon rains have caused damage to the road leading up to the citadel, which may be closed as a result. Check the status of the route at Pune's MTDC tourist information desk, on the concourse of the train station (Mon–Sat 9am–7pm, Sun 9am–3pm; tel: 020-261 2686).

Bibi ka Maqbara, Aurangabad.

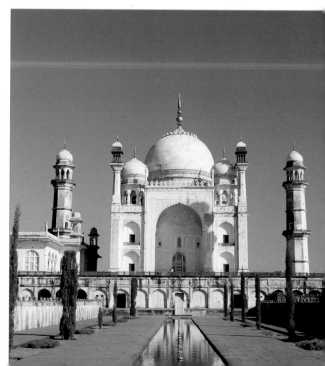

TIP

An ancient pilgrimage trail featuring hundreds of rock-cut steps climbs through the escarpments lining the lower flanks of Brahmagiri hill at Trimbakesvar. Taking you past a string of shrines, the climb gives access to the source of the Godavari, encircled by a sacred *parikrama* path – a wonderful three-hour hike affording matchless views over the surrounding peaks.

Aurangabad caves.

particularly fine, though all are worth a look. (See page 266.)

The far northeast

Nagpur , in Maharashtra's far northeast, was the capital of the Bhonsle branch of the Maratha Empire. Each winter its imperial status is faintly recalled when today's rulers – that is, the provincial government – relocate here from Mumbai. At the geographical centre of India, the region is also famous for its oranges.

Ramtek, a hilltop temple 40km (25 miles) northeast of Nagpur, is so named because Rama, the popular incarnation of Lord Vishnu, stopped here with his wife Sita and brother Lakshmana when they were banished from Ayodhya. It is also associated with the India's greatest Sanskrit poet and playwright, Kalidasa, who wrote his 5th-century epic *Meghdoota* ('The Cloud Messenger'). A modern memorial to the bard has been erected on the hilltop.

To the southwest of Nagpur, **Wardha** is the alighting point for **Sevagram** and **Paunar**. The village of Sevagram is where Mahatma Gandhi lived in an ashram. This has been well preserved and is a place of modern pilgrimage. Paunar was made famous by one of Gandhi's disciples, Acharya Vinoba Bhave, who lived and died there. He is famous for his *bhudan* (land-gift) movement, which encouraged landowners to give away portions of their estates to landless labourers.

This part of India was until relatively recently covered with a vast swathe of jungle teeming with tigers and other wildlife, and although large areas have been cleared, some wild forests remain. East of Nagpur, **Navegaon National Park** protects one such area.

Chandrapur, 160km (100 miles) south of Nagpur, has a fort, several temples and makes a convenient base for a visit to **Tadoba**, Maharashtra's best-known sanctuary. In the park is a lake held to be sacred by local Adivasis; crocodiles thrive in large numbers. **Chikhalda**, 220km (135 miles) west of Nagpur, is the hill station of the region. The nearby

Melghat Wildlife Sanctuary protects an area of thick jungle rich in wildlife.

MADHYA PRADESH

In the heart of the Subcontinent, the large state of Madhya Pradesh – the name means 'middle land' – is primarily comprised of upland plateaux and hills, interspersed with the deep valleys of rivers that flow east into the Bay of Bengal and west into the Arabian Sea. A large proportion of India's remaining forest is located here, with some of the finest deciduous hardwoods in the world – teak, sal, hardwickia, Indian ebony and rosewood. Bamboo is prolific in the hills, and there are magnificent fruit and flowering trees. The Mahadeo Hills of the Satpura Range are the home of the tiger, leopard and other forest animals. Madhya Pradesh is one of the hottest parts of India; in May and June temperatures regularly climb to 45°C (113°F) or more.

The state is also home to many Adivasi groups. Among the most populous are the Gonds, found across central and eastern parts. Western Madhya Pradesh is inhabited by the Bhils, a group of warriors who once held the powerful Mughal army at bay, while the east is dominated by the Oraons, now largely Christian.

Madhya Pradesh is known for its handicrafts, from the weaving of Chanderi and Maheshwar, to the carpet-making of Vidisha, Mandsaur and Sarguja. Other crafts include carpentry, pottery, textile printing and dyeing, metalworking, woodcarving and leather work.

Ancient monuments and sacred sites dominate most tourist itineraries. Approaching from the north, Gwalior's spectacular clifftop fort is the first sight worth pausing at en route to the exquisite medieval ruins of Orcha, from where a four-hour road trip takes you across rolling river plains to remote Khajuraho, site of some of India's most illustrious stone temples, famed for their erotic sculpture. Bhopal, the busy state capital, provides the best base for visits to the ancient Buddhist remains of Sanchi – like Khajuraho, a Unesco World Heritage monument – and to the prehistoric rock art of Bhimbetka. The other great archaeological site in the region is Mandu, where some remarkable, derelict Afghan-style palaces and tombs, dating from the early phase of Islamic expansion into peninsular India, sprawl over a high plateau above the Narmada River.

For wildlife enthusiasts, the state also offers a better than average chance of sighting tigers. In the far east along the border with neighbouring Chattisgarh, the national parks of Kanha and Bandhavgarh inspired the writings of Rudyard Kipling, and hold the largest populations of tigers in the country, as well as an abundance of other wildlife roaming one of the Subcontinent's last surviving areas of pristine *sal* forest.

Gwalior

In the far north of Madhya Pradesh (within easy reach of Agra), **Gwalior** ⓬ was established in the 8th century

---

TRANSPORT

Bhopal, Indore, Jabalpur, Khajuraho and Raipur have domestic airports, aiding travel around the states of Madhya Pradesh and Chattisgarh. Most areas are roughly equidistant from Delhi and Mumbai.

Bhopal: Trains to Delhi (27 daily; 8–12hrs); Gwalior (21 daily; 4hrs 30mins–6hrs 45mins); Indore (3–6 daily; 4–6hrs); Mumbai (6–12 daily; 12–16hrs); Nagpur (12 daily; 6–8hrs); Sanchi (3 daily; 1hr).

Gwalior: Trains to Delhi (28 daily; 5–6hrs 30mins); Indore (2 daily; 12hrs 15mins); Mumbai (3–6 daily; 18hrs 30mins–24hrs); Ujjain (3 daily; 9–11hrs).

Raipur: Trains to Delhi (3 daily; 24–27hrs 30mins); Kolkata (5–7 daily 13–15hrs 30mins); Puri (3 daily; 13–16hrs).

TIP

Tours of Ajanta and Ellora are easy to arrange from Aurangabad. Many itineraries take in both sites in a single day. A bus or taxi from Aurangabad to Ajanta takes around 2.5 hours, while Aurangabad to Ellora is just 45 minutes. Take a hat, mosquito repellent, comfortable shoes and a torch. Flash photography is not allowed inside the caves as it damages the pigment in the paintings.

TIP

A great place to soak up the religious atmosphere of the Narmada is the town of Maheshwar, 91km (56 miles) southwest of Indore, where an 18th-century riverside palace has been converted into a heritage hotel, the *Ahilya Fort (see page 464).* Maheshwar is also famous as a hand-loom centre, producing some of the country's finest hand-woven silk saris.

A sadhu (holy man) sits under the tree in front of Orcha's Ram Raj Temple.

AD and named after Saint Gwalipa, a holy man who cured Prince Swaraj Sen of leprosy. The city is dominated by its hilltop **fort** (daily 6am–7pm; charge), one of the most impressive in India. The Rajput palace of Raja Mansingh, the Gujuri Mahal, built 1486–1516, is the best-preserved section. Located at the northern end of the citadel, it retains much of its original Afghan-style turquoise, blue and green tiling, inlaid in intricate bands of geometric patterns and animal figures above domed kiosks and pierced-stone *jali* windows. The fort also has one of the finest museums of sculpture in the country (Tue–Sun 10am–5pm; charge); its prize exhibit, now on display after years of being locked in the vaults for safekeeping, is a sensuously carved sandstone figurine of a smiling *salabhanjika* ('tree nymph') – often dubbed as 'India's Mona Lisa'.

At the southern end of the fort is the wonderful 8th-century **Teli-ka-Mandir** ('oil man's temple'), while close by is the modern **Sikh *gurudwara*** commemorating Guru Gobind Singh (1595–1644), who was imprisoned here. The steep road up to the Urwahi Gate passes a series of Jain sculptures dating from the 7th to 15th centuries, and the view from the battlements near the ornate pair of 11th-century **Sas Bahu temples** is simply breathtaking.

The current maharaja, Jyotiraditya Rao Scindia, inhabits part of the enormous **Jai Vilas Palace**, built in 1875 on a vast scale that drew on elements of Buckingham Palace, Versailles and various Baroque stately homes visited by its British architect, Colonel Michael Filose. No expense was spared when it came to fitting out the interiors, and you can see some of the more extravagant family heirlooms at the **palace museum** (Thur–Tue 9.30am–5pm; charge), where exhibits range from the usual depressing array of dead tigers to some fine stone carving, Mughal miniatures, Persian rugs and Louis XVI furniture. The real pièce de résistance, however, is the cavernous durbar hall, where the Scindias received King Edward VII and his 1,000-strong entourage in 1875. It features a silver train set with which the maharaja used to serve brandy and cigars.

Gwalior has long been an important centre of Indian classical music. **Tansen**, the great musician of the court of Akbar, is buried in a 16th-century domed tomb, set in the pleasant grounds of his guru, Afghan prince **Ghaus Muhammad's mausoleum**, a kilometre or so east of the fort in the Old City. At the opposite (west) side of town, on Ustad Hafiz Ali Khan Road, is the **Sarod Ghar museum** (Tue–Sun 10am–1pm, 2–4pm; free), dedicated to the most ethereal of India's stringed instruments, the *sarod*. The mansion in which the museum is housed – itself a beautiful monument embellished with sandstone and marble courtyards – belonged to a family who produced a dynasty of virtuosos, among them Ajmad Ali Khan, one of India's great living musicians.

Datia, Orcha and Shivpuri

South of Gwalior are three of the loveliest places in Madhya Pradesh; Datia, Orcha and Shivpuri. Built in the early 17th century by the Bundela Rajput king, Bir Singh Deo, an ally of the Mughal emperor Akbar, **Datia**'s Narsing Dev Palace (dawn–dusk; free) towers over a small town on the main Delhi–Mumbai train line, 30km (18 miles) from the nearest big town, Jhansi. A maze of flying walkways, domed pavilions, hidden passages and terraces looking across the flat rooftops of the old quarter at its base, the palace is one of the most beautiful medieval monuments in India, though one that sees few visitors.

On the other side of Jhansi, **Orcha** ⑬ served as the Bundelas capital until Bir Singh Deo was killed by bandits in 1627, after which it went into sharp decline. Ransacked by various marauding armies over the years, it was finally deserted in the 18th century, since when little has changed. The undulating landscape is dotted with palace and fortress, temple and cenotaph. The architecture is a synthesis of traditional Hindu, hybrid Indo-Saracenic and ornate Mughal. One of the finest sights is the view of the stunning *chatris*, or cenotaphs, from across the blue river with green hills in the background.

About 100km (60 miles) from Gwalior is **Shivpuri** ⑭, the former summer capital of the Scindias of Gwalior. Located on the Vindhyan plateau, the contrast with the Gangetic Plain is immediate. Here are the two lakes of Sakhia Sagar and Madhav Sagar. Surrounding them is the **Madhav National Park**, home to deer, *chinkara* or Indian gazelle, sambar, blue bull, blackbuck, barking deer and four-horned antelope. Also seen are wild dog, and sloth bear. Bird life abounds and peacocks are to be seen in their hundreds.

Khajuraho

Deep in the Indian countryside to the southeast of Orcha lie the famous temples of **Khajuraho** ⑮. Over the course of the period from 950 to 1050 AD, the rulers of the Chandela dynasty built 85 temples, of which 22

WHERE

Evocative sound and light shows are held nightly in Gwalior Fort, near the Gujuri Mahal (Man Singh Palace). From November to February, the English versions start at 7.30pm (or an hour later from March until October), and last for just under an hour. Guides for tours of the fort wait for clients at the main Urwahi Gate.

Gwalior's magnificent fort overlooks the plain.

FACT

The memory of the legendary singer Tansen is celebrated each year in November, when some of India's most acclaimed classical musicians perform in the grounds next to his tomb, with the cliffs and turreted ramparts of Gwalior's fort looming in the background. Several recitals are always devoted to *drupad* – a particularly sparse, intense form of vocal music that originated in Gwalior, and which is still taught in the city's music school, the *gharana*.

Adivasi winnowing rice.

survive, ornately carved with a staggering array of erotic sculptures. The sculptures depict the everyday life of the people and the court in the 10th and 11th centuries. This procession of life itself culminates in the inner sanctum sanctorum. The western enclosure houses the main temples (sunrise–sunset, charge), and the **Archaeological Museum** (10am–5pm; closed Fri; charge) is nearby. For more on Khajuraho, see page 286.

Indore and Ujjain

The rapidly growing industrial city of **Indore** is located on the Malwa plateau in western Madhya Pradesh, an area known for its cotton fields. On its periphery is **Devas**, where the novelist E.M. Forster lived while working as private secretary to the local maharaja, an experience that provided the material for his travelogue, *The Hill of Devi*.

The land of Malwa is sacred, and two of the 12 *jyotirlingam*, or naturally occurring lingam, are located at the **Mahakalesvar Temple** at **Ujjain**, 60km (35 miles) from Indore, and **Mandhata** at **Omkaresvar**. For

Hindus, these two places enjoy a sanctity equal to Varanasi. Every 12 years Ujjain has the great fair of *Kumbha Mela*, or *Simhastha* as it is called locally. The *mela* moves every three years between Ujjain, Allahabad and Haridwar on the Ganges, and Nasik on the Godavari River.

The sacred river at Ujjain is the **Sipra**. The gods and the *asuras* (demons) fought for 12 days for possession of the *kumbh*, or pot, of *amrit*, nectar of immortality, that came from the churning of the milk-ocean. As they fought, four drops fell on the places where the *Kumbha Melas* are now held. Every 12 years, millions of Hindus congregate to worship at these spots. Ujjain is also a centre for textile dyeing using vegetable dyes and hand-carved teak blocks. The *chipas*, or dyers and printers, are found at **Bherugarh**.

Mandu

Mandu , the capital of the Sultanate of Malwa, lies in hilly country 90km (55 miles) southwest of Indore. The approach is impressive; there is a chasm, a deep wooded ravine crossed by a narrow bridge, and on the skyline before you is the largest-standing fortified city in the world – its walls have a circumference of more than 75km (45 miles). The **Bhangi Gate**, a fearsome defensive bastion, leads to lakes and groves, gardens and palaces. The **Jahaz Mahal**, or ship palace, floats on its lake, and the **Hindola Mahal**, or swing palace, appears to sway gently in the breeze.

The **Jama Masjid** has acoustics so perfect that a whisper from the pulpit is heard clearly in the furthest corner of the huge courtyard. There is also the **Nikanth Temple**, a standing monument to the tolerance of Emperor Akbar.

Close by is the **Reva Kund**, said to be filled by the waters of the Narmada River, some 25km (16 miles) to the south and 600 metres (2,000ft) lower down. Legend has it that Sultan Baz Bahadur met his future queen, Rupmati, on the banks of the Narmada when out hunting. He married her on a promise that he would bring the Narmada to Mandu, and Reva Kund is the fulfilment of that promise. On its banks he built a palace for himself and, further up, at the very edge of the escarpment, a pavilion for Rupmati, from the terrace of which she could see the Narmada as a silver thread on the horizon. There is a sheer drop of 600 metres (2,000ft) from the pavilion terrace to the plains of Nimar below.

Bhopal and Sanchi

The state capital, **Bhopal ⑲**, was tragically put on the world map in 1984 by the gas leak from a pesticide plant owned by the US multinational Union Carbide, which killed at least 2,000 and affected hundreds of thousands of others. With compensation still not paid to the victims, the city remains under the disaster's shadow, yet, with its moderate climate, splendid situation on the shores of three lakes, and magnificent Muslim monuments and museums, holds plenty of interest to visitors. The architect Charles Correa designed **Bharat Bhavan**, a fabulous multi-arts centre; it contains a **Museum of Man** (Tue–Sun Sept–Feb 10am–5.30pm, Mar–Aug 11am–6.30pm; charge) that displays striking exhibits. Also noteworthy are the **Archaeological Museum** and **Birla Museum**, with good displays of sculpture. Bhopal is one of the greatest centres of art and culture in the country, and is well endowed with art galleries, museums and theatres. The city was founded in the 10th century by Raja Bhoj. The **Bhojpur Temple**, even in its ruined state, speaks of the greatness of this king, as do the remains of the magnificent **Tal** Lake, which once covered 600 sq km (230 sq miles) and whose destruction in the 15th century by Sultan Hosang Shah of Malwa altered the climate of the region. Thirty km (18 miles) south is **Bhimbethka**, where more than 500

caves with Neolithic rock paintings have been discovered. Five periods have been identified, from the prehistoric Upper Palaeolithic to the early historical and medieval.

At **Sanchi ⑳**, 46km (28 miles) northeast of Bhopal, a great stupa covers relics of Gautama Buddha. Noted for exquisite carvings in honey-coloured stone, Sanchi is classed as a Unesco World Heritage site. Aside from the hemispherical mounds still in place, the site's chief treasures are the finely carved railings adorning the entrance arches to the main monument, the Great Stupa, built by the Mauryan emperor Ashoka in the third century BC. Northeast of Sanchi are **Vidisha** and **Udaygir** (8km/5 miles) and **Gyaraspur** (50km/30 miles), the cradle of Mauryan civilisation.

Kanha National Park

The setting for Rudyard Kipling's *The Jungle Book*, **Kanha National Park ㉑** and its sister sanctuary, **Bandhavgarh ㉒**, in the far east of Madhya Pradesh, are perhaps the state's top attractions. These magnificent parks feature

FACT

In 1610, Sir Thomas Roe, British emissary to the court of Emperor Jehangir, believed he and his companions were the only Englishmen in the Subcontinent. Imagine their amazement when, amid the ruins of Mandu, they met a traveller called Thomas Coryate, who had walked all the way there from Somerset. Unlike Roe, Coryate never made it home again: he died the following year of dysentery in Surat.

SLOWLY DOWN THE NARMADA

From its source high on the Amarkantak plateau, the Narmada River flows for 1,282km (810 miles) across the state of Madhya Pradesh, via a giant rift valley through the Vindhya and Satpura ranges. It's held to be sacred by Hindus: a mere glimpse of its waters can cleanse the soul of sin. The holiest of the pilgrimage sites along its banks is **Omkaresvar**, a tiny islet, where one of the country's 12 most venerated Shiva lingams is enshrined.

The ultimate act of veneration that can be accorded the river, however, is its parikrama, or circumambulation. The great walk begins at the river mouth, near the Gujarati town of Bharuch on the Arabian Sea, and from there heads east to the source in the Maikal Mountains at Amarkantak, where it reverses direction to return to the sea – a trip that typically takes two years to complete on foot.

Recent decades have seen religious activity on the Narmada disrupted by a massive – and highly controversial – dam building project. Opponents of the **Sardar Sarovar** scheme point to the fact that, far from benefitting poor farmers in the region, the multi-billion-dollar development has in fact displaced millions of impoverished villagers, many of them Adivasi (aboriginal) people.

FACT

During the Hindu festival of Maha Shivratri (Feb–Mar), tens of thousands of pilgrims flock to Pachmarhi for the ascent of a sacred mountain, Chauragarh, 10km (6 miles) from town. The crush can make the climb perilous, but come outside the festival and the ancient 24km (15-mile) track to the summit makes a superb hike. The peak is crowned by a thicket of Shiva's tridents, and gives magnificent views over the Vindhya range.

Jahaz Mahal.

grassy meadows, home to chital deer, barasingha (swamp deer) and black-buck, and thick jungles teeming with leopards, bears, monkeys and a significant population of tigers. The best times to visit are from December to March, and comfortable accommodation is available in both parks (see page 464).

Pachmarhi and Bedaghat

Pachmarhi, a former British hill station in the Satpura range 210km (130 miles) southeast of Bhopal, offers some wonderful forest walks, some to remote prehistoric rock-art sites with sweeping views across the distant plains.

Bedaghat ❷❸ is 22km (14 miles) from Jabalpur, in eastern Madhya Pradesh. Here the Narmada River flows through a 5km (2-mile) gorge, between towering white marble cliffs, particularly spectacular on full-moon nights. Below the gorge are the **Dhuandhar Falls**, literally 'smoky falls' – a location beloved of Bollywood moviemakers. Jabalpur is the most convenient place to stay whilst visiting the gorge.

CHATTISGARH

One of the least known and least urbanised parts of India, the sizeable state of Chattisgarh came into being in 2000, when it was cleaved off from the eastern parts of Madhya Pradesh.

Some 44 percent of the land is covered by trees, accounting for around 12 percent of the remaining forest in India. Beneath the surface lie some of the richest mineral deposits in the world, and these deposits are starting to be exploited. Mining, huge power plants, steel mills, aluminium factories and copper-smelters are already here, with little benefit to Adivasi populations.

Around the state

Raipur ❷❹, capital of Chattisgarh, is located in the middle of the state and is the transport hub for the entire region. Largely industrial and expanding rapidly, the city is said to have been founded by the Kalchuri king Ram Chandra near the end of the 14th century, although there seems to have been a settlement on the site since the 9th century. Sights in Raipur include a ruined fortress and a 17th-century temple.

Some 80km (50 miles) east of Raipur is the important site of **Sirpur**. It is mentioned as early as the 5th century AD, and excavations in the area have revealed many ancient temples, as well as two Buddhist monasteries. Two of the most important buildings still standing are the brick-built Lakshmana, and the finely decorated Gandesesvara temples.

In the **Kanger Valley** around 140km (90 miles) south of Raipur en route to Jagdalpur, the hilly landscape is covered in some of India's most extensive forests. Close to the pleasant city of **Jagdalpur**, the **Tirathgarh Falls** decorate the hills with a 250-metre (820ft) lace of froth, before disappearing into **Kotamsar**, whose limestone rocks produce caves full of stalactites and stalagmites. This part of Chattisgarh is the home of the Bison Horn Marias, whose dances and drumming can be

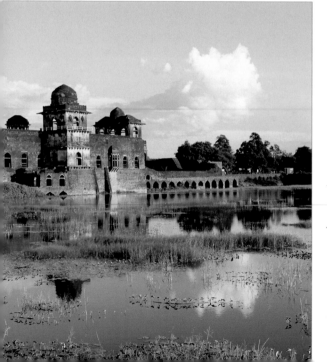

seen at festivals. West of Jagdalpur are the impressive **Chitrakut Falls** on the Indravati River.

In the same area west of Jagdalpur is the **Indravati National Park and Tiger Reserve** ㉕ (Dec–June) in the Dantewara region. This is one of the state's main attractions but, owing to the activities of Naxalite revolutionaries, entry is intermittently restricted; contact the state tourist office for more details (tel: 0771-4066 415; www. chhattisgarhtourism.net.).

Chattisgarh's Adivasi people

About one-third of the Chattisgarh's population are Adivasi. The most numerous are the Gonds, who once ruled much of central India. They inhabited the Satpura and Kymore ranges and their major branches, the Maria and the Muria Gonds, live in the Bastar region. Another numerous group are the Christian Oraons.

The Adivasis of Chattisgarh have retained their identities and customs, largely because previous state governments have treated them with sensitivity.

As a result, quality crafts may be found all over the state, from household and agricultural items made from bamboo to attractive jewellery made from a variety of metals, beads, cowries and feathers. Woodcarving is another widely practised skill. Similarly, wall and floor paintings display a high degree of skill, particularly traditional *pithora* paintings made to mark life-cycle ceremonies such as marriage and childbirth. These usually include the depiction of a horse, which in the past was considered an auspicious animal to sacrifice.

The Great Stupa at Sanchi.

Chitrakut Falls.

RESTAURANTS

PRICE CATEGORIES

Average price for dinner, up to three courses for one person, excluding alcoholic drinks:
£ = under Rs200
££ = Rs200–500
£££ = Rs500–1,000
££££ = over Rs1,000

The food of western Central India, with notable exceptions, is very much the same as that of the central plains, with dishes such as *palak panir* and *puri* with *chana dal* found almost everywhere. Bhopal has a long tradition of good, meat-based, Muslim cuisine that is similar to that of Lucknow. Along the Maharashtran coast there are firery fish curries, laden with chillies and some including coconut milk, while the beach snacks of Mumbai have spread everywhere. The distinctive foods of Mumbai, especially the Gujarati and Parsi communities, are also popular elsewhere in the state.

Maharashtra

Matheran
Most people eat as part of a full- or half-board deal at their hotel, but there are plenty of decent cafés and restaurants dotted along M.G. Road,

in the main bazaar. And be sure to sample the local *tikki* toffee.
Hookahs'n'Tikkas
MG Road. **££**
Tasty kebab and tikka dishes, which you can eat alfresco on a terrace overlooking the bazaar or in a more cosy dining room.

Lonavala
Kumar's
Mumbai–Pune Road. **££**
English-theme murals form the backdrop for this busy Mughlai tandoori restaurant: try the delicious *murg handi* (boneless chicken) with hot naan bread. Beers are served all day, and it does creamy, fruit-filled lassis for dessert.
Shabri
Hotel Rama Krishna, Mumbai–Pune Road. **£££**
This is the affluent Mumbaikars' finedining option, serving a wide range of North and South Indian dishes, and chilled beer.

Pune
The largest concentration of bars, cafés and restaurants in Pune lies to the northeast of the city centre, in an enclave called ABC Farms.
Fish Curry Rice
Narayan Peth, Near Kanya Shala.
££–£££

Lovers of Konkan and Mangalorean cuisine should not miss the trek southwest across town to this fine little seafood joint, where you can tuck into melt-in-the-mouth deep-fried pomfret, kingfish coconut curry, clams and prawns, all served with piping hot bhakri rotis and sour kokum dips. Everything's spotless, and the food is impeccably fresh.
Koyla
Mira Nagar Corner, North Main Road, Koregaon Park.
Tel: 020-2566 2656. **£££**
Extravagantly decorated Hyderabadi restaurant, where the waiters wear *djellabas* and fez caps. Rich curries and slow-baked biryanis are the mainstay, rounded off with desserts crammed with saffron, cardamom and pistachio nuts.
The Place (Touche the Sizzler)
7 Moledina Road. **£££**
Sizzlers (fish, pork, beef or vegetable) and steaks are the house specialities of this old Parsi restaurant in the city centre.
Shisha Café
ABC Farms, Koregaon Park. **££–£££**
Pune's coolest gastro-bar is a thatched structure on stilts. Irani food dominates the menu, with bebop background music. In addition to beer, you can order hookahs with fruit-flavoured tobacco.
Yogi Tree
Ground floor, Hotel Surya Villa, 284/1 Koregaon Park. **£**
Juices, grilled sandwiches, tofu steaks and delicious koftas, as well as some slightly more sinful deserts. Popular mainly with Osho devotees from the nearby ashram.

Kolhapur
Padma
Padma Guest House, near Padma Talkies, Laxmipuri. **££**
If you like your Indian food authentic and spicy, don't miss the special mutton thali at the Padma, a city institution and bastion of Kolhapuri cooking. The curries come in two colours (white and red) and both are as firey as each other, plus you get a plate of biriyani rice and, the piece de résistance, a bowl of their legendary mutton stew.
Shalini Palace
On banks of Rankala Lake. **£££**

Bhel Puri, a delicious snack common in Mumbai.

This was the summer residence of the maharaja, and is still a splendid place to eat. Housed in the former Durbar Hall, the restaurant and bar are evocative of a bygone era, and the multi-cuisine menu and superior service only add to the experience.

Subraya
Station Square. £
Swanky air-conditioned place where you can enjoy the best Maharashtran *thalis* in town, as well as a standard South Indian snack menu (*dosas*, *vada pao*, etc).

Aurangabad
Bhoj
CBS Road ££
Unlimited thalis of fragrant, spicy, pure-veg Marwari food dished up by a legion of busy waiters in pink tunics and orange turbans. Everything's freshly cooked each morning and delicious – especially the traditional sweets.

Food Lovers
Station Road East, opposite MTDC office. £££
A kitsch concoction of bamboo, waterfalls and fish tanks where the Indian and Manchurian food is consistently good.

Ellora
Roadside food stalls (dhabas) opposite the bus stop sell pakoras and other fried snacks, as well as cheap bowls of vegetable curry and rice.
Kailas
Opposite Ellora Caves. ££
Situated close to the caves, this midrange hotel offers the best dining option in Ellora. The multi-cuisine menu is extensive and staff helpful.

Ajanta
MTDC Ajanta Restaurant
Near the main entrance to the caves. £
Slightly run-down but has a reasonable selection of Indian and Chinese dishes.

Madhya Pradesh

Gwalior
Most of Gwalior's best restaurants are in its top hotels. For cheaper eats, try one of the simple *dhabas* outside the railway station.
Indian Coffee House
Station Road. £
Good South Indian meals and snacks, and decent breakfasts (opens early).
Silver Saloon
Usha Kiran Palace Hotel. ££££
Royal banquet fare, as enjoyed by the Maratha and Nepali maharajahs,

served on tables overlooking a lush courtyard. Meals are accompanied by classical music in the Gwalior *gharana* style.

Khajuraho
Bella Italia
Jain Temple Road.
Tel: 989-345 4795. ££
Anyone hankering for proper Italian cuisine will love this cosy rooftop place on the outskirts of the village. The pizzas and pasta sauces are knock-out, they offer free wifi, the prices are restrained and the views over the bustling street below and western temple group full of interest.
Blue Sky
Main Road. ££
The big plus of this popular tourist restaurant, which specialises in Japanese and Italian dishes, is its tree-house terrace, from where you get a sweeping view over the temple complex below.
Raja Café
Main Square. £
Popular Swiss-run travellers' hangout serving Western and Indian dishes (including rösti potatoes, goulash and waffles) in a well-shaded courtyard; also has a book and curio shop.

Indore
In addition to the mid- and upscale restaurants listed below, inexpensive meals are rustled up at numerous *dhabas* around the Sarawate bus stop, and at snack stalls near Raj Wada, in the market area. Try the fiery local nibbles, *ratlami sev* and *namkeen*.
Ambrosia
Fortune Landmark Hotel, Adjoining Meghdoot Gardens.
Tel: 0731-398 8444. ££££
The town's top place to eat: smart, snappy service and glacial air-con. The multi-cuisine menu has dozens of Indian, Continental and Chinese options, but everyone comes for the sumptuous Mughlai specialities.
Ginger Ganesha
13 DM Tower, New Palasia, nr Janjeerwala Circle.
www.gingerganesha.com. ££
Classy south Indian and Chinese dishes, served in an immaculate air-con dining hall in the city centre. All the udipi standards are on offer, only more beautifully presented than usual, and in novel combos. Try their crispy paneer and mushroom garlic dosa or veg hakka noodles.
Status
565 M.G. Road, below Hotel Purva. £
A good budget option. Excellent vegetarian food and *thalis* at lunch.

Bhopal
Bagicha Restaurant
3 Hamidia Road, New Market. ££
A popular restaurant with a strong reputation for its grilled dishes. Bring plenty of mosquito repellent if you plan to eat in the garden.
Greek Food & Beyond
R-8, 3rd Floor, DB City, Arera Hills.
www.greekfoodandbeyond.com. £££
Mediterranean food is all the rage in India these days, and this place up in the swanky Arera Hills suburb serves up some of the most authentic in central India, with dishes drawn from Lebanon, Turkey and Morocco as well as Italy and Greece. On offer are a sunny array of salads, mezzes, paninis, wraps, pastas and sizzlers, and flavoursome roasted red pepper and cashew nut hummus – though be sure to leave room for the chocolate and walnut brownie served hot with vanilla ice cream.
India Coffee House
Hamidia Road, New Market. £
South Indian *dosas*, *wadas* and biryanis, dished up by waiters in grubby white overalls and ice-cream-wafer *pagris*.

Chattisgarh

Raipur
As well as the smart restaurants reviewed below, there is a row of inexpensive snack places opposite the bus and train stations. The city's most popular *poha* stall is at Phool Chowk (7–9am), and also serves delicious *jalebi*.
Hotel Babylon
VIP Road, Rajiv Gandhi Marg. £££–££££
The state's swankiest hotel boasts three top-class restaurants, all air-conditioned. The Shells is the multi-cuisine option, serving Indian, Continental and Chinese; Oriental Kitchen is pan-Asian; and Frontier specialises in Indo-Muslim-style kebabs, tandoori and creamy Mughlai curries.
Deep Rupa
Near the City Kotwali. £
Best place in town for crunchy South Indian *dosas* and other snacks.
Girnar
Ramji Building, G.E. Road, Jaistambh Chowk.
Tel: 0771-253 4776. ££
Old established place near the clocktower where local middle-class families come for classy *thalis* and Bengali sweets – though they also offer a multi-cuisine menu featuring the usual range of north Indian dishes.

KHAJURAHO

The temple complex of Khajuraho in
northern Madhya Pradesh comprises
one of the greatest collections of
medieval Indian temple art.

The astounding temples at Khajuraho were built
under the reign of the Chandellas, who controlled
a large area of the northern Deccan between AD
950 and 1310. Important not only for their exquisite sense of architectural form and proportion,
their facades are fabulously decorated with a myriad of deities, nymphs and, most famously, erotic
carvings depicting a mind-boggling variety of sexual acts. Although the Chandellas were a Hindu
dynasty, there are both Hindu and Jain temples
at the site; the latter are almost all concentrated
in a compound at the eastern end of the site and
tend to be more modest in size and less highly
decorated than the major Hindu shrines.

Many of the surviving 22 temples (there were
originally around 85 scattered across the surrounding countryside) are in a remarkable state
of preservation. This is due mainly to their relative isolation. When the early Muslim invaders of
the Delhi Sultanates arrived in the 10th century
they destroyed or defaced many Hindu shrines.
Khajuraho was at the time far removed from the
centres of conflict, and so was ignored, and the
temples were gradually forgotten by the outside
world. By the time they were 'rediscovered' by
British scholars in the late 19th century, they had
been surrounded by thick jungle for centuries.

This isolation also posed problems for tourists until a new railway line opened in late 2008
between the site and Mahoba (63km/39 miles
away), making access much easier. In addition to
local services, trains run straight through from
Delhi five times a week, taking around eight hours
to reach Nizamuddin overnight.

*The temples are designed to lead one's eyes from ground level
ever upwards to the ultimate heaven, Kailasa.*

*Covered with exquisite carvings, the lofty, square bulk of the
Duladeo Temple, dedicated to Shiva, is an impressive sight,
especially at sunset. It is believed to date from around 1130,
making it one of the latest Hindu shrines at the site.*

*Dating from c.1025, the Lakshmana
Temple was the first built in the
Khajuraho style, where all
elements of the temple
are architecturally
unified.*

Erotic carvings at the Kandariya Mahadeva Temple.

EROTIC SCULPTURES

The Kandariya Mahadeva Temple is considered to be the greatest achievement of the Khararaho temple builders' art. It, more than any other, demonstrates a perfection of form and silhouette that seems scarcely credible on first sight. However, it is also famed for its exceptional decoration and particularly its erotic sculpture.

When the British first encountered the temples they were shocked (and, no doubt, secretly titillated) by such flagrant displays of what, to their eyes, was pornography. This was, of course, to misunderstand the intention behind the sculpture. To the medieval Hindu mind the unity of the male and female principles bound the universe together; sexual union was not only considered a manifestation of this perfect union but also a homage to the creation of the universe itself. Related to this metaphysical ideal was Tantra, a form of physical devotion, akin to yoga, that sought this unity through sex. Above all, however, these are very humane carvings, celebrating an essential part of human existence and can be, at times, a little tongue-in-cheek: look out for the nymph who part hides her face in either amusement or embarrassment, and for the man having sex with a horse.

e towers of the shrines seem almost fantastical as they rise
m the archaeological park.

e Lakshmana temple is dedicated to Rama's brother and
mpanion in his fight against the demon Ravana.

A good time to visit Khajuraho is
in March during the annual
10-day dance festival, when
India's leading classical dancers
perform on the podium of the
largest temple, Kandariya
Mahadeva.

A beach hut at Palolem.

GOA

Home to India's most popular and renowned beach resorts, the former linchpin of Portugal's vast Asian trade empire has evolved a uniquely hybrid culture that still lures Europeans to its shores.

Until the arrival off its shores in 1510 of Alfonso Albuquerque's fleet of Portuguese *caravelas*, Goa was merely one among many small ports dotted along India's southwest coast that owed its existence to the trade in horses with Arabia. For many centuries, the warring Hindu and Muslim empires inland had imported stallions bred in the Persian Gulf, exchanging them for Indian spices and diamonds. Albuquerque recognised that a huge fortune could be made by any country possessing a navy strong enough to control this trade. He promptly identified Goa as the perfect base for his country's expanding maritime empire, annexing it from Yusuf Adil Shah, the Sultan of Bijapur, in a ferocious battle at the mouth of the Mandovi River.

Over the ensuing century and a half, the tiny colony blossomed into Asia's most prosperous – the nexus of a trade network stretching from Macau to Brazil, with a population greater even than that of Rome or Lisbon. Glittering Baroque churches and high-roofed *palácios* rose above the palm canopy, and the bazaars of the old Rua Direita groaned under the weight of gold, silks and precious stones. But the boom was short-lived. Outmanoeuvred by rival European powers, the Portuguese eventually lost their grip on their sea-borne trade; the harbour silted up and thousands of Goans perished from disease.

Portugal, however, held on to their colony for 451 years (a much longer lifespan than that of the British Raj), only relinquishing control after Nehru sent in the Indian army in 1961. A tidal wave of changes were unleashed by the 'Liberation' (which some Goans still refer to as 'the Invasion'), but the state has nonetheless preserved its Indo-European identity.

Main Attractions
Panaji
Calangute
Anjuna Beach
Vagator Beach
Benaulim
Palolem
Old Goa

Panaji.

TIP

Juice from cashew fruit and palm sap, tapped two or three times daily and fermented in terracotta pots to make *todi*, provide the raw ingredients for Goa's special brand of hootch, *feni*. The Portuguese first introduced distillation to the region in the 16th century, since when villages in the Christian belt of Goa have resounded to the roar of the *feni* still. You can order it in most local bars – it makes a delicious cocktail when mixed with lemonade.

Goa's European influences

Although brutally imposed by the Portuguese, Christianity now coexists harmoniously with indigenous Hinduism, and the two have intermingled over the years, giving rise to unique forms of architecture, cuisine, dress and language. Wherever you travel in Goa you will come across whitewashed, gabled church facades, and as many flatteringly tailored, Catholic-style dresses as saris, while – most noticeably – every town and village sports an abundance of bars and liquor shops.

European-influenced attitudes to alcohol are only one reason why Goa has become a favourite holiday destination for sun-starved Europeans. Its exquisite beaches – washed by the warm surf of the Arabian Sea, and backed by ranks of swaying coconut trees – provide enough incentive in themselves. On the other hand, development has spiralled out of control in places, with whole villages smothered by luxury resorts. Yet while it's fair to say that none of Goa's beaches have come through the tourism revolution

entirely unscathed, a few relatively quiet stretches of coast survive where you can see what the place must have been like three or four decades ago, when it was visited only by homesick Goan expats and a handful of intrepid hippy travellers.

Regulations concerning the purchase of property in Goa were always considerably more liberal than elsewhere in India, leading to Europeans of all nationalities and professions making Goa their home.

Over time, however, these regulations were consistently abused, with the Russians in particular buying up huge swathes of shorefront property, leading eventually to a clamping down on foreign investment. The contrast between the high and low seasons couldn't be more marked. From October to February the state is inundated with tourists of all descriptions; trendy young Mumbaikars looking to party hard, backpackers, Russian package tourists and jet-setting celebs. Outside these months it is a different place: hotter and wetter but calmer and less frenetic, with only the permanent residents still around.

House at Fontainhas, Panaji.

Away from the beaches, the remains of the former Portuguese capital at Old Goa, in addition to pockets of decaying colonial architecture elsewhere, offer the most memorable day trips inland, with a glimpse of the 'real' Goa that was, and far fewer visitors throughout the year than on the coast.

Churches and carnivals

As you travel through Goa's villages, the imprint of four and a half centuries of Catholicism is evident. The Portuguese came not only to conquer, but also to preach. Presiding over every village, commanding the hilltops, hugging the shores of rivers, are sparkling white churches, crosses and small shrines, built mostly in the 16th and 17th centuries in the Gothic and Baroque styles.

On the feast day of the patron saint – and every village has one – the whole village is in attendance. The image of the saint, brightly decorated, is carried in procession by priests and laity to the chanting of prayers and litanies, recited or sung, accompanied by a violin or even a brass band.

Goa's Carnival takes place in February, and towns and villages celebrate for three days. Processions of floats and dancers attract huge crowds of revellers from out of state, and the Kingfisheer beer and Indian whiskey flow freely.

Panaji

Panaji (Panjim) ❶, the capital of Goa, situated on the southern bank of the Mandovi River, is centred on a church and the square in front of it. **Largo da Igreja** (Church Square) is an impressive ensemble, dominated by the dazzling Baroque facade of the **Church of the Immaculate Conception**, its proportions emphasised by the white-balustraded stairway in front. Built in 1541, its twin towers were the first signs of 'home' for the sailors who made the long voyage from Lisbon.

Panaji has several squares, the houses lining them rising directly above the wide streets. Most of these villas, painted in pale yellow, green or deep rose, with their embellishments picked out in white or some contrasting colour, feature shell windows opening onto wrought-iron balconies. Particularly quaint is the old residential area of **Fontainhas**, where narrow cobbled alleys weave past closely knit houses with tiled roofs, overhanging balconies and carved pillars, much as one would expect to find in any provincial town in Portugal. Winding streets echo to the splutter of motorcycles and the chatter of locals. Given an expensive facelift in 2004, when Panaji was nominated as the permanent venue for India's international film festival, the broad riverside boulevard running along the Mandovi is fronted by some of the grandest public buildings, including the old **Secretariat**, converted by the Portuguese in 1615 from the Adil Shah's former palace.

Further west, the **Menezes-Braganza Institute** (Mon–Fri 9.30am–1pm,

Painted trees mark the site of a full-moon beach party. Goa used to be well known for its party scene, but this is now largely a thing of the past. The full-moon party at Christmas is the exception: all the local taxi drivers will know where, and when, the main event will take place.

GOA TRANSPORT

Flights: Goa's bustling airport, Dabolim, is a 45-minute drive south of Panaji. A fleet of new taxis are on hand to shuttle travellers to and from the large terminal building that replaced the one erected in the 1990s to serve charter tourists. The nearest railway station to the airport is in Vasco da Gama, around 5km (3 miles) away; it can be reached by local bus or taxi. In addition to a wealth of international flights from Europe (mainly Russia) and the Gulf, it is served by frequent daily flights from Mumbai (14–15 daily); Delhi (7–8 daily); Bengaluru (6–8 daily); Chennai (1 daily). There are also daily flights to Hyderabad, Jaipur, Kochi, Kolkata, Pune and Thiruvananthapuram.

Trains: Goa is on the scenic Konkan Railway, connecting it with Mumbai and Maharashtra to the north, and coastal Karnataka and Kerala to the south. There is also a broad-gauge line running east into the Deccan – handy for visits to the ruins of Hampi.

Trains run from Madgaon (Margao) station in south Goa to Delhi (4 daily; 30–38hrs); Ernakulam/Kochi (2 daily; 15hrs); Gokarna (1 daily; 1hr 50mins); Hospet (for Hampi; 4 weekly; 7–8hrs); Mangalore (7 daily; 5–6hrs); Mumbai (15 daily; 11hrs 15hrs 30mins); Pune (1–2 daily; 12hrs); Thiruvananthapuram (1–2 daily; 16–20hrs); and Udupi (4 daily; 4hrs).

TIP

Goa is unique in India for having motorcycle taxis. Riding bikes distinguished by yellow mudguards, 'pilots' – as they're better-known – charge less than autorickshaws for short trips across town, and cut more quickly through the rush-hour traffic jams. You'll find them waiting outside the bus stop in Panaji and at ranks around town.

2–5.45pm; free) is the most imposing of many civic structures erected during the governorship of Dom Manuel E'Castro (1826–35), Panaji's 'Founding Father'. Spectacular panels of traditional Portuguese *azulejos* (painted ceramic tiles) enliven the main entranceway, depicting scenes from the nationalistic epic of Luís Camões, *Os Luisadas*, including one where admiral Vasco Da Gama encounters the Zamorin of Calicut on his first voyage to India in 1498.

Margao and Mapusa

Headquarters of Goa's most fertile district (Salcete), **Margao ❷** is the second-largest town in Goa. Some 27km (17 miles) south of Panaji, an indication of its former prominence is the number and size of Portuguese-era *palácios* surviving in the well-to-do north of town. The grandest, boasting deep-pillared verandas, high pitched roofs and huge oyster-shell windows, line the streets radiating from the **Largo da Igreja**, a red-dirt square where the massive **Church of the Holy Spirit** (daily 6.30am–noon, 4–9pm) stands as one of the finest

surviving late-Baroque churches in India.

Keep heading west from the rear of the church along Lourenço Road for around 200 metres/yds and you will arrive at the granddaddy of all Margao's colonial mansions, **Sat Banzam Gor**. Built in 1790 by a private secretary of the Portuguese viceroy, the house boasts an elegant Rococo facade, colour-washed in oxide-red and white, and five textbook Goan roof gables. The Da Silva family, descendants of the original owners, still live in the house, but do not encourage casual visits.

Goa's beach culture

Strung along Goa's 100km (60-mile) coastline are some superb beaches – stunning stretches of golden sand and surf edging the aquamarine expanse of the Arabian Sea. **Fort Aguada ❸**, 10km (6 miles) west of Panaji, is near the luxury resorts at **Sinquerim** beach and the popular package resort of **Candolim**. North along the coast 6km (4 miles) from Fort Aguada is **Calangute ❹** beach, favoured by bus-loads of day

Mapusa market.

trippers from other Indian states. This long stretch of beach, lined with restaurant shacks, ends at the mouth of a small river in **Baga**, around which sprawls the liveliest of the state's resorts, attracting a mainly young, hard-drinking crowd. Across the river are a few good cafés and restaurants.

A walk along a cliff-side path that skirts the ocean leads to **Anjuna beach ❺**, also approachable by road, 4km (2.5 miles) north of Calangute. Traditionally popular with hippies, this beautiful beachfront is fringed with coconut palms, and the gentle sea makes it ideal for bathing, except in the afternoons when local tourist groups descend to view the 'naked foreigners', or during the famous Wednesday flea market.

Around the corner from Anjuna are the superb white-sand beaches of **Vagator**, centre of Goa's vestigial trance-dance scene. For excellent views of the coastline, climb up to the ruined Portuguese fort at the fishing village of **Chapora**.

Further north still, the broad Chapora River marks the border with

Goa's northernmost district, reached via an impressive concrete bridge. The first village in this area, Morjim, has been colonized by long-staying, big-spending Russians and consequently has an unwelcoming atmosphere, but a more relaxed vibe holds sway at nearby Aswem and Mandrem, where a row of chic beach restaurants, lounge bars and boutiques have become the first choice of international A-listers and celebs (Brad and Angelina, Paris Hilton and Kate Moss have all dodged the paparazzi here in recent years).

Finally, in the far north, **Arambol ❻** is where all the alternative types migrated to when Anjuna became too hectic. Fronted by a wonderful white sand beach, the village is the place to come to dabble in yoga and other holistic therapies, and offers accommodation and top local seafood at a fraction of the price of spots further south down the coast.

Colva beach, 25km (15 miles) south of Panaji, with a 25km (15-mile) stretch of silver-grey sand running to Cabo de Rama, is a remarkable sight. Dozens of super-luxurious hotel resorts have

SHOP

Margao market is a great place to shop for textiles. You can buy high-quality hand-loom cotton and silk at the Khadi Gramodiyog store on the east side of the Municipal Gardens square, and have it made into shirts, dresses and suits at any number of tailors. One that's highly recommended is Señor Tailors, just off the square near the Khadi Gramodiyog shop. This is where local Catholic families have their wedding suits and dresses made.

Anjuna.

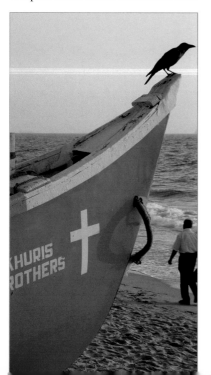

GOAN PALÁCIOS

Nothing encapsulates the elegant hybrid nature of Goan culture quite as well as the architecture of its colonial-era mansions, or *palácios*. While many fine specimens line the older streets of Panaji, Margao and Mapusa, the most photogenic nestle amid the paddy fields and palm groves further inland. They date from the middle phase of Portuguese rule, a time when high-ranking, Goan-born officials and merchants were making profits from trade in opium and gemstones, as well as commercial interests in Portugal's African colonies. Many amassed vast fortunes, which they spent converting their ancestral homes according to the fashionable European styles of the day.

Around traditional Hindu courtyards would be piled sumptuous Classical facades with fancy Rococo mouldings. Flights of formal steps would lead to gabled entranceways, where long stone seats were set along deep verandas. Inside, Belgian crystal chandeliers, Macau porcelain and ornately carved furniture embellished sumptuous salons and ballrooms.

Of the few surviving ancestral Goan homes open to the public, by far the most impressive is the Braganza-Perreira/Menezes-Braganza house, in **Chandor**, 13km (8 miles) east of Margao in south Goa and the wonderful Palacio do Deao in Quepem (www.palaciododeao.com), half an hour further southeast. Both are open to the public.

mushroomed here, and the formerly pristine beach is no longer tranquil. **Benaulim**, 2km (1.25 miles) south, has a better beachfront, while a further 40km (25 miles) south in **Canacona** district the rocky coast harbours beautiful beaches such as **Agonda**, currently the quietest resort in the state, and **Palolem** ❼, now the destination of choice for most backpackers who winter in Goa.

The full-moon party scene for which Goa was once famous has, thanks to a clampdown by the local government and police, all but fizzled out over the past decade. Instead, you can party at one of several nightclubs dotting the north coast. Tito's, in Baga, is the most famous, but Cuba Cubana, on a hilltop at nearby Arpora, is more popular with foreigners. Further north in Vagator, the Nine Bar and Hilltop's DJs spin textbook Goa trance, the brand of techno that grew out of the 1990s beach raves – for a mainly Indian and Russian crowd.

Old Goa

No trip to this corner of India is complete without a visit to the 16th- and 17th-century delights of **Old Goa** ❽, 'Rome of the Orient', with its magnificent churches, sumptuous buildings, stately mansions and broad streets.

The **Sé Cathedral** Ⓐ (Cathedral of St Catherine) remains one of the greatest monuments of the Portuguese colonial period. Completed in 1619, it is the largest Christian church in South Asia, and a grand example of Renaissance architecture. The cathedral's 80-metre (260ft) aisle culminates in a richly carved gilt altarpiece – one of the finest in India. There is a font in the church, possibly a vessel of Hindu origin, said to have been used by Goa's patron saint, St Francis Xavier. Within the compound of the cathedral, but facing the opposite direction, is the **Church of St Francis of Assisi** Ⓑ, with a stucco ceiling and a profusion of carvings.

The majestic **Basilica of Bom Jesus** Ⓒ is famous as the site of St Francis Xavier's mausoleum. It's a beautiful building, blending neoclassical restraint with Baroque exuberance and a flamboyant late-Renaissance

Traditional boat at Palolem beach.

facade. The Jesuits were the first Christians to undertake large-scale missionary activity in Portugal's new Asian possessions – the *Estado da India* – and Francis Xavier, a Basque priest, was their most successful emissary. Housed in a small chapel in the basilica's south transept, his supposedly incorruptible remains are Old Goa's most revered relic

The **Church of St Cajetan** 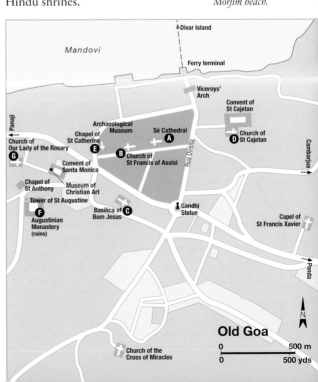, near the ferry wharf, complete with two belfries and a cupola, was modelled on the Basilica of St Peter in Rome by its Italian architect. Also near the riverbank stands the **Chapel of St Catherine** 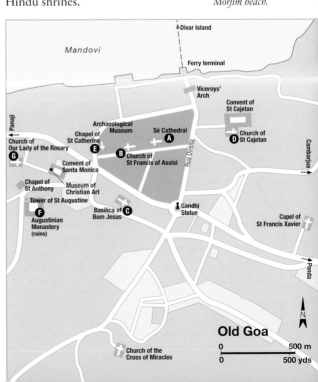, built on the site of the bitterest fighting during Albuquerque's conquest of Goa in 1510.

A few minutes' walk up the road from the basilica is **Monte Santo** (Holy Hill) where one, allegedly haunted, tower of the **Church of the Augustinian Monastery** 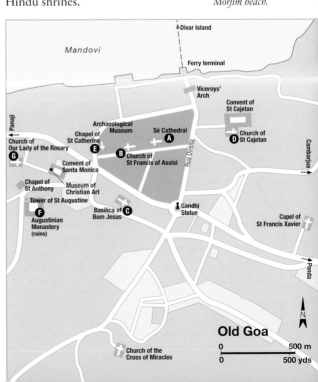 is all that remains of a once-splendid vaulted structure. Adjacent to the ruins stands the **Convent of St Monica**, once one of the largest nunneries in the Portuguese Empire.

Past the convent's buttresses, on a grassy mound at the edge of a steep slope, is the shell of the **Church of Our Lady of the Rosary** 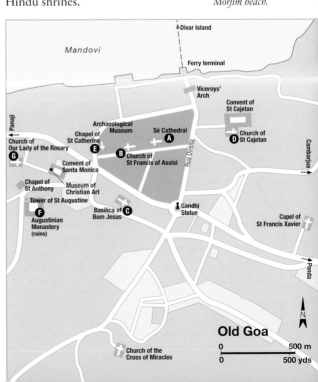, one of the earliest to be built in Goa. It contains the intricately carved alabaster tomb of Dona Caterina, wife of the 10th viceroy and the first Portuguese woman to hazard the arduous voyage to India.

The Goan interior

The interior of Goa is quite different from the coastal areas, and sees very few tourists. Those who were determined to preserve their ancient faith in the face of Portuguese proselytisation removed their deities from the coastal shrines and fled to the mountainous interior.

The **Sri Mangesh Temple** 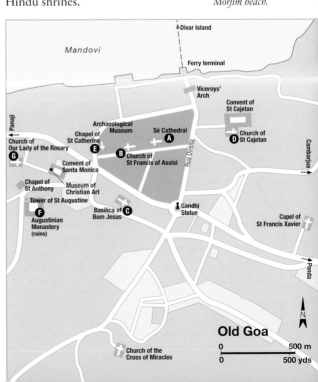 (dedicated to Lord Shiva) and the **Shanta-Durga** (to goddess Parvati) and **Nagesh** temples, 22km (13 miles) east of Panaji near Ponda, are among the most frequented in Goa. Ornate, Baroque interiors and several-storey *dipmals* – elaborate lamp towers – are unique features of these fine Goan Hindu shrines.

FACT

For the week preceding the Feast of St Francis on 3 December, Catholics from across the state, and beyond, travel to Old Goa to worship at the mausoleum of St Francis Xavier. Many families sleep under the stars to bag the best pews for Mass, held at dawn in the Basilica. Every 10 years, the event takes on a more intense complexion when the incorruptible corpse of the saint is displayed for veneration: the next 'Exposition' will be in 2014.

Morjim beach.

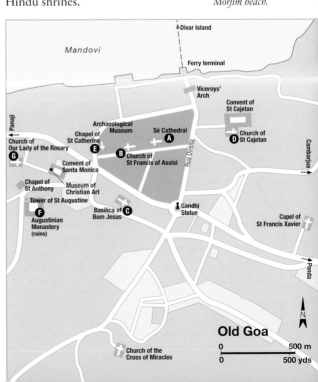

RESTAURANTS

PRICE CATEGORIES

Average price for dinner, up to three courses for one person, excluding alcoholic drinks:

£ = under Rs200
££ = Rs200–500
£££ = Rs500–1,000
££££ = over Rs1,000

The contribution of Goa to Indian cuisine is considerable. As well as coconut milk- and fish-based curries that are similar to elsewhere in coastal India, the most distinctive dishes are those drawn from its Portuguese heritage. This means that Goa is one of the few places where pork is widely eaten (among the Christian community), and it crops up in such dishes as *vindaloo*, a curry made with chilli and vinegar and spicy sausages.

Panaji

Mum's Kitchen
Dr D Bandodkar (DB) Marg (Panjim–Miramar Rd).
Tel: 901-109 5557, wwww.mumskitchengoa.com. £££
Authentic, wonderfully tasty Goan-Catholic food, prepared according to recipes collected from the owners' elderly relatives. Owners Ronnie and Suzette rustle up everything from standard fish curry to festival favourites such as cafreal and xacuti – with juicy tiger prawns if you feel like pushing the boat out.

Shiv Sagar
MG Road. £–££
The capital's slickest South Indian fast-food joint, or *udipi*, though you still have to squeeze into formica booths to eat here. The crunchy *masala dosas* (which you can order with spinach mixed into the batter), *idly-wada-sambar* and samosas are excellent, as is its popular Bombay-style *bhaji-pao*; and they make wonderful freshly squeezed fruit juices and lassis.

Vivanta by Taj
Off D.B.Bandodjar Road. £££–££££
Goa's finest pan-Asian eating experience, complete with a live teppanyaki counter. If you're in Panjim and feeling the need for air conditioning and sushi then this is the place to head for.

Viva Panjim!
178 Rua 31 de Janeiro, behind Mary

Immaculate High School, Fontainhas. ££
Crammed into an alleyway amid the colour-washed backstreets of the capital's 19th-century enclave, Fontainhas, this is the perfect spot to sample traditional Indo-Portuguese and Goan food: prawn *xacutis*, *ambot tik* and grilled kingfish *rechead*.

Margao

Banjara
££
A smart basement restaurant near the main market area serving quality Mughlai food.

Mapusa

F.R. Xavier's
Municipal Market complex. £
The perfect pit stop if you've worked up an appetite shopping in Mapusa's market. The vegetable and beef flaky-pastry 'patties', prawn curry and Goan-style samosas are all delicious, but the old-world atmosphere is the main appeal here.

Candolim

Bomra's
247 CHOGM (Fort Aguada) Road
Tel: 982-214 9633, www.bomras.com. ££££
Fine dining with a Burmese twist: spinach wraps in tahini sauce and snapper with lime and chill are just two of the gastro delights on offer at this gem of a restaurant, tucked away on the south side of Candolim. And they do knock-out mojitos.

Pete's Shack
Escrivao Waddo. ££
Beach cafés tend to have their ups and downs, but this one, near Shanu's guesthouse at the north end of Candolim beach, has been steadily improving for years. Choose from its ever-expanding repertoire of hygienic salads or main dishes of seafood sizzlers and tandoori specialities. For dessert, they also serve a knockout chocolate mousse.

Sheetal
Murrod Waddo. £££
The best place in north Goa for quality Mughlai cuisine. Served in shiny copper *karais* on charcoal braziers, the chicken, mutton and vegetable dishes bubble in creamy concoctions that will put your local Bangladeshi takeaway in the shade. If hot spices aren't really your thing, try the milder *murg malai*

– chicken in delicious cashew-nut sauce.

Stone House
Fort Aguada–Chogm Road. £££
Groaning portions of beef steak and kingfish fillets, accompanied by baked potatoes, are the trademarks of this lively restaurant in south Candolim. It has a great location and loads of atmosphere, staying open late most nights, when owner Chris D'Souza cranks up his beloved blues music at the bar.

Calangute

A Reverie
Near Goan Heritage Resort, Gauro Waddo.
Tel: 982-317 4927. ££££
This extravagantly decorated gastro place on the south side of Calangute is famous across the country for its innovative a menu, featuring delights that range from sophisticate pan-Asian (Himalayan trout with local herbs) to downright wacky (beef with mustard ice cream). Reservation essential.

Florentine's
Saligao, 4km (2½ miles) inland from Calangute, next door to the Ayurvedic Natural Health Centre (ANHC). ££
The reputation of this no-frills Goan eatery at Saligao, a short drive inland from Calangute, rests on just one dish: Mrs D'Costa's famous chicken *cafreal*. With prices as down to earth as the ambience, this is an absolute must.

I-95
1/115 Gauravado.
Tel: 988-130 1184, www.i95goa.com. £££–££££
Another excellent eatery, with a hip, funky vibe, outstanding Mediterranean food and a relaxed outdoor setting, as well as an art gallery that generally has an interesting range of exhibits.

Infantaria Pastelaria
Next to St John's Chapel. £££
A sub-venture of the famous Souza Lobo restaurant on the seafront, Calangute's busiest bakery pulls in streams of locals and tourists for its croissants, apple pies and traditional Goan sweets and cakes (including *dodol* and *bebinca*). You can eat under paddle fans on the open-sided ground-floor terrace, or on the first floor, where they serve main meals in the evenings.

Souza Lobo
Calangute beach. £££
One of the oldest restaurants in Goa,

and still one of the best. Does all the seafood staples exceptionally well, without seeming too full of itself. If you're in the mood for fried calamari, a cold beer and some people-watching this is hard, if not impossible, to beat.

Baga

Fiesta
Tito's Road, above the beach
Tel: 0832-227 9894, www.fiestagoa.com.
££££
Twinkling with fairy lights and lanterns, Fiesta has been Baga's most extravagantly dressed (and highly rated) restaurant since its glamorous owners, Maneck and Yellow Contractor, first came here from Mumbai in the late 1990s. The Mediterranean-Portuguese menu has stood the test of time: house specialities include carpaccio of beef and juicy wood-baked pizzas topped with fresh herbs and real mozzarella.

J&A Little Italy
Little Baga, opposite the river.
Tel: 982-313 9488, www.italyingoa.com.
££££
This Italian restaurant serves beautifully presented dishes alfresco in front of an old fisherman's cottage beside Baga Creek. Start with one of their innovative antipasti, and take your time over their whopping steaks or a seafood lasagne, but make sure you leave room for the hot chocolate soufflé.

Le Poisson Rouge
Opposite Baga bridge.
Tel: 982-385 9276. **£££**
Outstandingly authentic French cuisine prepared by a French chef and served in an intimate outdoor setting, this place has been getting rave reviews ever since it opened and is still going strong. An excellent wine list is the icing on the cake.

Anjuna

Artjuna
972 Monteiro Waddo, on the flea market road.
www.artjuna.com. **££**
This cute little garden cafe dishes up delicious salads, sandwiches and gourmet desserts as well as terrific coffee.

Villa Blanche
Assagao
Tel: 982 215 5099, www.villablanche-goa.com.
£££
It's well worth making the short drive out of the village on the Mapusa road to reach this trendy bistro-cum-bakery, where you can order everything from healthy sprout salads to homemade ice creams. On Sundays there's a popular brunch featuring pastas and sushi (advance booking essential).

Chapora

Bean Me Up
Near the petrol pump.
www.beanmeup.in. **££**
Refined wholefood cuisine that's as healthy as it is tasty. Home-made *tempeh* in cashew sauce and spicy tofu stew are the house specialities, served with steamed organic spinach and home-baked breads with dips. Also a tempting range of desserts.

Aswem-Mandrem

Nu
Junnaswada, near D'Souzas Residency
Tel: 985-065 8568. **£££**
Gourmet light bites from local celeb chef Chris Saleem Agha Bee, served in a chilled restaurant set back from the beach in a pretty garden. Go for the famous house hamburger or bumper organic salad, rounded off with the 'bon bon' desert.

La Plage
Beachfront. **£££**
Goa's most stylish beach shack. With a menu that boasts a range of dishes including kingfish carpaccio and seared tuna with wasabi mash, you know this isn't the regular Goa shack experience. French-run, this is not to be missed if you're up in north Goa – though expect to have to wait for a seat. Reservation essential on weekends

Arambol

Double Dutch
Main Street. **££**
Lounge under the palm canopy enjoying delights such as the famous 'mixed stuff' (stuffed mushrooms and capsicums with sesame potato), sublime Dutch apple pie, delicious cakes and South Indian coffee.

Fellini's
Beachfront. **£**
Most of the tourist population of Arambol converges on this Italian-run restaurant each evening for its wonderful pasta dishes, pizzas and gnocchi, served with a choice of over 20 different sauces at backpacker-friendly prices.

Benaulim

Palmira's
Beach Road. **£**
Homely roadside shack restaurant run by a delightful local family who serve up delicious all-day breakfasts. Palmira's creamy curd, dolloped on mounds of fresh papaya, pineapple and grated coconut, is a legend.

Palolem

Droopadi
Palolem beach. **£££**
Sophisticated North Indian dishes prepared right on the beach by a top-class Mughlai chef. The tandoori fish, chicken tikka masala and lamb kebabs are mouth-watering, and the creamy curries, laced with saffron and dry-roasted almonds, are sublime when scooped up with a naan bread crisp from the oven.

Ourem 88
South side of beach (behind Rococo Pelton Bar).
Tel: 869-882 7679. **£££**
Expat Brits, Jodie and Brett, are currently the darlings of the resident European scene for their superb steak with béarnaise sauce, chicken Kiev and oven-baked barramundi filet. Jodie sweats it out in the kitchen while Brett works front of house. The finest dining in Palolem by a long chalk.

Betalbatim

Martin's Corner
Close to Betalbatim beach, north of Colva.
Tel: 0832-288 0413, www.martinscornergoa.com. **£££**
Rammed every night with big-spending foreigners from the nearby luxury resorts, the restaurant has come a long way since its humble beginnings, but Mrs M remains at the helm, personally overseeing the preparation of her famous *masalas*. The menu is vast, but stick to the Goan favourites such as chicken *cafreal*, fish *caldin*, *xacuti*, pomfret *rechead* or lobster in butter-garlic sauce. Reservations recommended.

Goan fish curry.

Tea plantations near Darjeeling.

Haora Bridge, Kolkata.

EAST AND NORTHEAST INDIA

Bordering the Bay of Bengal, India's eastern corner is a distinctive and colourful part of the country, anchored by the city of Kolkata. Almost cut off from the rest of India, the remote northeast features on few visitors' itineraries.

Temple decoration, Sikkim.

East and northeast India might be the least visited regions in the country, but that is merely a result of their geographical isolation, rather than any lack of appeal. The teeming flood plains of the Ganges River in Jharkhand and the great Brahmaputra in Assam contrast with the sparsely populated, forested hills of the northeastern borderlands, the Himalayan north and the wild Odishan hinterland. In coastal Odisha (Orissa), startlingly ornate temples attract throngs of worshippers, notably at the Konark Sun Temple with its great carved chariot and annual dance festival. The original juggernauts (giant, hand-hauled chariots that carry the gods through the streets) come from the main temple in Puri and continue to rumble through the city once a year. Adivasi tribal groups in Odisha, though usually isolated from outsiders, add spice to weekly markets near the Adivasi crossroads of Koraput.

On the Ganges delta south of Kolkata, and bordering Bangladesh, is one of India's great wilderness areas: the extensive Sunderbans swamps, protected by national park status, and a major draw for adventurous wildlife-lovers. Fishermen wear masks on the back of their heads to fool swimming tigers, who reputedly will only pounce on a prey's back.

View at Darjeeling.

Kolkata (formerly Calcutta), despite its undeserved, and now outdated, reputation for misery, has gracious mansions, a horseracing track and cricket pitches dating from the British Raj. Pavement hawkers, rickshaw pullers, and political activists help to give the city of Kali a chaotic frenzy. Conversations are easy to strike up with opinionated and widely read Bengalis. To the north, where the plains give way suddenly to the foothills of the Himalaya, is Darjeeling. The largest hill station in the east, it is reached by an 88km (55-mile) journey on a 'toy' train that provides dramatic Himalayan views and steaming cups of home-grown tea. Sikkim adds orchids to this compelling list of attractions.

The northeastern states are almost cut off from the rest of the country by Bangladesh, and are remote in other ways. Away from the Brahmaputra lowlands this is a remote region of forested hills and Christian tribes.

Street scene in downtown Kolkata.

KOLKATA (CALCUTTA)

From its beginnings as a small east-coast trading settlement, Kolkata (formerly Calcutta) became a city of palaces in the heyday of the Raj. Today it is recognised as a vibrant cultural centre.

U ntil 1999, when it took on the local Bengali name of Kolkata, the capital of West Bengal was known to the world as Calcutta. Its history dates back to 1686, when Job Charnock, chief of the East India Company's factory in nearby Hugli was looking for new factory sites and selected a group of three villages – Kalikata, Govindapur and Sutanuti – where Armenian and Portuguese traders had already settled. A factory was established in Kalikata on 24 August 1690, and Calcutta was born. A fort was built, named after King William I.

The community's lifestyle was marked by the profile of the European population, most of whom were young bachelors. Punch houses, brawls and duels were common. The young 'writers', as Company employees were called, usually lived with local mistresses, their 'sleeping dictionaries.'

In 1773, Calcutta became the headquarters and nascent capital of the British administration in India. By that time, the European population had swollen from a few hundred to 100,000 through the arrival of new writers, traders, soldiers and what the administration called 'cargoes of females.' The city was flourishing, a home away from England with an Esplanade and a Strand.

Decline set in after 1911, when Delhi usurped Calcutta as the British Indian

capital. Following Independence, and the flow of refugees across the newly created borders, the city suddenly had more people than it could house. The 1971 Bangladesh War brought a further, rapid influx which brought the city's infrastructure to the verge of collapse. Since then, the overcrowding situation has gradually improved.

Kolkata today

Kolkata is the third-largest city in India, with a population of around between 4.5 and 14.2 million

Main Attractions
Fort William
The Maidan
Victoria Memorial
St Paul's Cathedral
Indian Museum
Kali Temple
Botanical Gardens
Salt Lake

Market by Haora Bridge.

Kolkata (Calcutta)

0 _____ 1000 m
0 _____ 1000 yds

N

HAORA

Howrah
(Haora)

Howrah Jetty

Railway
Museum

Telkal Ghat

Ramakrishnapur
Ghat

Chandpal Ghat

Babu Ghat

Outram
Ghat

Shibpur Ghat

Princep Ghat

Bidhan
Ghat

Gwalior
Monument

Botanical
Gardens

HASTINGS

Fort
William A

Eden
Gardens

Ranji
Stadium

Saheed
Minar F

Haora Bridge

Flower
Market

Armenian
Ghat

Strand Road

Writers'
Building J

St John's
Church I

High
Court

Town Hall,
Kolkata Museum

Rajya
Sabha

Raj
Bhavan H

Kali Krishna Tagore St

Rabindra Mancha

Tagore's
Castle N   Girish Park

JORASHANKHO

Marble
Palace O

**BARA
BAZAR**

American Church
Magen
David

St Andrew's
Kirk

Nakhoda Mosque L

CHINATOWN

Tiretta Market K

TIRETTA

Writers'
Building

BBD Bagh
(Dalhousie
Square)

Chandni
Chawk

Tipu Sultan's Mosque

Esplanade

MACHUABAZAR

Mahajati Sadan

Kolkata
University P

BAITAKKHANA

Sealdah

Tipu Sultan's Mosque

TALTALA

Oberoi
Grand
Hotel

Indian Museum G

Asiatic Society

Mother Teresa's
Mission

ENTALI

MAIDAN

Maidan B

Victoria
Memorial C

Academy
of Fine Arts E

Rabindra
Sadan

St Paul's
Cathedral D

Birla
Planetarium

Nehru
Children's
Museum

Rabindra
Sadan

Netaji
Bhavan

Racecourse
Polo Grounds

**ZOOLOGICAL
GARDENS**

National
Library Q

ALIPUR

BHAWANIPUR

Kala
Mandir

Mother
House

La Martinière College

BENIAPUKUR

South Park Street
Cemetery

**PARK
CIRCUS
MAIDAN**

Birla Industrial and
Technological Museum

BALIGANJA

Baliganja

Mother Teresa's
Home for the
Destitute and Dying

Kali
Temple R
S

KALIGHAT

Kalighat

CHETLA

**NEW
ALIPUR**

MAJERHAT

TOLLYGUNGE

Birla Academy
of Art and Culture U

Tollygunge
Club T

Ramakrishna Mission
Institute of Culture

C.I.T.
Open Theatre

(depending on where you draw its boundaries). Something of a byword in the West for third-world poverty, descriptions of its misery, however, are somewhat exaggerated these days. With its Soviet-designed metro and an efficient one-way system for traffic, Kolkata has the feeling of a well-run city. There are also a large number of well-maintained parks, especially the huge Maidan in the heart of the city.

Kolkata is a lively place: there is always something happening, be it a religious celebration, concert, cricket match, theatre or movie festival, or political demonstration; and although decaying, the architectural heritage is still there. Most of the city's main attractions are on the east side of the Hugli River, between the two bridges. The budget accommodation is centred around Sudder Street, while the more upmarket hotels are slightly further south on Park Street, but both are within walking distance of the town centre.

The city's reputation as a city of intellectuals and culture is unrivalled in South Asia. It was the home not only of India's first, and so far, only Nobel laureate for literature, Rabindranath Tagore in 1913, but also its first Oscar winner, Satyajit Ray in 1991, 'in recognition of his rare mastery of the art of motion pictures, and of his profound humanitarian outlook...' During the 20th century, the city also produced some of India's most important painters and sculptors, including Jamini Roy and Nandalal Bose. It retains a strong tradition of left-wing politics and, until 2011, was ruled by one of the world's longest-standing Communist administrations, the Left Front, which led the city's municipal and state administrations for 34 years. Marxist rule has always been a very pragmatic form of Communism, however, with the Bengali Party adopting some of the most free-market- and multinational-friendly policies in India. Although not a Communist political party, the current government, headed by the Trinamool Congress, is also left-leaning.

The Saheed Minar. In the 19th century, the monument was used by Young Bengal nationalists to hoist the French flag as a sign of rebellion against the British Raj.

The Edward VII statue in front of the Victoria Memorial.

GETTING TO KOLKATA

Buses: Long-distance buses depart from the Esplanade Bus Terminal near the Shahid Minar at the northern end of the Maidan, but the journey by rail is safer and far more comfortable.

Flights: Netaji Subhash Chandra Bose international airport, still widely known by its old name, Dum Dum, is the main gateway into eastern India. The domestic terminal is adjacent to the international one and serves almost all other areas of the country,

Trains: Regular trains run from Haora (Howrah), Kolkata and Sealdah stations to most other destinations in India. To: Delhi (6–9 daily; 16hrs 20 mins–26hrs); Chennai (2–3 daily; 26hrs 30mins–28hrs); Mumbai (4–5 daily; 26hrs 30mins–35hrs); New Jalpaiguri, for Darjeeling (6–10 daily; 8–12hrs); Guwahati (3–4 daily; 17–22hrs).

The Maidan

Kolkata was built around **Fort William** . On its western side is the **Strand** and the **Hugli River**, a branch of the Ganges. On the eastern side is the **Maidan** ➌, a huge open park established in 1758 by Robert Clive, who cleared tracts of forest around the new Fort (now the eastern head-quarters of the Indian army) in order to open up lines of fire for the guns.

The main construction on the Maidan is the **Victoria Memorial** ➍ (Tue–Sun 10am–5pm, gardens 5.30am–7pm daily; charge), an awe-inspiring domed building made from white marble quarried in Rajasthan. It has been beautifully maintained and sits in some of the most attractive gardens in the city. Inaugurated in 1921 by the then Prince of Wales, it houses an excellent collection of Victorian memorabilia as well as a huge number of items on Bengal and elsewhere in India, including paintings (the *Elephant Procession at Jaipur* is among the best), miniatures and manuscripts. The most interesting display, however, is the new **Calcutta Gallery**, describing the history of Kolkata from a small village to its inception as a trading port, and up to the Independence struggle. There are lots of fascinating documents and models, including a mock-up of an entire 19th-century street. In the park in which the memorial stands are statues of Queen Victoria and Lord Curzon. Here people picnic, couples hold hands beneath the trees and tourists squint through the strong light at the magnificent building.

Behind the memorial, on AJC Bose Road, is the **Presidency General Hospital** where, in 1898, Sir Ronald Ross identified the carrier of malaria, the female anopheles mosquito. South of the Maidan is the **Racecourse**, opened in 1819, and in its central oval are the **Kolkata Polo Club** grounds where the game has been played since 1861.

To the southeast is Cathedral Road starting at **Rabindra Sadan**, a concert hall named after Rabindranath Tagore. The nearby **Academy of Fine Arts** ➎ (daily 10am–5pm; free) has a collection of textiles, miniatures, Mughal swords, Tagore memorabilia and some examples of modern Bengali art.

The adjacent **St Paul's Cathedral** ➏ (daily 9am–noon, 3–6pm, Sunday services 6.30 and 7.30am, 6.30pm) was consecrated in 1847. It is a tall Gothic building with rows of fans hanging from a wooden ceiling, stalls and pews of heavy wood, and a stained-glass window by Edward Burne-Jones, *The Destruction of Sodom*. On the walls are commemorative slabs to the British killed during the 1857 Uprising and those who lost their lives in various wars. Near the cathedral are two attractions that children might find interesting. The **Birla Planetarium** (daily, shows in English 1.30pm and 6.30pm; charge) is one of the largest in the world. The **Nehru Children's Museum** (Wed–Sun 11am–7pm; charge) is also worth a look. The latter displays a collection of toys and

Birla Planetarium.

two dioramas of the *Ramayana* and *Mahabharata* shown in 61 scenes.

At the northern end of the Maidan, just behind the noisy bus terminal, is the 48-metre (158ft) high **Saheed Minar** ⓕ (Ochterlony Monument). It was erected to celebrate Sir David Ochterlony's victories in the Nepal Wars, but has been renamed Saheed Minar to honour martyred freedom fighters.

Nowadays the Maidan is a 24-hour show. At sunrise joggers appear, as do the West Bengal Mounted Police on their horses; army units perform their morning drills; goats and sheep browse on the course of the **Calcutta Golf Club**. Later, the trams start bringing people to work. Football or cricket then takes over, and people gather under trees near the **Gandhi Statue** and the **War Memorial**. At night, crowds congregate around **Sri Aurobindo's Statue** opposite the Victoria Memorial.

Eden Gardens, north of the Maidan, is the famous site of test-match cricket, and as the venue for the World Cup of 2011. It is festooned with banners proclaiming the Kolkata Knight Riders, the new Indian Premier League team part-owned by Bollywood heart-throb Shahrukh Khan. The park was laid out on the site of Respondentia Walk, a fashionable promenade, and the pagoda here was brought to Kolkata from Prome in Burma by Lord Curzon. Not far away, in the middle of a roundabout, is a statue to Bengal's most famous freedom fighter, Subhas Chandra Bose. His life is celebrated in Netaji Bhavan on Elgin Road (see page 312).

Chowringhee

To the east of the Maidan, **Chowringhee** (now Jawaharlal Nehru Road, although many people still use the old name) was once a jungle path leading to the Kali Temple. Together with the **Esplanade** at the Maidan's northern edge, it is home to late 19th-century buildings such as the **Oberoi Grand** and the Indian Museum. Chowringhee's glory is no more: many of the facades are decaying and the elegant old buildings are being displaced by modern high-rise

The festival of Durga puja in September or October is a big event in the city calendar.

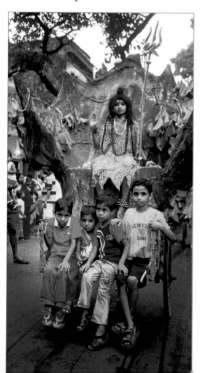

SATYAJIT RAY

One of Kolkata's most famous sons is the film director Satyajit Ray (1921–92). So far the only Indian director to win an Oscar, which he received in 1991 for Lifetime Achievement, Ray was a visionary, almost single-handedly responsible for developing an Indian 'new wave' of art-house cinema.

Born in Calcutta in 1921 to a family of prominent artists, Ray started his working life as a graphic designer for an advertising agency, then moved on to produce book jackets for a local publisher. His move into cinema came in the late 1940s after he served as a location scout for the French director, Jean Renoir, who was filming in his movie The River in Bengal. Renoir encouraged Ray to film, on a shoestring budget, his first feature, *Pather Panchali* (1955). The story of a young boy, Apu, growing up in a Bengali village was a great success, both in India and abroad, and Ray and his cameraman Subrata Mitra went on to complete what became known as the *Apu Trilogy* with *Aparajito* and *Apu Sansar*.

Although this is considered his greatest work, Ray subsequently made many other films, including Charulata (1964), the *Calcutta Trilogy* (1970–5) and his first Hindi/Urdu film *Shatranj ke Khilai* (The Chess Players, 1977). For detailed information on the great director's life and individual films, see www.satyajitray.org.

developments. Hawkers, shoe-shine boys, beggars and touts crowd the pavement.

The huge **Indian Museum** (www.indianmuseumkolkata.org; Tue–Sun, Mar–Nov 10am–5pm, Dec–Feb 10am–4.30pm; charge), certainly the largest in the country if not all of Asia, lies at the northern end of Jawaharlal Nehru Road. It was founded in 1814 but was not opened to the public until 1878. Also known as the *jadu ghar*, 'house of magic', the sprawling complex is dreadfully run-down (be warned that the toilets are un-usable), but it is still worth the effort to visit.

The 36 galleries contain a large variety of exhibits, and you will need to put aside a whole morning or afternoon to see the best of them. Prize archaeological items include a 3rd-century BC Mauryan lion capital, artefacts from Mohenjadaro and Harappa, and pieces from the 2nd-century BC stupa at Bharut in Madhya Pradesh. The museum also contains extensive geological and natural history galleries (although these are a legacy of rather unenlightened research methods).

In addition there are collections of textiles, Kalighat paintings, miniatures and sculpture, including many Gandharan works and some impressive Pala bronzes. The new painting galleries are particularly good, with collections of Bengali art.

Raj Bhavan on Esplanade Row East was built in 1803 by Governor-General Wellesley, who believed that India should be governed 'from a palace, not from a counting-house'. Towards the river are the **Rajya Sabha** (Assembly House), the old **Town Hall** and the **High Court** built in 1872 on the model of the Gothic belfry of Ypres in Flanders. The Town Hall has been restored and now houses the **Kolkata Museum** (Mon–Fri 11am–6pm; charge), which outlines the history of the city through models, paintings and interactive displays.

To the north of Raj Bhavan is **St John's Church** , built in 1784. Inside is a celebrated *Last Supper* by Zoffany. Job Charnock, the founder of the city, was buried in the cemetery here. In the garden stands the monument to the victims of the infamous

Visiting the Indian Museum.

SPORTING POWER

Kolkata produces a disproportionate number of India's greatest sports stars. It is home to that great crucible of Indian cricket, Eden Gardens, and excels at the national sport, with one of India's most successful Test cricket captain, Sourav Ganguly, among the city's favourite sons. But unlike other cities in the country, it doesn't end with bat and ball – Kolkata is India's most football-mad metropolis, home to many of the country's top clubs as well as the oldest football league in Asia. And the list goes on: Leander Paes, with 12 tennis Grand Slam doubles titles to his name, is Calcuttan; the oldest golf club in the world outside Britain is here, as is the world's oldest polo club. Even rugby union, that most un-Indian of sports, gets a look in, with the oldest international tournament, the Calcutta Cup, named after the city.

'Black Hole', when 146 British prisoners were crammed into a small room after Fort William was stormed in 1756, and 113 suffocated and died.

BBD Bagh

Beyond St John's is **Dalhousie Square**, renamed **BBD Bagh** in memory of three brothers, Binoy, Badal and Dinesh, who were hanged for having conspired to kill Lord Dalhousie, the Lieutenant-Governor of Bengal.

Facing the tank that once used to be Kolkata's only source of drinking water stands the **Writers' Building ❶**, seat of the West Bengal government. It was built in the late 19th century. The first buildings that stood here – constructed as far back as 1690 – housed 'writers' (clerks) of the East India Company, hence the name. Security is tight, and photography strictly forbidden. Opposite stands **St Andrew's Kirk**, opened in 1818 and built on the site of the old Court House. A cool retreat from the baking square outside, it is reputed to have the best church organ in India.

The offices of Kolkata's most prestigious companies – tall Victorian buildings, with Art Nouveau staircases, brass signs, marble floors and wood panelling – form a gracious parade along the old Clive Row, now **Netaji Subhas Road**. These streets are now choked with hawkers, cars and taxis. Even the **Stock Exchange** has spilled over onto the street opposite Jardine Henderson's. The Stock Exchange building on the corner of Lyon's Range, erected in 1917, houses a number of official bodies and associations. In India Exchange Lane, near the **Jute Balers Association**, speculators on the jute market operate from booths equipped with telephones projecting from the buildings along the street. Buyers shout their orders to sellers who stand in the street.

Chinatown

Starting at the northeastern corner of the Maidan, in **Bentinck Street** there is a succession of Chinese shoemakers, Muslim tailors and sweet and tea shops. **Tiretta Market** nearby, named after its former owner, a friend of Casanova who had to flee Venice, sells dried fish, vegetables and meat.

Chinatown ❸ is in Tangra, where the Chinese settled at the end of the 18th century. This area was a Cantonese town, but since 1962, when Indian and Chinese troops clashed at the frontier, it has been greatly reduced. There are still some 5,000 Chinese citizens – though the community has been greatly depleted by emigration – and most of the Chinese buildings have disappeared along with the Chinese-language newspapers that used to be printed here. Tangra still has a different feel to other areas of the city, and there are a number of Chinese restaurants, mostly producing a *Chinjabi* fusion of Indian and Chinese dishes.

In **Old China Bazaar**, west of Brabourne Road, Parsis have an *agiary* (fire temple), the Ismailis have a mosque, and the Gujarati Jains a **temple** (daily 6am–noon, 3–7pm),

Kolkata has a greater number of churches than any other large Indian city.

KOLKATA TRANSPORT

Travelling north–south between Dum Dum and Tollygunge through central Kolkata is easy on the metro. India's first mass rapid transport system, the Russian-designed network was inaugurated in 1984 and now has six constantly expanding lines in addition to its central axis

This main line was recently extended further south to Garia, and another new line opened in 2011 connecting Salt Lake and Haora (Howrah). Kolkatans are justly proud of their metro which, although showing signs of age, still manages to be cheap and punctual. Trains run from 7am–9.45pm Monday–Saturday and from 3pm–9.45pm on Sundays. For more info, visit www.kolmetro.com. Suburban rail services, by contrast, are of little use to most visitors.

Kolkata is currently the only city in India with a tram network and this can be a good way to get around the city centre. Most routes run between around 6am and 9pm.

Elsewhere in the city there is an extensive, if crowded, bus service, but it is generally best to pick up a taxi or autorickshaw. As elsewhere in India, these are supposed to use their meters, but it can be very hard to persuade them to do so. Negotiate hard and you will soon get a feel for what is a reasonable fare.

To cross over from Kolkata proper to Haora (Howrah), numerous ferries operate from various ghats along the river.

EAT

While you're in the University District, be sure to drop by the famous Indian Coffee House at 15 Bankim Chatterjee St, a favourite meeting place for generations of freedom fighter, revolutionaries and poets.

Street life on the Strand.

manuscripts, prints and paintings that can be visited on request.

Park Street used to be called European Burial Road and once ended at the **South Park Street Cemetery**, the oldest in Kolkata. Here are buried Major General Charles 'Hindoo' Stuart, an Irishman who adopted the Hindu religion; Robert Kyd, founder of the Botanical Gardens; William Makepeace, Thackeray's father; Rose Aylmer, 'who died of eating too many pineapples'; the poet Henry Derozio, founder of the Young Bengal movement; and Sir William Jones, the father of the Asiatic Society.

Another landmark is **La Martinière College** on Acharya Jagadish Chandra Bose Road, founded by a Frenchman, Claude Martin. A former bodyguard to the French Governor of Pondicherry, Martin later joined the service of the East India Company and ended his career as a Major General. He died in 1800, bequeathing his fortune to set up schools in Lyon (France), Kolkata and Lucknow, and donated a sum of Rs50,000 to the Church of the Sacred Heart in Chandernagore. Nearby, in

Bhawanipur, is **Netaji Bhavan** (Tue–Sun 11am–4.30pm; free) on Elgin Road, the house from which Subhas Chandra Bose, the nationalist leader, escaped during World War II to establish the Indian National Army in Japanese-occupied Southeast Asia. It is now a museum with a collection of photographs and letters written during his campaign to rid India of the British.

On Gurusady Road is the **Birla Industrial and Technological Museum** (Tue–Sun 10am–5.30pm; charge). The well-displayed galleries are arranged by theme (Life Sciences, Transport and Electricity, for example) and have interactive models.

South Kolkata

The south of the city is essentially residential, with several wealthy neighbourhoods. Warren Hastings's first residence, at Alipur, now an institute of education, is said to be haunted by its former owner.

The **National Library ○**, on Belvedere Road, was once the Winter Viceregal Lodge (www.nationallibrary.

On Muktaram Babu Street at Chorebagan ('the thieves' garden') is the **Marble Palace** Ⓞ (Tue, Wed, Fri and Sun 10am–4pm; free; visits must be arranged in advance from the Deputy Director of Tourism, 3/2 BBD Bagh, tel: 033-2248 8271, or from a regional tourist office). This charming, eccentric building was commissioned in 1835 by Raja Mullick and built in Italian marble. The raja's descendants still live here, but most of it can be visited. In its dark halls are assembled paintings, clocks, statues, crystal and china. Among them there is said to be a Napoleon by Houdin, one Arnold, one Gainsborough, three Rubens and a statue by Michelangelo. In the yard is the family temple, and a collection of parrots, doves and mynahs.

Kolkata University Ⓟ on College Square was founded in 1857 and moved to this location in 1873. It has, in the past, been the scene of many demonstrations, and many of its walls are periodically covered with political graffiti. In the **University Senate** building is the **Ashutosh Museum** (Mon–Fri 10am–5pm, Sat 10.30am–1.30pm; free), presenting a collection of Pala sculptures, terracotta pieces, bronzes and examples of Bengali traditional art.

The **Indian Coffee House**, on Bankim Chatterjee Street, is the traditional meeting place for the city's intellectual and student circles.

On R.N. Mukharji Road, to the west of BBD Bagh, is the **Old Mission**. This was built in 1770 by a Swedish missionary and is the oldest church in Kolkata.

Behind Chowringhee is the old European quarter. It is an area of mansions slowly being replaced by modern buildings. **Park Street**, the main thoroughfare, was laid during the first quarter of the last century. The **Freemasons' Hall** on this street was built in the 19th century and houses the oldest Lodge outside Britain.

The **Asiatic Society** (Tel: 033-2229 0779; Mon–Fri 10.30am–6pm, Sat–Sun 10am–5pm; free), also at the beginning of Park Street, was founded in 1784 by Sir William Jones. It houses a permanent exhibition of oriental

FACT

Kumartuli's god effigy workshops are busiest between August and November, over the period covering the city's popular Durga and Kali festivals.

Grandiose imperial architecture at the Writers' Building.

EAT

While you're in the University District, be sure to drop by the famous Indian Coffee House at 15 Bankim Chatterjee St, a favourite meeting place for generations of freedom fighter, revolutionaries and poets.

manuscripts, prints and paintings that can be visited on request.

Park Street used to be called European Burial Road and once ended at the **South Park Street Cemetery**, the oldest in Kolkata. Here are buried Major General Charles 'Hindoo' Stuart, an Irishman who adopted the Hindu religion; Robert Kyd, founder of the Botanical Gardens; William Makepeace, Thackeray's father; Rose Aylmer, 'who died of eating too many pineapples'; the poet Henry Derozio, founder of the Young Bengal movement; and Sir William Jones, the father of the Asiatic Society.

Another landmark is **La Martinière College** on Acharya Jagadish Chandra Bose Road, founded by a Frenchman, Claude Martin. A former bodyguard to the French Governor of Pondicherry, Martin later joined the service of the East India Company and ended his career as a Major General. He died in 1800, bequeathing his fortune to set up schools in Lyon (France), Kolkata and Lucknow, and donated a sum of Rs50,000 to the Church of the Sacred Heart in Chandernagore. Nearby, in

Street life on the Strand.

Bhawanipur, is **Netaji Bhavan** (Tue–Sun 11am–4.30pm; free) on Elgin Road, the house from which Subhas Chandra Bose, the nationalist leader, escaped during World War II to establish the Indian National Army in Japanese-occupied Southeast Asia. It is now a museum with a collection of photographs and letters written during his campaign to rid India of the British.

On Gurusady Road is the **Birla Industrial and Technological Museum** (Tue–Sun 10am–5.30pm; charge). The well-displayed galleries are arranged by theme (Life Sciences, Transport and Electricity, for example) and have interactive models.

South Kolkata

The south of the city is essentially residential, with several wealthy neighbourhoods. Warren Hastings's first residence, at Alipur, now an institute of education, is said to be haunted by its former owner.

The **National Library Q**, on Belvedere Road, was once the Winter Viceregal Lodge (www.nationallibrary.

'Black Hole', when 146 British prisoners were crammed into a small room after Fort William was stormed in 1756, and 113 suffocated and died.

BBD Bagh

Beyond St John's is **Dalhousie Square**, renamed **BBD Bagh** in memory of three brothers, Binoy, Badal and Dinesh, who were hanged for having conspired to kill Lord Dalhousie, the Lieutenant-Governor of Bengal.

Facing the tank that once used to be Kolkata's only source of drinking water stands the **Writers' Building ❶**, seat of the West Bengal government. It was built in the late 19th century. The first buildings that stood here – constructed as far back as 1690 – housed 'writers' (clerks) of the East India Company, hence the name. Security is tight, and photography strictly forbidden. Opposite stands **St Andrew's Kirk**, opened in 1818 and built on the site of the old Court House. A cool retreat from the baking square outside, it is reputed to have the best church organ in India.

The offices of Kolkata's most prestigious companies – tall Victorian buildings, with Art Nouveau staircases, brass signs, marble floors and wood panelling – form a gracious parade along the old Clive Row, now **Netaji Subhas Road**. These streets are now choked with hawkers, cars and taxis. Even the **Stock Exchange** has spilled over onto the street opposite Jardine Henderson's. The Stock Exchange building on the corner of Lyon's Range, erected in 1917, houses a number of official bodies and associations. In India Exchange Lane, near the **Jute Balers Association**, speculators on the jute market operate from booths equipped with telephones projecting from the buildings along the street. Buyers shout their orders to sellers who stand in the street.

Chinatown

Starting at the northeastern corner of the Maidan, in **Bentinck Street** there is a succession of Chinese shoemakers, Muslim tailors and sweet and tea shops. **Tiretta Market** nearby, named after its former owner, a friend of Casanova who had to flee Venice, sells dried fish, vegetables and meat.

Chinatown ⓚ is in Tangra, where the Chinese settled at the end of the 18th century. This area was a Cantonese town, but since 1962, when Indian and Chinese troops clashed at the frontier, it has been greatly reduced. There are still some 5,000 Chinese citizens – though the community has been greatly depleted by emigration – and most of the Chinese buildings have disappeared along with the Chinese-language newspapers that used to be printed here. Tangra still has a different feel to other areas of the city, and there are a number of Chinese restaurants, mostly producing a *Chinjabi* fusion of Indian and Chinese dishes.

In **Old China Bazaar**, west of Brabourne Road, Parsis have an *agiary* (fire temple), the Ismailis have a mosque, and the Gujarati Jains a **temple** (daily 6am–noon, 3–7pm),

Kolkata has a greater number of churches than any other large Indian city.

KOLKATA TRANSPORT

Travelling north–south between Dum Dum and Tollygunge through central Kolkata is easy on the metro. India's first mass rapid transport system, the Russian-designed network was inaugurated in 1984 and now has six constantly expanding lines in addition to its central axis

This main line was recently extended further south to Garia, and another new line opened in 2011 connecting Salt Lake and Haora (Howrah). Kolkatans are justly proud of their metro which, although showing signs of age, still manages to be cheap and punctual. Trains run from 7am–9.45pm Monday–Saturday and from 3pm–9.45pm on Sundays. For more info, visit www.kolmetro.com. Suburban rail services, by contrast, are of little use to most visitors.

Kolkata is currently the only city in India with a tram network and this can be a good way to get around the city centre. Most routes run between around 6am and 9pm.

Elsewhere in the city there is an extensive, if crowded, bus service, but it is generally best to pick up a taxi or autorickshaw. As elsewhere in India, these are supposed to use their meters, but it can be very hard to persuade them to do so. Negotiate hard and you will soon get a feel for what is a reasonable fare.

To cross over from Kolkata proper to Haora (Howrah), numerous ferries operate from various ghats along the river.

EAT

The dishes found in the small local restaurants of Chinatown bear little resemblance to authentic Chinese regional creations. A very Indian mix of spices is added to noodles and fried rice, resulting in what has become an exceptionally popular fusion of Indian and Chinese cooking. For authentic Chinese food, try Beijing or Mainland China (see page 316 and page 317).

one of the most charming in Kolkata. There are also two synagogues, one of which, **Magen David**, was built in 1884. Kolkata's Jews came from Iraq in the 19th century and formed a prosperous community, but emigration to Israel, the US and the UK since the end of World War II has left less than 100 Jewish families in the city.

Off Old China Bazaar Lane stands the **Armenian Church of Our Lady of Nazareth**. It was built in 1724 and is said to have the oldest working clock in Kolkata. Arriving as traders from the Persian city of Isfahan in the 17th century, the Armenians were already here and in Chinsura, upriver on the Hugli, when Job Charnock founded the city. A grave in the church cemetery is dated 1630. In and around Kolkata, the Armenians, of which there are now only a few hundred, have several churches, a school, a club and also one of India's best rugby teams.

Along Chitpur Road, now Rabindra Sarani, stands the **Nakhoda Mosque** ⑥, built in red sandstone with four floors. The model was Akbar's tomb at Sikandra near Agra. It has room for a congregation of 10,000. The area around the mosque is full of Muslim shops and some good restaurants.

North Kolkata

The adjacent areas of Jorashankho and Pathuriagata, in north Kolkata, are two of the oldest in the city, with streets lined by grand, colonnaded mansions and other buildings dating from the hey day of the Raj. Among them on Darpanarain Tagore Lane is **Tagore's Castle** Ⓜ, built in 1867 and originally a theatre, whose extravagant towers, turrets and crenellations were inspired by those of the fairytale Bavarian castle of Neuschwanstein. Overbuilt structures and tenements have, unfortunately, altered its silhouette.

At the end of Dwarkanath Tagore Lane is **Rabindra Mancha** Ⓝ (Tue–Sun 10.30am–4.30pm; charge), an 18th-century house where the poet Rabindranath Tagore was born in 1861, and where he died in 1941. Tagore House also puts on Bengali music and dance performances. Adjoining the house is a library and **Rabindra Bharati University**, the Tagore Academy. The university's museum (45-minute tours in English Nov–Jan 7pm, Feb–June 8pm; charge) is devoted to the poet's life and to the Young Bengal movement, as well as a collection of almost 2,000 of Tagore's paintings.

In **Kumartuli**, further north, lives a community of artisans making clay images of the goddesses Durga, Lakshmi and Sarasvati for festivals. In **Rajabazar** on Badni Das Temple Road are four Jain temples of the Digamber sect, built at the end of the 19th century. Known collectively as the **Parasnath Mandir**, the best-known is that dedicated to Sital Nath. Its architecture is a mixture of Mughal, Baroque, neoclassical and local styles, and its interior is decorated with mosaics, coloured glass, mirrors, coloured stones, crystal and marble.

Courtyard at the Indian Museum. The Italianate building dates from 1878.

gov.in; Mon–Fri 9am–8pm, Sat–Sun 9.30am–6pm) The collections are extensive and are divided into sections corresponding to the major Indian languages. The **Zoological Gardens**, close to the National Library, were established in 1876. Like all Indian zoos, a visit here can be a very depressing experience.

Kalighat is a pleasantly traditional middle-class neighbourhood on **Tolly's Nullah**. In 1775 Colonel Tolly drained the silted canal to bring Ganges water to the **Kali Temple ®**. The present *mandir* was built in 1809 by Sobarna Chowdhury on the site of a 16th-century Kali temple, although some kind of shrine has probably been here since early times. The Kali Temple is said to stand on the spot where Sati's little toe landed after her dead body had been dismembered by Vishnu and scattered across the earth; this was to stop Shiva's destructive dance of mourning.

The temple is still owned by the founder's descendants, the *paladas*, who have a monopoly over rituals. Pilgrims make offerings to Kali (an *avatar* of Sati) of milk mixed with Ganges water and *bhang* (cannabis). Human sacrifices are known to have taken place, but today only goats are sacrificed. Kali's image, inside the central shrine, is made of black marble, and the goddess is seen with four arms, garlanded with a chain of human heads, and with a hand, tongue and eyebrows made of gold; her eyes and tongue are painted blood-red.

The temple is closed to non-Hindus, and at times the streets around the shrine can feel slightly unsafe to visitors. The fervour of the devotees is fascinating, but with the animal sacrifices that take place daily, those of a sensitive disposition might want to observe the goings-on from a distance. The market outside the temple is very lively, and there is a huge amount of religious paraphernalia on display.

Next door, the late Mother Teresa's (1910–97) **Home for the Destitute and Dying ⑤**, or Nirmal Hriday, is the first of several missions run by her Sisters of Charity in the city. The nuns, in their white saris, can be seen all across town. Mother Teresa is well on her way to sainthood – given a big push after being beatified in 2003 by Pope John Paul II – but she remains a controversial figure both in India and abroad.

One of the numerous shrines at the Kali Temple.

Tollygunge

There are more temples further south on Chetla and Tollygunge roads. Nearby is the **Tollygunge Club ⑦**. An indigo plantation was laid out here in 1781 by the Johnson family. Later the exiled family of Tipu Sultan lived in the Johnson mansion, which was subsequently converted into the club. It became the Tollygunge Club in 1895 and offers its facilities (golf, tennis, squash and a swimming pool) to visitors on a daily basis. Come in

Shoe shining and repairs outside the main bus station.

TIP

People interested in volunteering at the Home for the Destitute and Dying (Nirmal Hriday) should contact the Mother's House in advance at: Missionaries of Charity, 54 A.J.C. Bose Road, tel: 033-2244 7115.

the evening to see Kolkata's 'great and good' having a drink and eating the somewhat institutional food; it offers a real insight into how the city's middle class operates and interacts. It is also possible to stay here (contact the club secretary in advance at: 120, Deshapran Sasmal Road, tel: 033-2417 6022, www.tollygungeclub.org).

Those of the middle class not enjoying themselves in the verdant surrounds of the Tolly are likely to be found not far away at Kolkata's largest shopping complex, **South City Mall**. Rather incongruous given the rundown surroundings, this is a large, glass-fronted, air-conditioned mall, complete with food court and international chains.

Northeast of Tollygunge, around **Rabindra Sarovar Lake**, are rowing clubs and the **Birla Academy of Art and Culture** ⓤ (Wed–Mon 4–8pm; free) on Southern Avenue, a museum that is never crowded, with a whole floor of miniatures from all the major schools, a modern art gallery and a collection of old statues.

The **Ramakrishna Mission Institute of Culture** on Gol Park, near the lake, is a branch of the Ramakrishna Mission of Belur Math. It has a school of languages, a library, a museum of Indian art and a Universal Prayer Room.

Along the Ganges

From the ghat near the Garden Reach shipyard, a ferry periodically crosses to the **Botanical Gardens** ⓥ (daily 7am–5pm; charge). Set up in 1787, these once boasted the largest banyan tree in the world. The trunk was struck by lightning in 1919 and was subsequently removed. About 1,500 offshoots remain, forming a circle with a diameter of more than 10 metres (33ft). It is also the location of the Central National Herbarium of India.

The **Metiaburuz Shi'ite Mosque**, where the last nawab, Wajid Ali Shah, was exiled, on Garden Reach Road was built and lavishly decorated by the royal family of Avadh in the 19th century.

The riverside ghats off Strand Road, like any on the Ganges, are most active at dawn and sunset. During festivals thousands of devotees converge on **Babu**, **Outram** and **Princep ghats** to immerse clay images of Durga, Kali, Lakshmi or Sarasvati into the river. Other communities hold festivals too. On Chat, Biharis dip fruit in the river and Sindhis, on Chetti Chand, immerse statues of the god Jhulelal. On Strand Road, in January, a transit camp is arranged for the thousands of pilgrims on their way to the holy island of Sagardwip. Every morning the ghats swarm with people washing and praying.

On the riverfront promenade is the **Gwalior Monument**, called the 'Pepper Pot' because of its shape, and erected to commemorate a British victory in the Maratha Wars. At Princep Ghat dinghies are available for hire on an hourly basis.

Stalls in the market outside the Kali Temple.

The 1941 **Haora Bridge** over the Hugli has eight traffic lanes, which is not enough for the daily flow of trams, buses, trucks, rickshaws, pedestrians, buffaloes, sheep, goats, taxis and bullock carts. On hot days its length can increase by 1 metre (3ft). It has been supplemented by a new **Vidyasagar Setu** suspension bridge at Hastings, 3km (2 miles) south.

Salt Lake

On the northeastern edge of Kolkata, on the way to the airport, is the new town of Bidhannagar, which is more popularly known as **Salt Lake**. Initially laid out in the 1950s, it has developed into one of the most attractive parts of the city, at the heart of which is a large park. Mostly comprising blocks of middle-class residences, it is also the location of the very swish Hyatt Regency, and one of the city's largest shopping malls, City Centre. **Nicco Park** (daily Oct–Mar 11am–8pm, Apr–Sept 11am–9pm; charge) is an amusement park on the south side of Salt Lake.

The somewhat optimistically named **Wet-o-Wild Beach Tropicana** (daily 11am–7pm; charge), the city's best public swimming complex, is entered through Nicco Park.

Not far away, where the Eastern Bypass crosses J.B.S. Halden Avenue, is another good destination for families, **Science City** (daily 9am–9pm; charge). The striking complex of rounded buildings accommodates a large interactive museum of science and technology, including a state-of-the-art planetarium. Look out for a particularly good display on tectonics and earthquakes.

A rather different complex is found in a large park just across from the Salt Lake Stadium. **Swabhumi** (daily 10am–7pm; charge) has a tempting food court serving dishes from all parts of India, a crafts village, heritage shopping complex and an auditorium which puts on performances of traditional music and dance.

Shaving on the street.

The great banyan tree at the Botanical Gardens.

RESTAURANTS AND BARS

PRICE CATEGORIES

Average price for dinner, up to three courses for one person, excluding alcoholic drinks:

£ = under Rs200
££ = Rs200–500
£££ = Rs500–1,000
££££ = over Rs1,000

Until recently authentic Bengali food was relatively unknown outside of Kolkata and West Bengal, partly because it was hard to find outside of the home. Thankfully this has now changed, and there are some excellent Bengali restaurants in the city that showcase one of India's most distinctive and delicious local cuisines. Kolkata has long been home to a successful Chinese community, and this has left its mark on the city with a number of fine restaurants.

Restaurants

BBD Bagh and Chandni Chowk

Amber
11 Waterloo Street.
Tel: 033-2248 6520. **££**
A city institution, little changed since the 1950s, and renowned above all for its North Indian dishes, especially the tandoori chicken specialities.

Delectable Bengali dishes at the Taj Bengal's Sonargaon restaurant.

Subhash Chandra Bose international airport

Eau Chew
P32 Mission Row Extension, Gandesh Chandra Avenue.
Tel : 9830-141857. **£££**
One of the last surviving, family-run and genuinely authentic Chinese restaurants in the city. Don't be put off by the seedy entrance, above a defunct petrol pump. The cooking is terrific, especially the show-stopping chimney soup (served in a smouldering brazier), honey-lemon chicken and Josephine noodles (Chicken, fish, egg, carrots and green veggies in pan-fried noodles).

Tangra

Beijing
77/1 Christopher Road.
Tel: 033-2328 1011. **££–£££**
Tangra, in east Kolkata, is home to the city's Chinatown, and this bar/restaurant is one of the best in the area. It serves a wide variety of authentic Chinese dishes.

Chowringhee

Aheli
Peerless Inn, 12 Jawaharlal Nehru Road.
Tel: 033-2228 0301. **£££**
Excellent, if slightly overpriced, traditional Bengali cuisine. One of Kolkata's oldest and most authentic

Bengali restaurants. Try one of the river fish options: hilsa, or bekti steamed in banana leaf.

Baan Thai
Oberoi Grand, 15 Jawaharlal Nehru Road.
Tel: 033-2249 2323. **££££**
The best Thai in Kolkata, if not in the whole of India. Wonderful spicy food that picks out delicate flavours. Booking recommended.

Floatel
9/10 Kolkata Jetty, Strand Road.
Tel: 033-2213 7777. **£££**
India's only floating hotel; while the food and service are generally indifferent, this is a unique dining experience – both of Kolkata's iconic bridges, as well as a large expanse of river, are in plain view as you eat.

Flury's
18 Park Street.
Tel: 033-4000 7453, www.flurysindia.com. **££**
Popular coffee shop serving delicious pastries, sandwiches and filled croissants – as well as tasty Continental mains such as mushroom stroganoff and fish and chips – with great ice cream sundaes to round things off.

Golbari
Bidhan Sarani, Shyambazar. **£**
A venerable institution in north Kolkata that specialises in Kosha Mangsho (spicy goat curry) best had with *roti* or *parathas*. Very basic decor and very inexpensive.

Mocambo
25b Park Street.
Tel: 033-2217 2934. **££–£££**
Another old favourite that's been here for decades, with kitsch 1980s décor and a menu to match, offering a wide selection of dishes. Most people come for the fish and chips, or chicken kiev and other Continental options, but the Bengali specialities are equally commendable, and be sure to leave room for the famous baked Alaska!

La Terrasse
Oberoi Grand, 15 Jawaharlal Nehru Road.
Tel: 033-2249 2323. **££££**
The all-day Continental restaurant at the Oberoi has some mouth-watering food. The buffet (breakfast and lunch) is particularly good.

Zaranj
26 Jawaharlal Nehru Road.
Tel: 033-2249 5572. **£–££**
Top drawer North Indian cooking. The vegetarian food is tasty, but the meat kebabs and tandoori potato, steeped

in yoghurt and whipped cream, are excellent.

Zen
The Park, 17 Park Street.
Tel: 033-2249 9000, www.theparkhotels.com. **££££**
The über-trendy Zen at The Park is a Conran-designed restaurant serving up pan-East Asian food in a very cool interior. The open kitchen showing off the Japanese, Chinese and Thai chefs' skills was designed as a 'theatre of food'. Whether you buy this or not, the dishes are certainly world-class – especially the sushi.

Elgin Road Area

Bhojohori Manna
18/1A Hindustan Road, Sarat Bose Road, Ballygunge.
Tel: 033-2466 3941. **£££**
These are the people who made authentic Bengali food available at an affordable price. They've opened several branches across Kolkata now, but best to visit where they run their own kitchens arethose on Ekdalia Road and Hindustan Road. Basic decor, but excellent food and good service. Rely on the waiters to order dishes of the day.

Kewpie's Kitchen
2 Elgin Lane.
Tel: 033-2475 9880. **£££**
If you'd like to sample traditional Bengali cuisine in a homely environment, rather than a sterile air-con mall, jump in a taxi to this delightful family restaurant in south Kolkata. Tacked on to a suburban house, the dining room's tiny. Let the waiter select from their daily fish specials, which come in tiny terracotta dishes with lacci puris and mounds of fragrant rice, all neatly presented on banana leaves.

Mainland China
Uniworth House, 3a Gurusaday Road.
Tel: 033-2283 7964, www.mainlandchina.com. **£££**
The best lobster in black bean sauce you'll probably ever eat. Also features a 15-course buffet.

Oh! Calcutta
Lala Lajpat Rai Sarani.
Tel: 033-2283 7161. www.speciality.co.in. **££££**
Excellent Bengali food, one of the first restaurants to raise the profile of the cuisine on a country-wide basis. Favourites of *hilsa* and lots of ground mustard seed, all extremely tasty. Booking recommended.

Baitakkhana

The Indian Coffee House
15 Bankim Chatterjee Street. **£**
This famous coffee shop near the university has long been a meeting place for Bengali intellectuals. Snacks available, open all day.

Alipur

Chinoiserie
Taj Bengal, 34B Belvedere Road.
Tel: 033-2223 3939. **££££**
Chinese at the Taj in Kolkata is likely to be good, and this long-standing restaurant doesn't disappoint. Mostly Cantonese and Szechwan dishes, with particularly good duck and scallops.

The Hub
Taj Bengal, 34B Belvedere Road.
Tel: 033-2223 3939. **£££**
Said to be the best 24-hour restaurant in Kolkata, The Hub serves great Italian dishes of the filling and warming variety, including delicious thin-crust pizzas and focaccia bread.

Sonargaon
Taj Bengal, 34B Belvedere Road.
Tel: 033-2223 3939. **££££**
The Bengali restaurant at the Taj is superb, with a wide range of authentic local dishes. Whether you opt for the Bengali *thali* at lunch or go à la carte for dinner, expect delicious food and excellent service.

Kalighat and Ballygunge

6 Ballygunge Place
Ballygunge Place. Tel: 033-2460 3922 **£££**
Fine dining, Bengali style, in ultra swish surroundings. It's especially popular with well-heeled emigrants from the Gulf who've retained a nostalgia for the family dishes of old, and few leave disappointed. Everything's meticulously well prepared and the service is slick.

Banana Leaf
73 Rashbehari Avenue, Lake Market.
www.bananaleaf.in. **££–£££**
On weekends, they literally queue around the block for a table at this classy south Indian restaurant, which serves all the usual udupi treats (uttamapams, dosas, idli-wada etc) as well as copious rice place meals and thalis heaped on steel platters. For starters, be sure to order the kuzhi paniyaram (crunchy, deep-fried Keralan rice batter balls with onion) and leave room for a divine payasam desert at the end.

Salt Lake

La Cucina
Hyatt Regency, JA-1 Sector III.
Tel: 033-2335 1234. http://kolkata.regency.hyatt.com. **££££**
The best, and most authentic, Italian food in the city. Excellent pasta, pizza and risotto, but make sure you leave some room for chocolate melting centre dessert.

Guchhi
Hyatt Regency, JA-1 Sector III.
Tel: 033-2335 1234. **££££**
The Indian restaurant at the Hyatt serves some very fine food indeed. The emphasis is on tandoori and Kashmiri dishes.

Red Hot Chilli Pepper
Bengal Intelligent Park, Sector 5.
Tel: 033-2357 0326. **££**
A hangout that serves Chinese and Continental food in a fusion of East Asian and Western décor. Go for the crab in its shell or jumbo garlic pepper prawns. There's a branch on Ballygunge Circular Road as well.

Bars

Chowringhee

Oly Pub
21 Park Street.
Tel: 033-2229 9306. **££**
Legendary watering hole in Kolkata, dim and grotty, but booze and food don't get any better at these prices. Beef steak and mutton *burra* kebabs are must-try. The style of serving spirits at the bar is unique. Counts Satyajit Ray among its best-known patrons.

Tantra
The Park, 17 Park Street.
Tel: 033-2249 9000.
The Park's DJ bar/club is certainly the best in the city, beloved of the in-set, and is great for dancing and cocktails.

Palm-leaf wrapped treats.

Darjeeling houses.

WEST BENGAL, ODISHA AND JHARKHAND

From the swamps of the Sunderbans to the peaks of the Himalayas, this diverse region has attracted traders and colonisers, poets and philosophers, all of whom have left their mark.

Map on page 323

The three states that make up the eastern part of the Indian Peninsula, West Bengal, Orissa – now renamed Odisha – and Jharkhand, see relatively few visitors compared to other parts of the country, but are nonetheless full of interest. Among the attractions are ancient temples, wide beaches, the world's largest mangrove forest, centres of culture and tea gardens clinging to the lower slopes of the Himalayas.

Bengal is known for its strong intellectual tradition as well as important historical sites, many of which shed light on the early years of European trade and conquest in India. Odisha has some of the holiest places in Hinduism in the temples of Puri and Bhubaneshwar, as well as some important Buddhist sites. The extravagant size and coastal location of the Hindu temples give them an atmosphere all of their own: they seemingly blend in to the surrounding landscape, and more than warrant the journey to see them. Jharkhand, carved out of the forested tracts of the Chota Nagpur plateau, is the home of a number of Adivasi (tribal) groups, as well as being the location of heavy industry, with India's largest steelworks.

WEST BENGAL

West Bengal stretches from the Himalayas to the Bay of Bengal. Early

mention of Bengal can be found in the Mahabharata and in Ptolemy's *Geography*. Bengal was then a seafaring nation, sending traders to Sri Lanka, Sumatra and Java and being visited by Greeks, Chinese and Persians.

From the end of the 19th century onwards Bengal was one of the most prosperous territories of the British Empire. Temples were built, the Bengali language was enriched by poets and writers such as Bankim Chandra Chatterjee and Rabindranath Tagore, and religious

Main Attractions

Sunderbans
Darjeeling
Darjeeling Himalayan Railway
Druk Thupten Sangag Choling Monastery, Dali
Bhubaneshwar
Jagannath Temple, Puri
Sun Temple, Konark

Sikkimese man and child.

FACT

The Grand Trunk Road is one of the oldest major roads in South Asia, running from Bangladesh right across northern India to Peshawar In Pakistan and then on through the legendary Khyber Pass to Kabul, Afghanistan, over 2,500km (1,500 miles) in total. Kipling famously described it in *Kim* as 'such a river of life as nowhere else exists in the world'.

philosophers such as Ramakrishna and Vivekananda emerged.

Early colonisers

Along the Grand Trunk Road, on the right bank of the Hugli just north of **Kolkata ❶**, are sleepy little towns with palaces, old churches, riverfront promenades and colonial houses and cemeteries – remains of the old Danish, Dutch and French settlements. The Grand Trunk Road is reached by the Bally Bridge crossing the Hugli at **Dakshinesvar**, 20km (12 miles) north of Kolkata, where, on the left bank, stands the 9th-century **Kali Bhavatarini Temple** complex containing a central temple to Kali, one to Radha-Krishna and 12 small temples to Shiva. The philosopher Ramakrishna once lived here, and his room is now a museum.

Downstream across the river is **Belur Math**, headquarters of the Ramakrishna Mission, founded by Ramakrishna's disciple Vivekananda. The main building, the **Sri Ramakrishna Temple**, 75 metres (246ft) long and 35 metres (115ft) high, reflects Ramakrishna's

call for harmony between religions. The gate is Buddhist, the structure above the entrance South Indian, the windows and balconies Mughal and Rajput, and the floor plan is that of a Christian cross.

The first foreign settlement north of Kolkata was at **Serampore**, 25km (15 miles) from Kolkata. The Danish East India Company carried on trade here from the late 17th century until 1845, when the Danes sold all their possessions in India to Britain. In 1799 William Carey, an Englishman, and two fellow Baptist missionaries established a press here and were pioneers of printing in several Asian languages.

In 1819 Carey founded the **Serampore College**, which was incorporated in 1827 as a university by Danish Royal Charter. Still active, the college is now a Baptist theological institute. It stands on the banks of the Hugli, among other 18th- and 19th-century mansions. Slightly inland is **St Olaf's Church**, built in 1747.

A gate bearing the motto of the French Republic, *Liberté, Egalité, Fraternité*, marks the entrance to

Tea picking. Whereas some coarser grades of tea are cut with shears, Darjeeling teas are all hand-picked.

Chandernagore, a French *Etablissement* almost continuously from 1673 to 1952. A French atmosphere still persists along the shaded Quai Dupleix, now Strand Road, with its public benches exactly like those in Parisian parks.

The Dutch settled at **Chinsura**, 1km south of Hugli, in 1625 and ceded it to Britain in 1826 against Bencoolen in Sumatra. A Dutch barracks, church and cemetery still remain from that period. Chinsura's Armenian community constructed **St John's Church** in 1695 and, once a year, on St John's day, in January, the Armenians of Kolkata gather here to hold religious services. To the north, on the riverside, is the **Imambara**, a Shi'ite place of worship with a clock tower donated by Queen Victoria.

The Portuguese founded nearby Bandel de Ugolim, now **Hugli**, in 1580, and controlled most of the trade passing through Bengal, until the arrival of other European nations. The **Church of Our Lady of Bandel** is all that remains of the Portuguese past. Consecrated in 1599, it was rebuilt after being destroyed by Shah Jahan in 1632, but without the usual exuberance of Portuguese churches. It has remained a pilgrimage centre. Even today, each Christmas Eve, a Mass is celebrated.

Bengal's holy cities

There are two temples at **Bansberia** ❷, 6km (4 miles) north of Hugli. The small **Vasudeva Temple**, constructed in the 17th century, has sculptured terracotta tiles representing ships, Portuguese soldiers and scenes from the *Ramayana*. **Hangsesvari Temple**, with its 13 towers, was founded in the early 19th century. Rajah Deb started building it following a dream, but died before completion. His widow was about to commit *sati* (self-immolation), but was rescued at the last moment by the religious reformer Ram Mohan Roy, founder of the Brahmo Samaj movement. She lived on and completed the temple.

Tribeni, 50km (30 miles) north of Bansberia, is a holy place at the confluence of two rivers where twice a year, at Dussera and during the festival of Varuna, the god of water, pilgrims visit the little **Benimadhava Temple** complex and take a bath in the Ganges. On the southern side is the **Darya Zafar Khan**, Bengal's oldest Muslim building, erected in the 13th century using material from dismantled Buddhist and Hindu temples.

Nawadwip ❸, 125km (78 miles) north of Kolkata, also known as **Nadia**, is built on nine formerly distinct islands on the Ganges, called Bhagirathi here. It was the capital of Bengal in the 11th and 12th centuries and is among the holiest of places in West Bengal. Chaitanya Mahaprabhu, said to be an incarnation of Vishnu, taught the Vaishnava philosophy here in the 16th century. Every year in March, over 500,000 pilgrims come to Nadia for the *padikrama*, a pilgrimage on foot that takes them along a 50km (30-mile) loop around places and temples associated with Chaitanya. Nearby is Sri Mayapur, the headquarters of

FACT

The Hugli river, like the Severn in the UK, has a tidal bore, a wave triggered by an advancing tide, which in this case reaches heights of 2 metres (7ft) and has been known to destroy small boats as far inland as Kolkata.

REGIONAL TRANSPORT

Flights: The major hub for the region is Kolkata's Netaji Subhas Chandra Bose airport, but most large cities, such as Bhubaneshwar and Ranchi, have domestic airports served by low-cost airlines as well as the major carriers. The exception is Darjeeling, where the nearest airport is the military runway at Bagdogra near Siliguri (take a taxi from here). However, most places are easily reached by rail – the exceptions being areas subject to the ongoing Nazalite-Maoist insurgency, where any kind of travel is unadvisable.

Trains: West Bengal, Odisha and Jharkhand are well served by rail services. Bhubaneshwar is on the main line north–south along the east coast, Puri is on a branch line off the main line at Khurda Road, while Ranchi takes a little more time but is still straightforward to reach from Kolkata or, better still, Patna. West Bengal has numerous local services, while the narrow-gauge railway from New Jalpaiguri up to Darjeeling is one of the great experiences of travelling in India.

Bhubaneshwar: Kolkata (Haora) (15 daily; 7–8hrs 30mins); Puri (12 daily; 1hr 40mins–2hrs)

Ranchi: Kolkata (Haora) (2 daily; 7hrs 30mins–9hrs); Patna (4 daily; 9–12hrs)

New Jalpaiguri–Darjeeling: (1 daily, dept. 9am, arr. 3.55pm. From Darjeeling the train departs at 9am, arr. 4.15pm)

the International Society for Krishna Consciousness (ISKON).

Murshidabad and Malda

Some 50km (30 miles) north of the battlefield of Plassey, **Murshidabad** ❹ was the capital of Bengal in 1705, when the *diwan* (Mughal viceroy) of Bengal, Bihar and Odisha, Murshid Kuli Khan, transferred his capital here from Dacca. Most of the monuments are ruined, but Siraj-ud-Daula's grave at Khusbagh (across the river), Murshid Kuli Khan's tomb inside the Katra Mosque and the Jafarganj cemetery can still be seen. There are also palaces; the Jafarganj Deorhi, where Siraj-ud-Daula was assassinated; and **Hazarduari**, the nawab's palace, built in 1837 in Gothic style, now a museum containing old arms, china and special plates called *ghauri* used by the nawab that, it was believed, would crack if the food were poisoned (Sat–Thur 10am–4.30pm; charge). Murshidabad is still well known for its fine silk and ivory carving.

Nearby, at **Baranagar**, are a number of 18th-century terracotta temples. Further north, about 340km (210 miles) from Kolkata, is the town of **Malda** ❺, formerly called English Bazaar, a foreign settlement dating from 1680, where the Dutch, the French and then the East India Company carried on trade.

Gaur, nearby, was the capital of the Pala and Sen dynasties. The now deserted city was destroyed by the Afghan rulers of Bengal, and you can see the Barasona Baroduari Mosque completed in 1526; the Feroze Minar, a minaret built in 1486; the ruined Chika Mosque with Hindu idols on the doors and lintels; and the now dilapidated Lattan mosque. Portions of Hindu monuments from Malda were used to build the new capital of **Pandua,** where the most important building is the Adina mosque.

South to the Sunderbans

The **Sunderbans** ('beautiful forest' in Bengali) ❻ formed by the Ganges-Brahmaputra delta, start south of Kolkata and extend across the northern shore of the Bay of Bengal. A Unesco World Heritage Site, two-thirds of which is in Bangladesh, this

Sunrise in the Sundarbans.

is an area of marshy mangrove jungle, the largest estuarine forest in the world. It is also the land of the Royal Bengal Tiger, which swims and has been known to attack fishermen.

There are few roads, and water transport is often the only way of communication. A permit is required to enter the area. Check with the West Bengal Tourist Promotion Board for the latest information, particularly regarding the **Sudhanyakali** and **Sajankali** wildlife sanctuaries. The chances of seeing a tiger are slim, but there are estuarine crocodiles, the largest in the world, usually seen sleeping on mudflats along the river, as well as fishing cats, water monitors and turtles.

At **Bratacharingam**, 15km (9 miles) south of Kolkata, on the road to Diamond Harbour, is **Gurusaday Museum** (Tue–Sun 10am–5pm), a collection of Bengali traditional art: terracotta temple plaques, clay figurines, wood sculptures, Kalighat paintings, scroll painting and *kanthas*, which are used cotton saris, stitched together and embroidered.

On the Hugli, at the end of Budge-Budge Road, branching off Diamond Harbour Road, is **Achipur**, named after Ah-Chi, the first Chinese to migrate to Bengal in modern times (end of the 18th century). His red-painted grave facing the river is probably the only Chinese tomb along the Ganges. There is also a Taoist temple with inscriptions dating back to the 18th century. On every Lunar New Year, the Chinese community of Kolkata comes here on a pilgrimage, transforming this Bengali village into a Chinese community for one day.

Diamond Harbour ❼, 50km (30 miles) down the Hugli from Kolkata, a natural harbour, is a former stronghold of Portuguese pirates. Remains of their fort can be seen along the riverfront.

The last island before the ocean is **Sagardwip**, where the Ganges meets the sea. Every year, in mid-January, a religious festival, Gangasagar Mela,

West Bengal,
Odisha and Jharkhand

0   100 km
0   100 miles

is celebrated here. Over half a million pilgrims take a holy dip and then converge at the **Kapil Muni Temple**. On the west coast of the Bay of Bengal 240km (150 miles) southeast of Kolkata, on the Odisha border, is **Digha**, which has a good beach, and is very popular with Indian tourists.

West of Kolkata

The **Tarakeshwar Temple**, 57km (35 miles) west of Kolkata, is built around a black stone lingam of Tarakesvar Babu, an avatar (incarnation) of Shiva. It is of little architectural interest but is one of West Bengal's most active pilgrimage centres. At Sivaratri in February and Kastamela in August, barefooted pilgrims carry Ganges water from Kolkata to the temple in earthen pots decorated with flowers and pour it over the lingam.

Kamarpukur, 60km (37 miles) further west, a group of three hamlets surrounded by paddy fields, is religious philosopher Ramakrishna Paramhansdeb's birthplace. There is a temple with a marble statue of Ramakrishna.

THE GREAT HEDGE OF INDIA

The taxing of salt was controversial throughout the period of British rule in India. Having taken control of all salt production in the then 'presidency' of Bengal in 1788, the British East India Company decided to impose a tenfold increase in the salt tax. Naturally this was an unpopular move, and led to the widespread smuggling of salt into the region, mainly from the princely states which were not under direct British rule. The British response to this was to build a series of customs offices on the major transport routes into the state. When this proved ineffective, it was decided that the only solution was a continuous, impenetrable barrier. Initially running between Delhi and Agra, the line, which for the most part consisted of thick, live hedge, eventually covered over 4,000km (2,500 miles) and was patrolled by a staff of 14,000. It extended from the Punjab in the east to Odisha (Orissa) in the west, and eventually came to be known as the Inland Customs Line. The sums of money involved were colossal; by 1877 the salt tax was earning the British government £6.3 million per year, but meant that the average worker was having to spend at least a month's salary a year just to keep his family in salt. The line was abolished in 1879 but the tax lived on, instead imposed at the point of manufacture, and survived Gandhi's famous protest march of 1930 before eventually being rescinded post-Independence.

Visnupur ❽, 200km (125 miles) west of Kolkata, was the capital of the Malla kings. In the 17th and 18th centuries Visnupur became an important cultural centre, developing its own distinctive style of brick-built temple architecture, as well as being a centre for *dhrupad* singing.

The most impressive building in Visnupur is **Rashmancha**, a Vishnu shrine that takes the form of a flat pyramid-like structure resting on the arches of three circumambulatory galleries.

Nearby, opposite the Tourist Lodge, stands **Dalmadal**, a huge cannon almost 4 metres (13ft) long, whose boom saved the city from the Maratha armies in 1742. There are temples all over the city, most of them dedicated to Radha and Krishna. The most remarkable among them are: the **Kalachand Sri Mandir**; the **Shyam Rai Mandir**, perhaps the finest terracotta temple in Bengal, decorated with scenes from the *Ramayana* and the *Mahabharata*; **Jor Bangla**, covered with tiles depicting naval battles and hunting scenes; the **Madan Mohan**, dating from 1694; and **Madan Gopal**, almost resembling a church more than a temple, with its five towers.

North of Visnupur, 136km (85 miles) from Kolkata, is **Shantiniketan**. In 1861 Rabindranath Tagore's father founded an ashram here. The poet spent most of his Nobel Prize money to make it an educational institution. Here the poet revived the traditional Indian way of teaching in the open air, under a tree, in close contact with nature. Shantiniketan soon became one of the hubs of intellectual life; one of the university's most famous alumni is the late Indira Gandhi.

An annual festival is celebrated nearby at **Kendubilwa,** the birthplace of Jaidev, another great Bengali poet and keen propagator of Vaishnava philosophy. In mid-January, Bengali bards, known as *bauls*, gather for a four-day non-stop recital of the poet's work.

The pilgrimage centre, **Tarapith**, 80km (50 miles) from Shantiniketan, is a small village dominated by a temple to Tara, an avatar of Kali, whose third eye is said to have landed here.

North Bengal

North Bengal includes the hills and mountains of the Himalayas around Darjeeling as well as the district known as the Dooars that lies on the edge of the plains in the Terai. Having more in common with the Tibetan-influenced peoples to the north, it is culturally very different to the rest of Bengal. There has been unrest for a number of years, with the Gorkha Janmukti Morcha demanding separate statehood for the area under the name of Gorkhaland (you will see graffiti demanding this along with the yellow and green flags of the Gorkha indepedence movement everywhere). So far nothing has come of their agitations, but strikes and protests can shut down the district for weeks at a time.

Darjeeling Himalayan Railway

Every year at the beginning of the monsoon, the viceroys of India, and after 1911 the lieutenant governors of Bengal, would move to **Darjeeling** ❾ (also spelt Darjiling), situated at an altitude of 2,134 metres (7,000ft), facing the Himalayas. In the 1840s tea-planting was introduced in the area and Darjeeling 'orthodox' tea is now famous for its delicate flavour. Darjeeling is a three-hour drive up a winding road from Bagdogra airport near Siliguri (where there is also a railway station). It can also be reached from New Jalpaiguri railway station by the **Darjeeling Himalayan Railway**, a Unesco World Heritage Site.

Completed in 1881, the line climbs 1,500 metres (5,000ft) over 88km (54 miles) through mountains and tea gardens, reaching its highest point at the station of Ghoom (2,225 metres/7,300ft), before rounding the spectacular Batasia Loop with its amazing views and dropping down to its final station at Darjeeling.

The steep ride takes around seven hours – at one point the train goes so slowly that one can buy from hawkers alongside – and the train is now pulled by oil-fired locomotives, converted from the original coal-burning rolling stock. During the monsoon the service may be disrupted as the track can be in danger of being washed away. Another sporadic disruption comes from strikes demanding separate statehood for the region; these can stop services for days or even weeks.

Darjeeling

Darjeeling is an abrupt change from the plains, its population being largely Nepali, Lepcha, Tibetan and Bhutia. At the town centre is the **Mall**, Darjeeling's commercial street, lined with souvenir shops. The Mall leads to **Chaurastha**, a square where there are cafés, hotels and a good bookshop with many interesting books on India and Tibet. A Nyingmapa Buddhist monastery, Dorjeling, 'the place of the thunderbolt', once stood on **Observatory Hill** but was destroyed

The Toy Train at Darjeeling station.

Wall painting of a lama at Druk Thupten Sangag Choling Monastery.

by the Nepalis in the 19th century. A Shiva temple now occupies the site, although the central shrine is shared by both Hindu and Buddhist priests and the surrounding trees are festooned with prayer flags.

On Birch Hill to the north stands the Shrubbery, the residence of the governor of West Bengal, and further down along Birch Hill Road is the **Himalayan Mountaineering Institute**, once headed by the late Tenzing Norgay, the Sherpa guide who conquered Everest with Sir Edmund Hillary on 29 May 1953. A museum displays the equipment used (daily 8.30am–1pm, 2–4pm, entry through zoo; closed Thur during the winter).

The **Zoological Park** specialises in high-altitude wildlife – yaks, Himalayan black bears, pandas, but it also has four Siberian tigers. They are housed in open enclosures, but even so the conditions are very cramped and the animals look rather miserable (daily 10am–4pm; charge includes entry to the Mountaineering Institute).

Sherpa tea stall in the hills above Darjeeling.

Dominating the Mall is the **Planters' Club**, which visitors can join and where they can stay on a daily basis. The **Lloyd Botanical Gardens** (Mon–Sat 6am–5pm) were laid out in 1878 on land donated by the owners of Lloyd's Bank, and boast an impressive collection of Himalayan and Alpine flora. Nearby is the Tibetan Refugee Self-Help Centre with its temple, school, hospital, and a shop selling carpets, textiles and jewellery.

A little way out of town towards Ghoom is the **Druk Thupten Sangag Choling Monastery** at Dali. Although the building is only a little over 20 years old (it was founded by the lama Thuksay Rimpoche, who died in 1983), it is beautifully constructed, with a wonderfully decorated facade and an impressive prayer hall (ask one of the monks to show you inside if it is not too close to the evening prayer time at 5pm; donations to the monastery are appreciated).

South of Darjeeling

Mount Kanchenjunga can be seen from Observatory Hill, but a much better view of the peak is that from **Tiger Hill**, 10km (6 miles) south of Darjeeling. Taxis take visitors there to watch the sunrise. On most winter days the range can be clearly seen, with Kanchenjunga (8,598 metres/28,208ft) in the middle, flanked by **Kabru** (7,338 metres/24,074ft) and **Pandim** (6,691 metres/21,952ft). To the right are the Three Sisters, **Everest** (8,850 metres/29,035ft), **Makalu** (8,482 metres/27,828ft) and **Lhotse** (8,500 metres/27,887ft), and to the east, Tibetan peaks.

With a plunging view of the plains, **Kurseong** (1,458 metres/4,783ft), 35km (22 miles), marks the point where the Toy Train starts running parallel to the road. Southwest of Ghoom lies **Mirik**, a hill station set in attractive forests. It has an artificial lake in a small valley where boats can be hired.

Ghoom (perhaps more aptly called 'gloom', as it sits in the mist for much of the year) has an important Buddhist temple and one of the highest railway stations in Asia. The **Yiga Cholang Gelugpa Buddhist Temple** was built in 1875 and hosts a 5-metre (16ft) statue of Lord Buddha. To reach the temple, follow the signs leading up the narrow street off the main road, just down from the station on the Darjeeling side. There is another small Tibetan monastery on the left-hand side of the main road a little further on that is often confused with the older temple.

A five-hour drive (57km/35 miles to the west) from Darjeeling via Ghoom is the trekking centre **Sandakphu**, which is situated 130km (80 miles) from Everest as the crow flies. As well as being the most convenient place from which to start a trek, Sandakphu is worth a visit just to see its particularly fine view of the main Himalayan range. Make sure you take your passport if you wish to go any further as there is a checkpoint at the entrance to the village. Much of what lies beyond

runs along the Nepal border, and there are military checkpoints at regular intervals.

If you are in need refreshment – as you probably will be if you have come from Darjeeling – then the Hotel Khangchendzonga opposite the jeep-hire booth is a good place to eat noodles and *momos*.

Sandakphu is also the place to rent a jeep to take you up to **Phalut** (3,596 metres/11,700ft) for spectacular views of Kanchendzonga. Many of the vehicles here date back to the 1940s, left behind by General Slim's army at the end of World War II. The 'road' up to Phalut (22km/14 miles from Sandakphu) is very rough, indeed spine-breaking, but the views en route are wonderful, as are the moss-laden rhododendron forests you pass through. At the top is a small trekkers' guesthouse and a tea stall; take warm clothes, as the wind can be bitter.

Kalimpong

Kalimpong ❿, east of Darjeeling, is reached after a two-hour journey. Winding its way among forests and

Prayer flags adorn the trees outside a Buddhist temple in the Darjeeling hills.

Gorkha women carry heavy loads on the hill of Darjeeling Mall.

tea gardens, the road crosses the one-lane bridge over the Teesta River, near its confluence with the Rangeet at Pashoke, finally reaching Kalimpong, 51km (32 miles) from Darjeeling. The Lepchas say the two rivers are lovers who fled the mountains to hide their love. One came down in a straight line, led by a partridge, the other zigzagged, led by a cobra, and they were united at Pashoke. Kalimpong was once the starting point for the land route to Tibet. Twice a week, on Wednesday and Saturday, a *hat* (market) is still held here selling spices, fruit and traditional Tibetan medicines, textiles, wool and musk.

There are two Gelugpa Buddhist monasteries in Kalimpong. **Tharpa Choling** at Tirpai houses a library of Tibetan manuscripts and *thanka*, while **Zangdog Palrifo Brang Monastery**, on Durpin Dara Hill, is smaller and of more recent construction.

East of Kalimpong, along the Bhutan border, are the **Dooars**, a tea

Darjeeling barber.

garden and jungle area little-known to tourists, which can be reached by rail from New Jalpaiguri and by plane via Cooch Behar or Bagdogra. At **Jaldapara** there is a wildlife sanctuary, home to one-horned rhinos, elephants, deer, gaur and wild boar. The Tourist Lodge at nearby **Madarihat** is a villa on stilts built entirely in timber. Nearby is Phuntsholing, across the border in Bhutan.

ODISHA (ORISSA)

Most visitors to Odisha seek out the state's ancient temples, Adivasi villages or the wide beaches, although this part of eastern India is also known for its destructive cyclones, which move in off the Bay of Bengal; in 1999 a huge storm hit, killing thousands of people and destroying many buildings.

Ancient seafarers from Odisha set up colonies in Burma and Java. Buddhism became the religion of the kingdom of Kalinga, as Odisha was called, soon after the faith was established – spreading down from Bodh Gaya just to the north. Buddhist universities flourished at Nrusinghanath and Ratnagiri, near Cuttack.

Modern Odisha remains an intensely religious state where devotion is focused on Lord Jagannath, an incarnation of Vishnu. A visit to one of the state's major temples is like nowhere else in India; the sense of unflinching devoutness is unsurpassed, giving an immediate idea of the continuing importance of religion in daily Odishan life, and the impression that this is a practice that will continue for centuries to come. Not surprisingly, many elements of Odishan culture stemmed from its temples, where the most remarkable erotic statuary can be found and where Odissi, a style of religious dance, originated. Odissi was traditionally performed by resident temple dancers (*maharis*) devoting their lives to the temple god. When temple dance was outlawed the style began to disappear, but Odissi has been revived as a performing art.

Bhubaneshwar

Bhubaneshwar ⓫, capital of Odisha since 1956, is a city of temples. There were once more than 1,000 of them, and many are still active. Unlike in nearby Puri, most of the temples in the city, with a notable exception, will admit non-Hindus into the temple compound. A large number are located around **Bindu Sarovar**, a tank that is believed to receive water from all the holy rivers of India. The **Lingaraj Temple** to the south, built in 1014 to the glory of Shiva, is certainly the most impressive. A massive wall surrounds a 45-metre (150ft) high *deul* (temple), as well as minor temples to Parvati, Gopalini and Bhubanesvari. All are decorated with a profusion of sculptures of deities, nymphs and amorous couples. Entry is prohibited to non-Hindus.

Vaital Deul is a typical 8th-century temple with an oblong roof (*khakhara deul*). It is decorated with stone figures of Durga, such as the eight-armed Mahishasuramardini, on the northern wall, piercing the left shoulder of Mahisasura, the buffalo-headed demon, with her trident. Within the sanctum, another avatar (incarnation) of Durga, eight-armed Chamunda, often hidden by a drape, sits on a corpse, with an owl and a jackal on each side. She wears a garland of skulls.

Sisiresvara Temple, next to Vaital, is adorned with sculptures of lions, elephants, the gods Ganesh and Kartikeya, and the Avilokitesvara Buddha seated cross-legged and accompanied by a deer and a *nag* (cobra), illustrating the strength of the Buddhist influence in Odisha. The **Uttaresvara Temple** situated on the north bank of the lake has undergone extensive restoration.

Parasuramesvar is one of the oldest of a group of temples located east of the lake. Built in the 7th century, it is still well preserved and is decorated with a four-armed Ganesh, a two-armed Kartikeya mounted on a peacock and killing a snake, as well as amorous couples and rampant lions.

FACT

In 2007 and 2008 parts of rural Odisha, particularly the predominantly Adivasi Kandhamal District, saw terrible communal violence. While there has long been enmity between the two communities, the killing of the Hindu leader Swami Lakshmanananda in 2008 by Maoist insurgents unleashed attacks against the state's Christians, and the situation has remained tense, with sporadic outbreaks of violence in the years that have followed.

Druk Thupten Monastery.

FACT

Odishan temples in the Nagara style, seen at their best in Bhubaneshwar, have a distinctive architectural style. The *mandapa* (hall) that leads to the inner sanctum is decorated with horizontal lines called *pida*. This striated appearance also carries over to the temple tower (*rekha deul*) where the convex soaring lines of the building are decorated with sculpture and the characteristic horizontal divisions known as paga.

Siddhesvara Temple, Bhubaneshwar.

Muktesvara is the gem of Odishan architecture. The entrance to the temple compound is through a sculptured *torana* (gateway); the *jagamohana* (porch) has diamond-shaped latticed windows and a richly decorated interior. Temple, gateway and walls are covered with figures of female warriors, erotic scenes, elephants, women, monkeys in various comic scenes, women worshipping lingams and *naginis* (half-snakes, half-women). On each side of the *deul* is a grimacing lion face, flanked by smiling *ganas* (dwarfs). Just to the northwest is the more recent and less ornate **Siddhesvara Temple**.

Bhubaneshwar's **Rajarani Temple** (daily dawn to dusk; charge) is another fascinating place. Like the temples at Khajuraho (see page 286), it is particularly noted for its sculptures of women in sensuous poses, as well as the sculptures of the eight 'guardians' placed at cardinal points around the main structure.

Bhubaneshwar has two museums worth visiting. The **Odisha State Museum** (Tue–Sun 10am–1pm, 2–5pm; charge) displays Hindu, Buddhist and Jain sculptures, and early Odishan palm manuscripts. The **Handicrafts Museum** has a collection of traditional art, including Cuttack silver filigree. The **Tribal Research Museum** (Mon–Sat 10am–5pm) is in a cluttered government office, but has a decent bookshop of manuscripts and maps.

Around Bhubaneshwar

West of Bhubaneshwar, on the immediate outskirts, are two hills, **Udayagiri** and **Khandagiri**. Both were once inhabited by Jain ascetics who lived in cells excavated in the rock. Khandagiri has fewer caves than Udayagiri, but a small Jain temple still stands on top of this hill.

At **Dhauli**, a hill 8km (5 miles) south of Bhubaneshwar, there is an example of Emperor Ashoka's edicts. Sculpted elephants mark the site where in 262 BC, the Mauryan emperor defeated Kalinga troops, slaying 100,000 people and taking 150,000 captive. This scene of bloodshed is said to have turned Ashoka away from violence and led him to embrace Buddhism. To commemorate Ashoka's acceptance of Buddhism, substituting the ideal of *dharmavijaya*, spiritual victory, for *digvijaya*, military conquest, Japanese Buddhists have built a white **Peace Pagoda** on top of the hill.

At the former Buddhist university site of **Ratnagiri**, northeast of Bhubaneshwar, there are the remains of three monasteries, a number of ruined temples and several stupas.

South to Puri

Some 10km (6 miles) to the south of Bhubaneshwar is **Pipli**, a small village specialising in appliqué work in vivid colours unique to this area. Further on, **Puri** ⑫, 60km (37 miles) southeast of Bhubaneshwar, is the holiest place in Odisha for Hindus, and one of the biggest pilgrimage centres anywhere in India. The city was at one time a flourishing port identified with ancient Dantpur.

Puri is known for its cult of Jagannath, originating, some say, in the times when the people of Odisha worshipped trees, hence the practice of carving his image in wood. According to the more popular legend, however, the Lord appeared in King Indrodyumna's dream and commanded him to build a temple for him. The king complied, having the images carved out of a single log of wood found floating in the sea, as the Lord had enjoined in the dream. His temple lies in the midst of a huge complex of buildings housing more than 5,000 priests and temple staff.

The climax of Jagannath worship is the spectacular Rath Yatra festival (also known as the Car festival) celebrated every summer at the **Jagannath Temple**, said to commemorate Krishna's journey from Gokhul to Mathura.

Although the beach at Puri is one of the best in India, the seas can be very rough, with strong and erratic currents. Caution is advised. *Nolia*, lifeguards, easily recognisable by their white, cone-shaped straw hats, are not always alert. Be sure to watch the fishermen come ashore through the surf.

Muktesvara Temple, Bhubaneshwar.

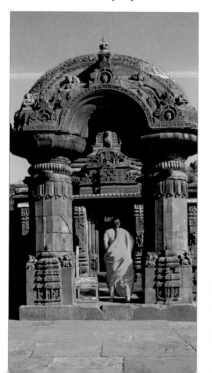

JAGANNATH TEMPLE, PURI

Known as the 'White Pagoda' by the mariners who used it in colonial times as a navigational aid while sailing between Madras and Calcutta, the Jagannath Temple was originally built in the 12th century. The main building is 65 metres (213ft) high, surmounted by the mystic wheel *(chakra)* and the flag of Vishnu. It is surrounded by a wall 6 metres (20ft) high. Non-Hindus are not permitted to enter the temple, although you're allowed to peek over the wall from the library opposite, whose roof terrace affords a bird's-eye view into the complex. About two weeks before the annual festival of Rath Yatra, held in June and July, the images of Jagannath and his brother, Balabhadra, and his sister, Subhadra, are given a ritual bath. On the first day of the festival, the deities are placed on *rathas*, chariots 12 metres (40ft) high, with wheels 2 metres (7ft) in diameter. Jagannath's chariot is decorated in yellow stripes; Subhadra has a red chariot; Balabhadra's is bright blue. All three are preceded by four wooden horses, but are actually drawn by hundreds of devotees from the temple to Gundicha Mandir (Garden House), 8km (5 miles) away, where they stay for seven days. The rituals completed, the deities ride back to their temple. Every 12 years, the images are replaced by new ones. The old images are then buried in a secret ceremony.

FACT

The Odishan coast is the world's most important nesting ground for the endangered Olive Ridley turtle. Thousands die every year, caught in fishing nets or hit by propellers, as they try to come inshore to breed. The state government has designated some protected zones along the coast, but illegal trawling still takes place. Local groups have set up the Odisha Marine Resources Conservations Consortium (www.omrcc. org) to protect the turtles.

Konark

Going north, 33km (20 miles) from Puri, is **Konark** (Konarak) , a former centre of Odishan Buddhism, an active port (now silted up) and, in ancient times, a centre for sun worship. A temple to the Sun God was built here in the 9th century. The present **Sun Temple** was erected in the 13th century and took 16 years to complete; 1,200 artisans were employed on the task. In its original form the temple consisted of a 70-metre (230ft) high *deul* with a 40-metre (130ft) *jagamohana*, representing the Chariot of the Sun; drawn by seven impetuous horses, the chariot rode on a dozen pairs of eight-spoke wheels.

Worship of the sun is thought to pre-date Hinduism, and still maintains a special reverence among Hindus, the sun being considered the only incarnation of God that can be seen on a daily basis. The sun god is known as Surya, the lord of excellence and wisdom; yoga practitioners will be familiar with the *surya namaskar*, a series of stretches designed to greet the rising of the sun.

A fishing village along the coast from Puri.

The *deul* collapsed in the middle of the 19th century and one horse is missing. The temple no longer stands on the shore since the sea has receded 3km (2 miles). Despite its dilapidated state the Sun Temple stands out as a fine example of Odishan architecture. Two lions guard the pyramidal entrance of the Sun Temple, and on each side of the temple stands a colossal war elephant and a warhorse trampling fallen warriors. Gentler scenes – erotic sculptures of couples in sensuous contortions, depictions of nymphs and court scenes, musicians, floral motifs and elephants – are also carved on the ruins.

South along the Odishan coast

Along the coast south of Bhubaneshwar is **Chilka Lake**, a 1,100-sq-km (425-sq-mile) shallow inland sea, separated from the Bay of Bengal by a sandy ridge, and spreading over 75km (47 miles) from north to south. From Barkul, the Odisha Tourist Development Corporation operates a two-hour cruise to Kalijai Temple offshore, and to Nalabar Island. The lake supports an abundance of fish and shellfish, and from mid-December to mid-January migratory birds spend the winter here. Further south, 95km (59 miles) from Bhubaneshwar, **Gopalpur-on-Sea** was, during the time of the British Raj, one of the finest beach resorts in eastern India.

Adivasis live in the district of **Koraput**, the Southern Hills area, and come mostly from the Austro-Asiatic Munda group. In the Northern Hills bordering West Bengal and Bihar, **Simlipal National Park** is one of India's most attractive forests; its 2,750 sq km (1,062 sq miles) are populated with tigers and wild elephants.

Northern Odisha

About 15km (10 miles) north from Bhubaneshwar is **Nandanakanan**, a park set in the Chandka Forest, where animals are kept in natural surroundings. The main attractions are four white tigers, one-horned rhinos, white-browed gibbons and African lions. There is also a **Botanical Garden**, with a rosarium, Zen temple and a cactus house.

Cuttack ⑯, the former capital of Odisha, is situated on a narrow river island 19km (12 miles) north of Bhubaneshwar. There are a few historical remains, including the blue granite **Barabati** Maratha fort, stormed by the British in 1803; **Qadmam-i-Rasul**, a walled compound with corner towers, containing three 18th-century mosques and a domed building housing footprints of the Prophet Muhammad engraved on a circular stone. The shrine is visited by both Muslim and Hindu worshippers.

Further north, **Balasore ⑰** is one of the earliest British settlements in India, granted to the East India Company in 1633. The Kutopokhari Temple at Remuna is a seat of Vaisnava culture and has an 18-arm granite statue of Durga. Bhudhara Chandi at Sajanagarh, built in the 16th century, contains a three-faced image of Shakti. Panchalingeswar on Devagiri Hill is a temple with five stone lingams. To the east is the small resort of **Chandipur-on-Sea ⑱**, with a beach where the sea recedes by 5km (3 miles) at low tide. This is a good place from which to visit Simlipal National Park.

JHARKHAND

To the east of Odisha and the south of Bihar is (along with Chattisgarh) the most recently created state of Jharkhand, cleaved off from Bihar in November 2000 and largely comprising the mineral-rich Chota Nagpur plateau. A large part of the population is Adivasi (over a quarter of the population are classified as 'tribals'), speaking Mon-Khmer languages. The main peoples are the Santhal, Bedia, Birhor, No, Khond, Munda and Oraon. Some still lead a hunter-gatherer existence, although the

majority have become sedentary and cultivate maize and millet, and raise cattle and fowl. About 60 percent are Christian. Many Adivasi groups face severe discrimination, and in desperation have left their traditional villages to find work in the state's new industrial cities. Enduring poverty in the region accounts for the long-running Naxalite-Maoist insurgency which has rendered the remote districts along Jharkhand's border with Odisha off-limits to outsiders for the past decade. In 2006, Prime Minister Manmohan Singh described the conflict as 'the single biggest internal security challenge ever faced by our country'. An estimated 12,000 people have been killed in violent encounters since the start of hostilities in 1990, yet little international attention has been attracted by what many regard as a de facto civil war.

Ornate sculptures adorn the Sun Temple at Konark.

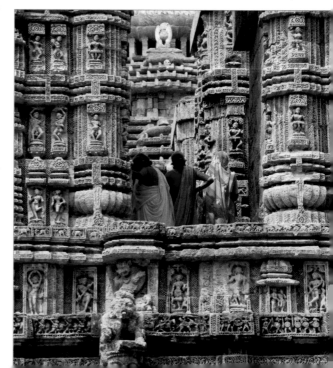

Konark's Sun Temple.

TIP

Parts of Odisha and Jharkhand, together with Bihar, are notorious for bandits, who have been known to target foreigners' hire cars. Avoid travelling on the road after dark be on your guard. These regions have also been affected by violence against certain minorities as well as the political Naxalite struggle against landlords.

Ranchi

Ranchi , the former summer capital of Bihar, suffered something of a loss of identity when its trees were cut to make room for a new industrial town. A few colonial buildings remain: the **Eastern Railway Hotel**, the **Lutheran Church** and **St Paul's Anglican Church**, and some eccentric villas on Kanke Road, near Ranchi Hill. Beyond the bazaar area, on top of Ranchi Hill, overlooking Ranchi Lake, stands a **Shiva Temple** of limited interest compared to the 17th-century fortified Jagannath Temple at Jagannathpur near the airport. It is open to non-Hindus. The city is also home to the **Tribal Research Institute and Museum** (Mon–Sat 10.30am–5pm), which has a large ethnographic collection open to the public.

Jharkhand has a great deal of forest cover (though this is being steadily depleted through logging), and there are many beautiful sites within easy reach of Ranchi. Three spectacular waterfalls lie within 40km (25 miles) of the capital, the **Hundru**, **Dassam** and **Johna falls**, and a little further

A woman performs morning rituals to celebrate Samba Dashami, a festival unique to Odisha.

are the **Panch Ghagh falls** (55km/35 miles from Ranchi; so called because it has five cascades in a row) and the **Hirni falls** (70km/44 miles away).

Rajrappa, situated at the confluence of the Damodar and Bhairavi rivers, is a lively pilgrimage site sacred to the goddess Chinamastika. Not too far away, **Palamau National Park**, 140km (87 miles) west of Ranchi, is both a Project Tiger site and a good place to spot elephants, particularly in the pre-monsoon months of March and April.

India's industrial heartland

Jharkhand's mineral wealth is the richest in India and accounts for most of the state's income. In addition to substantial deposits of coal and iron ore, there are also reserves of bauxite, copper and mica.

Jamshedpur , 170km (106 miles) southeast of Ranchi, is the property of the Tata Iron and Steel Company. The city has grown up around the first and most productive steel plant in India, built back in 1912 by the Parsi industrialist Sir Jamshedji Tata, after whom the city is named.

East of Ranchi is 'the Indian Ruhr', an industrial zone spreading along the Damodar River into West Bengal. In the northeast of Jharkhand is the city of **Dhanbad**; this sits on the largest coal reserves in India and is dominated by collieries, technical institutions and research centres. Just to the west is **Bokaro**, the site of India's largest steel complex. To the northwest of Dhanbad, the **Parasnath Hill** is a religious centre noted for its 24 Jain temples of both the Svetambara and Digambara sects, the most interesting ones being the **Samosavan**, **Bhomia Baba** and **Parasvanath**. Of the 24 Jain Tirthankaras, 20 attained nirvana here. Prospective visitors to this area should seek advice before travelling as many of the rural districts between the industrial centres are effectively held by Naxalite-Maoist rebels and too dangerous to cross.

RESTAURANTS

PRICE CATEGORIES

Average price for dinner, up to three courses for one person, excluding alcoholic drinks:
£ = under Rs200
££ = Rs200–500
£££ = Rs500–1,000
££££ = over Rs1,000

Eastern India has a surprisingly wide range of food. In the mountains some of the most popular dishes are Tibetan, such as noodle soups (*thukpa*) or *momos* (steamed vegetable or meat dumplings). Odishan food is influenced by both Bengali and Andhran food, and can often be fiery. Many of the best places to eat are in the pricier hotels, but local stalls serving simple rice- and *dhal*-based meals or Tibetan food can produce delicious, inexpensive and safe food.

West Bengal

Darjeeling
Hasty Tasty
Laden La Road. **£**
Quality, good value Indian thalis and side dishes (including dosas and pizzas) served to a discerning, and impatient, clientele in impeccably clean surroundings. Has the air of a school canteen at busy times, but still one of the best options in town for a quick meal.

Kunga
51 Gandhi Road.
Tel: 0354-225 3971. **£**
Understated roadside café close to the market area with heaps of mountain atmosphere and a menu of mostly Tibetan specialities to match. Try their huge bowls of steaming thukpa or juicy fried momos.

New Elgin
18 HD Lama Road. **£££**
A meal at this elegant Raj-era hotel is a quintessential Darjeeling experience. The dining hall is like a set from a Merchant Ivory film and the waiters wear white tunics, cummerbunds and ice-cream-wafer pagris on their heads. Drop by for High Tea or their popular lunchtime buffet; evenings à la carte only. And there's a cosy bare to retire to afterwards.

Odisha

Bhubaneshwar
Much of the best food in Bhubaneshwar is found in the hotel restaurants. Try the Indian eateries at Hotel Shishmo, on Gautam Nagar, and Hotel Swosti, on Janpath.
Bhuvanashree
Station Square. **££**
The bustle of this place reflects its popularity – pure veg local dishes, with a smattering of South Indian thrown in, all in a clean, efficiently run establishment.
Dalma
Sachivalaya Marg. **££**
One of the few places in town you can sample authentic, top-class Oriya cooking. Their filling lunchtime thalis feature the eponymous dalma (potato and aubergine simmered in dahl), traditional breads and curries, as well as fragrant chena poda for dessert, and there are plenty of non-veg rice meals (mutton, chicken or fish) for the less adventurous.

Mayfair Lagoon
8B Jaidev Vihar.
Tel: 0674-666 0101. **££–£££**
Choice of three quality eateries in this elegant hotel, a *dhaba*-style North Indian, Oriyan specialist 'Kanika' or a range of oriental cuisine at 'Lemongrass'.

Puri
Chanakya BNR
CT Road.
Tel: 06752-230 006, www.chanakyabnrpuri.com. **£££**
Puri's famous 'Railway Hotel' may have had a makeover, but the menu in its revamped restaurant still features the trademark Anglo-Indian dishes it's long been famous for – roast chicken, baked tomato tish and 'tipsy pudding' – alongside the usual multi-cuisine selection. Book a table in the old Bengal–Nagpur Railway dining car.
Peace Restaurant
CT Road. **£–££**
Does a good job of catering to the local traveller crowd; wide range of Western fare and a lovely garden.

Tibetan food such as momos (stuffed dumplings) is ubiquitous in Darjeeling.

Looking over Darjeeling and Kanchenjunga.

THE NORTHEAST

Situated in a sensitive border area with limited road access, the northeast is India's predominant Adivasi region. As restrictions ease, visitors have a greater chance to explore this fascinating region.

India's northeastern states, with the exception of Sikkim, are largely cut off from the rest of the country by Bangladesh, and as such form one of its most beautiful, spectacular and least visited areas. The landscape ranges from the steamy valley of the mighty Brahmaputra River with its World Heritage Site national parks, to the high mountains of Sikkim and the forested hills of the Adivasi states that border Burma (Myanmar) and Bangladesh.

Over the last few decades it has been difficult to gain access to the 'seven sisters' of Assam, Tripura, Meghalaya, Arunachal Pradesh, Nagaland, Manipur and Mizoram, but more recently the situation has improved. Although there are still the rumblings of insurgencies in Assam, Nagaland and, especially, Manipur, much of the region is free from trouble and more than repays the effort required to reach what is India's most remote region. Visitors require permits and forward planning is essential.

SIKKIM

Sikkim is India's highest state, with several peaks over 6,000 metres (19,700ft). Kanchenjunga, at 8,598 metres (28,208ft) the third-highest mountain in the world, is believed to be the abode of a god of the same

name, a fiery character with a red face who wears a crown made of five skulls and rides a snow lion.

Until the 18th century, the inhabitants of Sikkim were mainly Lepchas, cultivators of Mongol origin who came from Tibet in the 8th century. The first kings of Sikkim were the Namgyals, descended from the Minyaks of Tibet. Khye-Bumsa, a Namgyal prince, helped in the building of the Sakya Monastery in Tibet in 1268. He befriended the Lepchas and swore a blood brotherhood

Main Attractions
Gangtok
Rumtek Monastery
Kaziranga National Park
Shillong
Tawang
Kwairamband Bazaar, Imphal

Applying make-up for the Goshta Astami drama in Manipur.

TIP

Pelling is a small town in western Sikkim, just beyond Pemayangtse. It is becoming increasingly popular with visitors from the plains below, and has a large number of basic hotels. As well as Pemayangtse, there are a couple of other attractions nearby: the Sanga Choelling Monastery, thought to be the oldest in Sikkim, and the peaceful Khecheopalri Lake, which is said to be in the shape of the Buddha's foot.

with their chief, Thekongtek. When Thekongtek died, the Lepchas turned for leadership to Guru Tashi, Khye-Bumsa's fourth son, who was consecrated king (*chogyal*) in 1642. In 1700 the Bhutanese invaded Sikkim and the young *chogyal*, Chador, was forced into exile. He built monasteries at Pemayangtse and Tashiding and invented the Lepcha alphabet. He was assassinated in 1717 on the orders of his pro-Bhutanese half-sister, Pei Womgmo.

In the early 19th century the East India Company entered the Himalayas with a view to opening up trade with Tibet. In 1814, in the Anglo-Nepal Wars, Sikkim sided with the Company and received parts of the Nepali Terai (an area of grasslands, marshes and forests at the foot of the Himalayas) as a reward. As a friendly gesture, King Tsugphud Namgyal gave the East India Company the hill of Darjeeling for development as a resort. Relations soured and, following a quarrel over the illegal collection of taxes by the British in Sikkim, the British annexed the Terai

and established a protectorate over the kingdom. Since the 18th century, Nepalis have flowed into Sikkim, and now constitute 75 percent of the population.

When British rule in India ended, the government of independent India entered into a similar arrangement with the *chogyal*. Sikkim was not wholly merged with the Indian Union. In 1975, however, the Sikkim Parliament voted for the incorporation of the kingdom into India. The monarchy was abolished and Sikkim became a state.

Gangtok

The capital, **Gangtok ❶**, 'the hill made flat', lies at an altitude of 1,640 metres (5,400ft), facing Kanchenjunga. It is reached by road from Darjeeling, Bagdogra airport (110km/70 miles) or New Siliguri railway station (125km/77 miles). The most important building in the town is the **Chogyal's Palace**, usually closed to visitors except for the Tsuklakhang Royal Chapel, where ceremonies are held. The palace itself opens once a year, during the last week of December, for the Pong Labsal festival, during which lamas wearing masks perform a dance to Kanchenjunga around a banner-pole.

The **Research Institute of Tibetology**, built in 1958 by the last *chogyal* to preserve Tibetan culture, houses a library of more than 30,000 books on Buddhism, astrology, medicine and philosophy, as well as a collection of *thankas* (Tibetan religious paintings on cloth). The **Deer Park** was set up in homage to a Bodhisattva who was reincarnated as a musk deer. The **Orchid Sanctuary** is where 250 different types of orchids bloom. Nearby is a **Tibetan Refugee Craft Centre** and the well-known **Hotel Tashi Delek**.

Monastery treks

The **Rumtek Monastery**, 24km (14 miles) west of Gangtok, is one of the

ENTRY PERMITS

Entry to some areas of India's northeast can be problematic. Although the government is keen to open the region up to tourism, and restrictions are being eased all the time, it is wise to apply for any permits at least four weeks before you travel.

At present foreign travellers do not need permits to enter Assam, Tripura or Meghalaya, although they may be required to register on arrival and departure. In 2011, permit requirements were removed for Mizoram, Nagaland and Manipur. Although visitors need a permit to enter Sikkim, this is largely a formality, and it can be issued along with your visa or at the Sikkim border at Rangpo. For Arunachal Pradesh the regulations are less straightforward: you will need to apply for a Protected Area Permit and travel in a group of at least two people; the permit lasts for 30 days from the time of entry.

All permits are much easier to obtain through an agency. Alternatively you can apply in person to the Foreigners' Regional Registration Office, A.J.C. Bose Road, Kolkata. They might refer you to the Ministry of Home Affairs, Foreigners' Division, Lok Nayak Bhavan, Khan Market, Delhi. There are also registration offices in Siliguri and Darjeeling. Wherever you apply you will need passport photographs and a photocopy of your passport.

most famous in Sikkim. It belongs to the Karmapa school, a reformist branch of Tantric Buddhism founded in the 15th century. The monastery, built in the 1960s, is a replica of one in Tibet destroyed at the time of the Chinese takeover.

About 100km (62 miles) further west, **Pemayangtse** has a **Red Hat Ningmapa Monastery**, built in 1705. Its walls and ceilings bear frescoes of gods and demons. A one-day trek north leads to **Tashiding Ningmapa Monastery**, dating from 1706. A longer trek can be organised from Pemayangtse. As the path approaches **Kanchenjunga ❷**, the altitude rises to 4,270 metres (14,000ft) and terraced rice paddies and barley fields give way to apple orchards, then fir trees and mountain lakes. **Yakshun**, reached after six hours, is a small town where the first *chogyal* was crowned in 1642. The next stages are **Bakkhin** (five hours) and **Dzongri** (six hours), with a close-up view of Kanchenjunga.

ASSAM

Assam, meaning undulating, best describes this state of rolling plains dissected by the Brahmaputra and its many tributaries. One of the world's widest rivers, at places the Brahmaputra spills across several kilometres, making it impossible to see the opposite bank. The river often floods during the July monsoon, and in successive years recently Assam has experienced terrible deluges, due largely to excessive deforestation, in which more than a million people have been displaced.

Early Assamese history

The name Assam is probably derived from the Ahoms – the dynasty that ruled Kamrupa, as Assam was known, from the 13th to the early 19th century. Legend has it that the first king of Assam was Narakasur, son of the Hindu god Vishnu and Dharitiri (Mother Earth). Narakasur was killed

by Vishnu for his unreligious behaviour and was succeeded by his son Bhagadatta.

From the earliest times Assam has been a melting pot of peoples. In 1228, the Ahoms, a Buddhist people from northern Thailand, raided Assam and defeated the ruler of Kamrupa. They established their own kingdom with their capital in Charideo (now Sibsagar). The Ahoms converted to Hinduism, but there are isolated villages in Upper Assam where Buddhist customs are still practised and the inhabitants speak Shan Thai. The Ahoms established a powerful kingdom that flourished along the south bank of the Brahmaputra. On several occasions the Mughals tried to subdue the 'rats of Assam', but each time the Ahoms proved more than a match for the invaders.

British rule

The Ahom dynasty's grip on power started weakening from the 17th century. In 1792 Burma invaded Assam and the king, Gaurinath Singh, was forced to ask the East India Company

The fluttering of the flags in the breeze is considered by Buddhists to be an act of devotion.

The northeast is home to some 700 species of orchid.

for assistance. The Anglo-Burmese War of 1824–6 was followed by the Treaty of Yandaboo, whereby Burma ceded a large part of northeast India, including Assam, to the British. The colonists gradually established their hold over the region, and during World War II Assam played a strategic role as an important supply route to both China and Burma.

A testament to Assam's British legacy can be seen in the region's 300 tea estates. Braving the inhospitable terrain and climate, the British, with the help of labourers from central India, transformed large areas of malaria-infested tropical jungle into well-manicured carpets of tea for which the state is renowned.

Modern Assam

Since Independence in 1947 Assam has been fragmented into several smaller states. Today it only occupies the plains of the Brahmaputra Valley, south of Arunachal Pradesh and the kingdom of Bhutan. The fragmentation has deepened the crisis facing Assam. Its major problem is a growing imbalance between ethnic Assamese and immigrants – Bengali Hindus displaced by Partition in 1947 and Muslim immigrants fleeing poverty in Bangladesh.

The Northeast

0   100 km

0   100 miles

The fear of being swamped by outsiders triggered a popular student-led revolt in the 1980s, which snowballed into violent secessionist movements. The ULFA and Bodo militants now have a powerful presence in the state and are waging wars against Indian Army soldiers. As a result, Assam was shut to foreign tourists until the 1990s. The state is now open, but visitors should be aware of the political situation and take reasonable care when travelling around.

Guwahati

Pragjyotishpur, the ancient capital of the Kamrup kings, is now **Guwahati** ❸, a city with a population of around 600,000 people. Despite its dramatic location on the south bank of the Brahmaputra, Guwahati is not a pretty city. However, there are spectacular views of the river from the hill 3km (2 miles) southeast of the centre where **Raj Bhavan**, the governor's residence, and **Belle Vue Hotel** are situated.

Close to the railway station, opposite the Dighali Pukhuri tank, is the **State Museum** (Tue–Sat 10am–4pm, closed alternate Sats; charge), housing rare stone sculptures from the Kamrup period. Guwahati features some unusual temples: on a small promontory along the river is the 10th-century **Sukhlesvar Janardhan Temple**, which was rebuilt in the 17th century. It has a statue of Lord Buddha in a rare coexistence with Hindu deities. Nearby, in the middle of the river on **Umananda** (Peacock Island), is a small Shiva temple, which can be reached by boat from one of the ghats along the bank. During the winter months there's a daily sound and light show on Assamese history on the adjoining island.

Navagraha Mandir, the Temple of Nine Planets, is located on Chitrachala Hill. The temple was an astrological centre, hence the city's earlier name of Pragjyotishpur, the 'Eastern City of Astrology'.

Guwahati's most important temple is **Kamakhya Mandir**, 10km (6 miles) southwest of the city centre along the banks of the Brahmaputra on Nilachal Hill. Legend goes that to stop Lord Shiva's fearful dance of destruction, provoked by the sight of the dead body of his consort, goddess Shakti, the lesser gods dismembered and scattered her body far and wide. Shakti's *yoni* (reproductive organ) landed on Nilachal Hill. Kamakhya is one of India's main centres of the Tantric cult, and human sacrifices were once common here.

Along Guwahati's boundary wall and water tank one can still see the ruins of the original temple destroyed in 1553 by Kalapahar, a powerful Brahman who converted to Islam after being ostracised by his community for marrying a Muslim princess. The present structure, with its high beehive spire and long turtle-back hall, is typical of early Assamese religious architecture.

The pilgrimage to the hillside mosque of **Pao Mekkam** 25km (15 miles) to the southwest of Guwahati,

Numerous varieties of local tea: over half of India's tea comes from Assam. The best known is the strong, black tea, but other varieties are also grown.

Indian Tea

Although tea has only been grown on a commercial basis in India since the early 19th century, it is a vital part of Indian life

Chinese tradition points to India as the original home of tea. A Brahman, Dharma, went as a missionary to China. He was so tired that he fell asleep on reaching his destination. When he awoke, he was so angry at his own weakness that he tore out his eyebrows. The hair took root and became tea plants. He ate the leaves and fell into meditation.

The early tea trade

Tea had been identified in Assam by English travellers as early as in the last years of the 18th century. When the East Indian Company's monopoly of importing tea into Britain from China was abolished in 1823, the Honourable Company decided to look into the possibility of growing tea in India.

Expeditions were sent to Assam, and in 1826, following the Burmese Wars, the Company's troops brought back a tea bush as evidence of the

Picking tea on an estate near Darjeeling.

existence of tea in the area. On Christmas Eve 1844, the Governor General, Lord Bentinck, officially announced the discovery of tea in India and called for the development of the industry. Production started in Assam in 1836, in Bengal in 1839, and in the Nilgiris in the south in 1863. Plantations were introduced around Darjeeling in the early 1840s. The bushes were not indigenous; they had been smuggled out of China.

Workers for the plantations, which the Assamese were not keen to work on, were imported from Central India. Many of them were Adivasis and hired as indentured labourers, effectively slaves. The conditions were terrible, and a huge number of workers died from hunger and disease. Even today the overwhelmingly female tea workers are poorly treated.

The first Indian teas were of low quality, and Chinese experts were brought to Assam to supervise the processing of tea leaves. India became a major grower and, by 1900, was supplying Britain with 150 million pounds of tea against 15 million brought from China.

Modern tea production

Today, India is the world's largest producer of the fragrant leaf, with an output of 635,000 tonnes (total world production, 2 million tonnes). India's area under tea (400,000 hectares/990,000 acres) is the largest in the world. More than half of Indian tea is grown in Assam, one-quarter in West Bengal and one-fifth in the southern Nilgiris.

There are two sorts of Indian tea. CTC tea, the most common, takes its name from the Cut-Twist-Curl process in which the leaf is broken. It gives a strong liquid of dark colour. Most CTC production is for the home market. "Orthodox" teas have a lighter colour (they are said to be "bright") and yield a weaker liquid: one kilo makes 350 cups against 500 for CTC tea. Most of the Orthodox tea is exported, the best varieties being Darjeeling and Assam Golden Flower Orange Pekoe.

Some 60 percent of the Indian production is sold through auctions, including all export teas. There are auction centres at Guwahati, in Assam; Kochi, Coimbatore and Coonoor, in the south; and at Siliguri and Kolkata, in West Bengal. The Kolkata centre has two auction rooms, and the largest tea-tasting room in the world.

From having been consumed only by the hill peoples 150 years ago, tea has become the national drink of India. However, on average, each cup of tea consumed by an Indian is matched by approximately six consumed by an English person.

is said to be the equivalent to one-quarter, or a *pao*, of a Haj to Mecca. The state's Buddhist heritage can be seen at the site of Hajo's Hayagribha Maghadeva Mahadap temple, west of Guwahati. It is believed by some devotees that this was the place where the Buddha attained enlightenment.

Around Assam

Some 175km (108 miles) to the northeast of Guwahati lies **Tezpur**, widely regarded as the cultural capital of Assam. Historical ruins here date back as far as the 4th century, and the local orchid sanctuary has an amazing collection of rare species.

Travelling east, about 370km (230 miles) from Guwahati along the south bank of the Brahmaputra is the old Ahom capital of **Charideo**, now called **Sibsagar** ❹. Few monuments have survived Assam's monsoons and the tropical undergrowth that threatens to overrun every abandoned structure. Among those still standing are the water tank along with adjoining Devi, Shiva and Vishnu temples, an oval-shaped pavilion from where the kings watched elephant fights and the *charideo* (necropolis) of the Ahom kings.

Around 100km (62 miles) northeast of Sibsagar, surrounded by dense forests, are the oil towns of **Duliajan** and **Digboi** ❺. The British struck oil here in 1867 and built India's first refinery at Digboi.

Assam also has what may be the largest river island in the world, **Majuli**. The centre of Assamese Vaisnaivism, the island is dotted with *satras*, monasteries whose white-turbaned monks are renowned for their chimeric dance-plays and music. The island is also a haven for many species of birds.

National parks

Kaziranga National Park ❻, 230km (145 miles) northeast of Guwahati, is the principal sanctuary for the Indian one-horned rhinoceros. Nearing extinction at the turn of the 20th century, it's now being rehabilitated, with numbers now up to 2,100 and rising. Despite stringent protective measures, a number are still poached every year, and their horns

FACT

Outbreaks of ethnic violence between the Bodo minority and Assamese Muslims periodically results in the closure of entire districts and disruption to travel. In the monsoon in 2012, while 70,000 people sheltered from terrible flooding in government relief camps, widespread conflict between the two communities sent an additional 40,000 villagers into the camps. Around 20,000 passengers were also attacked after mainline trains were attacked by mobs during the disturbances.

Majuli Island in the Brahmaputra River.

TIP

Shillong Peak, not far from Shillong on the way to Cherrapunji, is 1,961 metres (6,430ft) high, the highest point in the district. Outside of the monsoon (May–September) and when not shrouded in mist and fog it gives magnificent views over the city and surrounding area.

are smuggled to traditional medicine markets in East Asia.

The majority of visitors are restricted to visiting only the central of the three ranges that make up the park, and while much of it is covered in tall grass, making sightings difficult, there are enough clearings to make a visit worthwhile. In addition to the rhinos, elephants, deer, bison and a variety of bird life can also be seen. The closest railway station is at **Furkating**, 75km (46 miles) away, or alternatively plenty of buses come here from Guwahati, 220km (136 miles) away.

To the northwest, 176km (109 miles) from Guwahati, is the **Manas Wildlife Sanctuary ❼**, a thick tropical jungle set along the Bhutan border. The park is a sanctuary for several endangered species, including tigers, leopards and elephants as well as rhinos. The river flowing through the park is an angler's paradise for *mahaseer*, a local variety of carp. Angling camps are also organised on the Jia Bharali River in the **Nameri Sanctuary**, 200km (124 miles) from Guwahati, also a good

place to see wild elephants, rare turtles and even tigers.

MEGHALAYA

Meghalaya, 'the abode of clouds', south of Assam, was previously part of Assam. It became a separate state of the Indian Union in 1972. It is a hilly region, and very foggy in winter, causing the traffic police to dress in fluorescent clothing. It is inhabited by three Adivasi groups: the Garos in the west, the Khasis in the centre, and the Jaintias in the east. They originally constituted independent little township kingdoms, the Seiyams, which the British annexed one by one to British India in the 19th century.

The Garos are Tibetan. They once practised human sacrifice as part of their local religion. In 1848, under a treaty with the British, they agreed to stop displaying skulls in their houses. Archery stakes, a peculiar local form of gambling using arrows, is still a common amusement.

The Khasis are Mon-Khmers related to the Shans of Burma. Their

An Indian one-horned rhinoceros cools off in a water hole at Kaziranga National Park.

NORTHEAST TRANSPORT

Buses: In many areas you will have to rely on the local bus service, or hire a jeep and driver. Buses are usually quite reliable, but for most northeastern states you must travel as an organised group: transport is usually organised as part of the package.

Flights: The gateway for travel into the northeast is Kolkata,. There are airports in Guwahati, Argartala, Dibrugarh, Imphal and Shillong,. The airport for Sikkim is Bagdogra, from where you must take a taxi up to Gangtok (there is a pre-paid counter in the airport).

Trains: Rail services are limited to the Brahmaputra Valley and run, via Guwahati, on broad-gauge tracks as far as Dibrugarh. A narrow-gauge line runs north of the broad-gauge line from Guwahati to Murkongselek.

religion, Seng Khasi, holds that God is everywhere and should not be represented or adored in a specific form. There are no temples, just prayer halls for specific celebrations. The Khasis adorn themselves in jewellery made of gold and amber. To commemorate their dead, they erect *mawbyn-nas*, monoliths arranged in groups of three or more that can be seen in most villages. The Pnars, generally known as Jaintias, are closely related to the Khasis. The three peoples have matrilineal and matrilocal family systems. Missionaries in the 19th century converted most of them to Christianity but old traditions persist, especially their dances. A major dance festival, the *Shat Suk Myasiem*, the Festival of the Joyful Heart, is held in Shillong in April. In November, the Garo 100-drum festival in Tura celebrates the end of the harvesting season.

Shillong ❽, the capital of Assam until 1972 and of Meghalaya since then, lies 100km (60 miles) south of Guwahati, a three-hour drive through hills covered with pineapple and betel plantations, and pine forests. It passes along **Bara Pani** (Umian Lake).

Shillong has been called the 'Scotland of the East' because of its climate and its location at an altitude of 1,500 metres (4,900ft). Here the British and rich Bengalis built cottages, a golf course and polo grounds. It is a small city with a market, **Bara Bazaar**, selling Nepali silver and Khasi gold jewellery, spices and textiles. Shillong spreads across hills covered with English-style country houses, the largest being **Raj Bhavan**, the summer residence of the governor of Assam and Meghalaya, and the **Pinewood Hotel**. Nearby are the **Ward Lake** and **Botanical Garden**. The highest point in the state is **Shillong Peak** (1,965 metres/6,440ft), which offers a fine view of the neighbouring hills.

Cherrapunji ❾, 56km (35 miles) to the south, was infamous as the world's wettest place, until the record was broken by nearby **Mawsynram, 15km (9 miles) northwest**, which on average receives just under 12 metres (470ins) of rain annually. The most

Religious art in a Vishnu Monastery.

interesting spot is **Mawphluang**, 24km (15 miles) further south, a barren and windy plateau covered with monoliths. The road takes you along the side of a spectacular gorge. This whole region is riddled with caves, many with spectacular formations and river passages.

Access to **Garo hill country** from Shillong is difficult, via Guwahati and then southwest to **Tura**. The villages in this region have retained their traditional architecture and some traditional buildings, like the bachelors' dormitory at Rongreng (Williamnagar). The highest point in the Garo Hills is Nokrek Peak (1,412 metres/4,630ft); the rich flora in this area is now protected as part of a biosphere reserve. The hill region is also home to a variety of fauna, including India's only ape, the Hullock gibbon, as well as elephants and tigers.

TRIPURA

Well-forested Tripura was the former princely state of Tipperah. The population, mostly of Tibeto-Burmese origin, took up Vaishnava Hinduism early,

Shillong's Bara Bazaar.

and was ruled by rajas until Indian Independence. Other major groups in Tripura are the Kukis – related to the Shans of Burma – Chakmas, Moghs, Lusharis and Riangs. Tripura had been at war with her neighbours when the British, taking advantage of a feud between Maharajah Krishna Manikya and the nawabs of Bengal, intervened and established a protectorate. Following Independence, Tripura joined the Indian Union in 1949 and became a state in 1972.

Agartala ⑩, the capital, is a burgeoning city town of 400,000 people, surrounded by hills on three sides. One of the main sights is the large **Ujjayanta Palace**, built 1899–1901 by Maharaja Radha Kishore Manikya. Much of the building is very fine and is set in pleasant Mughal-style gardens; it is now the home of the State Legislature. The **Pushbanta Palace** was erected in 1917 by Maharaja Birendra, a philanthropist who helped Rabindranath Tagore to finance the Shantiniketan University in Bengal. The palace is now the residence of the governor of Tripura. The **Tripura**

Government Museum (Mon–Sat 10am–1pm, 2–5pm; charge) has an interesting array of archaeological finds as well as a good display of Tripura crafts.

In Udaipur (55km/34 miles from Agartala), the ancient capital of Tripura, is the temple to **Tripura Sundari**. Said to be built on the spot where the right foot of Sati fell, it is also known as Kurma ('turtle') Pith as its shape resembles a turtle's back. By the temple is a pool containing enormous turtles which you can feed.

ARUNACHAL PRADESH

North of Assam lies Arunachal Pradesh, kept isolated for years by its strategic location on the frontier between India and China. The area has 1.4 million inhabitants divided into 82 different peoples, the largest groups being the Apatanis, Khamptis, Padmas and Miris. Most are Buddhists. It can get very cold in Arunachal, even in the summer, so it is advisable to take plenty of warm clothing.

Itanagar, the state capital, has a couple of interesting sights, including Itar

Fort, a brick-built citadel said to have been constructed by the Ahoms, and the Jawaharlal Nehru Museum, which has good coverage of the state's customs and peoples.

At **Tawang ⓫**, over the Sela Pass (4,215 metres/13,820ft), is India's largest Buddhist monastery. Founded in 1642, this Gelugpa *gompa* (monastery) is where the 6th Dalai Lama was born. The monastery is very similar to those in Tibet, with colourfully painted

Joss sticks at a Buddhist temple in Arunachal Pradesh.

Khasi archers, Meghalaya.

windows and murals, and there is also a huge gilded statue of the Buddha. The monastery celebrates its major festival in December/January. However, perhaps the main attraction is its spectacular location, at an altitude of 3,050 metres (10,000ft); the views and surrounding scenery are breathtaking.

To the east, near the border with China and Burma, the Brahmaputra forms a lake, **Brahmakund**, before entering the plains of Assam. Bathing here is believed to wash away one's sins, and Hindus come by the thousands on Makar Sankranti Day in mid-January. The old road to Mandalay begins at **Ledo**.

In the south of the state is the **Namdapha National Park**, which has retained much of its pristine state due to its inaccessibility. It covers a wide variety of environments, ranging from around 200 metres (650ft) to 4,500 metres (14,750ft) above sea level. The remote sanctuary is home to the very rare Hoolock gibbon, and four cat species – tigers, leopards, clouded leopards and snow leopards – as well as a population of red pandas.

Red pandas are an endangered species found in the Himalayan foothills of northeastern India at altitudes between 2,000 and 4,000 metres (6,500–13,000ft).

NAGALAND

Remote Nagaland is inhabited by a variety of Tibeto-Burmese peoples, speaking more than 20 different dialects, the largest groups being the Aos, Angamis and Konyaks. These Nagas were once headhunters, however, the practice was abandoned two generations ago.

The Cacharis, one of the Naga peoples, once established a Hindu kingdom at **Dimapur** from where they used to raid Assam and Burma. The Ahoms of Assam established their authority over the Cacharis at the end of the 17th century. However, as soon as Burma invaded Assam in 1816, the Naga raids on the plains were resumed. In 1832, the British, while establishing a road link between Assam and Manipur, met the Nagas for the first time. For a few years they made attempts to control them, Naga raids being followed by punitive expeditions. In 1879 the British outpost at **Kohima** came under Naga siege for a month. A state of permanent peace was finally reached in 1889.

During World War II the Japanese and the Indian National Army launched an attack on Kohima, taking half of the city in 1943. The objective was to reach Dimapur, a vital railhead for supplies to British Army units in forward areas. Kohima proved to be the furthest point west reached by the Japanese. The War Cemetery at Kohima contains Commonwealth graves, and a memorial with the inscription: 'When you go home tell them of us and say, "For your tomorrow we gave our today."'

In the war against the Japanese, the Nagas were of great help to the Allied forces, carrying supplies to the front, evacuating the wounded and spying behind enemy lines. Following Indian Independence, some Nagas grouped in a Naga National Council and demanded autonomy. But soon successionist elements were asking for independence, with the aim of uniting the estimated four million

Nagas living on both sides of the Indo-Burma frontier. In November 1975, at Shillong, the government of India and Naga leaders reached an agreement whereby the Nagas accepted the Indian Constitution, but there are still occasional outbreaks of violence, and visitors may encounter army checkpoints.

Naga villages are usually perched on hills and are surrounded by a stone wall. One, **Barra Basti**, is a suburb of Kohima. To the east of Kohima, at the railhead of Dimapur, are the remains of the former capital of the Cachar Hills razed by the Ahoms in 1536.

The best way to see the region is on foot between November and May. You have to apply for a Protected Areas Permit, and stick to officially designated circuits, visiting sanctioned sights. Chief among the attractions is the annual Hornbill festival, held in a village near Kohima in the first week of December. Sponsored by the government as an attempt to foster social integration between the state's indigenous inhabitants, it attracts Naga tribes people from across the region, dressed in traditional finery. Expect displays of dance, song, wrestling and archery competitions, as well as a chilli-eating contest, beauty pageant, rock concert and car rally.

MANIPUR

This is another former Princely State on the Burmese border. Meitheis, a Tibeto-Burmese people related to the Shans, form 60 percent of the population. They live in the valleys and have developed *Jagoi*, a Manipuri dance style which is performed at festivals and is accompanied by the *pung* (a double-headed barrel drum). The 29 other peoples, most of them Tibeto-Burmese and now mostly Christian, form one-third of the population and live in the hills. The largest of these groups are the Lotha, the Konyak and the Nagas.

Manipuris are reputedly fierce fighters. They excel in martial arts, including: *thangta*, practised by both men and women, and accompanied by drumming; the spear dance *(takhousarol)*; the sword fight *(thanghaicol)*; and wrestling *(mukna)*. The

Striking a bargain at Imphal's Kwairamband Bazaar – a large market run entirely by women.

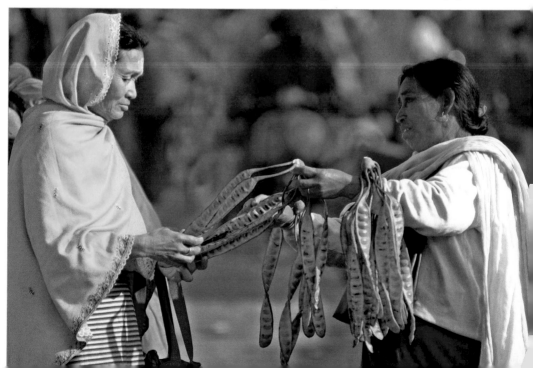

Manipuris have a history of conflict with their neighbours in Arakan and other border regions of Burma, which they invaded in 1738. In 1819, the raja of Manipur, who previously had paid tribute to the Burmese crown, did not attend the coronation of Burma's new king, Bagyidaw. The Burmese sent out a punitive expedition. The Anglo-Burmese War was caused partly by this incursion.

Burma was defeated, and by the Treaty of Yandaboo, on 24 February 1826, recognised British sovereignty over Manipur. After years of relative peace, a revolt took place in 1891 during which the British chief commissioner of Assam was killed. The rising was crushed and its leader, Tikenderjit Singh, the maharaja's brother, hanged. There was trouble again in 1930, when a self-styled prophet, Jadonang, announced the imminent departure of the British. He was executed and the priestess of his cult, Rani Gaidiniliou, who was only 17, was sentenced to life imprisonment. She was released when India gained its independence.

Yongchak (bitter gourd) is a highly prized local vegetable. Together with chillis and fermented fish, it forms a major part of yongchak eronba, Manipur's best-known dish.

In 1944, the Indian National Army and the Japanese put Imphal under siege from March to June. They were repulsed, and in March 1945, General Slim's 14th Army marched to Mandalay from the Manipur hills. The war cemeteries that commemorate those who died are outside of Imphal on the Dimapur road and are kept in a very good condition. In 1949 Manipur became a Union Territory and a fully fledged state of the Indian Union in 1972, although secessionists still continue to fight for independence.

Imphal ⓭, the capital, can be reached by road from Kohima after a 130km (80-mile) drive. The most impressive sight is the huge **Kwairamband Bazaar**, a women's market selling food and crafts. The **Manipur State Museum** (Tue–Sun 10am–4.30pm; charge) has a good display of Adivasi artefacts. Also worth seeing are the two well-maintained war cemeteries, the Raja's Palace and Royal Polo Grounds. Nearby, at **Langthabal**, is the Raja's Summer Palace. **Moirang**, 45km (28 miles) from Imphal, has the **Thankgjing**

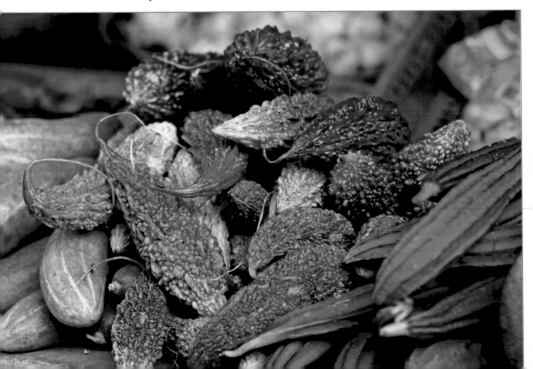

Temple, dedicated to a forest god, and is also known as the headquarters of the Indian National Army.

MIZORAM

The former Lushai Hills District, Mizoram is bordered by Bangladesh on one side and Burma on the other. The region has deep river gorges, the sides of which are densely forested with bamboo. Related to the Shan, Mizos are a group of peoples (Lushais, Hmars, Pawis) that came relatively recently to India. They started raiding tea plantations in 1871. The British retaliated and established control over the area in 1872, but could not establish peace until 1892. The British then introduced the Inner Line system. Only missionaries were allowed through. As a result, 95 percent of the population is Christian, and literacy has reached 86 percent in some areas. At Indian Independence Mizoram became a Union Territory, and was granted full statehood in 1987.

The capital, **Aizawl** ⑭, is built along a ridge. In town is Bara Bazaar, the central shopping area where local

Thukpa, Tibetan noodle soup. Tibetan cultural influences are in evidence in parts of Arunachal Pradesh.

people in traditional costume sell their produce, including river crabs in small wicker baskets. The small **Mizoram State Museum** (Mon–Fri 9am–5pm, Sat 9am–1pm; charge) has an interesting collection of local artefacts. Other places of interest include the **Dampha Wildlife Sanctuary** on the Bangladesh border, and the busy town of **Champhai**, from where you can visit the traditional Mizo village of **Ruantlang**.

RESTAURANTS

PRICE CATEGORIES

Average price for dinner, up to three courses for one person, excluding alcoholic drinks:
£ = under Rs200
££ = Rs200–500
£££ = Rs500–1,000
££££ = over Rs1,000

The food in Sikkim and Arunachal Pradesh is strongly influenced by Tibetan dishes. Elsewhere in the region, the diet is dependent on rice, and there is a great deal of freshwater fish on menus. Unlike most other areas of India, people in the northeast eat lots of pork and, in some places, duck. For Assamese dishes, try local 'meals' restaurants or food stalls (just make sure the turnover is quick and that things seem fairly hygienic). Be aware that in Nagaland dog meat is widely eaten.

Sikkim

Gangtok
9'INE
New Market, MG Marg. Tel: 3592 205061. ££
Proper Sikkimese cuisine can be hard to find outside family homes, but this tiny café serves wonderful local cooking – from chicken momos and thukpa, to full set meals. Everything's cooked fresh to order, so expect a bit of a wait. Only four tables, with a great view.
Baker's Café
MG Marg. £–££
The best place in town for light Continental bites: freshly baked croissants, paninis, toasties, pizzas, cakes and pastries, served in a modern café space with proper espresso coffee and a selection of delicious 'mocktails'.
Rasoi (Blue Sheep)
Above the tourist office, MG Marg. ££

Tasty vegetarian food, with a full range of dishes from both north and south. For a quick pitstop, try their mellow dahi kadhi with pakora. Or choose from a selection of different thalis at lunchtime.

Assam

Guwahati
Gam's Delicacy
GS Road, Ganeshguri.
Tel: 0361-223 3402. ££–£££
Indisputably the top place in town for non-veg northeastern cuisine, from duck, pigeon and pork to local river fish. Don't be put off by the unprepossessing location under a noisy bypass flyover – the interior's a delight and food superb.
Royal Woodland
GNB Road, near State Museum. £
A clean, vegetarian chain serving South Indian food; including good valvue *thalis and crunchy dosas*.

Fishermen in a dugout canoe at Kovalam.

View across the Western Ghats near Munnar.

THE SOUTH

India's steamy tropical south is the most relaxed part of the country. Wonderful food, cool green hill stations, a smattering of sandy beaches and an exuberant culture are all reasons to visit.

Schoolgirl with jasmine flowers in her hair.

All four states of South India, as well as the Lakshadweep and Andaman Islands, lie deep within the tropics, a possible reason for the more languid pace of life; on the whole, this is a laid-back region in comparison with the hustle of the north.

South Indian women twine fragrant jasmine blossoms into their hair, while many of the men still wear the traditional *lunghi*. Patterns made from flower petals or crushed and coloured rice, known as *kolam*, enhance the entrances of temples and households. Rice is the staple grain here, and people devour heaps of the stuff from clean banana leaves. Phrasebook Hindi won't get you very far in this region, where most languages are Dravidian. Linguists would need Telugu in Hyderabad, Kannada in Bangalore, Tamil in Chennai (Madras), and Malayalam in Kochi, but English is widely understood.

The vast Deccan plains, the rainforests of the Ghats, and two long coastlines distinguish the south. Temples are truly colourful: each deity is brushed with a vibrant hue, and the steep temple tops look as chaotic and crowded as a bazaar. Kerala is noted for its elephants and exuberant festivals. Hyderabad, the gateway to South India, has been famous since Marco Polo's time for the skills of its Islamic craftsmen and the grandeur of Golconda Fort. This glory is almost surpassed by Hampi, a deserted stone city in the

The Shore Temple at Mamallapuram

midst of rural Karnataka. The pubs of Bengaluru (Bangalore) resemble those anywhere in the world, reflecting the city's status as India's most forward-looking city. Chennai values, and strives to preserve, its heritage of music, dance and commerce. While it has retained its charm, the South is now throwing off its slightly dreamy traditional image and is the driving force behind India's thriving new technology and software industries.

Across the waters of the Bay of Bengal lie the scattered islands of Andaman and Nicobar, home to indigenous peoples, tropical jungles full of exotic birds and clear blue seas teeming with aquatic wildlife. Off the west coast is the beautiful, remote island chain of Lakshadweep, complete with perfect white-sand beaches.

The view from the Charminar, Hyderabad.

KARNATAKA AND ANDHRA PRADESH

Karnataka is one of the most appealing states in India, with beautiful scenery, evocative ruins and some fascinating cities. Less visited by tourists, Andhra Pradesh has some impressive sights including temples, palaces and ruined forts.

The states of Karnataka and Andhra Pradesh lie on the threshold of India's deep south, straddling the Subcontinent from the lush Malabar and Coromandel coasts via the largely inhospitable Deccan plateau. This huge area encompasses a little of everything that India has to offer, from the pulsating, high-tech megacities of Bengaluru and Hyderabad to the dry, arid expanses of the Deccan plateau and the lush greenery of the Nilgiri Hills.

Parts of both these states are devastatingly poor and underdeveloped, in great contrast with the finest residences of the states' capitals, which could rival those anywhere in the world. This has always been a region of enormous strategic importance, and has been home to some of the country's greatest dynasties, including the Nizams of Hyderabad and Wodeyars of Mysore. The resulting historical legacy can be seen in the stunning array of palaces, forts, monuments and museums that dot these two states; although Andhra Pradesh in particular sees relatively few visitors, this region is one of India's most colourful, and is not to be missed.

KARNATAKA

Created in 1956 from the former state of Mysore, Karnataka is one of India's most varied states, with a series of distinct regional landscapes. A narrow fertile coastal strip to the west – the so-called Konkan coast – is flanked by the hills of the Western Ghats, their well-watered slopes sustaining dense tropical forests famed for their teak, rosewood and bamboo. With much of the moisture from the rain-bearing monsoon expended on the ghats, the Deccan plateau to the east is a much drier region. In the southwest lie the hills and valleys of the Kodagu (Coorg) district. Amid the profusion of dense tropical rainforests in the

Main Attractions

Bengaluru (Bangalore)
Mysore
Somnathpur
Belur
Halebid
Sravanabelagola
Hampi
Gokarna
Charminar, Hyderabad
Golconda Fort

Mysore resident.

Karnataka and Andhra Pradesh

0   100 km
0   100 miles

N

Southern Ghats roams the Indian elephant, the gaur and the long-tailed langur, the last frequently breaking into the silence of the sun-freckled forest with gossipy chatter.

Karnataka has a population of around 61 million, and its people are as varied as its land. The northerners are predominantly Lingayats, followers of the 12th-century scholar-saint Basavanna. A Hindu reformer, his message was spread through rhythmic prose called *vachanas*. In the south around Mysore, the rich farming community of Vokkaligas dominates. Their rivalry continues in Karnataka's politics today. The state has one of India's most noticeable wealth gaps between well-off urbanites (notably in Bengaluru) and impoverished village dwellers.

Coastal Karnataka is inhabited by fisherfolk whose forebears traded with ancient Mesopotamia, Persia and Greece. Portuguese colonial influence can be seen in Mangalore, where the Christian community and its churches were established in the 16th century. Chikmanglur, along the border with Kerala, is a major coffee-growing district. Adivasi communities live mostly in the north and the west. The Coorgs of the Kodagu region on the border with Kerala have a distinctive culture of their own.

The principal language, Kannada, has a rich tradition of poetry and prose. The earliest classic, *Kavirajamarga* (9th century), and Kannada inscriptions from the 5th century, indicate its antiquity.

Karnataka's traditional theatre, *bayalata* (see page 367) has many forms, the best-known of which is *yakshagana*. These dance-dramas take their themes from Hindu epics, and the performers appear in elaborate costumes.

The traditional crafts of Karnataka include silk weaving, sandalwood- and ivory-carving, Bidri work from Bidar and the popular red clay tiles of Mangalore.

Regional history

Successive Buddhist, Hindu and Muslim rulers dominated this part of southern India, leaving a trail of architectural wonders such as Bijapur, Hampi, Aihole and Badami. Chandragupta Maurya, India's first emperor, was believed to have converted to Jainism in the 4th century BC at Sravanabelagola (see page 364).

The Hindu Chalukyas (6th–8th century AD) were followed by the Rashtra-kutas and other princely houses before the Hoysalas of the Vijayanagar Empire established the capital of their vast empire at Hampi (see page 378) in the central eastern region of the state.

The demise of the Vijayanagar Empire in the 16th century was followed by a period of Muslim rule. Hyder Ali and his son Tipu Sultan, rulers of the Kingdom of Mysore in the south, were defeated by the British in a battle at Srirangapatnam (see page 363) in 1799, and the British restored the former Wodiyar Rajas of Mysore as governors. The

FACT

Karnataka's hill forests are the source of 90 percent of India's sandalwood, a rare kind of timber that yields a delicate perfume used in Hindu ritual and ayurvedic medicine. The government Forest Department has a monopoly on production, but with prices reaching US$300 per kilo on the international market, illegal logging is decimating much of the remaining forest.

The Bull Temple in the southwest of Bengaluru is in south Indian Dravidian style.

FACT

On 1 November 2006, Bangalore's name was changed to its Kannada equivalent, 'Bengaluru'. The move – the latest in a series of name changes to have been imposed by nationalist politicians on major Indian cities – sparked a degree of controversy. Business leaders claimed it was a huge waste of money that gave entirely the wrong message to potential investors in India's hi-tech capital. Supporters insisted the re-branding would boost local pride.

Downtown Bengaluru.

present state government meets at the Vidhana Soudha in the capital, Bengaluru.

Bengaluru (Bangalore)

The booming city of **Bengaluru** ❶ (formerly Bangalore) derives its name from *Benda Kaluru*, 'place of boiled beans". It was originally founded in 1531 by a local chieftain, Kempe Gowda, who built a mud fortress here that was later extended by Hyder Ali and Tipu Sultan. During the British Raj the pleasant climate – Bengaluru's altitude of 920 metres (3,020ft) means temperatures are relatively low – made it a popular garrison town with attractive parks and gardens. In recent times the city has become a research centre for science and technology and the vibrant hub of India's dynamic hi-tech industries. The addition of the computer software industry attracted people from all parts of India and, with a population approaching 6 million, Bengaluru is rapidly becoming overcrowded and congested; it is now India's third-largest city.

A major transport centre, Bengaluru presents the modern face of India and has some of the country's best accommodation, some excellent restaurants and lively bars. These abound in the area around M.G. Road, Brigade Road and St Mark's Road. The shopping is good, too: try **Commercial Street** for clothes and jewellery, and for contrast visit the colourful city **vegetable and fruit market** on Avenue Road, and the Old Town with its narrow lanes and bazaars. Bengaluru is also famous for its cinema halls. **The Plaza** on M.G. Road and the **Galaxy** on Residency Road show first-run English films. As a university town, it has several music festivals, usually featuring local bands.

The few local sights include public buildings such as the 46-metre (150ft) **Vidhana Soudha** (Secretariat and State Legislature) at the northwest corner of **Cubbon Park** ❹, which is floodlit during weekends and holidays. The peaceful 1,200-hectare (3,000-acre) park was laid out by the British viceroy in 1864. Other notable buildings including the red Gothic

KARNATAKA TRANSPORT

Flights: Bengaluru (Bangalore) is one of India's busiest airports, with direct flights to many cities in Asia, Europe and North America, and domestic connections to most large cities in India. There are smaller domestic airports at Mysore and Mangalore. Goa airport gives access to the north of the state.

Train: Karnataka is well served by train, with fast main lines fanning out from Bengaluru westwards to Mangalore, southwest to Mysore, south into Tamil Nadu and north towards Hyderabad in neighbouring Andhra Pradesh. A major line also dissects the north of the state, with slower metre-gauge tracks branching northwards from it to Bijapur, Gulbarga and other towns on the Deccan. Along the coast, the new Konkan Railway forms a super-fast link between Mangalore and Kerala, and all points north, from Gokarna to Goa and, eventually, Mumbai. Bus routes fill in the gaps.

Bengaluru (Bangalore): Trains run to: Chennai (11 daily; 5–7hrs); Gulbarga (4–6 daily; 10–12hrs); Hospet (1–2 daily; 10–13hrs); Hyderabad (6 daily; 10–13hrs 15mins); Kochi-Ernakulam (5 daily; 10hrs 35mins–12hrs 30mins); Mumbai (6 daily; 23–29hrs); Mysore (daily; 2–3hrs 30mins).

Mysore: There are trains to Bengaluru (10 daily; 2–3hrs 30mins); Chennai (2 daily; 9–11hrs); Hassan (4–5 daily; 1hr 50mins).

High Court and **State Central Public Library** stand at its edge.

Another park, the **Lalbagh Botanical Gardens** (daily sunrise–sunset; charge) in the south of the city, was laid out in the 18th century by Tipu Sultan and Hyder Ali, and contains India's largest collection of rare tropical and subtropical plants, with trees from Iran, Afghanistan and Europe, and a glasshouse similar to the former Crystal Palace in London. Lalbagh is the venue for flower shows in January and August. The low hill at its centre affords tremendous views over the city. **Tipu Sultan's Palace** on Avenue Road southwest of the market is now a museum (daily 9am–5pm; charge).

The ultra-modern **ISKCON Sri Radha Krishna Mandir** (daily 4.15–5am, 7.15am–12.50pm, 4–8.20pm), a Hare Krishna temple, is located on Chord Road, 8km (5 miles) north of the centre. Long queues form to enter the colossal structure, said to be the largest temple complex in the world. Its main hall – surmounted by a pyramid of tinted glass, four huge, Dravidian-style *gopura* towers and an enormous golden dome and finial – centres on a suitably massive gilded chandelier, protruding from the ceiling in the form of an inverted lotus flower.

Also in Bengaluru is the headquarters of the **Art of Living Foundation**, the spiritual and humanitarian organisation founded by New Age guru and Hindu evangelist Sri Sri Ravi Shankar (not to be confused with the classical sitar player). The focal point of the state-of-the-art Ved Vignan Mahahvidyapeeth, or VVM campus, is a massive, five-storey meditation hall, built entirely of marble in the shape of a lotus, with 1,008 stone petals encrusting its exterior. Inside, adoring audiences, drawn mostly from the city's English-speaking elite, gather on the polished marble floor to listen to the teachings of their long-haired, bearded *guruji*, who sits on a stage in flowing silk robes – a British journalist, Edward Luce, once remarked that the scene 'looked as if Jesus were shooting a shampoo advertisement.'

Venkataramanasvami Temple next to Tipu Sultan's palace.

FACT

For the duration of Mysore's Dasara (Dusshera) festival, the royal palace is illuminated by around 97,000 electric light bulbs. Recent years have seen the old 40-watt bulbs replaced by a more environmentally responsible 30-watt variety, but the impact of the city's most splendid edifice reflected in the waters of specially filled tanks remains utterly mesmerising.

The Karnataka State Tourism Development Corporation (KSTDC) at Badami House, N.R. Square, offers city tours and excursions to **Bannarghatta National Park**, 21km (13 miles) to the south, which runs a wildlife safari and has a crocodile and snake farm (Wed–Mon), and to the **Sai Baba Ashram** 20km (12 miles) to the east at Whitefield.

Princely Mysore

The town of **Mysore** ❷ lies 140km (86 miles) southwest of Bengaluru. Once the capital of a former Princely State, it is now a busy city but retains an undeniable character and charm. The moderate climate adds to the appeal, as does the pride that the city seems to take in both its past and its present – Mysore is often referred to as the cleanest city in India. In October the festival of Dasara (Dusshera) is celebrated with royal splendour, and has become synonymous with the city, as the maharaja leads a richly decorated procession that includes elephants and horses, flowers and incense, through the city streets.

THE TIGER OF MYSORE

Tipu Sultan (1750–99), the redoubtable Muslim ruler of Mysore state, became infamous in the annals of British India for his audacious military campaigns, which – along with those of his father, Hyder Ali – proved a perennial menace to East India Company ambitions in the far south. Tipu learnt early in his career that the way to defeat European armies was to dish out a taste of their own medicine, and consciously emulated his adversaries' military tactics. With support from the French, he deployed well-drilled, well-equipped infantry, cavalry and artillery (including much-feared ranks of 'rocket men'), notching up a series of crushing victories over the course of four 'Mysore Wars'.

Tipu ranked among the very few Indian leaders ever able to dictate terms in a treaty to defeated British generals. His nemesis, however, came just short of his 50th birthday in 1799, when an army of 30,000 East India Company regulars and sepoys, led by Lord Wellesley and his brother Arthur (later the Duke of Wellington of Waterloo fame) descended on his capital at Srirangapatnam, 14km (9 miles) from Mysore. Badly let down by his French allies at the last minute, 'the Tiger of Mysore' died defending a breach in the fort's walls – a scene immortalised in Wilkie Collins's novel *The Moonstone*. The British then plundered his palace; numerous artefacts are on display at the Victoria and Albert Museum in London.

The former Wodiyar maharaja's huge, fairytale-castle **palace** (daily 10.30am–5.30pm; charge) was built at great cost by a British architect in 1912 in the Indo-Saracenic style. A part of it is still the residence of the current maharaja. The interior is an amazing medley of striped pillars, stained glass, carved doors (including one made of solid silver) and mosaic floors. An extravagant mural depicting the great Mysore Dasara procession of 1930 lines the walls of the octagonal Kalyana Mandapa, the royal wedding hall. It took a team of four artists 15 years to paint, and presides over a vast hall filled with crystal chandeliers and gaudy Belgian stained glass. An adjacent room features a magnificent ceiling carved from teak. The palace's pièce de résistance, however, is its open-sided, colonnaded Durbar Hall, where the maharaja once hosted audiences while seated on a throne made from 280kg (615lb) of solid Karnatakan gold. Mughal-style inlaid marble adorns the ceiling arches, and fine views over the city and surrounding hills extend from an outer balcony, raised on heavy circular pillars. Every Sunday night, and all through Dusshera, the contours of the palace's exterior are illuminated by 97,000 light bulbs, to mesmerising effect.

The **Sri Jayachamarajendra Art Gallery** (daily 8am–5pm; charge), housed in the Jaganmohan Palace to the west of Mysore Palace, features paintings dating from the 19th century, including works of Raja Ravi Varma and traditional Mysore gold-leaf paintings. **St Philomenas' Church**, built in Gothic style during the 1930s, has beautiful stained-glass windows. It is one of the largest churches in India.

For the best panoramic views over the city scale the 1,000 steps leading to the top of **Chamundi Hill**, 3km (2 miles) southeast of the centre, where a 12th-century temple dedicated to Durga (the Mysore royal family's patron goddess) houses a deity made of solid gold. En route, you pass a succession of minor shrines and, at around the halfway point, a stately 5-metre (16ft) -tall Nandi bull, Shiva's vehicle, sculpted from a single block of black granite – an object of popular veneration.

The central area around Sayaji Rao Road is full of places to eat and shops selling the sandalwood and incense for which Mysore is famous. It's a pleasant walk from here to **Devaraja Market**, which sells flowers, fruit, spices and conical piles of vibrantly coloured *kumkum* powders. The city is also renowned as a silk-weaving centre, and visitors are welcome to visit the government-run **Karnataka Silk Industries Factory**, 4km (2.5 miles) from the centre (Mon–Sat 10am–noon, 2–4pm) to watch the weavers and giant looms in action. Finely brocaded, gold-edged saris are sold in the factory showroom, and at many emporia clustered around K.R. Circle and along Mandavadi Road.

Srirangapatnam

The remains of Tipu Sultan's capital, **Srirangapatnam** ❸, occupy an islet in the Kaveri River, 14km (9 miles) from Mysore. The site was originally named after the Sri Ranganaswamy Temple, built in the 8th century and, miraculously, untouched by the devastating battles fought around it in later years.

The summer palace of the royal family, **Daria Daulat**, stands 1km (½ mile) east of the temple. Built as a guesthouse, the low colonnaded structure boasts elaborately decorated interiors, with tiger-striped pillars and lavish murals, including one showing Tipu's historic victory over the British at Polliore in 1780. The great leader and his father were both entombed 3km (2 miles) east in the Bijapuri-style **Gumbaz Mausoleum** (Sat–Thur 10am–5pm), a square granite structure topped by a whitewashed brick-and-plaster dome. Carved rosewood doors, exquisitely inlaid with ivory, lead into

the tomb's hushed inner sanctum, which is lined with Tipu's trademark tiger stripes.

The Hoysalas, who ruled over central Karnataka between the 11th and 13th centuries, erected a series of distinctive, richly decorated temples across their domain, blending northern and southern styles of Hindu architecture. The **Keshava Vishnu Temple** (daily 9am–5pm), outside the rural village of **Somnathpur** ❹, a couple of hours' bus ride east of Mysore, is widely regarded as the finest of the crop. Like its counterparts elsewhere in the state, it's built on a star-shaped plan and mounted on a high plinth, though here the bewilderingly ornate sculpture is what most impresses. Resplendent images of deities, hewn from lustrous steatite (soapstone), adorn the upper walkway surrounding the shrine, which is encrusted from top to bottom with delicate stonework.

Nilgiri Biosphere Reserve

The remote **hill country** in the far southwest of Karnataka, straddling

Descending the stairs to the open loggia at the front of Tipu Sultan's Palace.

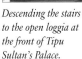

On the streets of Mysore.

The giant, 80-metre (260ft) figure at Sravanabelagola.

Mysore's Royal Palace.

the state border with Kerala, encompasses an area of extraordinarily rich biodiversity. Although under threat from hydroelectricity projects, overgrazing, road-building and illegal logging, the dense evergreen and mixed deciduous forests of the Western Ghats hold around one-third of all India's flowering species, as well as an array of large fauna, including jungle civets, Indian bison (gaur), elephants and vestigial population of tigers.

The vast **Nilgiri Biosphere Reserve** ❺, encompassing the Subcontinent's largest area of protected forest, was created from an amalgam of five separate national parks abutting the watershed of the range. Two of these – **Nagarhole** and **Bandipur** – lie within Karnataka, within easy reach of Mysore. At Bandipur, the more frequented of the pair, you can trek or take jeep safaris around the lower slopes of Gopalswamy Betta peak (1,455 metres/4,770ft), though sightings of large animals are only likely towards the end of the dry season, from late February through to May. Nagarhole, to the north, was decimated by fire in 1990s after disputes between the Forest Department and local tribal people over grazing rights erupted in a spate of arson attacks from which the wildlife population has yet fully to recover.

North of this area lies the Kodagu, or **Coorg**, region, dubbed the "Scotland of India". It is an extraordinarily beautiful place, famed for its abundant tea and coffee estates which have traditionally brought much prosperity to the region, and have turned the hills into waves of vibrant green. Many of the estates have now opened guesthouses which offer a supremely relaxing experience in stunning surroundings. The **Chikmagalur** region to the north of Coorg is equally beautiful and, in addition to the greenery, boasts the picturesque and historical town of **Sringeri**.

Sravanabelagola

Hassan (118km/73 miles northwest of Mysore) provides a base for exploring the region's top Hoysala temple towns, **Belur** and **Halebid** ❻, whose medi-eval shrines are embellished with some of India's most intricate Hindu sculpture. Belur's main draw is the painstakingly decorated **Channekeshava Temple**, the only remaining Hoysala temple still in use. Make sure you look up and take the time to appreciate the exquisitely fine ornamentation higher up the building. Arguably the most outstanding example of Hoysala temple architecture is **Hoysaleswara Temple** in Halebid; its uniquely extravagant exterior is a major work of art in itself. The third place worth heading to for Hoysala temple exuberance is **Somnathpur**, just 33km (20 miles) east of Mysore. The **Keshava Temple** here is the only example of a complete temple, and is again a marvel of decorative design.

The sacred Jain site of **Sravanabelagola** ❼, by contrast, holds monuments whose power to impress lies more in their jaw-dropping scale than decoration. Revered as the place where the Mauryan emperor Chandragupta starved himself to death in 300BC, the pilgrimage town, located around 50km (31 miles) east of Hassan, is dominated by a gigantic, 80-metre (260ft) colossus depicting the naked male figure of Gomateshwara. Said to be the largest free-standing sculpture in the world, it dates from the 10th century and provides the focus for the extraordinary **Mahamastakabhisheka festival**, held every 12 years (the next one is scheduled for 2017). At the end of the celebrations, a week of increasingly intense rituals culminates with the pouring of a vast quantity of holy water, sandalwood paste, spices, milk, flowers, ground jewels and gold dust over the statue's head from a specially erected scaffold or even, as in 2005, from a helicopter.

Hampi

In northern Karnataka, on the banks of the Tungabadhra River close to **Hospet**, lies the deserted city of **Hampi** ❽, capital of the great Vijayanagar Empire from the 14th century and one of India's archaeological highlights (Vittala Temple 8am–4pm; Royal Enclosure 6am–6pm; charge). Hampi was destroyed in 1565 after the Battle of Talikota, in which the Vijayanagar army was defeated by the Bijapur confederacy. Its many temples and palaces are a World Heritage Site. It made its fabulous wealth from the spice and cotton trade, and at one time had a population of half a million people. The spectacular landscape is dotted with ruins and huge boulders, and is best explored by bicycle.

Among its many sights, the **Vittala Temple** is noted for its sculptural details; the **Royal Enclosure** houses the remains of the **Lotus Mahal**. For more on Hampi, see page 378.

Badami and Aihole

The boulder-studded tableland to the northwest is scattered with remnants of the Chalukyas, a powerful and expansionist dynasty which ruled the region, indeed most of southern India, between the 6th and 8th centuries. At **Badami**, a five-hour bus ride north of Hospet, the cliff faces of a gorge slicing between two low sandstone hills are pock-marked with cave temples (daily sunrise–sunset; charge). More evocative ruined temples, decorated with accomplished carvings, are piled around the shores of Agastya Lake, an artificial tank at the foot of the gorge east of town, which is thought to date from the 5th century.

Archaeological remains spanning 600 years, including no less than 125 ancient shrines, lie around the village of **Aihole** ❾, an hour and a half's bus ride north of Badami. Founded on an age-old cultural fault line between the Brahmanical north and Dravidian south of peninsular India, the temples exhibit traits from both traditions. They also cover a long period and therefore plot the evolution of Hindu

TIP

Badami is connected to Bijapur (132km/82 miles north) and Hubli-Gadag (128km/80 miles south) by a metre-gauge line, covered by five or six trains daily. You can also get there by direct bus from Hospet (near Hampi) – a bumpy six-hour ride across Karantaka's central cotton belt.

Intricate sculpture at Halebid.

temple architecture, from the simpler designs such as the **Lad Khen Temple** to the more sophisticated style of the village's main draw, the **Durga Temple.**

The same is true of nearby **Pattadakal**, 25km (16 miles) from Badami, which served as a coronation site for its Chalukayn rulers from the 6th century onwards. Its finest vestiges are a group of temples inspired by the Pallava shrines of Kanchipuram, in Tamil Nadu, and were probably the grandest and most ornate in all of India at the time of their construction.

Karnataka's far north

The northernmost region of Karnataka, beyond the Krishna and Tungabhadra rivers, comprises a high, arid plateau – the Deccan or 'Desh' – whose dark volcanic soils today provide the Subcontinent with most of its cotton. From the late 14th century, renegade Muslim dynasties fled into this hostile border zone to carve out kingdoms beyond the reach of their tyrannical overlords, the Delhi Sultans, and later, the Mughals, who never

managed fully to subjugate the area but would, by the death of Aurangzeb in 1707, all but exhaust their imperial coffers attempting to do so.

Over time, control of the Konkan's maritime trade, coupled with successful campaigns against the wealthy Vijayanagar Empire (whose capital was only a short march to the south at Hampi), furnished vast fortunes which the Deccani Sultanates lavished on splendid fortifications, palaces, mosques and tombs in their stronghold cities.

The most impressive and best-preserved of these is **Bijapur** ❿, capital of the Adil Shahis, often dubbed in tourist literature as 'the Agra of the South' or 'Palmyra of the Deccan' for the scale and ornate style of its monuments. Bijapur's heyday extended over the reign of Adil Shah II (1627–57), a time when the dynasty's treasuries filled with booty from the plunder of Vijayanagar. His tomb, the mighty **Gol Gumbaz**, is the most conspicuous building in the city, if not in all of southern India, and stands as an eloquent reminder of the dynasty's

The view from Sravanabelagola, a sacred site for Jains.

formidable power – which extended at its height across most of the south. At almost 40 metres (132ft) in diameter, the great dome surmounting the mausoleum is the second-biggest in the world after St Peter's in Rome.

Bijapur's other famous tomb is an architectural gem conceived on a much smaller scale. Set in a walled compound on the opposite side of the city, the **Ibrahim Rauza** (daily dawn–dusk; charge) is believed to have been commissioned by the wife of the Sultan Ibrahim Adil Shah (1580–1626), and certainly possesses a more delicate, feminine aura, with slender minarets, fountains and finely domed cupolas embellishing a pair of twin tombs that face each other from opposite sides of a raised plinth.

The first dynasty to establish supremacy on the Deccan, after migrating into the region from Afghanistan, were the Bahmanis. At their former capital, **Gulbarga** ⑪, 160km (100 miles) northeast of Bijapur, remnants of a fort developed by Allauddin Bahmani cover several hectares and include the **Jami Mosque**, an expansive structure in the style of the mosque at Córdoba in Spain. The interior arches are so designed and the pillars so placed that the pulpit can be seen unobstructed from any part of the hall. Gulbarga's most visited monument, however, is the **tomb of Saiyid Muhammad Husaini Gisu Daras** on the northeast edge of town. 'Bandah Nawaz', as the the Sufi saint is today affectionately known, was the spiritual mentor of the Bahmanis, and his tomb has, ever since his death in 1422 at the ripe old age of well over 100, been the most important object of Muslim veneration in the Deccan.

Few travellers make it as far northeast as **Bidar** ⑫, another important Muslim capital, which emerged in the 1420s following the death of Bandah Nawaz and the ensuing break-up of the Bahmani dynasty. But the town, 284km (176 miles) northeast of

Bijapur and 136km (84 miles) from Hyderabad, holds some of the most beautiful Islamic relics in all of southern India. On its northern edge, 10km (6 miles) of ramparts and fortifications enclose a campus of crumbling palaces and mosques, some of which boast fine mother-of-pearl inlaid stonework, sumptuous woodcarving and magnificent views over the surrounding countryside. The old quarter to its south is dominated by the tile-encrusted minaret of a 15th-century madrasa, its facade enlivened with bands of Islamic calligraphy and patches of green, blue and yellow ceramics.

The Konkan coast

The narrow coastal strip dividing the Western Ghats from the Arabian Sea, known as the Konkan or *Dakshini Kannada*, is in many ways a region apart from the rest of Karnataka, boasting its own language (Konkani), seafood-rich cuisine and a long history of contact with foreign traders and invaders. Thanks to the high-spec NH-17 Highway and Konkan Railway, travel along the coast is these days a

SHOP

In the bazaar occupying the back streets of Bidar's old quarter, south of the fort, are workshops of metal-workers specialising in a now rare form of art called *bidri*. A Damascene technique originally devised by Persian silversmiths, it first arrived in the region with the Bahmanis in the 15th century. Deccani *bidri*, nowadays used to embellish everything from vases to betel nut boxes, is distinguished by swirling floral motifs in silver on dark backgrounds. Bidar's most famous workshops line Siddiq Talim Road.

KARNATAKAN ENTERTAINMENT

One of the most memorable experiences that Karnataka has to offer is an evening spent outdoors, sitting on a straw mat watching a *bayalata* (field play). These traditional dramas, which depict the exploits of heroes and heroines from Hindu epics such as the Ramayana and Mahabharata), may run from early evening until sunrise. The performances are an amalgam of music, dance and drama, featuring spectacular costumes and make up. An easygoing atmosphere prevails throughout: local people will be delighted to see a foreigner attend and any of them who speak English will ensure you understand the intricacies of plot and character.

When the fields are flush with water, there is another sight popular in Karnataka and not to be missed: the annual *kambala* (buffalo race). Held in a paddy field, the race is contested by pairs of specially trained racing buffaloes, egged on by men riding behind them. To start the race the driver jumps up, his hand cocked, his whip held high, and the huge animals lunge forward, bellowing, their hooves churning the muddy waters and sending their wet spray into the hot air, their eyes wide, wild and white. The races are a good excuse for some serious gambling, and a highly charged atmosphere is guaranteed.

EAT

The Brahmin cooks of Udupi's Krishna Temple are credited with originating India's best-loved snack – the *masala dosa*. Made of semi-fermented rice- and lentil-flour batter, which is griddle-fried into a crispy pancake, *dosas* are one of many delicious, but labour-intensive, dishes served in 'Udupi' (aka Udipi) cafés in towns and cities across the country. They're nearly always clean and food served in them scrupulously vegetarian and tasty.

Om beach, Gokarna.

far more straightforward affair than it used to be, when progress was hampered by frequent river crossings on slow, flat-bottomed ferries.

Beyond the largely uninteresting port city of **Mangalore**, close to the Keralan border, the first essential stop on any journey along the Konkan should be **Udupi** ⑬, a pilgrimage town par excellence. Its heart, surrounded by a square and broad bazaar, is the Krishna Temple founded by the Hindu saint Madhva in the 13th century. The site is famed above all for the spectacular festivals held within it in January and February, when gigantic wooden chariots capped with bulbous domes made of brightly coloured pennants are dragged by devotees around the sacred precinct.

A similar ritual is staged several times each year at **Gokarna** ⑭, another ancient Hindu temple town to the north of the coastal belt, not far from Goa. Unlike Udupi (a *vaishnava* site), most of Gokarna's shrines are dedicated to Shiva or to his associated deities. Top of most pilgrims' hit list, after they have taken a purificatory dip in the step-lined **Kooti Theerta tank** on the east side of town, is the **Mahabaleshwar Temple** on the western side of the town's main street. Within its smoke-blackened core resides one of India's most revered Shivalinga, said to have been dropped here by the arch-demon Ravana during his epic struggle with Rama.

Gokarna is also a place of refuge for long-staying hippie travellers from Western countries, thanks to the presence over the headland from town of a string of delightful sandy coves, reachable on foot or by fishing boat. In recent years, a handful of luxury hotels have started to mushroom on the bare laterite hillsides overlooking **Om Beach**, the most picturesque of the string (its name derives from the shape of its twin bays, thought to replicate the auspicious Hindu Om symbol). Otherwise, the pace of change in this staunchly traditional corner of India is slow, allowing visitors to savour what much of the country must have been like before Independence.

South of Gokarna, accessed by taking the road heading inland from the

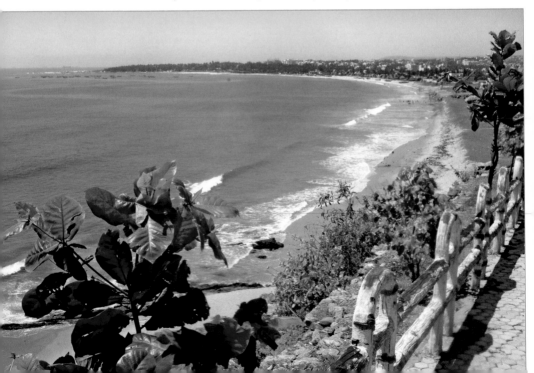

village of Honavar, are the **Jog Falls** ⓯. The Sharavati River plunges over four cataracts here as it descends from the heights of the Western Ghats to the coast.

ANDHRA PRADESH

Geologically one of the oldest parts of South Asia, Andhra Pradesh has stunning landscapes of hilly, rock-strewn plateaux, fertile river valleys, and a long coastline to its east. Yet it can be difficult to explore. The harsh climate – hot and dry for most of the year, interrupted by the flooding of rivers during the monsoon months – can make life very difficult. Cyclones frequently hit the coastal areas during May, October and November, paralysing transportation; the pre-monsoon period from April to June is baking hot, with temperatures regularly topping 45°C (113°F).

The present state of Andhra Pradesh, the first formed on a linguistic basis, was created in 1956 after a period of considerable political agitation. The predominantly Hindu Telugu-speaking parts of the Presidency of Madras were combined with the former territories of the Princely State of Hyderabad, hitherto ruled by a Muslim nawab. Recently there have been calls to create a separate state ('Telengana') out of the poorer northern districts, where people feel that their interests are often ignored by politicians from the coast and the southern parts of the state.

Buddhism, Hinduism and Islam have all flourished in Andhra. Ashokan accounts from the 3rd century BC refer to a people called the 'Andhras'. Later, the Satyavanas ruled from Amaravati and were Buddhist patrons.

Andhran culture

Telugu, the principal language of the state, has a rich literature that can be heard in its *padyams*; rolling, sonorous prose narrations of rural life, customs and festivities. Andhra has strong traditions of music and dance, too. *Kuchipudi*, a dance drama originating in the fertile delta of the Krishna and Godavari rivers, is thought to have developed out of the local *yaksagana* theatre. Of the skilled craft workers of Andhra some of the finest specialise in wood-carving; those from Kondapalli near Vijayawada fashion colourful toys and figures that portray village life. *Bidri* workers from Bidar create delicate designs, inlaid in silver or gold on matt-black gunmetal hookahs, vases, boxes and jewellery. The weavers use distinctive weaves and dye techniques, and are famous for their rich brocades, *ikats*, silks and *himru* fabric – a mixture of silk and cotton.

Hyderabad-Secunderabad

Hyderabad ⓰ is the capital of Andhra Pradesh and India's fifth-largest city. It has a population of around 6.8 million, although the figure is closer to 7.7 million when the entire urban area is included. An acute scarcity of water and overcrowding at **Golconda**, 11km (7 miles) to the west, led Muhammad Quli of the Qutb Shahi dynasty to

---

ANDHRA PRADESH TRANSPORT

Flights: Hyderabad's impressive Rajiv Gandhi International Airport, 22km south of the city, is widely regarded as the most modern and efficient in India. Inaugurated in 2008, it has direct flights to/from the UK, a few other European destinations and all large Indian cities, including Delhi, Mumbai, Chennai and Kolkata. AeroExpress shuttle buses run to and from the centre every 30mins.

Rail: The major **rail** hubs in the state are Secunderabad (for Hyderabad) and Vijayawada. Most important sites are reachable by rail, apart from Amaravati and Nagarjunakonda (bus tours run from Hyderabad and Vijayawada; see www.aptourism.com for details). The line that runs over the Eastern Ghats into the Araku Valley (twice daily from Vizag) is one of the most scenic journeys in South India – the tourist office in Vizag offers daily guided tours. Tirupati is most easily reached from Chennai (3 daily; 3–4hrs). Trains also run from Hyderabad but it's a long haul.

Hyderabad: Trains run to Mumbai (8 daily; 14–17hrs 30mins). From **Secunderabad** trains run to Bengaluru (1–2 daily; 12–13hrs); Chennai (2 daily, 12–14hrs); Tirupati (3–4 daily; 12–15hrs 30mins); Visakhapatnam (9 daily; 12hrs 30min–19hrs 30mins).

Vijayawada: Trains connect with Chennai (23 daily; 7–9hrs), Secunderabad (22–26 daily; 5–7hrs); Visakhapatnam (23 daily; 5–7hrs).

Hyderabad's Charminar is surrounded by busy streets.

build the new capital of Hyderabad on the banks of the Musi River in 1591. In 1687 the Mughal emperor Aurangzeb overthrew the dynasty and appointed his former general as viceroy. This dynasty of Asaf Jahi, which declared its independence after Aurangzeb's death, ruled as the Nizams of Hyderabad until 1949. The seventh and last ruling Nizam, Osman Ali Khan (1911–50), was famous for his eccentricities and enormous wealth, said to have been derived from diamonds and other gems mined by his ancestors around Golconda – which, in the 17th century, was the diamond centre of the world. At Independence in 1947 he expressed a wish to join Pakistan, a position he managed to maintain until 1949, when riots in the city gave the Indian army the excuse they needed to invade.

Traditionally a cosmopolitan centre of learning and the arts with a reputation for friendliness and hospitality that still exists today, the old town of Hyderabad and its twin city, the modern Secunderabad, are separated by **Hussain Sagar Lake**. Besides being a

Locals in Hyderabad.

major centre of commerce and industry, transport and communication, Hyderabad is also a processing centre for pearls from the Middle East, Japan and China. It is considered the centre for Islam in South India and yet on the lake is the world's largest statue of Buddha.

In recent years Hyderabad has become, along with Bengaluru, the centre of India's software and hi-tech service industries. The districts of Banjara and Jubilee Hills are now full of expensive villas and flashy shopping malls where the newly wealthy middle class congregate. Hitec City, a little further out, is where many of the multinational companies, including Microsoft and Oracle, have their headquarters in large, modern glass-fronted buildings. This is in striking contrast to the narrow backstreets around the Charminar and the relentless poverty of the surrounding countryside.

The Old City

The main Mahatma Gandhi Road cuts straight through Hyderabad City, past the central shopping area around

Abids Circle, and across the Tank Bund (a popular local promenade overlooking the lake) to continue onwards into Secunderabad. The old walled city area is anchored by Hyderabad's most famous landmark, the **Charminar** Ⓐ (literally 'four towers'; Tue–Sun 9am–5.30pm; charge). Floodlit in the evenings, this magnificent square archway supported by four 56-metre (184ft) towers was built in 1591 to commemorate the end of a local plague. It is covered with a yellow stucco mixed from powdered marble, gram flour and egg yolk. There is a tiny mosque on the second floor where royal children studied the *Qur'an*.

Nearby stands one of the largest mosques in India, the black granite **Mecca Masjid**, said to have bricks made of red clay from Mecca over the central archway. Old bazaars with narrow cobbled lanes lined with rows of tiny shops selling spices, grain, perfume oils and Hyderabadi specialities such as seedless Anabshahi grapes, surround the Charminar. The **pearl market** has

varieties of seed pearl, rice pearl and round pearl, sold loose by weight, or strung into jewellery. **Lad Bazaar**, a narrow street, is the traditional centre for bridal accessories and bangles (Hyderabad is particularly noted for its glass bangles). To its east is a quadrangular complex of palaces built by the nizams.

The **Salar Jung Museum** Ⓑ (www.salarjungmuseum.in; Sat–Thur 10am–5pm; charge), on the southern bank of the Musi River, is the largest single-person collection of art and artefacts in the world. Salar Jung was a minister at the court of the Nizams, and his collection of over 43,000 objects and 50,000 rare books and manuscripts includes a good selection of European artworks and some wonderful decorated manuscripts from all over the Islamic world. The large Mughal jade collection in the museum is outstanding.

The neoclassical **Falaknuma Palace**, about 4km (3 miles) south of the Charminar, served as the royal guesthouse for the Nizams. Built in 1884, it is an imposing structure (set

Pearls and traditional bangles for sale in a Hyderabad bazaar. The city is famous for its glass bangles.

Hyderabad

on a hill to maximise its impact) with an opulent interior that has now been fully restored by the Taj group and opened as a luxury hotel, see hotel listings.

Elsewhere in the city

Other places of interest include the **Bagh-e-Aam** (Public Gardens), which are the location of the ornate **Legislative Assembly** building, dating from the early 20th century. The **State Archaeological Museum G** (Tue–Sun 10.30am–5pm; charge) is also located here. The collections of Chalukyan, Buddhist and Kakatiya sculpture are particularly fine.

A good spot for sunset views is **Kala Pahad** (Black Mountain), where the **Birla Venkatesvara Temple** is perched on the hilltop. On the adjacent hill, Naubat Pahad, is the **Planetarium** (daily 10.30am–8.30pm; charge), with regular shows in English. Hyderabad's **Nehru Zoological Park**, in the southwest of the city, is said to be one of the better zoos in India, but the condition of the animals is still depressing.

GOLCONDA FORT

The huge and once-impregnable **Golconda Fort** (daily 10am–4.30pm; charge), situated on a steep granite hill 11km (7 miles) west of Hyderabad, was built by the Qutb Shahi dynasty of the 16th and 17th centuries. It was their capital until 1590, when the king moved to his new city of Hyderabad, and was used by the last of the Qutb Kings in the 17th century as a bastion against Mughal attack. The fort was encircled by walls with 87 semicircular bastions and eight gates with elephant-proof spikes. Famous for its ingenious acoustics, a hot-and-cold-water supply system, natural air conditioning and Turkish baths, the remains of its once-splendid palaces and gardens give an idea of its former grandeur, when diamonds and rubies embellished the walls of the Queen's Palace – a hint at where the Qutb Shahi dynasty's extraordinary wealth originated. In their day, the mines of Golconda were the only known source of diamonds in the world, and merchants from as far afield as Persia, Africa and Europe travelled here to purchase them. World famous gems that originated in the kingdom, and which were once stored in the Golconda sultans' treasuries include the Koh-i-Noor and exquisite blue Hope Diamond.

The views over the city from the topmost point are truly spectacular. Golconda is easily reached by local bus or autorickshaw from central Hyderabad.

Leaving the city in the direction of Golconda Fort brings you to the burial ground of the Qutb Shahi rulers. Despite being built over a long period of time, their **tombs D** (Sat–Thur 9am–4.30pm; charge) are remarkable for the unity of their design. They all have a central dome, more or less onion-shaped, rising from a lotus-petal calyx, a small dome, minarets and stucco decoration. Most graves are of black basalt with calligraphic inscriptions. At the centre of the enclosure is the **hamam**, the baths built by Sultan Quli. The simple interior space is impressive, with a beautiful inlaid platform.

In the furthest outskirts of the city is **Ramoji Film City**, centre of the Telugu film industry and the largest production complex in the world. It is possible to visit on guided tours (www.ramojifilmcity.com; 9am–5.30pm) which give a fascinating insight into the gaudy, glamorous world of Indian cinema. Elsewhere are the new **Botanical Gardens**, covering 48 hectares (120 acres) and opening in stages, and the **Shilparamam Crafts Village** out in Madhapur. The latter has stalls and workshops of craft workers from all over India.

Around Hyderabad

The major sight outside Hyderabad is magnificent **Golconda Fort E**. **Pochampalli**, a village east of the city, is noted for its silk saris and ikat weaves.

Further afield is **Warangal ⑰**, 145km (90 miles) to the northeast. This 12th- to 13th-century capital of the Hindu Kakatiyas was renowned for its now abandoned brick-and-mud fort, a massive structure protected by two rings of walls and a moat. There are a few Chalukyan Shiva temples in the hills around Warangal and, some 30km (19 miles) east of Warangal, the **Ramappa Temple** in Palampet is said to be the best-preserved example of Kakatiya temple architecture in India.

Also interesting is the **Nagarjun-akonda Sagar and Dam** ⑱, around 170km (106 miles) southeast of Hyderabad. Built in 1960, this reservoir submerged an entire valley, which had been home to a series of ancient civilisations. Important Buddhist monuments have been reconstructed at a museum within the ruins of a fort on an island, which was once the top of a 200-metre (650ft) hill. Boats leave three times daily from Vijayapuri between 9.30am and 1.30pm, the last boat returning at 4.30pm, and the trip takes about 45 minutes. The entrance charge covers the boat journey and access to the site and **museum** (Sat–Thur 9am–4pm).

In the area to the east of Nagarjuna is the important pilgrimage site of **Srisailam** (the 'holy hill'). Within the walls of a moated fort on the south bank of the Tungabhadra River, just before it joins the Krishna, are eight temples and a **museum** (Sat–Thur 10.30am–5pm; charge). The latter has a good collection of Alampuri sculpture.

Vijayawada and Amaravati

On the banks of the Krishna river, the ancient city of **Vijayawada** ⑲, 240km (150 miles) east of Hyderabad, was once visited by the Chinese traveller Hieun Tsang. It shows traces of its past in the two ancient Jain temples and the cave temples nearby, and also the hilltop **Kanakadurga Temple**, devoted to the patron deity of the city. It is now a busy commercial centre, and most travellers only pass through in transit along the east coast.

Vijayawada is useful to the visitor as a base from which to visit **Amaravati** ⑳, 30km (19 miles) to the west, the site of early Buddhist settlements. Here the remains of a 2,000-year-old Great Stupa are embellished with carvings depicting the life of the Buddha. A small **museum** (Sat–Thur 9am–5pm; charge) displays statues of the Buddha, although most of the sculptures are kept in either the Government Museum in Chennai or the British Museum, London.

A journey across the beautiful Krishna-Godavari delta to the coastal town of **Machilipatnam**, 70km (43

Golconda Fort.

FACT

The guru Sai Baba, born in the village of Puttaparthi, was a controversial figure. This is partly due to allegations ranging from sexual misconduct to murder, and partly because of the huge amount of money his brand of Hinduism generates from its thousands of loyal followers.

Paddy fields in the Araku Valley.

miles) to the east, makes an interesting excursion. Here you can still see the *kalamkari* process of printing cloth using a *kalam* (pen) and woodblocks. Also within striking distance of Vijaywada is **Kondapalli**, famous for its production of wooden toys, painted with vegetable dyes to stunning effect; there's also an impressive 14th-century fort.

The northeastern coast

The naval base and shipbuilding centre of **Vishakapatnam** (known as 'Vizag') on Andhra Pradesh's northeast coast is the fourth-largest port in India. Its twin city, **Waltair**, was built as a resort town by the British and still retains shady avenues, charming bungalows and marvellous views. Set on a beautiful curving bay, Vizag is delineated by two hills to the north and south. **Kailasa Hill** (to the north) is topped by well-maintained gardens, at the centre of which is a monumental pair of statues of Shiva and Parvati. There is also a small tourist train that runs around the park. While you can take the winding road up (toll fee), it

might be more fun to take the cable car to the top (daily 11am–1pm, 2–8pm, (closed every 19th day of the month); charge).

The view from **Dolphin's Nose** (so called because of its shape), the southern hill, is even more spectacular – especially from the **lighthouse** at the end of the road (daily 3–5pm; charge), although there are plans to convert this to a private hotel.

Unfortunately, apart from the beach at **Rushikonda** (11km/7 miles north of Vizag) swimming is extremely dangerous along this stretch of coast. At the quiet former Dutch settlement of **Bhimunipatnam** (24km/15 miles from Vizag) there are some striking colonial graves by the seashore. Between Vizag and Bhimunipatnam are a number of Buddhist sites, while the **Godavari River** provides some worthwhile sites, most noticeably the scenery close to the gorge and the temple architecture at **Draksharaman.**

There is a 13th-century Orissan-style Hindu temple and hot springs at **Simhachalam** up in the forested Eastern Ghats nearby, and **Mukhalingam**, close to the border with Odisha (Orissa), has some superb examples of Orissan-style temple architecture. A 70km (43-mile) journey inland (best done by train) brings you to the Adivasi area of the **Araku Valley** on the border with Odisha. There are coffee estates around the towns of Ananthagiri and Chintapalli that lie at the entrance to the valley. Also here are the impressive **Borra caves** (daily 10am–1pm, 2–5.30pm; charge). Discovered in 1807 by the British geologist William King, they are one of the natural wonders of Andhra. The Gosthani river that flows from the caves takes its name ('cow's udder') from the colour of the milky calcium carbonate in the water.

The Adivasi heritage of the region is celebrated in Araku with the **Museum of Habitat** (daily 10am–1pm, 2–5pm; charge). The collections here have a large array of fascinating Adivasi

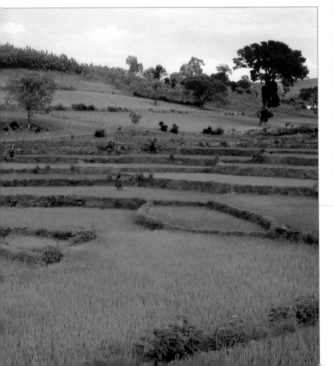

household objects, jewellery and musical instruments, many displayed in recreations of traditional housing.

Southern Andhra

Tirupati ㉓ is famous for the **Lord Venkatesvara Temple**, which stands on nearby Tirumala Hill. Receiving between 30 and 40 million pilgrims annually, this is officially world's busiest pilgrimage sites, as well as one of the wealthiest. The efficient temple administration (www.tirumala.org) deals with between 60,000 and 100,000 visitors daily, and operates an 18-hour-a-day *darsan* (view of the deity) regulated by a token system: pilgrims receive a token from one of several offices, which tells them which time to enter the queue, after which it takes about two hours to enter the temple. Many pilgrims shave their heads as a pledge, or to thank the deity. The hair is used to make wigs, which are sold locally and exported. The steep road up the hill has 57 hairpin bends and lovely views.

At **Chandragiri** (Sat–Thur 10am–5pm, sound and light show at 7.30pm; charge), 11km (7 miles) from Tirupati, are the Raja Mahal and Rani Mahal, late Vijayanagara structures of the 17th century. These palaces lie within a moat and formidable battlements. 25km (15 miles) in the other direction from Tirupati are the stunning temples of **Sri Kalahasti**, a place that really comes alive during the Mahashivaratri festival but which is worth a visit any time.

Thirteen kilometres (8 miles) east of Hindupur is the temple town of **Lepaksi**. On a little hill is the **Virabhadra Temple**, built in 1530, famous for its frescoes of deities. A monumental **Nandi**, the biggest in India, proudly raises its head 1km (2/3 mile) away.

The barren landscape can be surveyed from a number of impressive forts, including **Penukonda** about 35km (22 miles) north of Hindupur. Here there is a massive encircling wall

and a pavilion on the hilltop. Nearby is the elegant Gagan Mahal (a royal pavilion), still in good repair. The fort at **Gandikota**, to the east of Anantapur, is poised above a gorge carved out by the Pennar River.

Northeast of Penukonda is the small village of **Puttaparthi**, location of the ashram of the controversial spiritual teacher, mystic and self-proclaimed philapnthropist Sai Baba (*see* www. srisathyasai.org.in). Large crowds visit the site to attend rituals and bhajan (sacred hymn) sessions, despite the fact the guru passed away in 2012.

About 25km (15 miles) on from Gandikota are the temples at **Tadpatri**, easily reached by rail from Chennai. The **Ramalingesvara Temple** was built in the 15th century and the **Venkataramana** in the early 16th century. They are a mix of Chalukyan and Chola architecture, with exuberant Vijayanaga decoration.

Red-hot chilli harvest in the Andhran countryside.

Making an omelette at Vijaypuri.

RESTAURANTS

PRICE CATEGORIES

Average price for dinner, up to three courses for one person, excluding alcoholic drinks:
£ = under Rs200
££ = Rs200–500
£££ = Rs500–1,000
££££ = over Rs1,000

Karnatakan cuisine includes the usual South Indian *dosas* (said to have been invented in Udupi), *idlis* and the staple *thali*, but also offers such specialities as *bisi bele bath*, a delicacy of rice seasoned with lentils, spices and tamarind, and *hoalige*, a flat pancake-like wafer filled with molasses, shredded coconut and lentils.

Karnataka

Bengaluru
Brahmin's Coffee Bar
Ranga Rao Road, Shankarapuram. £
An idly-wada breakfast at Brahmin's, a sidewalk Udupi joint famous across the city for nearly five decades, is a quintessential 'Old Bangalore' experience. The idlys are fluffy and full of flavour, the wada scrumptious and coconut chatni the stuff of legends. If you're lucky you'll get a space on the stainless steel bar; otherwise, eat standing up like everyone else. The clientele ranges from crisp-shirted Infosystem execs to local market stallholders.
Caperberry
48/1 The Estate Building, 121 Dickenson Road.
Tel: 080-2559 4567, www.caperberry.in.
£££–££££
Bengaluru at its most cutting-edge; this place offers avant-garde Euro-gastro cuisine inspired by the molecular gastronomy of modern Spanish cooking. The minimal interior, menu and service are all world-class, and excellent value relative to comparable restaurants elsewhere.
Ebony
18th Floor, Barton Centre, 84 M.G. Road.
Tel: 080-4178 3344, www.ebonywithaview.com. £££
Fabulous-value pan-Indian cuisine, which you can enjoy on an outdoor terrace with a panoramic view of the city. It's worth trying the Parsi mutton *pulao*, delicately flavoured with saffron

and rose petals, or vegetarian *paneer kairi dopiaza*, soured Goan-style with green mangoes. They also do spectacular buffet breakfasts.
Karavalli
Taj Gateway Hotel, 66 Residency Road.
Tel: 080-6660 4545. £££–££££
Award-winning gourmet coastal cuisine, from Mangalorean pomfret to grilled seer fish, tiger prawns, butter-garlic crab, and pearlspot fresh from the Keralan backwaters, all served alfresco under a giant rain tree.
Koshy's
39 St Mark's Road. ££
An old-fashioned, relaxed café that's a Bengaluru institution, with split-cane blinds and drinks served in pewter tumblers and teapots. The varied menu features Indian and Continental options.
Mavalli Tiffin Rooms (aka 'MTR')
Lalbagh Road, www.mavallitiffinrooms.com. £
Open since 1924, MTR serves definitive Udupi-Brahmin food – notably *masala dosas*, for which queues regularly stretch out of the door (the management boasts that the Chief Minister of Karnataka even stood in line for one once). Always busy, but crammed at lunchtime for its *thalis*. The restaurant claims to hold a world record for a fast-food joint, having on one occasion fed 21,000 customers in just seven hours.
Miller's 46
46 Miller's Road, Vasanthnagar.
Tel: 080-4113 1746, www.millers46.com.
£££–££££
Wild West-themed steakhouse, the perfect escape for anyone missing their meat fix. In addition to excellent steaks, there are also burgers, Tex-Mex and a vegetarian menu on offer.
Nagarjuna
44/1 Residency Road. £–££
Hot and spicy non-vegetarian Andhran food, including excellent Hyderabadi biriyanis, served at breakneck pace on fresh banana leaves.
Toscano
UB City, 24 Vital Mallya Road.
Tel: 080-4173 8800. £££–££££
Perhaps Bengaluru's most authentic Mediterranean cuisine, served in a lively atmosphere and often accompanied by live music. The duck and the tiramisu are stand-outs; the general standard is high; book early to make sure you get a table, as

this place is deservedly popular.
Vidyarthi Bhavan
Gandhi Bazaar Main Road. £
It may not look like much from the outside, but this simple Udupi canteen in the vibrant fresh produce market district serves what many aficionados describe as the city's finest masala dosa – an accolade indeed. The waiters carry 20 at one go, and the queues wind out the door at peak times.
Zen
Leela Palace Kempinski, 23 Airport Road.
Tel: 080-2521 1234. £££–££££
This refined restaurant serves a good range of pan-Asian cuisine, but is best known for its sumptuous sushi. Not the cheapest Japanese joint in town, but arguably the best.

Mysore
Anu's Bamboo Hut
367 2nd Main, 3rd Stage, Gokulam.
Tel: 0821-4289492. ££
A haunt of Mysore's health-conscious Ashtanga yoga students, Anu's little rooftop restaurant offers buffets of freshly cooked, fragrant Indian cuisine, as well as superb salads of sprouts, crunchy carrots and kosumbari, as well as shakes, smoothies and herb teas. And leave room for the vegan chocolate-banana cake.
Lalitha Mahal Palace Hotel
Siddhartha Nagar.
Tel: 0821-252 6600. £££–££££
Superb food, try the biriyanis, served in opulent surroundings accompanied by live Hindustani music.
Olive Garden
Windflower Spa, Maharanapratap Road, Nazarbad.
Tel: 0821-252 2500, www.thewindflower.com.
££££
Relaxing, atmospheric place to eat in the bucolic grounds of the hideaway boutique hotel at the foot of Chamundi Hill. You can dine on Indian, Chinese or Continental dishes to a backdrop of babbling streams and birds. A far cry from the racket of the market area.
RRR
Gandhi Square. £
Andhra-style *thalis* dished up to hungry local workers in busy, no-frills canteen on banana leaves. One of the most enduringly popular cheap places to eat in the city, and it's handy for the shops and palace.

Vinayaka Mylari
769 Mazabad Main Road. **£**
Mysore has its own, particularly delicious brand of dosa, and this tiny place, 5 minutes' walk northeast of Harding Circle, is the place to try one, ideally with a side plate of their famous sago (spicy vegetable mush).

Hospet
Naivedyam/Manasa
Hotel Priyadarshini, V-45, Station Road. **££–£££**
Garden restaurant looking out on sugarcane and banana plantations. Good vegetarian and non-vegetarian food; also serves beer.

The Waves
Hotel Malligi, 10-90, Jambunath Road. **££–£££**
Pleasant terrace restaurant serving tasty tandoori, South Indian and Chinese dishes, along with chilled beers (the last from 7–11pm only). Bring mosquito repellent.

Andhra Pradesh

The cuisine of Andhra Pradesh is known for its fiery hot curries served with rice or parathas. Hyderabad has its own distinct *nawabi* cuisine, essentially Mughal but adapted to the tastes of the local royalty. Aromatic biryanis, *halim* (a spiced mixture of wheat and mutton) and *mirch ka salan* (green chilli curry) are some specialities.

Hyderabad-Secunderabad
Firdaus
Taj Krishna, Road No.1, Banjara Hills, Hyderabad.
Tel: 040-6666 2323. **££££**
Perhaps the best place in town to get real Hyderabadi food, with some of the more unusual Muslim dishes and live ghazals most evenings. Reservations recommended.

Hotel Ista
Road 2, I.T. Park, Nanakramguda Gachi Bowli.
Tel: 040-4450 8888. **££££**
One of the best places in town for foodies with the Deori serving excellent Andhran food and the Collage for international dishes. They often run special events.

Kamat's
Ramalaya and Alladin complexes, Sarojini Devi Road, Secunderabad; Secretariat Road and Station Road, Nampally. **£–££**
There are several outlets of this clean and inexpensive Udupi-style vegetarian chain in the city.

Kebabs and Kurries
ITC Kakatiya, 6-3-1187 Begumpet.
Tel: 040-2340 0132. **££££**

Reputedly serving the best biryani in Hyderabad, this is Indian fine dining taken to the next level. The food, service and surroundings are all equally sumptuous; highly recommended, book in advance.

Paradise
Annexe Persis, M.G. Road, Secunderabad. **£**
Paradise gets packed throughout the week for its melt-in-the-mouth kebabs and aromatic Hyderabdi-style biryanis. For dessert, everyone has kubaani ka meetha, a kind of stewed apricot in rose syrup with ice-cream.

Pickles
Baseraa Hotel, 9/1–167/8 Sarojini Devi Road, Secunderabad. **£££**
The 24-hour coffee shop at the Baseraa Hotel is one of the most popular late-night eateries in town; the midnight biryani is particularly good.

Rayalaseema Ruchulu
Level 4, Saboo Arcade, Next to HDFC Bank, Himayath Nagar.
Tel: 040-6461 5252, www.rayalaseemaruchulu.com. **£££–££££**
There are four branches of this smart, award-winning restaurant around the city, but the one in Himayath Nagar is the most central. Forget the north Indian menu; everyone comes for the Andhran cuisine: rabbits, quail, chicken and mutton, steeped in cashew-rich, creamy gravies, as favoured by the Nawabs of old.

Udipi Anand Bhavan
Machli Kaman, Pathar Gatti, Hyderabad. **£**
A good vegetarian 'meals' and dosa place right in the heart of the Old Town. Very popular and clean, with an air-conditioned section if you are desperate to escape the heat.

Utsav
221 Tivoli Road, Secunderabad. **££**
Excellent North Indian vegetarian food served in pleasant surroundings.

Nagarjunakonda
Punnami Ethipothala
Punnami Vihar. **£**
A small place about 11km (7 miles) from Nagarjuna Sagar, though many tour buses stop here. It is in a wonderful position beside a gorge with an impressive waterfall.

Vijayawada
Babai Idli
NRP Road, Gandhinagar. **£**
The town's most famous Udupi joint, now entering its eighth decade and still going strong. Order a plate of piping hot idly, topped with green chilli chatni, and a drizzle of ghee.

Punnami
Berm Park. **£**
A riverside restaurant attached to

a large government-run hotel. The multi-cuisine menu is decent and the position is lovely.

Sree Lakshmi Vilas Modern Café
Besant Road, Govenorpet. **£–££**
Good vegetarian restaurant attached to a hotel.

Vishakhapatnam
Dakshin
Hotel Daspalla, Suryabagh. **££–£££**
Very tasty – and spicy – non-vegetarian Andhran food. The lamb dishes are particularly good.

Punnami Yatri Niwas
Opposite the Appu Ghar Site, Beach Road, M.V.P. Colony. **£**
A decent restaurant attached to a government-run hotel. Wide-ranging, well-prepared menu.

Venkatadri Vantillu
CBM Compound, Siripuram, 9-14/5 Praveen Plaza, VIP Road. **££**
Authentic Andhran vegetarian meals, famed above all for its coconut and green chilli chatni.

Tirupati
Punnami Srinivasam
Tirupati. **£**
Good vegetarian restaurant attached to a government-run hotel.

Vadai, common south India snacks

HAMPI

The ruined capital of the Vijayanagar rulers is one of the greatest sights in South India, the location being as much part of the magic of the place as its historical remains.

The Vijayanagar Empire (1336–1565) was one of the largest in India, spreading across much of the South, and its rulers accrued a great deal of wealth. This helped build one of the medieval world's most opulent cities, Hampi, described by the Muslim envoy Abdul Razaq in 1443 as 'such that the pupil of the eye has never seen a place like it and the ear of the intelligence has never been informed that there existed anything to equal it in the world.' As well as being a centre for trade and crafts, its rulers were also great patrons of the arts, contributing much to the development of South Indian music, sculpture and architecture.

The Vijayanagar kings were Hindu, although they allowed the practice of other religions, and they themselves followed a variety of deities (including Virupaksa and Vittala, whose temples remain as important monuments). This cosmopolitan city was, however, to be wiped out in 1565 following the declaration of war by the Muslim sultanates to the north. The court fled and the city was sacked, never to be reoccupied. The remains were listed as a Unesco World Heritage Site in 1986 and they still conjure up an idea of the one-time splendour here.

Hampi's monuments are spread across a magical landscape strewn with granite boulders, and fall into three main areas: the sacred centre around the Virupaksa Temple, where recently shops and other businesses were bulldozed as part of a government attempt to 'sanitize' the site; the Royal Enclosure and the Vittala Temple. The site was naturally well defended, protected by rocky hills on three sides and to the north bounded by the River Tungabhadra, which also provided water for the city.

The elephant stables of the Royal Enclosure.

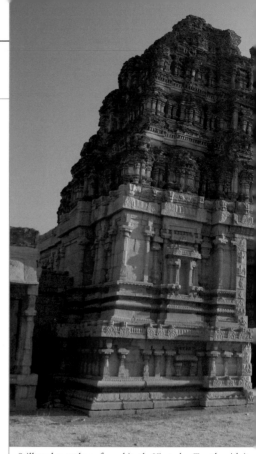

Still used as a place of worship, the Virupaksa Temple with its towering gopuram (temple gateway) dates back to the earlier Chalukyas and Hoysalas, and is dedicated to the consort of Pampa, goddess of the Tungabhadra river.

This huge monumental sculpture of Vishnu in his incarnation as a lion is carved from a single boulder.

The Vittala Temple complex is considered to contain some of the finest sculpture from the Vijayanagar period. It is particularly noted for its stone rath (temple chariot), which forms a small shrine

Devotees who come to Hampi take a ritual bath in the Tungabhadra river.

The Lotus Mahal, a skilful blend of Hindu and Islamic architecture.

THE ROYAL ENCLOSURE

This area in the south of the site was the location of the palaces of the Vijayanagar rulers, and also where the administrative functions of the state were carried out. Perhaps the most notable monument here is the Ramachandra Temple, the place of worship of the ruler and located between the royal court and the residence. As well as some beautifully carved pillars, in three bands around the outside wall of the temple are reliefs that tell the story of the Ramayana. There are a number of step wells and tanks on the site, but the most lovely is the Queen's Bath, a square basin overlooked by cantilevered balconies. The women of the court had their own quarters and the most famous structure of these is the Lotus Mahal, pictured above. The final notable monument in the Royal Enclosure is the elephant stables, a row of 10 chambers with high vaulted entrances in different architectural styles.

CHENNAI (MADRAS)

Chennai (formerly Madras), capital of Tamil Nadu, hugs India's sandy southeast shore. The least pressured of the country's four big urban hubs, it is a stronghold of Tamil culture.

The major metropolis of the South, Chennai – known as Madras until 1996 – is India's fourth-largest city, home to around 4.7 million inhabitants and sprawling for miles along the coast of northern Tamil Nadu. The area has been inhabited since as early as the 1st century, but really came to prominence as a major port from the 1500s onwards. The Portuguese and the Dutch both had bases here, but it wasn't until the arrival of the British East India Company in 1639 that the city began to take shape.

The city today is a curious mixture. While it retains the legacy of the British Raj, and is, in some ways, a conservative bastion in social and religious matters, it is also the Bollywood of South India and, simultaneously, a stronghold of traditional Tamil culture. There are churchyards, staid residential areas and prim gardens side by side with giant-size cut-outs of cinema heroes and heroines, painted in bright colours and dotted with flashing sequins.

As if this contrast were not enough, Chennai has reinvented itself over the last few years. Now one of the south's booming software and call-centre hubs (rivalling Bengaluru and Hyderabad), the centre is sprouting glossy new high-rise buildings and shopping malls,

patronised by the city's middle class. Not quite so fortunate, however, are Chennai's poor and lower castes, still greatly in evidence on the city streets.

Most of the city's sights are easily reached from the city centre, which is also where most of the accommodation options are to be found. The colonial Fort area is just to the north of the city centre, while the wider, more open spaces tend to be found to the south, with a number of attractions, particularly for children, dotted

Main Attractions

Fort St George
The Marina
M.G.R. Memorial
Anna Salai
Chennai Music Academy
St Andrew's Kirk
Kapalesvara Shiva Temple

A Mylapore jeweller.

As in most Indian cities, Chennai's buses are frequently overcrowded and difficult for foreigners to use.

along the scenic East Coast Road to Mammallapuram.

Climatically, this corner of India goes from hot to hotter and hottest, with relief brought by the northwest monsoon in June and July, and the southeast monsoon in November and December, when sea breezes bring a cool freshness to the land and the beaches are beautiful in the early hours and late evenings. The sea here, on the east coast – romantically named the Coromandel Coast – is not as inviting for the swimmer as India's western Malabar coast (the wicked undertow making it very dangerous), but the city beaches hum with groups of picnickers and strolling families. At night, lights from fishing boats can be seen glowing over the dark waters.

Chennai is also the gateway to Tamil Nadu, and makes an excellent introduction to Tamil culture, food, customs and people. Vegetarian food is available in restaurants serving delicious hot 'meals' with boiled rice, lentil curries and tiny portions of vegetables, while the famous fried *dosa* and steamed *idli* have come to be identified with Tamil Nadu.

Fort St George

The British East India Company established one of its earliest seats of power in India in the former Madras, and the construction of **Fort St George** ⒶA was begun around 1640 – making it the oldest colonial structure in the country. The fort was often attacked by Indian and French forces, yet it continued to expand. Today its buildings house the Tamil Nadu Government **Secretariat** and the **Legislative Assembly**. A feature of the East India Company architecture is the use of Madras *chunam*, a glittering whitewash of limestone mixed with crushed seashells. The *chunam*-coated walls of the buildings are dazzling.

Within the fort, a number of other early buildings still stand, of which **St Mary's Church** (daily 9am–5pm) is the most interesting. It is the earliest

English building surviving intact in India and the oldest Anglican church in Asia, consecrated in 1680. The interior of the church is whitewashed, but there are also elaborate carved wooden panels. The church was the venue for the marriage of Robert Clive, victor of the Battle of Plassey in 1759 – which marked the beginning of formal British rule in India.

The **Fort St George Museum** (Sat–Thur 10am–5.30pm; charge), housed in what was built as the Public Exchange, gives a good overview of the early British colonial lifestyle. A marble statue of Cornwallis by Thomas Banks greets visitors, with various storehouses and the city's first bank occupying the ground floor. The first floor, now a gallery of colonial portrait art, was once the coffee shop where merchants and officials met for gossip and trade. Other items on display include uniforms, coins, weapons and books. Perhaps the most intriguing artefact is Anstruther's Cage, a small wooden box used by the Chinese to imprison a British army officer captured in 1840 during the First Opium

GETTING TO CHENNAI

Chennai is one of India's major international airports, as well as a important hub for internal flights on a variety of domestic airlines.

There are two main railway stations, Chennai Central and Chennai Egmore, so check on your ticket where your train departs from. **Trains** run from Chennai to: Bengaluru (12 daily; 5–7hrs); Delhi (3–4 daily; 27–36hrs); Hyderabad (2 daily; 12–14hrs); Kanniyakumari (1 daily; 13hrs); Madurai (12 daily; 8–12hrs); Thanjavur (7 daily; 6–9hrs);; Tirupati (3 daily; 3–4hrs).

Long-distance **buses**, including those to Mamallapuram, depart from Mofussil Bus Terminus in southern Chennai – one of the largest in Asia, it is well-run and clearly signposted. Use it to reach Mamallapuram (2.5 hrs, over 20 departures daily).

War, who was subsequently kept in the cramped space for six months.

Other fort buildings of note include the **Old Government House** and the **Banqueting Hall** (Rajaji Hall), built for the governor's official entertainment during the Clive period. The architectural style drew inspiration from the classical Greeks and Romans – with Doric, Corinthian and Tuscan pillars, entablatures and friezes much in evidence.

The **Marina**, extending almost 13km (8 miles), is a wide, sandy – and in places rather dirty – beach and one of Chennai's most popular meeting places. A 2010 renovation and litter drive went a long way to tidying up the beachfront. It's worth coming down here at sunset to witness the crowds and the entertainment – **Elliot's Beach** in Besant Nagar is a slightly more low-key alternative. Facing the sea are the 19th-century **Presidency College** and the **Senate House** of the **University** ❸. The university building and its grounds are noted examples of the Indo-Islamic style popular in Indian public architecture in the late 19th century.

Opposite the university is the **Anna Samadhi**, a large marble-clad lotus commemorating C.N. Annadurai, who led the Dravidian movement to political power and changed the social and political structure of Tamil Nadu. Beside it is a memorial to **M.G. Ramachandran**, a much-loved film star and chief minister.

Anna Salai and environs

Anna Salai ❸ (previously Mount Road) is Chennai's main shopping street. Higginbotham's, one of India's best-known bookshops, is here. There are other bookshops worth checking out nearby: Landmark Books in Spencer Plaza is said to be one of Asia's largest bookstores, while Giggles in the Connemara is recommended for its knowledgeable owner and eclectic stock.

Chennai is famous for its silk emporia where silk saris, scarves, and material for suiting and dresses are available by the yard. The Government-run Co-optex shops have an extensive range of fabrics, and Poompuhar, the Government Handicrafts Emporium, has good bronzes. Both these are on Anna Salai, along with a number of other state emporia. At the junction of Anna Salai and Binny Road is Spencer Plaza, an air-conditioned complex with a large number of different shops. On Binny Road itself is the Art Deco Taj Connemara hotel.

To the north of the busiest part of Anna Salai are many of the newer landmarks of the city, most of them 100–150 years old. On Pantheon Road, where the **Pantheon** was home to public entertainments in Arthur Wellesley's (later the Duke of Wellington) day, is the magnificent, though dreadfully run-down, **State Government Museum** ❶ (www. chennaimuseum.org; Sat–Thur 9.30am–5pm; charge). Established in 1846, it has one of the finest collections in the country including a rare collection of

FACT

Chennai has a large Christian population. The British occupation from the 17th century left an Anglo-Indian population. Though well integrated into Indian society, their religion, clothes and culture make them distinct.

Traffic in the Anna Salai district.

sculptures from Amaravati in Andhra Pradesh, belonging to the Buddhist period, 2nd century AD. The white limestone sculptured medallions and panels tell the story of the life of the Buddha. The Bronze Gallery has a superb collection of Chola bronzes (9th–13th century AD). Some are barely 4cm (1.5 ins) tall, while others measure over half a metre (1.5ft). All are iconographically sophisticated. The dancing Shivas, Durgas and Ganapatis and the famous Rama, Lakshmana and Sita group are the pride of the museum.

Next door to the State Government Museum is the **National Art Gallery** (Sat–Thur 9.30am–5pm; admission included with State Government Museum), with a permanent exhibition of Indian painting. In the newer wings is a gallery of contemporary art where temporary shows are held. The nearby **Connemara Public Library** is one of the country's four national libraries to which every book published in India must be sent.

In performing arts, of all the city's concert halls, the **Music Academy E** is the most renowned. It puts on music and dance programmes by eminent artists for discerning audiences, which inspires the performers, whether of Karnatak music or *Bharata-natyam*,

Chennai
(Madras)

to memorable heights. Check out other venues, such as the **Krishna Gana Sabha**, particularly during the Chennai Festival in December and January, when you can see performances by South India's finest dancers and Karnatak musicians. The **Sangita Vadyalaya** (759 Anna Salai, behind the Tamil Nadu Handicrafts Centre; Mon–Fri 9.30am–5pm; charge) has an interesting collection of musical instruments.

Beyond, at no. 601, is **The Park** hotel – set in what was once the city's Gemini Film Studios, where a number of classic Tamil movies have been shot. Now a luxurious design hotel, its bar, club and rooftop pool are a magnet for Chennai's young middle class looking to spend their call-centre salaries.

Egmore and George Town

Beyond the Government Museum is **Egmore**, once the Indian town that complemented the colonial town of Fort St George. Now a commerical centre, it has a number of interesting colonial buildings. Egmore Railway Station, the Chennai Medical College, the Ripon Building and Victoria Public Hall are all worth seeking out. Perhaps the most magnificent Indo-Saracenic complex in the city, however, is the **High Court** and **Law College** campus to the northeast of Egmore, bordering on George Town. Its large, ornately-domed towers are surmounted on *chatris* (pavilions), while the windows are given a characteristic arch striking a nice balance between imperial pomp and local architectural forms.

Not far from Egmore Station is **St Andrew's Kirk** ❻. It bears a passing resemblance to St Martin-in-the-Fields in London and was built by James Gibbs in 1818–21. The towering steeples and the strength of the pillars of the facade make it a city landmark.

North of both Egmore and Fort St George is the district of **George Town**. Now quite run-down, its tightly packed grid of streets is nonetheless worth exploring. Within this trading district are some of the oldest temples and mosques of British Chennai and the churches of the first Protestant missionaries. The twin **Chennakesavara** and **Chennammallikesvara** temples, and the beautifully maintained **Armenian Church**, are among the most interesting places of worship in the city.

Mylapore

One of the most interesting parts of Chennai lies just south of the city centre. This is **Mylapore**, with a tank, market area and old Brahman houses. At the evening bazaar, crowds of people, freshly bathed, make their way to the **Kapalesvara Shiva Temple** ❼. The vibrantly colourful sculptures inside and all over its towering *gopuram* (temple tower)

The M.G.R. memorial commemorates Maruthur Gopala Ramachandran, film star, prominent Tamil nationalist and political leader who died in 1987.

THE "SEASON"

The most popular classical music and dance festival in India is the Chennai 'season', an annual event that began 65 years ago, when the Chennai Music Academy was founded and began organising conferences at which various aspects of Karnatak music and *Bharata-natyam* were the chief topics of discussion. The conferences were accompanied by day-long programmes comprising instrumental and vocal concerts and dance recitals. It is still held at the Academy today, running for three weeks from mid-December to early January. Artists consider it an honour to be invited to perform at its concerts, and devotees of South Indian music and dance come from all over the country to attend.

Several other art-promoting societies *(sabhas)* have sprung up in Chennai, and all now organise 'seasons' during the same period. They include the Tamil Isai Sangam, Brahma Gana Sabha, Narada Gana Sabha, Krishna Gana Sabha and the Mylapore Fine Arts Club. Listings of what's on are published every day in *The Hindu*.

Finally, if you're in the region any time in January, try to catch the annual Chennai Sangamam arts festival, which sees performances of south Indian folk music and dance, martial arts and street plays taking places at various open-air venues across the city; admission to all events is free.

EAT

The drink of the south is coffee, rather than tea, and there are innumerable small places serving frothy, milky coffee in small stainless steel cups. Recently, Western-style coffee chains have started to appear, the two most widespread being **Barista** and **Café Coffee Day**, which both have branches dotted around the city.

Gopuram detail at Kapalesvara Shiva Temple.

are among the most spectacular sights in Chennai. The temple is dedicated to Shiva in the form of a peacock (*mayil*) from which the town receives its name (*mayil-puram*, 'peacock town', which became Mylapore). The central shrine (closed to non-Hindus) has a Shiva lingam, behind which is the large temple tank. Timings can be sporadic – afternoon is the best bet. Almost as old is the **Krishna Paratasaraty Temple** on Triplicane High Road further to the north.

Mylapore is well known for its jewellers, who specialise in making gold-plated 'dance jewellery sets'. Silver ornaments are dipped into a gold solution, and bright-pink tissue paper is then placed into pre-moulded grooves before being capped with a pale pink stone. The result mimics the ruby-studded gold traditional patterns required for classical dance. The classic headpiece comprises a *rakodi*, worn just above the flowers in the hair, flanked by a stylised sun and moon. Ear ornaments come in three parts: a chain,

a dangler, and a support for the lobe. Around the neck is a choker, plus a half-moon-shaped pendant (*padakkam*) suspended from a longer chain. A *vanki* bracelet grips the upper arm and is heavier than the standard gold bangles jingling at the wrist. A broad ornamental belt, called an *odyanan*, completes the costume. Sometimes a *sarpam* hair ornament snakes around the long plait for a final golden touch.

San Thome and Adyar

On the coast to the east of Mylapore lies the district of San Thome, named after the St Thomas the Apostle. **San Thome Basilica** is on the Main Beach Road: it is believed that Thomas was martyred on what is called **St Thomas's Mount** and that his remains were enshrined in this church. The modern crypt marks where he is thought to have been buried and is an important pilgrimage spot for Indian Christians.

The **Theosophical Society** (Mon–Fri 8–10am, 2–4pm) has its headquarters on the banks of the Adyar

CHENNAI TRANSPORT

Chennai's new metro, a massive $2.7 billion project due for completion in phases between 2013–15, was still under construction at the time of writing. Comprising two lines and 32 stations, its opening is bound to transform travel in the city, which at present is bedevilled by the usual Indian traffic nightmares. In the meantime there exists a serviceable suburban railway, albeit one that's of little use to foreign visitors as its lines do not run near the major sights. Buses are cheap and crowded.

Taxis are difficult to flag down on the streets and it is best to make arrangements with your hotel if you're planning a day trip. For short hops, most people generally use autorickshaws. Chennai rickshaw drivers are well known for driving a hard bargain (and will generally refuse to use the meter).

River south of Mylapore. It houses a vast library of books on religion; in the gardens that lead up to the river and the sea is a sprawling banyan tree, said to be one of the largest in India.

Local attractions

The places described below are easily reached by bus from Chennai's new, and very well-organised, **Mofussil Bus Terminal**, which lies in the west of the city at Koyambedu.

South of the city in Thiruvanmiyur is **Kalakshetra** (www.kalashetra.net), an academy of music and dance set up by Rukmini Devi, the doyenne of Indian dance. Her efforts to re-establish temple dance after it had been banned led to the creation of *Bharatya-natyam*, now India's most prominent classical dance form. The academy organises dance programmes.

On the East Coast Road (ECR) south of Chennai is **Cholamandalam**, the artists' village, where exhibitions, poetry readings and other programmes take place. At Muttukkadu, 28km (17 miles) from Chennai, is

Dakshina Chitra (Wed–Mon 10am–6pm; charge). This is an exemplary museum featuring a number of rescued examples of South Indian village architecture. It aims to preserve and promote traditional crafts.

Outdoors, the attractions in the area immediately south of Chennai include the **Guindy Deer Park** and the **Snake Park** (Wed–Mon 9am–5.30pm; charge; no bags allowed inside). The former has species of black buck, chital (spotted deer) and numerous monkeys. The Snake Park is the only major reptilium in India, founded by the American conservationist Romulus Whitaker. Beside the Deer Park is the large campus of Chennai's branch of IIT (the Indian Institute of Technology). These are the most prestigious science universities in the country, and competition for admission to the courses is extremely fierce. Continuing south down the coast you'll come to **Madras Crocodile Bank** (Tue–Sun 8.30am–5.30pm; charge), an incredibly large collection of different varieties of crocodiles, well worth a visit.

TIP

Try to catch a *Bharata-natyam* performance while you're in Chennai, a contemporary interpretation of one of South Asia's oldest dance traditions. The dancers once came from a highly trained community of temple dancers, known as *devadasis* or 'servants of god', but are now mostly from urban middle-class backgrounds.

Indo-Saracenic architecture near Egmore Railway Station.

RESTAURANTS AND BARS

PRICE CATEGORIES

Average price for dinner, up to three courses for one person, excluding alcoholic drinks:

£ = under Rs200
££ = Rs200–500
£££ = Rs500–1,000
££££ = over Rs1,000

Restaurants

Rice is the mainstay of Tamil cuisine, often served with *sambar*, made of *dal* (lentils) and vegetables, plenty of tamarind for taste and *rasam*, a thin, peppery soup, as well as assorted vegetables called *kutus* and followed by a generous helping of curd (yoghurt), to be mixed with the rice as the last course. A south Indian peculiarity you will see is the crunching of a *pappad* (small *poppadam*) into the rice and *sambar* mixture. The feel of the food is held as very important by the Tamils, and this adds an extra texture to the mixture. Meals are traditionally served on fresh

Chennai food.

banana leaves, which are thrown away afterwards – a hygienically sound custom. The Tamils also have their Chettinad style of cooking, originating in the south of the state, in which a variety of meat and fish dishes are cooked with chillies and ground coriander. This style of cooking has undergone a renaissance and is available in many restaurants in Chennai.

Confusingly, eating halls in Tamil Nadu are traditionally referred to as 'hotels'. An age-old distinction is the one between non-vegetarian and vegetarian 'civil' food. If you want to avoid meat, South India has one of the best vegetarian cuisines in the world. Look out for vegetarian 'meals' halls or Udupi restaurants (serving snacks such as *dosa* and *idli*). There is a concentration of these places in Mylapore, although they can be found all over town. Some of them might appear a little worn around the edges, but despite appearances they are generally very hygienic.

The most expensive (and some

of the best) restaurants in Chennai are – like in all major Indian cities – in the five-star hotels, particularly The Park and the Taj Hotels, found on or near Anna Salai. Most are open for lunch and dinner, usually from around noon–3pm, and then 6pm–10.30pm, though cheaper places are generally open all day.

Central Chennai

Amethyst
Padmavathi Road, Next to Corporation Bank, White's Road.
http://amethystchennai.com. **£££**
Relaxing garden café, a real oasis in the heart of Chennai, down the road from the new Express Avenue Mall. The menu is broadly European, simple but very well executed. This is a great place to meet friends and linger over coffee and cake, or browse in the adjoining designer boutique.

Dahlia
93 Kauvery Complex, Nungumbakkam High Road.
Tel: 044-2826 5240. **£££**
Wonderfully authentic Japanese restaurant, tucked away at the back of an unprepossessing shopping centre. The menu has photos of every dish, and the service is welcoming, swift and sincere. Almost feels like eating in someone's living room, and extremely charming as a result.

Lotus
The Park, 601 Anna Salai.
Tel: 044-4214 4000. **££££**
Great Thai food in chic designer surroundings – very cold air conditioning though. Six-O-One, also at The Park, has an excellent buffet of Indian dishes as well as great Italian food.

Saravana Bhavan
Many branches including Shanti Theatre Complex, 44 Anna Salai; Central Railway Station; 77–9 Usman Road, Theagaraya Nagar; 209 N.S.C. Bose Road, George Town. **£–££**
An excellent chain of clean, cheap and tasty South Indian vegetarian meal halls. Open all day.

Zara
74 Cathedral Road.
www.orientalcuisines.in. **£££**
Lively tapas bar, with a good range of both veg and non-veg options. Fills up quickly in the evening, so arrive early or book ahead for a table.

Egmore

Annalakshmi Restaurant
18/3 Rukmani Lakshmipathy Road.
Tel: 044-2852 5109, www.
annalakshmichennai.co.in. ££–£££
'Where food is for the not just for the body but for the soul' runs the motto of this famous south Indian restaurant, where all the food preparation and service is carried out by local Sivananda yoga centre volunteers. The cooking's pure veg and delicious, the dining hall beautifully decorated and proceeds support local arts and the needy.

Vasanta Bhavan
33 Gandhi Irwin Street. £
By far the most hygienic and dependable south Indian 'meals' canteen close the train station. The menu features 248 items, including lots of north Indian options, but nearly everyone comes for the set 'Chennai Meal', rava masala dosa or utthapam. They also do plenty of cooling ice creams and faloodas for dessert.

Alwarpet

Benjarong
146 T.T.K. Road.
Tel: 044-2432 2640. ££££
Said to be Chennai's finest Thai restaurant – although the Lotus gives it a run for its money. The food here is authentic and extremely tasty. Advance booking is recommended.

Dakshin
ITC Park Sheraton, 132 TTK Road.
Tel: 044-2499 4101. £££
This south Indian restaurant is one of the best in the country, with unusual dishes from all four states, but a particularly strong showing from Thanjavur and the Chettinad region. Anyone with a sweet tooth shouldn't miss the Keralan-style coconut payasam. Exquisite Tanjore paintings hang on the walls and there's live Carnatic music every day except Monday.

Ente Keralam
1 Kasturi Estate, First Street, Poes Garden.
Tel: 044-4232 8585, www.entekeralam.in.
£££
This fabulous Keralan restaurant is the best in the city. They fly in the Pear Spot, banana blossom and other Malayali ingredients fresh each day, and offer the full gamut of dishes – from everyday pootu and parotta to sumptuous Syrian Christian duck dishes you'd normally only find on festival days.

Kabul's
35 TTK Road. £££
Expensive but very good northwest frontier and Mughlai food, served in bright, comfortable surroundings. The service is can be indifferent, though the waiters happily do 'special tea' in large porcelain jugs.

Midnight Express
115 TTK Road. £
The only late-night eatery outside of the posh hotels. Good for a fix of *dosa* or *idli* when everything else is shut.

Mylapore

Kaaraikudi
Vijayraghava Road. £
Excellent Chettinad food, including traditional chicken curries packed with flavour, and a wonderful biryani.

Nungambakkam

The Cascade
15 Khader Nawaz Khan Road. £££
Expensive but very tasty Chinese, Japanese and Thai food.

Krypto
Basement, Yafa Towers, Khader Nawaz Khan Road.
Tel: 044-4503 8001, http://www.kryptosbywilli.com. £££
Chennai's first Greek restaurant is a sophisticated dining experience, with a good assortment of Mediterranean favourites; the vegetarian meze buffet is particularly good value, and a sampler of what Chef Willi can do.

Southern Spice
Taj Coromandel Hotel, 37 MG Road.
Tel: 044-6600 2827. ££££
One of the top pan-South Indian restaurants in Chennai. Prego, also at the Taj Coromandel, serves up excellent Italian dishes.

Tuscana Pizzeria
No.19, 3rd Street, Wallace Gardens.
Tel: 044-4503 8008, www.tuscana.in. £££
Admittedly, with all the south Indian gastronomic talent in the city, no-one comes to Chennai to eat thin-crust pizza and pana cotta, but if you're hankering for a night off curry, this place is a safe bet. Authentic flavours, great service and a lively atmosphere, especially on weekends, when reservation is essential.

Theagaraya Nagar

Mavalli Tiffin Room
G.N. Chetty Road. £
The first branch of this long-established restaurant outside of Bengaluru serves up wonderful Udupi-style vegetarian dishes – you can also buy spices and pickles to take away.

R.A. Puram

Peppers
105 Chamiers Road. £££
Popular vegetarian restaurant serving good-quality Indian and Chinese dishes. Prominent on the menu is *panir* (fresh cheese) cooked in a multitude of ways.

Besant Nagar

Bella Ciao
East Coast Road, Kottivakkam Beach.
Tel: 044-2451 1130, www.bellaciao.in. £££
Authentic Italian cuisine served alfresco in the pleasant garden or in the air-conditioned interior. The wood-fired pizzas are a speciality, but they also serve perfect home-made pasta and a mean steak. Ciro, the Italian owner, is always on hand to help out.

Bars

Distil
Taj Connemara Hotel, Binny Road.
Tel: 044-6600 0000.
One of the nicer – and quieter – bars in Chennai but still with a contemporary edge. Good for cocktails. Open 6pm–midnight.

The Leather Bar
The Park, 601 Anna Salai.
Tel: 044-4214 4000.
Very popular with Chennai's young and fashionable, who come here to be seen. The outside decking area is a relief after the crush inside. The Park's nightclub, Pasha, on the side of the building is also worth checking out.

Ornate dessert at a five-star hotel.

Gopuram at Murugan Temple, Madurai.

TAMIL NADU

South India's outstanding temple architecture is just one of the highlights of Tamil Nadu, which stretches from the sand dunes of the east coast to the cool Nilgiri Hills in the west.

Tamil Nadu has a reputation for being conservative, devoutly religious and fiercely proud of its ancient culture, and while this may still largely hold true, a gradual transformation is taking place as the state increasingly deals with the outside world. There is a definite 'otherness' to Tamil Nadu, its language and culture unlike anywhere else in India. **Chennai** ❶ (see page 381) is the usual starting point for a tour of this most southerly of Indian states.

Tamil politics

A feature of Tamil temples is the presiding orthodox Brahmins, who still dress in white dhotis and display forehead markings, half-shaven scalps and long hair at the back twisted into single plaits. A sacred thread always stands out against their bare chests. Although a minority community, Tamil Brahmins continue to exert much influence in national and international affairs.

In reaction to centuries of Brahmin rule, a pan-Dravidian movement gathered pace after Independence, claiming that Brahmanical rule and influence were a symbol of northern domination. In 1967, a party championing the lower castes, the DMK, won power under C.N. Annadurai. The DMK was a breakaway party

from the DK of P.E.V. Ramaswamy which initially campaigned for a separate country of 'South India.' The film star M.G. Ramachandran (known by his initials as M.G.R.) took over as Chief Minister a decade later, controlling the splinter-party AIADMK and attracting a huge level of support. On his death he was succeeded by his former co-star and 'companion,' Jayalalitha Jayaram. Voted out in 1996 over allegations of corruption, undaunted, and still attracting fierce loyalty from her

Main Attractions

Mamallapuram
Puducherry
Kanchipuram
Thanjavur
Minakshi Sundaresvara Temple
  Madurai
Karaikkudi
Udhagamandalam
Blue Mountain Railway
Mudumalai Wildlife Sanctuary

A typical convenience store in Tamil Nadu.

supporters, she entered parliament and led her party into coalition with the BJP in 1998. This relationship soon soured, and when she withdrew her support the central government fell. She regained power in Tamil Nadu but her party, the AIADMK, was trounced by its bitter rival, the DMK under M. Karunanidhi, in the 2004 general election. In a further blow, he also took control of the state during the elections to the legislative assembly in 2006. Despite his advancing years, Karunanidhi continues to contest the chief minister's post with his arch adversary Jayalalitha, who has been in power four times since 1991.

Language was an important element in the pan-Dravidian movement and today still remains a vital part of Tamil politics. The adoption of Hindi as the 'national language' (seen as another manifestation of northern arrogance) was greeted with horror in the south, and its official imposition can still spark off riots.

Tamil Nadu has a long coastline, stretching down to Kanniyakumari at the very southern tip of India. The tsunami that hit Southeast Asia at the end of 2004 badly affected the Tamil Nadu coast, but most of the obvious damage has now been cleared up. Generally the major

Tamil Nadu and Kerala

tourist sights – including the Shore Temple at Mamallapuram and the city of Puducherry – escaped largely unscathed.

Mamallapuram

The first major destination south of Chennai is **Mamallapuram ➋** (daily, ticket sales 6.30am–5.30pm, sites until 6pm; charge, one ticket covers all sites), a tiny village by the sea and an extraordinary showcase for Tamil art. One of the great highlights is **Arjuna's Penance** or the **Descent of the Ganges**, the world's largest bas-relief, 27 by 9 metres (764 by 288ft) and one of the major masterpieces of Indian art. It is a beautiful composition of hundreds of deities, humans and animals, set around a natural cleft in the rock. Dominating the scene is a 5-metre (16ft) -long elephant leading a procession of elephants to the scene of the penance by the cleft, where Arjuna stands on one leg to propitiate Shiva to help him win back the kingdom of the Pandavas.

The best-known landmark of Mamallapuram, however, is the

Shore Temple (daily 6am–6pm). Standing by the sea, now protected by a wall that hides its facade but saves it from the elements that are fast eroding it, this twin granite spire has perfect proportions and a wealth of sculpture. It is also unique in that it includes shrines for both Shiva and Vishnu. The temple's architecture, much of which dates to the 7th century AD, has been declared a World Heritage Site.

The 2004 tsunami that hit the coast here particularly hard did not damage the Shore Temple but did carry off an enormous amount of sand. In the process it has uncovered the foundations of another huge monument, lying a few hundred metres to

The Krishna Mandapam at Mamallapuram.

Cycle rickshaws are becoming increasingly rare all over India.

TAMIL NADU TRANSPORT

Flights: Aside from the international airport in Chennai (see page 382), Tamil Nadu is well served by internal flights, with airports at Coimbatore, Salem, Puducherry, Madurai and Tiruchirapalli.

Trains: Railways wind throughout the state from the principal hubstations at Madurai, Erode, Tiruchirapalli and Nagercoil. Tamil Nadu's Blue Mountain Railway, built by the British in the 19th century to form a year round, narrow-guage link between the Tamil plains and hill station of Ootacamund, is now listed by Unesco as a World Heritage Site, along with the one running up to Darjeeling in northeastern India.

Madurai: Chennai (10 daily; 9–12 hours); Mumbai (1 daily; 33hrs); Mysore (1 daily; 14hrs 20mins); Tiruchirapalli (12 daily 3hrs).

Kanniyakumari: Chennai (2 daily; 13hrs 30mins).

Nagercoil: Chennai (3–4 daily; 13–15hrs); Madurai (8 daily; 4–5hrs).

Puducherry: Chennai (2 daily; 3hrs 30mins–4hrs).

Buses: The Tamil Nadu network is one of the best in the country. Some places in the state, especially in the hills, are only accessible by road. Useful services include those between Udhagamandalam and Coonoor (11 daily; 1hr) and Kodaikanal and Mettupalayam (2 daily; 7.5hrs). Another important route is that between Chennai and Mamallapuram (4 daily; 3hrs).

the south of the Shore Temple, apparently also dating from the Pallava era. The huge waves also uncovered a long wall running north of the Shore Temple, and in the moments before it formed, exposed traces of even more intriguing ruins on the sea-bed approximately 400 metres/yards off shore which, when explored later, turned out to date from AD 500–800,

The monkeys at Mamallapuram are very bold, and have been known to steal food and drink from visitors hands.

the height of the Pallava period. This has led to renewed speculation about the old belief that the Shore Temple was originally one of seven 'pagodas'– an assertion seemingly confirmed by reports by early European travellers to this coast.

Arjuna's Penance, the world's largest bas relief, at Mamallapuram.

The other wonders of Mamalla-puram are the *mandapams* – caves scooped from the hillsides and ornamented with pillars and great sculptured panels that are an integral part of the excavation – and the *rathas*, monolithic rock-cut shrines that have inspired generations of South Indian temple-builders. In the **Krishna Mandapam**, the seren-ity of a pastoral scene is ensured by Krishna protecting the earth from a storm's fury with his massive umbrella, the Govardhana mountain. In the **Varaha Mandapam**, Vishnu in his incarnation as Varaha the boar bursts from the ocean clutching the rescued Earth Goddess. Lastly, in the **Mahisasuramardini Mandapam**, the goddess Durga, astride a lion, battles the powerful buffalo-headed demon Mahisasura.

To the south of the Shore Temple, along a road lined with stalls selling stone carvings for which Mamalla-puram is famous, are the **Five Rathas** (daily 6am–6pm), named after the Pandava brothers, the heroes of the *Mahabharata*, and their wife Draupadi. These carved structures are thought to have been used as small shrines. They are in the shape of wooden *rathas* (temple chariots), and each is incomplete, yet remains an architectural gem. Also in this arena are a magnificent free-standing elephant and an exquisite Nandi, the sacred bull. There are four other *rathas* elsewhere in Mamallapuram.

Other notable sights include the **Trimurti Cave** and the **Adivaraha Temple**, where worship still continues, and scores of individual pieces of sculpture, of *yalis*, monkeys and other mythical and living creatures. There is also a smaller, open-air museum of scattered sculptural treasures from around the site. In tribute to the skills of the ancient sculptors, a college of sculpture is run in the township, not only granting degrees but turning out some excellent work.

Tamil Nadu's European enclaves

Tamil Nadu's long coastline is washed by diverse influences. **Puducherry** ❸ (previously Pondicherry), the former French colony, is listed as a Union Territory for administrative purposes (although it is now lobbying for full statehood). In addition to Le Club – one of the best French restaurants in South India – Puducherry has French-speaking rickshaw drivers, Vietnamese restaurants, the tastiest bottled water in India and Goubert Salai, the cleanest seaside promenade in the country. In parts of the town you'd be mistaken for thinking you were in France – a visit here is a definite contrast to anywhere else in the state, and also has some excellent shopping opportunities.

Just north of Puducherry lies the New Age community of Auroville, founded in 1968. The city is made up of attractive, experimental housing, and at its centre is the huge Maitri Mandir meditation centre. Travellers can stay in Auroville to learn more about the place and to participate in voluntary development projects.

Outside Puducherry is **Arikamedu**, an historic site where the famous British archaeologist, Mortimer Wheeler conducted excavations in

the 1940s, revealing a Graeco-Roman trading centre of the early Christian era. The discovery proved what Roman texts had already suggested: that a flourishing trade in dyed muslins and spices (particularly pepper) existed between Rome and this stretch of the Coromandel coast in ancient times.

Some European settlements on the Tamil Nadu coast are more obscure. The adventurous traveller can experience what is left of the former Danish settlement of **Tranquebar** ❹ (100km/62 miles south of Puducherry) by walking through the old gate, with its coat of arms, down to the sea. A memorial to the first Protestant missionaries to visit India remembers Bartholomew Ziegenbalg and Heinrich Plutschau, while overlooking the deserted beach, the remnants of Dansborg Fort and a Lutheran church, the oldest in India, recall this almost forgotten episode in European colonization of India's southeast coast. The former Governor's bungalow has been converted into a delightful heritage hotel,

Cave temple (mandapam) at Mamallapuram.

the Neemrana Group's Bungalow on the Beach.

Tamil temples by the sea

The **Ramalingesvara Temple** on **Rameswaram Island** ❺, 150km (93 miles) southeast from Madurai, severed from the mainland by a cyclone in the 15th century, is one of the holiest spots in India. This is believed to be the place where Rama stopped to worship Shiva after his conquest of Lanka. It is believed that the two lingams in the sanctum of the magnificently sculpted **Ramanatasvami Temple** were installed on this spot by Rama himself. The temple, it is said, took 350 years to complete; its crowning glory is a magnificent 1,220-metre (4,000ft) -long pillared corridor that surrounds the main quadrangle.

Walk away from blaring, devotional songs playing on loudspeakers and catch a bus as far as it will go to the extreme tip of the island for a holy bath at **Dhanushkodi**. Walk back to the bus stop, 3km (2 miles) across a perfect circle of sand dunes. A pilgrimage to Varanasi is said to be complete only after bathing at Dhanushkodi. The town was once a thriving port linking India to Sri Lanka, only 20km (12 miles) away across the Gulf of Mannar, until it was devastated by a cyclone in 1964. At the time of writing in early 2013 plans were afoot to reintroduce the ferry service between the two countries following the cessation of hostilities in the long-running civil war in Sri Lanka, though no precise date for the resumption of the service has yet been decided.

Tamil temple towns

Those with an interest in temple architecture could travel on to Kanchipuram, Tiruvannamalai, Chidambaram, Thanjavur and Tiruvarur, Tiruchirapalli (Trichy) and Srirangam or Madurai. Although each temple town has a distinct character, they share common elements. Processions of the god or goddess are accompanied by the loud temple ensemble of *nagasvaram* (a long oboe with a piercing tone) and *tavil* (barrel drum, played with a stick in the left hand

Street dogs are numerous all over India.

FRENCH INDIA

Puducherry lies on the coast of Tamil Nadu, 150km (93 miles) south of Chennai. It came under French rule in the mid-18th century and was finally returned to India in 1954. The town was originally divided by a canal. On one side was the **Ville Blanche** for the French inhabitants and on the other the **Ville Noire** for the Indian population. **Government Park** formed the heart of the city, around which the **Raj Nivas** (residence of the lieutenant governor) and other official buildings are now located.

Near the railway station is the Gothic-style **Sacred Heart Church**. The streets of the old French area are cobbled, and the waterfront is designed to resemble Nice. A great way to savour the faded Gallic ambiance is to stay at one of the handful of lovely heritage hotels that have opened up in the French enclave.

Ten kilometres (6 miles) from the town are the **Sri Aurobindo Ashram** and the international community of **Auroville**, which was designed by the French architect Roger Auger as an "universal city" devoted to realising "human unity". The ashram was set up by the Bengali philosopher Sri Aurobindo, who played an active role in the Indian independence movement. His teachings were preserved by his French-born spiritual companion, Mirra Alfassa, who became known as "The Mother".

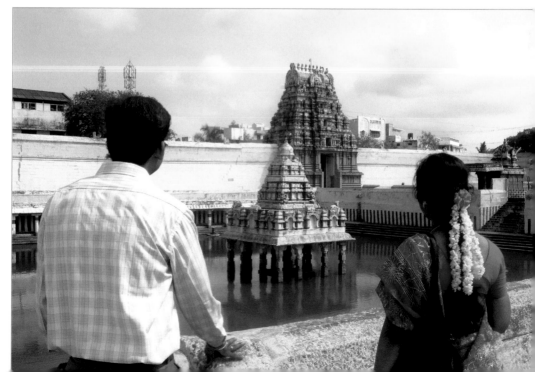

and fingers clad in plaster 'thimbles' on the right). The music from the procession is considered very auspicious. The overpowering fragrance of incense and jasmine and marigold garlands, the sight of hundreds of slippers piled up outside temple *gopurams* and the thousands of pilgrims pressing forward for a better view of an idol being paraded on a palanquin are common to all temples during festivals. Visitors should note that many Tamil temples forbid non-Hindus to enter the inner sanctum, although they are usually free to wander around the rest of the complex.

Kanchipuram

Known as the 'golden town of a thousand temples', **Kanchipuram ❻** has about 125 officially recognised shrines, all of them centuries old. Dating back to the early Jain kingdoms, Kanchipuram was successively capital of the Pallavas, the Cholas and the Rajas of Vijayanagara. The height of Kanchi's glory was as the capital of the Pallavas Empire from the 6th to the 8th century, when Mamallapuram

and Mylapore were its great ports. All that is left of that era are its magnificent temples.

The **Kailasanatha** Temple has an added courtyard, and a high *vimana* crowning the inner sanctum. Prototype carvings of Shiva, accompanied by his consort and mythical beasts known as *yalis*, set the standard for carvers. The largest of the town's temples is **Ekambaresvara**, dedicated to Shiva and with a famous '1,000-pillar' *mandapam* (columned hall). The town's silk weavers are renowned for their skill and their use of colour and intricate patterns.

Vellore, with its impressive 16th-century fort, lies a further 60km (40 miles) west of Kanchipuram, while **Tiruvannamalai ❼**, 100km (63 miles) to the southwest of Chennai, is one of the holiest sites in South India, and certainly one of the largest temple complexes, sprawling over 10 hectares (25 acres). The earliest part of the temple, the inner sanctum, dates back to the 11th century, while the huge *gopuram* was built during the Vijayanagar period (14th–16th century).

The tank at the Kamakshi Temple, Kanchipuram.

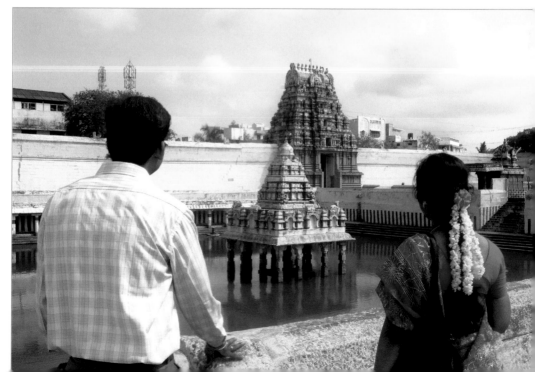

FACT

Before the 12th century, a temple's gateway, or *gopura*, was far less dominant than the towering, highly ornate edifices we see on the best-known temples today, some of which rise to heights of 60 metres (197ft) and beyond.

East of Tiruvannamalai is the 700-year-old **Gingee Fort**, with its battlements stretching over three hills. A Vijayanagara fort that the Marathas, the Mughals and the French added to over the years, Gingee has within its walls several richly carved temples, a palace, a harem and a mosque. It had an interesting system of plumbing and water storage, the remnants of which can still be seen. Towering over all of them is Rajagiri, a steep hill 150 metres (500ft) high.

Chidambaram

Beyond Gingee you begin to enter the heartland of Tamil Nadu, and especially the Chola, the fertile Kaveri delta. The temple at **Chidambaram** ❽, the Chola capital from the 10th to the 14th century, is dedicated to Shiva in his form as Nataraja (Lord of the Dance). The temple management is the sole preserve of a group of Brahmins known as Diksitars, recognisable by a single tuft of hair over their foreheads.

Much of the temple as seen today was built by the Chola emperors.

Ekambaresvara Temple, Kanchipuram.

Massive *gopurams* soar over great entrances. There are several shrines in the temple complex, including one for the god Vishnu. The inner sanctum enshrines the god in his dance pose. Adjacent to it is the sanctum of the goddess, whose name here is Shivakamasundari, 'the beautiful woman who evoked the love of Shiva.' An unusual shrine is one without an image in it; this is known as the secret of Chidambaram – the implication being that god is to be found everywhere. The roof of the temple is gold-plated. As befits a temple dedicated to the god of dance, poses now adopted by the classical *Bharata-natyam* style are sculpted around the shrines and on the gateways.

Tamil Nadu's World Heritage sites

In **Thanjavur** (**Tanjore**) ❾ (260km/ 160 miles southwest of Chennai), the former Chola capital set in the Kaveri delta paddy fields, the **Brihadesvara** Temple dominates the landscape. This, along with two further Chola temples at Gangaikondacholapuram and

---

THE DANCE OF SHIVA

As one of the holiest sites in South India, it is fitting that Chidambaram should have an origins story to match. It is said that the god Shiva performed his cosmic dance – or tandava – here after humbling several conceited *rishis* (sages) who believed they had acquired extraordinary powers through their rigorous austerities. Other sages, as well as the gods and goddesses, begged to see the dance, and Shiva agreed to perform for them in the forest of Thillai (another name for Chidambaram). The situation acquired an additional piquancy when the guardian of the forest, Kalika Devi (in reality Sakti, the consort of Shiva), challenged him to a dance contest. By performing movements which she as a modest woman could not, Shiva defeated her. He concluded his performance with the dance of bliss. In response to the *rishis*' request, Shiva dances the cosmic dance for all time to come in Chidambaram, as depicted in the beautiful bronze image in the temple. Some of the finest of all the Chola idols show Shiva in this distinctive pose, with his four harms gracefully raised, standing on one leg crushing the demon Apasmara, which signifies victory over ignorance. The surrounding flames represent the Universe, the snake writhing around his waist the divine force residing in all life, and calm expression on his face indicates detachment from the world.

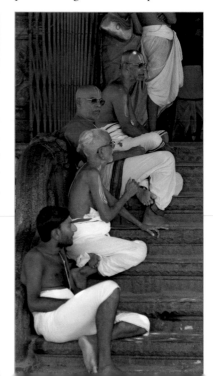

Darasuram, was added to the Unesco World Heritage List in 1987, cited for their importance not only as architectural gems but also their continued significance as places of worship.

The Brihadesvara Temple was constructed in the 10th century by Rajaraja I and features a *vimana* (sanctuary of the god) more than 60 metres (200ft) high (the tallest in India) and entrance towers (*gopurams*). Subsequent Chola temples add subsidiary shrines and extended *mandapams* or pavilions to the architectural plan. Unlike other temples in the south, the *gopurams* of this temple (aptly called the 'Big Temple') are dwarfed by the *vimana* over the sanctum. The exquisitely sculpted *gopurams* lead to a vast courtyard in which the main temple stands, guarded by two enormous *dvarapalakas* (sentries) carved out of single stones. Separated by a corridor and facing the sanctum is a Nandi (Shiva's bull).

Inside the sanctum stands a *lingam*, symbol of the god Shiva, which is reputed to be the largest in the country. The corridors around the sanctum in which devotees circumambulate, going from left to right, have many sculptures; some wonderful Chola frescoes have also been discovered here.

Close by, to the northeast, is the **palace** (daily 9am–6pm; charge). Remnants of the fort that surrounded the palace can still be seen, and a 58-metre (190ft) -high lookout remains in good shape. Members of the former royal family of Thanjavur continue to occupy some apartments in the inner recesses, but the palace is now used mainly as an art gallery and to house the Saraswathi Mahal Library. The Sangita Mahal is a music hall with great acoustics.

The **art gallery** (daily 9am–1pm, 3–6pm; charge) was set up in 1951. Initially established by the district collector who rescued many pieces from surrounding villages, the gallery houses some of the most beautiful sculptures of the Chola period, mainly from the 9th to the 14th century, and a magnificent collection of Chola bronzes, including some unique representations of Shiva Nataraja. The sculptures include freestanding pieces (many of them from Darasuram) as well as groupings. One of the most beautiful of the ensembles shows Shiva as a handsome mendicant, making the chaste wives of several *rishis* fall in love with him.

Within the art gallery is the **Rajaraja Museum** (daily 9am–6pm) which houses Chola artefacts, many excavated from the site of the palace of Rajendra Chola at Gangaikondacholapuram. These exhibits include coins, terracotta objects, carved conch shells and metal vessels and measures.

One of the greatest collections in India is in the **Saraswathi Mahal Library** (open to researchers Thur–Tue 10am–1pm, 1.30–5.30pm), housed in another part of the palace. The Maratha rulers of Thanjavur in the 17th and 18th centuries were enlightened monarchs who patronised art and culture. The greatest of

Eye-poppingly bright garlands of flowers are given as offerings to deities in Hindu

Traditional kitchen knives for sale in Karaikkudi.

Coconuts and bananas, sold as offerings outside the Minakshi Sundaresvara Temple, Madurai.

them, King Serfoji, started the library. An engaging and infinitely curious intellectual, he collected not only manuscripts and illuminations but also books in many European languages. There are over 40,000 items in the collection, and they include rare books on the arts and sciences, many of them written on palm leaves.

More Tamil temple towns

Close to Thanjavur is the town of **Tiruvarur**, birthplace of the South Indian 'trinity' of composers, Tyagaraja, Muttusvami Diksitar and Syama Sastri. **Gangaikondacholapuram** ❿ is about 64km (40 miles) northeast of Thanjavur. This elaborate name means 'the City of the King Who Conquered the Ganges', and commemorates the triumph of Rajaraja's son Rajendra. He invaded the north and conquered

many territories, reaching the Ganges in the process. On his return he built a city, and a **Brihadesvara Temple** which is almost the equal of the eponymous temple in Thanjavur. Some even assert that the sculptures in this temple are superior. This small village is all that remains of a grand 11th-century city, but the temple is a remarkable monument. Modelled on the Thanjavur Temple, it too has a large enclosure, at the centre of which is a shrine containing a huge Shiva lingam. Close by is a small museum with finds from local excavations (daily; charge).

Darasuram ⓫, close to Kumbakonum, has a magnificent Shiva Temple, the **Airavatesvara Temple** built by the Chola king Raja Raja II in the 12th century. Because of neglect over the centuries, much of the temple has crumbled, but what remains reveals a gem of Chola architecture and sculpture. The main shrine with a 26-metre (85ft) -tall *vimana* (superstructure) and the shrine of the goddess are in a fair state of preservation. The entrance hall is shaped like a chariot, and the steps leading up to it give a musical ring when struck. The exuberance of the sculptures makes one wonder what the temple must have been like in its heyday. Sculptures and remnants of paintings create a whole world of dancers and acrobats, and depict a variety of scenes from everyday life. It was known as 'the temple of perpetual entertainment.'

Tiruchirappalli (Trichy)

Tiruchirapalli ⑫ is dominated by a 90-metre (300ft) -high rock fort containing 7th-century rock-cut temples. At the top of 437 steps is the Tayumanasvami Temple, crowned with a golden *vimana*. From the fort there are remarkable panoramic views (daily 6am–8pm).

The **Sriranganathasvami Temple** in nearby **Srirangam** is one of the holiest temples for devotees of Vishnu, and its annual winter festival (December to January) attracts thousands of people. It is a rather confusing complex since it was built over the centuries. Surrounded by crumbling granite walls, with 21 ornamental towers, most parts of the temple are open to non-Hindus. The main charm of Srirangam is that it is a living temple – much like Madurai's Minaksi Temple.

Madurai

Madurai ⑬, a bustling town to the south of Tirucharapalli, is Tamil Nadu's main transport hub after Chennai, and as such tends to end up featuring in most visitors' itineraries at some point. This is no bad thing – it is the site of another great Vijayanagar temple, the **Minakshi Sundaresvara Temple,** perhaps Tamil Nadu's most popular, with thousands of visitors from all over the world coming to it every day. Dedicated to the goddess, and consort of Shiva, this is said to be the biggest temple in the country. Its four towering *gopurams* with their brightly painted sculptures are spectacular. The 1,000-pillar *mandapam* here has some beautifully carved

columns and displays of art. Other special sights include a monolithic statue of Ganapati, and the temple tank, where the god Indra is believed to have bathed.

The splendour of the Nayak rule in Madurai is evident in the remains of the **palace of Tirumalai Nayak** (daily 9am–1pm, 2–5pm; charge), the most famous king of the Nayak dynasty. The palace originally occupied an area of approximately 210 by 300 metres (700 by 1,000ft), and consisted of many fine apartments and galleries, as well as gardens, tanks and fountains. Much of it is gone now, except for the great audience hall, a three-sided pavilion; the courtyard, supported by pillars 18 metres (60ft) high and 4 metres (12ft) in circumference; and an unsupported dome over 18 metres (60ft) high.

Also worth a visit is the **Gandhi Memorial Museum** (www.gandhimmm.org; Tue–Thur 9am–1pm, 2–6.30pm; charge), located in the historic Tamukkam Palace. It contains a comprehensive account of the struggle for independence in India, and of course a more specific collection on

EAT

To dismiss the notion that only mild vegetarian *thalis* are available in South India, try fiery Chettinad cuisine, which uses lamb, quail, crab and many spices and lichens for flavouring. The Chettinad area of southeastern Tamil Nadu is also famous for its merchant traders' palatial houses with woodwork in carved Burma teak.

Inside Minakshi Sundaresvara Temple.

TIP

For more on the life of
Swami Vivekananda, pay
a visit to Kanniyakumari's
Wandering Monk
Museum, on Main Road,
where 41 panels give a
detailed account of his
travels and philosophies.

the life of Mahatma Gandhi. On the road out to the airport is a **Murugan Temple** that backs onto a large granite hill. The brightly painted facade and *gopuram* are especially fine. Young trainee Brahmins can be seen racing from their school behind the temple in time for *pujas*. Further around the monolith is a small **rock-cut temple** dating back to the Pallavas. This is an especially calm and peaceful spot with monkeys playing in the trees that grow below the towering rock.

Chettinad

On the coastal plain between Tiruchirapalli and Madurai is the **Chettinad** region, homeland of the Chettiar merchant community. Their ancestral villages, now partly deserted, have some of the finest family mansions in South India. In the 19th century the Chettiars were known as the bankers of South India, and their immense wealth was poured into gold, jewellery and, most impressively, their houses. Covering entire blocks, their interiors contain pillars of teak, satin wood and granite, intricately carved

Devotees at Minakshi Sundaresvara Temple.

teak doors, and Italian marble floors. The walls are gleaming white, covered with a paste made from lime, egg white and *myrobalam* fruit.

Some of the finest mansions can be found in **Karaikkudi** , the largest village in the region, and nearby **Kanadukathan**. After Independence, the wealth of the community diminished and the money was no longer available to maintain these luxurious dwellings, and now many of them are uninhabited. The Chettiars have, however, left a culinary legacy of peppery meat-based dishes, flavoured with unusual spices and dried fruits. While it is impossible to gain access to most of the houses, even those that have been well maintained, one or two enterprising families have begun to open up their mansions as attractive hotels, giving visitors a peek into what was an extraordinary world.

Kanniyakumari

At the southermost tip of India, **Kanniyakumari** occupies a unique position in the mythology, as well as the geography, of the Subcontinent.

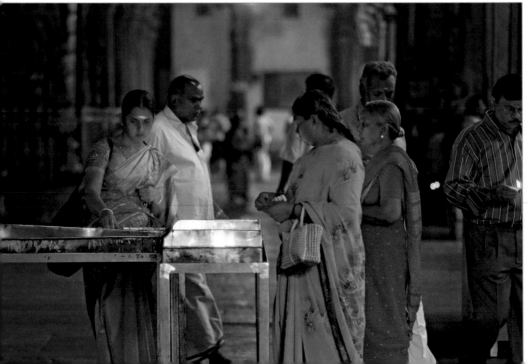

Close to 2 million Hindu pilgrims travel here each year to worship at the temple dedicated to the Virgin Goddess, Kanya Devi, whose weathered stone walls overlook the place where the waters of the Bay of Bengal, Indian Ocean and Arabian Sea merge. It's considered particularly auspicious to bathe at the ghats extending into the waves below the shrine during the full-moon phase of April, when you can watch the sun set and moon rise on the same horizon.

Standing offshore, their bases lashed by surf, is a pair of rocky islets, one of which sports a giant, 29-metre (92ft) image of the Tamil poet-saint Thiruvalluvar. The colossus, inaugurated in 2000, took 150 workmen more than a decade to build, at a cost of more than US$1 million. On the other island rests a memorial to the 19th-century spiritual leader and Hindu reformer, Swami Vivekananda, one of the figures responsible for introducing yoga and Vedic philosophy to the West. The spot marked the culmination of the two-year journey which the sage made across the length and breadth of India in 1890: on reaching Kanniyakumari, he plunged into the sea and swam out to the rock, meditating for three days on the country's past, present and future. Just over a century later, 400 people were stranded on the islet after the Boxing Day tsunami laid waste to much of the coast hereabouts.

Kanniyakumari's religious associations aside, the town can – thanks to its crowds, ugly concrete architecture and overzealous hawkers – come as a bit of a disappointment if you've travelled here expecting a mystical atmosphere. However, there's plenty of old-world ambience on offer at **Suchindram**, 12km (7.5 miles) northwest, whose spectacular Sithanumalayan Temple was founded 1,000 years ago in Chola times; its most famous monuments are a collection of exquisitely carved musical pillars, which emit notes when struck. Ancient Tamil epigraphs may also been seen on a boulder in the main *mandapa* assembly hall. Unlike most shrines in the region, the inner sanctum – unique in India for holding a

19th-century Chettiar mansions at Kanadukathan.

TODAS

The Todas are an isolated tribal people living on the Nilgiri plateau on the Kerala–Tamil Nadu border. Despite their relatively low number, which has been around 800 for the last century or so, their extreme isolation has made them the subject of much anthropological research. The central focus of their religion, and therefore much of their life, is the buffalo; they have traditionally made their living as dairy farmers. Their sociological framework was originally based on a model of fraternal polyandry, wherein the same woman would be married to all the brothers in a family, although the practice is now thought to have largely died out. Although they had started to abandon their traditional bamboo huts, called *munds*, in favour of concrete houses, recent years have seen a resurgence in *mund* building.

Yoga, Spas and Retreats

Whether you are looking to find yourself or your figure, or just want to get away from it all – India offers all manner of yoga programmes, health spas, ashrams and retreats.

Yoga originated in India, and while it is now practised worldwide, the Subcontinent is still seen as the centre of the discipline. Thought to have developed from the Buddhist/Hindu tradition of meditation, yoga strives to enhance both physical and mental well-being, with the intake and exhalation of air also playing a vital role. In the strictest interpretations of both the Hindu and Jain faiths, the ultimate goal of yoga is the achievement of *moksha*, meaning liberation from suffering, the only way to break the cycle of life and death.

The benefits of yoga are myriad, from improved strength, flexibility and tone to reduced symptoms in osteoarthritis and rheumatoid arthritis patients. Balance and core strength are enhanced through the holding of the various *asanas*, or poses, and the weight-bearing nature of some of the exercises has

Yoga on the beach.

been shown to benefit women approaching menopause, delaying the onset of osteoporosis (thinning of the bones). The psychological benefits are equally wide-ranging; yoga is often prescribed to those dealing with depression, anxiety or stress; many practitioners report a heightened sense of well-being, improved powers of concentration and deeper sleep.

Schools of yoga

There is now a vast array of different schools of yoga, each emphasising a slightly different aspect of its practice. At the most energetic end of the scale is 'power yoga', of which the most common form is *Ashtanga*, in which participants are encouraged to keep moving throughout the class, using a selection of *vinayasas* sequences of movements that link the principal poses together without pause. This makes for a strenuous, fitness-orientated workout. At the milder end comes *Hatha* yoga, which concentrates on far gentler poses, with a significant proportion of the class dedicated to exercises in breathing and meditation.

There are a huge number of opportunities to practise yoga in India, from informal drop-in classes in local parks, sample classes at gyms and hotel spas to ashrams and retreats and even university-level courses. While some type of yoga will be accessible almost wherever you go in India, anyone looking for a specific type of course should plan in advance, as the best-known institutes tend to be oversubscribed.

Ashrams and spas

However, ashrams and retreats are not exclusively yoga-based, with many different experiences on offer – from super-luxurious spa-type places where pampering is the main aim, to a more general focus on well-being which may include some yoga but will also offer activities such as ayurvedic spa treatments, meditation, exercise and diet control. These are dotted all over the country, often run in conjunction with an established hotel or spa centre.

At the other end of the scale are bare-bones ashrams, which can be austere, with basic accommodation, a strictly no-frills vegetarian diet and a high level of reverence expected for the residing guru; some even forbid talking. But for an authentic, grassroots experience, they are hard to beat.

In North India, Rishikesh is the place to go, its location on the banks of India's most spiritual river, the Ganges, providing the perfect setting. Head south and you will be spoilt for choice, with well-established centres of learning in Pune, Mumbai, Mysore, Trivandrum and Chennai.

deity that represents all three gods of the Hindu Trinity – is also open to non-Hindus.

Interesting stopping-off points on the way down to Kanniyakumari include **Tirunelveli**, 70km (44 miles) to the north. Reputed to be one of the oldest cities on the Subcontinent, Tirunelveli is home to Tamil Nadu's largest Shiva temple. Fifty kilometres (31 miles) east of Tirunelveli lies the largely industrial port town of **Tuticorin,** which is home to India's foremost pigeon-racing club.

West of Kanniyakumari lies **Nagercoil**, with its temples and churches, and beyond Nagercoil the palace at **Padmanabhapuram** (Tue–Sun 9am–1pm, 2–4.30pm; charge). The splendid fort and palace set out around four courtyards were once the seat of the maharajas of Travancore, before the capital moved to Thiruvananthapuram, in modern-day Kerala, in 1790.

Inside, slatted screens and window panes of mica cast a magical light into the carved rooms cooled with natural air conditioning created by the use of inner courtyards. An imposing royal bed, formed from a single granite slab, is placed on a gleaming black floor made from egg whites and burnt coconut shell. Murals adorn many of the walls (though the best of them, in the raja's former meditation room, are closed to the public), and in several of the larger rooms collections of antique furniture and miniature paintings are displayed. The **palace museum** (Tue–Sun 9am–5pm) has a fine collection of murals, stone sculptures and beautiful woodcarvings.

The Southern Ghats

Forming a mighty barrier between the Tamil plains and the Malabar coast, the Southern Ghats are the last major manifestation of a 1,400km (870-mile) chain of mountains running along the flank of peninsular India. The range reaches its highest in the far south around the conjunction

of the Karnataka, Tamil Nadu and Kerala borders, where it's known as the Nilgiris, or 'Blue Mountains.'

Peaks nudging 2,700 metres (8,850ft) soar above a vast tract of evergreen forest and inaccessible valleys, falling to a belt of tea gardens. Because they block the eastward march of the monsoon clouds billowing off the Arabian Sea between June and October, the Nilgiris soak up a huge amount of rain – around 2.5 metres (8ft) in less than six months. This ensures an exceptional biodiversity: one-third of all the Subcontinent's flowering plants are present in the forests here, along with elephant, bison (guar), panther, viable populations of tiger and dozens of other rare mammals, birds, reptiles and insects.

Fresh coconut water makes a refreshing drink in the heat of South India.

Decoration on Sri Ranganathaswamy Temple in Tiruchirapalli.

TIP

There are four trains that make the journey down the Nilgiri Blue Mountain Railway to Conoor. Passengers wishing to travel on to Chennai should take the one that continues to Mettupalayam, a main-line station served by regular connections to the Tamil Nadu capital.

It was to hunt and collect these magnificent animals that the first British explorers ventured into the area in the early 19th century. Until then it had remained the exclusive territory of Adivasi (aboriginal) tribes such as the Todas, who inhabited the upper valleys, rarely descending to the plains. When John Sullivan, Collector of Coimbatore, and his detachment of Indian sepoys hacked their way to the head of the Hulikal Ravine in 1819, they discovered a huge, saucer-shaped depression ringed by high ridges and fed by rivers crashing through virgin forest. Sullivan was quick to see the potential of this lost Eden and, after purchasing land of the local Toda for Rs1 per acre, moved there with his family in 1822 to establish a tea estate.

Snooty Ooty and the Blue Mountain Railway

Within a couple of decades, Ootacamund had mushroomed into a prosperous settlement, to which increasing numbers of Brits started to flee to escape the heat and humidity of the plains. By the 1880s it had acquired all the trappings of a Home Counties Victorian town, complete with Anglican church, botanical gardens, a racecourse and, most infamously, a Members' Club whose verandas and lawns became synonymous with the Raj at its snobbiest.

'Snooty Ooty', now known as **Udhagamandalam** (its original Toda name), survived Independence and, thanks to its cool climate, continues to thrive as a hill resort, though little of the British era's stiff-upper-lipped gentility has endured in the centre of town. Plenty of evocative Raj-era bungalows, however, nestle on the outskirts, while the surrounding hills offer limitless scope for walkers, with treks leading into the high Nilgiris, where isolated Toda outposts lie scattered in the forest. The more traditional of these, comprising wagon-shaped huts of bamboo and thatch, attract a trickle of curious visitors, but the Todas remain for the most part suspicious of outsiders, most of their land having been taken from them

Granite rock formation near Madurai.

by successive governments, and their numbers decimated by disease, poverty and alcoholism.

Perhaps the best way to spend your time in downtown Ooty is simply to wander around, taking in the semi-ordered, tourist-tinged chaos of it all. There are, however, several worthwhile sights; the **Botanical Gardens** (daily 8am–8pm; charge) are exceptional, with a wide range of plants, and fossils, from both the local vicinity and elsewhere. The museum at the **Tribal Research Centre** (Mon–Fri 10am–5pm; free) gives a good insight into the lives and cultures of the local tribes, and the quirky **Thread Garden**, (daily 8.30am–7.30pm; charge) featuring a collection of extremely realistic-looking plants made entirely from coloured thread, has to be seen to be believed.

A busy highway winds up to Ooty from the industrial city of Coimbatore on the plains, but the authentic way to travel there is on the **Blue Mountain Railway**. Built between 1890 and 1908, the narrow-gauge line today functions as one of the Subcontinent's last steam railways, retaining its original locomotives and rolling stock intact. The secret of its survival is the old 'Swiss Rack' system of cogs and bars by means of which it ascends 1:12 gradients, unmanageable for more modern machines. Passing through 16 tunnels in the course of its 46km (28-mile) journey from the railhead at Mettuppalaiyam, the rattling ride ascends for four and a half hours across misty tea gardens and *shola* forest.

Its principal stop en route is Conoor, a dishevelled plantation town whose scruffy bazaar of tin-and-stone houses clusters in a valley at the top of the Hulikal Ravine. There's nothing much to see or do here, beyond shop for top-grade Orange Pekoe tea and pungent essential oils in the market, but Conoor's high fringes hold several attractive heritage hotels and homestays in British-era buildings. One of the great pleasures of the Nilgiris is to sit in flower-filled gardens, sipping fine Orange Pekoe and gazing across the valley to the tea estates, while the engines of the Blue Mountain Railway

Verdant landscape around Udhagamandalam (Ooty).

chuff, wheeze and screech their way to and from Ooty.

Kodaikanal

Further south, the Palani Hills form a spur of the Southern Ghats projecting into the Vagai plain, some 120km (75 miles) northwest of Madurai. At an altitude of 2,000 metres (6,560ft), the massif's principal hill station is **Kodaikanal** ('Princess of Hill Stations'), a less brash, greener version of Ooty, surrounded by beautiful forest. It was founded by American missionaries in the 1840s around an artificial, star-shaped lake, now known as **Kodai Lake**, and remains a popular destination particularly among Tamil honeymooners, who enjoy pedalo rides and strolls along the escarpment enfolding the southeastern edge of town. **Coaker's Walk** is the main path, and the views across the plains from the lip of the cliffs here are breathtaking, stretching most of the way to Madurai. The attractive **Bryant Gardens** (daily sunrise–sunset; free) are close to the start of Coaker's Walk, and also the place to start the 7km (4-mile) trek to **Pillar Rocks**, another stunning viewpoint.

Kodai is also renowned for its prestigious International School, whose students hang out in the cafés around the bazaar. One of India's premier educational establishments, offering International Baccalaureat diplomas to pupils drawn from more than 30 countries, KIS boasts a trademark hiking and outdoor programme that makes great use of the many trails winding through the wilder corners of the Palani Hills. In recent years these have started to attract the attention of trekkers: numerous guides nowadays work out of local beauty spots, offering routes ranging from half-day rambles around the town to more adventurous forays involving overnight says in Forest Rest Houses.

A lesser known but perhaps more relaxing hill station is **Yercaud**, just north of Salem which is 150km (93 miles) north of Kodaikanal. There's not an awful lot to do here, which is the whole point of coming – there are some good hotels and the surrounding hills are stunning.

High in the hills above Ooty.

Tamil Nadu's wildlife sanctuaries

As might be expected from a state bounded by mountains and the Coromandel coast, there are still a few pockets of natural jungle, coastal wetland and coral islands where wild animals and birds can thrive. On the coast, **Vedanthangla** and **Point Calimere**, 315km (196 miles) south of Chennai, play host to a large number of migratory birds during the winter monsoon. **Mudumalai**, in the Nilgiri foothills, 67km (42 miles) northwest of Ooty, is home to the gaur (Indian bison), wild elephants and a handful of tigers. The **Annamalai Sanctuary**, 70km (43 miles) northwest of Kodaikanal, harbours lion-tailed macaques. Access to these sanctuaries is easily granted upon arrival, though it is wise to book accommodation, elephant rides and jeeps in advance.

Lesser-known sanctuaries (which require special government permits) offer the naturalist an extraordinary chance to view rare species. **Mannar National Marine Park**, for example, is clustered around 21 low-lying, uninhabited coral islands in the Gulf of Mannar. The sanctuary is the home of the endangered sea cow, the dugong. Myriad other aquatic life forms are also supported by the park's coral reef, as well as more than 100 varieties of seaweed and grass, which change the depths of green in the seabed. Permission to land on the islands can be granted only by the Chief Conservator of Forests in Chennai, if you convince him that you have a genuine professional reason for visiting. Fears have recently been raised about the long-term survival of the islands, which seem to be slipping into the sea, possibly due to illegal sand extraction.

The **Mukurti National Park**, home of the Nilgiri tahr (an endangered species of mountain goat) and a few tigers, located high in the Nilgiris, also has restricted access. Permission may be obtained from the Nilgiri Wildlife Association in Ooty, but can take a few days. Clefts of tropical rainforest (*shola*) combine with grassland. The altitude (1,800 metres/6,000ft) gives the park a temperate climate while supporting a variety of tropical wildlife.

Wild elephants at Mudumalai.

RESTAURANTS

PRICE CATEGORIES

Average price for dinner, up to three
courses for one person, excluding
alcoholic drinks:
£ = under Rs200
££ = Rs200–500
£££ = Rs500–1,000
££££ = over Rs1,000

The vegetarian food of Tamil Nadu
is one of the world's great cuisines.
Dishes such as the *dosa*,a crisp thin
pancake made with fermented lentil
dough, and *uttappam*, similar but
thicker and served with vegetables
such as onions, as well as the dry
curries known as *poriyals*, are popular
all over India. Perhaps the best option
is to visit a busy 'meals' place, where
at lunchtime a banana leaf is used
as a plate and the huge pile of rice

deposited in the middle is surrounded
with *poriyals*, *sambar* and *rasam* (lentil-
based soups), *chatni* (chutney, a little
like a salsa) and pickles. The food of
the Chettinad region, now gaining great
popularity across the state, stands out
for its use of meat and unusual spicing,
taken from a wide variety of local herbs.

Mamallapuram

Good Luck Cafe
Bajanaikoil Street. **££**
This rooftop restaurant above the Sri
Harul guest house is the best of the
budget travellers' joints facing the
beach – both for its consistently great
cooking (they do wonderful butter-
garlic kingfish with lemon rice) and
fine views, which extend as far as the
Shore Temple. Order ahead for lobster.
Moonrakers
34 Othavadai Street. **££–£££**

The original, and still the best, of the
many eateries along Mamallapuram's
main drag. Renowned for its seafood,
but the vegetarian coconut curry is
also pretty special, and the *parathas*
are to die for. The same team runs the
plusher place opposite.
The Wharf
Radisson Resort Temple Bay, 57 Covelong
Road (on the way out of town towards
Chennai).
Tel: 044-2744 3636. **£££**
The food can be hit and miss, although
the fish tikka is always a good bet
and the setting is superb. Come for
dinner to feel the sea breeze and
watch the floodlit waves roll in over the
fastidiously clean beach.

Puducherry

Ashram Dining Hall
North of Government Place. **£**

Rice with vegatables and sambar on banana leaf.

You'll need to buy a ticket at one of the Ashram guesthouses to eat here, and the meals are served at set times, but the experience is worth the hassle. Sitting at low tables on floor cushions you'll be served simple, wholesome Indian food. Incredibly good value.

Le Club
38 Rue Dumas. **££–£££**
Never quite as good as its reputation, but meat-eaters in particular will find something to enjoy at this French-styled favourite. There's a good range of wine and spirits, and the service is professional and prompt.

Hotel de L'Orient
17 Rue Romain Rolland. **£££**
The standard of food here can be a little inconsistent, but the Creole dishes make for an interesting change, the ambience is pleasant and the wine list is one of the best in town.

La Maison Rose
8 Romain Rolland Street.
Tel 041-3421 0806 **£££**
Delightful European-run place in the courtyard of a pink-painted French mansion. Grab a table in the shade of the mango tree for a heavenly milles feuilles with aubergines and real buffalo mozzarella, veg couscous with butter semolina or, their signature dish, a 100 percent pure-beef hamburger.

La Terrasse
5 Subbiyah Salai. **££**
Generous portions of good-value Continental cuisine, as well as popular patisserie items such as croissants and pains au chocolat. The semi-open atmosphere is pleasant, but there's no alcohol.

Kanchipuram

Saravana Bhavan
504 Gandhi Road; 66 Anna Indira Gandhi Road, close to the bus station. **£**
Two branches of the excellent, cheap and very clean chain of South Indian vegetarian restaurants.

Chidambaram

Krishna Vilas
West Car Street. **£**
Deservedly the most popular of the pure vegetarian South Indian places ranged around the temple. Pilgrims pile in for crunchy dosas, tasty utthapam, and light, fluffy idli, served with particularly good sambar and green chatni.

Hotel Saradharam
19 VGP Street. **£**
A run-down hotel with a popular restaurant serving a wide range of dishes.

Thanjavur

Ananda Bhavan
Gandhiji Road, close to the Hotel Tamil Nadu. **£**
Clean, with extremely cheap and very tasty vegetarian meals.

Coffee Palace
Eliamman Kovil Street. **£**
The best place in Thanjavur for real South Indian coffee and snacks.

Hotel Parisutham
55 GA Canal Road.
Tel: 04362-231 801. **££**
Wide range of both Indian vegetarian and non-vegetarian specialities, as well as a variety of international cuisine, served in plush surroundings. Recommended.

Trichy

Jenny's Residency
3/14 MacDonald's Road. **£££**
Good Chinese served in distinctly chilled surroundings, with the added attraction of the Wild West Bar.

Kannappa Chettinadu
Grand Gardenia Hotel, 22-25 Mannapuram Junction.
Tel: 0431-404 5005. **£££**
As with all Hindu pilgrimage towns, Trichy is dominated by pure vegetarian places, but at this hotel restaurant on the edge of town you can enjoy more meat-based Chettinad dishes, such as mutton biryani, kheema balls and spicy chicken curry, mopped up with chilli parottas and wonderfully spongy appam.

Madurai

Bell Jumbo
Kochadai. **££**
The largest eating hall in the city, spotlessly clean and serving an array of tasty and well-cooked North and South Indian food (including vegetarian and non-vegetarian).

Meenakshi Bhawan
West Perumal Maistry Street, near the Anna bus stop. **£–££**
Excellent and locally popular South Indian food, including a few Chettinad dishes.

Murugan Idli Shop
196 West Massi Street. www.muruganidlyshop.com. **£**
No trip to Madurai should be considered complete with a stop at Murugan's to sample their famous 'jasmine flower idlis' – so-called because they're so lightly steamed, fluffy and aromatic. The onion utthapam is not bad, either.

Only Appam
Town Hall Road. **£**
A tiny place serving some of the best local dishes in Madurai.

Kanniyakumari

Sravana Bhavan
Near Jetty and on Sannathi. **££**
The best of the vegetarian places in town. Efficiently run and better than average food – thalis (meals) are particularly good.

Udhagamandalam

Most hotels in Ooty have restaurants attached, and push full-board packages in season. But plenty of independent places vie for custom around the town centre.

Chandan
Nahar Hotel, Commercial Road. **££**
Good-value North Indian cuisine, including Ooty's top tandoori and a paneer-butter masala to die for, which you can enjoy on a smart lawn. They also do a full snack, lassi and ice-cream menu, and unbeatable thalis at lunchtime.

Sidewalk Café
Nahar Hotel, Commercial Road. **£–££**
Wood-fired pizzas, toasties, veggie burgers and crunchy salads are the specialities of this snazzy, Mumbai-style fast-food joint. It's also a good spot for a pit stop, serving cool shakes, fresh fruit juices and proper cappuccinos.

Kodaikanal

Frequented by students of the famous International School, PT Road is the place to head for cheap eats, with a string of bright, pleasant cafés and snack joints.

Manna Bake
Bear Shola Falls Road. **£**
Tasty, nourishing vegetarian wholefoods, prepared fresh each day by a friendly local family. Expats and travellers come from miles away for their wholemeal bread, and the apple crumble and custard are sublime. The whole enterprise is studiously 'green', though some find the grey concrete café walls a bit bleak.

Royal Tibet
PT Road. **£**
This is the place to come for steaming bowls of thukpa and momos, mopped up with delicious fried rice or real brown bread.

Tava
PT Road, 7 Roads Junction. **£**
Kodai's most popular place to eat by a long chalk. It doesn't look like anything special from the outside, but serves wonderfully tasty north Indian dishes, including alloo paratha, spicy, Mumbai-style pau bhaji and – to ease the chilli burn afterwards – soothing Gujarati buttermilk.

KERALA

Between the ancient creation myth of Kerala and the modern political fact is a land of lush, physical beauty that contains a rich storehouse of legend, history, culture and tradition.

When the victorious warrior-goddess Bhadrakali selected a place on Earth where she would reside she chose Kerala in the southwestern corner of India, and today the *thattakkam*, Kerala's local equivalent of a parish, is always under the divine jurisdiction of a goddess. Although legend declares that the land of Kerala was formed when Parsurama, an incarnation of Lord Vishnu, threw his mighty battle-axe into the Arabian Sea, the fertile land that emerged was not established as an Indian state until 1956, with the integration of three Malayalam-speaking areas, Malabar and the two former Princely States of Cochin and Travancore.

Kerala's main attractions are found principally in the south, within easy distance of the capital, Thiruvananthapuram, where the wealth of beautiful white-sand beaches around the resort of Kovalam attract streams of sun worshippers throughout the European winter months. Further north, the densely populated backwaters area forms a distinctive tropical environment, its tangled canals, rivulets and lakes screened from the main transport routes of the coastal strip by a wall of intense greenery. A fleet of converted rice boats cruise these idyllic waterways, allowing you to explore

the region in great comfort and style from towns such as Kollam and Alappuzha.

The backwaters peter out as they approach Kerala's biggest city, Kochi (formerly Cochin), a sprawling metropolis divided between modern Ernakulam on the mainland, and the historic district of Fort Cochin across the water. Lined by some of India's oldest colonial buildings, the fort's narrow streets are packed with visitors from all over the world, just as they were 400 years ago, when they

Main Attractions

Padmanabhapuram
Kovalam
Varkala
Kuttanad (backwaters)
Periyar Wildlife Sanctuary
Eravikulam National Park
Munnar
Kochi-Ernakulam

Vizhinjam.

TIP

Recitals of Kathakali, specially tailored for the short attention spans of foreign audiences, are staged each evening at several locations around Fort Cochin. Two of the most popular are those laid on by the Cochin Cultural Centre (www. cochinculturalcentre.com) and Kathakali Centre (www.kathakalicentre.com). Performances start at 6.30pm.

formed the hub of India's maritime spice trade.

Spices, tea and coffee

Spices such as cardamom and turmeric – along with tea and coffee – remain the economic mainstay of the interior, where thick forests and river valleys give way to grassy summits approaching 3,000 metres (9,800ft). Coffee plantations spread across the foothills of the Western Ghats, tea grows at higher altitudes and, in southern Kerala, there are acres of rubber trees.

On the coastal plains the landscape is dominated by tall, elegant coconut palms. No part of this tree is wasted, and the state has a flourishing coir (fibre) industry. The Malabar coast grows the world's best pepper, and half of Europe engaged in power struggles to command supplies of this small, pungent berry. Cardamom and cashew nuts are other important cash crops, and no compound is without a few banana trees. The fertile land also supports two or three annual harvests of rice.

Nilgiri thar at Eravikulam National Park.

Modern values

Kerala made its impact on modern India when, in the state's first elections in 1957, it formed the world's first democratically elected communist government – controversially dismissed by the Congress government in Delhi after intense lobbying by Indira Gandhi. The CPI (M), which soon regained power with a huge popular mandate, was led by the great E.M.S. Namboodiripad, who pushed through sweeping land reform, educational and health care programmes. As a result, Kerala has the most equitable land distribution in India, near-total literacy and low rates of poverty, which is remarkable considering it is the Indian state with the least natural resources.

This high level of literacy (which is also due to the enlightened educational policies of the hereditary rulers of Travancore), coupled with relatively few employment opportunities in Kerala itself, has led to Keralites finding work all over India and in the Gulf States. Gulf workers are an important source of income for the state, sending much of their money home to their families – as seen in the proliferation of 'Gulf houses', some of them extraordinary fantasies built of concrete in defiance of the climate and environment; towns such as Chavakad have become 'little Dubais'.

Women in Kerala have traditionally had a higher profile than elsewhere in India. The Nambudiri Brahmans and Nairs practised matrilineal inheritance, and women were in charge of running family property. Although this system has now largely broken down, high literacy levels have empowered Keralan women, and they tend to have more freedom than their counterparts in other states.

Multi-faith Kerala

Kerala not only has Hindus, Muslims, Christians and Jews, but many different castes and communities – all with their own customs and traditions and styles of dress, food, jewellery and marriage. Perhaps these contrasting elements explain the genuine religious tolerance found in Kerala, a state remarkably free from the communal violence that haunts other parts of India.

Here a Marxist politician might prostrate before a Hindu shrine, a Muslim contribute to a temple festival or a Christian make a Hindu pilgrimage, and buses display the religious icons of three faiths. Saint George is particularly popular across all communities, as he is thought to offer protection against snake bites.

Performance arts

Kerala has extraordinarily rich theatre. There is the Sanskrit drama of *Kutiyattam*, the lyrical dance of *Mohiniattam*, the religious fervour of *Krishnattam* and, above all, the spectacular magnificence of *Kathakali*. All these dramas evolved out of the religious beliefs of their participants and, despite their highly dramatic presentation, are less a theatrical performance than an act of worship. The

spectacular *theyyams* of Malabar demonstrate this concept when the fantastically costumed god-actors dance before shrines, possessed with the spirit and power of their Dravidian deities.

Costume and make-up play an important part in these ritual dramas. It is worth arriving early at a *Kathakali* dance drama to watch the pre-show transformation of the actors as they apply bright make-up, and don masks and ornate skirted costumes weighing up to 35kg (77lbs).

Only during the monsoon months of June to August is it difficult to find some ritual, ceremony or festival taking place. Although non-Hindus are not usually permitted to enter Keralan temples, temple festivals are accessible and visible to all. In central Kerala the use of

Local village festivals in Kerala often involve the use of ornate and bizarre costumes and headdresses.

KERALA TRANSPORT

Flights: Kerala has three civil airports (at Kochi, Thiruvananthapuram and Kozhikode). Although most flights passing through them are services to and from hubs in the Gulf States, domestic carriers maintain links with cities elsewhere in India. Book as far in advance as possible, especially if you intend to fly to Goa. Direct flights do not run daily and are in particularly high demand, meaning travellers frequently have to make the long trip to Hyderabad, or even all the way north to Mumbai, to catch a connecting flight.

Trains: Along Kerala's main railway line, which runs the length of the state via the coastal strip, trains are fast and frequent. Many continue north to the Konkan Railway and Mumbai. In addition, a couple of branch lines peel east across the Ghats into neighbouring Tamil Nadu, and a line also links Alappuzha and the backwaters. South of Kerala, the main line skirts the tip of the peninsula at Kanniyakumari before bending north into the Tamil plains and Chennai. Tickets should ideally be booked in either Thiruvananthapuram or Kochi, where dedicated tourist reservation facilities exist, allowing foreign travellers to access special ticket quotas.

Buses: Long-distance bus services tend to be much slower than the train, but seats are easier to come by at short notice than on popular rail services. As elsewhere in the country, buses are better for shorter journeys.

Trains

Kochi/Ernakulam to: Alappuzha (16 daily; 45mins–1hr 50mins); Bengaluru (3–5 daily; 10–14hrs); Chennai (7 daily; 11hrs 45mins–16hrs); Kanyakumari (2–3 daily; 7hrs 25mins–10hrs); Kozhikode (18–21 daily; 4hrs–5hrs 30mins); Mumbai (8 daily; 27–39hrs); Thiruvananthapuram (every 30mins; 3hrs 30mins–5hrs 30mins).

Kozhikode to: Kochi/Ernakulam(18–21 daily; 4hrs–5hrs 30mins); Mumbai (4–6 daily; 17–22hrs).

Thiruvananthapuram to: Alappuzha (10 daily; 2hrs 40min–3hrs 15mins); Bengaluru (2 daily; 16–18hrs); Chennai (4–5 daily; 16hrs 30mins–18hrs 45mins); Kanyakumari (3 daily; 2hrs 45mins–4hrs); Kochi/Ernakulam (every 30mins; 3hrs 30mins–5hrs 30mins); Kozhikode (11 daily; 7hrs–10hrs 30mins); Madurai (3 daily; 6hrs 40mins–9hrs); Mumbai (3–5 daily; 25–30hrs); Varkala (15–20 daily; 45–1hr 25mins).

Cochin centa players.

elephants brings a regal quality; there can be few sights to beat 50 or more caparisoned tuskers assembled before the Vadakkunathan Temple in Thrissur on the day of the Thrissur Pooram. Temple festivals are invariably accompanied by traditional music. Look out for the *panchavadyam* (literally 'five instruments') drum and trumpet ensembles that accompany processions, the loud but virtuosic *cenda melam* drum-orchestras and the drumming genre *tyampaka*.

Southern Kerala

Attractions are plentiful in the capital, **Thiruvananthapuram** ⑱ (Trivandrum), former seat of the maharajas of Travancore, and set around seven low, wooded hills. The temple of **Sri Padmanabhasvami**

that the maharajas built to honour Lord Vishnu physically dominates the bustling Old City. Reflected images of its majestic gateway towers, designed not according to traditional Keralan principles but in typical Tamil-Chola style, shimmer in the waters of the adjacent bathing tank, where devout worshippers bathe before entering. Unfortunately, the complex is closed to non-Hindus – a rule enforced by bare-chested *ambalavasis* guards – which means few foreign visitors get to peek inside at the temple's main deity, a massive image of a reclining Vishnu which worshippers peer at through openings in the floor of a special stone platform. Sri Padmanabhaswami made international headlines in 2011 when the state's high court ruled that its custodians should conduct an inventory of the valuables sealed inside the temple's treasury. A vast hoard of antique gold and precious stones was duly discovered, valued at a staggering $40–200 billion, making this the world's richest place of worship. A decision has yet to be made on what to do with the treasure – many in Kerala would like to see it displayed in a special museum – but its most likely resting place will be the secret vault under the deity where it was discovered.

The Travancore family's rather more dowdy royal heirlooms are displayed in their former residence, the **Puttan Malika Palace** (Tue–Sun 8.30am–12.30pm, 3–5.30pm; charge), next to the temple. With its elegant gables, elaborately carved pillars and enclosed courtyards, the complex is a wonderful example of regal Keralan architecture. A fine collection of musical instruments and dance costumes bears witness to the fact the Travancores were passionate patrons of the region's arts, particularly music. A festival held annually in the grounds here celebrates the memory of one member of the dynasty, Raja Swathi Thirunal (1813–46), renowned as one of Kerala's greatest composers. Singers

AYAPPAN

Between December and January each winter, the roads and holy places of Kerala are thronged by bus parties of bare-chested, barefooted men and boys, wrapped in distinctive black *lunghis*. Punching the air and shouting sacred chants as they walk around (in a manner not unlike football fans), these noisy groups are devotees of Lord Ayappan, a Hindu deity whose principal shrine is a remote forest temple at Sabarimala in the Western Ghat mountains, 200km (124 miles) inland. Also known as Shasta, the temple is only open for these two months each year and cannot be reached by motor vehicle. It has been estimated that around 1.5 million people make the journey to it on foot, walking 61km (38 miles) from the nearest village. This massive event, held to be the world's second-largest pilgrimage after the Muslim Haj, culminates on the night of Makara Sankranti, when a 'celestial pillar of light', or *makara jyoti*, mysteriously appears on a hilltop on the opposite side of the valley.

Men of any age may participate in the march, but females between the ages of nine and 50 aren't allowed. Before embarking on the trip, Ayappan devotees must make a 41-day penance, wearing the trademark black *lunghi* and necklace of *tulsi* seeds, and abstaining from sex, eating meat and cursing.

and instrumentalists from all over the country perform in the grounds, with Puttan Malika's illuminated walls as an atmospheric backdrop.

Fort, the old quarter around the temple and palace, remains a bastion of traditional arts. At the **Margi School** (www.margitheatre.org), in the west of the district, you can watch students learning Kathakali dance drama. Regular performances are also held here of the more archaic *kutiyattam*. Many of the rigorous physical exercises you'll see the students being put through here originated in Kerala's own form of martial art, *kalarippayattu*. The CVN Kalari Sangam, southeast of the temple, ranks among the state's most highly reputed teaching institutes; visitors are welcome to attend early morning training sessions (daily from 7am; free) in the gym's traditional red-earth-floored sparring pit.

North of the city centre, in a park popular with picnickers and strollers, stands Thiruvananthapuram's **Napier Museum of Arts and Crafts** (Tue–Sun 10am–5pm; charge), housed in an extraordinary Indo-Saracenic building designed by Robert Fellowes Chisholm for Lord Napier (a former governor) in 1880. Inside, its lavishly patterned walls, cases of jewellery, ivorywork, Chola bronzes and Keralan woodcarvings are somewhat upstaged by the showy Raj-era architecture. Also worth a visit, in the northern corner of the park, beyond the city zoo and botanical gardens, the **Shri Chitra Art Gallery** (Tue–Sun 10am–5pm; charge) features paintings by Raja Ravi Varma – a minor Keralan royal who became hugely popular in the late 19th century for his realist depictions of curvy, sari-clad women and mythological scenes – alongside some luminous Himalayan landscapes by Russian mystic Nicholas Roerich.

Before the Travancores shifted the capital to Thiruvananthapuram at the end of the 19th century, their principal palace lay 63km (39 miles) further south, across the modern Kerala-Tamil Nadu state border. Reachable in a half-day trip by bus or taxi, **Padmanabhapuram** is regarded as the finest surviving example of Keralan architecture (see page 405).

The Krishna Temple at Guruvayur.

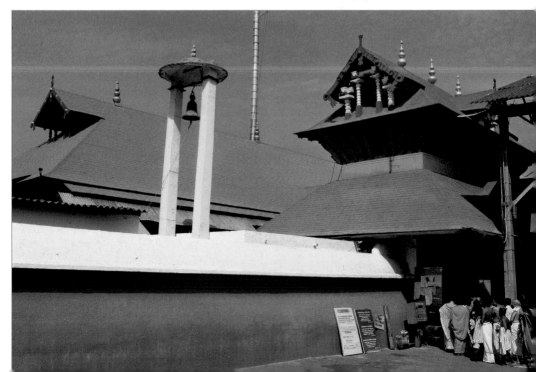

TIP

Buses run to
Padmanambhapuram
Palace from
Thiruvananthapuram's
Thampanoor bus stop,
via Kovalam junction. All
services heading to
Nagercoil or Kanniyaku-
mari pass the site. Aim
to arrive as early in the
morning as possible,
before the heat builds.
Taxis also run the route,
for pre-fixed routes
displayed on boards at
taxi ranks.

Sixty-three kilometres (40 miles) to the northeast of Trivandrum city lies **Ponmudi**, the closest hill station to the Keralan capital. The drive to get there is stunningly scenic, winding its way past tea estates and waterfalls, and the town itself, although small, makes an excellent trekking base.

Kerala's best beaches

Among Kerala's excellent beaches, the best-known is **Kovalam ⑲**, located 16km (10 miles) south of Thiru-vananthapuram, where facilities at all levels are available. Except for the tourist trade near the beach itself, life in the surrounding countryside and the fishing settlements in the area goes on very much as in the rest of rural Kerala. Ayurvedic massage is relaxing after a swim in rough waters, and masseurs are ready on shore to oblige. Massage using herbal oils is said to be most effective at the moment the monsoon breaks in early June.

A ramshackle agglomeration of hastily erected hotels, the resort extends across the paddy fields and palm groves inland from a trio of

separate coves, each with their own distinct character. Most foreign tourists, including an ever-increasing number of charter holidaymakers from Russia, congregate on Lighthouse beach, whose arc of golden sand is overlooked by the red-and-white-striped tower of the eponymous Kovalam lighthouse. At night, the revolving lamp casts its beam across a strip of brightly lit café-restaurants and the crashing surf to a horizon dotted with the lamps of tiny inshore fishing boats.

Get up early enough in the morning and walk around the low, rocky promontory dividing Lighthouse beach from its neighbour, Hawa beach, and you'll be treated to one of the quintessential spectacles of the Keralan coast: teams of local fishermen, dressed in cotton turbans and Madras-chequed *mundus (lunghis)*, hauling huge nets ashore with ropes.

Hawa beach comes to an abrupt end at a sheer-sided headland, crowned by the five-star Leela hotel, but the sands – empty save for a few fishing boats – continue on the

Cochin fishing nets.

opposite side, spreading north for as far as the eye can see.

Heading in the other direction, south from Kovalam, tourism development is more marked once you're past the port of **Vizhinjam**, a former regional capital divided between low-caste Hindu and Christian fishing communities. The shoreline beyond Vizhinjam breaks into a succession of small coves, backed by a large, gated hotel complexes specialising in Ayurvedic therapies. Eventually, the cliffs yield to the shimmering expanse of Chowara beach, which stretches south for 17km (10.5 miles) to the mouth of the Neyyar River, where a large island in the backwaters shelters another cluster of luxury hotels.

Varkala ❷⓪, 54km (32 miles) north of Thiruvananthapuram, is an attractive village with a less commercialised, fine sandy beach at the base of dramatic red cliffs. Though tourists come for the beach, it is also one of Kerala's major Hindu pilgrim centres: guided by local priests, families immerse the ashes of recently deceased relatives in the waves, while ranks of foreign sun worshippers slurp tropical fruit cocktails, play volleyball and practise yoga poses nearby. High above them, a row of bamboo and palm-leaf cafés noses over the cliff edge, offering ideal spots to gaze at the sunsets over the Arabian Sea.

To escape Varkala's tourist scene you can amble 4km (2.5 miles) north along the laterite-paved coast path leading to neighbouring Odayam, where a handful of small guesthouses huddle in the coconut groves behind a small, black-sand cove. Fishing is still an important part of the economy in these parts. The mostly Muslim fishing villages are conservative, and it is important not to cause offence by bearing too much flesh. Even in Varkala, topless sunbathing is definitely taboo.

Kuttanad: the backwaters

About 20km (12 miles) north of Varkala is **Kollam** ❷① (Quilon), a cashew-nut port that once served as the hub of the Malabar Coast's spice trade, attracting Arab, Greek, Roman and Chinese ships. These

TIP

Lifeguards patrol Lighthouse beach to ensure swimmers do not fall foul of the treacherous currents that rip through the bay at certain phases of the tide. Fatalities occur every season. Always stay within the limits of the safety flags and obey the whistles of the lifeguards.

Theyyam dance.

FACT

One of Kerala's most renowned holy men and social reformers, Sri Narayana Guru, spent much of his life in Varkala. At Sivagiri Hill, 3km (2miles) inland from the beach, the ashram he founded remains an important regional pilgrimage site. Its centrepiece is a samadhi where the guru's remains are enshrined. Rabindranath Tagore and Mahatma Gandhi numbered among Sri Narayana's devotees.

Kovalam is Kerala's main beach resort.

days, however, most of the boats passing through here are en route to the **Kuttanad** backwater region to the north, for which Kollam serves as a gateway. Many visitors also stop over on their way to the famous ashram of Amma, 'the hugging saint', and Amritpuri, 33km (20 miles) north.

Among the few surviving relics of the town's former prominence is the British Residency, on the shores of Ashtamudi Lake, just north of the centre. A stately 250-year-old mansion, it was built in an idiosyncratic, Keralan-British fusion style typical of the mid-18th century, when attitudes to local traditions were still more respectful rather than dismissive. Inside the building, which nowadays houses an atmospheric Government guesthouse, a vast teak table, giant Chinese pickle jars and walls hung with military lithographs gather dust.

The most popular cruise in the backwaters is the eight-hour trip between Kollam and **Alappuzha** ㉒ (Alleppey). Two companies run the route: the District Tourism Promotion Council (DTPC) and Alappuzha Tourism Development Council (ATDC), both of which have offices at Kollam's main boat jetty (on the west side of town) where you can purchase tickets. The boats depart at 10.30am sharp, and stop for lunch at **Karunagapalli**, where shipbuilders construct *kettuvallam* rice barges out of jackwood planks sewn together with coir rope. Halfway through the journey, 10km (6 miles) east of Chengannur, is **Aranmula**, famed for both its **Parthasarathi Temple** and its unique metal mirrors. Equally unique is the boat 'race' held here every year on the last day of Onam (Aug–Sept) as part of the Vallamkali festival. It commemorates the crossing of the river by Krishna, who is thought to be present in all the boats taking part, meaning they are all obliged to cross the finish line at the same time in deference to the god.

Alappuzha itself is a bustling, typically Keralan market town, set on a grid plan formed by intersecting canals. In colonial times, these formed an important link between the interior and the sea. Coir, cashews, spices, rubber, tea and coffee were transported via the backwaters to the *godown* warehouses lining the town's waterways and shipped to Europe from a long pier, whose rusting remnants still preside over Alappuzha's desultory beach. These days, hotels and cruises form the mainstay of the area's economy, with over 400 tourist barges plying the backwaters.

Vembanad and Kottayam

The northeastern fringes of Alappuzha are dominated by a vast inland lake, whose waters stretch for almost 100km (62 miles) to the edge of Kochi. Encompassing more than 1,500 sq km (580 sq miles), Vembanad Lake is one of India's largest bodies of water and is also a busy transport artery, connecting the coastal strip and backwaters with the foothills. During the winter, literally hundreds of rice barges may be seen drifting across its glasslike surface, and local ferries chug between the towns and villages lining its shores.

Vembanad's eastern flank was chosen by the British missionary Henry Baker as the site of an experimental rubber and fruit farm in the 1820s. After Independence, this estate was ceded to the government and turned into the **Kumarakom Bird Santuary** (dawn–dusk; charge), an important nesting site for winter migrants, while Baker's residence was converted into the first of the many luxury hotels that now encrust the shoreline. Arundhati Roy's Booker Prize-winning novel *The God of Small Things* was set in this area; and both Baker and his former home feature in the book.

One of the reasons for Kumarakom's success as a tourist destination is its proximity to **Kottayam ㉓**, 10km (6 miles) further inland. Rubber plantations in the surrounding countryside form the bedrock of the town's legendary prosperity, which has fuelled exceptionally high rates of literacy – high-earning expats now account for as much income hereabouts as rubber. The majority of local estates, and the booming Kottayam publishing industry, are dominated by Syrian Christians, for whom this is an important centre. A pair of ancient

FACT

Arundhati Roy, author of the Booker Prize-winning novel The God of Small Things, was born and raised in Kerala. Many of the characters and places that appear in the book were derived from real-life people and locations in the backwaters near Kottayam, including the infamous 'History House', the residence of a former rubber planter and now a luxury hotel.

Vizhinjam harbour.

TIP

Kottayam is famous as the source of Kerala's most widely read daily, the *Malayalam Monorama*, published here since 1890 and boasting a state-wide readership of around 1.5 million. Non-Malayalam speakers can browse its English edition online at www.manoramaonline.com.

churches, 5km (3 miles) northwest at Valliapalli and Cheriapalli, testify to their long presence in the area.

Thirty kilometres (18 miles) east of Kottayam is **Palai**, commonly known as the Vatican of India. It holds a Guinness world record for being the Christian parish with the largest number of priests in the world: 101 and counting! There are naturally a large number of churches in the area, including Alphonsa Church, a popular pilgrimage destination which houses the mortal remains of St Alphonsa of India, the first person of Indian origin to be canonised as a saint by the Catholic Church.

The Ghats

Inland from Kottayam, the flat country of the backwaters is soon interrupted by tracts of low, wooded hills and rubber plantations, which gradually steepen as they approach the shirt-tails of the Western Ghats – the highest mountain range in South India. Because it blocks the eastward advance of the monsoon weather systems, this chain of peaks,

Toddy tapper at Alappuzha.

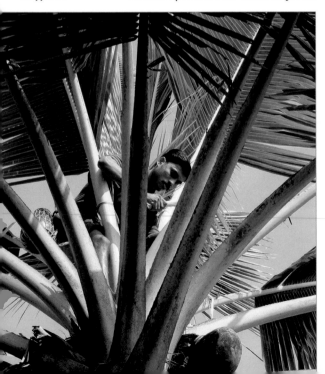

culminating at an altitude of 2,695 metres (8,840ft), soak up astonishing levels of rainfall between June and November; most regions receive 3–4 metres (10–13ft) over these six months, and some get as much as 9 metres (30ft). The result is one of the planet's richest eco-systems: 4,000 species of plants thrive on the Ghats' western flanks, where stands of giant teak trees give way to montane rainforest and deciduous woodland, before finally yielding to open grassland. In high valleys, the British took advantage of the moist weather and cooler temperatures to plant vast coffee and tea estates, and these – together with cardamom and spice plantations – still dominate the landscape of many districts.

For visitors, however, the main incentive to travel into the Keralan mountains is the chance to spot wildlife in one of several reserves established in the region. By far the best-known of these is **Periyar Wildlife Sanctuary**, near the market town of Kumily, close to the Tamil Nadu border, where the former hunting reserve of a maharaja is now protected as an official sanctuary. The park, among the most visited in India, centres on a convoluted reservoir where, from the comfort of a boat deck or bamboo raft, you can sight grazing herds of wild elephant, and even, on rare occasions, one of the handful of tigers that survive in the surrounding forests. In an attempt to protect its fragile populations of fauna from poachers, the Periyar Tiger Reserve has implemented a radical scheme whereby local forest-dwelling minority people are employed as guides, wardens and hotel staff in the park – the idea being that if local villagers gain direct financial benefit from the sanctuary, they are less likely to indulge in illegal hunting. So far, the initiative seem to have been extremely successful, with animal numbers on the increase and local poverty on the wane. For details of the reserve's tips, go to www.periyar tigerreserve.org.

Another sanctuary worth making a detour to visit is **Eravikulam National Park** (daily 7am–6pm; charge), a four-hour drive north of Periyar, not far from the tea station of Munnar. High up near the watershed of the Ghats, the reserve is the last bastion of the Nilgiri tahr, a rare species of mountain goat that survives on the grasslands of the range's uppermost ridges and peaks. The tahr was almost wiped out by hunters during the colonial era, but revived after American biologist Clifford Rice attracted herds to his camp using salt licks; dozens of semi-tame tahr hang around outside the park gates at Vaguvarai.

As the site of the Western Ghats' most beautiful tea gardens, **Munnar** ㉔ fully deserves a couple of days out of anyone's itinerary. The stiff-upper-lipped gentility of the Raj still very much holds sway at the famous High Range Club, on the south side of town, where you can sip gin and tonics in a bar lined with hunting trophies and the dusty pith-helmets of long-deceased British tea-planters.

Kochi-Ernakulam

One of the most atmospheric old cities in the south, **Kochi-Ernakulam** ㉕ (Cochin) is well worth a day or more's exploration. It can be reached from Alappuzha by water, but boat traffic on the way to this major port and naval base is heavy, and many prefer to travel by road or rail. Ferries connect the islands of **Willingdon**, **Bolgatty**, **Gundu** and **Vypeen** to the southern peninsula of Fort Cochin and Matancherry and to the commercial centre, **Ernakulam**, on the mainland. Semitic traders from Yemen and Babylon used to import dates and olive oil in exchange for peacocks and spices, and Kochi is still an important spice port – its *godowns*

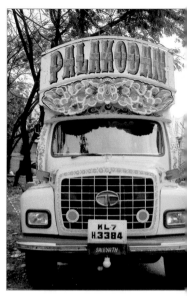

Colourfully decorated trucks are a common sight on India's highways.

Fertile land in the Western Ghats.

FACT

India is the world's third-largest producer of pepper, and most of the 70,000 tonnes it ships annually are either grown or sold in Kerala. Mantancherry, Kochi, used to be the site of the Inter-national Pepper Exchange, whose functions were recently superseded by the online India Pepper and spice Trade Assocation (IPSTA).

(warehouses), smelling of pungent spices, are a hive of activity.

Most of the interest is concentrated in the Fort area. **Matancherry Palace** (Sat–Thur 10am–5pm; charge), on the eastern side of the peninsula, was built in 1557 by the Portuguese in exchange for trading rights, and then repaired by the Dutch (renaming it the Dutch Palace) in 1663, although its architectural style is Keralan. Its frescoes, dating from the 17th century, depict Indian epics in extraordinary vegetable colours. The Royal Bedroom is particularly splendid, featuring a series of 45 murals relating the tale of the *Ramayana.* In the heart of the Fort area is the oldest European church in India, **St Francis's**, dating all the way back to 1506. Vasco de Gama died here, and was originally buried in the cemetery before his remains were removed to Portugal 14 years later.

Jew Town, a settlement that dates back a millennium, still thrives with antiques and spice shops. Lying to the south of Matancherry Palace, the small Pardesi synagogue here is used by the diminishing Jewish community; most families have left for Israel. The synagogue is floored with blue-and-white tiles from Canton, no two of which are the same.

There is little trace of the Arabs, Phoenicians, Romans and Greeks who traded at the port. Old colonial churches and warehouses recall the Portuguese, Dutch and British settlers with faded elegance, while the Chinese fishing nets that line Fort Kochi's northern shore hark back to the era when the harbour was jammed with massive junks from Canton. The nets are operated by a cantilevered system of counterweights and they have become a visitor attraction in their own right.

The **Chottanikkara Temple** 30km (18 miles) west of Kochi attracts a growing number of pilgrims who seek release from evil spirits, and the long iron nails driven into the huge tree near the sanctum of the goddess testify to their successful exorcism.

Northern Kerala

Leaving Kochi by crossing to Vypeen island and heading north, you pass a pair of Portuguese forts before rejoining the mainland. Just beyond Azhikod is **Kodungallur**. Steeped in history, this settlement is thought to have been the ancient port of Muziris, visited by the Romans. The followers of the Prophet Mohammed also came early to Kerala, and although the **mosque** at Kodungallur is a brash, modern concrete structure, its interior is still the cool and serene original of India's oldest mosque.

Travelling further north up the coast from Kochi takes you past the turn-off to the **Palakkad Gap** (Palghat), the lowest point in the Western Ghats, at **Thrissur** ㉖. This is the site of one of Kerala's most important temples, **Vadakkunnatham**, which legend says was founded by Parasurama. Each year in May, the broad avenues outside it host the annual Pooram festival, the largest and most exuberant temple festival in the state, featuring dozens of

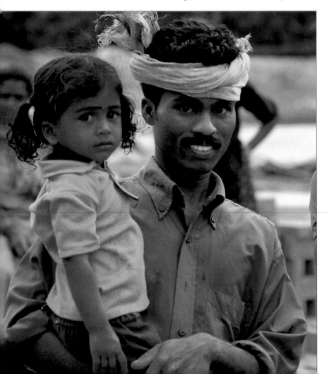

Hill people.

lavishly caparisoned elephants and ear-splitting drum orchestras. Thrissur's small **Archaeological Museum** on Town Hall Road (Tue–Sun 9am–5pm; charge) has interesting examples of temple art. The Krishna Temple at **Guruvayur**, 30km (18 miles) from Thrissur, is the most sacred place in Kerala. The temple painters from this town are particularly skilled. Like most Keralan temples, access is for Hindus only.

Kozhikode ❷❼ (Calicut), capital of northern Kerala, was known to the Phoenicians and ancient Greeks, who both traded spices here. These days, the town's economy rests not on exports, but on the remittance cheques of its many emigrants resident in the Gulf States. The **Pazhassi Raja Museum** (Tue–Sun 10am–1pm, 2–4pm) and **Krishna Menon Art Gallery and Museum** both have interesting displays. Krishna Menon was a prominent Keralan politician after Independence.

Close by, at **Kappad**, 16km (10 miles) from Kozhikode, is the place where Vasco da Gama first landed in India in 1498. Further north, past the French enclave of **Mahé**, is the attractive coastal town of **Kannur** (Cannanore). The town is home to the Mopplah community, originally of Arab descent; the picturesque streets of **Mopplah Town**, just south of **Fort St Angelo**, are well worth exploring, as is nearby **Payyambalam beach**. The town's other claim to fame is its weavers, of whom many work at the **Kanhirode Weavers' Cooperative Society** (www.weaveco.com), which welcomes visitors. Further north again is the atmospheric **Bekal Fort** ❷❽, overlooking a beautiful beach. Although often referred to as Tipu Sultan's Fort, it was originally built by the Kadamba Kings before coming under Tipu Sultan's control, and then finally passed into the hands of the East India Company.

Roughly 60km (37 miles) inland from Kannur is the **Waynad** district,

Heavy load.

EAT

The food stalls lined up next to Fort Cochin's Chinese fishing nets are a great source of delicious local seafood. You can pick the fish you want straight from the nets, and watch it grilled or pan-fried in front of you. The quayside is busiest just after sunset.

an area of rainforest interspersed with tea and coffee plantations, many of which now operate as guesthouses and offer a supremely tranquil experience. The journey there from the coast, and continuing on to Mysore, is one of India's most scenic.

Munnar street life.

RESTAURANTS

PRICE CATEGORIES

Average price for dinner, up to three courses for one person, excluding alcoholic drinks:
£ = under Rs200
££ = Rs200–500
£££ = Rs500–1,000
££££ = over Rs1,000

Kerala's food reflects the mix of its communities, Hindu, Christian and Muslim. As elsewhere in the south 'meals' predominate, but with the use of the characteristic fat-grained Keralan rice; flecked with red, it is parboiled while in the husk to retain its vitamin D. In some places you may find tapioca root replaces rice as a staple. Coconut milk and oil are ubiquitous and Keralan fish curries, and fried fish, are especially good.

The Christian community especially is fond of beef (a strict taboo for Hindus) and it can be widely found as 'beef fry' (a dry curry), while the Mapillas (Keralan Muslims) have spicy meat and seafood curries flavoured with cloves and pepper. Bananas are deep-fried as crisps or steamed and in used curries.

Thiruvananthapuram

Arya Niwas
Aristo Road, near the railway station. £
Keralan thalis don't come fresher, more fragrant, or beautifully presented than at this hugely popular banana-leaf 'meals' joint. It gets packed out at lunchtime. Thereafter, a standard Udupi menu of dosas and other snacks holds sway. The dining hall upstairs is air-conditioned and only slightly pricier.

Maveli Café (Indian Coffee House II)
Central Station Road, beside the bus stop. £
Coffee and snacks served by waiters in the trademark ICH ice-cream-wafer turbans in a spiral building designed by Laurie Baker. A popular spot for breakfast.

Kovalam

The best option outside of the bigger hotels, and certainly the most atmospheric, is to eat at one of the many beachfront cafés/restaurants serving freshly caught fish, grilled or fried and served with chips and salad. Make sure you choose your fish carefully. Finish off with fruit from the women selling mango, pineapple and papaya along the beach.

Fusion
Lighthouse Beach. ££
Kovalam's most sophisticated menu, featuring dishes that combine the best of Kerala and Europe. Try its scrumptious house tagliatelle with home-made chilli pesto, rounded off with a cooling mint lassis, which you can sip while enjoying panoramic views across the beach and out to sea.

Waves
South end of Lighthouse Beach. ££
Something of a Kovalam institution, the 'German bakery' sells strudel and bread, as well as a good selection of Thai and European dishes (mainly pasta).

Varkala

Most of the restaurants along the clifftop at Varkala have great views out to sea, and the food is all of a similar standard (the usual combination of North Indian dishes, noodles and fresh seafood).

Shri Padman
Temple Junction. £
Overlooking the temple tank, the rear terrace of this simple local café, which serves basic travellers' grub as well as Keralan vegetarian 'meals', is a great place for crowd-watching, especially early in the morning, when half the village comes for a propitious dip.

Suprabhatam
Varkala Village, 4km (2½ miles) east of the beach. £
This is where all the locals go for filling, eat-all-you-can Keralan 'meals', and the usual selection of dosas.

Kollam

Prasadam
Hotel Nani, opposite the clock tower. Tel: 0474-275 11412, www.hotelnani.com. £££
Decent places to eat are like hens' teeth in Kollam, but thankfully the smart air-con restaurant in the Hotel Nani more than makes up for the shortfall, offering an extensive multi-cuisine menu of pan-Indian, Chinese and Continental dishes – at honest prices.

Alappuzha

Chakara
Hotel Raheem Residency, Beach Road. ££££
This is the top place to eat in Alappuzha, and a first-floor, open-sided restaurant that makes the most of the breezes blowing off the nearby beach. Keralan seafood, masala-fried or simmered in coconut-rich gravies, is the house speciality. There is also menu also a wide choice of healthy Western alternatives.

Dreamers
Alappuzha beach. ££–£££
Italian run café-restaurant down on the beach, with a kind of travellers-beach-shack vibe and an eclectic menu of pasta and pizza, Thai curries, grilled local seafood and chips, and tandoori chicken that falls off the bone. The sea-facing location can't be beaten and the service is flawless. Get there before sunset for a seat on the first floor deck.

The Harbour
Beach Road. £££
Alappuzha-style seafood and backwater delicacies, such as Kuttanadi chicken and karimeen pollichathu, served in a spick and span beachfront restaurant, along with a selection of freshly prepared Continental sandwiches and snacks.

Kottayam

Kottayam's hotels all have dependable restaurants, and there are plenty of simple 'meals' canteens ranged around Gandhi Square (the best of these is the Anand, just off KK Road).

Karimpunkala
6km (3½ miles) south of Kottayam at Nattakom-Palam, on the MC Road. £
Rustic-style roadside diner, where elaborate thalis featuring oysters, tapioca and more-ish appam number among the delicious, staunchly traditional specialities.

Meenachil
Homestead Hotel, KK Road. £–££
Quality non-vegetarian Keralan food, including delicious kuttanadi-style chicken curry and meen pollicahattu, in a cosy air-conditioned restaurant close to the centre of town. There's also a vegetarian annexe where you tuck into standard rice-plate 'meals'.

Kochi-Ernakulam

In Ernakulam, a row of popular, inexpensive cafés and restaurants line up along Shanmukam Road. Over in Fort Cochin, you can opt for one of many atmospheric tourist restaurants in the district's heritage hotels.

Arca Nova

Fort House Hotel, 2/6A Calvathy Road, Fort Cochin.
Tel:0484-221 7103. **£££**
Deliciously spicy Keralan fish steaks, millet-fried or steamed in banana leaves, served at a prime location on a jetty jutting into the harbour – a great spot for watching the ships come and go.

Dal Roti

1/293 Lily Street. **£–££**
First choice among the enclave's backpackers, this shabby-chic diner is renowned for its smokey, flavour-packed north Indian specialities. They do all kinds of curries here, but nearly everyone comes for the more-ish kati rolls.

The Old Courtyard

The Old Courtyard Hotel, 1/371–2 Princess Street, Fort Cochin.
Tel: 0484-221 6302. **££££**
Enjoy gourmet delicacies, such as the famous house seafood spaghetti or grilled seer fish in coriander butter, served on candlelit tables against a backdrop of 17th-century Portuguese arches. The Courtyard provides the most atmospheric fine dining in the Fort; and its desserts are to die for.

Subhishka

Bharat Tourist Home, Durbar Hall Rd, Ernakulam. **££**
Sumptuous Keralan sadya thalis (vegetarian only) served on fresh banana leaves in a smart hotel restaurant. Pricier than average, but the curries, pickles and papadoms are top drawer and just keep on coming. It's a great place for people watching too – especially on weekends.

Thrissur

The town's hub, the Round, is lined with dozens of busy 'meals' places, which serve standard Keralan thalis at lunchtime, and dosas, uttapams and other South Indian snacks thereafter. There's also a workers' tattukada food market that opens after office hours on Round South, opposite the Medical College Hospital.

Bharath Hotel

Chembottil Lane. **£**
The best pure-veg place in Thrissur. It's more of a canteen than a restaurant, but scrupulously clean and bustling all day from early morning till late evening. Queues frequently stretch out the door at lunchtime.

Kozhikode

A great source of fresh, tasty and inexpensive food is the tattukada night market on Beach Road, where rows of stalls lit by kerosene lamps rustle up local fish steaks and rice-plate meals.

Paragon

Off Kannur Road. **£–££**
One of the region's hallmark Mapilla dishes is fish kombathu, eaten with proper local pathiri rice cakes, and there's no better place to sample it than here. They also serve a range of other Malabari seafood staples (including succulent local mussels) in addition to a full South Indian vegetarian menu.

Sopanam

Delma Complex, Mavoor/IG Road. **£**
A good, and cheap, vegetarian 'meals' hall in the centre of town serving a particularly tasty coconut korma.

A typical Keralan breakfast

CRUISING KERALA'S GREEN BACKWATERS

In these southern lagoons women catch mudfish with their bare toes and Chinese fishing nets leave phosphorescent streaks across night waters.

'It was warm, the water. Greygreen. Like rippled silk./With fish in it./With the sky and trees in it./ And at night, the broken yellow moon in it.' In these lines from her novel *The God of Small Things*, Keralite author Arundhati Roy evokes a sense of the reflective pace of life beyond the mainstream.

The backwaters of Kerala are a tangle of brackish channels fed by rivers just inland from the Arabian Sea. They extend from Kochi south to Allapuzha, where peppercorns are still traded silently, using hand signals beneath a kerchief.

Progress here can be slow as the shallow waterways are often choked with water lilies and duckweed. A recent menace has been the proliferation of the water hyacinth, which has bred so successfully it now makes passage through some of the canals impossible and starves the life underneath of light. Sadly, this is only one indicator of the ecological threat this lovely landscape faces. Many of the lakes are now polluted and have been reduced in area through land-reclamation projects.

Life on the waterfront

The backwaters are neither an untamed wilderness like Florida's Everglades, nor are they a waterfront cityscape like Venice. They are a bustling tropical townscape, lined with tidy gardens and interlaced by slender canals. Housewives trim the hibiscus, schoolgirls walk two by two up the nearest gangplank, and livestock travels downstream. Local industries such as rope-making can be viewed from on deck, and you may see post and newspapers delivered by skiff.

With trademark woven mats protecting their cargo, backwater boats cater to everyone from commuting locals to pleasure cruising, multi-day trippers.

Nearly one third of Keralans are Christian, and stunningly preserved churches dot the dark green landscape. Their architecture is a reminder of the Portuguese presence along the Malabar coast.

Travelling the backwaters of Kerala on a converted rice barge allows visitors an authentic view of life at water level.

Nature's energy drink, coconuts and their water are a mainstay of Keralan cuisine and one of the best ways to beat the heat.

COCONUT PALMS

The rural and urban landscape of the Malabar coast is dominated by the coconut palm. The trees that sway over these backwaters are put to use in a dozen ways – virtually nothing is wasted.

Each tree produces around 80 nuts a year. Copra is the dried coconut flesh from which workers extract cooking oil and soap. Coir is the fibrous outer husk, which is stripped and kept for months in unsightly heaps, soaking in the shallows. It is then dried stiff and beaten. The short fibres are twisted into rope or woven into mats for the table or floor. Family coir workshops abound in the backwaters.

Coconut palm fronds are prized for thatching roofs against the rain, or are fashioned into sun hats or baskets. The liquid is drunk fresh or fermented into a potent liquor. Coconut milk, prepared with the white flesh, is often used for cooking, and the grated flesh is a staple for sweets. Tree trunks are sawn into boards for boatbuilding or house construction. If they are not burnt as fuel, the hard shells are polished and made into salad bowls or carved hair ornaments.

Found nowhere else in India, these cantilevered fishing nets were introduced to the region by Chinese seamen in the 16th century.

Boat racing is a serious business in Kerala. The biggest snakeboats require 100 oarsmen to row to a chanted beat.

Children on coracles on the backwaters

Elephant with calf, Andaman Islands.

OFFSHORE ISLANDS

India's offshore archipelagos, the Lakshadweep group in the Arabian Sea and the Andaman and Nicobar Islands in the Bay of Bengal, are fringed with coral reefs and mangrove swamps, and are home to unique groups of indigenous peoples.

The myriad small islands which make up the Lakshadweep and Andaman archipelagos are remote, entrancingly beautiful and way off the beaten tourist trail. Anyone seeking the quintessential white-sand, palm-fringed, turquoise-watered tropical beach experience – without the tourist crowds – will not be disappointed. The Nicobar group is off-limits to tourists.

LAKSHADWEEP

Scattered some 200–400km (124–248 miles) west of the Keralan coast are the Lakshadweep Islands. Some speculate that the name derives from the estimates of early sailors, who imagined at least 100,000 (one *lakh*) of these coral islands and atolls. In fact, there are only 22 (depending on how they are counted), of which just 11 are inhabited by some 64,400 people. The group is a continuation of the Maldives, and the small islands are similarly characterised by beautiful white-sand beaches fringed with palm trees and translucent lagoons; the islanders of Minicoy, further to the south than the main group, have a great deal in common culturally with the Maldives.

From the 13th century, the islands were ruled by the rajas of the Keralan kingdom of Kannur, and a large proportion of the population are

descendants of the settlers who came here from that part of Kerala. To the Portuguese and other European mariners, these were the Laccadive Islands. They were under British control from 1877 until Independence.

The climate is tropical throughout the year, with daytime maximum temperatures ranging from 32° to 35°C (90° to 95°F). The southwest monsoon arrives in May and it rains, on and off, until the end of September. During this period, the islands are harder to reach, and

Main Attractions

Kavaratti
Kalpeni
Agatti
Bangaram
Kadmat
Port Blair

Agatti Resort, Lakshadweep.

transit between islands may have to be by helicopter as the sea can become extremely rough.

Being largely of Keralan descent, the islanders were originally Hindu, as the prevalent systems of caste and of matrilineal inheritance bear out. However, most converted to Sunni Islam, which had been established on the islands from as early as the 7th century. Today the vast majority of islanders are Muslims. The people speak a dialect of Malayalam, the only exception being Minicoy island, where Mahl (the language of the Maldives) is spoken. Coconut farming and fishing are the main occupations, along with some dairy and poultry farming.

These are some of the few unspoilt coral islands left in the Indian Ocean, and they have an exceptionally sensitive environment. Tourism by non-Indian nationals is officially restricted to the islands of Bangaram and Kadmat. It may, at times, also be possible to stay at the tourist resort close to the airport on Agatti. Transfer from Agatti to Bangaram and Kadmat is by boat.

Around the islands

The capital of the island chain is **Kavaratti ❶**, headquarters of the administration of Lakshadweep and home to around 10,000 people. The Ujra Mosque here has an ornately carved ceiling, said to be made of driftwood. **Kalpeni**, to the southeast, has a spectacular lagoon containing three uninhabited islands, Tilakkam, Pitti and Cheriyam; Kalpeni has been developed for internal tourism and has watersports facilities and tourist huts. Evidence can still be seen of a huge storm that devastated the island in 1847. The southernmost island is **Minicoy**. The predominant industry here is tuna fishing and canning. There is also a 50-metre (165ft) lighthouse built by the British in the 19th century.

The three islands likely to be of most interest to foreign tourists are Agatti and its minuscule neighbour Bangaram, northwest of Kavaratti, and Kadmat further to the northeast.

Agatti ❷, on the edge of a stunning lagoon, is the location of the only

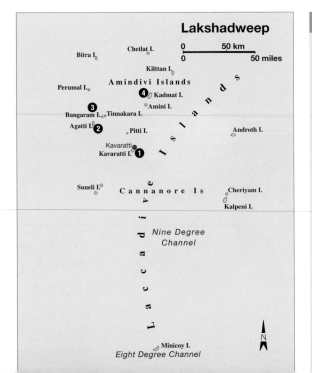

Lakshadweep

LAKSHADWEEP TRAVEL

As access to the Lakshadweep islands is controlled and limited by the Indian government, foreign tourists must book through one of two tour operators. The only airport is at Agatti, from where onward travel is by helicopter or boat.

For Bangaram Island Resort, contact CGH Earth (previously the Casino Group), tel: 00 91-0484 301 1711, www.cghearth.com; for Kadmat, contact Lacadives, tel: 00 91-022 666 27 381, www.lacadives.com. Both operators offer PADI-registered diving packages for experts as well as those for beginners.

Indian Airlines operate six flights weekly between Agatti and Kochi. The other option is to take the ship from Kochi (see www.lakshadweep.nic.in for details of tours and latest schedules), stopping off at several islands en route. Journey time is between 14 and 20 hours.

airport in the island chain. A 20-seater Indian Airlines plane connects with Kochi. Visitors who are heading to Bangaram either take a helicopter or embark on a two-hour boat ride. **Bangaram ❸** is uninhabited apart from its resort complex, and is also situated on a beautiful clear lagoon. **Kadmat ❹**, usually reached by helicopter, has small-scale tourist development and a breathtaking beach with superb diving.

The marine life on the reefs and within the lagoons is impressive. As well as a huge variety of corals, there are over 1,000 species of fish, including butterflyfish, clownfish, wrasses, parrotfish, goatfish and lionfish. Among the more spectacular sights are the turtles, harmless sharks and manta rays, and visitors may also encounter dolphins in the lagoons.

Glass-bottomed boats, snorkels or scuba gear are available for close-up encounters, and the resorts offer scuba and snorkel training. If you are planning on diving you will need a certificate of health from your doctor.

THE ANDAMAN AND NICOBAR ISLANDS

The Andaman and Nicobar islands lie 1,220km (760 miles) southeast of Kolkata across the Bay of Bengal, or 'Kala Pani' (Black Water), as this cyclone-prone sea was traditionally known. Their existence was reported in the 9th century AD by Arab merchants sailing towards the Straits of Sumatra, but with dense forests, mangrove swamps and shark-infested seas, the 572 islands were considered fit only for political prisoners and Malay pirates. Their development as a tourist destination, attracting scuba-divers, birdwatchers and honeymooners, has happened only in the past three decades. Most of the islands, however, are Adivasi (tribal) reserves and only a limited number are open to visitors – and the Nicobar group remains off-limits. The best time to visit is from December to April.

The aboriginal inhabitants of the Andamans, comprising several independent tribes known collectively as the Andamese, are among the most isolated peoples on earth. The exact

The vast majority of islanders are Muslim.

ANDAMANS TRAVEL

Flights: Port Blair is connected to Chennai and Kolkata by direct daily flights on Indian Airlines and Jet (2hrs).
By sea: It takes between three and five days to travel from Kolkata (departures once a fortnight) and Vishakapatnam (monthly); conditions on board the poorly maintained government vessels are often extremely uncomfortable, the food poor and sanitation less than ideal.

Within the islands, government ferries run from Port Blair to Havelock Island (2–3 daily; 2hrs–2hrs 45min); Little Andaman (5 weekly; 8–12hrs); Long Island (4 weekly; 7hrs); Neil Island (1–2 daily; 3hrs); Rangat Bay (1 daily; 8hrs). There is also a private catamaran service between Port Blair and Havelock which leaves Port Blair at 8.30am and returns at 4pm; see www.makruzz.com for details.

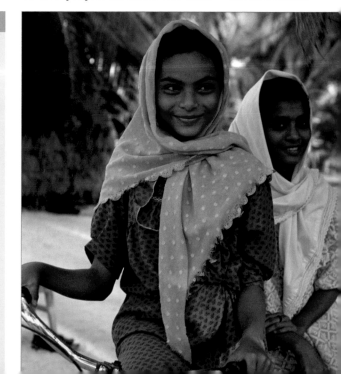

TIP

It's worth remembering that although the Andamans are 1,000km (620 miles) east of the Indian mainland, they are still within the same time zone as the rest of the country. This means that sunrise and sunset are disconcertingly early – at around 5.30am and 5.30pm respectively, which makes for an early start to the day if you want to enjoy the fleeting cool hours of morning, and correspondingly long evenings.

Traffic moves along a street in Port Blair.

date of their arrival on the islands is not known, but is thought to have been at least 60,000 years ago, and in all likelihood formed part of the large-scale migration of humans from Africa to Asia, which began some 100,000 years ago. From that time until the arrival of the British in 1789, they lived in complete isolation, with no contact with the outside world or even each other – they lived so separately that they don't understand each other's languages.

The largest group on Little Andaman are the Onges. They are hunter-gatherers, who collect honey and spear fish, and ritually paint their bodies with clay. The Sentinelese are an elusive group of 200 people, who have been known to fight off intruders with poisoned arrows. They adorn themselves with body paint, beads and bone. The Jarawa, with a population of 240, have a large reserve on South Andaman.

The first Westerners to set foot on the islands were the Danes, who established a settlement in the Nicobars, but left in 1768 due to poor health

conditions. The British Indian government annexed both groups of islands in 1872 and built a prison at Port Blair for prisoners serving life terms. The jail was used mainly for political prisoners engaged in the Independence struggle, and it was in Port Blair, while under Japanese occupation during World War II, that the Indian flag was first raised.

The arrival of the British saw many of the indigenous people perish through disease, alcoholism and, according to some sources, deliberate attempts to wipe them out. There were approximately 5,000 Andamese when the British arrived, but this number had fallen to just 600 by 1901. Throughout the 20th century, the tribes were known for their fierce attempts to maintain independence; a European anthropological party that attempted to land on one of the islands in the 1970s was repelled by a flurry of arrows. They left gifts of modern appliances, including metal buckets and spades, only to find that upon their return some time later they were subjected to the same

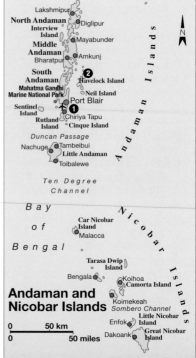

aerial bombardment; only this time the arrows had metal tips.

The Jarawa tribe, who live closest to Port Blair, began to initiate contact with the settled population in 1997, and have slowly increased their interaction with the capital – some Jarawan children are now attending schools outside their reserve. The building of the Great Andaman Trunk Road in the 1970s, which runs straight through the Jarawa reserve, has had a huge impact on the lives of this tribe, including several outbreaks of common diseases such as measles. In reaction to this, a law was passed to try to protect the Jarawa from such contact, and from the widespread encroachment on their land. All visits to Jarawa territory are forbidden by government law, a law unfortunately flouted by government travel agencies, which take Indian tourists to visit the Jarawa on a daily basis.

On 26 December 2004 the islands were hit by the enormous tsunami that also devastated parts of Southeast Asia. The damage was overwhelming, particularly in the Nicobars and on Little Andaman. More than 3,000 are officially listed as having been killed, and thousands more displaced, but the main areas visited by tourists, including Port Blair and Havelock, although affected by the earthquake, were protected from the tsunami itself.

Port Blair and South Andaman

Port Blair ❶, on the island of South Andaman, is the capital and only sizeable town (population 100,000) in the archipelago. It was named after Lt Reginald Blair, who conducted a survey of the area in 1789. The British, however, only gained control over the Andamans after 1857, and used this outpost of empire as a penal colony right through to 1947.

The **Cellular Jail**, where 400 freedom fighters were held during the struggle for Independence, is now a museum (Tue–Sun 9am–noon, 2–5pm; charge). There is also an **Anthropological Museum** (Tue–Sun 10am–12.30pm, 2–4pm; charge), which has mini-reproductions of villages of local peoples. Across the

TIP

A permit is required by all foreign travellers to the Andaman islands. These are issued on arrival and are valid for 30 days (extendable to 45 days), allowing travel and overnight stays to a strictly designated list of destinations in the archipelago. Permits and passports are checked on disembarkation at all islands. For current restrictions, see http://tourism.andaman.nic.in/entry.htm.

Casting a net.

Nicobar pigeons are easily identified by their beautifully coloured, iridescent plumage. They are resident in parts of Indonesia and, as the name suggests, the Nicobar islands.

Andaman rainforest damaged by the 2004 tsunami.

harbour is **Viper Island**, where executions used to take place, and **Ross Island**, guarded by World War II Japanese bunkers, and now a peaceful spot grazed by numerous chital deer.

Around one hour south from Port Blair (there are four daily buses), **Chiriya Tapu** has a beautiful beach and some good snorkelling. For truly spectacular snorkelling and scuba-diving, the village of Wandoor is the gateway to the **Mahatma Gandhi Marine National Park**: it is likely you will have to sign up for a tour in Port Blair. If you want to experience the pristine tropical forest, **Mount Harriet** has some superb walking trails: take the ferry from Port Blair to Hope Town, from where the starting point is a short bus ride. Alternatively, it is easy to hire a scooter, but extreme caution is advised on the unpredictable roads.

Elsewhere in the Andamans

Havelock Island ❷, around 2.5 hours by boat to the northeast of Port Blair, has an abundance of fabulous beaches, and is the main focus of tourism in

the archipelago. Unsurprisingly given its location much closer to Thailand than India, Havelock is reminiscent of many of the Thai islands, not just in its physical beauty but also in the way that tourism seems poised to take off – think Koh Samui in the mid-1990s. There is still a very relaxed feel to the place, with the majority of the island still uncultivated jungle – the drive from the west to east coasts is spectacular. The choice and range of accommodation is expanding every year, and the diving is superb, with costs amongst the lowest anywhere in the world, encompassing anything from one-off dives to officially recognised courses, right up to instructor level.

The stunning sea life is not solely the preserve of the certified diver – snorkelling excursions are plentiful, and there's even a glass-bottomed boat at **Elephant Beach**, one of the most popular snorkelling sites. Access is either via a 3km (2-mile) trek through the jungle or by boat – there are generally wooden longtail motorboats, known as *dunghis*, on most of the more popular beaches, with the owners open to offers for excursions around the island. Be warned, however, that these are noisy contraptions, and have very little stability at low speeds!

Although most of the accommodation is strung out along the east coast, between beaches No. 2 and No. 5, the shoreline here is not as enticing as on the west coast – the beaches are narrow, and the water shallow and rocky underfoot.

Make the trip to the west coast, though, and the stunning **Radhanagar beach** (or Beach No. 7) awaits you. Wide and long, with squeaky clean sand and pristine, aquamarine waters, this is a beach that bares comparison with the best in the world. The only downside to this paradise is the sandflies, but a liberal application of baby oil seems to stop the little critters grabbing hold and biting. If you are there at sunset, you might even see an elephant belonging to the nearby Barefoot Resort strolling on the beach returning from the jungle where it spends its day feeding.

Another great place to spot elephants is the **Elephant Training Camp**, on the east coast just south of Kalapathar village. Follow the sandy trail through the forest to reach the enclosure – again these elephants tend to be feeding in the forest by day, so early morning or late evening are the best times to visit. There are an increasing number of options for excursions from Havelock, some of which include overnight camping on other islands. Check out www.barefoot-andaman.com for more details.

Just to the south, **Neil Island** is quieter, but just as beautiful, with an increasing number of backpacker-type hotels, as well as snorkelling and diving sites every bit as good as on Havelock.

The large islands of **Middle Andaman** and **North Andaman** are further off the beaten track, covered in thick

Havelock Island.

forests. Some tribal areas are off-limits. The island of **Little Andaman**, devastated by the 2004 tsunami, has rebuilt its small-scale settlements and has started to make a few tentative steps into the world of tourism, with package tours from Port Blair including elephant safaris to remote waterfall sites in the interior organized by the snappily titled Andaman and Nicobar Islands Forest Plantation Development Corporation Limited (ANIFPDCL).

TIP

If you are staying on the east coast of Havelock Island, away from the main market, finding a rickshaw to take you anywhere can be tricky – consider hiring a scooter; rates are reasonable, there is very little traffic and the roads are generally well surfaced.

RESTAURANTS

PRICE CATEGORIES

Average price for dinner, up to three courses for one person, excluding alcoholic drinks:
£ = under Rs200
££ = Rs200–500
£££ = Rs500–1,000
££££ = over Rs1,000

Food on these islands is traditionally restricted to the ingredients that are immediately available. In general this means a lot of fish, and seafood, often cooked with grated coconut and coconut milk.

Lakshadweep

As visitors are only permitted as part of a package tour, the only restaurants are at the holiday resorts.

Andaman Islands

Port Blair
Eating options in Port Blair consist of a handful of rough-and-ready

South Indian-style cafés in and around Aberdeen Bazaar – the town's main drag – and three or four more congenial hotel restaurants on the outskirts. While the former are recommended for cheap and filling breakfasts or *thali* lunches, the latter tend to be more enjoyable places to spend the evening.

Annapurna Café
Aberdeen Bazaar, near the Post Office.
£
The best Indian food in town, including the usual Udupi snacks, and some tasty Chinese and North Indian alternatives. Resident Tamils stream in at breakfast for hot *pongal*, a rice dish made with *moong dal* (split beans) and coconut.

Mandalay
Fortune Resort, Marine Hill. ££
This is about as swanky as Port Blair gets: a breezy alfresco deck restaurant with fine views over the bay and good value buffets at lunchtime. The Nico Bar next door serves alcohol.

New Lighthouse
Aberdeen Jetty. ££
Great place down on the waterfront for inexpensive local seafood. Order a crab masala and you won't be disappointed – and there's a tank of live lobster for the thick-skinned.

Havelock

Most of the resorts have restaurants serving a reasonable selection of both Western and Indian fare, generally with fish and seafood prominent on the menu. Service can be slow, and limited availability of certain ingredients can mean not everything on the menu is available.

Barefoot at Havelock
Radhanagar/Beach No. 7. £££
Barefoot's Italian-run kitchen is strong on wood-fired pizzas and other Italian specialities, but also has a good Indian selection, including a tandoor oven.

Temples and palaces line the banks
of the Ganges at Varanasi.

INSIGHT GUIDES TRAVEL TIPS
INDIA

Transport

Getting There 440
  By Air................................. 440
  Overland 440
Getting Around..................... 440
  Air Travel within India........ 440
  Boats 441
  Buses................................ 441
  Cars and Taxis 441
  Driving in India 442
  Railways............................ 442
  Rickshaws and Tongas 445

Accommodation

Choosing a Hotel 446
Delhi.. 447
Punjab and Haryana............... 449
Uttar Pradesh......................... 449
Bihar.. 451
Uttarakhand............................ 451
Himachal Pradesh.................. 453
Ladakh 454
Rajasthan 455
Gujarat 460
Mumbai 461
Maharashtra 463
Madhya Pradesh 463
Goa.. 465
Kolkata 467
West Bengal............................ 467
Odisha (Orissa) 468
Sikkim 468
Assam 469
Karnataka 469
Andhra Pradesh...................... 471
Tamil Nadu.............................. 471
Kerala...................................... 473
Lakshadweep 476
Andaman Islands 476

Activities

The Arts................................... 477
  Cinemas 477
  Music and Dance 477
Nightlife................................... 478
  Delhi 478
  Mumbai 478
  Goa 479
  Kolkata 479
  Bengaluru (Bangalore)...... 479
  Chennai 479
Outdoor Activities 480
  Trekking 480
  Watersports....................... 480
Shopping................................. 481
  What to Buy 481
  Where to Shop................... 481
Spas and Retreats.................. 484
  The North........................... 484
  The Northern Plains 484
  Himalayas.......................... 484
  Rajasthan 485
  Mumbai 485
  Goa 485
  Kerala 485
Wildlife Parks......................... 485

A – Z

Admission Charges 487
Begging 487
Budgeting for Your Trip 487
Children................................... 487
Climate.................................... 487
Crime and Safety.................... 487
Customs 488
Disabled Travellers 488
Electricity 488
Embassies and Consulates ... 489
Etiquette 489
Gay and Lesbian Travellers 489
Health and Medical Care 490
Insurance................................ 492
Internet 492
Maps 492

Media 492
Money Matters 493
Opening Hours........................ 493
Photography 494
Postal/Courier Services.......... 494
Public Holidays 494
Restricted/Protected Areas... 494
Telephones 494
Time Zone 495
Tipping..................................... 495
Toilets...................................... 495
Tourist Information 495
Visas and Passports............... 496
Water....................................... 496
What to Bring........................... 496
Women Travellers................... 496

Language

Traveller's Hindi 497
  Basics................................ 497
  Pronouns 497
  Verbs................................. 497
  Questions 497
  Days of the week............... 497
  Months 498
  Relatives............................ 498
  Health 498
  Travel 498
  Food.................................. 498
Traveller's Tamil 498
  Basics................................ 498
  Verbs................................. 499
  Days of the week............... 499
  Questions and 'and'.......... 499
  Pronouns and relatives...... 499
  Health 499
  Food (Sappadu)................. 499

Further Reading

History..................................... 501
Fiction 502
Travel....................................... 503
Wildlife 503

TRANSPORT   ACCOMMODATION   ACTIVITIES   A – Z   LANGUAGE

TRANSPORT

GETTING THERE
AND GETTING AROUND

By Air

The vast majority of visitors arrive in India by air. Mumbai and Delhi airports are the major entry points, although a few international flights from Europe use Kolkata (Calcutta), Chennai (Madras) and Bengaluru (Bangalore). There are direct, non-stop flights between India and the UK (where many transatlantic passengers can change) on Air India (www.airindia.com), British Airways (www.ba.com), Virgin Atlantic (www.virgin-atlantic.com) and Jet Airways (www.jetairways.com), and one-stop flights on a number of other carriers, including Emirates, Qatar, Gulf, Etihad and KLM. There are also charter flights in season from UK airports to Goa. These flights are laid on for package tourists, but spare tickets are sometimes sold off to independent travellers, often at bargain prices.

India also has extensive air connections with other countries in Asia and the Gulf, with international flights from Sri Lanka, Nepal, Pakistan, the UAE and many other places. There are also direct non-stop flights from New York to Delhi and Mumbai on Air India (and also to Delhi on Continental), and from Sydney to Mumbai on Qantas.

The major airports all have left-luggage facilities, porters and licensed taxis, as well as duty-free shops in both the arrival and departure halls and banks (open 24hrs).

International airport contacts

Indira Gandhi International (IGI) Airport, Delhi
www.newdelhiairport.in

Tel: 0124-337 6000
Chhatrapati Shivaji International Airport, Mumbai
www.csia.in
Tel: 022-6685 1010
Netaji Subhash (Dum Dum) International Airport, Kolkata
Tel: 033-2232 0501
Anna International Airport, Chennai
Tel: 044-2556 0551
International Airport, Bengaluru
www.bengaluruairport.com
Tel: 080-6678 2425

Overland

India shares land borders with Pakistan, Nepal, Bangladesh, Bhutan, China and Burma. There are currently five border posts where visitors can cross between India and Nepal, four with Bangladesh, one with Pakistan, and one with Bhutan. The borders with China have long been closed to travellers. The same is true of Myanmar (Burma), although this may well change over the coming years if the promised opening of the Ledo Road across the mountains from Assam goes ahead.

For the adventurous, it is theoretically possible to take the train from the UK to India (there's a comprehensive overview of the route at www.seat61.com/India-overland. htm, which is also an excellent resource for all train information about India). The route is via Istanbul, Tehran to the end of the rail line at Bam, from where you would need to get a bus to Zahedan, from where a very basic twice-monthly train travels to the Pakistani border at Quetta, from where you can travel on to Lahore or Karachi. There is currently only one train service between India and Pakistan. It runs twice a week (usually Monday and Thursday) from Delhi via Amritsar to Lahore, crossing the border at Wagah/Atari.

Air Travel within India

There's been an incredible explosion in domestic air routes within India in recent years, with new operators entering the fray on a regular basis (and going bust just as reguarly). Almost every city of any size is now served by frequent flights, and there is fierce competition on more popular routes. Fares vary widely. Those on the more upmarket carriers, like Jet Airways, can be relatively expensive, although fares on the low-cost carriers can often be an absolute bargain.

The domestic airline market is in an almost constant state of turbulence at present, as airlines swallow one another up, re-brand, or simply go bust. In addition, the two government-owned airlines, the flagship international carrier, Air India and the domestic operator, Indian Airlines, merged in February 2011, which has led to a certain amount of confusion in terms of services and schedules. Just how volatile the Indian airline industry has become was underlined in October 2012 after Kingfisher, backed by the liquor tycoon Vijay Malia, was forced by spiralling debts to ground all its flights, leaving passengers stranded and crew unpaid across the country.

Tickets for all the following airlines can be booked online.

Domestic airlines in India

Air India
www.airindia.com
Tel: 011-2462 4074
The national carrier operates a
small number of domestic services
between Mumbai and Delhi,
Kolkata, Bengaluru, Chennai and
Thiruvananthapuram.

Air India Express
www.airindiaexpress.in
Mumbai head office tel: 022-2279
6330 (for other offices see website).
Low-cost subsidiary of Air India, with a
good range of domestic services.

Go Air
www.goair.in
Tel: 1800-222 111 or 09223-222
111
Low-cost airline based in Mumbai,
with flights to Goa, Kochi, Delhi,
Srinagar and Ahmadabad.

IndiGo
http://book.goindigo.in
Tel: 1-800-180 3838 or 0124-661
3838
Low fares and an impressive number
of destinations nationwide.

Jet Konnect
www.jetkonnect.co.in
Tel: 3989 3333 prefixed with nearest
city code (eg in Delhi, call 011-3989
3333).
India's leading private airline,
with a huge network and high
standards – although tends to be
more expensive than other domestic
carriers.

Spicejet
www.spicejet.com
Tel: 1800-180 3333 (mobile users
tel: 0987-180 3333)
Low-cost carrier, based in Delhi,
serving around 20 destinations
across the country.

Cut Your Carbon

Air travel produces a huge amount
of carbon dioxide and is one of
the main contributors to global
warming. Where possible, take the
train while in the country, as this
produces less CO_2. It is possible
to offset your 'carbon load' by, for
example, having trees planted
as a 'carbon sink'. A number of
organisations can do this for
you, and many have online
'carbon calculators'
which tell you how much you
need to donate. In the UK,
travellers can try www.climatecare.
org or www.carbonneutral.
com; in the US, log on to www.
climatefriendly.com or www.
sustainabletravelinternational.org.

Buses are frequently crowded.

Boats

Apart from river ferries there are
very few boat services in India. The
Andaman Islands are connected to
Kolkata, Chennai and Vishakapatnam
by boat, as well as to each other.
Kerala has a regular passenger
boat system, and a number of
services operate from Alappuzha
and Kollam (formerly Alleppey and
Quilon), including the backwater
trip between the two. In addition,
luxury cruises on the Brahmaputra
and Ganges Rivers are operated by
the Indo-British outfit, the Assam
Bengal Navigation Company (www.
assambengalnavigation.com; tel (UK):
44-1572-821121).

Buses

Virtually every part of the country is
connected to India's extensive and
well-developed bus system, which
complements the railway system
and also goes to places where trains
can't reach (especially up in the
mountains). Services range from
clapped-out old rust buckets on more
rural routes to deluxe, state-of-the-art
air-conditioned express coaches on
the major highways.

Although it's difficult to generalise,
buses can often be a bit faster and
more convenient than trains –
services are often more frequent,
and frequently don't have to bother
buying tickets or making reservations
in advance. On the downside,
they're generally less comfortable,
particularly for long journeys, and not
quite as safe either.

Buses are either operated by
private companies or by the local
state government. Again, it's tricky

to generalise, but private buses tend
to be a bit more comfortable, with
padded seats and tinted windows,
and the drivers more reckless.

On many buses you can just buy a
ticket on board, although on others
you'll have to purchase a ticket
before getting on. Bus terminals in
larger cities can sometimes be a bit
confusing, with numerous different
counters for different destinations.
It's also possible to reserve a seat on
many buses.

Baggage is usually carried in the
boot or squeezed under your seat,
although it sometimes ends up on the
roof, in which case it's worth keeping
an eye on it during stops en route (or
better still, attach it to the roof rack
with a small lock and chain).

Local city buses are generally
less useful. All the major cities have
their own services, but it's usually
hard work to figure out which buses
go where, and they can often be
unbearably crowded too, particularly
during the rush hours. It's generally
much easier just to catch a rickshaw
or taxi.

Cars and Taxis

For longer tours, you might consider
hiring a **car with driver**. These
generally cost about US$35–50 a
day and can be arranged through
tourist offices, hotels or travel agents.
Costs vary depending on the size
and condition of the vehicle and
whether or not it's air-conditioned.
Alternatively, you can usually hire
a car with driver for a day – again,
easily arranged through local tourist
offices and hotels.

The local yellow-top black **city
taxis** are metered, although with

constant hikes in fuel prices, charges may be higher than indicated on the meter. If so, this will be prominently stated in the taxi and the driver will – in theory – have a card showing the excess over the meter reading that can be legitimately charged.

When arriving in India, most international airports (including Delhi, Mumbai, Chennai and Bengaluru) offer a system of **prepaid taxis**, running to fixed prices, which will save you the bother of having to haggle a fare yourself or dealing with unscrupulous drivers. Elsewhere, enquire at the information desk for the going rate for a journey to your destination before getting into the taxi; and make sure the meter is 'down' before you embark. In some cities, for example Mumbai, taxis have fare charts which, when applied to the amount on the meter, give the correct fare.

Driving in India

Driving in India is not for the faint-hearted. Roads can be congested and dangerous, and there are many unwritten rules which you'll need to be aware of. City roads can often be (or appear to be) totally anarchic, and although things are a lot more peaceful in the countryside, route-finding can often be a problem. In general, it's far better, and quite often even cheaper, to hire a car and driver. If you do decide to drive, you should have an international driving licence (although this might not be insisted on if you have your driving licence from home).

Information regarding road conditions can be obtained from

national and state automobile associations. Useful **contacts** include: the Automobile Association of Upper India (AAUI), C-8 Qutab Institutional Area, Behind Qutab Hotel, New Delhi 110 016, tel: 011-2696 5397, www.aaui.org; the Western India Automobile Association Lalji Narainji Memorial Building, 76 Veer Nariman Road, Churchgate, Mumbai 400 020, tel: 022-2204 1085, www.wiaaindia. com; the Automobile Association of Eastern India, 13 Promothesh Barua Sarani, Kolkata 700 019, tel: 033-2486 5131, www.uraaei.org; and the Automobile Association of Southern India, 187 Anna Salai, Chennai 600 006, tel: 044-2852 1162, www. aasindia.in.

Railways

Rail travel is by far the most enjoyable way to get around the country – although standards of cleanliness in some classes, and punctuality, may not be what you're used to back home. There are three basic types of train. The best are the 'Super-fast' services: air-conditioned trains on major inter-city routes. These include the excellent 'Shatabdi' daytime-only expresses, and 'Rajdhani' services, which link Delhi with cities nationwide. The second category are the 'Express' or 'mail' inter-city services, which are also generally fast and – if you book a seat in one of the more expensive carriages – comfortable. It's generally best to avoid the third category of train, the painfully slow 'passenger' services, which tend to take forever to get anywhere. There are also a number of special tourist trains. For an excellent

Urban Metros

The **Delhi Metro** (www. delhimetrorail.com) opened in 2002 and has revolutionised transport in the city. Services run from 6am to 11pm and there are currently three lines, although the network is set to expand enormously by 2020.

India's first metro system, far smaller than Delhi's, was inaugurated in **Kolkata** way back in 1984. An underground system is also being built in **Mumbai**, a massive, fifteen-year construction project whose first phase is set to complete in 2013. It will link up with the already extensive – but appallingly overburdened – suburban rail network. Bangalore also recently acquired a new line, and work is scheduled to start on brace of others in Chennai, Hyderabad, Jaipur, Kochi, Ahmedabad, Lucknow and Pune, to name but a few cities.

overview of Indian railway services, check out the authoritative website www.seat61.com/India.htm.

Fares are generally low, especially if you travel in a non-A/C class, although the price of a long-haul first-class ticket can often be as much as (or even more than) the comparable air fare.

Comprehensive **timetable** and fare information is available at www. indianrail.gov.in, or the more user-friendly www.cleartrip.com.

Retiring rooms (for short-term occupation only) are available at over 1,100 stations on a first-come first-served basis, but these are usually heavily booked. All first-class waiting rooms have couches for passengers using their own bedding. At New Delhi and Howrah stations, a Rail Yatri Niwas offers accommodation for transit passengers which can be booked in advance.

Cloakrooms are available at most stations where travellers may leave their luggage, but bags must be locked and may be subject to an x-ray scan for security purposes. Be sure not to lose your reclaim ticket and check opening times of the cloakroom for collection.

Very useful prepaid **taxi** and/or **auto-rickshaw** services are available at some of the largest stations.

Remember to check which station your train departs from and allow at least half an hour to find your seat/berth. Lists of passengers with the compartment and seat/

Delhi's rapidly expanding Metro is a great way to get around the city.

berth numbers allotted to them are displayed on platforms and on each carriage an hour before departure. The station superintendent and the conductor attached to the train are usually available for assistance.

On Shatabdi and Rajdhani trains the fare includes **food**, drinks and snacks. In other classes (except second class unreserved) veg and non-veg meals (often surprisingly good) can be ordered from the carriage attendant. Failing that, whenever the train stops the carriages are invaded by itinerant hawkers selling all sorts of food, while roving hawkers also dish up endless supplies of tea and coffee – the endless calls of *chai-chai-chai* or *kafi-kafi-kafi* providing an emblematic soundtrack to all Indian railway journeys.

Travelling by train is a unique Indian experience.

Classes of travel

Indian Railways has no fewer than eight different **classes**, of varying degrees of comfort (although most trains will only have three or four different types of class). Sleeper compartments consist of two- or three-tier bunks: during the day, the bottom bunk is used for seating; reserving a top-bunk means you can lie down even in the middle of the day if you want to.

In descending order of price, the various classes are:

First class AC (AC1) Very comfortable compartments with lockable cabins of two or four berths each, arranged in two tiers.

AC 2-tier (AC2) Two-tier bunks in open-plan carriages (not compartments) arranged in groups of six berths with curtains that pull across to provide privacy.

AC 3-tier (AC3) Like AC 2-tier carriages, but with three-tier bunks. The middle berths fold down when not used for sleeping.

AC executive chair class Found only on the most important Shatabdi services. Spacious seating (four seats across) in A/C carriages.

AC chair class The standard class on Shatabdi services. Like executive chair class, but with slightly more cramped seating (six seats across, rather than four) and plainer carriages.

First class (non A/C) This type of compartment is being phased out, and is increasingly rare. They consist of non A/C lockable compartments containing two or four berths.

Sleeper class The most common class, with open-plan carriages divided into partitions of six berths with ceiling fans.

Second class unreserved Open-plan carriages of hard seats (no bunks). Can get horribly crowded.

Obviously, in the hot summer months A/C can be a worthwhile option. The major drawback with A/C carriages is that they usually have tinted and/or scratched/dirty windows, which means you don't get a great view of the countryside outside. Sleeper class and second class unreserved, by contrast, just have metal grilles over open windows, which means you'll get a better view, and also benefit from pleasant breezes when the train is in motion.

Carriages have a mix of Western and Indian-style toilets – the latter are usually cleaner and less unpleasant, assuming you can keep your balance while squatting in a moving train.

Basic bedding (two sheets, a pillow and a blanket) is provided in first class AC, AC 2-tier and 3-tier, and is also available from the attendant for Rs20 in first class. No bedding is provided in sleeper class, so you might want to take your own.

Reservations

Reservations are required for all classes other than second class unreserved, and reserving well in advance is strongly recommended. Reservations may be made up to 60 days in advance. Many stations now have very efficient computerised booking counters from where you can book any ticket for any route. In

Indian Railways Online

The excellent Indian Railways website at www.indianrail.gov.in is a comprehensive, if unwieldy, source of information. You can check timetables for all trains here, as well as fares and current availability, and find out what classes are available on which trains.

It's also now theoretically possible to buy tickets online at www.irctc.co.in, though in practise you'll need book weeks in advance: Indian Railways require customers wishing to pay using credit or debit cards registered abroad have to send a photocopy (or scan) of their passport to India for verification first. A code will then be sent to you which you'll need to key in when you book online – a cumbersome process outlined in fine-grain detail at http://www.seat61.com/India.

htm#book – from outside India. The private travel booking site Clear Trip (www.cleartrip.com) is much better set up than Indian Railways, with a clearer, faster interface, but again, foreign tourists are subject to Indian Railways arcane booking rules and required to verify their identity by sending passport copies in advance. All in all, you're invariably better off advance booking by means of an Inrail Pass which buys you access to special quotas on popular trains and thus nearly always ensures reservations on your desired day of travel – especially worthwhile for onward journeys by rail shortly after arrival in India.

If you really fall in love with the railways and want to learn more, try the excellent Indian Railways Fan Club site at www.irfca.org.

the larger cities, the major stations have tourist sections with English-speaking staff to reduce the queues for foreigners and non-resident Indians buying tickets. Tourist offices at railway reservation centres are helpful in planning itineraries and obtaining reservations (International Tourist Bureau, New Delhi railway station, tel: 011-2334 6804). There are tourist offices at New Delhi, Mumbai Churchgate, Kolkata Fairlie Place, Chennai Central, and some other popular tourist destinations.

The bottom line, however, is that reserving a railway ticket can be a pain, given the fact that you've got to visit the station in person and then probably queue, often for a long time. One good option is to get a local travel agent or your guesthouse/hotel to send someone to the station to buy a ticket for you. They'll charge you for this, of course, but the sums involved are usually fairly modest (typically around Rs250), and are well worth it for what they'll save you in terms of time and hassle.

If there are no available places on the train you want, then you have a couple of options. Certain trains have a tourist quota that may be available. Other options are to take a wait-listed ticket or the more assured reservation against cancellation (RAC). There's also an 'emergency' quota, available only on the day of travel. The booking clerk should be able to advise you on how likely you are to get a reservation.

Your best option, however, is to try for a ticket under the Taktal scheme. This operates on trains (marked with a 'T' in timetables) on major inter-city routes, with 10 percent of the seats only being released for sale five days before departure. The catch is the price. You'll pay a surcharge for a Taktal ticket, but more importantly you'll also have to pay for the cost of a ticket for the whole of the train's journey from originating

to terminating stations, regardless of how much of this route you intend to use.

Cancellations (for which you will need to fill in the same form as for a reservation) can be made with varying degrees of penalty, depending on the class and how close the cancellation is made to the time of departure.

Luxury trains

Since the advent of the Palace on Wheels in the early 1990s, luxury trains have proved an enduringly popular option with highend visitors to India. Half a dozen of these super-swish locomotives now operate around the country. All adopt a similar formula, taking opulent carriages formerly used by local maharajas – or ersatz versions of them – and following routes around the tourist highlights of a given region. They're all government run by state tourism development corporations, but can be booked abroad through private agents – in fact, it's often cheaper to do just that as agents benefit from discounts which they usually (but not always) hand a part of back to customers. One thoroughly dependable London-based operator who offers the most competitive rates is SD Enterprises (103 Wembley Park Drive, Wembley, Middlesex HA9 8HG; tel: 0208-903 3411, www.indiarail. co.uk). In India itself, a recommended specialist is Indian Luxury Trains (tel: +0091-971-797 9498; www. indianluxurytrains.com).

The Deccan Odyssey (www.deccan-odyssey-india.com)
This plush train starts in Mumbai, and heads south down the Konkan coast, pausing at Ratnagiri and the Maratha fort at Sindhudurg en route to Goa, before swinging north again through Kolhapur to Aurangabad, for Ellora and Ajanta Caves. Tariffs hover around US$425/night, making this a among the least expensive options.

To reserve a ticket you must first fill out a Reservation Requisition Form, which will be available from one of the windows in the booking office. The form is in the local language on one side and English on the reverse. In addition to the obvious information such as where you wish to leave from and go to and when, to fill in the form you also need to know:

The train number and name. You can get this from a timetable, or, if the train departs from the station you are booking from, it is usually displayed on a board in the booking office.

The class you wish to travel and whether you require a berth (for overnight journeys, or any journey between 9pm and 6am), or only a seat.

Whether you require a lower, middle or upper berth. An upper berth is a good idea as it can be used throughout the day, whereas the other two may only be used for sleeping 9pm–6am.

Foreign travellers should also fill in their passport numbers in the column that asks for your Concession Travel Authority Number, which is needed if the ticket is issued under the foreign tourist quota.

The Golden Chariot (www.thegolden chariot.co.in)
Taking in the highlights on the southern Indian state of Karnataka, the Golden Chariot follows a varied route through some fabulous scenery, and stops at some memorable locations. Rather than start at Bengaluru, we recommend you skip the first, rather dull couple of stages and pick the train up in Mysore, from where it calls at the Hoysala temple sites around Hassan, the ruined city of Hampi, the ancient Hindu capitals of Badami and Aihole, then arrives at Goa. The same train also follows a longer route stringing together the highlights of Karnataka with those of Kerala and Tamil Nadu, the 'Splendor of the South' tour. Tariffs for both start at around US$440/night.
The Indian Maharaja (www. theindianmaharaja.co.in)
Operated by Maharashtra Tourism Corporation, the Indian Maharaja also travels from Mumbai to Delhi but via the famous cave sites of Ellora and Ajanta, then on to Udaipur,

Indrail Pass Fares in US Dollars						
	First Class AC		**Other AC and FC**		**Sleeper Class**	
	Adult	Child	Adult	Child	Adult	Child
Half-day	57	29	26	13	11	6
1 day	95	47	43	22	19	10
2 days	160	80	70	35	30	15
4 days	220	110	110	55	50	25
7 days	270	135	135	68	80	40
15 days	370	185	185	95	90	45
21 days	396	198	198	99	100	50
30 days	495	248	248	126	125	65
60 days	800	400	400	200	185	95
90 days	1,060	530	530	265	235	120

Ranthambore tiger reserve and Jaipur in Rajasthan, before stopping at Agra en route to Delhi. Tariffs are US$600/night.

Maharaja's Express
An über-luxurious alternative to the Palace on Wheels is the Maharaja's Express, which offers weekly departures on a range of five inter-city routes across India. Tours last between four and eight days and cost from around US$600/night

The Palace on Wheels (www.rtdc. in). India's original and most famous luxury train, the Palace on Wheels, leaves Delhi every Wednesday afternoon from September to April and stops at Jaipur, Bharatpur, Chittaurgarh, Udaipur, Sawai Madhopur, Jaisalmer, Jodhpur, Bharatpur and Agra, returning to Delhi on the eighth day. Tariffs range from around US $4,275–5,750 depending on the season, or $US520/night.

Royal Rajasthan On Wheels (www. royalrajasthanonwheels.com) This lavishly appointed train is run by the same outfit as the Palace on Wheels, and follows a similar route around the highlights of Rajasthan, only with a detour east to Varanasi via the temples at Khajuraho. Prices from $2,000–4,500 depending on length of the tour.

India also has a number of charming 'toy trains' which run from the plains up to certain hill stations. These include the narrow-gauge tracks up to Udhagamandalam (Ooty) in the Nilgiris, the line from New Jalpaiguri to Darjeeling, and the track between Neral and Matheran near Mumbai, as well as the broad-gauge service (known as the Himalayan Queen) between Kalka and Simla.

Rickshaws and Tongas

The most convenient, and typically Indian, way of getting around is by

A Delhi cycle-rickshaw.

rickshaw. These come in two types: a cycle rickshaw (an oversized tricycle-type contraption with a seat for two people on the back), and motorised three-wheelers, known as autorickshaws or simply '**autos**'.

Autos are, like taxis, supposed to use a meter, although you'll only very rarely find one that's working, or a driver who's prepared to use it. In practice this means haggling every time you use an auto. *Always* agree a **fare** with the rickshaw driver before you set off to avoid arguments later. It's often tricky to know what a good fare is – and you'll inevitably pay a bit more than the locals (and possibly a lot more if you're not keen on bargaining). It's a good idea to check the latest going rates at your hotel or guesthouse to get an idea of what it should cost to get wherever you're going. And if the first auto driver won't agree to the fare you want, just walk away. There will probably be 10 more just around the corner.

As well as one-off journeys, you might also want to hire a rickshaw (either auto or cycle) for the day in order to make a tour of the local sights. Again, check the going rate at your hotel and make it clear that you only want to visit the sights, and don't want to be dragged off to endless local shops where he will earn commission en route.

Auto-rickshaw rides can be fun but noisy – and sometimes decidedly hair-raising, as the driver ducks kamikaze-fashion through the traffic, dodging buses and lorries. **Cycle-rickshaws**, by contrast, are significantly slower than autos, but can be a lot more peaceful – if you're not in any particular hurry. Again, make sure you agree a fare before you set off. Many visitors are unhappy at the thought of being pedalled along by cycle-rickshaw

Indrail Passes

The Indrail Pass gives unlimited travel on the entire rail network for periods of between 12 hours and 90 days and can be good value if you plan on travelling nearly every day – or if you wish to gain access to seats or berths at busy times through the special tourist rail pass quota. They are available to foreign nationals and Indians resident abroad and are paid for in foreign currency. Inrail passes considerably reduce time getting reservations; you pay no fees and no sleeper berth surcharge for night journeys for any class of accommodation.

In the UK the pass can be obtained through the very efficient S.D. Enterprises Ltd, 103 Wembley Park Drive, Wembley, Middlesex HA9 8HG; tel: 020-8903 3411, www.indiarail.co.uk. They can also book single-journey tickets in advance for you. In India, the Indrail pass can be bought at Railway Central Reservations Offices in Chennai, Kolkata, Mumbai Central, Mumbai CST and New Delhi.

wallahs, many of whom are clearly under-nourished and pitifully thin, although of course the fact is that they need your custom – and you can always give them a good tip at the end.

Note that rickshaws are not allowed into central Mumbai; the only transport options are the well-developed bus service or the reasonably priced taxis.

There are also an increasingly tiny number of hand-pulled rickshaws in central Kolkata – that is, rickshaws pulled by men on foot. The idea of being pulled along by another human being might seem distasteful to many visitors, but these rickshaws perform a useful function during the monsoon when the streets flood and the other rickshaws will not work – and also provide a living for the impoverished pavement-dwellers who pull them).

Finally, in quite a few towns it's still possible to travel by tonga. These traditional horse-drawn carts can be pretty to look at, although many of the horses are in a pitiable condition and are clearly mistreated by their (often equally impoverished) owners. Agree the fare before you set off, and expect to pay roughly what you would in a cycle-rickshaw.

ACCOMMODATION

HOTELS, YOUTH HOSTELS, BED & BREAKFAST

Choosing a Hotel

Accommodation in India ranges from ultra-cheap flophouses to opulent palaces of former maharajas. At the bottom of the scale are plenty of small-scale **budget guesthouses** and cheap **tourist hotels**. Those catering to foreign tourists are usually reasonably clean and cheap, though the mattresses tend to be thin and lumpy and plumbing limited to a squat loo and bucket bath . Away from tourist hotspots there are plenty of **mid-range hotels** aimed at local business travellers – again usually with good standards of comfort and cleanliness, though often lacking character. Air-conditioning will be optional. In addition to standard rooms, they'll also offer a 'deluxe' category, with greater space and comfier beds, and possibly frills such as a minbar-fridge and large, flat-screen TV. The air-con units will also be more modern and quiet. Many of the state tourist corporations run similarly bland but comfortable mid-range establishments, often described as tourist bungalows. Rates will be relatively low, but standards of maintenance and service in these places not comparable with hotels in the private sector.

While other mid-range options had been something of a rarity, there are now an increasing number of places catering to the older, or more discerning traveller who has perhaps done the backpacking thing once upon a time but doesn't want to go the five-star route, as well as to the well-travelled Indian middle classes. Be aware, though, that mid-range pricing does not always mean the standard will be better than the budget place next door – watch out, in particular, for the trick of naming a new hotel after a popular older one.

Going upmarket, India has some of the world's most memorable places to stay, many of them occupying the former palaces, forts and havelis of the country's erstwhile maharajas and other ruling elites, as well as many fine old Raj-era piles such as the Taj in Mumbai. These places include world-famous **heritage hotels** like the Taj Lake Palace in Udaipur. Expect to spend several hundred dollars a night or more in such establishments. The two leading chains, Taj and Oberoi, boast dozens of superb properties countrywide. Heritage doesn't always equate with expense, however, and there are innumerable less ostentatious boutique options, particularly in Rajasthan and Kerala, ranging from old havelis through to rustic hilltop forts to former hunting lodges and tea planters' bungalows in the hills many of which offer oodles of atmosphere.

National Parks

When it comes to national parks and tiger reserves, choice has expanded considerably over the past decade. In addition to lower-mid-range government motels, you now also have a broad range of highend safari lodges, with accommodation offered in luxury tents, boutique-style mud-and-thatch huts and honeymoon lovenests with their own plunge pools and deep verandahs. Prices tend to be top whack, running to hundreds of dollars per night, but will include the services of a qualified guide, as well as a Jeep and driver for safaris.

Beach resorts

On-beach resorts have also become much more sophisticated in past years. At the top of the scale are uber-luxurious complexes centered on huge, curvi-form pools, where the rooms recreational facilities and sports provision are international quality, and restaurants gourmet standard. Essentially five-stars-on-sea, such places do, however, possess much less character than boutique hotels of a comparable standard, where the décor will be more stylish and individual. Here, the vibe will be less formal and designer interiors like something out of a magazine.

Heritage homestays

Well-to-do families with beautiful old country mansions dominate the so-called heritage homestay market. Like boutique hotels, these tend to be far less anonymous than five stars. You will be welcomed as part of the family by your hosts, who'll chat with you at meal times and show you around their estate or local village – all of which can make for a very memorable and rewarding time, particularly if you have children in tow.

Top tips

Wherever you stay, when checking in, ask to see two or three rooms before handing over your money. Check that lights, hot water and the fan or A/C work, and that the complete price is clear. Be sure to double-check for taxes and hidden extras. And finally, it is always worth trying to haggle a discount.

DELHI

Ahuja Residency
193 Golf Links, New Delhi
Tel: 011-2462 2255
www.ahujaresidency.com
Clean, friendly and quiet, this well-located guesthouse is one of Delhi's hidden gems. Great value to boot, make sure you book well in advance. The owners have another, smaller and slightly cheaper, property in Defence Colony a short distance away, plus a newly opened property in Sunder Nagar. **£££**

Ajay
5084A Paharganj Main Bazaar
Tel: 011-2358 3125
www.ajayguesthouse.com
Patronized mainly by foreign backpackers, Ajay offers some of the best value accommodation in the bustling Paharganj enclave, close to New Delhi Railway station. The rooms are very well maintained by the standards of the area, and there's a pool room, bakery-cum-café, travel desk and internet access on the ground floor. **£**

The Aman
Lodi Road, Nizamuddin West
Tel: 011-4363 3333
www.amanresorts.com
Opened in 2008, this very chic designer hotel is now one of the city's finest. With local stone floors and *jali* screens it aims at a contemporary Indian ambience. Rooms and suites (some of which are truly luxurious) have their own private plunge-pools, and the hotel also has a state-of-the-art spa. **££££**

Amarya Haveli
P5 Haus Khas Enclave, New Delhi
Tel: 011-4175 9268
www.amaryagroup.com

This gorgeous little French-owned boutique hotel in trendy Haus Khas village occupies an antique haveli, close to one of India's best shopping districts and within easy range of south Delhi's many sights. The decor's très chic – fusing sumptuous traditional craft, textiles and ornaments with Hindi pop and contemporary art; the tariffs are very reasonable considering the location and level of comfort. Plus there's a spa on site. Or there's the similarly attractive sister hotel, Amarya Villa, in the posh suburb of Safdarjung. **£££**

Bajaj Indian Home Stay
8A/34 WEA, Karol Bagh
Tel: 011-2573 6509
www.bajajindianhomestay.com
Promising an experience that's 'Indian, altogether', this place prides itself on its homely ambience, treating each guest as one of their own. With 10 rooms it is a little bigger than the usual 'home stay' but it still stands out from the crowd, and the rooms are spotlessly clean. **££££**

Hotel Broadway
4/15a Asaf Ali Road
Tel: 011-4366 3600
www.hotelbroadwaydelhi.com
A old-favourite midrange hotel close to the sights of Old Delhi, offering great value for money in its bracket. The rooms are well maintained, the service snappy and there are two famous restaurants on site. **££**

The Claridges
12 Aurangzeb Road, New Delhi
Tel: 011-3955 5000
www.claridges.com
A refined hotel in the heart of New Delhi. The rooms have an understated elegance and are very comfortable,

and the service is excellent. There are also a couple of good restaurants. The Aura bar is one of the best places in the city for a drink. **££££**

Geet Deluxe
8570 Arakashan Road, Ram Nagar
Tel: 011-2361 6140
The district of Ram Nagar, just north of Paharganj, is marginally less frenetic than New Delhi's Main Bazaar, and this lower-midrange hotel ranks among its more dependable options. It lacks any aspect, and is tucked down a narrow lane, but the rooms are spacious and clean for the price, and the staff courteous. **£**

Hyatt Regency
Bhikaiji Cama Place, Ring Road, New Delhi
Tel: 011-2679 1234
www.delhi.regency.hyatt.com
What's big and swish and found on the Ring Road? Answer, the Hyatt Regency. Not a shrinking violet this one; the impressive bulk of the exterior prepares you for the equally brash lobby. The rooms, while aimed at business travellers, have a cool contemporary feel and the restaurants are superb. **££££**

Imperial Hotel
1 Janpath, New Delhi
Tel: 011-2334 1234
www.theimperialindia.com
Pretty much the best hotel in Delhi, this place oozes Art Deco charm. Built in 1933, it was the only hotel included in Lutyens's plans for New Delhi. The entrance drive is flanked by huge palm trees, behind which is the pool. The rooms are decorated with lithographs and engravings from the owner's private collection, and it has one of Delhi's best restaurants (the Spice Route). **££££**

ITC Maurya
Sardar Patel Marg, Diplomatic Enclave, Chanakyapuri
Tel: 011-2611 2233
www.itcwelcomgroup.in
Like the Taj Palace, this highly luxurious hotel not only attracts the travelling 'great and good' but also scores on account of its two fabulous Indian restaurants, the Bukhara and the Dum Phukt. Cheap? No (it's

Luxury at the Claridges Hotel.

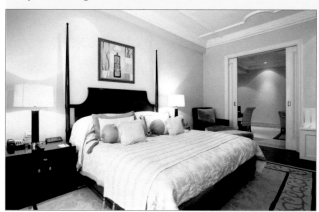

PRICE CATEGORIES

Price categories are for a double room (A/C where available) in high season, including taxes:
£ = under Rs2,000
££ = Rs2,000–5,000
£££ = Rs5,000–10,000
££££ = over Rs10,000

TRANSPORT

ACCOMMODATION

ACTIVITIES

A – Z

LANGUAGE

one of the most expensive places in Delhi), but the service and rooms are second to none. **££££**

Jorbagh '27'
27 Jorbagh
Tel: 011-2469 8647
www.jorbagh27.com
Set in a residential area, but run more as a hotel then a guesthouse, this 18-room property lacks some of the charm of the more homely establishments, but is efficiently run, clean and well located, with the proximity of Lodi Gardens a real bonus. **£££**

Lutyens Bungalow
39 Prithviraj Road, New Delhi
Tel: 011-2461 1341
www.lutyensbungalow.co.in
Set in a Lutyens-designed bungalow on one of the capital's most exclusive roads, this guesthouse retains the building's original charm, has a very friendly but unobtrusive feel and a swimming pool in the lovely gardens. A real chance to experience part of New Delhi's history at first hand; book well in advance. **£££**

The Maidens Hotel
7 Sham Nath Marg, Old Delhi
Tel: 011-2397 5464
www.maidenshotel.com
A classic Raj-era hotel with loads of period character, the Maidens first opened in 1903 and was where visiting VIPs used to stay before Lutyen's New Delhi was built – hence its slightly tucked away location near Kashmiri Gate, mid-way between Old and New Delhi. The rooms are huge, with typically British high ceilings and luxurious bathrooms, and there's a three-hectare (eight-acre) garden where you can enjoy a cold beer on the lawn watching the buzzards flit through the branches of trees that have been here for 100 years. **££££**

Major's Den
2314 Lakshmi Narain Street, Paharganj, New Delhi
Tel: 011-2358 9010
A safe, well-run backpacker's hotel with clean-ish, air-cooled rooms and attached bathrooms. Some of the best-value accommodation in Paharganj. **£**

The Manor
77 Friends Colony (West), New Delhi
Tel: 011-2692 5151
www.themanordelhi.com
One of Delhi's most sleek and attractive luxury places to stay. Twelve nicely thought-out rooms, with lots of natural fabrics and wonderful bathrooms. Although it might lack the facilities (such as a pool) of the large five-stars, it does have a beautiful garden and makes a wonderfully

quiet place to stay. The rates for the standard rooms are surprisingly low. **££££**

Master Paying Guest House
R-500 New Rajendar Nagar
Tel: 011-2874 1089
www.master-guesthouse.com
Cosy, friendly B&B in a leafy suburb of south Delhi that's been getting rave reviews since it opened nearly two decades ago. It's run by a genuinely hospitable couple, Ushi and Avnish, and boasts relaxing common areas and outdoor terrace, with a library created by guests' contributions. **££**

Hotel New City Palace
726 Jama Masjid, Old Delhi
Tel: 011-2327 9548
www.hotelnewcitypalace.in
Just behind the mosque in Old Delhi, in the same building as the post office. Basic but clean, air-cooled rooms with attached bath. Go for room 307 for a fabulous view of the Jama Masjid's iconic marble. **£**

The Oberoi
Dr Zakir Hussain Marg, New Delhi
Tel: 011-2436 3030
www.oberoihotels.com
Once the standard bearer for Delhi's five-star hotels, the Oberoi is still elegant, exclusive and expensive. Rooms have spectacular views over Delhi golf course on one side and Humayun's Tomb on the other. As well as a great spa and the justly famous pool, the hotel's multi-cuisine Threesixty restaurant offers some of the capital's finest dining, with its own sushi station and wood-fired pizza oven. **££££**

The Park
15 Sansad Marg (Parliament St)
Tel: 011-2374 3000
www.theparkhotels.com
The Park pioneered the design hotel concept in India and they remain some of the best. Perhaps the funkiest contemporary-style rooms in town, plus an interesting restaurant, poolside bar and great location make this a winner. Agni, the hotel's DJ bar, is one of the liveliest in the city. **££££**

Rak International
820 Main Bazaar, Chowk Baoli
Tel: 011-2358 6508
www.hotelrakinternational.com
Another dependable cheapy in the Paharganj area; clean, relatively quiet and with a pleasant rooftop restaurant. **£**

Ringo Guest House
17 Scindia House, Connaught Lane (off Janpath)
Tel: 011-2331 0605
The pick of the backpacker options in Connaught Place, Ringo's has tiny but well-scrubbed rooms, a passable

restaurant and friendly staff. Overall, it's a notch superior to nearby Sunny's. **£**

La Sagrita
14 Sunder Nagar
Tel: 011-4150 7013
www.lasagrita.com
Near the zoo in a quiet residential area, this welcoming midscale guesthouse offers rooms with comfortable beds and hot water. The staff are great and the food good and relatively inexpensive. The shopping area just around the corner has an excellent vegetarian restaurant, sweet corner and some good antique shops. **££**

Shangri La's Eros
19 Ashoka Road
Tel: 011-4119 1919
www.shangri-la.com
Amazing panoramic views over New Delhi unfold from the upper floors of the Shangri La's Eros, an international-grade five-star occupying a floodlit skyscraper at the heart of the historic government district, close to India Gate. The lobby's a dazzling expanse of polished marble and crystal chandeliers, and there's a wide choice of multi-cuisine restaurants, a large curvi-form pool in the garden, in-house art gallery and top-notch spa. **££££**

Shanti Home
A-1/300 Janakpuri
Tel: 011-4157 3366
www.shantihome.com
Located close to the international airport, within 300 metres/yards of the metro station, Shanti Home is a beautifully set up boutique hotel that makes a soft first landfall in India if you're arriving, or launch pad for the flight home. Its 17 rooms are filled with delightful repro antiques – each one themed (we loved the 'Bollywood Masala' with its antique film prints). Most have carved wood four- posters. Carefully prepared meals are served on a rooftop terrace. **£££**

Taj Palace
Sardar Patel Marg, Diplomatic Enclave, Chanakyapuri
Tel: 011-2611 0202
www.tajhotels.com
While its luxurious suites are much loved, this well-designed hotel caters for all visitors and sits in beautiful grounds. Three exceptional restaurants (Masala Art, Orient Express and Blue Ginger) provide other reasons to stay. **££££**

Treetops
R 8b Hauz Khas Enclave
Tel: 9899-555704
https://sites.google.com/site/treetopsbedandbreakfast/home

TRANSPORT
ACCOMMODATION
ACTIVITIES
A – Z
LANGUAGE

Run by a retired journalist, Murud Ali Baig, and his cookery writer wife, Tannie, Treetops is a homely B&B in one of south Delhi's most leafy and atmospheric neighbourhoods. The house is swathed in greenery, the rooms are spacious and comfortable, the traditional north Indian cuisine gourmet standard and the rates restrained. Guests can also sign up for cookery courses at a reduced rate. **££**

Wongdhen House
15A New Tibetan Colony, Manju-ka-Tilla
Tel: 011-2381 6689
wongdhenhouse@hotmail.com
About 2km (1.25 miles) north of Old Delhi, this predominantly Tibetan colony offers a more peaceful range of backpacker accommodation than Pahar Ganj. Wongdhen House is deservedly the most popular of the

bunch, offering clean, well-priced rooms and sweeping rooftop views over the Jamuna River. **£**

Yatri House
Corner of Panchkuian and Mandir Margs
Tel: 011-2362 5563
www.yatrihouse.com
Situated down a small lane, set well back from the main road, this is a clean, well-run guesthouse in a modern family home. Although in somewhat uninspiring surroundings, it's only 1km (2/3 mile) from Connaught Place, so amounts to one of the quietest options this close to the city centre. **£££**

Youth Hostel
5 Naya Marg, Chanakyapuri,
New Delhi
Tel: 011-2611 6285
www.yhaindia.org
Modern, eco-friendly and good value,

YHA India's flagship property is set in the green and pleasant diplomatic quarter, with its wide, tree-lined streets and sparse traffic. You must be a member to stay (membership is issued on the spot for Rs250) – well worth it. Dorms and rooms available. **£**

YWCA International Guest House
10 Sansad Marg, New Delhi
Tel: 011-2336 1662
www.ywcaindia.org
A recommended, well-run and safe place to stay for both sexes, in a convenient New Delhi location. The spotless A/C rooms with attached bath come with a complimentary breakfast at the very good attached restaurant. There is an STD booth and an efficient travel service on site. Profits go towards project helping women in India. **£**

PUNJAB AND HARYANA

Amritsar

Hotel Indus
Opposite Langar Hall, nr Galiara
Tel: 0183-252 5900
www.hotelindus.com
Located bang opposite the Golden Temple, this place boasts the finest views from any of the city's hotels of the Harmandir. The rooms are well maintained and excellent value, but you'll probably spend most of your time on the rooftop terrace gazing at the gilded vision below. **£**

Mrs Bhandari's
10 Cantonment
Tel/fax: 0183-222 8509
http://bhandari_guesthouse.tripod.com
Quirky, delightfully old-fashioned guesthouse on the outskirts with a colonial-era ambiance, garden, pool and fireplaces in the rooms. You can arrange to be picked up from the train station. **££**

Hotel Ritz Plaza
45 The Mall
Tel: 0183-256 2836

www.ritzhotel.in
An grand, elegant hotel in a quiet but convenient location with lawns and a pool. The rooms are clean and functional. Friendly management and a restaurant. **£££**

Chandigarh

CITCO Hotel Parkview
Sector 24
Tel: 0172-270 0050
www.citcochandigarh.com/parkview
Great value, clean A/C and non-A/C (**£**) rooms, and a decent restaurant. Conveniently central and – because it's government-run – there's no shortage of eager taff. Tariffs include breakfast. **£–££**

The Kaptain's Retreat
SCO 303–304,
Sector 35B
Tel: 0172-500 5594
www.kaptainsretreat.com
Owned by former Indian cricket captain, Kapil Dev, this small

boutique hotel in the city centre is crammed with cricketing memorabilia and has the atmosphere of a gentlemen's club. All the rooms are individually styled. The furnishings could do with an upgrade, but the tariffs are low for the location and level of comfort. **££**

The Manor Hotel, Delhi.

UTTAR PRADESH

Agra

Amarvilas
Taj East Gate Road
Tel: 0562-223 1515
www.oberoihotels.com
By far the most luxurious of the five-stars, Amarvilas is up to the usual Oberoi standards. Located just 600 metres/yards from the Taj, it boasts the best views of the tomb of any

hotel in the city. You can gaze at the fabled white domes and minarets from all the rooms, as well as the lobby, lounge and bar. To the rear, terraced lawns, reflection ponds and pillared pavilions frame a spectacular pool. **££££**

Atithi
Tourist Complex Area, Fatehabad Road
Tel: 0562-233 0878

PRICE CATEGORIES

Price categories are for a double room (A/C where available) in high season, including taxes:
£ = under Rs2,000
££ = Rs2,000–5,000
£££ = Rs5,000–10,000
££££ = over Rs10,000

www.hotelatithiagra.com
Forty-four clean A/C rooms in modern hotel with pool and attentive staff; good value for Agra. **££**

The Grand Imperial
MG Road
Tel: 0562-225 1190
www.hotelgrandimperial.com
Beautifully restored heritage property, slightly further from the Taj Mahal than other five-stars but oozes charm and sophistication. **££££**

Hotel Maya
18/184 Purani Mandi Circle,
Fatehabad Road
Tel: 9719-107691
www.mayainmagic.com
Extremely friendly and well-run backpackers' hotel within walking distance of the Taj. Great food, good value. **£**

Mughal Sheraton
Taj Ganj
Tel: 0562-402 1700
www.itchotels.in
Popular mainly with tour groups, this luxury hotel, with its Mughal-inspired architecture and interiors, makes a very pleasant base for the Taj and Fatehpur Sikri. Nice gardens with a good pool; the pricier rooms have a view of the distant Taj. **££££**

Sheela
Taj East Gate Road
Tel: 0562-233 1194
www.hotelsheelaagra.com
Pick of the budget bunch in Taj Ganj, the *Sheela* offers immaculate rooms ranged around a leafy central courtyard, only a few minutes' walk from the Taj. It's great value, and correspondingly popular so book at least a week ahead. **£**

Taj Gateway
Fatehabad Road
Tel: 0562-660 2000
www.thegatewayhotels.com
From this luxury hotel on the outskirts of town you can enjoy a view of the famous mausoleum from your bed. Its rooms, ranged over seven floors, are decorated in modern-Mughal style, and the Islamic-tiled pool is set amid neatly lawns. **££££**

Tourist Rest House
Kachahari Road, Baluganj
Tel: 0562-246 3961
www.dontworrychickencurry.com
The best budget option in Agra. Clean rooms with attached bath around a courtyard. Friendly owners and good vegetarian food. **£**

Trident Hotel
Fatehabad Road
Tel: 0562-223 5000
www.tridenthotels.com
Extensive use of Fatehpur Sikri sandstone, offset by cream-painted

walls, lend a touch of Mughal style to the Trident, whose interiors are modern and minimalist. The pleasantly furnished rooms all face a central landscaped courtyard garden featuring a large swimming pool, where you can dine in the evenings by babbling fountains. **££££**

Allahabad

Hotel Allahabad Regency
16 Tashkent Marg, Civil Lines
Tel: 0532-258 9675
www.hotelallahabadregency.com
Elegantly furnished colonial-era bungalow in the former British enclave, with a smart coffee shop, restaurant, health suite and pool. **£££**

Kanha Shyam
Civil Lines
Tel: 0532-2560123
www.hotelkanhashyam.com
Modern, multi-storey hotel in the commercial centre that's popular mainly with business visitors, though tour groups also use it. Rooms range from average to quite plush, but the beds are comfy, the showers hot and the multi-cuisine restaurant dependable. **£££**

Hotel Yatrik
33 Sardar Patel Marg, Civil Lines
Tel: 0532-226 0921
www.hotelyatrik.com
A popular, well-managed midrange hotel with A/C rooms and a lovely tropical garden and restaurant. **££**

Jhansi

Hotel Samrat
Elite Road
Tel: 0510-244 2943
Easily the nicest of the budget options, and within walking distance of the train station. Some A/C rooms, and a good restaurant. **£**

Kanpur

Attic
15/198 V. Singh Road, Civil Lines
Tel: 0512-230 6691
www.theattickanpur.com
Charming heritage hotel, created from a former British barracks (c.1830). Peaceful and secluded, and with simple modern comforts including a/c, but it's definitely on the decline. **££**

Hotel Gaurav
18/56 The Mall
Tel: 0512-233 3456
www.gauravhotel.com
Good-value, comfortable A/C rooms in a well-maintained midscale hotel that serves as a sanctuary for visiting businessmen. Also has a restaurant and a nice garden. **£**

The Landmark
10 Somdatt Plaza, The Mall
Tel: 0512-230 5305
www.thehotellandmark.com
The best, and most expensive, hotel in Kanpur. Comfortable, modern rooms, as well as good restaurants, a coffee shop and pool (the only one in the city). **£££**

Lucknow

Hotel Clarks Avadh
8 Mahatma Gandhi Marg
Tel: 0522-262 0131
www.hotelclarks.com
A comfortable, if rather dated, luxury hotel only a few minutes' drive from the airport. Helpful, courteous staff and quality dining, especially the rooftop Falaknuma, which serves rich Avadhi dishes – see restaurant listings. **£££**

Lucknow Homestay
110-D Mall Avenue
Tel: 0522-646 0592
lucknowhomestay.wordpress.com
This family-run B&B is a godsend for the few backpackers who make it to Lucknow. It's welcoming, clean, quiet and great value, offering complimentary internet access and laundry – though you might need to phone ahead for directions. **£**

Taj Residency Hotel
Vipin Khand, Gomti Nagar
Tel: 0522-239 3939
www.tajhotels.com
Lucknow's top hotel, very luxurious and peaceful with lovely gardens. Excellent restaurant specialising in traditional Avadhi food. **££££**

Mathura

Hotel Madhuvan
Krishna Nagar
Tel: 0565-242 0064
bhtul@nde.vsnl.net.in
Clean, air-conditioned rooms with attached bath; the hotel also has a swimming pool and pleasant restaurant. **££**

Muskan Hotel
Mayur Vihar, Dhauli Pyau
Tel: 0565-240 8310
www.muskanhotel.com
Well managed, pleasantly furnished budget hotel close to the centre of town, with simple but clean rooms in a modern building and helpful staff. **£**

Radha Ashok
Masani By-Pass Road (NH-2), Chatikara
Tel: 0565-253 0395
www.radhaashok.com
A very well-kept and attractive, modern hotel featuring comfortable rooms, pleasant gardens with a swimming pool and a very good vegetarian restaurant. **££**

Sarnath

Jain Paying Guest House
Tel: 0542-259 5621
jpgh@rediffmail.com
A small but very friendly guesthouse.
The clean rooms, doubles with
attached shower and toilet (singles
have attached shower and shared
toilet). Good, home-cooked
vegetarian food. **£**

Namo Buddha
S10/81 C-2 Mohalla Baraipur, 3rd house
behind Mishra General Store
chrisnehrulal@yahoo.com
A small guesthouse with simple,
comfortable rooms. The atmosphere
is friendly and the accommodation
good value. **£**

Varanasi

Alka
Meer Ghat
Tel: 0542-240 1681
www.hotelalkavns.com
Impeccably well scrubbed, attached
rooms in a three-storey complex
ranged around a leafy inner courtyard.
One of the best views of the riverfront
extends from its terrace. Among the
most dependable budget choices in
Varanasi. **£**

Diamond Hotel
Bhelpur
Tel: 0542-227 6696
www.hotel-diamond.com

Good-value A/C and non-A/C rooms
in comfortable hotel with a restaurant
and garden. **££**

Hotel Ganges View
Assi Ghat
Tel: 0542-231 3128
www.hotelgangesview.com
A beautiful old colonial-era mansion
converted into an atmospheric
heritage hotel. Comfortable, very
clean A/C rooms, furnished with
carved wood four-posters and
decorated with antique prints. Great
views over the river through cusp-
arched windows of a raised terrace
where drinks, snacks and vegetarian
suppers are served. **£££**

Hotel Pradeep
C-27/153 Jagatganj
Tel: 0542-220 4963
www.hotelpradeep.com
A friendly hotel with well-maintained
and clean A/C rooms. Very good value
for money and also has the excellent
Poonam restaurant. **££**

Hotel Surya
S20/51 5a Nepali Kothi, Varuna Bridge,
Cantonment
Tel: 0542-250 8466
www.hotelsuryavns.com
Recently refurbished rooms in a
characterful old palace of a former
Nepali king. All of the rooms are a/c
and have balconies overlooking a
lawned garden that doubles as a

quality restaurant; and there's a pool
and funky hookah bar. **££**

Taj Ganges Gateway
Nadesar Palace Grounds
Tel: 0542-666 0001
www.tajhotels.com
Luxury five-star located 6km (4
miles) north of the centre in the
grounds of a former royal palace
(see Nadesar, below). Set amid 16
hectares (40 acres) of landscaped
gardens, the modern multi-storey
building's a relatively bland one
by local standards, and worn
around the edges, but the decor is
pleasantly old fashioned and rooms
impeccably smart and comfortable
– and the outdoor pool is great.
££££

Taj Nadesar
Nadesar Palace Grounds
Tel: 0542-666 0002
This former palace, originally a
British mint, has hosted royalty and
visiting bigwigs, including Emperor
Hale Selassie, Mountbatten, Nehru
and Queen Elizabeth II, since 1835,
and was recently restored to its
past glory, with splendid outdoor
pool, spa and small golf course. Set
amid mango orchards and fields
of marigolds, it's sumptuously
furnished with antiques from the
Maharaja of Varanasi's collection.
££££

BIHAR

Bodhgaya

Root Institute
Near the Thai Temple
Tel: 0631-220 0714
www.rootinstitute.com
The root institute is an organisation
that runs a Buddhist meditation
retreat. As well as attending courses,
it is possible to stay in the huts and
dormitories as an independent visitor.
Consistently good vegetarian meals
are provided; retreat rules to be
followed at all times. **£**

Taj Darbar
Bodhgaya Rd

Tel: 0631-220 0053
www.hoteltajdarbar.com
Large, modern, efficient and
comfortable hotel 6km (4 miles)
from the airport, with plush
interiors and central a/c, as well
as a restaurant serving meals
alfresco on the front lawn.
££–£££

Patna

Maurya Patna
South Gandhi Maidan
Tel: 0612-220 3040
www.maurya.com

Patna's poshest hotel is set in
sprawling grounds, and boasts all
the facilities you'd expect of an
international grade 5 star, including
a crystline pool, gourmet restaurants
and fitness centre. **££££**

Hotel Windsor
Exhibition Rd
Tel: 0612-220 3250
Great-value budget hotel in the
centre of the city, popular mainly
with visiting businessmen. All the
rooms are a/c and have comfy
beds and clean bathrooms.
£–££

UTTARAKHAND

Almora

Hotel Himsagar
The Mall
Tel: 05962-230 711
http://hotelhimsagar.com
Friendly hotel in middle of town, range
of rooms, reasonable value. And it's
one of the few places in this bracket

offering parking – always a problem
in hill stations. **£**

Corbett National Park

Corbett Aroma Park
Dhikuli
Tel: 05947-284 122
www.corbettaromapark.com

PRICE CATEGORIES

**Price categories are for a double
room (A/C where available) in high
season, including taxes:**
£ = under Rs2,000
££ = Rs2,000–5,000
£££ = Rs5,000–10,000
££££ = over Rs10,000

Modern hotel on the main road opposite the sanctuary, comprising only 20 'cottages' in double storey blocks. Better value than many of the camp-style properties. **£££**

Hideaway
Book through tel: 011-4652 0000
www.corbetthideaway.com
The Hideaway's USP is its fabulously leafy setting, under giant mango and guava trees, amid gardens full of vibrant azaleas and hibiscus blooms. Over fifty red-tiled cottages are dotted around the grounds, with contemporary interiors and outside seating. There's also a pool on site, and large wood-panelled lounge to relax in. **££££**

Infinity Wilderness
Dhikuli
Tel: 05947-251 279
www.infinityresorts.com
Astride a bluff overlooking the Ramganga River, the Infinity Wilderness is the best situated of the luxury lodges. From its sun deck you can gaze up a sweeping S-bend of bleached pebbles and rushing water, flanked by forested Himalayan foothills. The rooms are spacious and high-ceilinged, with safari-style dark-wood furniture and comfy beds. Buffet meals are served in a splendid circular dining hall made of river stones and giant teak trunks. **££££**

Tiger Camp
Book through tel: 011-4112 8785
www.tiger-camp.com
Attractive, local-style cottages and rooms with en suite bathrooms. There is a good restaurant and well-run jeep tours. **£££**

Dehra Dun

Hotel President
6 Astley Hall, Rajpur Road
Tel: 0135-265 7082
www.hotelpresidentdehradun.com
Twenty-two A/C rooms in a well-run hotel. Friendly, with a good restaurant and an efficient travel desk. **££**

Samar Niwas
M-16 Chanderlok Colony, Rajpur Rd
Tel: 0135-274 0299
www.samarniwas.com
Welcoming guesthouse run by descendents of the Tehri-Garwahl royal family. The rooms are spacious and comfortable. Antiques and other collectables lend an old-world feel to the 1980s building, and there's a relaxing garden to lounge in. Great value. **£**

Haridwar

Haveli Hari Ganga
Pilibhit House, 21 Ramghat
Tel: 01334-226 443

www.havelihariganga.com
A beautifully restored, atmospheric *haveli* with 20 characterful rooms overlooking the Ganges and a good vegetarian restaurant, easily the best place in town. **£££**

Midtown
Railway Road, Laltarao Pull
Tel: 01334-223674 /
www.midtownhotel.in
Well set up midrange place a stone's throw from the station and famous Har-ki-Pauri Ghat, though it's tucked away up an alley so surprisingly quiet. Most rooms have balconies and a/c. Restaurant on site. **£–££**

Uttaranchal Tourism Rahi
Station Road
Tel: 01334-226 430
Rooms and dormitories set amid pleasant gardens. Centrally located, this is a good budget option. Book ahead. **£–££**

Mussoorie

Carlton's Plaisance
Off Charleville Road
Tel: 0135-263 2800
www.carltonplaisance.com
Quiet and relaxing, family-run heritage hotel with period furnishings and breathtaking views over flower-filled apple orchards to the mountains. There's pleasant lawn, verandah restaurant and friendly St Bernard. **£££**

The Claridges Nabha
Air Field, Barlowganj Road
Tel: 0135-263 1426
www.claridges-hotels.com
Summer residence of the former Maharaja of Nabha, now a fully refurbished and extremely elegant hotel surrounded by a lovely garden. Quiet and peaceful, with oodles of Raj-era charm and fine foothill views. **££££**

Kasmanda Palace
The Mall
Tel: 0135-263 2424
www.welcomheritagehotels.com
Originally built in 1836 for a high-ranking British army officer, this stately whitewashed mansion now serves as an atmospheric heritage hotel. Set amid a pine forest, it boasts superb views over the Doon Valley. **££££**

Joshimath

GMVN Tourist Bungalow
Joshimath
Tel: 01389-222 118
Small and basic and clean, recently renovated rooms managed by the tourism development corporation. Very cheap dormitory beds are also available. **£**

Mount View Hotel
Joshimath
Tel: 01389-221 993
www.hotelmountview.in
Splendid old colonial-era hotel with typically Victorian green tin roof and white walls that's been in the same family since the 1890s. Set in spacious grounds, it boats sweeping valley views. Rooms in various categories – some dowdier than others, though easily the best option in this neck of the woods. **££**

Nainital

Alka Hotel
The Mall
Tel: 05942-235 220
www.alkahotel.com
A curiously-styled hotel with pleasant themed rooms ('middle Eastern', 'Log Cabin' and 'Baroque') and lake view. Well managed, with a good restaurant. **£££**

Belvedere Palace
Awagarh Estate, Mallital
Tel: 05942-237 434
www.welcomheritagehotels.com
A converted palace with large rooms and views over the lake. Lovely gardens and a pleasant restaurant. **££££**

YHA
Ardwell, Mallital
Tel: 05942-235 194
www.yhaindia.org
Great-value dormitories and rooms in a peaceful location. Book ahead. **£**

Naukuchiyatal

The Lake Village
Tel: 05942-279 224
www.thelakevillage.com
Beautifully landscaped upmarket resort overlooking the lake, offering rooms tented accommodation in ersatz thatched Kumaoni 'huts' and 'gazebos', plus a great swimming pool. Recommended for families. Rates for half board only. **££££**

Tourist Rest House
Tel: 05942-247 138
www.kmvn.org
Fantastic location right on the water's edge, reasonable rooms, great place to relax. **££**

Ranikhet

Chevron Rosemount
Tel: 05966-221391
www.chevronhotels.com
Fairy-tale views of distant snow peaks are to be had from the balconies and neatly clipped lawns of this charismatic hotel on the outskirts of town, which first opened in 1900. Its teak-lined rooms are spacious and fragrant, and there are swathes of

pinewoods to roam in nearby. One of the loveliest addresses in the Indian Himalaya. **£££–££££**

Rishikesh
Ananda in the Himalayas
Palace Estate, Narendra Nagar
Tel: 01378-227 500
www.anandaspa.com
A very expensive but fabulous spa 18km (11 miles) from Rishikesh. Set in an old palace, it has elegant rooms with wonderful views– and a gorgeous pool. **££££**
Bhandari Swiss Cottage
High Banks

Tel: 0135-243 2939
Well-run hotel in quiet area above town, outdoor café/bakery with superb views over the Ganges from its (pricier) rooms on the upper floors; yoga and music classes also on offer. **£–££**
GMVN Rishilok
Badrinath Road, Muni ki Reti
Tel: 0135-243 0373
www.gmvnl.com/newgmvn
Good-value mid-budget cottages and rooms, which are set in pleasant grounds. Quiet, if a little austere, with a decent restaurant. **£**

High in the hills.

HIMACHAL PRADESH

Dalhousie
Aroma-n-Claire
Court Road
Tel: 01899-242 199
A sprawling old-fashioned hotel with character. The rooms are a little basic but some have great views and there is a restaurant and small library. **££**
Hotel Grand View
Tel: 01899-240 760
www.grandviewdalhousie.in
For once the name's no understatement. The British army colonel who built this stately wooden mansion as a military sanatorium in the 1850s picked the sweetest of spots, on a forest plateau gazing across the ridge tops to the snow peaks of the Pir Panjal. The architecture's straight out of the Far Pavilions and refurbished interiors equally charming. **££££**
Youth Hostel
Near the bus stand
Tel: 01899-242 189
www.yhaindia.com
Good budget accommodation with meals available. Reservations are recommended. **£**

Dharamsala
Chonor House
Lower Dharamsala
Tel: 01892-221 006
Located close to the Norbulingka Institue for Tibetan arts and Dalai Lama's residence, Chonor House is set under old cedar trees beside a pretty garden. Colourful Buddhist murals, appliqué work and carved-wood furniture add a dash of romantic Himalayan character to the rooms, which have great views over the valley and surrounding snow peaks from their balconies. Also on site is a cosy restaurant serving authentic mountain cuisine. **£££**

Glenmoor Cottages
Mall Road, McLeod Ganj
Tel: 01892-221 010
www.glenmoorcottages.com
Five self-contained cottages in a forest location. The setting is lovely and quiet, and meals are available on request. **£££**
Norbulingka
Lower Dharamsala
Tel: 01892-246 405
www.norbulingka.org
This is a quiet and comfortable hotel, decorated with Tibetan wall paintings. Popular with visiting celebrities, it's the most upmarket hotel in town. Booking is essential. There is also a good Tibetan restaurant. **££££**
Om
Near the bus stand, McLeod Ganj
Tel: 01892-221 313
A few good-value budget rooms, all very clean, with attached showers. A good restaurant and lovely views complete the picture. **£**
Pema Thang Guesthouse
Hotel Bhagsu Road
Tel: 01892-221 871
www.pemathang.net
Friendly and well-run hotel, many of the rooms with small kitchens. There's also a great restaurant. **£–££**
Surya Resorts
South End, McLeod Ganj
Tel: 01892-221 418
www.suryamcleod.com
Modern, comfortable, large rooms, many with excellent views. The service is helpful and friendly, and the attached restaurant has good food. **££–£££**

Kangra
The Judge's Court
Jhagwan Bhawan, Pragpur
Tel: 01970-245 035
www.judgescourt.com
Charming period hotel in the middle

of this restored heritage village, hugely atmospheric and a unique experience. **£££**
Taragarh Palace Hotel
Taragarh
Tel: 01894-242 034
www.taragarh.com
Built in the 1930s, this was formerly a palace of the Maharaja of Kashmir. It has 16 pleasant rooms with period furniture. There is a good restaurant and a pool in lovely gardens. **£££**

Kasauli
HPTDC Ros Common
Lower Mall
Tel: 01793-272 005
http://hptdc.nic.in
The best hotel and restaurant in town, in lovely surroundings. All rooms have baths with hot water. Book ahead. **££**

Kullu
Shobla International
Dhalpur
Tel: 01902-222 800
The smartest option in Kullu, in a modern building overlooking the river, with a decent restaurant. **££**
Span Resorts
PO Katrain, National Highway
Tel: 01902-240 138
http://spanresorts.com
A series of quiet and secluded cottages with comfortable rooms, about 12km (7.5 miles) from Kullu. The five-star resort offers various

PRICE CATEGORIES

Price categories are for a double room (A/C where available) in high season, including taxes:
£ = under Rs2,000
££ = Rs2,000–5,000
£££ = Rs5,000–10,000
££££ = over Rs10,000

activities, including yoga. Good food is on offer in the restaurant. **££££**

Manali

Banon Resorts
New Hope Orchards
Tel: 01902-253026
Situated on the leafy outskirts of Manali, with views across apple orchards and deodar forests to the distant peaks, Banon Resorts comprises rooms in a large main block, and smaller cottages dotted around landscaped grounds. Although modern, the buildings are made of traditional pahari-style cedar and stone layers. Wood-burning stoves keep the cottages cosy in winter; and there's a pleasant restaurant on site. **£££**

HPTDC Hotel Beas
On the riverbank, towards Vashisht
Tel: 01902-252 832
http://hptdc.nic.in
An excellent-value hotel in a splendid location. Well run, with decent rooms; meals available on request. **£–££**

HPTDC Hotel Rohtang Manalsu
The Mall
Tel: 01902-252 332
http://hptdc.nic.in
A quiet hotel set in lovely grounds, out towards the Hadimba Temple. The large rooms have good views across the valley. **£–££**

Johnson's Lodge
Circuit House Road
Tel: 01902-251 523
www.johnsonslodge.com
Smart, well furnished rooms in a

modern hotel with rooms in three- and four-storey stone-and-cedar blocks, close to the centre. Relaxing grounds and quality restaurant serving trout. **££–£££**

Tiger Eye
Old Manali
Tel: 01902-251 092
www.tigereyeadventure.com
Outstandingly pleasant budget hotel run by an Indian-Dutch couple. Its 15 rooms are spread over three floors and all have verandahs decorated with potted plants and flowers. A notch pricier than the competition but worth it. **£**

Simla

Dreamland
The Mall
Tel: 0177-2653005
www.hoteldreamlandshimla.com
It's worth shelling out a little extra at this outstanding lower-midrange hotel, set just above the Mall in the heart of Simla, for a room on one of the upper floors, which boast magnificent views of the distant Himalayas. The rooms are large for the price and restaurant one of the most dependable in town. **£**

Chapslee House
Lakkar Bazaar
Tel: 0177-280 2542
www.chapslee.com
A Simla institution. A very elegant manor house with wonderful suites, period furnishings and antiques, as well as excellent food. Book in advance. **££££**

Hotel Combermere
The Mall, opposite the lift
Tel: 0177-265 1246
www.hotelcombermere.com
A friendly, modern hotel near the centre of town. Comfortable rooms and helpful staff give the hotel a pleasant air. **££££**

Hotel Willow Banks
The Mall, near the lift
Tel: 0177-265 8125
www.willowbanks.com
One of Simla's newest hotels, bright, modern and well equipped, all mod cons and more. **£££**

Oberoi Cecil
Chaura Maidan
Tel: 0177-280 4848
www.oberoicecil.com
A stylish and luxurious Simla landmark, with a fabulous pool, restaurant and well-appointed rooms with excellent views. **££££**

Wildflower Hall
Mashroba, Charabra
Tel: 0177-264 8585
www.oberoiwildflowerhall.com
A fabulous hilltop resort, formerly the residence of Lord Kitchener. Stunning views, luxurious surroundings and a world-class spa make this one of India's finest hotels. **££££**

YMCA
The Ridge
Tel: 0177-225 2375
Large, old-fashioned rooms with shared bathrooms. There is also a dining hall. Open to both sexes, though book well ahead as it's very popular. **£**

LADAKH

Alchi

Choksor Guest House
1km (0.5 mile) from the temple complex off the main road to Leh.
Tel: 01982-227 084
Best fall back if the Heritage (above) is full, with a traditional Ladakhi courtyard and rooftop terrace with great mountain views. **£**

Heritage Guest House
Tel: 01982-227 125
This small, family run place opposite the entrance to the temple complex offers the village's most comfortable rooms, with marble floors and tiled bathrooms. Meals available. **£**

Leh

Indus
Malpak Alley
Tel: 01892-252502
The warren-like Old Town below the fort is jammed with ancient mud-walled houses, and the Indus is

in the thick of the action. Ranged around a tree-lined inner courtyard, its sixteen rooms have tiny balconies overlooking the roofscape and are immaculately clean and well heated (with green fuels). Meals available. **£**

Hotel K-sar Palace
Fort Road, next door to theLha-ri-mo
Tel: 01982-252 348
A largish hotel with good-sized rooms in a quiet spot. Lovely surroundings and views over the valley. **££**

Oriental
Changspa Lane
Tel: 01982-253 153
www.orientalguesthouse.com
Located just below the Shanti Stupa at the end of Changspa Lane, this is one of the most welcoming and pleasant places to stay in the region, if not all India. Lovely rooms, great local food, flower filled garden and internet access. Open during the winter. **£**

Padma
Fort Road
Tel: 01982-252 630
www.padmaladakh.net
A pleasant guesthouse with very clean rooms and great views. The pricier rooms in the new wing have en-suite baths. **£–££**

Hotel Shambhala
Skara
Tel: 01982-253 500
www.hotelshambhala.com
Nestled under a stand of shimmering poplars on the town's outskirts, the Shambhala comprises 26 simply furnished, generously sized rooms, opening on to walkways with Tibetan-style pillars. Chill out in hammocks on a terrace strung with fluttering prayer flags, gazing across the valley to the snow peaks of Stok Kangri. The food's unfailingly delicious, and location tranquil. **££**

RAJASTHAN

Ajmer

Haveli Heritage Inn
Kutchery Road
Tel: 0145-262 1607
www.haveliheritageinn.com
Set in a 100-year-old haveli in the city centre, this family-run *heritage hotel* is best midscale option in Ajmer. The rooms, opening to a sociable inner courtyard where delicious meals are served, are basic, but the welcome is warm and the staff go out of their way to help. **££**

Mansingh Palace
Vaishali Nagar
Tel: 0145-242 5702
Error! Hyperlink reference not valid.
Though showing signs of age, this is the top hotel in town – a striking modern building designed to replicate an 18th-century fortress, with large, comfortable rooms, and a decent, but expensive, restaurant. **££££**

RTDC Khadim
College Road
Tel: 0145-262 7536
www.rtdc.in/khadim
Much the same as other government hotels in the state but, given Ajmer's relative lack of decent accommodation, a welcome fallback option if the Hvaeli Heritage is full, with the usual wide range of rooms, restaurant and bar. **££–£££**

Alwar

Hotel Alwar
26 Manu Marg
Tel: 0144-270 0012
www.alwarhotel.com
Spacious, well-maintained rooms (A/C and non-A/C) with attached bath. Restaurant and pleasant garden. **££**

Hill Fort Kesroli
Kesroli, 12km (7.5 miles) from Alwar
Tel: 01468-289 352
www.neemranahotels.com
Ranged around a lush inner courtyard full of bougainvillea and palm trees, this 14th-century fort has been sensitively converted into an atmospheric hotel, deep in the Aravalli countryside. The views from its ramparts over the surrounding fields and hills are the main attraction, though the rooms have retained plenty of traditional flair. **£££–££££**

Bharatpur

The Bagh
Agra–Achnera Road, Bharatpur 321 001
Tel: 05644-225 415
www.thebagh.com
Bharatpur's only boutique hotel, beautifully situated amid former royal orchards and gardens. The decor in its 14 rooms combines modern design elements with traditional Rajput style. Views of the grounds unfold from cusped arched windows. Easily the nicest upscale option in this area. **£££**

Falcon Guest House
Saras
Tel: 05644-223 815
www.falconguesthouse.com
A peaceful and homely budget guesthouse run by the amiable Mrs Rajni Singh. The rooms are clean, and the larger ones have private balconies and softer mattresses. The owner's husband is a keen ornithologist willing to share his knowledge. Home-cooked meals are served in the garden restaurant. **£–££**

Jungle Lodge
Gori Shankar
Tel: 05644-225 622
Clean rooms, hot running water, shady marble-floored verandas, a beautiful green garden and a library make this one of the best budget choices within easy walking distance of the park. The service is great and there is a small but nice restaurant. Cycles, binoculars and two motorcycles can be hired. **£**

Kiran Guest House
364 Rajendra Nagar
Tel: 05644-223 845
www.kiranguesthouse.com
Has five spacious and immaculate rooms with a lovely terrace-top restaurant serving tasty meals and chilled beer. Great personal service, homely and good value for money. The hotel arranges rides to and from town, and bikes and binoculars are available. **£**

Laxmi Vilas Palace
Kakaji ki Kothi
Tel: 05644-231 199
www.laxmivilas.com
This former palace on the outskirts of the city dates from 1887 and was built for the brother of the Maharaja of Bharatpur. It holds 25 attractive suites and rooms, combining Mughal and Rajput architectural styles, with colonial furniture, colourful murals and carved wood beds. Buffet meals are made with locally grown produce, and there's a Jacuzzi, pool and croquet lawn. **£££**

Bikaner

Bhairon Vilas
Next to Junagadh Fort
Tel: 0151-254 4751
http://hotelbhaironvilas.tripod.com
This eccentric heritage hotel, owned and run by a bohemian cousin of the maharaja, is a real one off. The usual family heirlooms and 19th-century Rajasthani architecture are stylishly juxtaposed with funky modern decor, and there are frequent parties in the garden. **£**

Gajner Palace
Gajner
Tel: 01534-275 061
www.hrhhotels.com
A typically Rajput mansion of ornately carved, dark-red sandstone situated on the shores of a dreamy lake, this former hunting lodge was where the Maharaja of Bikaner used to entertain visiting dignitaries in Edwardian times. It's a great place to rekindle the spirit of a bygone era. Wild peacocks and spotted deer still graze in abundance on the banks, and local folk troupes dance in the evenings against a backdrop of filigreed domes. **££££**

Karni Bhawan Palace
Gandhi Colony
Tel: 0151-252 4701
www.hrhindia.com
Previously the residence of the Maharaja of Bikaner. Wonderful period rooms in a late Art Deco (1950s) house; antique photos, furniture and curios add to the atmosphere, and there's a quality restaurant serving local specialities. **£££**

Laxmi Niwas Palace
Lalgarh Palace
Tel: 0151-220 2777
www.laxminiwaspalace.com
The more congenial of the two heritage hotels occupying Bikaner's old royal palace, boasting very large rooms, all with original furniture and fittings. Queen Victoria was the first of three British monarchs to stay in No. 108. **££££**

Hotel Shri Ram
A-228 Sadul Ganj
Tel: 0151-252 2651
www.hotelshriram.com
Impeccable budget accommodation, with very clean attached rooms (some

PRICE CATEGORIES

Price categories are for a double room (A/C where available) in high season, including taxes:
£ = under Rs2,000
££ = Rs2,000–5,000
£££ = Rs5,000–10,000
££££ = over Rs10,000

A/C) and cheaper dormitories, run by the family of a former brigadier in the Indian camel corps. All meals are available. **£–££**

Bundi

Hotel Braj Bhushanjee
Below the palace
Tel: 0747-244 2322
www.kiplingsbundi.com
Cavernous 250-year-old *haveli* belonging to the family of a former prime minister, sandwiched between the old walled town and the palace. The views from its various roof terraces and pavilions are superb, as are the antique furniture and original murals. Room rates vary widely according to size and levels of comfort. **££**

Bundi Haveli
Tel: 0747-244 6716
www.hotelbundihaveli.com
Beautiful modern boutique hotel in a lovingly restored old *haveli* on the shores of the lake and the in-house restaurant is the nicest place to eat in town. Bargain tariffs too. **££**

Lake View
Bohra Meghwahan, Ji-ki-Haveli
Tel: 0747-244 2342
This friendly, rather ramshackle guesthouse on the lakeside, occupying a small 200-year-old *haveli*, offers a great chance for budget travellers to stay in a period house that still holds heaps of traditional charm – though it is far from a luxury palace, and prone to pilfering raids by monkeys if windows are left open. A couple of the pricier rear-side rooms have lovely views over the Nawal Sagar tank. **£**

Dungarpur

Udai Bilas Palace
Tel: 02964-230 808
www.udaibilaspalace.com
A fascinating mid-19th century palace, now a hotel, in a wonderful lakeside location. Art Deco rooms and bathrooms, and eccentric decor, featuring elaborate pebble murals and mirrorwork. **£££–££££**

Jaipur

Alsisar Haveli
Sansar Chandra Road
Tel: 0141-236 8290
www.alsisar.com
A sumptuous converted mansion with 47 clean, elegant and atmospheric rooms (all A/C), decorated in high Rajput style. There is a wonderful rooftop swimming pool, surrounded by graceful domed pavilions. **£££**

Athiti Guest House
1 Park House Scheme Road, opposite All

India Radio
Tel: 0141-237 8679
www.athitiguesthouse.com
This family-run hotel-cum-guesthouse is one of the cleanest, brightest, most welcoming places in the state. The rooms, which open onto a courtyard, are modern and simple, but spacious, and there's a great rooftop terrace for lounging on, plus a popular residents-only restaurant on the ground floor. **£**

Bissau Palace
Chand Pol, near the Saroj Cinema
Tel: 0141-230 4391
www.bissaupalace.com
Former summer home of the Thakurs of Bissau, dating from the late 18th century and still in possession of its original furniture and fittings: the wood-panelled library is particularly evocative of the period. **£££**

Dera Mandawa
New Mandawa House, Adjoining Punjab National Bank, Sansar Chandra Road
Tel: 0141-511 8490
www.deramandawa.com
Welcoming heritage homestay in a wonderful old haveli that's been added to over successive generations, with multi-storey apartments ranged around a central courtyard. The air-conditioned guest suites ooze traditional style, but aren't overly grand. Meals are served al fresco, while a troupe of traditional musicians provide the entertainment. **£££**

Diggi Palace
Diggi House, S.M.S. Hospital Road
Tel: 0141-237 3091
www.hoteldiggipalace.com
A beautiful old palace, centrally located close to Ajmeri Gate, with lawns and a pleasant terrace restaurant. **£££**

The Oberoi Rajvilas
Goner Road
Tel: 0141-268 0101
www.oberoihotels.com
This is as opulent as Rajasthan gets: an ultra-luxurious and ultra-expensive 13-hectare (32-acre) complex, 12km (7.5 miles) outside the city. Elegant rooms and suites in beautiful gardens with every conceivable amenity. Gourmet food and a beautiful pool. **££££**

Pearl Palace
Hathroi Fort
Tel: 0141-237 3700
www.hotelpearlpalace.com
Probably the best budget hotel in Rajasthan, with spotless and superb-value modern rooms, super-efficient service and a lovely rooftop restaurant. Book well in advance as it's very popular. **£**

Raj Mahal Palace Hotel
Sardar Patel Marg, C Scheme
Tel: 0141-510 5665
www.rajmahalpalacejaipur.com
Built in 1729 by Jai Singh for his favourite Maharani, the Raj Mahal served as a residence of the British Agent and temporary palace of Man Singh II. Set in 4 hectares (10 acres) of grounds enclosed by a high wall, it still exudes colonial style, though less grandeur than some of Jaipur's heritage hotels. **£££**

Rambagh Palace Hotel
Bhawani Singh Road
Tel: 0141-221 1919
www.tajhotels.com
The ultimate Art Deco palace for film-star fantasies. Plush interiors, beautifully decorated rooms and suites, and an indoor pool. Good food and lovely gardens. **££££**

Samode Haveli
Ganga Pol
Tel: 0141-263 2407
www.samode.com
Wonderfully romantic *haveli* of a former prime minister, comprising a mass of ornate mirror work, mural-plastered alcoves, arches and pillared courtyards, plus a pool with its own wet bar. **££££**

Sunder Palace
Hathroi Fort
Tel: 0141-236 0878
www.sunderpalace.com
Rivalling the nearby Pearl Palace, with spacious and spotless modern rooms, a friendly atmosphere and faultless service. Phone on arrival for complementary pick up from the train station. **£**

Jaisalmer

Fort Rajwada
Hotel complex, Jodhpur–Barmer Link Road
Tel: 02992-254 608
www.fortrajwada.com
An impressive modern complex on the outskirts of town, built using filigreed sandstone fragments from old *havelis*, with attractively furnished, cool rooms. Fabulous pool and the rates are unbelievably low given the levels of comfort. **£££**

Jawahar Niwas Palace
1 Bada Bagh Road
Tel: 02992-252 208
www.jawaharniwaspalace.co.in
A beautiful old *haveli* on the quiet west side of Jaisalmer, converted into a traditional-style heritage hotel. The spacious rooms are quiet, with wonderful views. There is a restaurant in the garden and an outdoor pool. Good value. **£££**

Narayan Niwas Palace
Tel: 011-2619 5951

www.narayanniwas.in
A delicately carved 19th-century haveli with simple A/C rooms of mixed quality – the only bona fide heritage hotel in the heart of the Old City. Good Indian food and pleasant surroundings. £££

Shahi Palace
Tel: 02992-255 920
www.shahipalacehotel.com
Well run modern hotel made of traditional sandstone, with glorious fort views and beautifully decorated rooms. ££

Simla
Fort
Tel: 02992-253 061
www.simlahaveli.com
Six romantically furnished rooms with divan beds in a quiet north corner of the fort. Recently restored and a model conservation project of its kind, with environmentally friendly plumbing and waste disposal. ££

Suraj
Southeast corner of the fort
Tel: 09414-391 149
Richly carved yellow sandstone *haveli* that's among the most attractive budget hotels in the fort. The interiors are decked out in traditional style, but its real plus is a sublime roof terrace close to the Jain temples, with amazing desert views. £

Suryagarh
Kahala Phata, Sam Road
Tel: 09001-995 819
www.suryagarh.com
Set amid magnificent desert scenery a 20-minute drive out of Jaisalmer, Suryagarh (literally 'Sun Fort') opened only in late 2010, since when it's become the first-choice luxury hotel in the region, combining the glitz of a five star with the style of a gorgeous boutique hideaway. If you can stretch to it, book the Jaisalmer Suite, which comes with its own private terrace, romantic plunge pool and exclusive desert views. ££££

Jodhpur

Ajit Bhawan Hotel
Opposite the Circuit House
Tel: 0291-251 3333
www.ajitbhawan.com
Ersatz village 'huts' grouped around a curvi-form pool behind the facade of a 19th-century royal palace, on the southern edge of town. They also offer luxury tents as cheaper alternatives to the roundhouses. ££££

Bal Samand Lake Palace
Off the Mandor Road, 8km (5 miles) north of town
Tel: 0291-257 2321
www.welcomheritagehotels.com
Former royal lakeside summer palace,

Looking out over Jodhpur, the blue city.

beautifully converted into one of the most gorgeous heritage hotels in the state. Set amid expansive gardens, with croquet lawns and a huge pool, the rooms come in two categories: if your budget can stretch to it, go for the suites in the main block. £££

Cosy Guest House
Novechokiya Road, Brahm Puri
Tel: 0291-261 2066
www.cosyguesthouse.com
Spread over a hamster-run of levels interconnected by external steps, this house, in the thick of Jodhpur's old city, is as blue as they come, and from its terraces the views over the cuboid rooftops below are wonderful. Its rooms are on the small side, and a touch overpriced, but clean and comfy, and both the location and warm hospitality are first-rate. £

Indrashan
593 High Court Colony, 3km (2 miles) south of town
Tel: 0291-244 0665
www.mahindrahomestays.com
Model homestay place in a smart suburb of the old city, with hospitable owners (who host internationally acclaimed cookery courses as a sideline). Just five rooms (all en suite). A bit of a trek from the centre, but correspondingly peaceful. ££

Hotel Karni Bhawan
Defence Lab. Road, Ratanada
Tel: 0291-251 2101
www.karnihotels.com
A charming 1940s sandstone bungalow with attractive rooms done out in homey local textiles. There is a lovely pool and dhani huts for dining

in the gardens. Excellent food and good value. ££–£££

Raas
Tunwarji ka Jhalara, Makrana Mohalla
Tel: 0291-263 6455
www.raasjodhpur.com
A fusion of traditional Rajput panache and global designer style, Raas is the last word in Indian boutique chic. Its 18th and 19th-century sandstone havelis have been fused with some cutting-edge interiors that wouldn't look out of place in LA. But this hotel's real USP is its location. From the poolside, you've an uninterrupted view of Meherangarh's fairy-tale fort-palaces lining the rim of the cliffs above. ££££

Rohetgarh
Off SH 64, Rohet, Pali
Tel: 02936-268 531
www.rohetgarh.com
Resting beside an idyllic lake 40km (25 miles) north of Jodhpur, Rohetgarh was one of Rajasthan's first true heritage hotels and has a great pedigree (it's where Bruce Chatwin stayed while he wrote Songlines, and where William Dalrymple holed up to write City of Djinns). Decorated and furnished in traditional style, the rooms are beautiful, fronted by semi-

PRICE CATEGORIES

Price categories are for a double room (A/C where available) in high season, including taxes:
£ = under Rs2,000
££ = Rs2,000–5,000
£££ = Rs5,000–10,000
££££ = over Rs10,000

circular verandahs where guests gaze through cusp-arched windows at wild peacocks in the lawned garden. They also run great equestrian safaris to visit local villages and wildlife spots. **££££**

Shahi
Gandhi Street, opposite Nursingh temple, Old City
Tel: 0291-262 3802
www.shahiguesthouse.net
Small, intimate guesthouse in a 350-year-old *haveli* overshadowed by the Meherangarh cliffs, deep in the blue city. Its rooms are simply furnished, but the terrace is a superb place to hang out, and the host family especially warm. Rickshaw-wallahs will tell you it's closed, or some such nonsense, because they don't get commission. **£–££**

Umaid Bhawan Palace
Tel: 0291-251 0101
www.tajhotels.com
A magnificent, ultra-luxurious hotel set in India's most spectacular Art Deco palace, the 347-room home of the Jodhpur royal family. Spacious rooms with original furniture, large gardens, restaurants and a superb underground pool. **££££**

Kota

Brijraj Bhawan Palace Hotel
Civil Lines
Tel: 0744-245 0529
www.indianheritagehotels.com
A former British Residency rising from the banks of the Chambal, now run by the royal family (who live on the top floor) as a pleasantly informal heritage hotel. Spacious rooms with their original Victorian furniture and antique prints on the walls overlook lush gardens, which fall away to the river. Most of the food served in the multi-cuisine restaurant is made from home-grown ingredients. All in all, exceptional value for money. **£££**

Umed Bhavan Palace
Station Road
Tel: 0744-232 5262
www.welcomheritagehotels.com
A palace built in 1905 and designed by the British architect Swinton Jacob. A splendid Indo-Sarcenic building a little way out of town with lovely Raj-era interiors, though it hasn't preserved its period feel as keenly as the Brijraj Bhawan. **£££**

Mount Abu

Cama Rajputana Club Resort
Adhar Devi Road
Tel: 02974-238 205
www.camahotelsindia.com
This former British club, dating from the 1870s, occupies a stalwart

granite building ensconced amid manicured grounds on the leafy northern fringe of the hill station. Its rooms are large and well aired, many of them opening onto verandas and lawns. Facilities include tennis courts, an antique billiards room and an exclusive outdoor pool. **££££**

Connaught House
Rajendra Marg
Tel: 02974-238 560
www.welcomheritagehotels.com
This British-era bungalow, which used to belong to the Prime Minister (Diwan) of Mewar (Jodhpur), has the edge over the competition thanks to its homely, compact scale, wonderful period architecture and understated decor. Nowhere else in the hill station conjours up the feel of British times as vividly, and the views are superb. **£££**

Jaipur House
Tel: 02974-235 176
www.hotelsmountabu.net
Enjoying a fabulous hilltop vantage point overlooking the town and lake, the Maharaja of Jaipur's former summer palace and hunting lodge retains heaps of colonial-era charm, with extensive views from its elegantly furnished rooms and salons. The furniture and decor are mostly original, and the walls plastered with evocative photos, prints and trophies. Avoid the overpriced modern wing further down the driveway if possible. **£££**

Palace Hotel (Bikaner House)
Dilwara Road
Tel: 02974-238 673
www.palacehotelbikanerhouse.com
Built in 1893 for the Raj of Bikaner by Sir Swinton Jacob, in stately mock-Scottish-baronial style, the Palace Hotel has its own private lake and tree-shaded grounds. Each of the 33 rooms and suites are individually styled, in keeping with the colonial period; some are positively vast. **£££**

Shri Ganesh Hotel
Near Sophia High School
Tel: 02974-237 292
Clean, efficient, friendly budget travellers' guesthouse on the outskirts of Mount Abu, with variously priced en-suite rooms, rooftop terrace and a good kitchen serving tasty Rajasthani curries and travellers' grub. Owners Lalit and his Irish wife offer Rajasthani cookery lessons and lead guided walks into the rocky terrain around the hill station. **£**

Nagaur

Ranvas
Nagaur Fort
Tel: 0291-2572321

www.ranvasnagaur.com
This fabulous hotel, midway between Jodhpur and Jaisalmer, occupies the former zenana (womens' quarters) of a medieval fort – a feast of delicately sculpted, salmon-coloured sandstone and interlocking courtyards. Inside, bougainvillea-pink silk cushions and indigo-blockprint bedspreads provide splashes of colour against the whitewashed walls and dark-wood furniture. You can lounge by a gorgeous courtyard pool and dine on gourmet Mughal-Sufi dishes, served by turbaned staff in a domed pavilion to a backdrop of tiny oil lamps. **££££**

Pushkar

Jagat Palace
Ajmer Road
Tel: 0145-277 2001
www.hotelpushkarpalace.com
Assembled from fragments of traditional Rajasthani houses, the Jagat Palace offers Pushkar's most luxurious, elegantly styled accommodation, in a pair of four-storeyed towers rising from the sandy edges of town. The interiors are a mass of intricate murals, mosaics, reproduction antique furniture and art. There's also a secluded pool, screened from prying eyes in its own walled garden, and fine views over Nag Pahar mountain from the rooftop terraces. **£££**

New Park
Panch Kund Road
Tel: 0145-277 2464
www.newparkpushkar.com
A secluded, modern, mid-scale place, set 4km (2.5 miles) out of town amid its own rose gardens, close to the hills. The marble-lined and tiled rooms on two storeys are all kept fastidiously clean and tidy, plus there is a small pool (residents only) and a couple of restaurants decorated with gorgeous local textiles. **£**

Pushkar Resorts
Motisar Road, Village Ganhera
Tel: 011-2649 4531
www.sewara.com
Out-of-town accommodation in attractive and comfortable cottages. Good pool and restaurant in extensive grounds. The helpful staff will arrange tours. **£££**

Seventh Heaven
Near Mali-ki-Mandir, Chotti Basti
Tel: 0145-510 5455
www.inn-seventh-heaven.com
Beautifully converted 100-year-old *haveli*, tucked away in the backstreets northeast of the lake, and a real haven for budget travellers. The lovingly decorated rooms, filled with crazy patchwork quilts and rugs, open onto

a Mughal arched courtyard centred around fountains and fruit trees, and you can lounge on swing chairs at a choice of raised terraces overlooking the rooftops. Meals are served in a snug second-storey restaurant. And the rates represent great value. Their sister concern, Dia, slightly out of town, is also recommended. **£**

Ranthambore National Park

Khem Vilas
Tel: 0941-403 0262
www.khemvilas.com
Brainchild of Ranthambore legend Goverdhan Singh Rathore and his wife, veggie chef Usha, Khem Vilas is a luxury camp with a difference. You can stay in individual thatched cottages with colonial-style interiors, private plunge pools and verandahs; opulent Rajasthani hunting tents; or conventional rooms. Either way, great forest views are standard, and a percentage of the profits go to innovative local development schemes. **££££**

Ranthambore Bagh
Ranthambore Road
Tel: 07462-221 728
www.ranthambhorebagh.com
There's a choice of either simple, tastefully decorated en suite rooms or luxury tents here, plus excellent food, a great atmosphere and one of Ranthambore's most convivial hosts. Dicky knows everything there is to know about tigers and the park, and if you're keen on photography this is the place to be. **££**

Sher Bagh
Park edge
Tel: 07462-252 119
www.sherbagh.com
Originally designed for the Maharaja of Jaipur and his guests' hunting expeditions, this forest-friendly camp has 12 luxury tents with attached bathrooms. The food is first-class, and the special evening talks with conservationists who have dedicated their lives to Ranthambore and its animals are a real treat. **££££**

Taj Sawai Madhopur Lodge
Tel: 07462-220 541
www.vivantabytaj.com
Managed by the five-star Taj chain, the former Art Deco hunting lodge of the Maharaja of Jaipur retains plenty of 1930s charm. Both rooms and suites are spacious, featuring private courtyard gardens where bonfires blaze in the evenings, and there's a lovely pool in the garden. A luxurious base for tiger-spotting trips into the adjacent forest. **££££**

Tiger Safari
Ranthambore Road
Tel: 07462-221 137
www.tigersafariresort.com
Most of Sawai Madhopur's budget accommodation leaves a lot to be desired, so it is worth splashing out a little more than you might normally for a room in this friendly, comfortable mid-range hotel, 4km (2.5 miles) from the train station on the way to the park. Its centrepiece is a well-tended garden, and there's a breezy rooftop terrace restaurant offering fine forest views. **£**

Samode

Samode Palace and Bagh
Tel: 01423-240 014/240 235
www.samode.com
A sister concern of the Samode Haveli, this country palace of Jai Singh II's finance minister was built on a much grander scale than his town house, and is the main attraction of this small village. Towering above a warren of cobbled streets, it is a fairytale Rajput pile, with interconnected courtyards on several levels, a lavishly decorated Durbar Hall and Sheeh Mahal mirror pavilion. The rooms are luxurious and beautifully furnished, and it has a great pool. Excellent service and a fine attention to detail; 3km (2 miles) from Samode village is the cheaper Bagh ('garden'). Run by the owners of the palace, accommodation is in luxury 'tents', with attached bath, set in beautiful gardens. Lovely swimming pool. **££££**

Shekhavati

Apani Dhani
Nawalgarh (Samode village, 50km/30 miles north of Jaipur)
Tel: 01594-222 239
www.apanidhani.com
Low-impact eco-resort of traditional mud and thatch huts, fitted out with Western amenities (including miraculously odourless compost loos) around a bougainvillea-filled central yard. Most of the produce used in the kitchen comes from their own organic garden. **££**

Hotel Castle Mandawa
Mandawa
Tel: 0141-371 194
www.castlemandawa.com
Castle Mandawa has tastefully furnished heritage rooms, in an 18th-century, high-walled fortress, centred on a large, sandy courtyard where nightly shows of local folk dances and music are staged most evenings. **£££**

Narayan Niwas Castle
Mahansar
Tel: 01595-264 322
www.mehansarcastle.com
One of Rajasthan's quirkier, more down-to-earth heritage hotels, in a labyrinthine mansion still occupied by the 'royal family'. It has a dozen rooms of various sizes, from simple backpackers' cells to 'Arabian Nights' suites with old carved wood doors and windows – all at affordable prices; book No. 1 if it's available. Excellent food. **£**

Roop Niwas Palace
Nawalgarh
Tel: 01594-222 008
www.roopniwaskothi.com
A colonial-era mansion holding pleasantly old-fashioned rooms, decorated with authentic furniture, old photos and block-printed wall hangings. The gardens are lovely, and there is a good restaurant and pool. Friendly service. **££**

Shekhawati Guest House
Near the Roop Niwas Palace, Nalwalgarh
Tel: 01594-224 658
www.shekhawatirestaurant.com
This delightful guesthouse tries to limit its environmental impact, and the restaurant serves excellent vegetarian food, mostly using organic, home-grown ingredients. The rooms are in the rather dingy main building or in brighter cottages in the garden. **£**

Udaipur

Amet Haveli
Hanuman Ghat
Tel: 0294-243 1085
www.amethaveliudaipur.com
Exquisite 350-year-old *haveli* with romantic rooms, whose carpeted window seats look through delicate arches across Pichola Lake to the City Palace and Lal Ghat – Udaipur's trademark view. A prime spot, with architecture and service that do it justice. The hotel also hosts a top-notch restaurant, Ambrai. **£££**

Devi Garh
Delvara, Nathdvara
Tel: 02953-289 211
www.deviresorts.in
This magnificent 18th-century fort, an hour's drive north of Udaipur, has been converted in a cool, minimalist style, fusing modern furnishings with

PRICE CATEGORIES

Price categories are for a double room (A/C where available) in high season, including taxes:
£ = under Rs2,000
££ = Rs2,000–5,000
£££ = Rs5,000–10,000
££££ = over Rs10,000

antique stonework. The views over the surrounding countryside are dreamy, and facilities (including an ayurvedic spa, gourmet restaurant and heated outdoor pool) are top-notch. One of India's benchmark hotels, with tariffs to match. **££££**

Fateh Garh
Sisarma
Tel: 0869-694 5101
www.fatehgarh.in
Wonderful new boutique hotel on the outskirts, which surveys the whitewashed palaces of the lake city from a hilltop swathed in mustard fields. The vistas are loveliest from the hotel's infinity pool. Antique materials feature prominently in the main building, where the rooms are suave and minimalist, with dark woods, pale marble and silk upholstery. **££££**

Hotel Hilltop Palace
5 Ambavgarh, Fatehsagar
Tel: 0294-243 2245
www.udaipurhotelhilltoppalace.com
An efficient, modern hotel with comfortable rooms and friendly staff. Great views and decent food from the rooftop restaurant. **£££**

Jaiwana Haveli
14 Lal Ghat
Tel: 0294-241 1103
www.jaiwanahaveli.com
Terrific value accommodation in a historic lakeside *haveli* hotel that enjoys a plum position on the waterfront. The rooms are all gleaming, and from the rooftop restaurant you get an unrivalled view across the lake to the palaces and distant Aravalli Hills. **££**

Kankarwa Haveli
26 Lal Ghat
Tel: 0294-241 1457
www.kankarwahaveli.com
The rooms inside this old *haveli*, located on the lakeside next to the Jagat Niwas Palace, are straight off the pages of an interiors magazine, with bolsters, patchwork wall-hangings and carpeted sitting platforms. Superb value for money, and they offer some budget options with the same decor but minus the lake views. **££**

Lalghat Guest House
33 Lalghat
Tel: 0294-252 5301
www.lalghat.com
A well-known budget travellers' haunt that's showing signs of age but retains its romantic feel thanks to an unrivalled position on the ghats. A wide range of rooms and dormitory beds are on offer, some with attached baths; snacks are available on the terrace, from which views extend through Mughal arched windows onto the water. **£**

Shiv Niwas
City Palace
Tel: 0294-252 8016
www.hrhindia.com
The Rana of Udaipur's former guest wing rivals the Lake Palace as Udaipur's most swanky address. While the standard rooms aren't particularly special, the pricier suites, jammed with silver furniture, Persian carpets and original 17th-century murals, are the last word in Rajput splendour (some even have their own fountains). **££££**

Taj Lake Palace Hotel
Pichola Lake
Tel: 0294-242 8800
www.tajhotels.com
Few luxury hotels in the world can claim as irresistible a position as this one, slap in the middle of Pichola Lake. When water levels are low, you have to squelch there by camel, otherwise launches ferry guests to the boat jetty of the palace: a fantasy of whitewashed Mughal domes and arches, stained glass, twinkling mirror work and expensive textiles. It even has a pool inside, shaded by a stately old mango tree. **££££**

Udaivilas
Haridasji ki Magri
Tel: 0294-243 3300
www.oberoihotels.com
Oberoi Udai Vilas, Udaipur
Just when you thought Rajasthani palace hotels couldn't get any more opulent, Oberoi build the Udaivilas. Set amid verdant countryside on the western shores of Lake Pichola, the building was designed as modern take on traditional Rajput splendour, and for once delivers without a trace of pastiche. The interiors are crammed with traditional arts and crafts: murals, marble inlay, wood carving and mirror work. Some of the luxury suites even have their own private pools. Most lovely of all, though, are the grounds – a dreamscape of interconnecting courtyards, watercourses and lawns that look especially gorgeous at night, illuminated by flickering lanterns. **££££**

GUJARAT

Ahmedabad

Hotel Royal Highness
Near Roopali Cinema, Ahmedabad
Tel: 079- 2550 7450
www.hotelroyalhighness.com
This recently built, business-oriented place in the city centre offers a range of bright, spacious and comfortable rooms, with impeccably clean bathrooms and some whacky retro interior decor. There's a multi-cuisine restaurant and 24-hr coffee shop. **££–£££**

The House of Mangaldas Girdhardas
Opposite the Sidi Sayid Mosque
Tel: 079-2550 6946
www.houseofmg.com
This heritage-boutique hotel in a 20th-century *haveli* has a range of beautifully refurbished room and

suites – all very elegant, with four-posters and floaty mosquito nets. Also in the building is an indoor pool and health club, and a choice of fine dining. **£££–££££**

Taj Residency Ummed
International Airport Circle, Hansol
Tel: 079-6666 1234
www.tajhotels.com
Located on the outskirts close to the airport, this is Ahmedabad's top business hotel: a swish, modern, efficient and with a large outdoor pool. The rooms are pleasant, overlooking the green belt, and there are several multi-cuisine restaurants. **££££**

Volga
Lal Darwaza, off Relief Road
Tel: 079-2550 9497
Among the snappiest, brightest

mid-range options in the city, in thick of the action near Siddi Saiyad's mosque. **£**

Bhavnagar

Nilambag Palace
Tel: 0278-242 4241
www.nilambagpalace.com
A charming heritage hotel, formerly the royal palace, dating from 1859, with large, comfortable A/C rooms, beautiful gardens and an outdoor, rather kitsch, Roman-style swimming pool surrounded by woodland. **£££**

Bhuj

Gangaram
Behind the Aina Mahal
Tel: 02832-222 948
The best of a generally ropey bunch of hotels in Bhuj, run with great

enthusiasm by the amiable Mr Jethi. Gangaram occupies the lower floors of a modern tower block, just behind the palace, it was virtually the only structure left standing after the 2001 earthquake. The rooms (all attached) are basic, but well scrubbed and well aired, and there is a small in-house kitchen serving delicious Gujarati and Bengali food. **£–££**

Daman

Hotel Gurukripa
Seaface Road
Tel: 0260-645 2494
www.hotelgurukripa.com
The best in town. Good rooms, roof garden, bar and good restaurant serving seafood, tandoori and Chinese dishes. **£–££**

Diu

Hotel Samrat
Collectorate Road
Tel: 02875-252 354
www.hotelsamratdiu.com
The most comfortable option in Diu. A/C rooms with bath and balcony, and a good restaurant. **£–££**

Sanmaan Palace
Fort Road
Tel: 02875- 253 031
An old Portuguese house with oodles of old-world charm close to the main market area. Go for a room in the main building, and grab a table on the rooftop terrace restaurant for a view over the waterfront at sundown. **£**

Sao Tomé Retiro
Next to Diu Museum, Firangi Wada
Tel: 02875-253 137
Laid-back pension housed in a former church (with great panoramic views from the top of the tower). You can crash in huts on the roof, or in breezy doubles opening onto the Old Town. Host George D'Souza hosts regular barbecues of home-cooked, Portuguese-style seafood. **£**

Little Rann of Kutch

Rann Riders
Dasada
Tel: 02757-280 257
www.rannriders.com
Comprising well-equipped, kutchi-style kooba huts grouped around a pool and dining are, this hotel offers a/c comfort on the edge of the Rann – a true oasis. Packages include meals and safaris to the Wild Ass Sanctuary. **£££**

Sasan Gir

Gir Birding Lodge
Bambhafod Naka, Sasan,
Gujarat
Tel: 02877-2630 2019
www.girnationalpark.com
Pleasant, well-maintained accommodation set in a mango orchard close to the entrance of the Sasan Gir sanctuary. Enthusiastic, knowledgeable management and staff. **££–£££**

MUMBAI

Accord
Nehru Road, Santa Cruz (East)
Tel: 022-2611 0560
www.hotelaccordindia.com
Dependable budget hotels close to the airport are as rare as hen's teeth, which is why the Accord tends to be booked weeks in advance. Neither the roadside location nor the rooms are anything to write home about, but everything's well scrubbed and well maintained, the staff efficient and bookings can be made online. **££**

Ascot
38 Garden Road
Tel: 022-6638 5566
www.ascothotel.com
Spruce, stylish three-star hotel that offers great value in its bracket, with most of the mod cons you'd expect (including in-room internet access and safe deposits), though no pool. It's close to the action in Colaba, but tucked away down a quiet side street. **£££–££££**

Bentley's Hotel
17 Oliver Road, Colaba
Tel: 022-2284 1474
www.bentleyshotel.com
Bentley's is an institution in Mumbai which divides opinion among travellers. Some love its faded, old-world, worn-out charm; others consider it a rip off. Either way, it's one of the few affordable choices in this busy tourist enclave – and the location can't be beaten. Rates include breakfast. **£–££**

City Palace
121 City Terrace
Tel: 022-2261 5515
www.hotelcitypalace.net
Right opposite CST (VT) railway station, and clean enough, though its cheaper rooms lack windows – rather like a Japanese capsule hotel. A/C available. Convenient if you need to catch an early morning train – though its competitive tariffs and handy location ensure it's usually booked well in advance. **££**

Hotel Godwin
41 Garden Road, Colaba
Tel: 022-2287 2050
www.hotelgodwin.co.in
International-standard three-star in a good location, with great views from its upper rooms (ask for 804, 805 or 806). There's a rooftop terrace restaurant and well stocked bar. **£££**

Grand
17 Shri S.R. Marg, Ballard Estate
Tel: 022-5658 0500
www.grandhotelbombay.com
Charming old colonial-style hotel near the docks. It is one of the few places to have preserved an authentic pre-Independence atmosphere, and offers good value in its bracket. **£££**

Harbour View
Kerawalla Chambers, 25 P.J. Ramchandani Marg
Tel: 022-2284 1197
www.viewhotelsindia.com
At an unbeatable location on Apollo Bunder, the hotel has enormous rooms with some wonderful views, although these come at a premium. Some of the cheaper rooms aren't great, but the rooftop restaurant ranks among the most relaxing places to hang out in the city. **££££**

Intercontinental
135 Marine Drive
Tel: 022-3987 9999
www.mumbai.intercontinental.com
Ultra-slick boutique hotel fitted out with designer furniture, in-room broadband, plasma-screen TVs and other up-to-the-minute gadgets. The views over Back Bay from its sea-facing suites are superb; plus there's a fashionable terrace restaurant on the roof, and a very hip vodka bar on the ground floor. **££££** southeast Asian restaurant. It's also only a short drive from the airport. **££££**

Lawrence
3rd Floor, 33 Rope Walk Lane
Tel: 022-2284 3618
Opposite the Jehangir Art Gallery, this is a small, family-run hotel with only a handful of basic, non-a/c rooms

PRICE CATEGORIES

Price categories are for a double room (A/C where available) in high season, including taxes:
£ = under Rs2,000
££ = Rs2,000–5,000
£££ = Rs5,000–10,000
££££ = over Rs10,000

with shared bathroom, but they're always well scrubbed. Very popular (mainly with foreign backpackers) so reservations are essential. **£**

Marine Plaza
29 Marine Drive
Tel: 022-2285 1212
www.hotelmarineplaza.com
Overlooking the bay, this Art Deco-style five-star is famous for its glass-bottomed rooftop pool. With luxurious rooms and all the usual facilities, it's a good choice if you want the comfort but find larger five-star hotels too impersonal. **££££**

Midland
Jawaharlal Nehru Road, Santa Cruz East
Tel: 022-2611 0413
www.hotelmidland.com
Among the few reliable midrange hotels within striking distance of the airports. Room rates include a courtesy bus to and from the airports and breakfast. **££–£££**

Moti International
10 Best Marg
Tel: 022-2202 1654 or 022-2202 5714
hotelmotiinternational@yahoo.com.in
Small, friendly budget hotel, with a range of inexpensive rooms (from simple bathroom-less doubles to large A/C suites) in a colonial-era building. They're cool, quiet and clean (if showing signs of age) and the management is welcoming. **£**

New Bengal
Dr D.N. Marg
Tel: 022-2340 1951
www.hotelnewbengal.com
A good economy option if you want to be in the thick of things, close to Crawford Market and central Mumbai, but only a short taxi ride from Colaba. Aimed at visiting businessmen on low budgets, the accommodation is decidedly no-frills, ranging from low-ceilinged, airless dorms to more spacious A/C doubles. This is not somewhere for a long stay, but it's clean and safe. **£–££**

Orchid
70-C Nehru Road, Vile Parle East
Tel: 022-2616 4040
www.orchidhotel.com
Ground-breaking eco-five-star close to the international airport whose every feature, from the swimming pool right down to the laundry service and coathangers, has been designed to minimise environmental impact. **££££**

Regent
8 Best Road
Tel: 022-2287 1854
www.regenthotelcolaba.com
Efficient, modern place just off Colaba Causeway whose fully en suite, A/C rooms are on the small side, but perfectly comfortable, with soundproofed windows. **££££**

Residency
26 Rustom Sidhwa Marg, D.N. Road
Tel: 022-2262 5525
www.residencyhotel.com
The best-value mid-range place in the city centre, and correspondingly popular. Its standard rooms, all fully air-conditioned, soundproofed and en suite, are a steal for this area, but you'll have to book weeks ahead. **££**

Salvation Army Red Shield Hostel
Red Shield House, 30 Mereweather Road, Colaba
Tel: 022-2284 1824
Behind the Taj Mahal Hotel. Double rooms and (much cheaper) dormitories. Lockers and meals are available. Institutional and run-down, but you won't find a cheaper bed anywhere, and it's more secure than the druggy dives nearby. **£**

Sea Green South
145a Marine Drive
Tel: 022-2282 2294
www.seagreenhotel.com
Hotel in glamorous location with great views, though now showing its age. Most of the large and airy rooms have A/C and are well appointed. **££**

Sea Palace
Kerawalla Chambers, 26 P.J. Ramchandani Marg
Tel: 022-6112 8000
www.seapalacehotel.net
Old-fashioned hotel in a rather grand building facing the seafront where the P&O steamers used to tie up. The rooms, which a reasonably priced for the seafront location, are showing signs of wear, but equipped with internet connections, fridges and cable TVs as standard; there's a multi-cuisine restaurant. **£££**

Sea Princess
Tara Road, Juhu
Tel: 022-2661 1111
www.seaprincess.com
Most appealing among the rank of swish five-star hotels backing on to Juhu Beach with pleasantly furnished rooms and a small pool. Only a 30-minute drive from the airport. **££££**

Sea Shore
4th Floor, 1–49 Kamal Mansion, Arthur Bunder Road
Tel: 022-2287 4237
The most dependable and secure of the rock-bottom-budget hotels in Colaba. Only half of its rooms have windows and none are en suite, but everything is kept spick-and-span (it had a makeover in 2011) and the management is unfailingly courteous. Handy safe-deposit and left-luggage facilities available. **£**

Strand Hotel
30 P.J. Ramchandani Marg, Colaba Sea Face
Tel: 022-2288 2222
www.hotelstrand.com
At a prime location on the seafront, this old Art Deco place is one of the better value options in Colaba, though its rooms are in desperate need of a face lift these days. Avoid unless the others listed in this class are full. **£££**

Svenska Design Hotel
SAB TV Road, off Link Road, Andheri West
Tel: 022-4431 0000
www.svenskahotels.com
Inspired by Swedish interior design concepts, this luxury boutique hotel in the burgeoning north-central suburb of Andheri makes a relaxing base, close to the airports. The handsomely furnished rooms are wood floored and have soothing clean lines, as well as iPod docking stations and dedicated butler service. A Mediterranean restaurant provides quality in-house dining. **££££**

The Taj Mahal Palace and Tower
P.J. Ramchandani Marg
Tel: 022-6665 3366
www.tajhotels.com
Located opposite the Gateway of India, the country's most illustrious hotel has bounced back after the terror attack of 2010, when a large portion of it was destroyed by fire. The refurbishment has been a triumph. Both the old and new (tower block) wings are as glamorous as ever. Top notch restaurants and bar, and a great outdoor pool. **££££**

The Waterstones
Across the road from The Leela Mumbai, Andheri East
Tel: 022-4090 6633
www.waterstoneshotel.com
Revamped and rebranded in 2012, the Waterstones holds 89 stylish, spacious rooms with cutting-edge designer interiors and furniture, but owes its success to the fact guests get the run of the adjacent clubhouse, with its outdoor pool, movie lounge, state-of-the-art fitness centre and gastro bistro. **££££**

YWCA International Guest House
18 Madam Cama Road, Fort
Tel: 022-2202 5053
www.ywcaic.info
A good place to stay for both women and men. Very clean and safe rooms and dormitories. Rates include Rs50 temporary membership, breakfast and dinner. Make a reservation with deposit (by international money order) well in advance. **£**

MAHARASHTRA

Aurangabad

Lemon Tree
Chikaltana, Airport Road
This bright, cheerful new chain hotel on the city's outskirts offers blissfully cool, spacious and attractively furnished rooms spread around a magnificent pool. All the style and comfort of a five-star at a fraction of the price. So nice you'll find it hard to drag yourself into the heat and around the caves. **£££**

Panchavati
Off Station Road West, Padampura
Tel: 0240-232 8755
www.hotelpanchavati.com
A well-run, lower mid-scale place on the western edge of Aurangabad's centre, opposite the YHA. The best option in its bracket as it's cleaner than the competition, and more welcoming. **£**

Taj Residency
Ajanta Road
Tel: 0240-661 3737
www.tajhotels.com
A predictably plush hotel with large rooms, 8km (5 miles) out of town. Lovely gardens and pool, and excellent restaurant. **££££**

Lonavala

Ferreira Resort
D. Shahani Road, Ward C, near Telephone Exchange
Tel: 02114-272 689
A five-minute rickshaw ride from the train station, set in a peaceful backstreet, with large, clean rooms, attached bathrooms and balconies. Transport to the caves may be arranged on request. **£**

Matheran

Lord's Central
M.G. Road
Tel: 02148-230 228
www.matheranhotels.com
Little seems to have changed at Lord's since its 1930s heyday, down to the custard pudding desserts and plaid blankets on the beds. Spectacular views extend from the garden (where there's a small pool). The rooms are dowdier than you might expect for the price, but that's all part of the appeal. Full board is obligatory. **££–£££**

The Verandah in the Forest
2km (1.25 miles) southwest of the station, above Charlotte Lake
Tel: 02148-230 296
www.neemranahotels.com
Beautifully restored 19th-century bungalow filled with gorgeous period decor and furnishings. Its huge veranda literally looks through the forest canopy and is a delightful spot for afternoon tea (though beware of the thieving monkeys). **£££**

Admiring the view at Matheran.

Pune

Happy Home
294 Koregaon Park
Tel: 020-2612 2933
happyhomehostel@yahoo.co.im
Pune's best budget option. The rooms are clean and have attached bathrooms and balconies. **££**

Samrat
17 Wilson Garden, opposite railway station
Tel: 020-2613 7964
thesamrathotel@vsnl.com
Air-conditioned tower block, whose spacious, impeccably clean rooms are ranged around a central atrium. Unbeatable value in this bracket, and very close to the station. **££££**

Surya Villa
284/1 Koregaon Park
Tel: 020-2612 4501
www.hotelsuryavilla.com
Pleasant en suite rooms spread in a quiet suburban backstreet near Osho Ashram. **££**

MADHYA PRADESH

Bandhavgarh National Park

Bandhavgarh Jungle Lodge
Umaria
Tel: 011-2685 3760
www.tiger-resorts.com
A complex of ersatz Rajasthani mud-brick cottages set in pleasant grounds with a central dining area. Located very close to the park entrance. Nature tours and excursions can be arranged through the lodge. **££££**

Camp Mewar On Ketkiya
Tala
Tel: 011-2757 0446
www.tigersafariindia.com
On the boundary of the tiger reserve, this exclusive camp of traditional aodhi hunting cottages, thatched huts and sumptuously furnished safari tents raised on stone plinths is the last word in safari style and comfort. **££££**

Bhopal

Noor-us-Sabah Palace
V.I.P. Road, Kho-e-Fiza
Tel: 0755-422 3333
www.noorussabahpalace.com
A luxury heritage hotel occupying a 1920s palace. The rooms, some with a lake view, are beautifully furnished and there are three restaurants, one on a terrace where you're serenaded with live Indian classical music. **£££–££££**

Hotel Sonali Regency
Radha Talkies Road, off Hamidia Road
Tel: 0755-274 0880

PRICE CATEGORIES

Price categories are for a double room (A/C where available) in high season, including taxes:
£ = under Rs2,000
££ = Rs2,000–5,000
£££ = Rs5,000–10,000
££££ = over Rs10,000

TRANSPORT

ACCOMMODATION

ACTIVITIES

A – Z

LANGUAGE

www.hotelsoanliregency.com
A brisk, modern, efficient and clean hotel slap in the centre. The best budget option in the city. **£**

Gwalior

Hotel Shelter
Padav, opposite Indian Airlines
Tel: 0751-237 6209
www.hotelshelter.in
A modern hotel with clean A/C rooms and a good restaurant. Good value and close to the railway station. **££**

Usha Kiran Palace
Jayendraganj, Lakshar
Tel: 0751-244 4000
www.tajhotels.com
This was formerly the maharaja's guesthouse, but is now a luxury heritage hotel owned by the Taj Group. It has retained its historic splendour but is equipped with all modern facilities. **££££**

Indore

Hotel President
163 R.N.T. Marg
Tel: 0731-252 8866
www.hotelpresidentindore.com
A ritzy, mid-budget hotel with a good vegetarian restaurant. The A/C rooms are comfortable, and there is a pool and health club. **££**

Rashid Kothi
22 Yeshwant Niwas Road
Tel: 0731-243 4377
Delightful homestay in an elegant 1940s suburban house, set in gardens filled with neem trees, frangipani flowers and jasmine bushes, 2km (1¼ miles) northeast of the city centre. **££££**

Kanha National Park

Earth Lodge
Tel: 0124-422 2657
www.kanhaearthlodge.com
Locally sourced materials and labour were used extensively in the construction of this beautiful new resort, set at a distance from the main tourist hub at Kahna, yet close to the park gates. Exposed stone, split-cane and earthy hues dominate the luxurious interiors, decorated with tribal textiles and metalwork. There's also a lovely infinity pool, set under leafy mahua trees, and the food is top notch. **££££**

Kipling Camp
Morcha Village, Kisli, Mandla 481 768
Tel: 07649-277 218
www.kiplingcamp.com
Charming accommodation in cosy two- to four-room cottages, each with its own verandah offering views of the camp and the surrounding forest. The staff are expert naturalists,

the wildlife-watching is excellent and the resident elephant, Tara, one of India's most famous pachyderms (she was the heroine of Mark Shand's hit travelogue Travels On My Elephant). **££££**

MPTDC Lodges
Bhagira Log Huts, Mukki; Tourist Hostel, Kisli; Kanha Safari Lodge, Mukki
Tel: 07649-277 227; Kanha Safari Lodge 07637-226 029
www.mptourism.com
A range of simple but clean and decent accommodation, from dormitories to double rooms. All of the lodges have restaurants, and offer exceptional value for money given the high tariffs elsewhere in the park. **£–££**

Royal Tiger Resort
Mukki 481 111, Balaghat
Tel: 011-2237 3389
www.royaltiger.com
Locally inspired cottages in large, wooded grounds. Good amenities, including excellent, locally grown organic food. **££££**

Shergarh
Bahmi village
Tel: 0909-818 7346
www.shergarh.com
Extremely well run and professional camp, with knowledgeable guides and comfortable, eco-friendly accommodation in luxury tents. **££££**

Khajuraho

The Lalit Temple View
Opposite Circuit House
Tel: 07686-272 111
The only luxury hotel in Khajuraho boasting a view of the temples themselves – you actually gaze at the carved towers of the Western Group from the garden. The building itself is on a modest scale by five-star standards, though the interiors are unstintingly glamorous, while the clover-shaped outdoor pool provides a relaxing escape from the heat. Bikes are available for rent should you wish to shake loose and explore the quieter, outlying sites. **££££**

Siddarth
Opposite the Western Group, Main Road
Tel: 07686-274 627
One of the few budget places that can boast temple views from its balconies – and the roof terrace restaurant makes the most of the location. The rooms are a good size for the price, and well furnished, with bath tubs and 24hr hot water. **£**

Surya
Jain Temples Road
Tel: 07686-274 145
www.hotelsuryakhajuraho.com
The best budget option in Khajuraho, offering large, well-aired rooms,

all freshly whitewashed and with balconies overlooking the grounds. Free yoga sessions are held each morning, and there's broadband internet access on site. Credit cards accepted. **£**

Taj Chandela
Airport Road
Tel: 07686-272 355
www.tajhotels.com
Favoured by tour groups, and with all the class you'd expect from a Taj Group hotel, with a huge outdoor pool, swish restaurants, coffee shops and glittering souvenir arcades. **££££**

Maheshwar

Ahilya Fort
Maheshwar
Tel: 011-4155 1575 (Delhi)
www.ahilyafort.com
A real gem of a heritage hotel, hidden in a pilgrimage town on the north banks of the Narmada. The former palace, built of ornately carved, honey-coloured sandstone, has been exquisitely restored. From its traditionally furnished rooms, draped with locally woven silk, you can lounge on bolsters and gaze through delicate cusp-arched windows across the river. **£££**

Mandu

MPTDC Tourist Cottages
2km (1¼ miles) south of main square
Tel: 07292-263 235
www.mptourism.com
Pleasant, spacious rooms with bath and a view of the Sagar Talao Tank. There is also a nice open-air restaurant. Book in advance. **£**

MPTDC Traveller's Lodge
Near the SADA barrier
Tel: 07292-263 221
www.mptourism.com
Clean, pleasantly furnished rooms with a good view and a small restaurant. Book in advance. **£**

Hotel Rupmati
Main Rd
Tel: 07292-263 270
The rooms in this small midrange place, a short walk from the Royal Enclave, are average, but the views over the adjacent ravine are superb. Enjoy them over dinner on the lawn – they serve some of the tastiest food in central India. Bargain rates, too. **£**

Sanchi

MPTDC Traveller's Lodge
Bhopal Road
Tel: 07592-262 723
www.mptourism.com
The best option: clean, simple rooms, a decent restaurant, and lovely gardens. Book in advance. **£**

GOA

Agonda

H2O
Agonda Beach
Tel: 0832-264 7143
www.h2oagonda.com
A boutique hut camp, complete with funky black-painted chalets with red-tiled roofs and silk cushions, slap on the beach – though you pay handsomely for the hip decor and prime location. **£££**

Palm Beach Lifestyle Resort
Agonda Beach
Tel: 0832-264 7783
www.palmbeachgoa.com
Wood-floored chalets on a low hillside overlooking the beach. Relaxing, impeccably clean and well run: the most comfortable option in this unspoilt village in the deep south. **££**

Anjuna

Anjuna Beach Resort
De Mello Vaddo
Tel: 0832-227 4499
www.anjunabeachresort.com
Comfortable rooms with attached baths, some A/C, all of which have balconies overlooking the garden. There is also an outdoor, palm thatched, restaurant. Good discounts are available in low season. **£–££**

Casa Anjuna
D'Mello Waddo
Tel: 0832-227 4123
www.casaboutiquehotels.com
Beautiful boutique hotel occupying a converted 200-year-old *palácio*. Fitted with Indo-Portuguese-style furniture, tile work and textiles, the interiors are gorgeous, and so are the garden and roof terrace (the latter doubles as a residents-only restaurant). There's also a large outdoor pool. **£££**

Granpa's Inn
Gaun Waddo, Anjuna
Tel: 0832-227 3270
www.granpasinn.com
The pleasant rooms of this hotel are set around the bougainvillea-filled courtyard of an old Portuguese mansion. The hotel is friendly and well run, with a good restaurant and pool. Great value. **££–£££**

Laguna Anjuna
De Mello Waddo
Tel: 0832-227 4131
www.lagunaanjuna.com
Designed by prominent local architect Dean D'Cruz, the resort consists of spacious villas, each one different, set amid palm trees. A very attractive pool is set in lush gardens. The price drops considerably during the monsoon. **££–£££**

Peaceland
Soronto Waddo, Anjuna
Tel: 0832-227 3700
Anjuna's best-value budget place, with clean, well-aired rooms fitted with mosquito nets and backpack racks. The couple who run it are very hospitable. It's a 15-minute walk to the seafront, in one of the quieter corners of the village. **£**

Villa Anjuna
Near Anjuna beachfront, Anjuna
Tel: 0832-227 3443
www.anjunavilla.com
Modern, well-run hotels are a rarity in Anjuna; this one is closer to the beach than any of the competition, and has a pool and gym, but it's also only a stone's throw away from Club Paradiso's thumping sound system (the reason most of its clientele stay here). **££**

Yoga Magic
www.yogamagic.net
Funky canvas 'ecotel', set back in the paddy fields around 1km (0.5 mile) inland, run by British yoga crew. The 'tents' (the term doesn't nearly do the bamboo-and-thatch lodges justice) are text-book hippy chic inside: all silk curtains and cushions, with low beds to lounge on while the fans whir overhead. There's also a gorgeous pool. **££**

Baga

Nilaya Hermitage
On a hillside 3km (2 miles) inland
Tel: 0832-227 6793
www.nilaya.com
Very exclusive, with 12 uniquely designed rooms in a startling building. The slightly new-agey interiors have lots of organic curves, and there is a wonderful pool out front. Hideously expensive over Christmas but half-price in low season. **££££**

Villa Fatima
Baga Road, Baga
Tel: 0832-227 7418
Popular backpackers' hotel in the thick of Baga's busy strip, only a short stroll across the dunes from the sea. Fifty clean, en suite rooms (single, double and family-sized) at low rates for the area. **£**

Benaulim

Heaven Goa
1 Sernabatim
Tel: 0832-275 8442
This Swiss-Keralan-run place comprises a block of a dozen simply furnished rooms opening on to a leafy lily pond, around 10 minutes' walk

from the beach. The beds are comfy and bathrooms spotless, and they serve succulent wood-fired pizzas in the sociable garden area to the rear. Great value. **£**

Palm Grove
Tamdi Marti, Vas Vaddo
Tel: 0834-277 5509
www.palmgrovegoa.com
Surrounded by a lovely garden, this is a clean, atmospheric and pleasant place to stay. The restaurant serves mainly Goan dishes and seafood. **££**

Succorina
1711/A Vas Waddo
Tel: 0832-277 0365
A homely little guesthouse on the south side of the village, next to the fishing quarter. It's clean, welcoming and barely five minutes' walk across empty paddy fields to the beach – although it's a bicycle or scooter ride to the village shops and restaurants. **£**

Taj Exotica
Cal Waddo
Tel: 0832-668 3333
www.tajhotels.co
Along with the Park Hyatt, this is Goa's flagship luxury hotel: a low-rise palace set amid 22 hectares (56 acres) of lush gardens and flower-filled patios right next to the beach. The facilities of this award-winning complex include a golf course, ayurvedic spa, four restaurants and kids' clubs. **££££**

Bogmalo Beach

Coconut Creek Resort
Bimmut
Tel: 0832-255 6100
www.coconutcreekgoa.com
This complex of double-storeyed chalets, built with laterite and old-style terracotta tiled roofs around a lagoon-shaped pool, ranks among south Goa's most desirable places to stay. As a base for trips further down the coast, it's a stylish and convenient option, though Bogmalo beach itself is no great shakes. **££**

Calangute

Pousada Tauma
Porba Vaddo

PRICE CATEGORIES

Price categories are for a double room (A/C where available) in high season, including taxes:
£ = under Rs2,000
££ = Rs2,000–5,000
£££ = Rs5,000–10,000
££££ = over Rs10,000

TRANSPORT

ACCOMMODATION

ACTIVITIES

A – Z

LANGUAGE

Tel: 0832-227 9061
www.pousada-tauma.com
Ultra-stylish boutique hotel
constructed entirely from local red
laterite. The decor's low-key and the
pool magical, with waterfalls and teak
loungers scattered around a relaxing
sun terrace. Also has a top-notch
ayurvedic spa. **££££**

Candolim

Aashyana Lakanpal
Sequeira Waddo
Tel: 0832-248 9335
www.aashyanalakhanpal.com
Très exclusive boutique hotel hidden
under the palms at the north end
of Candolim Beach, featuring eye-
poppingly pricy five-bedroom villas or
more affordable 'casinhas' (cottages),
ranged around a divine diamond-
shaped pool. An army of masseurs,
gourmet chefs and liveried butlers
man the pumps. Recent A-list guests
include Kate Moss, Daniel Craig and
Mick Jagger. **££££**
Casa Seashell
Fort Aguada Road
Tel: 0832-247 9879
www.seashellgoa.com
A conveniently located place with a
small pool. The rooms are large and
clean with gbalconies and quality
bathrooms, and the restaurant is
recommended for its seafood. **££**
Shanu
Sequeria Waddo
Tel: 0832-227 9606
Well-kept rooms in a great location
– right on the most peaceful stretch
of Candolim beach. Reasonable
tariffs, although it's quite a walk to
the main strip without some form of
transport. **£**

Cavelossim

Dona Sa Maria
Tamborim Vaddo
Tel: 0834-274 5290
www.donasamaria.com
This small, friendly place is good
value. Helpful service and simple but
clean rooms, and there is a swimming
pool in the peaceful grounds. **££**

Mandrem

Elsewhere/Otter Creek
Mandrem, Pernem
Tel: 0832-253 8451 or 9820-037 387
www.aseascape.com
Arguably the most beautifully situated
and elegantly restored period property
in Goa, Elsewhere is a 19th-century
bolt-hole with gorgeous pillared
veranda looking across empty dunes
to a stretch of undeveloped beach.
You generally have to rent the house
on a weekly basis: three bedrooms

accommodate up to six adults, or a
family. Hidden from view behind it,
along the banks of a tidal inlet, is a
row of architectural tents called Otter
Creek, offering comparable peace,
seclusion and comfort. Friendly staff
are on site to serve meals. **££££**
River Cat Villa
438/1 Junasavaddo
Tel: 0832-224 7928
www.villarivercat.com
Set up by a local artist on the banks
of a quiet river, the River Cat Villa has
good, clean rooms with bath, and an
attractive veranda. **££**

Palolem

Bhakti Kutir
Tel: 0834-264 3469
www.bhaktikutir.com
An eco-friendly resort of 22
individually styled cottages made
from locally available materials. The
open-air bathrooms have stone floors
inlaid with shells and decorated with
plants. The restaurant dishes up tasty
Western food. **££**
Dream Catcher
Palolem Beach
Tel: 0834-264 4873
www.dreamcatcher.in
Attractive hut camp which has better
beds and decor than most of the
other places hereabouts, and is
situated right next to the river at the
north end of Palolem beach. This
place is a good fall-back if nearby
Cozy Nook (see above) doesn't
have any vacancies – and it's much
cheaper. **£–££**
Oceanic
Tembi Waddo, Colom, Palolem
Tel: 0834-264 3059
www.hotel-oceanic.com
Thanks to the local municipality's
ban on construction near Palolem
beach, proper rooms are like gold
dust in this area. These are the most
pleasantly furnished of the bunch,
with a small pool and restaurant. Also
one of the best places to stay with
kids. **££–£££**
Ordo Sounsar
North end of the beach
Tel: 9822-488 769
www.ordosounsar.com
The nicest and best value of the
dozens of camps, not least for
its off-track location – you have
to cross a rickety bamboo bridge
over the creek at the far end of
Palolem beach to reach it. The huts
themselves, all on stilts, have comfy
beds (a rarity), proper electric fans
and are well spaced; some are even
en suite. And the restaurant serves
terrific Goan-style seafood and
tandoori dishes. **£**

Panaji/Panjim

Afonso
St Sebastian Chapel Square, Fontainhas
Tel: 0832-222 2359
Handsomely restored Portuguese-era
house in the heart of Panjim's most
picturesque quarter, with a range
of clean budget rooms and an airy
rooftop terrace. **£**
Casa Britona
Britona, near Panjim
Tel: 0832-241 0962 or 9850-557 665
www.casaboutiquehotels.com
Set amid the mangroves 4km (2.5
miles) up the Mandovi from town,
this luxury hotel combines old-world
elegance with modern amenities
such as a swimming pool and smart
restaurant. **£££**
**Panjim Inn/Panjim Pousada/
Panjim Peoples**
E-212, 31 Janeiro Road, Fontainhas
Tel: 0832-243 5628
www.panjiminn.com
Three converted old town houses,
run by the same owners. All rooms
have period furniture, but those
overlooking the Pousada's interior
courtyard are the most attractive. **£££**

Sinquerim

Marbella Guest House
Tel: 0832-247 9551
www.marbellagoa.com
One of Goa's more stylish and
romantic small hotels, hidden under
a giant mango tree on the hillside
above Sinquerim beach. The interiors
are all beautifully furnished with
traditional textiles and reproduction
antiques, and most of the rooms have
private verandas. **££–£££**

Siolim

Siolim House
Opposite Wadi Chapel, Siolim, Bardez
Tel: 0832-227 2138
www.siolimhouse.com
A 300-year-old house, restored using
traditional materials, with mother-
of-pearl window panes and walls of
shell and lime plaster. The traditional
architecture doesn't allow for a/c, but
there's a sparkling pool in the leafy
rear garden. **££££**

Tiracol

Tiracol Fort Heritage
Tel: 0832-652 9653
www.forttiracol.com
Goa's finest view unfolds from
the ramparts of this old fort, now
beautifully renovated by expat
European designers to serve as
a stylish outpost in the state's
most northerly enclave. The quiet,
comfortable rooms are set around
the courtyard, with suites above. You

can also enjoy the sea vistas from a breezy terrace restaurant. **££££**

Vagator
Bethany Inn
Tel: 0832-227 3731
www.bethanyinn.com

The best budget option. Spotless rooms with attached baths and fridges – though it's a fair old plod to the beach. **£**
Leoney Resort
Ozram Beach Road
Tel: 0832-227 3634

www.leoneyresort.com
Small-scale resort hotel comprising double-bedded chalets and larger octagonal 'cottages', all with A/C facing a central pool. Set in a peaceful corner, around 15 minutes' walk from Ozran-Vagator beach. **£££**

KOLKATA

The Astor
15 Shakespeare Sarani
Tel: 033-2282 9957
www.astorkolkata.com
A very popular Victorian house with comfortable and characterful rooms. Centrally located with a garden and a couple of good restaurants and a bar, this is a good option for the centre of town. **£££**
Bodhi Tree
48/44 Swiss Park
Tel: 033-2424 6534
www.bodhitreekolkata.com
Buddha-themed boutique B&B near Sarovar Metro station. The rooms are beautifully furnished and decorated in earthy colours, with subdued lighting and serene art objects creating the feel of a stylish oasis. The district is crammed with art galleries, old temples and quirky shops to discover. Great value, too. **££**
Fairlawn Hotel
13a Sudder Street
Tel: 033-2252 1510
www.fairlawnhotel.com
A legendary hotel which seeks to maintain a Raj-era ambience (for example, the full English breakfast). Well run and not without a certain eccentric charm, it has comfortable rooms and a pleasant garden. **££**
Hotel Hindustan International
235/1 J. C. Bose Road
Tel: 033-2280 5353

www.hhihotels.com
A long-standing Kolkata five-star, one of the more traditional luxury hotels but very comfortable and with good amenities. The pool is particularly nice, and the trendy new bar gives the hotel a bit of a design lift. **££££**
Lytton Hotel
14–14/1 Sudder Street
Tel: 033-2249 1875
www.lyttonhotelindia.com
A well-established decent hotel with comfortable, if slightly old fashioned, rooms. As well as being clean and safe, the staff are friendly and efficient as it is good value for its central location. **£££**
The Oberoi Grand
15 Jawaharlal Nehru Road
Tel: 033-2249 2323
www.oberoihotels.com
A Kolkata landmark. A very elegant hotel with extremely luxurious rooms and suites. Excellent restaurants including La Terrasse (French), and the Baan Thai. **££££**
The Park Hotel
17 Park Street
Tel: 033-2249 9000
www.theparkhotels.com
A central five-star, flagship of the swish design hotel group with very chic rooms and public areas. The latest coup is the Conran-designed Zen restaurant. **££££**

Taj Bengal
34b Belvedere Road, Alipore
Tel: 033-2223 3939
www.tajhotels.com
One of the city's best-run hotels, wonderfully comfortable and luxurious. The rooms, arranged around the impressive entrance atrium, have a contemporary feel. The service is second to none and the pool and restaurants are wonderful. **££££**
Tollygunge Club
120 Deshapran Sasmal Road
Tel: 033-2477 6022
www.tollygungeclub.org
The accommodation at Kolkata's most famous club, dating back to 1895, is a bizarre cross of Butlins and Fawlty Towers. It does, however, have beautiful grounds and excellent sports facilities; in South Kolkata close to a metro station and the city's largest shopping mall. Advance booking is essential through the reservations secretary. **££££**
YWCA
1 Middleton Row
Tel: 033-2229 7033
www.ywcaindia.org
This very quiet and pleasant YWCA admits men and women. Very clean rooms and a dormitory; all meals are included in the price. An excellent option. **££**

WEST BENGAL

Darjeeling
The Darjeeling Club
7 Nehru Road
Tel: 0354-225 4348
Set in a rundown but atmospheric old building, with 20 suites that haven't seen a lick of paint for decades. There is a billiards room, naturally, and a great bar as well as superb views over the mountains. A commendable option if you can't afford to stay at the Windamere but love the old-world vibe of the Raj era. **£££**
Dekeling Hotel
51 Gandhi Road

Tel: 0354-225 3298
www.dekeling.com
A friendly and attractive Tibetan-run hotel with pleasant rooms (the ones in the wood-lined attic are best), some with a good view; all have an attached bath and hot water. **£–££**
Dekeling Resort at Hawk's Nest
2 A.J.C. Bose Road
Tel: 0354-225 3092
www.dekeling.com
A late 19th-century building in a fabulous position. Lovely wood panelled rooms – open fires are set in the rooms during the evening – with

excellent views. Friendly staff and good food. Book well in advance. **£££**
Glenburn Estate
Tel: 9830-070 213
www.glenburnteaestate.com

PRICE CATEGORIES
Price categories are for a double room (A/C where available) in high season, including taxes:
£ = under Rs2,000
££ = Rs2,000–5,000
£££ = Rs5,000–10,000
££££ = over Rs10,000

Savour the atmosphere of a traditional British tea estate in the hills, just over an hour out of Darjeeling town, at this luxury B&B, whose flower-filled varandahs have an uninterrupted view of Kanchenjunga. Everything's effortlessly refined, from the toile de jouy upholstery to the low-slung wicker chairs and open fires. Guided treks, fishing trips and river rafting expeditions are optional extras. **££££**

Revolver
110Gandhi Rd
Tel: 0354-225 370
Beatles-themed budget boutique hotel offering comfortable rooms that are packed with Fab Four memorabilia. Great Naga food served in the dining room, and cookery lessons are of offer. **£**

Windamere Hotel
Observatory Hill
Tel: 0354-225 4041

www.windamerehotel.com
A legendary hotel with famous clientele and an old-fashioned grandeur. Plenty of nostalgia; not as comfortable as it might be, but worth it for the experience. **££££**

Youth Hostel
Dr Zakir Hussain Road
Tel: 0354-252 290
www.wbtourism.com
This is a very popular place for budget travellers. Very good value, with pleasant views. **£**

Kalimpong

Elgin Silver Oaks
Upper Cast Road
Tel: 03552-255 296
www.elginhotels.com
The 1930s home of a British jute planter, now a delightful hotel. Surrounded by lovely gardens and with characterful rooms. **££££**

Himalayan Hotel
Upper Cart Road

Tel: 03552-255 248
www.himalayanhotel.biz
This famous old guest house in the hills, built in the 1920s by a retired British governor, was once the last outpost of civilization for Everest-bound mountaineers. Its present incumbents have lovingly retained the original feel, with red Nepalese rugs over wood-floored corridors, verandahs draped in wisteria and fireplaces in the bedrooms. The food is fresh and delicious, the staff charming and gardens a wonderland of exotic plants. **££**

Sunderbans National Park

WBTDC Tourist Lodge
Sajnekhali, Gosaba, South 24 Parganas 743 331
Tel: 03219-252 560
www.wbtourism.com
Basic rooms and a dormitory in a secluded building. Food is available. **£**

ODISHA (ORISSA)

Bhubaneshwar

The Royale Midtown
52–3 Janpath
Tel: 0674-253 6138
www.royalehotels.com
One of the better-value hotels in Bhubaneswar. Clean and pleasant A/C rooms with attached baths and hot water. **££**

Hotel Sishmo
86a/1 Gautam Nagar
Tel: 0674-243 3600
www.hotelsishmo.com
Very comfortable hotel with modern amenities including pool and restaurants. Price includes tea in bed and breakfast. **££**

Konark

Lotus Eco Village
Ramchandi Beach,
off Marine Drive
Tel: 06758-236 161
www.lotusresorthotels.com
This campus of cedar-clad, eco-friendly, air-conditioned cottages and 'villas', 7km (4 miles) away from Konark, offers comfortable

accommodation on a blissfully quiet, clean stretch of beach that's safe to swim on. What's not to like? **£££**

OTDC Panthanivas Konark
By the temple
Tel: 06758-236 831
www.panthanivas.com
Basic but reasonable and convenient accommodation with a restaurant. Clean rooms with A/C and bath. **£**

Puri

Chanakya BNR (formerly Railway) Hotel
CT Road
Tel: 06752-230 006
www.chanakyabnrpuri.com
Puri's venerable old Railway Hotel has finally had the refit it's deserved for decades, and the results are splendid. The oxide floored, pillared walkways, louvred galleries, holed mozzie nets and lacquer murals are still there, only now they're framed by polished wood and plush furniture. Fabulous antique photos culled from IR's vast collection underline its historic pedigree. Best of all, the

restaurant still serves the old Railway Hotel's trademark retro Raj-era fare. Bargain rates. **££**

Hans Coco Palms
Swargadwar, Goubada Sahi
Tel: 06752-230 951
www.hanshotels.com
Lovely sea-view rooms with balconies in a renovated modern hotel. There is also a nice restaurant and pretty gardens. **££££**

Hotel Samudra
CT Road, Balukhand, Sea Beach
Tel: 06752-224 155
A mid-range hotel with sea-facing rooms, some with A/C. Friendly and also has a restaurant. **££**

Z Hotel
C.T. Road
Tel: 06752-222 554
www.zhotelindia.com
The rooms in this old house, now a perennially popular backpackers' hotel, are straightforward but large and clean; some of them have sea views. An atmospheric and popular place to stay, with an attractive garden. **£**

SIKKIM

Gangtok

Denzong Inn
Denzong Cinema Chowk, Lall Bazaar Road
Tel: 03592-202 692
www.hoteltashidelek.com/denzong.html

Sister concern of the more upmarket Tashi Delek, offering a wide range of great value budget rooms, all with attached bath and hot water; there's also a restaurant and a relaxing

terrace. **£–££**

Denzong Regency
Cherry Banks
Tel: 03592-201 568
www.denzongregency.com

Spacious, luxurious modern rooms with Nepali rugs on polished hardwood floors ranged over four floors overlooking the town. Those on the front side have fabulous views of Kanchenjuna. **£££**

Elgin Nor-Khill
Paljore Stadium Road
Tel: 03592-205 637
www.elginhotels.com
Ambassadors, movie stars and even the Dalai Lama have stayed at this elegant heritage hotel on the edge of Gangtok. Touches of vibrant Sikkimese painted wood carving and furniture lend a traditional Himalayan feel to the interiors. And there's a relaxing garden where you can enjoy views of Kanchenjunga over a gin gimlet. **££££**

Hidden Forest
Middle Sichy Busty
Tel: 03592-203 196
www.hiddenforestretreat.org
Despite lying only 3km (2 miles)

from Gangtok centre, this delightful homestay is smothered in lush flower gardens, bamboo groves and woodland. Exposed stone walls and varnished wood floors lend a warm, earthy feel to the dozen rooms, whose verandahs look across the hills to Rumtek monastery. Meals are served to order in a cosy dining room, made from homegrown ingredients. **££**

Siniolchu Lodge
Enchay, near the Enchay Gompa
Tel: 03592-222 074
A very good budget option. A little out of town but with superb views. There is a restaurant and tours can be booked from the desk. **£**

Hotel Sonam Delek
Tibet Road
Tel: 03592-202 566
www.hotelsonamdelek.com
Well located, good value rooms, from bog-standard cheapies with no outlook to pricier suite with

far-reaching valley views. There is a pleasant garden and decent restaurant serving good local food. **£–££**

Hotel Tashi Delek
Mahatma Gandhi Marg
Tel: 03592-202 991
www.hoteltashidelek.com
Deservedly famous luxury hotel complex attractively furnished throughout with contemporary Tibetan touches. But the real show stopper here is a rooftop terrace café where guests can enjoy hot samosas and tea while admiring magnificent views over the valley and town. **£££**

Hotel Tibet
Paljor Stadium Road
Tel: 03592-203 468
www.hoteltibetgangtok.com
A comfortable and friendly hotel with plenty of Sikkimese flavour. Excellent local and Tibetan food in the restaurant. **££**

ASSAM

Guwahati

Dynasty
SS Rd, Lakhtokia
Tel: 0361-251 6021
www.dynastyhotel.in
Efficient four-star in the bazaar district of the Assamese capital, whose room have mellow wood floors, ultra-comfy beds and central air-con. Fine north Indian cuisine is served on the rooftop, from where views extend over the Brahmaputra River. Bar, gym and spa, but no pool. **£££**

Kaziranga National Park

Aranya Tourist Lodge
Book through: Tourist Information Officer, Kaziranga National Park, Golaghat, Assam
Tel: 03776-262 429
www.assamtourism.org
A mix of clean and simple rooms, all with en suite facilities. Helpful staff and a pretty good restaurant. **£**

Wild Grass
Kaziranga National Park, Golaghat, Assam

Tel: 03776-266 2085
www.oldassam.com
Wild Grass was the first jungle lodge to open near Kaziranga, and the atmosphere here remains essentially that of a 1940s country club in decline: creaky staircases, cavernous guest rooms, dark-wood furniture and lovely verandahs opening on to well tended gardens. A team of expert guides are on hand to answer any wildlife-related questions. **£££**

KARNATAKA

Bandipur National Park

Bandipur Safari Lodge
Melkamanahalli
Tel: 08229-2559 7021
www.junglelodges.com
Very well-managed basic accommodation in modern cottages (no air conditioning), most with panoramic views. Located close to the park entrance. Knowledgeable staff and good jeep safaris for observing the wildlife. **£££**

Forest Department Bungalows
For reservations contact:
The Field Director
Tel/fax: 0821-248 0901
www.karnatakatourism.org
Basic accommodation, some of it in very cheap dormitories, in good locations. **£–££**

Bengaluru (Bangalore)

Casa Piccola Cottage
2 Clapham Road
Tel: 080-2227 0754
www.casapiccola.com
Fans of quirky colonial architecture will love this homely heritage hotel, hidden down a quiet alley in Richmond Town. Its rooms are vast, airy and cool, and offer a welcome haven from the bustle of Bengaluru's chaotic centre, only a walk away. **£££**

The Oberoi
37–9 Mahatma Gandhi Road
Tel: 080-2558 5858
www.oberoibangalore.com
A very expensive but luxurious hotel with beautiful gardens. The rooms and suites all have private 'sit out'

areas overlooking the gardens. **££££**

The Park
14/7 Mahatma Gandhi Road
Tel: 080-2559 4666
www.theparkhotels.com
A very swish, modern hotel. The rooms are elegant and bright, and there is the gourmet i-t.ALIA restaurant – among the city's trendiest eateries. **££££**

PRICE CATEGORIES

Price categories are for a double room (A/C where available) in high season, including taxes:
£ = under Rs2,000
££ = Rs2,000–5,000
£££ = Rs5,000–10,000
££££ = over Rs10,000

TRANSPORT

ACCOMMODATION

ACTIVITIES

A – Z

LANGUAGE

The Taj West End
55 Race Course Road
Tel: 080-5660 5660
www.tajhotels.com
A beautiful old garden hotel. The lawn-side rooms and restaurants are recommended. The Taj Group also runs two business hotels in the centre of Bengaluru, the Taj Residency on M.G. Road, and the Gateway Hotel on Residency Road (see website above for details). **££££**
Tourist
Ananda Rao Circle, Race Course Road
Tel: 080-2226 2869
One of Bengaluru's few commendable budget lodges, but correspondingly popular. Its rooms aren't large, but they're well aired and open onto a long pillared veranda. No advance reservations. **£**
Villa Pottipati
142 4th Main, 8th Cross, Malleswaram
Tel: 080-2336 0777
www.neemranahotels.com
A rare heritage hotel, out in the suburbs, ensconced amid a fragrant garden of jacaranda trees and aromatic shrubs. Its rooms, decorated and furnished in period, have private verandas, deep baths and direct access to an outdoor swimming pool. **££££**

Gokarna

Gokarna International Hotel/Beach Resort
Kumta Taluk, Gokarna
Tel: 08386-256 622
http://gokarnbeachresort.com
Pair of jointly owned hotels: the first a basic midrange hotel at the entrance to town on the roadside (prone to traffic noise in the day); the other a

Hampi.

newer, and much more appealing, block set in its own garden behind Gokarna beach, with kitchenettes and seafacing verandahs. **£**

Hampi

Hotel Mayura Bhuvaneshwari
Kamalapur
Tel: 08394-241 574
www.karnatakatourism.com
Good-value A/C and non-A/C rooms a little distance from the site. Meals and beers are served in a congenial garden restaurant. **£–££**
Shanthi Guest House
Virupapur Gadi (north side of river from Bazaar)
Tel: 08394-325 352
www.shanthihampi.com
Beautifully conceived place with thatched rooms opening on to paddy fields or (pricier ones) facing the river. Swing beds on shady stone pillared verandahs provide respite from the heat, and there's a sociable travellers' restauarant and lounge terrace with views. **£**
Shanti Lodge
Near Virupaksha Temple
Tel: 08394-325 352
www.shanthihampi.com
Clean but worn rooms with rock hard beds and shared bathrooms, overlooking a shaded inner courtyard. The lodge's enduring popularity is down to its owner, a local yoga guru and cult figure among travellers. **£**

Hassan

Hoysala Village Resort
Belur Road
Tel: 08172-256 764
www.hoysalavillageresorts.com
Luxury resort, designed in ersatz

'village' style, 8km (5 miles) northwest of town. Set in peaceful countryside, it's by far the most relaxing base in this area from which to visit the temples. Facilities include a smart restaurant, pool and bullock rides for the kids. **£££**
Hotel Suvarna Regency
97 BM Road
Tel: 08172-266 774
www.suvarnaregency.com
A large business-style hotel with polished marble interiors and large, comfortable A/C rooms at unbelievably low prices. **£**

Hospet

Hotel Malligi
6/143 Jambunath Road
Tel: 08394-228 101
www.malligihotels.com
Close to MG Road. The nicest option in Hospet, with a wide choice of differently priced rooms (from basic economy options to fully A/C suites) a bar, multi-cuisine restaurant and a decent-sized pool. **£–££**
Hotel Priyadarshini
V-45 Station Road
Tel: 08394-228 838
A/C rooms with balconies, helpful and friendly service and a garden restaurant overlooking the sugarcane and paddy fields. **£–££**

Mysore

Green Hotel
Chittaranjan Palace, 2270 Vinoba Road, Jayalakshmipuram
Tel: 0821-425 5000
www.greenhotelindia.com
A charming palace conversion in its own gardens a little way out of town. A project in sustainable tourism through energy-saving and equal-opportunity employment, with profits funding local charities and environmental groups. Good value, attractive rooms and superb food. **£££**
Lalitha Mahal Palace Hotel
Siddhartha Nagar, 5km (3 miles) from city centre
Tel: 0821-252 6100
www.lalithamahalpalace.in
Sumptuous rooms with wonderful period bathrooms, in a neoclassical former royal palace sporting a dome modelled on St Paul's Cathedral in London. The service is excellent service and there is an impressive restaurant, as well as a pleasant outdoor pool and gardens. **££££**
Parklane
2720 Sri Harsha Road
Tel: 0821-400 3500
www.parklanemysore.com
Among the swankiest addresses in the city – though still great value. A

sky-lit atrium opens onto individually styled rooms, quirkily shaped and with balconies. There are two excellent restaurants, both with live classical music nightly, and a popular bar. **££**

Hotel Ritz
Regency Theatre Complex, near the Zoo
Tel: 0821-242 2668
www.hotelritzmysore.com
Centrally located hotel with a good bar-restaurant downstairs. The rooms have mosquito nets and attached bathroom with hot water. Advanced booking. **£**

Windflower
Maharanapratap Road, Nazarbad,
Tel: 0821-252 2500
www.thewindflower.com

Gorgeous boutique resort on the outskirts of Mysore whose main selling points are its huge gulmohar trees, award-winning spa and a fabulous rock pool. The rooms, which overlook a shimmering central pond, are huge, and have open-to-sky rain showers. **£££**

Nagarhole

Forest Department Cottages
Book through:
Conservator of Forests, Kodagu Circle,
Aranya Bhavan, Madikeri 571 201,
Karnataka
Tel: 08272-225 708
Basic lodges with simple but clean rooms; food is available, as are jeeps

for safaris. **££**

Kabini River Lodge
Karapur, Nissana Beltur, Mysore District 571 114, Karnataka
Tel: 08228-264 402
www.junglelodges.com
Nestled on the banks of the Kabini itself, this ranks among India's loveliest safari lodges, comprising a row of stylish stone-clad rooms with verandahs, and wood-beamed villas with sitouts facing the water. The luxurious interiors form a stark contrast to the nature on your doorstep, but don't feel over-done. A perfect base for safaris, nature walks, birdwatching trips and kayaking on the river. **££££**

ANDHRA PRADESH

Hyderabad-Secunderabad

Amrutha Castle
5/9–16, Saifabad, Opposite Secretariat, Hyderabad
Tel: 040-4443 3888
www.amruthacastle.com
Kitsch rules at this fantasy Bavarian castle, a cross between Trump Towers and Disneyland, now managed by the Best Western group. Good rooms and amenities including a 5th-floor open-air swimming pool. **££££**

Golden Glory
Road No3, Banjara Hills
Tel: 040-2355 4765
www.goldengloryguesthouse.com
Smart, spacious en-suite rooms in an impeccably well-run guest house up in the smart Banjara Hills neighbourhood, 5km (3 miles) out of the city centre. **£**

Golconda Fort.

Hotel Sai Prakash
Station Road, Nampally, Hyderabad
Tel: 040-2461 1726
www.hotelsaiprakash.chobs.in
A good option close to Hyderabad station. Clean, well-maintained rooms arranged around a large atrium. Two decent restaurants. **££**

Taj Falaknuma Palace
Engine Bowli, Falaknuma
Tel: 040-6629 8585
www.tajhotels.com
The last word in heritage luxury; the Taj group, in consultation with the Hyderabadi Royal Family, have spent the last 10 years refurbishing the Nizam of Hyderabad's palace to its former glory. There are 60 bedrooms and a plethora of stunning halls, of which the Durbar Hall is the most magnificent, but the whole place has to be seen to be believed. **££££**

Tirupati

Bhimas Paradise
34–38 G. Car Street
Tel: 0877-223 7271
www.hotelbhimas.com
A lovely, very well-run hotel just around the corner from the railway station. Friendly, helpful staff and management. There is an excellent vegetarian restaurant. **££**

Vijayawada

Hotel D.V. Manor
M G Road
Tel: 0866-663 4455
www.hoteldvmanor.com
The business hotel is the best option in Vijayawada. Comfortable rooms, all with bathrooms, lead off the main atrium. Two good restaurants. **££–£££**

TAMIL NADU

Chennai

Chandra Park
9 Gandhi Irwin Road
Tel: 044-2819 1177
Directly opposite Egmore Station, so very well placed for early morning train departures. Consistently the best value cheapie in the city centre,

PRICE CATEGORIES

Price categories are for a double room (A/C where available) in high season, including taxes:
£ = under Rs2,000
££ = Rs2,000–5,000
£££ = Rs5,000–10,000
££££ = over Rs10,000

TRANSPORT

ACCOMMODATION

ACTIVITIES

A – Z

LANGUAGE

though no palace and the service is often surly. **£**

Hotel Kanchi
28 Ethiraj Salai, Egmore
Tel: 044-2827 1100
www.hotelkanchi.com
Large and light rooms that are starting to show their age, but still with a certain charm. Great views and North Indian dishes in the rooftop restaurant. **£**

Hotel New Woodlands
72–75 Dr Radhakrishnan Road, Mylapore
Tel: 044-2811 3111
www.newwoodlands.com
A large hotel with excellent vegetarian restaurant. The large, clean rooms are popular so book ahead. **££**

The Park
601 Anna Salai
Tel: 044-4267 6000
www.theparkhotels.com
The swishest address in town. Set in the old film studios – where many Tamil classics were born – it has become one of modern Chennai's landmarks. The rooms are chic, if a little small, but it is the public areas that shine. One highlight is the rooftop pool with its views over the city. A real taste of modern India. **££££**

Taj Connemara
2 Binny Road
Tel: 044-6600 0000
www.tajhotels.com
A charming, relatively small-scale five-star, set in an Art Deco building. Excellent value and service. It has a lovely pool and good restaurants, as well as a chic cocktail bar. The coffee shop is a great place for breakfast or lunch. **££££**

YWCA International Guest House
1086 E.V.R. Periyar High Road
Tel: 044-2532 4234
ywcaigh@indiainfo.com
Rooms with attached baths, some

Porter at The Park.

with A/C, and also camping facilities. Handy for Egmore Station. A small membership fee is payable. Breakfast included. **£**

Coimbatore

Heritage Inn
38 Sivasamy Road, Ramnagar
Tel: 0422-233 1451
www.hotelheritageinn.in
Modern, comfortable and well-maintained rooms. A clean hotel with good restaurants. **££**

The Residency
1076 Avinashi Road
Tel: 422-224 1414
www.theresidency.com
This landmark four-star in the city centre is Coimbatore's top hotel. Rooms, which come in three categories, are ranged over seven floors and are plush for the price tag. There's a fitness centre and small pool but no sun terrace; dining options include an alfresco Afghan bbq, Chinese restaurant and smart Pavilion buffet. **£££**

Kanniyakumari

TTDC Hotel Tamilnadu
Beach Road
Tel: 04652-246 257
www.tamilnadutourism.org
A wide range of cottages, rooms, dormitories, some A/C. Decent food available and in a good location, though being a government-run place, standards of service aren't great. **£–££**

Vivekananda Kendra
Vivekanandapuram, 2km (1¼ miles) north
Tel: 04652-246 250
www.vkendra.org/english/accommodations
A bit of a trek from town, but easily the most pleasant budget option: go for one of its more spacious triple-bed A/C rooms, rather than the functional dorms. Excellent value, and they run shuttle buses to town on the hour. **£**

Kodaikanal

Elephant Valley
Ganesh Puram, Vilpatti, 20km (12 miles) from Kodai
Tel: 0413-265 5751
www.elephantvalleyhotel.com
A 100-acre (40-hectare) organic plantation and eco lodge, on the edge of pristine forest, 1,300 metres (4,260ft) up in the Nilgiris. The cottages with exposed brick walls and cosy wood burners around their garden are stylish, contemporary and comfortable. **££–£££**

Greenland's Youth Hostel
St Mary's Road, near Coaker's Walk
Tel: 04542-241 336
www.greenlandskodaikanal.com

The best budget option – thanks to the fabulous views across the plains from its pleasant gardens. Clean, but very basic, rooms and dormitories. **£**

Madurai

Heritage Madurai
11 Melakkal Main Road, Kochadai
Tel : 0452-238 5455
www.heritagemadurai.com
This boutique place on the outskirts scores highly for its Indo-Fusion chic: bright, airy interiors juxtaposed with reclaimed temple pillars, antique carved wood and bell metal. Tamil specialities also feature prominently on the restaurant menu, and there's a good-sized pool to lounge by between trips to the temple. **£££**

Hotel Sree Devi
20 W. Avani Moola Street
Tel: 0452-234 7431
Good-value, clean rooms (some A/C, non-A/C **£**) with attached bath. Great views of the temple gopurams from the roof. **£–££**

Taj Gateway Pasumalai
40 T.P.K. Road, Pasumalai
Tel: 0452-237 1601
www.thegatewayhotels.com
Madurai's top hotel, and part of the Taj group, set on top of a hill overlooking the city in the midst of wonderful grounds, many of the rooms have lovely views, as do the two restaurants. **££££**

Mudumalai National Park

Jungle Hut
Bokkapuram, Masinagudi
Tel: 0423-252 6463
www.junglehut.in
Simply furnished, but perfectly comfortable, stone cottages dotted around a forested plot. They've got a small pool with a view, and wide range of activities on offer. **££–£££**

Jungle Retreat
Bokkapuram, Masinagudi
Tel: 0423-252 6469
www.jungleretreat.com
Straightforward and pleasant accommodation to suit every pocket, in dorms, bamboo cottages, tree houses or deluxe rooms. Wonderful views from the grounds (which also have a small curviform pool). **£–£££**

Puducherry

Dune
Off the East Coast Road, Pudhukuppam
Tel: 0413-265 5751
www.thedunehotel.com
Wonderfully unique, French-owned funkfest 15km (9 miles) out of town, close to Auroville. Each room is completely different, but all share exquisite styling, artistry and

ambience. Most are in separate buildings, so bicycles are provided to get around the sizeable site. There's a farm, a swimming pool and two superb restaurants. **££££**

Maison Perumal
44 (Old No. 58) Perumal Koil Street,
Tel: 0413-222 7519
www.cghearth.com
This beautifully restored boutique property in the old Tamil quarter holds just ten rooms, opening on to a pair of inner courtyards with whitewashed walls and balconies shaded by stained glass windows. A great place to soak up the colonial elegance of this former French enclave. **££££**

Hotel de l'Orient
17 rue Romain Rolland
Tel: 0413-234 3067

www.neemranahotels.com
An 18th-century neoclassical mansion, now an elegant heritage hotel. It has lovely rooms and a Creole restaurant. **££££**

Seaside Guest House
14 Goubert Salai
Tel: 0413-233 6494
www.aurosociety.org/visiting/accommodation.aspx
A spotlessly clean Sri Aurobindo Ashram guesthouse bang on the seafront. The view is magnificent, and there is a good vegetarian cafeteria. **£–££**

Fernhills Palace
High Level Road

Tel: 0423-244 3910
www.welcomheritagehotels.com
This sumptuous heritage hotel is set in the expansive grounds of the former British Country Club. Accommodation is in richly furnished suites. **££££**

Hotel Seekar
236 Raceview Road, Dasaprakash Complex
Tel: 0423-224 2348
Best budget option in town: a low-slung, red-tiled cottage with only a handful of basic rooms at bargain rates, though they can get decidedly chilly in winter. The elderly manager who runs it is a gem. Handy for the Blue Mountain Railway station. **£**

KERALA

Akkarakalam Memoirs
Chennamkary, 3km (2 miles) southeast of Alappuzha
Tel: 0477-276 2345
www.akkarakalammemoirs.com
The feel of this backwater heritage property is as close to that of the original ancestral home as a small hotel can get, down to the black-and-white family photos on the walls. With their whitewashed walls and darkwood furniture, the rooms offer traditional comfort (and quiet a/c units if the humidity gets too much), while the waterfront location is perfectly placed for deeper explorations of this fascinating area by canoe or houseboat. **£££**

Emerald Isle Heritage Villa
Kanjooparambil–Manimalathara
Tel: 0477-2703 899
Mobile: 94470 77555
www.emeraldislekerala.com
A peaceful retreat 12km (7 miles) from Alappuzha. Five A/C guest rooms with lovely 'outdoor' bathrooms, in a traditional house set in idyllic tropical surroundings. Excellent Keralan meals. Call in advance so the boat is waiting for you at the jetty to take you to the island. **££££**

Keralite
Vadakekalam House, North of Dutch Square
Tel: 0477-224 3569
Run by the amiable Mrs Alice Thomas, this B&B set in a quiet back road, is a real gem, both for the traditional atmosphere of the house, and warm hospitality (and

superb Syrian Christian cooking) of its hostess. Some of the rooms have shared bathrooms, though, hence the bargain tariffs. **£**

Palmy Lake Resort
Thathampally, 2km (1¼ miles) north of the boat jetty
Tel: 0477-223 5938
www.palmyresort.com.
Spacious terracotta-tiled chalets scattered around a leafy garden, within walking distance of the lakeside, but well away from the bustle of the town centre. Relaxing, secluded, hospitable and exceptional value for money. Phone ahead for free pick-up. **£**

Raheem Residency
Beach Rd
Tel: 0477-223 9767
www.raheemresidency.com
There's only one heritage hotel in India owned by an Irish TV personality, and it's quite something: a grand, 140-year-old merchant's house on the beachfront beautifully restored and furnished in high Keralan style. The décor is gorgeous; the pool inside a dream; and the restaurant services sumptuous south Indian dishes. **£££–££££**

Gitanjali Heritage
Panayal
Tel: 0467-223 4159
www.gitanjaliheritage.com
A traditional, 70-year-old kodoth house set in a delightful garden, this is a wonderful place to base yourself in the far north. Mr Jagannathan and his family are very welcoming, and can direct you to local theyyem

dances during the winter season. **£££**

Costa Malabari
Thottada, 10km (6 miles) south of Kannur
Tel: 0484-237 18761 (Cochin)
www.costamalabari.com
Five comfortable rooms in an efficiently-run guesthouse, pleasantly screened by cashew groves, close to a string of gorgeous, deserted beaches. Backwater trips can be arranged, and the guesthouse manager is an expert on local theyyem rituals. **££**

Kannur Beach House
Thottada, 10km (6 miles) south of Kannur
Tel: 9847-186 330
www.kannurbeachhouse.com
Beautifully sited guesthouse, perched on a sandy strip between the beach and a backwater. Simple and stylish, with antique carved wood doors and white walls, its rooms catch the sea breezes, and owners Nazir adn Rosie are perfect hosts. Meals available. **£££**

Biju's Tourist Home
Corner of Canonshed and Market roads, Ernakulam
Tel: 0484-238 1881

PRICE CATEGORIES

Price categories are for a double room (A/C where available) in high season, including taxes:
£ = under Rs2,000
££ = Rs2,000–5,000
£££ = Rs5,000–10,000
££££ = over Rs10,000

www.bijustouristhome.com
Unbeatable-value budget hotel close to the main boat jetty in Ernakulam. All the rooms are immaculate, and there's a same-day laundry service. Friendly management. **£–££**

The Brunton Boatyard
Calvetty Road, Fort Cochin
Tel: 0484-221 5461
www.cghearth.com
A luxury hotel in a splendid location, built in the style of early Portugese and Dutch colonial architecture. Elegant and beautifully appointed rooms and bathrooms. A restaurant serves local dishes recreated from historical recipes, and the waterfront pool is the finest in the city. **££££**

Delight Tourist Resort
Parade Ground, Fort Kochi
Tel: 0484-221 7658
www.delighthomestay.com
A quiet little guesthouse with spotless rooms right in the centre of Fort Kochi. Comfy beds, a lovely garden and a helpful travel desk. **£–££**

The Old Courtyard
1/371–2 Princess Street, Fort Cochin
Tel: 0484-221 6302
www.oldcourtyard.com
Opening onto an elegant Portuguese courtyard, the eight rooms in this landmark heritage hotel, in the thick of the old fort, preserve their original 17th-century wood floors and antique furniture. Those on the upper storey are less bothered by noise from the (excellent) restaurant below. **££–£££**

The Old Harbour
1/328 Tower Road, Fort Cochin
Tel: 0484-221 8006
www.oldharbourhotel.com
Smartest of the fort's upscale heritage hotels, blending modern amenities with exquisitely restored original architecture and features. You can stay in individually styled rooms in the main block, or in garden cottages by the poolside. **££££**

The Tower House
1/320-321 Tower Road
Tel: 0484-221 6960
www.neemranahotels.com
If you're looking for old-world atmosphere from your hotel rather than mod cons and snappy service, this place is hard to beat. Exquisitely restored by the French Neemrana people, its wood-floored suites overlook the square, a stone's throw from the Chinese fishing nets. The pool's small but adequate. Superb value. **£££**

Kollam

Government Guest House
Ashramom
Tel: 0474-274 3620

This former British Residency on Ashtamudi Lake is one of the oldest-surviving colonial buildings in India. It's falling apart, but offers memorable budget accommodation in rooms the size of dance halls. Meals available on request. No advance bookings. **£**

Palm Lagoon
Vellimon West, 18km (11 miles) north of Kollam
Tel: 079-3984 1111
www.thecambay.com
Lost deep in the backwaters, this compact lakeside resort comprises traditional-style Keralan cottages, with carved wood gabled roofs and pillared verandas, plus a quality ayurvedic centre, right on the water's edge. Fishing and boat trips are laid on for guests. **£££**

Kottayam and Kumarakom

Hotel Aida
Aida Junction, M.C. Road
Tel: 0481-256 8391
www.hotelaidakerala.com
Good-value, comfortable rooms, all with en suite bath and hot water; the restaurant serves Indian dishes. **££**

Akkara
Mariathuruthu, 5km (3 miles) northwest of Kottayam
Tel: 0481-251 6951
www.akkara.in
The Akkara is a wonderful heritage homestay in an old-fashioned Syrian-Christian house, astride a bend in the Meenachil river. The backwater setting, straight out of *The God of Small Things*, is as idyllic as the architecture. Access is by dugout canoe. **££**

Coconut Lagoon
Vembanad Lake
Tel: 0481-252 4491
www.cghearth.com
One of the finest resorts in Kerala, about 10km (6 miles) from Kottayam and only accessible by boat. The facilities are first-class, including the ayurvedic treatments, and the rooms are tasteful and luxurious. **££££**

Philip Kutty's
Pallivathukal, Vechoor, 20km (12 miles) northwest of Kottayam
Tel: 04829-276 529
www.philipkuttysfarm.com.
This upscale homestay, on a 50-acre (20-hectare) spice and fruit plantation, was one of the first in the state to offer simple, but stylish, accommodation on a working farm. From the privacy of your own veranda you can watch backwater life at close quarters; and the food is sumptuous. **££££**

Kovalam

Amrutham

Pannagodu, near Venganoor
Tel: 0471-645 5423
www.amrutham.in
Not even the local taxi drivers know where to find this hidden gem of a guest house, tucked away deep in the palm forest inland from Kovalam. It was set up as an Ayurveda centre, but welcomes casual guests. Large, comfortable, octagonal rooms. Lovely rural views from the verandahs and rooftop terrace, where delicious home-cooked meals are served. Plus there's a big pool and sun terrace. Great value. **££**

Friday's Place
Poovar Island, 25km (15.5 miles) south of Kovalam
Tel: 0974-416 1636 (Nov–Feb)
www.fridaysplacekerala.com
Luxury mahogany huts, set deep in the backwaters on an island only accessible by launch. British-Sri Lankan couple. Great local cuisine, a telescope and tsunami-proof tower are other attractions. **££££**

Karikkathi Beach House
Pulinkudi, 8km (5 miles) south of Kovalam
Tel: 0471-240 0956
www.karikkathibeachhouse.com.
A whitewashed, red-tiled cottage nestled under the palm terraces above a secluded cove – the area's most exclusive hideaway. Book both rooms for maximum privacy. **££££**

The Leela Kovalam
Tel: 0471-248 0101
www.theleela.com
Striking hotel complex (previously the Kovalam Ashok), designed in part by Charles Correa. The hotel now includes the Halcyon Castle, summer palace of the Maharajas of Travancore. Expensive but exceptionally luxurious, with a great overflow pool and in a superb location. **££££**

Surya
Lighthouse Beach
Tel: 0471-248 1012
kovsurya@yahoo.co.in
One of the few genuinely pleasant budget guesthouses packed into the narrow sandy lanes running back from Lighthouse Beach. Quiet, secluded and efficiently run; and there are several good fallbacks in the same row if it's full. **£**

Kozhikode

Alakapuri Hotel
Moulana Mohammed Ali Road
Tel: 0495-272 3451
An excellent-value colonial-style guesthouse, ranged around a central courtyard. The large rooms with bath are full of character. The restaurant serves good Indian food. **£–££**

TRANSPORT

ACCOMMODATION

ACTIVITIES

A – Z

LANGUAGE

Beach Heritage
Beach Road
Tel: 0495-276 2056
www.beachheritage.com
Somerset Maugham and Jawaharlal Nehru stayed in this former British club in the 1950s, and little has changed here since. Whitewashed walls, dark wood furniture and verandas opening onto expansive lawns set the tone; and the tariffs are amazingly restrained. **££**

Harivihar
4km (2.5 miles) north of Kozhikode in Bilathikulam village
Tel: 0495-276 5865
www.harivihar.com
Occupying a beautifully converted royal palace, Harivihar ranks among Kerala's most traditinoal heritage hotels. Landscaped gardens dotted with lotus ponds enfold the family mansion, which is crammed with heirlooms. In addition to quality ayurvedic treatments, courses are offered in Indian mythology and cookery. **£££**

Kadavu Resort
15km southeast on NhH-17
Tel: 0483-283 0023
www.kadavuresorts.com
Huge 120-room five-star overlooking a spectacular bend in the Chaliyar River. For the best views and most Keralan ambiance, one of the their 'deluxe' or 'superior' options. The Ayurveda centre's especially lovely, and there's a lagoon pool. **££££**

Munnar

High Range Club
Kanan Devan Hills Road
Tel: 04865-230 253
www.highrangeclubmunnar.com
The clock stopped in August 1947 at the High Range Club. You'll need a stiff upper lip and neatly creased trousers to stay here, but the pretence is all part of the fun. Turbaned bearers greet arrivals, and the bar, with its topees and hunting trophies on the walls, is a true bastion of the patriarchal Raj ('No Women Allowed'). Accommodation comes in rooms or cottages. Tennis, golf, billiards and meals are included. **££**

The Olive Brook
In the Tata Tea Estate, Pothamedu
Tel: 04865-230 588
www.olivebrookmunnar.com
These two bungalows set high above the town are a lovely retreat. The staff are great and there are cooking demonstrations in the evening. **££££**

The Windermere Estate
PO Box 21, Pothamedu
Tel: 91486-523 0512

www.windermeremunnar.com
Attractive, simple rooms in secluded planters' cottages with stunning views over the hills. It is beautifully quiet and very relaxing. **£££**

Zina Cottage
Kad, 3km (2 miles) south of Munnar Bazaar
Tel: 04865-230 349
By far the most congenial budget option in Munnar. The stone-walled rooms of the Raj-era bungalow can get rather chilly in mid-winter, but the views from its flower garden across the valley to Anamudi, and hospitality of its owner, Joseph Iype, more than compensate. Joseph is a mine of advice and information on the region. **£**

Periyar Wildlife Sanctuary

Chrissie's
Bypass Road, Kumily
Tel: 04869-224 155
http://chrissies.in
Recently built, four-storey hotel in Kumily village, owned by expats from the UK and Egypt. You get fabulous forest views from the rooms, which are all impeccably clean and comfortable. There's also a sunny yoga practice room on the rooftop, and a buzzing little café-restaurant on the ground floor. **£–££**

Forest Department Jungle Inn
3km (2 miles) east of Kumily at Kokkara
Book through the Eco-Tourism Centre, Ambadi Junction
Tel: 04869-224 571
www.periyartigerreserve.org
A rare opportunity to spend a night in amongst the wildlife of the park. A small, secluded hut that is ideally placed for forest treks. **££**

Jungle View
On the east edge of Kumily
Tel: 04869-223 582
Jungleview8@yahoo.co,
Great little budget homestay whose rooms literally open on to wild forest. Friendly family, home-cooked food and a relaxing, sociable verandah – through beware the marauding monkeys. **£**

Lake Palace
Thekkady, Idukki 685 536, Kerala
Tel: 04869-223 888
www.ktdc.com
Previously belonging to the Maharaja of Travancore, this small heritage resort is a great base for wildlife-spotting trips. **££££**

Shalimar Spice Garden
Murikaddy, 6km (4 miles) from Kumily
Tel: 04869-222 132
www.shalimarkerala.net
Stylish teak huts with elephant-grass roofs and designer interiors,

set on the edge of old cardamom plantations. A stylish hideaway, and the luxury extends to a top-notch ayurvedic spa, shaded outdoor pool and gourmet restaurant. More of a boutique hotel than a five-star. **££££**

Thiruvananthapuram

The Grand Central
M.G. Road, Thirvananathapuram
Tel: 0471-247 1286
www.grandcentral.in
Polished business hotel opposite the Secretariat, offering two classes of rooms, equipped with most mod cons, including Wi-fi; those to the rear are quieter and have greener views. **£££**

Greenland Lodging
Aristo Road
Tel: 0471-232 8114
A decent budget lodge with clean rooms. Very convenient for the railway and bus stations. **£**

KTDC Mascot Hotel
P.M.G. Junction
Tel: 0471-231 8990
www.ktdc.com
Pleasant, quiet hotel, originally built to house British officers during World War I. Competitively priced rooms and a quality restaurant. **£££**

Varikatt Heritage
Poonen Road, near Cantonment Police Station, behind the Secretariat (look for the brown gates)
Tel: 0471-233 6057
www.varikattheritage.com
The Varikatt is a wonderful old British-era residence, run as an evocative heritage homestay by a retired army colonel. The three front-side suites open onto a deep veranda, cooled by paddle fans, where you can sip gin slings under the watchful eye of moth-eaten hunting trophies. **£££**

Thrissur

Kuruppath Heritage
Mannadiara Lane, off Kuruppam Road
Tel: 0487-645 0001
www.kuruppathheritage.com
Five cool, traditionally styled rooms in a restored period house, one of the few remaining in central Thrissur. A haven of Keralan elegance in the heart of this bustling city, only a skip from the temple.

PRICE CATEGORIES
Price categories are for a double room (A/C where available) in high season, including taxes:
£ = under Rs2,000
££ = Rs2,000–5,000
£££ = Rs5,000–10,000
££££ = over Rs10,000

Rates include full board. **£££**

Varkala

Bohemian Masala
Thiruvambadi, North Cliff
Tel: 9287-215 567
www.thebohemianmasala.com
Tribal mud cottages, done out with
floaty mosquito nets and hand-
printed textiles, in a haven of greenery
behind the main tourist strip on North
Cliff. Ayurveda, yoga on site; and
nutritious Keralan cuisine served in
a funky dining hall. A cut (well) above
the competition. **££**
Taj Gateway Hotel
Near Government Guesthouse, Janardana

Puram
Tel: 0470-260 3000
www.thegatewayhotels.com
A luxury resort hotel near to the
beach. There are great views from its
hilltop position. Good restaurants and
pool. **££££**
Villa Jacaranda
Temple Road West
Tel: 0470-261 0296
www.villa-jacaranda.biz
Beautifully designed rooms in a
modern guesthouse near the temple.
The surrounding gardens
are delightful, and the views of
sunset over the sea breathtaking.
£££

Waynad

Tranquil
Kappamudi Estate, Kolaggappara
Tel: 04936-220 224
www.tranquilresort.com
Set amid a vast acreage of
coffee, cardamom and vanilla
plantations, this is the benchmark
luxury homestay in Kerala, with
accommodation in former
planter's bungalows or a spectacular
treehouse. The food is of five-star
quality and the hospitality of the
Dey family legendary. You'll
be expected to dress for
dinner. Minimum two nights stay.
££££

LAKSHADWEEP

Bangaram

Bangaram Island Resort
Book through: CGH Earth,
CasinoBuilding, Willingdon Island,
Kochi 682 003

Tel: 0484-301 1711
www.cghearth.com
All-inclusive board and lodging.
Accommodation is in simple huts
set back from the beach. There are

facilities for snorkelling, scuba-
diving and sailing. The shallow
lagoon here is fabulously clear and
clean, and perfect for swimming.
££££

ANDAMAN ISLANDS

Havelock

Barefoot at Havelock
Beach No. 7, Radhanagar Village
Tel: 044-2434 1001
www.barefootindia.com
Easily Havelock's finest resort, and
for now the only one situated on the
stunningly picturesque Beach No. 7.
The elegant wooden cottages and
villas, of varying degrees of luxury,
are all designed to be as eco-friendly
as possible, and the international
cuisine is both original and delicious.
Within a minute's walk from what
Time magazine decided was the best
beach in Asia. **££££**
Barefoot Scuba
Beach No.3
Tel: 044-2434 1001
www.diveandamans.com
Essentially a dive centre run by the
same group as Barefoot Resort, this
place also has a range of excellent

accommodation, a decent restaurant
and a relaxed, friendly atmosphere.
The duplex, sea-facing cottages and
de luxe tents are fantastic value, and
there are even barebones backpacker
huts for Rs250 a night. **£–£££**
Seashell
Beach No. 2
Tel: 03192-242 773
www.seashellhavelock.com
A development of 22 tasteful
wooden cottages and a multi-cuisine
restaurant, conveniently located
1km (0.6 mile) from the arrival jetty.
£££–££££

Port Blair

Aashiaanaa Rest Home
Marine Hill
Tel: 0947-421 7008
Spotless rooms in a welcoming family
home, the pricier ones with bay
views. **£**

Fortune Resort Bay Island
Marine Hill
Tel: 03192-234 101
www.fortunehotels.in
Port Blair's top hotel, situated
1km (.5 mile) south of town,
overlooks secluded Corbyn's
Cove with fine views over the bay.
Much of the building, designed by
Goan architect Charles Correa, is
made of local red padouk
hardwood, lending it a relaxed feel.
££££
Sun Sea Resort
M.G. Road,
Middle Point
Tel: 03192-238 330
www.sunsearesort-andamans.com
More comfortable than most of the
upscale competition at a fraction
of the price. A/C and modern
furnishings, but on a busy road.
££–£££

PRICE CATEGORIES

Price categories are for a double
room (A/C where available) in high
season, including taxes:
£ = under Rs2,000
££ = Rs2,000–5,000
£££ = Rs5,000–10,000
££££ = over Rs10,000

ACTIVITIES

THE ARTS, NIGHTLIFE, OUTDOOR ACTIVITIES, SHOPING, SPAS AND WILDLIFE PARKS

THE ARTS

Cinemas

Most cinemas in India show Bollywood films *(see page 96)*, although in larger cities you will also find several screening Hollywood releases, while Tamil-language ('Kollywood') films are also popular in the south.

Delhi

Plaza, Radial Road, Connaught Place, www.pvrcinemas.com. Gracious old cinema, dating from 1933 but recently renovated.

Jaipur

Raj Mandir, Bhagwan Das Road. This huge Art Deco cinema is one of the most famous in India, and a great place to experience the fun of Bollywood at first hand.

Mumbai

The Eros Opposite Churchgate Station, tel: 022-2282 6828, www.erostheatre.com. A famous old colonial-era Mumbai cinema.
The Regal Colaba, tel: 022-2202 1017. Built in 1933, this sumptuously decorated old Art Deco cinema is the oldest in Mumbai, and one of the finest in India.

Kolkata

Elite, S.N. Banerjee Road, tel: 033-2265 0383. This is one of the best of Kolkata's many fine old Art Deco-style colonial-era cinemas.
Nandan, 1/1, A.J.C. Bose Road, tel: 033-2223 1210. Inaugurated by the great Bengali film-maker Satyajit Ray in 1985, the government-sponsored

centre features three screens with regular showings of art-house productions. Also hosts the excellent Kolkata Film Festival (www.kff.in).

Music and Dance

India's rich classical dance and music heritage is showcased in a string of venues around the country, with recitals by leading musicians and performances of traditional dances such as Bharatnatyam, Odissi and Kathakali.

Delhi

Dances of India, Parsi Anjuman Hall, Bahadur Shah Zafar Marg, near Delhi Gate, Old Delhi, tel: 011-2323 1228. A mix of classical, tribal and folk dances from across India, including Bharatnatyam and Kathakali.
India Habitat Centre, Lodi Road

(near Safdarjang's Tomb), tel: 011-2468 2001, www.indiahabitat.org. This pioneering centre hosts cultural and entertainment events, including frequent performances of traditional and contemporary dance and music from around India.
Sangeet Natak Akademi, Rabindra Bhavan, 35 Firoz Shah Road, tel: 011-2338 7246, www.sangeetnatak.com. Delhi's 'National Academy of Music, Dance and Drama', with performances by some of India's top classical musicians and dancers. There is also a museum of musical instruments.

Mumbai

Bharatiya Vidya Bhavan, K.M. Munshi Marg, tel: 022-2363 1261, www.bhavans.info. Stages frequent concerts by leading Indian classical musicians.

Cocktails at Q'Ba, an upmarket bar in Connaught Place, Delhi.

National Centre for the Performing Arts, Nariman Point, tel: 022-6622 3737, www.ncpamumbai.com. One of India's premier performing arts venues, hosting a wide range of events including Indian and Western music, dance and theatre.

Kolkata

ITC Sangeet Research Academy, 1 Netaji Subash Chandra Bose Road, Tollygunge, tel: 033-2377 3395, www.itcsra.org. Founded in 1978 to preserve the rich heritage of Hindustani (North Indian) classical music. Hosts recitals every Wednesday, and also offers long-term courses.

Rabindra Sadan, 1/1, A.J.C. Bose Road, tel: 033-2248 9936. Kolkata's leading cultural centre and auditorium, hosting performances of music, dance and drama.

Bengaluru (Bangalore)

Nrityagram Dance Village, 30km (20 miles) west of Bengaluru, tel: 080-2846 6313, www.nrityagram.org. Famous model village and cultural centre, founded by leading Odissi performer Protima Gauri and hosting regular performances of Indian dance.

Festivals

There are many festivals in India but few public holidays. Here is a selection of the annual highlights in India's festival calendar. In addition, every town, village and temple celebrates its own during the year. *See also Festivals, page 90.*

Jan–Feb

Pongal. This is the most celebrated harvest festival in South India; typically lasting four days, it involves the painting of elaborate *kollams* (floor paintings) and the preparation of *pongal*, a rice, sugar and nuts confection which gives the festival its name.

Holi. Full-moon festival welcoming the arrival of spring. Indians typically celebrate by throwing vast quantities of dyed water and paint over one another. Not for the faint-hearted.

August

Raksha Bandhan. A festival dedicated to the brother-sister relationship, celebrated most prominently in North India, during which brothers and sisters tie coloured strings on each other's wrists.

Sept–Oct

Dussehra. Ten-day festival

Chennai

Kalakshetra Arts Village, Dr Muthulakshmi Road, Tiruvanmiyu, tel: 044-2452 4057, www.kalakshetra.net. Founded in 1936 with the intention of reviving traditional Indian music, dance and crafts, and hosting regular performances.

The Music Academy, corner TTK Road and Dr Radhakrishnan Salai, tel: 044-2811 2231, www.musicacademy madras.in. The leading venue for Carnatic classical music and Bharatnatyam dance.

NIGHTLIFE

Outside of the sometimes dubious pleasures of Goa, and the burgeoning prosperity of Mumbai, India is not famed for its nightlife. However, things are slowly changing in other large cities, too, as the young middle classes adopt more Western lifestyles. Many places are in the large, luxury hotels, all of which have strict admission policies. Bars are still largely a male preserve and lone women may find them intimidating. For up-to-date listings check out www. explocity.com.

celebrating the victory of good over evil, particularly Rama's triumph over Ravana and Durga's over Mahishasura.

Oct–Nov

Diwali. India's biggest national celebration, the 'Festival of Lights', commemorates the homecoming of Rama and Sita with the lighting of innumerable oil lamps and the setting-off of vast quantities of fireworks.

Nov–Dec

Pushkhar Camel Fair. One of India's most celebrated events, with thousands of camels converging in the Rajasthani Desert while a mass Hindu bathing ritual takes place in nearby Pushkar Lake.

Moveable

Kumbha Mela. India's greatest religious celebration, held every four years, leading up to the Maha Kumbha Mela, held every 144 years at Allahabad, the world's biggest festival – the last one, in Jan/Feb 2013, attracted tens of millions of pilgrims.

Eid-ul-Fitr. India's largest Muslim festival, celebrating the end of the holy month of Ramadan.

Delhi

Agni, The Park Hotel, 15 Parliament Street, Connaught Place, www. theparkhotels.com. Designed by London's Conran & Partners, this chic and sexy bar (plus small dance floor) is one of the fanciest places to party in the city, with a glam crowd to match.

Decibel, Hotel Samrat, Kautilya Marg, Chanakyapuri, tel: 011-2611 0606. Young expats and hip young things from south Delhi's beau monde are the mainstay of this wildly popular club, where you can order fancy cocktails and dance the night out on a large floor to mostly mainstream sounds.

Elevate, Centre Stage Mall, Sector 18, Noida. Four-floor, state-of-the-art super-club on the Jamuna's east bank, with local and international DJs playing a mix of Bollywood, Hip Hop and House. The dance floor accommodates 600 plus and literally shakes (hidden motors underfoot create the good vibes), and there's a breezy rooftop terrace to chill on.

Q'Ba E Block 42–43, Inner Circle, Connaught Place, www.qba.co.in. Slick-looking place with Q-shaped bar downstairs and dining upstairs, plus pleasant outdoor terraces and a DJ most evenings.

Urban Pind, N-4 N-Block Market, Greater Kailash I, tel: 011325146460; www.urbanpind.com. Chic lounge bar famous for its in-your-face, Khajuraho-temple-inspired erotica. They do great Italian cuisine, but the real draw among its mostly twenty-something clientele are the punchy, Indian-inflected cocktails.

Mumbai

Aer Lounge, Four Seasons Hotel, Worli. If they ever shoot a Bond movie in Mumbai, you can bet it will feature the Aer Lounge – a dreamy rooftop bar on the 34th floor of a skyscraper surveying central Mumbai. Crammed to the gunwhales with overpaid expats and local fashionistas sipping Lady Boy cocktails on weekends, but quiet during the week. The perfect venue for a sundowner.

Blue Frog, D2 Mathuradas Mills Compound, Lower Parel, www.bluefrog. co.in. India's most hip and happening venue, comprising live music, its own record label, recording studios and more. Get there early and prepare to meet India's cutting edge.

Café Mondegar, Metro House, Colaba Causeway. Popular drinking hole, with colourful cartoons on the walls, a lively mix of travellers and local students, and wall-to-wall Western rock classics on the sound system.

China House, Grand Hyatt, Off Western Express Highway, Santa Cruz East. Along with Trilogy, the most hip club in north Mumbai and the place to party after hours (closes 3am). House and Hip Hop are the music of choice. Big name DJs play on Fridays.

Cloud 9, Godwin Hotel, 41 Garden Rd, Colaba. Rooftop terrace bar with a sweeping 360-degrees panorama over south Mumbai and the harbour. Come on a week night and you'll have to place to yourself. Serves chilled beer at restrained prices, and great food.

Enigma, J.W. Marriott Hotel, Juhu Tara Road. Ultra-trendy and stylish club, favoured by Bollywood stars and Mumbai's filthy rich. The decor's as glam as the clientele and the music a mix of bangra, filmi dance tracks and house. Dress to impress, or you'll have a long wait to get in.

Ghetto, 30B Bhulabhai Desai Road, Breach Candy. Old established south Mumbai dive bar, with graffiti-covered walls, free popcorn and a sound system belting out classic rock.

Indigo, 4 Mandlik Road, Colaba, www.foodindigo.com. Uber-sophisticated fine dining experience, with a refined bar to match – this is one of the Mumbai glitterati's favourite haunts.

Trilogy, Hotel Sea Princess, Juhu Tara Road, Juhu Beach. Unquestionably Mumbai's sexiest night club. Wins in the glamour stakes for its lipstick- red staircase, velvet sofas and rainbow lighting on the dance floor. If you're out to impress, book one of the VIP tables upstairs overlooking the Arabian Sea.

Zenzi, Wakefield Riad, Bandra, www.zenzi-india.com. Hip Balinese-inspired interiors and top-notch pan-Asian menu are the hallmarks of this cool Dutch-owned club in the swanky suburb of Bandra.

Goa

Club Cubana Baga, www.clubcubanagoa.com. Cosmopolitan club with a two-storey dance floor, pool and visiting DJs playing R&B, garage and hip-hop.

Club Fresh, Aswem-Morjim, www.clubfreshgoa.com. New-ish arrival on the north Goa scene, this glam club-cum-restaurant offers a decent selection of sushi, live DJs and occasional fashion shows.

Hilltop, Vagator. An old-school club in the scrub behind Ozran Vagator

High end fashion at a Delhi Hauz Khas boutique.

beach, Hilltop recreates the vibe of a Goa rave circa 1990, down to the fluorescent-painted palm trees and Trance DJ sets. A mostly Russian and Israeli clientele fills the circular earth dance floor.

Mambo's Baga. Wildly popular open-air pub-cum-club right on Baga Beach, below the legendary (but rather seedy) Tito's.

Nine Bar, Vagator. Classic Goa trance blasts from a hefty PA across the open-air dance floor, with spacy views through the palm tops out to sea – this venue was at the epicentre of the Trance scene back in the 1990s, and still hosts kicking parties on Wednesdays evenings.

Tito's Baga. Legendary Goan nightclub – arguably the most famous in India – with an eclectic range of music and a rather down-at-heel atmosphere.

Kolkata

Afraa, 7th Floor, City Centre, Salt Lake, www.afraakolkata.com. All-white interiors and a global menu make for a sophisticated experience.

Fusion, Golden Park Hotel, 13 Ho Chi Minh Sarani, Park Street, www.goldenparkk.com. A relaxed restaurant at the beginning of the night, this place gets swinging later on, when the 20,000-watt sound system cranks up to full effect.

Tantra, Park Hotel, 17 Park Street, http://calcutta.theparkhotels.com. Kolkata's biggest club, spread over two floors and open until late. If the throbbing dance floors and celeb-studded bars fail to do it for you, try the 1960s-inspired Roxy cocktail bar in the same hotel.

Underground, Hotel Hindustan International, 235/1 A.J.C. Bose Road. Fun club, with Hard-Rock-style decor inspired by the London

Underground and a soundtrack that's big on electro and hip-hop.

Urban Desi, 9th Floor, 6 Carnac St. Laid-back lounge bar on a rooftop terrace surveying the skyline of central Kolkata. Serves Indian and pan-Asian cuisine, and there's a funky Moroccan tent with proper sheeshas.

Venom, 8th floor, Fort Knox, 6 Camac Street. Biggest dance floor in the city, with DJs pumping out a mix of rock, hip-hop, house and Bollywood.

Bengaluru (Bangalore)

13th Floor, Barton Centre, 84 MG Road, tel: 080-4178 3355. Great skyline panorama from this classy lounge bar, with its views over the city's iconic new metro station on MG Road.

B-Flat, 100ft Rd, Above ING Bank, Indiranagar. Live Jazz, Blues, Fusion, Retro and quiz nights feature at this cool music venue. Listings are posted on their busy Facebook page.

I-Bar, The Park, 14/7 M.G. Road, tel: 080-2559 4666. Trendy night-time venue for Bengaluru's hip crowd, with the added attraction of a poolside terrace.

Peco's, Rest House Road, off Brigade Road. Dark and entertainingly grungy rock dive with cheap draught beer and loud retro sets from the house DJs.

Shiro, 2nd Floor, UB City Mall, Vittal Mallaya Road, tel: 080-4173 8864. Stunning oriental-themed lounge bar atop Bengaluru's swankiest mall; food and drinks both top-class – and so is the decor, dominated by a gigantic, serene-faced Japanese Buddha.

Chennai

10 DS, Kences Inn, 50 BN Road, T. Nagar, tel: 044-2815 2152, www.10downingstreetindia.net. Perenially popular 'British-style' bar/

TRANSPORT   ACCOMMODATION   ACTIVITIES   A – Z   LANGUAGE club, where fish fingers feature on the menu and a smart dress code is enforced. More popular with expats and well-heeled locals than travellers. Ladies free on Wednesdays.

Distil, Taj Connemara, Binny Road, Anna Salai, tel: 044-6600 0000. Regarded by many as the classiest bar in town, with cutting edge designer decor and innovative cocktails (where 'fresh fruit and herbs are happily muddled' as the menu blurb puts it).

The Leather Bar, The Park, 601 Anna Salai, tel: 044-4267 6000. Leather-lined walls, pumping tunes and a vast array of drinks make this one of the top choices in the city – head to Pasha in the same hotel if you feel like going on.

No Sky Above, Tangy Resorts, off East Coast Rd, Nellankarai, tel: 044-4290 7500. One of the only places near town where you can enjoy a drink with a view of the ocean, and watch IPL cricket games live on a big screen. A nice, laid-back vibe, reasonable food and a cooling sea breeze make this a popular option for a relaxing drink.

OUTDOOR ACTIVITIES

Trekking

There's superb trekking throughout the Indian Himalayas and compared to neighbouring Nepal, routes are still pleasantly peaceful and un-touristed. The main starting points for treks are Leh, Darjeeling, Manali, Gangtok and Garhwal, and around Kinnaur in Himachal Pradesh, with a wide variety of routes. Possibilities include treks through the Singalili range near Darjeeling (taking in Kanchenjunga, the world's third-highest peak); between remote Buddhist monasteries and villages in the uplands around Leh; along the pilgrimage routes around Garhwal; or through Sikkim's high-altitude rhododendron forests.

There are also numerous trekking possibilities in the Western Ghats in southern India, particularly in the extensive highland forests of the Nilgiri Biosphere Reserve, which straddles the borders of Tamil Nadu, Kerala and Karnataka and offers many, still largely unexplored, hiking possibilities, including walks in or around the Bandipur, Nagarhole and Mudumalai wildlife sanctuaries. There are further trekking possibilities in Rajasthan, particularly up in the Aravalli Hills around Mount Abu.

High Places, UK tel: 0114-275 7500, www.highplaces.co.uk. Experienced UK operator running treks throughout the Indian Himalayas.

Mountain Kingdoms, UK tel: 01453-844 400, www.mountainkingdoms.com. Treks in Himachal Pradesh, Garhwal and Rajasthan.

Mountain Travel Sobek, US tel:

What's On

Time Out listings magazines are published fortnightly for Delhi, Mumbai and Bengaluru, and also at www.timeout.com. *First City* is a monthly magazine covering events in Delhi. *Mumbai This Fortnight* is a useful source of information – and it's free.

1-888-831 7526, www.mtsobek.com. Challenging treks in the Himalayas and elsewhere in India.

Watersports

Diving

The best diving in India is far away from the mainland in India's two tropical archipelagos. There are superb coral reefs at the **Andaman Islands** (trips can be arranged from Port Blair) and at the tiny **Lakshadweep Islands**. Unfortunately, the cost of getting to either of these places (and the expense of staying at Lakshadweep) is something of a deterrent. On the mainland, **Goa** is the principal diving spot, with several operators now offering trips, although the limited underwater visibility is a drawback (operators have to ferry divers four hours south down the coast by boat to dive off Anjevid Island, where there's less silt in the water).

Paragliding over Anjuna beach.

Whitewater rafting

A number of rivers in northern India
offer challenging and spectacular
whitewater rafting as they tumble
down through the Himalayas. Some
of the best places to go rafting are
Kullu, Manali, Leh, Risikesh and
Gangtok. The Indus River near Leh
offers a particularly scenic (although
fairly staid) ride, and you can also go
kayaking here. Rafting is best from
around June to August, when water
levels are at their highest.

Contact Himalayan River Runners,
Green Park, Delhi for expert advice,
tel: 011-2685 2602, www.hrrindia.
com.

SHOPPING

What to Buy

India can be a very rewarding place to
shop – perhaps no other country on
Earth produces such a dazzling array
of handicrafts in such a huge variety
of forms. **Textiles** are ubiquitous,
from the traditional *khadi* (homespun
cotton) garments championed by
Gandhi through to brilliantly coloured
mirrorwork Rajasthani fabrics and
sumptuous Mysore and Varanasi
silks. Clothes come in all shapes
and sizes, from beautiful traditional
saris (those from Kanchipuram in
Tamil Nadu are particularly famous)
and *shalwar kameez* through
to contemporary designs using
traditional fabrics, such as those sold
by the excellent Anokhi, Soma and
Fabindia chains.

Kashmir is the traditional centre of
India's carpet industry (made in both
wool and silk), producing world-class
rugs – sometimes at world-class
prices. Colourful **dhurries** (the Indian
version of the *kilim*) are made in many
parts of the country and are likely to
make less of a dent in the wallet.

Gold, silver and jewellery can be
found everywhere. Jaipur is famous
for its gems (although not all are
genuine – shop with caution), and is
also good for silver, as are many other
places in Rajasthan. Metalware is
popular, too: brass and copper trays,
plates, statues and enamel inlay-
work, or the beautiful *bidri* designs
made in Karnataka.

Carved sandalwood figures and
elaborately worked wooden panels
are a speciality of the south, while
superb marble inlay-work (*pietra
dura*) can be found in Agra. Pottery,
lacquerware and cane goods are

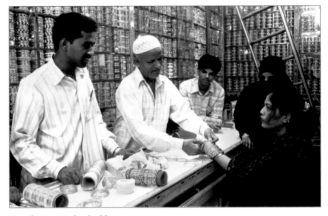
Bangles at a Hyderabad bazaar.

common, while leatherware is also
often excellent, either made into
bags or fashioned into traditional
shoes, or *jutis*. Miniature paintings
make particularly beautiful souvenirs,
ranging from Persian-style Rajasthani
miniatures on paper or silk through to
Tibetan *thangkas* (religious paintings).

There are thousands of shops
selling all manner of handicrafts all
over the country. Most states run their
own chains of handicrafts shops, and
these so-called **government emporia**
are usually a good place to see what's
on offer and get an idea of roughly
how much things should cost – prices
are fixed here, although generally a
bit more expensive than elsewhere.
Away from the government emporia,
bargaining is the order of the day.
Note that antiques and semi-antiques
are governed by strict laws limiting
their export; also beware of fakes.
The export of skins, furs and ivory is
strictly forbidden. Major **credit cards**
such as Visa and MasterCard are
widely accepted in shops, but don't let
your card out of sight as credit-card
fraud is common (multiple copies of
card receipts are often made and then
charged later on).

Where to Shop

Agra

Agra is a major craft centre,
particularly famous for its inlaid
marble work, or *pietra dura* (similar
to that which can be seen on the
facade of the Taj Mahal). Note,
though, that many items passed off
as marble are actually soapstone
or chalk. Check if the stone is
translucent (it will light up from the
other side) and whether it leaves
a mark when rubbed on a rough

surface; marble will light up and will
not leave a mark. The city is also good
for carpets and dhurries, as well as
traditional embroidery and leather.

There are handicraft emporia
scattered all over town. A good
starting point is along **Fatehabad
Road**, which has a long string of big
shops selling all the different crafts
made in the region. The large **Cottage
Industries Exposition** is one of the
largest, although also one of the most
expensive. **Shilpgram** crafts village,
near the Taj East Gate, has items from
all over India.

Bengaluru (Bangalore)

MG Road and Brigade Road are
Bengaluru's main shopping streets,
with the usual array of shops. The
main souvenir emporium is the
government-run Cauvery Arts and
Crafts Emporium, at the junction
of these two roads, which sells an
excellent range of wooden objects
including statues and assorted
toys and souvenirs finely carved in
sandalwood and rosewood.

The best selection of **bookshops**
is along MG Road and Church Street.
Alternatively, for India-related titles try
the excellent Motilal Banarsidas, at
16 Mark's Road near the junction with
MG Road. For more mainstream fare,
visit the big new Crossword store at
the ACR Towers, 32 Residency Road.

Chennai

The **Indian Arts Emporium** at 152
Anna Salai is a good place to look for
handicrafts and metalwork. Over the
road is **Spencer Plaza**, a large, air-
conditioned shopping centre, which
has a good range of clothes shops
and souvenir stalls.

Chennai is one of the best places
in India to buy **books**. The following

Backstreet workshops are found everywhere in Indian cities.

shops are all very helpful, have a good stock and will post books back for you: Landmark Books in Spencer Plaza is said to be Asia's largest bookstore, with a huge number of books and CDs; Bookpoint, 160 Anna Salai, is also recommended; Higginbothams, 814 Anna Salai, is one of the largest bookshops in India; and Giggles in the Taj Connemara Hotel is also recommended for its knowledgeable owner and eclectic stock.

Chennai is also a good place for **clothes and fabrics**, and is an excellent place to pick up the famous silks made in the nearby town of Kanchipuram. Try the government shops (and others) at the top end of Anna Salai, in particular the **Central Cottage Industries Emporium** at No. 476 and Poompuhar at No. 818. There's also a branch of the excellent Anokhi chain, specialising in contemporary takes on traditional block-printed fabrics, at 106 Chamiers Road, RA Puram.

Delhi

Central Delhi
The centre of New Delhi, Connaught Place, has a wide range of smart-looking but fairly uninteresting Western-style shops, although it's much more fun to rummage around in the touristy **Tibetan market** close by at the top of Janpath, which has stalls selling Tibetan curios alongside a wide range of other Indian and Western clothes and cheesy souvenirs. Opposite here, at Jawahar Vyapur Bhavan, Janpath, is the cavernous, government-run **Central Cottage Industries Emporium**, with a huge variety of goods from

across India spread over six floors – fabrics, jewellery, metalwork, woodcarvings and much more. The similarly huge **State Emporia** close by on Baba Kharak Singh Marg host branches of government-run handicraft shops from around the country. Among the best of the emporia are Cauvery (Karnataka) with good silks; Poompuhar (Tamil Nadu) with some exquisite, but expensive, bronzes; the Handicrafts Development Corporation, with lots of silks; Lepakshi (Andhra Pradesh) with good gold and pearl jewellery; Rajasthali (Rajasthan), with a very large and well-presented selection of everything from fabrics to jewellery; and Gurjari (Gujarat), with an excellent selection of cotton textiles. It's also worth visiting the **Khadi Gramodyog Bhawan** on Sansad Marg, which has a fine selection of traditional Indian *khadi* (homespun cloth) clothing.

Old Delhi
The heaving bazaars of Old Delhi, centred on the famous thoroughfare of Chandni Chowk, form the city's traditional commercial heart. Running south off Chandni Chowk, just past the Jain Mandir, is **Dariba Kalan**, the jewellers' street, once famous for its gold but now mostly selling silver. **Katra Neel**, west of the town hall on Chandni Chowk, is a warren of small shops selling fabrics, particularly silk, by the metre. **Nai Sarak**, which runs between Chandni Chowk and Chawri Bazaar, has various small bookshops, although they sell mainly Hindi-language and educational titles. By the Jama Masjid is the extraordinary **spare car-parts bazaar**.

The main bazaar in **Paharganj** is the principal backpacker hangout in

Delhi, lined with little shops and stalls selling all manner of clothes, fabrics, souvenirs and every conceivable type of kitsch. Prices tend to be fairly cheap (and very bargainable), although quality isn't always particularly high.

Karol Bagh Market is a much more local affair, aimed at middle-class Delhiites and selling a wide range of clothes and home ware, as well as being home to Delhi's main motorcycle and cycle markets.

South Delhi
The upwardly affluent suburbs of South Delhi are a world away from the old city bazaars – expect designer malls and posh markets. Just south of India Gate, **Sunder Nagar Market** has a number of good art and antique stores, while it's also worth visiting the shop at the nearby **Crafts Museum**. A short distance west from here, **Khan Market**, is where Delhi's diplomatic crowd goes to shop. It has good bookshops and some superb delis, plus a branch of Anokhi and an outlet for the Biotique range of ayurvedic skin-care products, as well as an increasing number of designer boutiques.

Further west, the chic **Santushti** shopping complex has another branch of Anokhi, and of Padakkam, which sells fabrics and accessories from South India, mostly Keralan. **Sarojini Nagar Market**, a bit further south, is good for export surplus clothes and shoes.

The swish, air-conditioned **Ansal** Plaza, on Khel Gaon Marg, has designer shops and a branch of Music World with a good range of Indian CDs. Another established stop on the South Delhi shopping circuit, the swish **Hauz Khas Village Complex** has numerous designer shops selling *shalwar* and *lehengas*. Try Nasreen Qureshi (26 Hauz Khas Village), a Pakistani designer from Lahore, now living in Delhi. Expressionist Designs (1A Hauz Khas Village, tel: 651 8913) stock the clothes of Delhi designer Jaspreet. For a large stock and the work of several Delhi designers, go to Marwari's (15 Hauz Khas Village).

Other good markets can be found at South Extension, Defence Colony, Greater Kailash (N and M Block Market), and Lajput Nagar Central Market. For **books**, try the Om Book Shop at E77 South Extension Part 1 (also at 45 Basant Lok, Vasant Vihar).

There has been an explosion in the number of malls in Delhi in recent years, most of them in Gurgaon, with the two notable exceptions being

TRANSPORT

Select City Walk near Saket and Ambience Mall in Vasant Kunj, both catering to the top end of the market and indistinguishable from malls the world over.

Gangtok

Gangtok is a good place to search for all things Tibetan and Sikkimese. The **Directorate of Handicrafts and Handloom Emporium** at Zero Point on the National Highway is a good first port of call, with a big stock including carpets and paintings of *thangkas*. Various shops on M.G. Road sell Tibetan and Sikkimese handicrafts, while cheaper artefacts can be found at Lal Market on Paljor Stadium Road.

Goa

As you'd expect, shops in Goa tend to specialise in colourful, flimsy clothes, beachware and sarongs, although many places also stock handicrafts from elsewhere in India, particularly colourful Rajasthani fabrics and jewellery.

The celebrated **flea market** held every Wednesday at **Anjuna beach** is one of India's most famous shopping experiences, attracting an eclectic array of sales folk from across India, with Tibetan and Kashmiri traders rubbing shoulders with Lamani tribal women from Karnataka along with sunburnt tourists and seasoned hippies. Stalls from different regions occupy different parts of the market, so although it's big, it's fairly easy to find what you think you might want – although expect to bargain like crazy to get a decent price if you decide to buy.

For something a little less frenetic, head to the **Saturday Night Bazaar** (also known as Ingo's Night Bazaar) on Arpora Hill, between Baga and Anjuna, which has a mix of Indian stalls alongside many run by Westerners selling party gear and various other quirky collectables. There's a third market, **Mackie's Saturday Night Market**, further up towards Baga.

Hyderabad

Hyderabad is the **pearl capital** of India, and pearl jewellery and silver filigree-work are the best buys in the city. Hyderabad is also famed for its glass and lacquer bangles and Lambadi silver jewellery. Venkatagiri and Pochampalli handloom saris, Dharmavaram silk fabrics, Kalamkari 'painted' cloths, and carpets from Warangal and Eluru are also good buys. Kondapalli wooden toys and inlaid *bidri*-ware are other well-

known Andhran handicrafts. All these products are available at **Lepakshi** in the Mayur Complex.

The **pearl market** is on Petherghati Road near the Charminar in Hyderabad. Nearby are the city's famed **bangle shops**, along with numerous silversmiths and *bidri*-ware craftsmen.

Jaipur

Jaipur makes a fair claim to being regarded as India's handicraft capital, with literally miles of bazaars showcasing brilliant Rajasthani artefacts, including textiles, gemstones, silver, pottery and more. Start at the cavernous **Rajasthali Government Emporium**, on M.I. Road opposite Ajmeri Gate, which offers a good overview of the state's handicrafts and approximate prices.

Textiles are a particular forte, such as the characteristic tie-dyed *bandhani* fabrics, as well as the block prints (a speciality of the nearby town of Sanganer), or the stunning appliqué-work fabrics inlaid with gold or silver thread, mirror work brocades, or patchwork designs. Bapu Bazaar is chock-full of shops selling all the above, as are the shops along Amber Road just beyond Zorawar Gate. Jaipur is also the home town of **Anokhi** (2nd floor, KK Square Mall, Prithviraj Road), which sells superb block-printed clothes, fabrics and home ware in beautiful block-printed designs, and **Soma** (5 Jacob Road), which sells similar products at slightly cheaper prices. If you want to get your own clothes made, try **Jodhpur Tailors**, behind the Neelam Hotel on M.I. Road, who count the Maharaja of Jaipur amongst their customers.

Jaipur is also famous as a centre for semi-precious **gemstones** – although fakes are common. There are numerous gem shops along M.I. Road and in Chameliwala Market (although this has a rather dubious reputation for fakes). **Johari Bazaar** is the place to head for if you're looking for jewellery, with a huge array of shops selling vast quantities of silverware, along with gemstones and gold.

You can have gems tested for authenticity at the government-sponsored Gem and Jewellery Export Promotion Council, 2nd Floor, Rajasthan Chamber Bhavan, M.I. Road (tel: 0141-256 8221; open Mon–Fri). Tests cost Rs441–772 per stone (overnight service) or Rs772–1,103 (same-day service), depending on the type of stone. They'll need to keep the stone for at least two hours, and for same-day tests you'll need to

get it to them by 2pm.

Another local speciality is '**blue pottery**', hand-painted vessels decorated with floral motifs and geometric patterns in combinations of blue, white and occasionally other colours. The best shops are on Amber Road, or head to the workshop of the late Kripal Singh on Shiv Marg, Bani Park. Traditional leather **shoes** (*jutis*) are also widely available.

Kerala

The state government emporium is known as **Kairali**, with branches in Ernakulam (on M.G. Road), Kozhikode (on M.M. Ali Road) and Thiruvananthapuram, where it is called the SMSM Handicrafts Emporium (just behind the Secretariat building).

Among Kerala's exports are items made from **coir** (coconut fibre), spun and made into all kinds of mats, carpets and bags. Alappuzha is the centre of the coir industry and is probably the best place to look.

All towns have their **fabric shops**. In Thiruvananthapuram try Partha's on Powerhouse Road (they also have a branch in Ernakulam on M.G. Road), which has a huge selection of dress fabrics and ready-made clothes, or Alapatt Silks in East Fort. In Kochi a lovely modern shop selling designer clothes and items for the home is **Cinnamon**, on Ridsdale Road, by the Parade Ground.

Traditional **gold jewellery** can be exquisite, with delicate interwoven strands and characteristic small bobbles. It is generally sold by weight, and the day's gold price should be displayed in the shop. Don't expect jewellery to be cheap, especially if gems are included in the piece. Do make sure, as well, that you buy from a reputable jeweller. One of the largest chains in the state is **Alukkas**. They have branches in Thiruvananthapuram (East Fort), Ernakulam (M.G. Road), Alapuzha (Boat Jetty Road) and Thrissur (Round East, by the temple). Another very reputable chain is Josco. They can be found in Thiruvananthapuram (East Fort), Kottayam (K.K. Road), Ernakulam (M.G. Road), Thrissur (M.O. Road) and Palakkad (G.B. Road).

Although the rules for exporting antiques from India are very strict, you can find some very fine items (all passed for export) at **Natesans** on M.G. Road in Thiruvananthapuram.

Kolkata

Kolkata's government emporium, the **Central Cottage Industries**

ACCOMMODATION · ACTIVITIES · A – Z · LANGUAGE

Emporium, is at 7 Chowringhee Road, with the usual range of local and India-wide handicrafts. Close by, antique shops sell Rajasthani jewellery, old prints and postcards. The city also hosts the Assam Craft Emporium at 8 Russell Street, and the Nagaland Emporium at 11 Shakespeare Sarani, featuring Naga artefacts such as traditional shawls and necklaces. There's also a good range of other government emporia at the **Dakshinapan Shopping Centre** on Gariahat Road. **Sasha**, at 27 Mirza Ghalib Street, showcases the productions of a women's self-help group, with good handicrafts and textiles. The colonial-era **New Market** on Chowringhee Road is home to further handicraft outlets. Silks can be purchased at **Indian Silk House**, Gangadeen Gupta, 1 Shakespeare Sarani, in the air-conditioned market, while for contemporary Indian art try Gallerie 88 (28B Shakespeare Sarani) and the Centre Art Gallery (87C Park Street).

The bazaar area in **North Kolkata** spreads over a third of the city, with individual streets devoted to particular types of goods. There are shops and gaddies with elevated floors where hawkers sit selling bags, second-hand books and records, pets and animals (Natibagan), second-hand furniture (Mullick Bazaar), electrical goods (Paddar Court), shoes (Bentinck Street), jewellery (P.B. Sarkar, P.C. Chandra, Dharamtola Street, Bow Bazaar).

Every year, at the end of January, the **Kolkata Book Fair** on Cathedral Road on the Maidan attracts more than a million visitors. Other books can be found at Oxford Book and Stationery, 17 Park Street, and at the Modern Book Depot, 15A Jawaharlal Nehru Road.

Lucknow

Lucknow is famous for its *chikan* embroidery, consisting of delicate floral patterns used to decorate male and female clothing. Examples can be found in the shops around Hazratganj (Janpath Market in particular), Nazirabad and Aminabad. Alternatively, visit **Gangotri**, the Uttar Pradesh Government Emporium, at Hazratganj.

The other local speciality is *ittar* (or *attar*), a type of perfume made by mixing extracts of flowers or spices with oil, and available in various forms like amber, *khus* and *gulab* (rose). Try Sungandcho in Janpath Market.

Mumbai

Mumbai doesn't boast any particularly distinctive artisanal traditions, but is a great place to pick up souvenirs from across the country, showcased in a huge array of shops.

Mumbai also produces much of India's clothing. For a cheap travelling wardrobe, head to '**Fashion Street**' on M.G. Road, specialising in reject and surplus export clothing. For traditional Indian clothing, the place to visit is the **Khadi Village Industries Emporium** at 286 Dr D.N. Marg, occupying the atmospheric premises of the venerable old Whiteaway & Laidlaw Victorian department store. The city also hosts branches of the excellent **Soma** (16 Madama Cama Road) and **Fabindia** (Jeero Building, 137 M.G. Road), retailing beautiful modern silk and cotton clothes made using traditional block-printing techniques. Alternatively, visit **Courtyard**, at SP Centre, Minoo Desai Marg in Colaba, Mumbai's fashionista central, with various boutiques showcasing the work of leading local couturiers and jewellers.

Chor Bazaar offers a great selection of Raj-era antiques, especially around Mutton Street, though check whether you'll be allowed to export anything you buy, and beware of fakes. Alternatively (but more expensively), head to the famous **Philip's** antique shop, in Colaba opposite the Regal Cinema, with a well-stocked selection of Victorian bric-a-brac. **Natesan's**, in the Jehangir Gallery Basement, also has some wonderful, if pricey, antiques and works of art.

For **handicrafts**, try the various state emporia in the World Trade Centre, Cuffe Parade, and Sir P.M. Road, Fort. The **Central Cottage Industries Emporium**, 34 Shivaji Marg (near the Gateway of India) has the widest range.

Mumbai is also a great place to hunt for **books**. Crossword, 22B Bhulabhai Desai Road, has a good range of books, as does Strand, off P.M. Road, Fort. Bookstalls line M.G. Road, from the museum to Hutatma Chowk, mostly selling novels and university and school textbooks. Planet M, Times of India Building, D.N. Road, has a huge range of **CDs**.

Mysore

Mysore is one of the south's leading shopping destinations, famous for silk and sandalwood. Good places to buy fabrics include the **Cauvery Arts and Crafts Emporium** on Sayyaji

Rao Road, and the **Government Silk Factory** on Mananthody Road – or check out the factory's showroom on KR Circle. If in doubt, you can check the purity of silk by burning a strand or two. If the fibres burn away to ash that just crumbles in your fingers then it is pure silk, but if there is a residue then the fabric is wholly or partly synthetic.

Sandalwood is found all over Mysore in various forms: sandalwood carvings, oil, incense and soap. For sandalwood carvings, visit the Cauvery Arts and Crafts Emporium. For sandalwood oil and incense, pay a visit to the **Sandalwood Oil Factory** at Ashokapuram, 2km (1.25 miles) southeast of town.

SPAS AND RETREATS

India has a sizeable, and rapidly growing, number of top-class spas – Kerala and Rajasthan are particularly well supplied; many are found within hotels run by India's two leading hotel chains, Taj and Oberoi. Most Indian spas feature at least some traditional ayurvedic treatments, the ancient system of holistic health care which has been around for at least 5,000 years, and which remains popular, particularly in Kerala, although most also offer various Western treatments as well.

The North

Amatrra Spa, Ashok Hotel, New Delhi, tel: 011-2412 2921, www. amatrraspa.com. Serene city spa offering unique treatments based on the principle of 'Astroveda' – a combination of ayurveda and astrology.

The Northern Plains

Amarvilas Spa, Oberoi Amarvillas, Agra, tel: 0562-223 1515, www. amarvilas.com. Sumptuous spa with views of the Taj outside and a range of treatments featuring ayurvedic techniques along with Thai, hot stone, and Western massage techniques within.

Himalayas

Ananda in the Himalayas, Rishikesh, tel: 01378-227 500, www. anandaspa.com. Serene Himalayan retreat, built in the estate of a maharaja's palace and focusing on ayurveda and yoga.

TRANSPORT

Wildflower Hall Spa, Oberoi Wildflower Hall Resort, Shimla, tel: 0177-264 8585, www.wildflowerhall. com. Superb Himalayan spa, regularly voted the best in India, with glorious mountain views and ayurvedic, Thai and Balinese massages.

Rajasthan

Rajvilas Spa, Oberoi Rajvilas, Jaipur, tel: 0141-268 0101, www.oberoirajvilas.com. This is a sumptuous spa with palatial decor and a wide range of ayurvedic and Western treatments.
Devi Garh, Delwara, 25km (15 miles) north of Udaipur, tel: 02953-289 211, www.deviresorts.in. Set in an imposing 17th-century hilltop palace in the Rajasthani countryside and offering holistic packages combining ayruveda, yoga and meditation with Western treatments.
Jiva Spa, Taj Lake Palace, Udaipur, tel: 0294-242 8800, www.tajhotels. com. In the stunning Lake Palace Hotel and offering a range of traditional treatments such as the signature 'Mewar Khas' royal bathing ritual.

Mumbai

Quan Spa, J.W. Marriott Hotel, Mumbai, tel: 022-6693 3000, www. quanspa.com. Funky urban spa attracting stressed-out executives,

A tiger in Kanha National Park.

Bollywood stars and the like with its menu of restoring (mainly Indian-style) massages and wraps.

Goa

Sereno Spa, Park Hyatt Goa Resort and Spa, Cansaulim, tel: 0832-272 1234, http://goa.park.hyatt. com. Stunning beachside spa, with treatment pavilions overlooking the ocean and a range of unique therapies based on ayurvedic and yogic principles.

Kerala

Coconut Lagoon, Kumarakom, Kerala, tel: 0481-252 4491, www. cghearth.com. The traditionally styled Ayurveda treatment centre of this luxury Keralan resort, which you can only reach by launch, overlooks the glassy waters of Vembanad Lake. Martial arts training and yoga are optional extras, and you sleep in beautifully reconstructed antique carved wood nallukettu houses. Kalari Kovalikom, Kollengode, Kerala. The ultimate Ayurveda spa, housed in a sumptuous 18th-century palace at the foot of the Western Ghat mountains. Its regime is strict – your bags are searched on arrival for cigarettes, alcohol and other forbidden substances. Everyone floats around in white cotton, and the food is pure veg.

WILDLIFE PARKS

There are about 70 national parks and more than 330 sanctuaries in India, home to hundreds of species of mammals, birds and reptiles. Of these, Corbett, Ranthambore, Bandhavgarh and Kanha are famous for tigers, Gujarat's Gir Forest for its population of Asiatic lions, Periyar and Wayanad (both in Kerala) for elephants, Manas and Kaziranga in Assam for one-horned rhinoceroses. A selection of some wildlife sanctuaries follows:
Dudhwa National Park (Uttar Pradesh)
Tiger, leopard, sloth bear, rhinoceros, swamp deer, hog deer, chital deer and an excellent range of bird life. Best time: Dec–June.
Nanda Devi National Park (Uttar Pradesh)
A World Biosphere Reserve and the site of India's second-highest mountain, Nanda Devi Peak (7,816 metres/25,643ft). Animals here include mountain goat, snow leopard and musk deer – though access permitted to only a handful of accredited mountaineering expeditions each year.Best time: Apr–Oct.
Corbett National Park (Uttarakhand)
One of India's oldest and most

ACCOMMODATION

ACTIVITIES

A – Z

LANGUAGE

famous national parks, Corbett is known for its tiger, mugger and gharial crocodile and various species of deer. Mahseer and other fish in the Ramganga River. Best time: Feb–May.

Valley of Flowers National Park (Uttarakhand)
Famous for the 300 species of Alpine flowers that carpet the high-altitude meadows in summer; also noteworthy for bears, tahr and snow leopard and other Himalayan species. Best time: June–Aug.

Great Himalayan National Park (Himachal Pradesh)
Lying southeast of the Kullu Valley, the park has a small population of snow leopards, brown bears, musk deer and thar (mountain goat). Altitudes range from 1,700–5,800 metres (5,700–19,000ft). Best time: Apr–June and Sept–Nov.

Rajasthan

Keoladeo Ghana National Park (Rajasthan)
Formerly known as Bharatpur, India's top ornithological destination, with huge and spectacular flocks of water birds and other resident and migratory species. Best time: Oct–Mar.

Kumbalgarh Sanctuary (Rajasthan)
This large sanctuary in the Aravalli Hills is perhaps the only area in India where the highly endangered wolf is breeding successfully. Other animals include leopard, sloth bear, chinkara, chousingha, ratel and flying squirrel. Best time: Sept–Nov.

Ranthambore National Park (Rajasthan)
Famous for its tigers, and one of the easiest places in the world to see these big cats. Also boasts sambar, chital, nilgair, monkey, hyena and abundant bird life. Best time: Oct–Apr.

Sariska Tiger Reserve (Rajasthan)
Sadly, and despite a recent scheme to re-introduce them, the Sariska tigers are no more, but the reserve retains populations of nilgai antelope, various deer, abundant bird life and beautiful scenery. Best time: Oct–Apr.

Thar Desert National Park (Rajasthan)
To the west of Jaisalmer, this park is a sanctuary for desert species such as the jackal and Indian bustard. Best time: Nov–Mar.

Sasan Gir Lion Sanctuary (Gujarat)
Last home of the Asiatic lion and one of the last of the Indian wild ass. The park has more than 40 species of animals and more than 300 species of birds, some migrant from Africa. Best time: Dec–Apr.

Velavadar National Park (Gujarat)
One of the best places to see blackbuck antelope. Best time: Nov–Mar.

Wild Ass Sanctuary (Gujarat)
This special sanctuary in the Little Rann of Kutch was set up for the Indian wild ass. Other animals include blackbuck, a few chinkara gazelle, wolf and desert cat. Best time: Jan–June.

Bandhavgarh National Park (Madhya Pradesh)
Sal and mixed forest with bamboo breaks. Excellent game-viewing and bird life. Tiger, leopard, gaur (India bison), chital and sambar deer, dhole (wild dog), nilgai antelope, wild boar, sloth bear, chinkara (Indian gazelle). Elephant riding. Best time: Nov–June.

Kanha National Park (Madhya Pradesh)
Considered by some to be India's greatest national park, and an inspiration for Rudyard Kipling's *Jungle Book*, Kanha is certainly an excellent place to see many species in their natural habitat. Barasingha (swamp deer), tiger and other species. Best time: Feb–June (closed July–Nov).

Indravati National Park and Tiger Reserve (Chattisgarh)
This park has perhaps the only viable population of wild buffalo in Central India and is also home to the barasingha (swamp deer), sambar deer, nilgai antelope, chausingha antelope, chinkara and blackbuck gazelles, gaur, sloth bear, wild boar, leopard, wolf, hyena and jackal. Best time: late Jan–Apr.

Sunderbans Tiger Reserve (West Bengal)
Most of the area is a vast estuarine mangrove forest and swamp inhabited by crocodiles and turtles. The Gangetic dolphin can also be seen. The park holds more tigers than any other reserve. Best time: Dec–Feb.

Khangchendzonga National Park (Sikkim)
Wet temperate forest rising to the rock and snow of the high Himalayan peaks on the Nepalese border. The park has an impressive range of animals and birds: leopard, clouded leopard, tahr, musk deer, bharal (blue sheep), serow, snow leopard, red panda and binturong (Asian bearcat). Best time: Apr–May, Aug–Oct.

Kaziranga National Park (Assam)
Famous for rhinoceros, wild buffalo, barasingha deer and hog deer. Tiger, wild boar, Hoolock gibbon, capped langur and ratel can also be seen.

Well-trained elephants can be hired for safaris – the only park in India where this is possible. Best time: Nov–Mar.

Manas National Park (Assam)
Together with Kaziranga, Manas is well known for its population of one-horned rhinoceros.

Namdapha National Park (Arunachal Pradesh)
This remote sanctuary in the eastern Himalayas shelters a fascinating mix of Indo-Burmese, Indo-Chinese and Himalayan wildlife. Leopard, clouded leopard, snow leopard, gaur, goral, takin, musk deer, Hoolock gibbon, slow loris, binturong and red panda. Hornbill and pheasant are among the great range of birds. Best time: Oct–Mar.

Bandipur National Park (Karnataka)
This park has one of the best-planned road systems among Indian parks, which provides excellent opportunities for game-viewing, especially for elephant, leopard and gaur. Best time: Nov–Feb.

Nagarhole National Park (Karnataka)
An extremely attractive park, separated from Bandipur by a large reservoir. Large groups of gaur, elephant, the occasional tiger and leopard, chital and sambar are seen. Over 250 species of birds have been recorded here. Best time: Oct–Apr.

Annamalai Sanctuary (Tamil Nadu)
Also known as the Indira Gandhi Sanctuary, this densely forested area in the Nilgiri Hills northwest of Kodaicanal is known for its lion-tailed macaques, leopards and a small number of tigers and elephants.

Mudumalai National Park (Tamil Nadu)
This sanctuary with mixed deciduous forests is bounded to the north by Bandipur National Park in Karnataka and to the west by the Wayanad Sanctuary in Kerala. It has good animal viewing and facilities. Best time: Mar–June, Sept–Oct.

Periyar Wildlife Sanctuary (Kerala)
India's southernmost tiger reserve. Elephant-viewing excellent, some tigers and monkeys. There are woodland birds in abundance. Boats and rafts available. Best time: Sept–May.

Silent Valley National Park (Kerala)
This was set up to protect the peninsula's last substantial area of primary tropical rainforest. Elephant, lion-tailed macaque and tiger are among the animals seen. Restricted access. Best time: Sept–Mar.

A – Z

A HANDY SUMMARY OF PRACTICAL INFORMATION

A

Admission Charges

Admission charges at India's museums and tourist attractions vary widely: from a couple of rupees at minor sites up to Rs750 for the Taj Mahal. Many of the country's major sites are run by the Archaeological Survey of India (ASI), with typical entrance fees between Rs100 and Rs250. Entrance to national parks is generally around Rs150–200, plus transport costs.

B

Begging

Visitors to India will encounter people asking for alms, especially in the cities, around holy shrines and on railway journeys. Many of them are physically disabled and have few other options for survival. Small amounts of money will be gratefully received. Try to give discreetly or you might attract unwanted attention. If you are unsure about whether to give or not, simply follow what other people are doing.

Budgeting for Your Trip

India can be either very cheap or incredibly expensive. Living on a shoestring, you could conceivably scrape by on as little as US$20 per day, although most backpackers probably spend around twice this amount or more. For around US$60–80 per day you can stay in comfortable mid-range hotels, eat well and perhaps hire your own car and driver. If you want to really push the boat out, however, you'll be looking at $150–200 per day (and possibly much more than this) – there are plenty of top hotels now charging US$500 per night, or more. Obviously, travelling as a couple is a lot cheaper than going solo, and the big cities are a lot more expensive than the countryside – Mumbai, in particular, is notoriously pricey.

C

Children

Indians love children and are very tolerant of them, making India a very easy place to travel with kids. Children will find the sights and sounds just as rewarding as adults. The problem is that little ones tend to be more easily affected by the heat, unsafe drinking water and unfamiliar food seasoned with chillies and spices. In case of diarrhoea, rehydration salts are vital. To avoid the risk of rabies, children should be vaccinated and kept away from stray animals, especially dogs and monkeys. It is difficult to find nappies and places to change them, so consider bringing a supply of disposables – though bear in mind if you do the absence in most of India of regular waste disposal. Washables may be messier, but at least you won't be leaving your mess behind you. A changing mat is essential. For touring, walking and hiking, a child-carrier backpack is well worth its weight, though you might consider a stroller if you plan to do much travelling in airports and train stations.

Climate

India's climate ranges from the permanent snows of the Himalayas and the tropical conditions along the coasts, to the continental climate of inland areas. There are also many regional and seasonal variations. In general, the best time to visit is after the southwest monsoon.

October to March is the cool season and the best time of year in Peninsular India. The weather is beautifully predictable in winter, with blue skies and bright sunshine in most areas. Parts of the south and east see a brief spell of rain from the northeast monsoon, while snow and sleet make the extreme north very cold and often inaccessible.

Summer, from April to June, is very hot and dry for most of the country, and humid along the coasts. The hills are particularly lovely at this time of the year.

The southwest monsoon begins to set in along the western coast towards the end of May, bringing respite from the heat and varying amounts of rain as it moves across the rest of the country through June and July and withdraws by late September. Northeastern India has heavy rain during this season, making it one of the wettest regions in the world.

Crime and Safety

Generally speaking, India is a safe place to travel, but a tourist is a natural target for thieves and pick-pockets, so take the usual precautions and keep money, credit cards, valuables and passport in a money belt or pouch well secured with a cord around your neck. A protective hand over this in a crowded place could save you a lot of heartache and hassle.

Do not leave belongings unattended, especially on a beach. Invest in good strong locks (available in India) for your bags. Chaining luggage to the berth on a train, or to your seat on a bus, is a precaution that travelling Indians often take. Watch your luggage, especially during loading and unloading.

Credit-card frauds do exist, so make sure that shops and restaurants process your card in front of you.

Another sensible precaution is to keep a photocopy of your passport and visa, traveller's cheque numbers and receipts, ticket details, insurance policy number and telephone claims number, and some emergency money in a bag or case separate from your other cash and documents. If you are robbed, report the incident immediately to a police station (be patient: this can take hours).

Parts of inland Odisha (Orissa), Jharkand and southern Bihar are known for their extreme poverty, persecution of Christian minorities and bandits and are notably less safe than other areas in India. Travel to remoter parts of Kashmir is also not advisable at the present time.

Customs

At present, currency declaration forms for amounts of cash in excess of US$10,000 must be completed at customs on arrival. Prohibited articles include certain drugs, live plants, gold and silver bullion, and coins not in current use. All checked luggage arriving at Delhi airport is X-rayed before reaching the baggage collection area in the arrival hall. Duty-free imports include 200 cigarettes (or 50 cigars), 0.95 litres (1.75 pints) of alcohol, and a reasonable amount of personal effects, including binoculars, laptop, sound recording instruments, etc. Professional equipment and high-value articles must be declared or listed on arrival with a written undertaking to re-export them. Both the list and the articles must be produced on departure. As this formality can be a lengthy process, allow extra time, both on arrival and at departure. For unaccompanied baggage or baggage misplaced by the airline, make sure you get a landing certificate from customs on arrival.

Export of antiques (over 100 years old), all animal products, and jewellery valued at over Rs2,000 (in the case of gold) and Rs10,000 (in the case of articles not made of gold) is banned. When in doubt about the age of semi-antiques, contact the office of the Archaeological Survey of India in Delhi, Mumbai, Kolkata or Chennai (www.asi.nic.in).

Disabled Travellers

Although disability is common in India, there are very few provisions for wheelchairs and special toilets. The roads are full of potholes, and kerbs are often high and without ramps. It may be hard to negotiate street obstacles, beggars, or steep staircases. On the other hand, Indians will always be willing to help you in and out of buses or cars, or up stairs. Taxis and rickshaws are cheap, and the driver, with a little tip, will probably help. You could employ a guide to help with obstacles. Another option is to go with a paid companion. In the UK, **Tourism For All** (7APixel Mill, 44 Appleby Road, Kendal Cumbria LA9 6ES; tel: 0845-124 9971; www.tourismforall.org.uk) can put you in touch with someone.

Some package holiday operators cater for travellers with disabilities, but ensure that your needs have been understood before making a booking.

E

Electricity

The voltage system in India is 220V AC, 50 cycles. DC supplies also exist, so check first. Sockets are normally of the two round-pin variety, but do vary. Take a universal adaptor for British, Irish and Australasian plugs. US and Canadian appliances will need a transformer. Be aware that both power

CLIMATE CHARTS

Delhi

°C J F M A M J J A S O N D mm

Maximum temperature
Minimum temperature
— Rainfall

Kolkata

°C J F M A M J J A S O N D mm

Maximum temperature
Minimum temperature
— Rainfall

Mumbai

°C J F M A M J J A S O N D mm

Maximum temperature
Minimum temperature
— Rainfall

Chennai

°C J F M A M J J A S O N D mm

Maximum temperature
Minimum temperature
— Rainfall

cuts and surges are not uncommon – more expensive hotels will have generator back-up, others will not.

Embassies and Consulates

Australia
www.india.embassy.gov.au
Delhi: Australian High Commission
1/50 G Shantipath, Chanakyapuri, Delhi
Tel: 011-4139 9900
Mumbai: Consulate General
36 Maker Chambers VI, 220 Nariman Point, Mumbai 400 021
Tel: 022-6116 7100

Canada
http://india.gc.ca
Delhi: Canadian High Commission
7–8 Shantipath, Chanakyapuri, New Delhi 110 021
Tel: 011-4178 2000
Mumbai: 6th Floor Fort House, 221 Dr Dn Marg, Mumbai
Tel: 022-6749 4444

Ireland
www.irelandinindia.com
Delhi: Embassy
230 Jor Bagh, New Delhi 110 003
Tel: 011-2462 6733

New Zealand
http://new-zealand.visahq.com/embassy/India
Delihi: High Commission
Sir Edmund Hillary Marg, Chanakyapuri, Delhi 110 021
Tel: 011-4688 3170
Mumbai: Consulate
Level 2, 3 North Avenue, Maker Maxity, Bandra Kurla complex, Mumbai
Tel: 022-6131-6668
Chennai: Consulate
Maithri, 132 Cathedral Road, Chennai 600 042
Tel: 044-2811 2472

UK
http://ukinindia.fco.gov.uk/en
Delhi: British High Commission

Emergency Numbers

As well as the following numbers, there is a new India-wide number covering all three emergency services on **108**. The following numbers, however, will continue to be in use.
Police 100
Fire 101
Ambulance 102
Directory enquiries 197

Sign in Kolkata.

Shantipath, Chanakyapuri
Tel: 011-2419 2100
Mumbai: British Deputy High Commissions
Naman Chambers, C/32 G Block
Bandra Kurla Complex
Bandra (East)
Tel: 022-6650 2222
Kolkata: 1A Ho Chi Minh Sarani
Tel: 033-2288 5172
Chennai: 20 Anderson Road
Tel: 044-4219 2151
Goa: Ms. Shilpa Caldeira
Head of Consular Section, 303-304
Casa del Sol, Opposite Marriott Hotel
Miramar, Panaji
Tel: 0832 2461110/

US
Delhi: Embassy
Shantipath, Chanakyapuri, New Delhi 110 021
Tel: 011-2419 8000
http://newdelhi.usembassy.gov
Mumbai: C-49, G-Block, Bandra Kurla Complex
Bandra East, Mumbai 400051
Tel: 022 2672-4000
http://mumbai.usconsulate.gov
Kolkata: Consulate Generals
5/1 Ho Chi Minh Sarani, Kolkata 700071
Tel: 033-3984 2400
http://kolkata.usconsulate.gov
Chennai :Gemini Circle, Chennai 600 006
Tel: 044-2857 4000
http://chennai.usconsulate.gov

Etiquette

Removing one's shoes before entering someone's house, or a temple, mosque or gurdwara (Sikh temple) is essential. Wearing socks or stockings is usually permissible.

The traditional *namaskaram* greeting with joined hands has been largely (if not completely) replaced by the Western handshake, particularly in cities, although women often prefer not to shake hands with men – don't offer to shake hands with a woman unless she first holds out a hand to you. Kissing and embracing in public is frowned upon; in rural areas, even men and women holding hands can provoke curious stares. (Although the sight of Indian men holding hands with other Indian men is common.)

Leather goods of any kind should not be taken into temples, as these are regarded as impure and can often cause offence. Menstruating women are also usually forbidden from entering Jain temples (although of course no one's going to check).

Photography is prohibited inside the inner sanctum of many places of worship. Do obtain permission before using a camera. Visitors are usually welcome to look around at their leisure and can sometimes stay during religious rituals. For visits to places of worship, modest clothing is essential. In Sikh temples, your head should be covered. In mosques, women should cover their head and arms and wear long skirts. A small contribution to the donation box *(hundi)* is customary.

When eating with your fingers, remember to use only the right hand.

Avoid pointing the soles of your feet towards anyone as this is considered a sign of disrespect. Don't point with your index finger: use either your extended hand or your chin.

G

Gay and Lesbian Travellers

Homosexuality is still a taboo subject for many Indians. Sexual relations between men are no longer punishable with long prison sentences since the regulations were relaxed in 2009, but cruising in public could come

TRANSPORT
ACCOMMODATION
ACTIVITIES
A – Z
LANGUAGE

under public disorder laws. There is no similar law against lesbians. While general attitudes are discriminatory, things are changing slowly, and at least the issue of gay and lesbian rights is starting to be discussed, due in no small part to Deepa Mehta's 1998 film *Fire*, which depicted an affair between two married women, and the 2004 film *Girlfriend*. Attacks on cinemas by the religious right brought counter-demonstrations onto the streets of major cities. However, gay and lesbian travellers should be discreet and avoid any public displays of affection (as should heterosexual couples). On the plus side, hotels will think nothing of two men or women sharing a room.

Good websites with useful information and links include (for gay men) www.indiandost.com, http://gaydelhi.tripod.com, www.bombaydost.co.in, www.humsafar.org and www.gaybombay.org, and (for lesbians) www.sanginii.org.

H

Health and Medical Care

Altitude sickness

This can occur above 2,500 metres (8,200ft). Watch for symptoms of breathlessness, palpitations, headache, insomnia and loss of appetite. With total rest, travellers usually acclimatise within 48 hours. It is important that fluid intake is maintained; at least 4 to 6 litres per day is recommended.

Inhaling a few breaths from an oxygen canister can provide immediate relief in a mild attack. A severe attack, brought on by climbing too high or quickly, is marked by dizziness, nausea, vomiting, convulsions, severe thirst, blurred vision, drowsiness, weakness or hearing difficulties.

The only cure is to descend to a lower altitude at once. Lung damage from lack of oxygen can be permanent if untreated. Allow several days to acclimatise before attempting to re-ascend in easy stages. In acute cases, seek medical advice.

A previous trip with no symptoms does not mean that a traveller is immune to altitude sickness. It can strike anyone, and being fit does not prevent the problem.

Two other, extremely serious and potentially fatal, conditions can occur at high altitude, primarily to

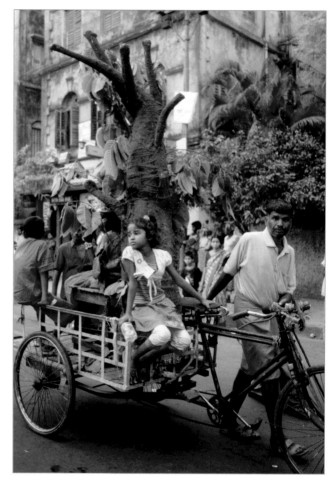

At a Kali festival in Kolkata.

mountaineers: pulmonary oedema and cerebral oedema. The first is the filling of the lungs with fluid (symptoms include coughing up frothy fluid, irrational behaviour and fatigue); the only cure and treatment is to descend immediately. The second is a swelling of the brain (symptoms here include headache, hallucinations and disorientation, eventually resulting in coma); immediate descent is essential to prevent death. To reduce the swelling it is also possible to give 4mg dexamethasone three times per day, although this is a powerful drug and should only be given with medical supervision or in an emergency.

Diarrhoeas

Traveller's diarrhoea is usually caused by low-level food poisoning and can be avoided with a little care. When you arrive, rest on your first day

and only eat simple food; well-cooked vegetarian dishes, a South Indian *thali* and peeled fruits are perhaps best. An upset stomach is often caused by eating too many rich Indian meat dishes (usually cooked with vast amounts of oil and spices) and failing to rest and let your body acclimatise.

Drink plenty of fluids (although it's best to avoid unboiled or unfiltered tap water). When in doubt, stick to soda, mineral water or aerated drinks of standard brands. Avoid ice as this is often made with unboiled water. All food should be cooked and eaten hot. Don't eat salads and always peel fruit.

With all cases of diarrhoea, including dysentery and giardia described below, it is not a good idea to use immobilising drugs such as loperamide (Imodium) and atropine (Lomotil), unless you absolutely need to bung yourself up for, say, the duration of a bus journey, as they prevent the body ridding itself of infection. The most important thing to do in cases of diarrhoea and/or vomiting is to rehydrate, preferably using oral rehydration salts.

Dysentery and giardia are more serious forms of stomach infection and should be suspected if the diarrhoea lasts for more than two days.

Dysentery is characterised by diarrhoea accompanied by the presence of mucus and blood in faeces. Other symptoms include severe stomach cramps and vomiting. Bacillic dysentery comes on quickly and is usually accompanied by fever. It may clear up by itself but its usual treatment is with 500mg of ciprofloxacin or tetracycline twice daily for five days. Do not take the powerful antibiotic chloramphenicol as it can have dangerous side effects. Amoebic dysentery has a slower onset and will not clear up on its own. If you suspect you have amoebic dysentery you should seek medical help as it can damage the gut. If this is not available then self-treat with 400mg of metronidazole (Flagyl) three times daily with food for seven days. Avoid alcohol when taking metronidazole.

Hospitals

In an emergency you can call an ambulance by dialling 102 (although depending on how ill you are, you might find it better just to jump in a taxi/rickshaw and make your own way to the nearest hospital). For other forms of assistance following an emergency, contact East West Rescue, 38 Golf Links, New Delhi, tel: 011-2469 8865, www.eastwestrescue.com. They operate over the whole country and have an extremely good reputation. As a rule of thumb, the new generation of modern, privately run hospitals, such as those founded by the Apollo chain, are better equipped and offer conditions and care closer to what you may be used to back home. Should you require any serious medical treatment in and Indian hosptial, proof of medical insurance cover will be handy.

Chennai
Apollo Hospital, 21–22 Greams Road
Tel: 044-2829 3333
Delhi
All India Institute of Medical Sciences, Ansari Nagar
Tel: 011-2658 8500
Safdarjang General Hospital, Sri Aurobindo Marg
Tel: 011-2616 5060
Hyderabad/Secunderabad

General Hospital, Nampally
Tel: 040-2234 344
Kolkata
Birla Heart Research Centre, 1-1 National Library Avenue
Tel: 033-2456 7777
Medical College Hospital, 88 College Street
Tel: 033-2241 1891
Mumbai
Prince Ali Khan Hospital, Nesbit Road
Tel: 022-2377 7900

Insect bites and stings

Bed bugs can be a problem in cheap hotels; look out for the marks of squashed insects on the walls and floor around the bed. Leeches can also be a problem in wet jungle areas; remove with a lighted match or cigarette, or salt.

Giardia is a similar infection caused by a parasite. Like amoebic dysentery, it comes on slowly and its symptoms include loose and foul-smelling diarrhoea, feeling bloated and nauseous, and stomach cramps. Giardia will not clear up on its own and will recur; its treatment is the same as for amoebic dysentery.

Malaria

This mosquito-borne disease is very serious and potentially fatal. There are two common strains in India, *P. falciparum* and *P. vivax*, both carried by the Anopheles mosquito. Symptoms are similar to acute flu (including some or all of fever, shivering, diarrhoea and muscle pains), and an outbreak may come on as much as a year after visiting a malarial area. If malaria is suspected then medical attention should be sought as soon as possible.

Malaria risk varies in different parts of the country (see the useful malaria map at www.fitfortravel.nhs.uk). Malaria prophylaxis is not always considered necessary (and will never be needed at high altitudes above 2,500 metres/8,200ft); discuss your needs with your doctor or health clinic before travel.

The usual anti-malarial protection for India consists of a combination of daily proguanil (Paludrine) and weekly chloroquine (Avoclar, Nivaquin) tablets. These can now be bought across the counter in the UK, and your pharmacist can advise you on the correct dosages (usually 200mg of proguanil daily and 300mg of chloroquin weekly). This is at present the only safe prophylaxis during pregnancy. However, the combination is at best 70 percent effective and doesn't always work in areas of high

risk. Another drawback with this regime is that you have to start taking these tablets a week before you arrive, and continue for a month after you've returned home.

An alternative and much stronger anti-malarial drug is mefloquine (Lariam), taken weekly. However, this should not be taken by people with a history of epilepsy or mental illness, and there has been much anecdotal evidence of long-lasting and serious side effects (although medical evidence suggests that these are no more likely than with the proguanil/chloroquin combination). In the UK mefloquine is only available as a private prescription.

Other anti-malarial drugs include doxycycline and the recently developed atavoquone-proguanil combination marketed as Malarone. This is recommended for areas of chloroquine resistance (such as Assam) and is taken once a day. Malarone is expensive, but has the great benefit that you only have to start taking it the day you arrive in a malarial area, and continue for a week after. Other drug regimes are not effective against both strains of the disease.

The best, and only certain, protection against malaria is not to get bitten. Sleep under a mosquito net impregnated with permethrin, cover up in the evenings and use an effective insect repellent such as DEET (diethyltoluamide). Burning mosquito coils, which are easily obtainable in India, is also a good idea.

Skin problems

Prickly heat is a common complaint caused by excessive perspiration. Try to keep the skin dry by using talcum powder and wearing loose-fitting cotton clothes. Fungal infections are also common, especially during the monsoon, and can be treated by exposure to the sun and/or by the application of Canesten cream.

Sun exposure

The power of the sun is obvious on the plains and in tropical India, but also be careful in the mountains, where thinner air makes the sun very powerful, even if it feels cooler. Cover up and use a high-factor sunscreen and lip balm, even if it is cloudy. Overexposure can also lead to the two conditions below:

Heat exhaustion is common, and indicated by shallow breathing, a rapid pulse or pallor, and is often accompanied by leg cramps,

TRANSPORT

ACCOMMODATION

ACTIVITIES

A – Z

LANGUAGE

headache or nausea. The body temperature remains normal. Lying down in a cool place and sipping water mixed with rehydration salts or plain table salt will prevent loss of consciousness.

Heatstroke is more serious, and more likely to occur when it is both hot and humid. Babies and elderly people are especially susceptible. The body temperature soars suddenly and the skin feels dry. The victim may feel confused, then pass out.

Take them quickly to a cool room, remove their clothes and cover them with a wet sheet or towels soaked in cold water. Call for medical help and fan them constantly until their body temperature drops to 38°C (100°F).

Vaccinations

No inoculations are legally required to enter India, but it is strongly advised that you get vaccinations against typhoid (Typhim Vi gives protection for 3 years), hepatitis A (Havrix gives immunity for 1 year, or up to 10 years if a 6-month booster is given), polio (a booster is needed every 5 years) and tetanus (booster injection every 10 years). You may need to show proof of a yellow fever inoculation if arriving from an infected area. Other diseases, against which vaccinations might be considered, particularly for longer trips, include meningitis, rabies and Japanese B encephalitis. There is no vaccination against Dengue fever, occasionally contracted in India. The only protection is to avoid being bitten (see also Malaria).

Bring along a personal medical kit to take care of minor ailments. This should include anti-diarrhoea medication, a broad-spectrum antibiotic, aspirin, clean needles, and something for throat infections and allergies would be a good idea. Take your regular medications, tampons, contraceptives and condoms, as these may be difficult to find in shops.

Also include plasters, antiseptic cream and water-purification tablets. All cuts, however minor, should be cleaned and sterilised immediately to prevent infection. Locally supplied oral rehydration powders (such as Vijay Electrolyte) containing salts and dextrose are an ideal additive to water, especially when travelling in the summer months or when suffering from diarrhoea. If oral rehydration salts are not available then one teaspoon each of salt and sugar in 500ml of water is a useful substitute.

Insurance

It is always advisable to obtain good travel insurance to cover the worst possible scenario, and make sure that your policy covers what you need (for instance, that it covers activities like trekking or whitewater rafting, if you're planning on doing these, or that it covers valuables such as expensive cameras or camcorders). Take a copy of your policy and keep a copy of the emergency medical numbers separately as a safeguard.

Internet

Internet access is widely available, either in guesthouses and hotels or in dedicated cybercafés – although away from the big cities connections can be slow and unreliable, with antiquated dial-up connections and frustrating service interruptions. Charges are usually around Rs50–60 per hour – or cheaper in larger cities.

Maps

Obtaining good maps of India can be difficult; the government forbids the sale of detailed maps in border areas, which includes the entire coastline, for security reasons; those which can be bought may not be exported.

Some good maps to bring along with you are: Bartholomew's 1:4,000,000 map of South Asia; Lascelles map of the same scale and Nelles Verlag maps. Other highly recommended maps are the Eicher series of detailed city maps, including those of Delhi, Chennai and Bengaluru, and their India Road Atlas.

Tourist offices can supply visitors with larger-scale city maps. The most detailed are held by the Survey of India, Janpath Barracks A, New Delhi 110 001.

Many of these maps are available from www.indiamapstore.com.

Google's map coverage of India is improving all the time, and provides the most accurate topographical reference tool, even if street labelling can be erratic. StreetView is still a distant dream, however. Attempts were made by Google India in 2012 to photograph go-ahead Bengaluru, but the initiative was stopped by the security-conscious government.

Media

An essential part of India's vibrant political and intellectual life, the press and broadcast media cover a wide political spectrum and have a long and honourable tradition of holding those in power to account. Star, Asia's biggest media company, provides news and entertainment channels.

Newspapers and magazines

The large number of English-language dailies and hundreds of newspapers in Indian languages provide a wide and critical coverage of national and international events.

Among the better-known national English-language dailies are the Times of India (www.timesofindia. indiatimes.com), the Indian Express (www.indianexpress.com), The Hindu (www.hinduonline.com) and The Hindustan Times (www.hindustantimes. com). All dailies have Sunday editions. The main newspapers in Delhi are the Asian Age (www.asianage.com; good for political gossip) and The Pioneer (www.dailypioneer.com), for which both Churchill and Kipling used to write.

The top news magazines include India Today (www.indiatoday.intoday. in), Outlook (www.outlookindia.com) and the exemplary Frontline (www. frontlineonnet.com). There are also excellent general-interest magazines such as Sanctuary (specialising in South Asian natural history), and travel magazines like Outlook Traveller and India Today Travel Plus, which give current information on local cultural events. Other useful news websites include www.samachar. com, with links to leading Indian newspapers, and the pioneering and irreverant www.tehelka.com, which has played a leading role in exposing government corruption scandals.

There are several glossy magazines in English, including Society, many flim magazines and city magazines such as First City, Delhi Diary and Hallo! Madras, plus women's magazines such as Femina, and Indian editions of Cosmopolitan and Elle.

Television and radio stations

Doordarshan is the government TV company and broadcasts programmes in English, Hindi and regional languages. Satellite television is available almost everywhere – hotel TVs usually provide 40-plus channels.

The main provider is Star TV (the Asian version of Sky), which incorporates the BBC World Service and MTV, as well as providing its own sports and movies channels. NDTV is a local 24hr news channel that provides good coverage of Indian news and politics. Other stations include Channel V (a local youth-oriented music channel) and the pop and youth culture-oriented Zee TV (in Hindi and other Indian languages).

All India Radio (AIR) broadcasts on the short wave, medium wave and, in Delhi, Mumbai and Chennai, on FM (VHF). The frequencies vary – you can check programmes online at http://allindiaradio.org/.

Money Matters

The Indian currency is the rupee (subdivided into 100 paise). Coins come in denominations of 10, 20, 25 and 50 paise (although these are increasingly rare) and 1, 2 and 5 rupees. Notes come in 5, 10, 20, 50, 100, 500 and 1,000 rupees. Officially, it's illegal to import or export Indian rupees, although you're unlikely to be checked. Indian banknotes often become incredibly ragged with use. Don't accept torn banknotes, which can prove almost impossible to get rid of (even beggars look upon them with scorn, and giving ruined notes to alms-seekers can be construed

Shopping in downtown Bengaluru.

as insulting). In addition, getting small change in India can be a real challenge. Break large-denomination notes wherever possible, and hoard small change.

The easiest way to access your money in India is via credit or debit card. Almost all towns now have at least one ATM which accepts foreign cards. Visa is the most widely accepted, followed by MasterCard and then American Express; Diners Club is less widely recognised. Credit cards are also increasingly accepted by hotels, restaurants, large shops, tourist emporia and airlines. A number of banks will issue rupees against Visa, MasterCard and (to a lesser extent) Amex. It's worth checking that your card will be valid in India, however. Credit-card fraud means that many banks now automatically block the use of their cards in foreign ATMs unless you call them and ask that they unblock your card for the duration of your visit.

Many tourists still opt to carry a small stock of traveller's cheques with them to guard against the loss of their credit card, or problems finding an ATM which will accept it. Stick to major brands such as American Express, Visa and Thomas Cook, preferably denominated in US dollars or pounds sterling.

O

Opening Hours

Government offices are officially open 9.30am–6pm Monday to Friday, but most business is done between 10am and 5pm with a long lunch break. Post offices open from 10am–4.30pm Monday to Friday, and until 12 noon on Saturday. However, in most of the larger cities, the Central Post Office is open until 6.30pm on weekdays, 4.30pm on Saturday. On Sunday some open until noon. Major telegraph offices are open 24hrs.

Banking hours are Monday to Friday 10am–2pm and Saturday 10am–noon for most foreign and nationalised Indian banks. Some operate evening branches, while others remain open on Sunday and close on another day of the week; some open 9am–1pm. In larger cities many banks now have 24hr ATMs, often guarded, which are very convenient and safe. All banks are closed on national holidays, on 30 June and 31 December for balancing the books.

Shops open from roughly 10am–7pm, some closing for lunch. Although Sunday is an official holiday, different localities in major cities have staggered days off so that there are always some shopping areas open.

Most businesses close on public holidays.

P

Photography

Digital photography is well supported in India, and virtually every town now has at least one photo lab where you can download and burn images to disc, purchase memory cards and get help with technical troubleshooting.

Colour print film, developing and digital printing facilities are available in all cities. Colour slide film has fast become a rarity and labs capable of processing can only be found in major cities,.

Protect your camera and film from excessive exposure to heat, dust and humidity, and note that there are strict restrictions on photography of military installations, bridges and dams, airports, border areas and Adivasi/restricted areas. In general, most Indians are delighted to have their picture taken, although it's still polite to ask permission (and, if using a digital camera, to show them the results afterwards). Note, too, that some people in more remote areas, women in particular, may be less enthusiastic about being snapped. Exercise caution and polite restraint.

Postal/Courier Services

The internal mail service is efficient in most areas. It is advisable to affix stamps to letters or postcards yourself and hand them over to the post office counter for immediate franking rather than to post them in a letter box, or to use one of the private courier services, which are generally efficient and amazing value.

Sending a registered parcel overseas is a complicated and time-consuming process. Most towns have only one main post office, but there is often confusion between Delhi and New Delhi. New Delhi's main post office is near Connaught Circus, while

Dialling Codes

To call India from abroad, dial the international access code, followed by 91 for India, the local code less the initial zero, then the number.

Delhi's main post office is between the Red Fort and Kashmir Gate in Old Delhi.

Courier services

An (expensive) alternative to regular post is to use a courier service. Both FedEx and DHL have offices in all major towns. An alternative to courier services is the government Speedpost service, which delivers parcels fractionally faster than airmail but at far cheaper rates than couriers.

Public Holidays

26 January: Republic Day.
15 August: Independence Day.
2 October: Mahatma Gandhi's Birthday.
25 December: Christmas Day.

R

Restricted/Protected Areas

Andaman and Nicobar Islands, and Lakshadweep

Significant parts of all these island archipelagos are out of bounds to foreign tourists in order to protect indigenous inhabitants (Andamans and Nicobar) or the marine environment (Lakshadweep).

Sikkim

Tourists need an Inner Line Permit to visit Sikkim (available at the border at Rangpo, or in advance from an Indian embassy). You'll need an additional Protected Area Permit (available from the Sikkim Tourism offices in Gangtok) to visit areas in East and North Sikkim (including Tsomgo Lake) and most high-altitude treks.

The northeast

Assam, Meghalaya and Tripura are currently free of restrictions. Permits are required to visit Arunachal Pradesh, Nagaland, Mizoram and Manipur. All visitors to these areas are officially required to travel in groups of at least four, although this rule is sometimes waived on payment of an additional fee. The best way of obtaining a permit is to book a tour through a local operator (see below). Alternatively, contact the Foreigners' Division of the Ministry of Home Affairs, Lok Nayak Bhavan, Khan Market, New Delhi, or the Foreigners' Regional Registration Office, A.J.C. Bose Road, Kolkata (apply four weeks

in advance). You may also be able to obtain a permit through Indian embassies abroad, though apply at least two months in advance.

Local tour operators include Gurudongma Tours (www.gurudongma. com), Jungle Travels India (www. jungletravelsindia.com), Purvi Discover (www.purviweb.com) and, for the south, Aadi Kerala (www.aadikerala. com)

T

Telephones

India's telephone system is improving year on year, and international calls can now be dialled direct to all parts of the world. Calling from hotels can be extremely expensive, with surcharges up to 300 percent, so check rates first. Mobile telephones are everywhere in India, and your own phone may well work while you are there (though you should check in advance with your network provider). If not, you can buy local pre-paid SIM cards from most of the local mobile phone companies, who have shops on every high street. The set-up process involves filing forms with passport photos, but can be completed in around half an hour.

Privately run telephone services with international direct-dialling facilities are widespread. Advertising themselves with the acronyms STD/ISD (standard trunk dialling/ international subscriber dialling), they are quick and easy to use. Some stay open 24hrs. Both national and international calls are dialled direct. To call abroad, dial the international access code (00), the code for the country you want (44 for the UK, 1 for the US or Canada), the area code (without any initial zeros) and the number. Some booths have an electronic screen that keeps time and calculates cost during the call. Prices are similar to those at official telecommunications centres.

Indian telephone numbers are all 10 digits long (including the area code minus the initial zero). Mobile phone numbers also consist of 10 digits, starting with a '9'.

Home country direct services are available from any telephone to the UK, US, Canada, Australia, New Zealand and most other countries. These allow you to make a reverse-charges or telephone credit-card call to that country via the operator there. If you cannot find a telephone with home country direct buttons, you can use any phone toll-free by dialling 000, your country code and 17 (except Canada, which is 000-167). US international access codes are: MCI 000 127; Sprint 000 137; and AT&T 000 117.

Time Zone

India is 5.5 hours ahead of Greenwich Mean Time; 10½ hours ahead Eastern Seaboard Time.

Tipping

There's no harm in expressing your appreciation with a small tip, although be aware that many upmarket hotels and restaurants automatically add a 10 percent service charge to their bills, so there's no need to tip further (unless you particularly want to). If service isn't included, a tip of around 10 percent is generally a good rule of thumb.

Porters at railway stations expect around Rs20 a bag. Rickshaw and taxi drivers won't expect to be tipped, although of course they'll appreciate it if you do – or just letting them keep the change, assuming it's not too much, does equally well. If you have been a house guest, check with your host whether you may tip his domestic helpers (for instance, the driver or cook) before doing so.

Toilets

Traditional Indian 'squat' toilets are becoming increasingly rare, with

Western-style sit-down toilets now the norm. It's still a good idea to carry your own supply of toilet paper, however. Public toilets (in Hindi, *sulabh*), are few and far between, and are almost always stomach-churningly horrible. If you get caught short it's best to head for the nearest reputable hotel.

Tourist Information

The Ministry of Tourism has a good website (www.incredibleindia.org), with a lot of useful information on obtaining visas, places to visit and tour operators. One excellent general site is www.indiamike.com, a popular travel forum run by US India-phile Mike Szewczyk, with lively chat rooms and a useful number of members' travel articles.

Indian government tourist offices abroad

Australia
Level 5, Glasshouse Shopping Complex, 135 King Street, Sydney, New South Wales – 2000
Tel: 61-2-92219555,
E-mail info@indiatourism.com.au.
Canada
60 Bloor Street (West), #1003, Toronto, Ontario M4W 3B8
tel: 416-962-3787
email: indiatourism@bellnet.ca.
South Africa
PO Box 412 542, Craighall 2024, Hyde Lane, Lancaster Gate, Johannesburg 2000
tel: 011-325 0880

email: goito@global.co.za
UK
7 Cork Street, London W1S 3LH
tel: 020-7437 3677
email: info@indiatouristoffice.org
US
3550 Wilshire Boulevard, Suite #204, Los Angeles, CA 90010
tel: 213-380 8855
email: indiatourismindla@aol.com;
Suite 1808, 1270 Avenue of the Americas, New York, NY 10020
tel: 212- 586 4901
email: rd@itonyc.com.

State tourism websites

Andaman and Nicobar Islands andaman-tourism.com
Andhra Pradesh www.aptourism.in
Arunachal Pradesh www. arunachaltourism.com
Assam www.assamtourism.org
Delhi delhitourism.nic.in
Goa www.goatourism.gov.in
Gujarat www.gujarattourism.com
Haryana http://haryanatourism.gov.in
Himachal Pradesh www.hptdc.nic.in
Karnataka www.karnatakatourism.org
Kerala www.keralatourism.org
Lakshadweep www. lakshadweeptourism.com
Madhya Pradesh www.mptourism. com
Maharashtra www. maharashtratourism.gov.in
Odisha (Orissa) www.orissatourism. gov.in
Rajasthan www.rajasthantourism. gov.in
Sikkim www.sikkimtourism.travel
Tamil Nadu www.tamilnadutourism.org

The phone system has improved.

Uttaranchal www.uttarkhandstate.com
Uttar Pradesh www.up-tourism.com
West Bengal www.westbengaltourism.
gov.in

Local tourist offices

Below is a list of government tourist
offices in the major cities:
Agra 191 The Mall Tel: 0562-222
6378
Aurangabad Tourist Reception
Centre, (1st Floor) MTDC Holiday
Resort, Near Goldie Cinema, Station
Road Tel: 0240-233 1217
Bengaluru KFC Building,
48 Church Street Tel: 080-2558 5417
Bhubaneshwar Paryatan Bhawan,
Lewis Road Tel: 0674-243 2203
Chennai 154 Anna Salai Tel: 044-
2846 1459
Delhi 88 Janpath Tel: 011-2332
0342
Hyderabad/Secunderabad Ground
Floor, Balayogi Paryatak bhavan No
6-3-870, Green Lands, Begumpet Tel:
040-2340 9199
Jaipur State Hotel, Khasa Kothi Tel/
fax: 0141-2237 2200
Kochi/Ernakulam Willingdon Island,
Kochi Tel: 0484-266 8352
Kolkata 4 Shakespeare Sarani Tel:
033-2282 1475
Lucknow P3 Nawal Kishore Road,
Chitrahar Building Tel: 052-2222
8349
Mumbai 123 Maharishi Karve Marg,
opposite Churchgate Tel: 022-2203
3144
Domestic Airport Tel: 022-2615 6920
International Airport Tel: 022-2832
5331
Varanasi 15B The Mall
Tel: 0542-250 1784

V

Visas and Passports

All visitors (apart from citizens of
Nepal and Bhutan) require a visa

Weights and Measures

The metric system is used
everywhere. Precious metals,
especially gold, are often sold
by the traditional tola, which is
equivalent to 11.5 grams. Gems
are weighed in carats (0.2 grams).
　　Two characteristically Indian
expressions which you'll probably
come across are *lakhs* (100,000)
and *crores* (100 *lakhs* or 10
million).

to enter India. Nationals of Finland,
Japan, Luxembourg, New Zealand
and Singapore will be granted a visa
on arrival; all other nationalities are
required to obtain a visa in advance.
Tourist visas are issued for six months
from the date of issue (not entry).
Note that anyone leaving India on
a tourist visa will not be allowed to
re-enter within two months, although
exceptions are made in certain
cases – these need to be arranged in
advance. To get a visa you'll need to
apply online (http://in.vfsglobal.co.uk/
onlineapplication.html), print off a copy
of your completed form, then either
deliver it by hand or send by post to
the Indian Visa Applicaton Bureau
in your country. Once submitted, the
application will take around three
to four days to process, or up to two
weeks by post. Some firms will also
arrange visas for you – try the India
Visa Office (www.indiavisaheadoffice.
co.uk).
　　Tourist visas cannot be extended;
you must leave the country and
re-enter on a new one two months
later. It may be difficult to apply for a
new visa from neighbouring countries.
Five-year visas are also issued
to businessmen and students. In
addition to visas, special permits are
required for certain areas, while other
areas are out of bounds to foreigners
altogether.
　　If you stay for more than 180
days, you must get a tax-clearance
certificate before leaving the country.
These can be obtained from the
foreigner's section of the income
tax department in every city. Tax-
clearance certificates are free, but
take bank receipts to demonstrate
that you have changed money legally.

W

Water

Tap water, especially in larger cities, is
generally chlorinated and (in theory, at
least) safe to drink, although it's best
to stick to bottled or filtered water,
since the unfamiliar micro-organisms
in tap water can precipitate mild
stomach upsets.

What to Bring

Clothing

Travelling in southern India, or the
North during summer, it is best to
wear cotton. Avoid synthetics. In the

North during winter, sweaters and
jackets are required. Cotton shirts,
blouses and skirts are inexpensive
and easily available throughout
the country. Remember to bring
swimwear.
　　In winter a sweater – preferably
two, one light and one heavy – as
well as a jacket or an anorak are
necessary, especially in the North,
where daily temperature differentials
can be quite wide. Lighter clothing
would be adequate in the South
and along the coast. Comfortable
footwear, trainers for winter and
sandals for summer, is essential.
'Trekking' sandals are excellent for
wearing in India as they are tough and
provide good protection to your feet.
Teva and Reef are good brands to look
out for.
　　For your own convenience,
women should not wear sleeveless
blouses, miniskirts and short,
revealing dresses. Cover up – it's a
good idea in the Indian sun anyway
– locally available *shalwar kamiz*
(also known as *churidar*), a long
tunic top worn over loose trousers,
are ideal.

Other Essentials

If travelling away from the major
cities or big hotels, take a sheet
sleeping bag, pillowcases and
medical kit among other items. Sun
block (vital in the mountains) are
not readily available, so they should
be brought with you, along with
cosmetics and tampons. A hat or
scarf to cover your head is a sensible
item. A mosquito net and a basin/
bath plug are also useful in smaller
hotels, which often do not have
them.

Women Travellers

'Eve-teasing' is the Indian
euphemism for sexual harassment.
Take the normal precautions,
especially on crowded local public
transport (crowds are a haven for
gropers). Do not wear clothes that
expose legs, arms and cleavage;
shalwar kamiz are ideal, and a
shawl is handy to use as a cover-
all when required. More serious
sexual assaults on tourists are rare
and tend to occur in popular tourist
areas such as Rajasthan, Goa and
Varanasi, but in case something
should happen, call for help from
passers-by. On the up-side, there are
'ladies-only' queues at train and bus
stations, and 'ladies-only' waiting
rooms at stations and compartments
on trains.

LANGUAGE

UNDERSTANDING THE LANGUAGE

With 18 official languages, hundreds of others and countless dialects, India can present a linguistic minefield. Luckily for the traveller, English is often understood, and it is usually possible to get by in all but remote, rural locations. However, attempts to speak the local language are always appreciated. The language most widely spoken in the North is Hindi, while in the South, Tamil is spoken in Tamil Nadu, Malayali in Kerala, Kanad in Karnataka and Marathi in Maharashtra.

Attempts to speak the local language are, however, always appreciated. The language most widely spoken in the North is Hindi, while in the South, Tamil has the highest profile.

Indian languages are phonetically regular, based on syllables rather than an alphabet. Important differences are made between long and short vowels, and reteroflex, palatal and labial consonants – listen hard to get a feel for the vocabulary below. There are various systems of transliteration, and you may see many of the words below spelt different ways in English. Where a consonant is followed by 'h' this is an aspirated sound, 'c' is usually pronounced 'ch' (followed by 'h', 'chh'), and 'zh' in Tamil stands for a sound somewhere between a reteroflex 'l' and 'r'.

TRAVELLER'S HINDI

Basics

Hello/goodbye Namaste
Yes Ji ha
No Ji nehi

Perhaps Shayad
Thank you Dhanyavad/shukriya
How are you? Ap kaise hai?/Ap thik hai?
I am well Me thik hu/thik hai
What is your name? Apka nam kya hai?
My name is (John/Jane) Mera nam (John/Jane) hai
Where do you come from? Ap kahan se aye?
From (England) (England) se
How much (money)? Kitna paise hai?
That is expensive Bahut mahenga hai
Cheap Sasta
I like (tea) Mujhe (chai) pasand hai
Is it possible? Kya ye sambhav hai?
I don't understand Mujhe samajh nehi
I don't know Mujhe malum nehi
Money Paisa
Newspaper Akhbar
Sheet Chadar
Blanket Kambal
Bed Palang
Room Kamra
Clothes Kapre
Cloth Kapra
Market Bajar

Pronouns

I am Mai hun
You are Ap hain
He/she/it is Voh hai
They are Ve hain

Verbs

To drink Pina
To eat Khanna
To do/make Karna
To buy Kharidna
To sleep Sona
To see Dekhna

To hear/listen to Sunna
To wash (clothes) Dhona
To wash (yourself) Nahana
To get Milna or pana

Prepositions, adverbs and adjectives

Now Ab
Right now Abhi
Quickly Jaldi
Slowly Dirhe se
A bit Bahut
A little Tora
Here Yaha/idhar
There Vaha/udhar
Open Khola
Closed Bund
Finished Khatam hai
Big/older Bara
Small/younger Chota
Beautiful Sundar
Old Purana
New Naya

Questions

What is? Kya hai?
Where is? Kahan hai?
Why? Kyun?
Who is? Kaun hai?
When is? Kab hai?
How? Kaisa?
Most straightforward sentences can easily be turned into a question by putting 'kya' on the front and raising the pitch of the voice at the end of the sentence, eg 'Dhobi hai', 'There is a washerman', 'Kya dhobi hai?', 'Is there a washerman?'

Days of the week

Monday Somvar
Tuesday Mangalvar
Wednesday Budhvar
Thursday Guruvar

Newspapers in a variety of languages.

Friday *Shukravar*
Saturday *Shanivar*
Sunday *Itvar*
Today *Aj*
Yesterday/tomorrow *kal*
Week *Hafta*

Months

January *Janvari*
February *Farvari*
March *March*
April *Aprail*
May *Mai*
June *Jun*
July *Julai*
August *Agast*
September *Sitambar*
October *Aktubar*
November *Navambar*
December *Disambar*
Month *Mahina*
Year *Sal*

Relatives

Mother *Mata-ji*
Father *Pita-ji*
Sister *Behen*
Brother *Bhai*
Husband *Pati*
Wife *Patni*
Maternal grandmother *Nani*
Maternal grandfather *Nana*
Paternal grandmother *Dadi*
Paternal grandfather *Dada*
Elder sister (term of respect) *Didi*
Daughter *Beti*
Son *Beta*
Girl *Larki*
Boy *Larka*
Are you married? *Kya ap shadishuda hai?*
Are you alone (male/female)? *Kya ap akela/akeli?*
How many children have you got? *Apke kitne bache hai?*
How many brothers and sisters have you got? *Apke kitne bhai behen hai?*

Health

Doctor *Daktar*
Hospital *Aspatal*
Dentist *Dentist*
Pain *Dard*
I am ill *Main bimar hun*
I have been vomiting *Mujhe ulti ho rahi thi*
I have a temperature *Mujhe bukhar hai*
I have a headache *Mere sir men dard hai*
I have a stomach ache *Mere pat men dard hai*
I have diarrhoea *Mujhe dast ar raha hai*
The English word 'motions' is a common expression for diarrhoea.

Travel

Where is (Delhi)? *(Dilli) kahan hai?*
Bus station *Bus adda*
Railway station *Tren stashan/railgari*
Airport *Hawai adda*
Car *Gari*
How far is it? *Kitni dur hai?*
In front of/opposite (the Taj Mahal) *(Taj Mahal) ke samne*
Near *Ke nazdik/ke pas*
Far *Dur*
Ticket *Tikat*
Stop *Rukh jaiye*
Let's go *Chele jao*
I have to go *Mujhe jana hai*
Come *Ayie*
Go *Jayie*

Food

I want (a thali) *Mujhe (thali) chahiye*
Without chilli *Mirch ke bina*
Little chilli *Kam mirch*
Hot *Garam*
Cold *Thanda*

Ripe/cooked *Pukka*
Unripe/raw *Kachcha*

Basics

Mirch Chilli
Namak Salt
Ghee Clarified butter
Dahi Yoghurt
Raita Yoghurt with cucumber
Chaval Rice
Panir Cheese
Pani Water
Dudh Milk
Lassi Yoghurt drink
Nimbu pani Lime water
Tandur Oven
Pilao Rice cooked with *ghee* and spices
Biriyani Rice cooked with vegetables or meat
Mithai Sweets

Breads (Roti)

Puri Deep-fried and puffed-up wheat bread
Chapatti Unleavened flat bread
Nan Leavened flat bread
Tandoori roti Similar to *nan*
Paratha Chapatti cooked with *ghee*

Vegetables (Sabzi)

Palak Spinach
Aloo Potato
Gobi Cauliflower
Bindi Okra
Pyaz Onion
Matter Peas
Tamata Tomato
Baingain/brinjal Aubergine
Dal Dried pulses

Meat

Gosht Lamb
Murg Chicken
Machli Fish

Fruit

Kela Banana
Santra Orange
Aum Mango

TRAVELLER'S TAMIL

Basics

Hello *Vanakkam*
Goodbye *Poyvituvarukiren* (Reply *Poyvituvarungal*)
Yes *Amam*
No *Illai*
Perhaps *Oruvelai*
Thank you *Nandri*
How are you? *Celakkiyama?*
What is your name? *Ungal peyar yenna?*

My name is (John/Jane) *Yen peyar (John/Jane)*
Where is the (hotel)? *(Hotel) yenge?*
What is this/that? *Idu/Adu yenna?*
What is the price? *Yenna vilai?*
That is very expensive *Anda vilai mikavum adikum*
I want (coffee) *(Kapi) Vendum*
I like (dosa) *(Dosai) Pudikkum*
Is it possible? *Mudiyuma?*
I don't understand *Puriyadu*
Enough *Podum*
Toilet *Tailet*
Bed *Kattil*
Room *Arai*
Train *Rayil*
Sari *Pudavai*
Dhoti *Vesti*
Towel *Tundu*
Sandals *Ceruppu*
Money *Punam*
Temple *Kovil*

Verbs

To come (imperative) *Varungal*
To go (imperative) *Pongal*
To stop (imperative) *Nillungal*
To sleep *Tungu*
To eat *Sappidu*
To drink *Kudi*
To buy *Vangu*
To pay (money) *Punam kodu*
To see *Par*
To wash (clothes) *Tuvai*
To wash (yourself) *Kazhavu*

Prepositions, adverbs and adjectives

Quickly *Sikkirum*
Slowly *Meduvaka*
A lot *Mikavum*
A little *Koncam*
Here *Inge*
There *Ange*
This *Idu*
That *Adu*
Now *Ippodu*
Same *Ade*
Good *Nalla*
Bad *Ketta*
Hot *Karam*
Cold *Kulirana*
Dirty *Acattam*
Clean *Cattam*
Beautiful *Azhakana*
Sweet *Inippu*
Big *Periya*
Small *Cinna*
Old *Pazhaiya*
New *Pudiya*

Days of the week

Monday *Tingal*
Tuesday *Cevvay*
Wednesday *Putam*
Thursday *Viyazhan*
Friday *Velli*
Saturday *Ceni*
Sunday *Nayiri*
Today *Inraikku*
Week *Varam*
Month *Matam*
Year *Varutam*

Questions and 'and'

How? *Yeppadi?*
What? *Yenna?*
Who? *Yar?*
Why? *Yen?*
Where? *Yenge?*
When? *Yeppodu?*
How much? *Yettanai/Yevvalavu?*
Questions in Tamil are usually formed by adding a long 'a' to the last word of a sentence (usually the verb), eg 'Ningal venduma?' 'What do you want?'. 'And' is formed by adding 'um' to the end of the nouns (with an extra 'y' if the noun ends in a vowel), eg 'Kapiyum, dosaiyum', 'Coffee and dosa'.

Pronouns and relatives

I *Nan*
You *Ningal*
He/she/it *Avan/Aval/Avar*
We (including addressee)/ (excluding addressee) *Nam/ Nangal*
They *Avakal*
Man *Manidan*
Woman/girl/daughter *Pen*
Boy/son *Paiyan*
Children *Pillaikal*
Baby *Pappu*
Mother *Amma*
Father *Appa*
Husband *Kanavan*
Wife *Manaivi*

Health

I am sick (vomiting) *Utampu cariyillai irukkiradu*
I have a pain *Vali irukkiradu*
I have diarrhoea *'Motions'*

Hindi Numbers

1 *ek*		**30** *tis*	
2 *do*		**40** *chalis*	
3 *tin*		**50** *pachas*	
4 *char*		**60** *sath*	
5 *panch*		**70** *setur*	
6 *che*		**80** *assi*	
7 *sat*		**90** *nabbe*	
8 *arth*		**100** *sau*	
9 *nau*		**1,000** *hazar*	
10 *das*		**100,000** *lakh*	
20 *bis*		**10,000,000** *kror*	

irrukkiradu
Doctor *Taktar*
Help! *Utavi cey!*

Food (Sappadu)

Tunnir Water
Sadum Rice
Puzham Fruit
Kaykuri Vegetables
Pal Milk
Mor Buttermilk
Minakay (iilamal) (without) chilli
Tengay Coconut
Mampazham Mango
Valaippazham Banana
Kapi Coffee
Ti Tea
Iddli Steamed rice cakes
Dosai Pancake made from fermented dough
Vadai Deep fried snack made of dal
Rasam Thin, spicy soup, usually with a tamarind base
Sampar Thick soup made from dal
Poriyal Dry vegetable curry
Kolikarri Chicken curry
Attukkari Lamb curry
Mils 'Meals', similar to a North Indian thali, traditionally served on a banana leaf
Payasam Sweet milk-based dish served at festivals

GLOSSARY OF COMMONLY USED TERMS

Acha OK, good, I understand, really?
Ahimsa Non-violence
Air cooler Fan that blows air through wet straw or similar
Angrez Foreigner
Ashram Spiritual retreat or community
Auto (rickshaw) Three-wheeled, scooter-engine conveyance, tuk tuk
Avatar Traditionally an incarnation of a god, but now used more broadly
Bagh Garden
Bandar Monkey

TRANSPORT

ACCOMMODATION

ACTIVITIES

A – Z

LANGUAGE

Tamil Numbers

1 *onru*
2 *irandu*
3 *munru*
4 *nanku*
5 *aindu*
6 *aru*
7 *yezhu*
8 *yettu*
9 *onpadu*
10 *pattu*
11 *patinonru*
12 *pannirandu*
20 *irupadu*
30 *muppadu*
40 *rarpadu*
50 *aimpadu*
60 *arupadu*
70 *alupadu*
80 *yenpadu*
90 *tonnuru*
100 *nuru*
100,000 *latcam*
10,000,000 *kodi*

Bandh General strike
Banian T-shirt or vest
Baori Step well, meaning a well accessed by an elaborate series of stairways
Bhang Dried marijuana, sometimes added to lassi
Bhangra Punjabi dance music
Bharat India
Bidi Small, leaf-rolled cigarette
Bindi Red dot worn on forehead
Brahmin Highest Hindu caste of priests
Burqha All-concealing dress worn by Muslim women
Basti Slum
Cantonment Military area of town
Caste Hindu equivalent of class system, based on occupation
Chalo Let's go
Charbagh Traditional Persian-style garden, divided into four quarters
Charpoi Traditional bed, made of rope woven across wooden frame
Choli Sari blouse
Chowk Junction
Chokidar Guard/caretaker
Coolie Porter
Crore 10 million
Dacoit Bandit
Dalit Lowest Hindu caste, previously known as 'untouchables'
Dhaba Basic restaurant, often at side of the road
Dharamsala Basic accommodation for pilgrims
Dhobi Clothes washer
Dhobi Ghat Area where clothes are washed, often next to a lake or river
Dhoti Long skirt worn by men, pulled up between legs and tucked in

Dhurrie Cotton, flat woven carpet
Diwan-i-Am Public audience hall
Diwan-i-khas Private audience hall
Dowry money or goods traditionally given to groom's family by bride's parents during wedding
Durgah Shrine of Muslim saint
Eve teasing Sexually harassing women
Fakir Muslim ascetic
Ganesh Elephant-headed god of good fortune
Ganj Market
Gaon Village
Garh Fort
Gari Vehicle, normally car but also bike, train, etc
Geyser Water heater
Ghat Either steps leading down to a lake or river or a range of hills
Ghazal Urdu devotional/love song
Godown Warehouse
Gompa Tibetan monastery
Gulli Alley
Gurudwara Sikh temple
Hanuman Monkey god
Hati Elephant
Haveli Elaborate old walled mansion
Hijra Eunuch
Hindola Swing
Imam Muslim leader
Imambara Shiite tomb
Jali Ornately carved screen
Jhuggi Slum
Kabaddi Traditional sport, a bit like tag
Kameez Long shirt worn by women
Khadi Homespun cloth
Khalsa Sikh botherhood
Khol Black eyeliner, often used on baby boys to ward off evil spirits
Kurta Long shirt worn by men
Lakh 100,000
Lok People
Lungi Skirt/sarong worn by men, particularly in South India
Mahabharata Epic Hindu poem of mythology
Mahal Room or palace
Mahout Elephant trainer
Maidan Open square in city
Mali Gardener
Mandala Circular painting

particularly popular in Buddhism
Mandi Market
Mandir Temple
Marg Street or road
Masjid Mosque
Mehndi Henna, often used to paint intricate designs on ladies' hands and feet, particularly for weddings
Mela Festival
Memsahib Madam
Nadi River
Namaskar/Namaste Traditional greeting
Namaz Muslim prayers
Namkeen Crunchy savoury snacks (often dubbed 'Bombay Mix' in the West).
Nilgai Blue bull, a type of antelope
NRI Non-Resident Indian
Nullah Small stream
Paise Penny, but more commonly used to mean money in general
Panchayat Village council
Pandit Priest or expert
Peon Office drudge
Prasad Sacred food which has been offered to and blessed by a deity in a Hindu temple
Puja Ritual in which offering is made as act of devotion
Qawwali Sufi singing
Qila Fort
Ramadan/Ramzan Annual Muslim month of daytime fasting
Sadhu Hindu ascetic
Sahib Sir
Salwar Kameez Shirt and trouser combo worn by women
Sambhar deer
Sati Traditional act of a wife setting fire to herself at her husband's funeral
Scheduled Castes Official term for members of Dalit castes
Singh Literally 'lion', common surname amongst Sikhs and Rajputs
Stupa Buddhist monument
Sufi Muslim mystic
Tabla Twin drums
Tal Lake
Wallah 'Man', used as suffix to denote occupation, eg chai wallah, dhobi wallah, etc
Yatra Pilgrimage

Knowing a smattering of the local language will enrich your experience.

FURTHER READING

HISTORY

The Discovery of India, by Jawaharlal Nehru (Asia Publishing House, 1966). Revealing history by India's first prime minister, which tells as much about the author as its subject.
Freedom at Midnight, by Larry Collins and Dominique Lapierre (Tarang, 1975). Gripping popular history of the birth of the Indian nation.
A History of India, Volume I, by Romila Thapar (Pelican, 2003). New edition of this highly acclaimed history. Volume 1 traces the history of South Asia from ancient times through to the Delhi Sultanate. Volume II, by Perceval Spear, continues from the Mughals to the assassination of M.K. Gandhi.
India: a History, by John Keay (HarperCollins, 2000). A one-volume history by a well-respected writer. Also by Keay is the brilliant **India Discovered** (HarperCollins, 1998) telling the story of how British scholars and adventurers helped India rediscover its ancient past.
The Last Mughal, by William Dalrymple (Bloomsbury 2009). Ground-breaking revisionist history of the 1857 Uprising in Delhi and its bloody aftermath, drawing on hitherto forgotten records in Urdu.
Liberty or Death: India's Journey to Independence and Division, by Patrick French (HarperCollins, 1997). Readable and well-researched account of the freedom struggle and Partition.
The Nehrus and the Gandhis: an Indian Dynasty, by Tariq Ali (Pan, 1985). A gripping account of India's famous political family. Now out of print, but second-hand copies can still be found.
Tea: Addiction, Exploitation and Empire, by Roy Moxham (Robinson, 2004). A fascinating history of the skulduggery and economics behind one of India's most valuable crops.
They Fight like Devils, by D.A. Kinsley (Da Capo 2002). Stories from Lucknow during the Great Uprising in 1857.

Traders and Nabobs: the British in Cawnpore 1765–1857, by Zoe Yalland (Michael Russell, 1988). Fascinating account of the early days of the Raj until the Uprising, focussing on the city of Kanpur.
Travels of Ibn Batuta, by Ibn Batuta and Tim Mackintosh-Smith (Picador, 2002). The story of a 14th-century adventurer.
White Mughals, by William Dalrymple (Harper 2004). This page-turning account of the controversial marriage between a high-ranking British official and a teenage Hyderabdi princess in 18th-century frames a sympathetic account of the early British Raj.
Wicked Women of the Raj, by Coralie Younger (**SOS** Freestock, 2005). Stories about the women who married Indian Rajas.
The Wonder That Was India, by A.L. Basham (Rupa, 1967). Learned

Send Us Your Thoughts

We do our best to ensure the information in our books is as accurate and up-to-date as possible. The books are updated on a regular basis using local contacts, who painstakingly add, amend and correct as required. However, some details (such as telephone numbers and opening times) are liable to change, and we are ultimately reliant on our readers to put us in the picture.

We welcome your feedback, especially your experience of using the book "on the road". Maybe we recommended a hotel that you liked (or another that you didn't), or you came across a great bar or new attraction we missed.

We will acknowledge all contributions, and we'll offer an Insight Guide to the best letters received.

Please write to us at:
Insight Guides
PO Box 7910
London SE1 1WE
Or email us at:
insight@apaguide.co.uk

historical classic in idiosyncratic, rapturous prose.

SOCIETY, CULTURE AND RELIGION

The Argumentative Indian, by Amartya Sen (Penguin, 2006). Reflections on culture, history and identity by India's Nobel Prize-winner.
A Book of India, by B.N. Pandey (Rupa, 1982). A real *masala* mix of philosophies, travellers' notes, poetry and literary trivia, revealing a quixotic India. **Changing Village, Changing Life**, by Prafulla Mohanti (Viking, 1990). Wry account of village life in Orissa (Odisha).
Everybody Loves a Good Drought, by P. Sainath (Penguin, 1996). Stories from India's poorest district, by an award-winning investigative reporter who looks at the human face of poverty.
Gods, Demons and Others, by R.K. Narayan (Heinemann, 1986). Retellings of some of India's most popular religious myths by one of the country's greatest writers. Also worth looking out for are his retellings of **The Ramayana** (Penguin, 1977), based on the Tamil Kamban version, and **The Mahabharata** (Heinemann, 1986).
India: A Literary Companion, by Bruce Palling (John Murray, 1992). Another compilation of impressions taken from literature, letters and unpublished diaries, skilfully presented.
Indira: the Life of Indira Nehru Gandhi, by Katherine Frank (HarperCollins, 2002). An in-depth biography of one of post-Independence India's most charismatic leaders.
In Spite of the Gods, by Edward Luce (Little, Brown 2006). Definitive but accessible account of the economic rise, against all the odds, of modern India.
An Introduction to Hinduism, by Gavin Flood (Cambridge University Press, 1996). Perhaps the best general introduction to the complexities of this diverse religion.

TRANSPORT ACCOMMODATION ACTIVITIES A–Z LANGUAGE

I Phoolan Devi, by Phoolan Devi with Marie-Thérèse Cuny and Paul Rambi (Little, Brown, 1996). The autobiography of an illiterate low-caste woman who fought convention, led a gang of bandits and surrendered to the Indian government after years on the run. When freed from prison, she went on to win a parliamentary seat. A controversial insight into caste politics.

India, by Patrick French (Penguin, 2011). Wide-ranging portrait of modern-day India, and how it came to be the country it is.

Maximum City, by Suketu Meta (Headline Review, 2005). A compelling anatomy of Mumbai depicted through a series of life stories of hitmen, dancing girls, cops, movie stars, poets, beggars and politicians.

May You Be the Mother of a Hundred Sons, by Elisabeth Bumiller (Penguin, 1990). Women's issues tackled head-on: everything from dowries to infanticide, with dozens of poignant interviews. Though its statistics may be somewhat out of date, the issues still hold as true as ever.

A Million Mutinies Now, by V.S. Naipul (Heinemann, 1990). The misanthropic scholar returns to seek his roots and finds a cast of characters not easily pigeon-holed. A more positive follow-up to his earlier, jaundiced, **India: A Wounded Civilisation** (Penguin, 1979).

Plain Tales from the Raj, ed. Charles Allen (Rupa, 1992). First-hand accounts from ex-colonialists.

South Asia: the Indian Subcontinent (The Garland Encyclopedia of World Music), ed. Alison Arnold (Garland Science, 1999). The ultimate reference work on the performance traditions of South Asia, written by leading academics.

Temptations of the West, or How to be Modern in India, Pakistan and Beyond, by Pankaj Mishra (Picador, 2006). Insightful travelogue by the author of *Butter Chicken in Ludhiana*.

FICTION

Calcutta Chromosome, by Amitav Ghosh (Harper Perennial, 2001). A scientific thriller set in India, New York and Egypt.

Clear Light of Day, by Anita Desai (Penguin, 1982). The difficulties of post-Partition India seen through the eyes of a Hindu family living in Old Delhi.

Delhi, A Novel, by Kushwant Singh (Viking, 1989). A bawdy saga that takes us through 600 years of temptresses and traitors to unravel the Indian capital's mystique. Narrated in turns by a eunuch, an irreverent wag, potentates and poets. Superb. (It took this popular author 20 years to write.)

The English Teacher, by R.K. Narayan (various editions). Narayan depicts infuriating and endearing characters which inhabit Malgudi, a composite South Indian village. Also, in various editions, **Malgudi Days**, a series of short stories.

A Fine Balance, by Rohinton Mistry (Faber & Faber, 1996). Beautifully written, sad story of two tailors who move from their village to the city.

The Gift of a Cow, by Premchand (Allen & Unwin, 1968). The great Hindi novelist's tragic classic about the hardships endured by a North Indian peasant.

The God of Small Things, by Arundhati Roy (Random House, 1997). The Kerala backwaters are evoked in a hauntingly personal novel set in a small village pickle factory in the 1960s. **Hungry Tide**, by Amitav Ghosh (HarperCollins, 2005). An atmospheric novel set in the Sunderbans swamps.

In Custody, by Anita Desai (Heinemann, 1984). The last days of an Urdu poet, made into a beautiful Merchant-Ivory film.

Kanthapura, by Raja Rao (Oxford University Press, 1947). A lyrical novel about a village in Karnataka which implements Gandhi's methods of non-violent resistance to British rule.

Kim, by Rudyard Kipling (Penguin Books, 2000, ed. Edward Said). The wonderful adventures of a boy who wanders across North India in search of the Great Game.

Midnight's Children, by Salman Rushdie (Jonathan Cape, 1981). Rushdie burst onto the literary scene with this dazzling novel of post-Independence India. **The Moor's Last Sigh**, on Mumbai, is another tour de force set in India's south (Jonathan Cape, 1995).

A New World, by Amit Chaudhuri (Picador, 2000). Naturalistic contemporary tale of divorced Indian man, resident in America, who takes his young son back to his parents in Kolkata for the holidays.

A Passage to India, by E.M. Forster (Penguin, 2000). The classic novel of the misunderstandings that arose out of the East–West encounter. After a mysterious incident in a cave Dr Aziz is accused of assaulting a naive

young Englishwoman, Adela Quested. The trial exposes the racism inherent in British colonialism.

Pather Panchali, by Bibhutibhushan Banerji (Rupa, 1990). Outstanding Indian novel which outdoes the film by Satyajit Ray, depicting richness of spirit amid poverty in Bengal.

The Raj Quartet, by Paul Scott (University of Chicago Press, 1998). Four novels – **The Jewel in the Crown**, **The Day of the Scorpion**, **The Towers of Silence** and **A Division of Spoils** – set during the last days of the British Raj and charting its decline and fall.

A River Sutra, by Gita Mehta (Viking, 1993). Gently wrought stories which linger in the imagination.

The Romantics, by Pankaj Mishra (Random House, 2000). East meets West in Banaras.

Samskara, by U.R. Anantha Murthy (Oxford University Press, 1976). A tale of a South Indian Brahman village in Karnataka, where one Brahman is forced to question his values. Beautifully translated by A.K. Ramanujan.

The Scent of Pepper, by Kavery Nambisan (Penguin, 1996). This beautifully written family saga is set in South India.

Shantaram, by Gregory David Roberts (Abacus, 2004). Epic tale of Mumbai slums and underworld, as well as rural Indian life – a real page-turner.

A Suitable Boy, by Vikram Seth (Phoenix Press, 1994). A huge and multifaceted novel set during the run-up to Independent India's first elections, which centres around a mother's search for a suitable husband for her daughter. Highly recommended.

Train to Pakistan, by Kushwant Singh (various editions). This is a gripping story of the excesses of Partition, penned when scars of the divided Subcontinent were still fresh.

2 States, by Chetan Bhagat (Rupa & Co., 2009) Humorous take on the difficulties of inter-community marriages in modern-day India, by India's most successful English-language novelist ever.

Untouchable, by Mulk Raj Anand (Penguin, 1986). Grinding tale of poverty and discrimination.

The White Tiger, by Aravind Adiga (Atlantic Books, 2008). Insightful account of the workings of modern India, as told in a series of letters to the Chinese premier. Winner of the 2008 Man Booker Prize.

Women Writing in India: 600 BC to the Present, ed. Susie Tharu and

K. Lalitha (Feminist Press, 1991).
Wonderful and eclectic anthology
bringing to light the neglected history
of Indian women. Volume 1 includes
writings from 600 BC to the early 20th
century; volume 2 concentrates on
the 20th century alone.
Yaarana: Gay Writing from India,
ed. Hoshang Merchant, and, **Facing
the Mirror: Lesbian Writing from
India**, ed. Ashwini Sukthankar (both
Penguin, 1999). Anthologies of short
stories, extracts from novels and
poetry from gay and lesbian Indian
writers.

TRAVEL

**Butter Chicken in Ludhiana: Travels
in Small Town India**, by Pankaj
Mishra (Penguin, 1995). An urban
Indian novelist casts a jaundiced eye
over modern Indian life.
City of Djinns, by William Dalrymple
(HarperCollins, 1993). The respected
travel writer's account of a year spent
in Delhi, full of historical references.
Desert Places, by Robyn Davidson
(Viking, 1996). A woman's story of
living and travelling with the desert
nomads of Rajasthan.
Exploring Indian Railways, by Bill
Aitken (Oxford University Press, 1996).
Highly informed and occasionally
idiosyncratic tour of the Indian railway
system written by a clear enthusiast.
A Goddess in the Stones, by Norman
Lewis (Cape, 1991). The founder of
Survival International travels among
the Adivasis of Bihar and Odisha
(Orissa). **The Great Hedge of India**,

by Roy Moxham (Constable, 2000).
One man's bizarre quest to find the
hedge that marked the old British
customs line. Very entertaining
and packed full of historical detail.
Recommended.
**Leaves from the Jungle: Life in
a Gond Village**, by Verrier Elwin
(Oxford University Press, 1992). Very
entertaining account of this early
anthropologist's stay with a Central
Indian Adivasi group.
The Smile of Murugan, by Michael
Wood (John Murray, 2002). Account
of a journey through Tamil Nadu,
which reveals the ancient roots of the
region's religious traditions.
Sorcerer's Apprentice, by Tahir Shah
(Penguin, 1998). Travelogue of the
author's attempts to learn the secrets
of illusion and fraud of India's street
magicians.

FOOD, LANGUAGE AND IMAGES

**Dakshin: Vegetarian Cuisine
from South India**, by Chandra
Padmanabhan (Angus and Robertson,
1999). An excellent guide to
wonderful foods of South India.
**Hanklyn-Janklin, or a Stranger's
Rumble Tumble Guide to some
Words, Customs and Quiddities
Indian and Indo-British**, by Nigel
B. Hankin (Banyan Books, 1992).
Lives up to its title and is a delightful
reference work.
Hobson-Jobson (Routledge & Kegan
Paul, 1968). The 1886 glossary on
which Hankin modelled his modern

etymology. The pair complement each
other.
India: Decoration, Interiors, Style, by
Henry Wilson (Watson-Gupthill, 2001).
Exquisite photography of a number of
North Indian palaces and houses (in
Delhi and Rajasthan), demonstrating
the inventiveness and sense of design
to be found in this part of India.
Lucknow City of Illusion, by Rosie
Llewellyn-Jones (Prestel Verlag,
2006). Historical survey of the
city with photos from the Alkazi
collections.
The Raj at Table, by David Burton
(Faber, 1994). This culinary history of
the Raj is one of the most entertaining
books on British India ever written,
approaching the subject via an
exploration of the ways in which the
formidable British memsahib made
her mark on Indian culture – and vice
versa.

WILDLIFE

A Book of Indian Birds, by Salim
Ali (Bombay Natural History Society.
2002). The classic guide to Indian
birds, suitable for novices and
experienced birdwatchers.
The Last Tiger, by Valmik Thapar
(Oxford University Press, 2006). A
history of conservation of the tiger
and Thapar's current views on how to
save it from extinction.
**Pocket Guide to the Birds of the
Indian Subcontinent**, by Richard
Grimmett, Carol Inskipp and Tim
Inskipp (New Delhi, 1999). Illustrated
guide for keen ornithologists.

TRANSPORT

ACCOMMODATION

ACTIVITIES

A – Z

LANGUAGE

CREDITS

Photo Credits

4Corners Images 287BL, 287ML
Abe Nowitz/Apa Publications 7BL, 7BR, 10T, 14/15, 28, 31, 35, 50, 72/73, 85, 89, 102, 103, 112/113, 246, 249, 251B, 251T, 253, 255, 259, 260, 261, 262, 263, 265, 266BL, 266/267T, 266BR, 267ML, 267BR, 267BL, 267TR, 268, 269, 271, 272B, 273, 274T, 275, 276, 463, 500
akg-images 55
Alamy 91BL, 110/111T, 111BR, 148, 149, 172BL, 178, 184, 186, 188, 200, 212, 231, 235, 242, 256, 257, 280, 284, 286BR, 330, 331, 333B, 345, 409, 430, 431, 433, 435
PA Photos 45, 67, 71
AWL 181T, 190B, 213
Axiom Photographic Agency 346, 347B
Bigstock.com 43B, 90Bl & BR, 91TR, 111TR, 177, 202, 203, 205, 208, 209, 210, 217B, 220, 223, 228BR, 278, 279, 322, 364B, 405B, 429BL, 445
Britta Jaschinski/Apa Publications 4/5, 6TR, 11MR, 16, 17B, 18, 19, 21, 34, 36, 37, 38, 39, 42L&R, 48, 49, 74, 75, 76, 77, 79, 80, 82, 83, 84, 87, 88, 91BR, 92, 93, 94, 95, 100, 101, 104, 105, 110BR, 111ML, 116/117, 118, 119B, 196, 197, 229BL, 272T, 298/299, 300,

301T, 301B, 302, 303, 305T&B, 306, 307, 308, 309, 310, 311, 312, 313T&B, 314, 315T&B, 316, 317, 319, 320, 325, 326T&B, 327, 328T&B, 329, 335, 339T, 342, 347T, 350, 354, 355T&B, 356, 357, 359, 361T&B, 363T&B, 364T, 365, 366, 368, 370T&B, 371, 373, 374, 375T&B, 377, 381, 382, 383, 385, 386, 387, 388, 389, 390, 391, 393T&B, 394T&B, 395, 396, 397, 398, 399, 400T&B, 401, 402, 403, 405T, 406, 412, 413, 414, 415, 416, 417, 418, 419, 420, 421, 422, 423T&B, 424, 425T&B, 427, 428/429T, 428BL, 428BR, 429BR, 429ML, 429TR, 440, 441, 443, 446, 453, 470, 471, 472, 481, 487, 489, 490, 493, 495, 497, 498
Bridgeman Art Library 59
Corbis 9TR, 58, 61, 62, 64, 65, 66, 68, 69, 70, 153, 164, 180, 181B, 198/199, 229BR, 248, 254, 282, 283B, 337, 349
David Abrams/Apa Publications 6BL, 10B, 11ML, 20, 32, 33, 52, 86, 96, 108, 233, 244/245, 247T, 247B, 288, 289, 290, 291, 292, 293, 294, 295, 378/379T, 378BL, 378BR, 379BL, 379ML, 379T, 380, 480
Dreamstime 8M, 8BL, 9BR, 22, 25L&R, 30, 90/91T, 97, 165, 201B, 221, 230, 274B, 334

Fotolia 243BR, 351
Getty 44T, 46, 54, 57, 99, 318, 336, 343, 352/353, 434
iStockphoto 6MR, 7MR, 7TL, 7TR, 11TR, 23, 24, 26, 27, 51, 91ML, 110BL, 166B, 168, 169, 173ML, 173BR, 173BL, 174, 175, 185T, 185B, 187B, 187T, 190T, 191, 192, 193, 195, 201T, 207, 211, 214, 216, 217T, 218, 219, 222, 224, 227, 228BL, 232, 240, 241, 283T, 286BL, 286/287T, 287BR, 287TR, 332, 333T, 339B, 344, 348, 404, 407, 408, 410, 436T, 437, 457, 485
Julian Love/Apa Publications 1, 2/3, 6BR, 7ML, 8BC, 9TL, 12/13, 17T, 29, 40/41, 43T, 47, 53, 78, 81, 106, 107, 109, 111BL, 114/115, 119T, 122, 123T, 123B, 126, 127, 129, 130, 132, 133, 134, 135, 136, 137, 138, 139, 140, 141, 143, 144, 145, 147, 150, 151, 152, 154, 155, 156, 157, 158, 159B, 159T, 160, 161, 162T, 162B, 163, 166T, 171, 172/173T, 172BR, 173TR, 234, 297, 341, 438, 442, 447, 449, 477T&B, 479, 482
Photolibrary 183, 436B
Picture Alliance/Photoshot 98R, 229ML, 238
Rex Features 44B, 98L, 228/229T
Robert Harding 236, 237, 239
TopFoto 56, 60, 63
Topham Picturepoint 189

Cover Credits

Front cover: Ceremonial elephant, Hawa Mahal, Jaipur *AWL Images*
Back cover: (top) Taj Mahal *Julian Love/Apa Publications*; (middle) Pupils at La Martinere, Lucknow *Julian Love/Apa Publications*

Front flap: (from top) Fishing boats on beach, Goa *iStockphoto*; Varanasi *Julian Love/Apa Publications*; Bara Imambara, Lucknow *Julian Love/Apa Publications*; Tea Estates, Darjeeling *Britta Jaschinski/Apa Publications*

Back flap: Fabindia in GK1, Delhi *Julian Love/Apa Publications*
Spine: Fatehpur Sikri detail *Julian Love/Apa Publications*

Insight Guide Credits

Distribution

UK
Dorling Kindersley Ltd
A Penguin Group company
80 Strand, London, WC2R ORL
customerservice@dk.com

United States
Ingram Publisher Services
1 Ingram Boulevard, PO Box 3006,
La Vergne, TN 37086-1986
ips@ingramcontent.com

Australia
Universal Publishers
PO Box 307
St Leonards NSW 1590
sales@universal
publishers.com.au

New Zealand
Brown Knows Publications
11 Artesia Close, Shamrock Park
Auckland, New Zealand 2016
sales@brownknows.co.nz

Worldwide
Apa Publications GmbH & Co. Verlag
KG (Singapore branch)
7030 Ang Mo Kio Avenue 5
08-65 Northstar @ AMK
Singapore 569880
apasin@singnet.com.sg

Printing
CTPS-China

© 2013 Apa Publications (UK) Ltd
All Rights Reserved

First Edition 1992
Tenth Edition 2013

No part of this book may be
reproduced, stored in a retrieval
system or transmitted in any form or
means electronic, mechanical,
photocopying, recording or
otherwise, without prior written
permission of Apa Publications.
Brief text quotations with use of
photographs are exempted for book
review purposes only. Information
has been obtained from sources
believed to be reliable, but its
accuracy and completeness, and
the opinions based thereon, are not
guaranteed.

www.insightguides.com

Project Editor
Sarah Sweeney

Series Manager
Carine Tracanelli

Picture Research/Art Editor
Ian Spick & Tom Smyth/Shahid
Mahmood

Map Production
Original cartography Berndtson &
Berndtson, updated by
Apa Cartography Department

Production
Tynan Dean and Rebeka Ellam

INDEX

Main references are in bold type

A

accommodation 446
  heritage hotels 205
  luxury tents 189, 205
Achabal (J & K) 191
Achipur (WB) 323
activities 477
admission charges 487
Advani, L.K. 80
Agartala (Tri) 346
  Pushbanta Palace 346
  Tripura Government Museum 347
  Ujjayanta Palace 346
Agatti (Lak) 432
Agonda (Goa) 294, 465
Agra (UP) 154
  accommodation 449
  Agra Fort 155, 156
  Chini ka Rauza 156
  Itimad-ud-Daula tomb 155
  Rambagh gardens 156
  Red Fort 106
  restaurants 170
  shopping 481
  Taj Mahal 52, 106, 107, **156**, **172**
agriculture 19, 147, 154
  coconuts 414, 432
  coffee 20, 359, 364, 414, 422
  rice 19, 21, 414
  rubber 422
  spices 414, 422, 424
  tea 20, 59, 325, 340, 342, 364,
    407, 414, 422
  wheat 19
Ahmedabad (Guj) 105, 231, **232**
  accommodation 460
  Calico Museum of Textiles 235
  Doshivada-ni-Pol 235
  Gujarat Vidyapith 235
  Hridey Kunj 235
  Jama Masjid 233
  Khadi Gramudyog Bhandar 236
  Manek Chowk 235
  restaurants 243
  Sidi Bashir's Mosque 235
  Sidi Saiyad's Mosque 235
  Teen Darwaza 233
  Tomb of Ahmed Shah I 235
Aihole (Kar) 365
  Durga Temple 366
  Lad Khen Temple 366
air travel 440
  to/from Andhra Pradesh 369
  to/from Bihar 165
  to/from Chennai (TN) 382
  to/from Delhi 128
  to/from Goa 291
  to/from Gujarat 231
  to/from Jammu and Kashmir 187
  to/from Karnataka 361
  to/from Kerala 415
  to/from Kolkata (WB) 305
  to/from Madhya Pradesh 277
  to/from Mumbai (Mah) 250
  to/from Punjab & Haryana 147
  to/from Rajasthan 204
  to/from Tamil Nadu 393
  to/from The Northeast 344

to/from Uttarakhand 177
to/from Uttar Pradesh 155
to/from West Bengal, Odisha and
  Jharkhand 321
Aizawl (Miz) 351
  Mizoram State Museum 351
Ajanta (Mah) 103, 247, **266**, **275**,
  285
  tours 277
Ajmer (Raj) 214
  accommodation 455
  Arhai din ka Jhonpra mosque 215
  Dargah Sharif 214
  Daulat Khana 215
  Nasiyan Jain Temple 215
  restaurants 226
Akal Fossil Park (Raj) 225
Akbar, Emperor 36, **52**, 102, 130,
  154, 155, 156, 205
Alappuzha (Ker) 420, 428, 483
  accommodation 473
  restaurants 426
Albuquerque, Alfonso 289
Alchi (J & K) 194
Alchi (Lad) 454
Alexander the Great 47
Alfassa, Mirra 396
Aligarh (UP) 159
Allahabad (UP) 162
  accommodation 450
  Anand Bhavan 162
  restaurants 170
All-India Muslim League 60
Almora (Utt) 178, 451
Alwar (Raj) 209, 455
  City Palace 210
Amaravati (AP) 373
Amarnath Cave (J & K) 191
Amba Mata temple (Guj) 240
Ambani, Mukesh 79
Ambedkar, B.K. 29
Amber (Raj) 107, 208
  Anokhi Museum of Hand Printing
    208
  Diwan i Am 208
  Jaigarh Fort 208
  Jaya Vana 208
  Shish Mahal 208
Amritsar (Pun) 147, 150
  accommodation 449
  Durgiana Temple 152
  Golden Temple 68, 69, 107, 147,
    150
  Jallianwala Bagh 152
  restaurants 170
amusement parks
  Nicco Park (Kolkata) 315
  Wet-o-Wild Beach Tropicana
    (Kolkata) 315
Anandpur Sahib (HP) 188
Anandpur Sahib (Pun) 148, 153
  Kesgarh 153
Andaman & Nicobar Islands 21, 355,
  433, 494
  transport 433
  visitor permits 435
Andhra Pradesh 369
  climate 369
  transport 369

Anjuna (Goa) 297
  accommodation 465
  beach 293
  flea market 483
Annadurai, C.N. 383, 391
Annamalai Sanctuary (TN) 409, 486
Annapurna 163
antiques, exporting 488
Apollonius Tyaneus 182
Araku Valley (AP) 374
Arambol (Goa) 293, 297
Aranmula (Ker) 420
Aravalli Hills (Raj) 204
archaeology 148, 236, 263
architecture 101
  Architecture Museum (Chandigarh)
    149
  British colonial 130, 181
  Goan 293
  havelis 211, 213, 218, 220, **225**,
    235
  Indo-Muslim 233
  Indo-Saracenic 108, 159, 258
  Islamic 161, 203
  modern 108
  religious buildings 101
  temples 330
  urban cubist 139
Arikamedu (TN) 395
art and crafts 101, 359
  ancient cave art 266
  bas relief art (Mamallapuram) 393
  Calico Museum of Textiles
    (Ahmedabad) 235
  Crafts Museum (Delhi) 137
  deity images 310
  Didarganji Yakshi (Patna) 165
  embroidery 234, 238
  fine art 101, 109, 305
  Kala Raksha Trust (Guj) 238
  Kanhirode Weavers' Cooperative
    Society (Kannur) 425
  metal-work 367, 369
  Napier Museum of Arts and Crafts
    (Thiruvananthapuram) 417
  of Madhya Pradesh 277
  of Rajasthan 204
  of the Adivasi people 283
  Shilparamam Crafts Village
    (Hyderabad) 372
  shipbuilding 236
  shopping for 481
  stone carving 241
  textiles 109, 209, **234**, 238, 278,
    293, 369, 374
  Tibetan Refugee Craft Centre
    (Gangtok) 338
  wood crafts 369, 374
art galleries. See museums and
  galleries
arts, performance 92, 477. See
  also theatres and performance
  venues
  arts season (Chennai) 385
  Bharata-natyam dance 387
  classical music and dance 92, 278,
    477
  devotional music 93
  film music 97

Natyasastra 95
Odissi dance 328
popular music and dance 92
raga and tala 92
Tibetan music and dance 186
traditional dance-dramas 95, 359, 367, 369, 415, 417
traditional music and dance 184, 201, 416
Arunachal Pradesh 347, 494
climate 347
Ashoka, Emperor 48, 166, 169, 238, 330
Assam 301, 339
Aswem (Goa) 293, 297
Aswem-Morjim (Goa) 479
Augnier, Gerald 251
Auli (Utt) 178
Aurangabad (Mah) 275
accommodation 463
Bibi ka Maqbara 275
Panchakki 275
restaurants 285
Aurangzeb, Emperor 36, 53, 55
Auroville (TN) 395, 396
autorickshaws 445
Delhi 131
Jaipur (Raj) 204
Avantipur (J & K) 191
Ayodhya (UP) 69, 80, 161
Hanumangarhi 161
Ayurveda 418. See also spas and retreats

B

Babur, Emperor 51, 102, 129
Backwaters (Ker) 413, **428**, 473
Badami (Kar) 365
Badkhal Lake (Har) 148
Badrinath (Utt) 177
Baga (Goa) 293, 297, 465, 479, 483
Bairath (Raj) 209
Baker, Herbert 108, 130
Bakkhin (Sik) 339
Balasore (Odi) 333
Bandhavgarh National Park (MP) 281, 463, 486
Bandipur National Park (Kar) 364, 469, 486
Bangalore. See Bengaluru
Bangaram (Lak) 433, 476
Bangladesh 301
creation of 68
Bannarghatta National Park (Kar) 362
Bansberia (WB) 321
Hangsesvari Temple 321
Vasudeva Temple 321
Baranagar (WB) 322
Bara Pani (Umian Lake) (Meg) 345
Barra Basti (Nag) 349
Bathinda (Pun) 148
Bay of Bengal 301, 21, 324
bazaars. See markets and bazaars
beaches 10, 20
Andaman & Nicobar Islands 436
Goa 290, 292
Gujarat 241
Karnataka 368
Kerala 20, 413, 418, 425
Konkan coast 247
Lakshadweep Islands 431, 433
Maharashtra 270, 271
Mumbai 260, 261
Odisha 331, 332, 333

Tamil Nadu 382, 383
Beatles, The 177
Bedaghat (MP) 282
Bedsa cave temple (Mah) 272
begging 261, 487
Bekal Fort (Ker) 425, 473
Belur (Kar) 105, 364
Channekeshava Temple 364
Belur Math (WB) 320
Sri Ramakrishna Temple 320
Benaulim (Goa) 294, 297
accommodation 465
Bengaluru (Kar) 355, 360
accommodation 469
Art of Living Foundation 361
cinemas 360
Commercial Street 360
Cubbon Park 360
High Court 361
ISKCON Sri Radha Krishna Mandir 361
Lalbagh Botanical Gardens 361
nightlife 479
Nrityagram Dance Village 478
restaurants 376
shopping 481
State Central Public Library 361
Tipu Sultan's Palace 361
vegetable and fruit market 360
Vidhana Soudha 360
Betalbatim (Goa) 297
Bhagavad Gita 34, 157
Bhaja cave temple (Mah) 272
Bharatpur (Raj) 216
accommodation 455
Bharatpur Fort 216
Bhavanagar (Guj) 241
Bhave, Acharya Vinoba 276
Bhavnagar (Guj) 460
Bhima River (Mah) 269
Bhimbethka (MP) 281
Bhimunipatnam (AP) 374
Bhindranwale, Jarnail Singh 68
Bhopal (MP) 281
accommodation 463
Archaeological Museum 281
Bharat Bhavan 281
Bhojpur Temple 281
Birla Museum 281
Museum of Man 281
restaurants 285
Tal Lake 281
Bhrugarh (MP) 280
Bhubaneshwar (Odi) 104, 319, **329**
accommodation 468
Bindu Sarovar 329
Handicrafts Museum 330
Lingaraj Temple 329
Muktesvara Temple 330
Odisha State Museum 330
Parasuramesvar Temple 329
Rajarani Temple 330
restaurants 335
Siddhesvara Temple 330
Sisiresvara Temple 329
Tribal Research Museum 330
Uttaresvara Temple 329
Vaital Deul 329
Bhuj (Guj) 237, 460
palace 237
restaurants 243
Bhutan, border with 328
Bidar (Kar) 367
Bihar 164
Bijapur (Kar) 366

Gol Gumbaz 105, 366
Ibrahim Rauza mosque 105, 367
Bijli Mahadeva temple (HP) 182
Bikaner (Raj) 213
accommodation 455
Anup Mahal 213
Durbar Hall 213
Junagarh Fort 213
Lalgarh Palace 213
Old City 213
Shri Sadul Museum 213
Bilaspur (HP) 188
Lakshmi Narayan Temple 188
Radheshyam Temple 188
Vyas Gufa cave 188
Binsar (Utt) 178
birdlife 25, 153, 216, 236, 409. See also national parks and wildlife sanctuaries
cranes 216
flamingos 241
owls 27
peacocks 25, 216, 218
waterfowl 25, 195
Bison Horn Marias 283
'Black Hole of Calcutta' 309
Blue Mountain Railway (TN) 407
boating 314
boat trips and cruises 441
Ganges 163
glass-bottom boat trips (Lak) 433
Kerala backwaters 413, 420
Bodhgaya (Bih) 102, 168
accommodation 451
archaeological museum 169
Chanka Ramana 169
Mahabodhi Temple 169
restaurants 171
Vajrasana (Diamond Throne) 169
Bokaro (Jha) 334
Bolgatty Island (Ker) 423
Bollywood 249
Borra caves (AP) 374
Bose, Nandalal 305
Bose, Subhas Chandra 63, 307, 312
Brahmagiri (Mah) 275
Brahmakund (ArP) 348
Brahmaputra 301
Brahmaputra River 19, 337, 339
Brahmaur (HP) 188
Brahmins 30, 47, 391
Braj (UP) 157
Bratacharingam (WB) 323
Gurusaday Museum 323
Buddha 38, 102, 154, 161, 164, 167, 168, 343
Bulsara, Farok. See Mercury, Freddie
Bundi (Raj) 216
accommodation 456
Chitra Shala 217
Naval Sagar 217
palace 217
Raniji-ki-Baori step well 218
Taragarh Fort 218
business hours. See opening hours
bus travel 441
Bihar 165
Delhi 128, 131
in Tamil Nadu 393
long-distance buses 305, 382, 415
to/from Jammu, Kashmir and Ladakh 187
to/from Nepal 167
Buxar (Bih) 167
Byron, Robert 259

C

Calangute (Goa) 292, 465
  restaurants 296
Calcutta. See Kolkata
Camel Fair. See Kartik Purnima, under
  festivals and events
camel treks 201, 213, 224, 225
Cameron, James 17
Canacona (Goa) 294
Candolim (Goa) 292
  accommodation 466
  restaurants 296
Carey, William 320
cathedrals. See churches
caves
  Ajanta (Mah) 266, 275
  Amarnath (J & K) 191
  Bhimbethka (MP) 281
  Borra (AP) 374
  Elephanta (Mumbai) 250, 262
  Ellora (Mah) 266, 275
  Kanheri (Mah) 263
  Kotamsar (Cha) 282
  mandapams (Mamallapuram) 394
  Trimurti (Mamallapuram) 395
  Vyas Gufa (Bilaspur) 188
Chail (HP) 181
Chamba (HP) 187
  Bhuri Singh Museum 187
Chamba Valley (HP) 187
Champaner (Guj) 242
Champhai (Miz) 351
Chandernagore (WB) 321
Chandigarh (Pun & Har) 148
  accommodation 449
  Architecture Museum 149
  Government Museum and Art
    Gallery 150
  High Court 149
  Legislative Assembly 149
  restaurants 170
  Rock Garden 150
  Rose Garden 150
  Secretariat 149
  Sukhna Lake 150
Chandipur-on-Sea (Odi) 333
Chand, Nek 150
Chandor (Goa) 293
Chandragiri (AP) 375
Chandrapur (Mah) 276
Changspa (J & K) 193
  Shanti Stupa 193
Chapora (Goa) 293, 297
Char Dham (Utt) 177
Charideo. See Sibsagar
Charnock, Job 308
Chatterjee, Bankim Chandra 319
Chattisgarh 247, 269, **282**
Chaul (Mah) 270
Chauragarh mountain (MP) 282
Chennai (TN) 355, **381**, 391
  accommodation 471
  Anna Salai 383
  Anna Samadhi 383
  Armenian Church 385
  Banqueting Hall 383
  bars 389
  Chennakesavara Temple 385
  Chennammallikesvara Temple 385
  Connemara Public Library 384
  Egmore 385
  Elliot's Beach 383
  Fort St George 382

Fort St George Museum 382
George Town 385
Government Museum 105
High Court and Law College 385
Kalakshetra 387
Kalakshetra Arts Village 478
Kapalesvara Shiva Temple 385
Krishna Gana Sabha 385
Krishna Paratasaraty Temple 386
Legislative Assembly 382
Marina 383
MGR Film City 96
Mofussil Bus Terminal 387
Music Academy 384, 478
Mylapore 385
National Art Gallery 384
nightlife 479
Old Government House 383
Pantheon 383
Park hotel 385
Presidency College 383
  restaurants 388
Sangita Vadyalaya 385
San Thome Basilica 386
Secretariat 382
Senate House 383
shopping 383, 481
St Andrew's Kirk 385
State Government Museum 383
St Mary's Church 382
St Thomas's Mount 386
Theosophical Society 386
transport 382, 386
University 385
Cherranpunji (Meg) 345
Chettinad (TN) 402
Chidambaram (TN) 398, 411
Chikhalda (Mah) 276
Chikmagalur (Kar) 364
children 487
Chilka Lake (Odi) 332
Chinsura (WB)
  Imambara 321
  St John's Church 321
Chinura (WB) 321
Chiriya Tapu (A & N) 436
Chitrakut Falls (Cha) 283
Chitrakut (UP) 158
Chittaurgarh (Raj) 221
Cholamandalam (TN) 387
Chota Nagpur plateau 20
Chottanikkara Temple (Ker) 424
churches 291
  Afghan Memorial (Mumbai) 255
  All Souls' Memorial Church (Kanpur)
    159
  Armenian (Chennai) 385
  Armenian Church of Our Lady of
    Nazareth (Kolkata) 310
  Augustinian Monastery (Old Goa)
    295
  Basilica of Bom Jesus (Old Goa)
    108, 294
  Basilica of Mount Mary (Mumbai)
    262
  Chapel of St Catherine (Old Goa)
    295
  Holy Spirit (Margao) 292
  Immaculate Conception (Panaji) 291
  Lutheran (Ranchi) 334
  Our Lady of Bandel (Hugli) 321
  Our Lady of the Rosary (Old Goa)
    295
  Padri-ki-Haveli (Patna) 166

  Sacred Heart (Puducherry) 396
  Saint Paul's Anglican (Ranchi) 334
  San Thome Basilica (Chennai) 386
  Sé (Cathedral of St Catherine) (Old
    Goa) 108, 294
  St Andrew's Kirk (Chennai) 385
  St Andrew's Kirk (Kolkata) 309
  St Andrew's (Mumbai) 251
  St Cajetan (Old Goa) 295
  St Francis (Kochi) 424
  St Francis of Assisi (Old Goa) 294
  St James's (Delhi) 133
  St John's (Chinsura) 321
  St John's (Kolkata) 308
  St Mary's (Chennai) 382
  St Olaf's (Serampore) 320
  St Paul's Cathedral (Kolkata) 306
  St Philomena's (Mysore) 362
  St Thomas" Cathedral (Mumbai)
    258
Churchill, Winston 61
cinema. See film and television
  industry
cinemas 477
climate 21, 250, 253
Clive, Robert 306, 382
clothing 496
  jodhpurs 221
  traditional dress 203
  turbans 152
Coimbatore plateau 21
Colva (Goa) 293
Coorg (Kar) 364
Corbett, Jim 27, 179
Corbett National Park (Utt) **178**, 451,
  485
Coromandel Coast (TN) 20, 382
Coryate, Thomas 281
cotton 58, 253
couriers. See postal and courier
  services
cricket 181, 256, 307, **308**
crime and safety 11, 71, 164, 183,
  487
  bandits 334
  civil unrest 325, 329, 341, 349
  ethnic violence 343
  Naxalite-Maoist insurgency 283,
    333, 334
  terrorism 69, **70**, 189, 190, 232,
    249
Curzon, Lord George 173, 240
customs regulations 488
Cuttack (Odi) 333
  Barabati fort 333
  Qadmam-i-Rasul 333

D

da Gama, Vasco 55, 425
Dakshina Kasi. See Kolhapur
Dakshinesvar (WB) 320
  Kali Bhavatarini Temple 320
Dalai Lama 179, 186
Dalhousie (HP) 188
  accommodation 453
  restaurants 196
Dal Lake (J & K) 190
Daman (Guj) 242, 461
Dampha Wildlife Sanctuary (Miz) 351
Darasuram (TN) 400
  Airavatesvara Temple 400
Darjeeling Himalayan Railway (WB)
  325

Darjeeling (WB) 301, 325
  accommodation 467
  Chaurastha 325
  Himalayan Mountaineering Institute
    326
  Lloyd Botanical Gardens 326
  Mall 325
  Observatory Hill 325
  Planters' Club 326
  restaurants 335
  Zoological Park 326
Dassam waterfall (Jha) 334
Datia (MP) 279
  Narsing Dev Palace 279
Daulatabad (Mah) 275
Deccan plateau 20, 357, 366
Deeg (Raj) 211
  Gopal Bhawan 211
  Keshar Bhawan 211
  palace 211
Dehra Dun (Utt) 176, 196, 452
Delhi 106, 127
  accommodation 447
  Adilabad ruins 141
  Akshardham Temple 101, 141
  Archaeological Museum 135
  Ashokan Pillars 133
  Baha'i Lotus Temple 139
  Bangla Sahib Gurudwara 131
  Baroda House 135
  bars 143
  Bhulbhulaiyan 140
  Bird Hospital 132
  Central Cottage Industries
    Emporium 131, 137
  Chanakyapuri 135
  Chandni Chowk 130, 132
  Chattarpur 140
  Civil Lines 133
  Connaught Place 130
  Crafts Museum 137
  Dances of India 477
  Dandi Statue 135
  Delhi Zoo 136
  Digambara Temple 132
  Dilli Haat Food and Crafts Bazaar
    139
  DLF Mall of India 128, 141
  Fatehpuri Masjid 132
  Feroz Shah Kotla 129
  Flagstaff Tower 133
  Gandhi Darshan 133
  Gandhi Smarak Sangrahalaya 133
  Gandhi Smriti 136
  Garden of the Five Senses 141
  Ghantewala 132
  Gurgaon 141
  Hanuman Mandir 130
  Hauz-i-Shamsi tomb 140
  Hauz Khas 129
  Hauz Khas Village 139
  history 129
  Humayun's Tomb 106, 138
  Hyderabad House 135
  India Gate 134
  India Habitat Centre 138, 141, 477
  India International Centre 138, 141
  India Islamic Cultural Centre 138
  Indira Gandhi Memorial Museum
    136
  Indira Gandhi National Centre for
    the Arts 135
  Iron Pillar 50
  Jahaz Mahal 140

Jamali Kamali tomb 140
Jama Masjid 130, 132
Janpath 131
Jantar Mantar 131
Jawaharlal Nehru Memorial
  Museum 136
Kamani Auditorium 141
Khan Market 137
Lakshmi Narayan Temple 131
Lalit Kala Akademi 134
Lal Kot ruins 140
Lal Qila 130, 131
Lodi Colony Market 137, 138
Lodi Gardens 129, 137
Mehrauli 140
Moti Masjid 140
Muhammad Shah tomb 137
Mutiny Memorial 133
National Gallery of Modern Art 109,
  136
National Museum 106, 136
National Rail Museum 137
New Delhi 127, 130
nightlife 478
Nila Gumbad 138
NOIDA 141
Old Delhi 127, 131
Paharganj Bazaar 130
Palika Bazaar 130
population 127
Pragati Maidan 135
Purana Qila 129, 135
Qudsia Bagh 131
Qutb Minar Complex 50, 105, 129,
  140
Qutbuddin Bakhtiyar Kaki 140
Quwwat-ul-Islam Mosque 140
Rabindra Kala Sangam 134
Raj Ghat 132
Rajpath 134
Rashtrapati Bhavan 108, 134
Red Fort 106
restaurants 142
Safdarjang's Tomb 138
Sangeet Natak Akademi 134, 141,
  477
Sansad Bhavan 134
Sanskriti Museums 141
Santushti Complex 135
Shahjahanabad. See Old Delhi
Sheikh Nizamuddin Aulia shrine 138
shopping 137, 141, 482
Siri Fort 139
Sispganj Gurudwara 132
South Delhi 139
St James's Church 133
St Stephen's College 133
Sulabh International Museum of
  Toilets 134
Sundar Nagar colony 136
Sunehri Masjid 132
Suraj Kund 141
taxis 131
The Ridge 133
Tibet House Museum 138
transport 128, 131, 140, 442
Tughlaqabad Fort 141
University 133
websites 131
Desai, Morarji 67
Desert States 201
Deshnok (Raj) 214
Devas (MP) 280
Devi, Rukmini 387

Dhanbad (Jha) 334
Dhanushkodi (TN) 396
Dharamsala (HP) 186
  accommodation 453
  McLeod Ganj 186
  Museum of Kangra Art 186
  Namgyal Monastery 186
  Norbulingka Institute 186
  restaurants 196
Dhauli (Odi) 330
  Peace Pagoda 331
Dholpur (Raj) 216
Dhuandhar Falls (MP) 282
Diamond Harbour (WB) 323
Digboi (Assam) 343
Digha (WB) 324
Dimapur (Nag) 348
disabled travellers 488
Diu island (Guj) 240
Diu town (Guj) 241, 461
diving and snorkelling 432, 433, 436,
  480
Dixit, Shiela 128
Dolphin's Nose (AP) 374
Dooars (WB) 328
Draksharaman (AP) 374
Drew, Jane 149
driving 442
**Druk Thupten Sangag Choling
  Monastery (WB)** 326
Dudhwa National Park (UP) 161,
  485
Duliajan (Assam) 343
Dundlod (Raj) 212
Dungarpur (Raj) 456
Dwarka (Guj) 238
  Temple of Dvarkadish 238
Dzongri (Sik) 339

E

earthquakes 237
Eastern Ghats 20
East and Northeast India 301
East India Company 52, **55**, 215,
  251, 303
eating out. See restaurants
economy 57, 66, 67, 69, 70, **75**
  outsourcing & IT boom 75
  special economic zones 78
electricity 488
Elephant Beach (A & N) 436
elephants 208
  elephant safaris 437
Elephant Training Camp (A & N) 437
Ellora (Mah) 104, 103, 247, **266**, 275
  restaurants 285
  tours 277
embassies and consulates 489
emergency numbers 489
environmental issues 27, 441
  air pollution 127, 240, 242, 273
  conservation 27
  endangered species 165
  illegal logging 359
  in the Kerala backwaters 428
  water pollution 261
  wildlife poaching 23, 24, 25, 27
Eravikulam National Park (Ker) 423
Ernakulam (Ker) 423, 426
etiquette 489
  at religious sites 150
  on beaches 419
Everest, Mount 326

F

Faizabad (UP) 161
Faridkot (Pun) 148
Fatehpur (Raj) 212
  Nadine Le Prince Haveli 212
Fatehpur Sikri (UP) 52, 106, 156
festivals and events 11, 90, 478
  Ardh Kumbh Mela 161
  art biennale (Kochi) 109
  Ayappan pilgrimage (Sabarimala)
    416
  Carnival (Goa) 291
  classical music and dance festival
    (Chennai) 385
  dance festival (Khajuraho) 286
  Dasara (Mysore) 362
  Dussera (Kullu) 182
  Festival of the Joyful Heart (Shat Suk
    Myasiem) (Shillong) 345
  Ganesh Chathurthi (Mumbai) 260,
    261
  Gangasagar Mela (Sagardwip) 323
  Garo 100-drum festival (Tura) 345
  Hola (Nahan) 188
  Hornbill festival (Nag) 349
  International Kite Festival
    (Ahmedabad) 233
  kambala (buffalo race) (Kar) 367
  Kartik Purnima (Pushkar) 215
  Khichri Mela (Gorakhpur) 161
  Kumbha Mela 176, 274
  Lavi (Rampur) 181
  Magh Mela (Allahabad) 162
  Maha Kumbh Mela (Allahabad) 161
  Mahamastakabhisheka
    (Sravanabelagola) 365
  Maha Shivratri 282
  Minjar fair (Chamba) 187
  Pandhapur Yatra pilgrimage
    (Kolhapur) 274
  Pong Labsal (Gangtok) 338
  Pooram (Thrissur) 424
  Purna Kumbha Mela (Allahabad)
    162
  Ramnagar Ram Lila (Varanasi) 164
  Rath Yatra (Puri) 331
  Sangamam arts festival (Chennai)
    385
  Shivrati Fair (Mandi) 188
  Urs Mela 214
  Vallamkali (Ker) 420
film and television industry 96, 249,
  305, 307
  MGR Film City (Chennai) 96
  Ramoji Film City (Hyderabad) 372
fishing 344
food and drink 85
  alcohol 89
  Bengali cuisine 316
  Bombay Duck 255, 258
  Chettinad cuisine 401, 402
  feni 290
  Goan cuisine 296
  Gujerati cuisine 243
  Himalayan cuisine 196
  Indian cuisines 85
  masala dosa 368
  Northern Plains 170
  street food 88, 262
  Tamil cuisine 388, 410
  tea 325, 342
football 308
Forrest, G.W, 256

Forster, E.M. 280
Fort Aguada (Goa) 292
forts 108
  Agra 155, 156
  Ajatasatru (Rajgir) 168
  Anandpur Sahib (Pun) 148
  Bahu (Jammu town) 190
  Barabati (Cuttack) 333
  Bathinda (Pun) 148
  Bekal (Ker) 425
  Bharatpur (Raj) 216
  Chittaurgarh (Raj) 221
  Daulatabad (Mah) 275
  Faridkot (Pun) 148
  Fort William (Kolkata) 306
  Gandikota (AP) 375
  Gingee (TN) 397
  Golconda (AP) 369, 372
  Gwalia (MP) 279
  Gwalior (MP) 278
  Jaigarh (Amber) 208
  Jaisalmer (Raj) 224
  Janjira (Mah) 271
  Jhansi 158
  Junagarh (Bikaner) 213
  Kangra (HP) 186
  Kausambi (UP) 162
  Kesgarh (Anandpur Sahib) 153
  Kumbalgarh (Raj) 220
  Lal Qila (Delhi) 130, 131
  Meherangarh (Jodhpur) 223
  Nahargarh (Jaipur) 208
  Penukonda (AP) 375
  Purana Qila (Delhi) 129, 135
  Rao Hamir (Raj) 216
  Red Fort (Agra) 106
  Red Fort (Delhi) 106
  Sindhudurg (Mah) 271
  Sinhagad (Mah) 273, 275
  Siri (Delhi) 139
  St Angelo (Kannur) 425
  St George (Chennai) 382
  Taragarh (Bundi) 218
  Tughlaqabad (Delhi) 141
  Vellore (TN) 397
  Vijaydurg (Mah) 271
Fry, Maxwell 149
Furkating (Assam) 344
further reading 501

G

Gaitor (Raj) 208
  Royal Cenotaphs 208
Galta (Raj) 208
  Monkey Temple 208
Gandhi, Indira 67, 80, 151, 189
  assassination 68
Gandhi, M.K. 29, 61, 133, 233, 235,
  260, 276
  assassination 66, 80
  birthplace 239
Gandhi, Rahul 70
Gandhi, Rajiv 68
  assassination 69
Gandhi, Sanjay 68
Gandhi, Sonia 70
Gangaikondacholapuram (TN) 400
  Brihadesvara Temple 400
Ganges, River 19, 145, 154, 162,
  175, 176, 301, 314
  estuary 323
  source of 177
Gangotri (Utt) 177

Gangtok (Sik) 338
  accommodation 468
  Chogyal's Palace 338
  Deer Park 338
  Hotel Tashi Delek 338
  Orchid Sanctuary 338
  Research Institute of Tibetology
    338
  restaurants 351
  shopping 483
  Tibetan Refugee Craft Centre 338
Ganguly, Sourav 308
Ganpathipule (Mah) 271
gardens. See parks and gardens
Garo hill country (Meg) 346
Gaumukh (Utt) 177
Gaur (WB) 322
Gaya (Bih) 168
  Visnupada Temple 168
gay and lesbian travellers 489
geography and geology 19
Ghoom (WB) 327
  Yiga Cholang Gelugpa Buddhist
    Temple 327
Ghrusnesvar Temple (Mah) 275
Gill, Robert 267
Gingee Fort (TN) 397
Gir Forest (Guj) 22, 240
Goa 55, 289, 479, 483
  transport 291, 292
Godavari River (Mah) 20, 269, 274,
  275, 276, 374
Gokarna (Kar) 368, 470
  Kooti Theerta tank 368
  Mahabaleshwar Temple 368
Golconda Fort (AP) 369, 372
golf 181, 307, 313
gompas. See monasteries
Gopalpur-on-Sea (Od) 332
Gorakhpur (UP) 161
Gorkha Janmukti Morcha 325
government. See politics and
  government
Govind Singh 38
Gowda, H.D. Deve 69
Gramphu (HP) 185
Grand Trunk Road 320
Great Himalayan National Park (HP)
  486
Guindy Deer Park (TN) 387
Gujarat 201, 231
  transport 231
Gujural, Inder Kumar 69
Gulbarga (Kar) 367
  Jami Mosque 367
  Saiyid Muhammad Husaini Gisu
    Daras tomb 367
Gulmarg (J & K) 191
Gundu Island (Ker) 423
Gurgaon. See Delhi
Guru Nanak 37, 38
Guru Shikhar (Raj) 222
Guruvayur (Ker) 425
  Krishna Temple 425
Guwahati (Assam) 341, 469
  Belle Vue Hotel 341
  Kamakhya Mandir 341
  Navagraha Mandir 341
  Raj Bhavan 341
  restaurants 351
  State Museum 341
  Sukhlesvar Janardhan Temple
    341
  Umananda (Peacock Island) 341

Gwalior (MP) 247, 277
  accommodation 464
  Ghaus Muhammad's mausoleum
    278
  Gwalior Fort 278, 279
  Jai Vilas Palace 278
  restaurants 285
  Sarod Ghar museum 278
  Sas Bahu temples 278
  Sikh gurudwara 278
  Teli-ka-Madir 278
Gyaraspur (MP) 281

H

Halebid (Kar) 105, 364
  Hoysaleswara Temple 364
Hampi (Kar) 51, 355, 365, **378**, 470
handicrafts. See art and crafts
Hanuman 164
Haridwar (Utt) 176, 196
  accommodation 452
  Har-ki-Pauri 177
Harihara I 51
Haryana 67, 146
  transport 147
Hassan (Kar) 364, 470
Havelock, General 159
Havelock Island (A & N) 436, 437,
  476
Hazare, Ana 71, 76
health and medical care 77, 490
  altitude sickness 192
  Ayurvedic therapies 418
Hemis (J &K) 194
Hemkund (Utt) 178
hiking. See trekking and hiking
hill stations 9, 123, **180**
  Almora (Utt) 178
  Dalhousie (HP) 188
  Darjeeling (WB) 301, 325
  Kodaikanal (TN) 408
  Mahabalesvar (Mah) 274
  Matheran (Mah) 272
  Mount Abu (Raj) 221
  Mussoorie (Utt) 176
  Nainital (Utt) 178
  Naukuchiyatal (Utt) 178
  Pachmarhi (MP) 282
  Panchgani (Mah) 274
  Ponmudi (Ker) 418
  Ranikhet (Utt) 178
  Udhagamandalam (TN) 406
  Yercaud (TN) 408
Himachal Pradesh 19, 146, 175, **179**
  climate 179, 185
  transport 179
Himalayas 19, **175**, 325
Hirni waterfall (Jha) 334
history 17
  2008 terrorist attacks 70
  ancient times 46
  British rule **56**, 130, 251, 272, 303,
    324
  Danish presence 320
  Delhi Sultanate 50, 129
  Dutch presence 56, 321
  French presence 321, 396
  Gupta Empire (Golden Age) 48, 50
  Independence movement 60
  Maratha Empire 271
  Mauryan Empire 47
  modern times 65
  Mughal Empire 51, 52, 129, 204

Partition 65, 145
Portuguese presence 55, 251, **289**,
  321
railways, building of 58
sectarian violence 69, 80
separatist insurrections 68
spice trade 55
Uprising of 1857 **57**, 123, 158
World War I 60
World War II 63, 348
horse racing 306
horseriding 274
Hospet (Kar) 365, 470
  restaurants 377
hotels. See accommodation
hot springs
  Manikaran (HP) 183
  Nubra Valley (J & K) 195
  Vashisht (HP) 184
Hugli river (WB) 306, 321
Hugli (WB) 321
  Church of Our Lady of Bandel 321
Humayan 102
Humayun 129
Hume, Allan Octavian 59
Hundru waterfall (Jha) 334
Huxley, Aldous 259
Hyderabad (AP) 355, 369
  accommodation 471
  Bagh-e-Aam gardens 372
  Birla Venkatesvara Temple 372
  Botanical Gardens 372
  British Residency 108
  Charminar 371
  Char Minar mosque 106
  Falaknuma Palace 371
  Hussain Sagar Lake 370
  Kala Pahad 372
  Lad Bazaar 371
  Legislative Assembly 372
  Mecca Masjid 371
  Nehru Zoological Park 372
  Old City 370
  pearl market 371
  Planetarium 372
  Qutb Shahi tombs 372
  Ramoji Film City 372
  restaurants 377
  Salar Jung Museum 371
  Shilparamam Crafts Village 372
  shopping 483
  State Archaeological Museum 372

I

Imphal (Man) 350
  Kwairamband Bazaar 350
  Manipur State Museum 350
Indian Institute of Technology (TN)
  387
Indian National Congress 59
Indore (MP) 280, 464
  restaurants 285
**Indravati National Park and Tiger
  Reserve (Cha)** 283, 486
Indus river 194
industry 66, **75**, 240, 319, 334, 360,
  370
  motor industry 147
  textiles 363
Inland Customs Line 324
insurance 492
internet 492
Itanagar (ArP) 347

J

Jagdalpur (Cha) 282
Jagesvar (Utt) 178
Jahangir, Emperor 52, 102, 154
Jaidev 324
Jaipur (Raj) 205
  accommodation 456
  Central Museum 208
  City Palace 206
  City Palace Museum 107
  Hawa Mahal 207
  Jantar Mantar 207
  Nahargarh Fort 208
  restaurants 226
  Sawai Man Singh II Museum 206
  shopping 483
  transport 204
Jaisalmer (Raj) 224
  accommodation 456
  Gadi Sagar Tank 225
  Main Chowk 225
  Nathmali-ki-Haveli 225
  Palace of the Maharawal 225
  Patwa Haveli 225
  Rani ki Mahal 225
  restaurants 227
  Salim Singh Haveli 225
  shopping 224
Jaldapara (WB) 328
Jalori Pass (HP) 183
Jammu and Kashmir 189
  transport 187
Jammu town (J & K) 190
  Amar Mahal Palace 190
  Bahu Fort 190
  Dogra Art Gallery 190
  Raghunath Temple 190
  Ranbireshwar Temple 190
Jamnagar (Guj) 238
  Lakhota Palace 238
Jamshedpur (Jha) 334
Janjira (Mah) 271
Jaunpur (UP) 161
Jawalamukhi (HP) 186
Jayaram, Jayalalitha 96, 391
Jhansi (UP) 158, 450
  fort 158
Jharkhand 301, 319, **333**
  transport 321
Jhunjhunu (Raj)
  Rani Sati Temple 212
Jinnah, Muhammad Ali 61, 65
Jodhpur (Raj) 222
  accommodation 457
  Meherangarh Fort 223
  restaurants 227
  Umaid Bhavan 108, 223
Jog Falls (Kar) 369
Johna waterfall (Jha) 334
Joshimath (Utt) 177, 196
  accommodation 452
  Narsingh Bhagwan temple 177
Junagadh (Guj) 239

K

Kabir 37
Kabru, Mount 326
Kadmat (Lak) 433
Kailasa Hill (AP) 374
Kala Raksha Trust (Guj) 238
Kalidasa 48
Kalimpong (WB) 327

accommodation 468
Tharpa Choling 328
Zangdog Palrifo Brang Monastery 328
Kalpa (HP) 182
Kalpeni (Lak) 432
Kamarpukur (WB) 324
Kanadukathan (TN) 402
Kanchenjunga, Mount (Sik) 19, 326
Kanchipuram (TN) 104, **397**, 411
Ekambaresvara Temple 397
Kailasanatha Temple 397
Kanger Valley (Cha) 282
Kangra (HP) 186, 453
Kangra Valley (HP) 186
Kanha National Park (MP) 281, 464, 486
accommodation 464
Kanheri Caves (Mah) 263
Kanniyakumari (TN) 402, 411, 472
Wandering Monk Museum 402
Kannur (Ker) 425
accommodation 473
Fort St Angelo 425
Kanhirode Weavers' Cooperative Society 425
Mopplah Town 425
Payyambalam beach 425
Kanpur (UP) 159
accommodation 450
All Souls' Memorial Church 159
restaurants 170
Kappad (Ker) 425
Karaikkudi (TN) 402
Karla cave temple (Mah) 272
Karnataka 357
transport 361
Karni Mata 214
Karunagapalli (Ker) 420
Karunanidhi, M. 392
Kasauli (HP) 453
Kashmir 66, 69, 71, **190**. See also Jammu & Kashmir
Kathiawar Peninsula (Guj) 232
Kausambi (UP) 162
Kavaratti (Lak) 432
Kaveri River 21
Kaza (HP) 185
Kaziranga National Park (Assam) 343, 469, 486
Kedarnath (Utt) 178
Kendubilwa (WB) 324
Keoladeo Ghana National Park (Raj) 25, **216**, 486
Kerala 20, 355, **413**, 483
climate 422
transport 415
Keylong (HP) 185
Khajuraho (MP) 103, 158, 247, **279**, **286**
accommodation 464
Archaeological Museum 280
restaurants 285
Khan, Ajmad Ali 278
Khandagiri (Odi) 330
Khangchendzonga National Park (Sik) 486
Khaziranga National Park (Assam) 27
Khecheopalri Lake (Sik) 338
Khuldabad (Mah) 275
Khuri (Raj) 225
Khushinagar (UP) 161
Muktabandhana stupa 162

Khusrau, Amir 37
Kinnaur (HP) 181
Kipling, Rudyard 181, 216, 277, 281, 320
Kochi (Ker) 423, 413
accommodation 473
Jew Town 424
Matancherry Palace 424
restaurants 426
shopping 483
St Francis's Church 424
Kodaikanal (TN) 408
accommodation 472
Bryant Gardens 408
Coaker's Walk 408
Kodai Lake 408
Pillar Rocks 408
Kodalkanal (TN)
restaurants 411
Kodungallur (Ker) 424
Kohima (Nag) 348
Kolhapur (Mah) 274
Kotiteerth temple 274
Malalaksmi Temple 274
New Palace 274
Pandhapur Yatra pilgrimage 274
Raj Wada 274
restaurants 284
Kolis 253
Kolkata Night Riders 307
Kolkata (WB) 301, 301, **303**, 320
Academy of Fine Arts 306
accommodation 467
Armenian Church of Our Lady of Nazareth 310
Ashutosh Museum 311
Asiatic Society 311
BBD Bagh (Dalhousie Square) 309
Bentinck Street 309
Birla Academy of Art and Culture 314
Birla Industrial and Technological Museum 312
Birla Planetarium 306
Botanical Gardens 314
Calcutta Gallery 306
Calcutta Golf Club 307
Chinatown 309
Chowringhee 307
Eden Gardens 307, 308
Esplanade 307
Fort William 306
Freemason's Hall 311
Gandhi Statue 307
ghats 314
Government House 108
Gwalior Monument 314
Haora Bridge 314
High Court 308
history 57, 65
Home for the Destitute and Dying (Nirmal Hriday) 313, 314
India Museum 308
Indian Coffee House 311
ITC Sangeet Research Academy 478
Jain temple 309
Jorashankho 310
Jute Balers Association 309
Kalighat 313
Kali Temple 313
Kolkata Museum 308
Kolkata Polo Club 306
Kolkata University 311
Kumartuli 310
La Martinière College 312

Magen David synagogue 310
Maidan 306
Marble Palace 311
Metiaburuz Shi'ite Mosque 314
Nakhoda Mosque 310
National Library 312
Nehru Children's Museum 306
Netaji Bhavan 312
Netaji Subhas Road 309
Nicco Park 315
nightlife 479
Oberoi Grand 307
Old China Bazaar 309
Old Mission 311
Parasnath Mandir 310
Park Street 311
Pathuriagata 310
Presidency General Hospital 306
Rabindra Bharati University 310
Rabindra Mancha 310
Rabindra Sadan 306, 478
Rabindra Sarovar Lake 314
Racecourse 306
Rajabazar 310
Raj Bhavan 308
Rajya Sabha 307
Ramakrishna Mission Institute of Culture 314
restaurants 310, 316
Saheed Minar 307
Salt Lake 315
Science City 315
shopping 483
South City Mall 314
South Park Street Cemetery 312
Sri Aurobindo's Statue 307
St Andrew's Kirk 309
St John's Church 308
Stock Exchange 309
St Paul's Cathedral 306
Strand 306
Swabhumi 315
Tagore's Castle 310
Tiretta Market 309
Tollygunge Club 313
Tolly's Nullah 313
Town Hall 308
transport 305, 309
Victoria Memorial 306
Vidyasagar Setu bridge 315
War Memorial 307
Wet-o-Wild Beach Tropicana 315
Writers' Building 309
Zoological Gardens 313
Kollam (Ker) 419, 426, 474
British Residency 420
Konark (Odi) 104, **332**, 468
Sun Temple 301, 332
Kondapali (AP) 374
Konkan coast (Mah) 247, **269**, 357, 367
Koraput (Odi) 301, 332
Kotamsar (Cha) 282
Kota (Raj) 218
accommodation 458
City Palace 218
Maharao Madho Singh Museum 218
Kottayam (Ker) 421
accommodation 474
restaurants 426
Kovalam (Ker) 413, 418
accommodation 474
restaurants 426

Kozhikode (Ker) 425
  accommodation 474
  Krishna Menon Art Gallery and
    Museum 425
  Pazhassi Raja Museum 425
  restaurants 427
Krishna 157
Krishna River (Mah) 20, 269
Kufri (Utt) 178
Kullu (HP) 182, 453
Kullu Valley (HP) 182
Kumarakom Bird Sanctuary (Ker)
  421
Kumari, Mayawati 154, 156
Kumar, Nitish 164
Kumbalgarh Fort (Raj) 220
Kumbalgarh Sanctuary (Raj) 486
Kunzam Pass (HP) 185
Kurseong (WB) 326
Kurukshetra (Har) 153
Kutch (Guj) 232, 237
Kuttanad (Ker) 420

L

Ladakh (J & K) 19, 123, 175, 189,
  192
Lahaul Valley (HP) 184
Lahori, Ustad Ahmad 172
Lakshadweep Islands 21, 355, **431**,
  494
  climate 431
  transport 432
Lakshmibai, Rani 158
Langthabal (Man) 350
language 250, 355, 359, 369, 392,
  432, **497**
Le Corbusier 149
Ledo (ArP) 348
Leh (J & K) 193
  accommodation 454
  Dzomsa 191, 193
  Ecology Centre 193
  Leh Palace 193
  Old Leh 193
  restaurants 197
  Soma Gompa 193
  Tsemo Gompa 193
Lepaksi (AP) 105, 375
  Birabhadra Temple 375
  Nandi 375
Lhotse, Mount 326
Likir (J & K) 195
literature 102, 254, 502
  Mahabharata 129
Little Andaman Island (A & N) 437
Loduvra (Raj) 225
Lonavala (Mah) 272, 463
  restaurants 284
Lothal (Guj) 236
Lucknow (UP) 123, 159
  accommodation 450
  Alambagh 159
  Bara Imambara 160
  Chowk 160
  Dilkusha 159
  Dr Ambedkar Memorial 160
  Hazratganj 160
  Hussainabad Imambara 160
  Imambara Sibtainabad 160
  Kurshid Manzil 160
  La Martinière College 159
  Residency Compound 160
  restaurants 171

Shah Najaf Imambara 160
  shopping 484
  Sikandarbargh 160
  Taron Wali Kothi 160
Ludhiana (Pun) 153
Lumbini (Nepal) 162
Lutyens, Sir Edwin 108, 130

M

Machilipatnam (AP) 373
Madarihat (WB) 328
Madhav National Park (MP) 279
Madhya Pradesh 247, 269, **277**
  climate 277
  transport 277
Madras. See Chennai
Madras Crocodile Bank (TN) 27, 387
Madurai (TN) 104, 401
  accommodation 472
  Gandhi Memorial Museum 401
  Minakshi Sundaresvara Temple 401
  Murugan Temple 402
  palace of Tirumalai Nayak 401
  restaurants 411
Mahabalesvar (Mah) 274
Mahabharata 34, 102
Mahadeo Hills (MP) 277
Mahanadi River 20
Mahaprabhu, Chaitanya 321
Maharashtra 247, 269
Maharishi Mahesh Yogi 177
Mahatma Gandhi Bridge (Bih) 167
Mahatma Gandhi Marine National
  Park (A & N) 436
Mahavira 39, 162, 167
Mahé (Ker) 425
Maheshwar (MP) 278, 464
Mahmud of Ghazni 50
Majuli island (Assam) 343
Makalu, Mount 326
Malda (WB) 322
Malvan (Mah) 271
Mamallapuram (TN) 103, 393
  Adivaraha Temple 395
  Arjuna's Penance (Descent of the
    Ganges) 393
  Five Rathas 394
  Krishna Mandapam 394
  Mahisasuramardini Mandapam 394
  restaurants 410
  Shore Temple 393
  Trimurti Cave 395
  Varaha Mandapam 394
Manali (HP) 123, 175, **184**
  accommodation 454
  Dhungri Temple 184
  restaurants 197
Manas National Park (Assam) 344,
  486
Mandawa (Raj) 212
Mandi (HP) 188
  Bhutnath Temple 188
  Raj Madhan Temple 188
Mandore (Raj) 224
  Hall of Heroes 224
  Mahavira temple 224
  Osian Temple 224
  Sachiya Mata Temple 224
Mandrem (Goa) 293, 297, 466
Mandu (MP) 247, 280
  accommodation 464
  Bhangi Gate 280
  Hindola Mahal 280

Jahaz Mahal 280
  Jama Masjid 280
  Nikanth Temple 280
  Reva Kund 280
Mandvi (Guj) 236
Maner (Bih) 167
  Bari Dargah 167
  Choti Dargah 167
Mangalore (Kar) 368
Manikaran (HP) 183
Manipur 349, 494
Mannar National Marine Park (TN)
  409
maps 492
Mapusa (Goa) 296
Margao (Goa) 292, 296
  Church of the Holy Spirit 292
  Largo da Igreja 292
  market 293
  Sat Banzam Gor 292
markets and bazaars. See
  also shopping
  Bara Bazaar (Shillong) 345
  Bengaluru (Kar) 360
  Bidar (Kar) 367
  Devaraja Market (Mysore) 363
  Dilli Haat Food and Crafts Bazaar
    (Delhi) 139
  Jyotiba Phule (Crawford) Market
    (Mumbai) 259
  Kalimpong (WB) 328
  Khan Market (Delhi) 137
  Kwairamband (Imphal) 350
  Lad Bazaar (Hyderabad) 371
  Leh (J & K) 193
  Lodi Colony Market (Delhi) 137, 138
  Margao (Goa) 293
  Old China Bazaar (Kolkata) 309
  Paharganj Bazaar (Delhi) 130
  Palika Bazaar (Delhi) 130
  pearl market (Hyderabad) 371
  Tiretta (Kolkata) 309
Martand Temple (J & K) 191
martial arts 349, 417
Martin, Claude 159, 312
Masrur (HP) 187
Matheran (Mah) 272, 463
  restaurants 284
Matho (J & K) 194
Mathura (UP) 102, 157
  accommodation 450
  Dvarkadhish shrine 158
  Government Museum 102
  Kesava Deo Mandir 158
  museum 158
  Potara Kund 158
  Vishram Ghat 158
Maurya, Chandragupta 47
mausoleums. See tombs
Mawphluang (Meg) 346
Mawsynram (Meg) 345
Mayawati 79
Mayer, Albert 149
media 492
Meghalaya 344
Melghat Wildlife Sanctuary (Mah)
  277
Mercury, Freddie 250
Middle Andaman Island (A & N) 437
minerals and mining 20, 334
Minicoy (Lak) 432
Mirik (WB) 326
Mistry, Rohinton 254
Mittal, Lakshmi 79

Mizoram 351, 494
Modhera (Guj) 236
  Sun Temple 236
Modi, Narendra 80, 232
Moirang (Man) 350
  Thankgjing Temple 351
monasteries 102, 175
  Alchi (J & K) 194
  Druk Thupten Sangag Choling (WB) 326
  Hemis (J & K) 194
  in Ladakh 194
  Jarasandha-ki-Baithak (Rajgir) 168
  Jetavana (Sravasti) 162
  Likir (J & K) 195
  Majuli island (Assam) 343
  Namgyal (Dharamsala) 186
  Phyang (J & K) 194
  Red Hat Ningmapa (Pemayangtse) 339
  Rizong (J & K) 195
  Rumtek (Sik) 338
  Sanga Choelling (Sik) 338
  Sankar (J & K) 194
  Shey Gompa (Shey) 194
  Spitok (J & K) 194
  Tashiding Ningmapa (Sik) 339
  Tawang (ArP) 347
  Tharpa Choling (Kalimpong) 328
  Tikse (J & K) 194
  Zangdog Palrifo Brang (Kalimpong) 328
money matters 493
  budgeting for your trip 487
  money-saving tips 11
Morjim (Goa) 293
Morris, Jan 256
mosques 105
  Arhai din ka Jhonpra (Ajmer) 215
  Char Minar (Hyderabad) 106
  Fatehpuri (Delhi) 132
  Ibrahim Rauza (Bijapur) 105
  Imambara (Chinsura) 321
  Jama Masjid (Ahmedabad) 233
  Jama Masjid (Delhi) 130, 132
  Jama Masjid (Mandu) 280
  Jama Masjid (Mumbai) 259
  Jama Masjid (Srinagar) 191
  Jami (Gulbarga) 367
  Kodungallur (Ker) 424
  Mecca Masjid (Hyderabad) 371
  Metiaburuz Shi'ite (Kolkata) 314
  Moti Masjid (Delhi) 140
  Nakhoda (Kolkata) 310
  Pao Mekkam (Assam) 341
  Pather Masjid (Srinagar) 191
  Patther-ki-Masjid (Patna) 166
  Qadmam-i-Rasul (Cuttack) 333
  Qutb Minar (Delhi) 50, 105
  Quwwat-ul-Islam (Delhi) 140
  Shah Hamadan (Srinagar) 191
  Sher Shah Masjid (Patna) 166
  Sidi Bashir's (Ahmedabad) 235
  Sidi Saiyad's (Ahmedabad) 235
  Sunehri Masjid (Delhi) 132
Mother Teresa 313
Motihari (Bih) 167
Mount Abu (Raj) 104, 221
  accommodation 458
  Dilwara Jain temples 222
  guided walks 220
  restaurants 227
Mountbatten, Lord Louis 65
Mount Girnar (Guj) 239

Mount Harriet (A & N) 436
Mudumalai National Park (TN) 472, 486
Mudumalai (TN) 409
Mukhalingam (AP) 374
Mukurti National Park (TN) 409
Mumbai (Mah) 108, 247, **249**, 269
  accommodation 461
  Afghan Memorial Church 255
  Bandra 262
  Banganga Tank 261
  Basilica of Mount Mary 262
  Bharatiya Vidya Bhavan 477
  Bhuleshwar 259
  Byculla 261
  Chathrapathi Shivaji Terminus 258
  Chhatrapati Shivaji Maharaj Vastu Sangrahalaya 106
  Chowpatti Beach 260, 261
  Churchgate station 258
  climate 250, 253
  Colaba 250, 253
  Dharavi 261
  Elephanta Island and Caves 103, 250, 262
  Flora Fountain 258
  Fort district 250, 257
  Gateway of India 250, 253
  General Post Office 258
  Haji Ali 261
  Horniman Circle 257
  Hutatma Chowk 258
  Jama Masjid Mosque 259
  Jehangir Art Gallery 256
  Jyotiba Phule (Crawford) Market 259
  Kala Ghoda 250, 256
  Kalbadevi 258
  Leopold Café 254, 264
  Mahalakshmi Temple 261
  Maharaja Chatrapati Sivaji Museum 256
  maidans 256
  Malabar Hill 260
  Mangaldas Lane 259
  Mani Bhavan 260
  Marine Drive 259
  Mumba Devi Temple 259
  Mumbai University 256
  Nariman Point 253, 260
  National Centre for the Performing Arts 260, 478
  nightlife 478
  Panjarapool animal sanctuary 259
  Portuguese Church areas 251
  restaurants 264
  Royal Asiatic Society Library 257
  Salsette 251
  Sassoon Docks 255
  S Dr Bhau Daji Lad Museum 261
  Secretariat 256
  shopping 255, 484
  slums 261
  St Andrew's Church 251
  street food 262
  St Thomas' Cathedral 258
  Taj Mahal Palace and Tower 255
  terrorist attacks of 2008 70
  tiffin wallahs 259
  transport 250, 258
  Victoria Terminus 258
Mumtaz Mahal 106, 156
Munnar (Ker) 423
  accommodation 475
Murshidabad (WB) 322

  Hazarduari 322
Murud (Mah) 271
museums and galleries
  Academy of Fine Arts (Kolkata) 306
  Anokhi Museum of Hand Printing (Amber) 208
  Anthropological Museum (Port Blair) 435
  Archaeological Museum (Bhopal) 281
  archaeological museum (Bodhgaya) 169
  Archaeological Museum (Delhi) 135
  Archaeological Museum (Khajuraho) 280
  Archaeological Museum (Thrissur) 425
  Architecture (Chandigarh) 149
  art gallery (Thanjavur) 399
  Art Museum (Tanjavur) 105
  Ashutosh Museum (Kolkata) 311
  Bhuri Singh Museum (Chamba) 187
  Birla Academy of Art and Culture (Kolkata) 314
  Birla Industrial and Technological Museum (Kolkata) 312
  Birla Museum (Bhopal) 281
  Calcutta Gallery (Kolkata) 306
  Calico Museum of Textiles (Ahmedabad) 235
  Central Museum (Jaipur) 208
  Chhatrapati Shivaji Maharaj Vastu Sangrahalaya (Mumbai) 106
  City Palace Museum (Jaipur) 107
  Crafts Museum (Delhhi) 137
  Dakshina Chitra (Muttukkadu) 387
  Dogra Art Gallery (Jammu town) 190
  Dr Ramnath A Podder Haveli Museum (Nawalgarh) 212
  Fort St George Museum (Chennai) 382
  Gandhi Darshan (Delhi) 133
  Gandhi Memorial Museum (Madurai) 401
  Gandhi Smarak Sangrahalaya (Delhi) 133
  Gandhi Smriti (Delhi) 136
  Government Museum and Art Gallery(Chandigarh) 150
  Government Museum (Chennai) 105
  Government Museum (Mathura) 102
  Gurusaday Museum (Bratacharingam) 323
  Handicrafts Museum (Bhubaneshwar) 330
  Hazarduari (Murshidabad) 322
  India Museum (Kolkata) 308
  Indira Gandhi Memorial Museum (Delhi) 136
  Jawaharlal Nehru Memorial Museum (Delhi) 136
  Jehangir Art Gallery (Mumbai) 256
  Kangra Art (Dharamsala) 186
  Kolkata Museum (Kolkata) 308
  Krishna Menon Art Gallery and Museum (Kozhikode) 425
  Lalit Kala Akademi (Delhi) 134
  Maharaja Chatrapati Sivaji Museum (Mumbai) 256
  Maharao Madho Singh Museum (Kota) 218
  Mani Bhavan (Mumbai) 260

Manipur State Museum (Imphal) 350
Mathura museum (Mathura) 158
Mizoram State Museum (Aizawl) 351
Museum of Habitat (AP) 374
Museum of Man (Bhopal) 281
museum of sculpture (Gwalior) 278
Nagarjunakonda Sagar (AP) 373
Napier Museum of Arts and Crafts (Thiruvananthapuram) 417
National Art Gallery (Chennai) 384
National Gallery of Modern Art (Delhi) 109, 136
National Museum (Delhi) 106, 136
National Rail Museum (Delhi) 137
Nehru Children's Museum (Kolkata) 306
Netaji Bhavan (Kolkata) 312
Nicholas Roerich gallery (Naggar) 184
Odisha State Museum (Bhubaneshwar) 330
Patna Museum (Patna) 165
Pazhassi Raja Museum (Kozhikode) 425
Raja Kelkar Museum (Pune) 273
Rajaraja Museum (Thanjavur) 399
Ramakrishna Mission Institute of Culture (Kolkata) 314
Salar Jung Museum (Hyderabad) 371
Sangeet Natak Akademi (Delhi) 134
Sangita Vadyalaya (Chennai) 385
Sanskriti Museums (Delhi) 141
Sarod Ghar (Gwalior) 278
Sawai Man Singh II Museum (Jaipur) 206
Science City (Kolkata) 315
S Dr Bhau Daji Lad Museum (Mumbai) 261
Shilpgram (Udaipur) 220
Shri Chitra Art Gallery (Thiruvananthapuram) 417
Shri Sadul Museum (Bikaner) 213
Sri Jayachamarajendra Art Gallery (Mysore) 362
Srisailam (AP) 373
State Archaeological Museum (Hyderabad) 372
State Government Museum (Chennai) 383
State Museum (Guwahati) 341
Sulabh International Museum of Toilets (Delhi) 134
Tibet House Museum (Delhi) 138
Tribal Research Centre (Udhagamandalam) 407
Tribal Research Institute and Museum (Ranchi) 334
Tribal Research Museum (Bhubaneshwar) 330
Tripura Government Museum (Agartala) 347
Wandering Monk Musum (Kanniyakumari) 402
Mussoorie (Utt) 176
accommodation 452
restaurants 196
Muttukkadu (TN) 387
Dakshina Chitra 387
Mysore (Kar) 362
accommodation 470
Chamundi Hill 362

Devaraja Market 363
Karnataka Silk Industries Factory 363
palace 362
restaurants 376
shopping 484
Sri Jayachamarajendra Art Gallery 362
St Philomena's Church 362

N

Naddi (HP) 186
Nadia (WB). See Nawadwip (WB)
Nagaland 348, 494
Nagarhole National Park (Kar) 364, 471, 486
Nagarjunakonda (AP) 377
Nagarjunakonda Sagar and Dam (AP) 373
Nagaur (Raj) 458
Nagercoil (TN) 405
Nagesh Temple (Goa) 295
Naggar (HP) 184
Nicholas Roerich gallery 184
Nagpur (Mah) 276
Nahan (HP) 188
Nainital (Utt) 178
accommodation 452
restaurants 196
Nal Sarovar Bird Sanctuary (Guj) 236
Namboodiripad, E.M.S. 414
Namdapha National Park (ArP) 348, 486
Nameri Sanctuary (Assam) 344
Nanda Devi National Park (Utt) 175, 485
Nandanakanan (Odi) 332
Naramada River (MP) 269
Narayan, J.P. 67
Narkanda (HP) 178, 181
Narmada River (MP) 281, 282
Nasik (Mah) 274
National Camel Research Centre (Raj) 214
national parks and wildlife sanctuaries 10, 27, 148, **485**
Annamalai (TN) 409, 486
Bandhavgarh (MP) **281**, 463, 486
Bandipur (Kar) **364**, 469, 486
Bannarghatta (Kar) 362
Corbett (Utt) **178**, 451, 485
Dampha (Miz) 351
Dudhwa (UP) 161, 485
Eravikulam (Ker) 423
Gir Forest Reserve (Guj) 22
Great Himalayan (HP) 486
Indravati National Park and Tiger Reserve (Cha) 283, 486
Jaldapara (WB) 328
Kanha (MP) **281**, 464, 486
Kaziranga (Assam) **343**, 469, 486
Keoladeo Ghana (Raj) 25, **216**, 486
Khangchendzonga (Sik) 486
Khaziranga (Assam) 27
Kumarakom Bird Sanctuary (Ker) 421
Kumbalgarh Sanctuary (Raj) 486
Madhav (MP) 279
Mahatma Gandhi Marine National Park (A & N) 436
Manas (Assam) 344, 486

Mannar National Marine Park (TN) 409
Melghat (Mah) 277
Mudumalai (TN) 472, 486
Mukurti (TN) 409
Nagarhole (Kar) **364**, 471, 486
Nal Sarovar Bird Sanctuary (Guj) 236
Namdapha (ArP) 348, 486
Nameri Sanctuary (Assam) 344
Nanda Devi (Utt) 175, 485
Navegaon (Mah) 276
Nilgiri Biosphere Reserve (Kar) 363
Palamau (Jha) 334
Periyar Wildlife Sanctuary (Ker) **422**, 475, 486
Ranthambore (Raj) **215**, 459, 486
Sajankali (WB) 323
Sanjay Gandhi National Park (Mah) 263
Sariska Tiger Reserve (Raj) 24, **210**, 486
Sasan Gir Lion Sanctuary (Guj) 240, 486
Silent Valley (Ker) 486
Simlipal (Odi) 332
Sudhanyakali (WB) 323
Sultanpur Bird Sanctuary (Har) 153
Sunderbans (WB) 20, 301, **322**, 468, 486
Tadoba (Mah) 276
Thar Desert (Raj) 486
Valley of Flowers (Utt) 178, 486
Velavadar (Guj) 486
Wild Ass Sanctuary (Guj) 238, 486
Naukuchiyatal (Utt) 178, 452
Navegaon National Park (Mah) 276
Nawadwip (WB) 321
Nawalgarh (Raj) 212
Dr Ramnath A Podder Haveli Museum 212
Nehru, Jawaharlal 65, 148, 189
Neil Island (A & N) 437
Nepal, border with 160, 167, 327
newspapers and magazines 492
Nicobar Islands. See Andaman and Nicobar Islands
nightlife 478
Goa 294
Nilgiri Biosphere Reserve (Kar) 363
Nilgiri Hills 20
Norgay, Tenzing 326
North Andaman Island (A & N) 437
Northeast, The 337
entry permits 338, 349
transport 344
Northern Plains 145
North, The 123
Nowicki, Matthew 149
Nubra Valley (J & K) 195
Nurpur (HP) 188

O

Odisha 301, 319, **328**
climate 328
transport 321
oil 343
Old Goa (Goa) 294
Basilica of Bom Jesus 108, 294
Chapel of St Catherine 295
Church of Our Lady of the Rosary 295
Church of St Cajetan 295

Church of St Francis of Assisi 294
Church of the Augustinian
    Monastery 295
Convent of St Monica 108, 295
Monte Santo 295
Sé (Cathedral of St Catherine) 108,
    294
Om Beach (Kar) 368
Omkaresvar (MP) 280, 281
    Mandhata Temple 280
opening hours 493
oracles 194
Orcha (MP) 279
Orissa. See Odisha
Orwell, George 167

P

Pachmarhi (MP) 282
Padmanabhapuram (Ker) 417
Padmanabhapuram (TN) 405
Padum (J & K) 195
Paes, Leander 308
Pahalgam (J & K) 191
Pakistan 145
    border with 153, 189
    creation of 65
    relations with 66, 68, 69, 82
palaces
    Agha Khan (Pune) 273
    Amar Mahal (Jammu town) 190
    Bhuj (Guj) 237
    Bundi (Raj) 217
    Chogyal's (Gangtok) 338
    City Palace (Alwar) 210
    City Palace (Jaipur) 206
    City Palace (Kota) 218
    City Palace (Udaipur) 219
    Daria Daulat (Srirangapatnam) 363
    Daulat Khana (Ajmer) 215
    Deeg (Raj) 211
    Falaknuma (Hyderabad) 371
    Hawa Mahal (Wadhwan) 241
    Hindola Mahal (Mandu) 280
    Jag Mandir (Udaipur) 220
    Jag Niwas (Udaipur) 220
    Jahaz Mahal (Mandu) 280
    Jai Vilas (Gwalior) 278
    Lakhota (Jamnagar) 238
    Lakshmi Vilas (Vadodara) 241
    Lalgarh (Bikaner) 213
    Leh (J & K) 193
    Marble Palace (Kolkata) 311
    Matancherry (Kochi) 424
    Mysore (Kar) 362
    Narsing Dev (Datia) 279
    New (Kolhapur) 274
    Padmanabhapuram (TN) 405
    Palace of the Maharawal (Jaisalmer)
        225
    Pushbanta (Agartala) 346
    Puttan Malika
        (Thiruvananthapuram) 416
    Raj Bhavan (Kolkata) 308
    Raj Wada (Kolhapur) 274
    Rani ki Mahal (Jaisalmer) 225
    Sajjangarh (Udaipur) 220
    Shanivarvada (Pune) 273
    Shey (J & K) 194
    Stok (J & K) 194
    Thanjavur (TN) 399
    Tipu Sultan's (Bengaluru) 361
    Ujjayanta (Agartala) 346
    Umaid Bhavan (Jodhpur) 223

Palai (Ker) 422
Palakkad Gap (Ker) 424
Palamau National Park (Jha) 334
Palani Hills 20
Palitana (Guj) 241
Palolem (Goa) 294, 297
    accommodation 466
Panaji (Goa) 291
    accommodation 466
    Church of the Immaculate
        Conception 291
    Fontainahas 291
    Largo da Igreja 291
    Menezes-Braganza Institute 291
    restaurants 296
    Secretariat 291
Panchgani (Mah) 274
Panch Ghagh waterfall (Jha) 334
Pandim, Mount 326
Pandua (WB) 322
Pangong Tso (J & K) 195
Panipat (Har) 148
Pao Mekkam mosque (Assam) 341
Paonta Sahib (HP) 188
paragliding 184
Parasnath Hill (Jha) 334
parks and gardens. See
    also amusement parks, national
    park and wildlife sanctuaries
    Bagh-e-Aam (Hyderabad) 372
    Botanical Garden (Nandanakanan)
        333
    Botanical Garden (Shillong) 345
    Botanical Gardens (Hyderabad)
        372
    Botanical Gardens (Kolkata) 314
    Botanical Gardens
        (Udhagamandalam) 407
    Bryant Gardens (Kodaikanal) 408
    Chasma Shahi (Srinagar) 191
    Cubbon Park (Bengaluru) 360
    Deer Park (Gangtok) 338
    Garden of the Five Senses (Delhi)
        141
    Harwan (Srinagar) 191
    Lalbagh Botanical Gardens
        (Bengaluru) 361
    Lloyd Botanical Gardens (Darjeeling)
        326
    Lodi Gardens (Delhi) 129, 137
    Maidan (Kolkata) 306
    maidans (Mumbai) 256
    Nishat (Srinagar) 191
    Orchid Sanctuary (Gangtok) 338
    Pinjore Gardens (Har) 147
    Qudsia Bagh (Delhi) 131
    Rambagh (Agra) 156
    Rock Garden (Chandigarh) 150
    Rose Garden (Chandigarh) 150
    Shalimar (Srinagar) 191
    Sikandarbargh (Lucknow) 160
    Thread Garden (Udhagamandalam)
        407
    Venuvana (Rajgir) 168
Parsis 254
Parthasarathi Temple (Ker) 420
Parvati Valley (HP) 183
Patel, Sardar Vallabhai 80
Patiala (Pun) 153
Patna (Bih) 165
    accommodation 451
    Bankipur 165
    Didarganji Yakshi 165
    Golghar 165

    Gulzaribagh 166
    Haramandirji 166
    High Court 165
    Khuda Baksh Oriental Library 166
    Kumhrar 166
    Maharaja's Palace 165
    Padri-ki-Haveli (St Mary's Church)
        166
    Pataliputra 166
    Patna Museum 165
    Patna Women's College 165
    Patther-ki-Masjid 166
    Qila House 166
    Raj Bhavan 165
    restaurants 171
    Sher Shah Masjid 166
Pattadakal (Kar) 104, 366
Paunar (Mah) 276
Pelling (Sik) 338
Pemayangtse (Sik) 338, 339
    Red Hat Ningmapa Monastery 339
people
    Adivasi **32**, 277, 283, 301, 333,
        344, 433
    Andamese 433
    Armenians 310, 321
    Chinese 309
    Kolis 253
    Nepalis 338
    Parsis 254, 261
    Tibeto-Burmese 348, 349
    Todas 403, 406
Periyar Wildlife Sanctuary (Ker) 422,
    475, 486
    accommodation 475
Phalgu River 168
Phalut, Mount 327
photography 489, 494
Phyang (J & K) 194
Pinjore Gardens (Har) 147
Pipli (Odi) 331
Piprahva (UP) 162
plantlife 26
    hardwood forests 20, 277
    mangrove jungle 323
    of the Southern Ghats 405
    of the Western Ghats 422
    orchids 301, 338
    sandalwood 359
    tropical rainforests **20**, 357, 409
Pochampalli (AP) 372
Point Calimere (TN) 409
politics and government 62, 154. See
    also economy
    Bahujan Samaj Party 79
    Bengali Party 305
    Bharatiya Janata Party 69
    Communist Party of India 78
    constitution 66
    corruption 67, 69, 71, 76, 154, 156,
        164, 168
    Indian Administrative Service 176
    in Kerala 414
    in Kolkata 305
    in Tamil Nadu 391
    Janata Party 68
    Left Front Party 305
    National Front Party 69
    of Gujarat 232
    Shiv Sena Party 249, 261
    socialism 67
    Trinamool Congress 305
polo 306
Ponmudi (Ker) 418

population
Delhi 127
Karnataka 359
Kolkata (WB) 303
Mumbai (Mah) 250
Uttar Pradesh 154
Porbandar (Guj) 239
Port Blair (A & N) 435
accommodation 476
Anthropological Museum 435
Cellular Jail 435
restaurants 437
postal and courier services 494
Pragpur (HP) 187
Prasad, Rajendra 80
Premiji, Azim 79
Prinsep, James 238
public holidays 494
Puducherry (TN) 395, 396
accommodation 472
Raj Nivas 396
restaurants 410
Sacred Heart Church 396
Pune (Mah) 247, 272
accommodation 463
Agha Khan Palace 273
Osho International Meditation
Resort 273
Parvati Temple 273
Qamarali Darvesh 273
Raja Kelkar Museum 273
restaurants 284
Shanivarvada 273
Shinde Chatri 273
Temple of Patalesvar 273
Punjab 67, 145
climate 20
history 68
transport 147
Puri (Odi) 104, 301, 319, **331**
accommodation 468
Jagannath Temple 331
restaurants 335
Pushkar (Raj) 215
accommodation 458
restaurants 226
Puttaparthi (AP) 375

R

Radcliffe, Sir Cyril 65
Radhanagar beach (A & N) 436
radio stations 492
Rahman, A.R. 98
rail travel 228, 442
development of 253
international 440
Konkan Railway 270, 291, 367
luxury rail tours 229, 444
rail passes 445
to/from Andhra Pradesh 369
to/from Bihar 165
to/from Chennai (TN) 382
to/from Delhi 128
to/from Goa 291
to/from Gujarat 231
to/from Himachal Pradesh 179
to/from Karnataka 361
to/from Kerala 415
to/from Kolkata (WB) 305
to/from Madhya Pradesh 277
to/from Mumbai (Mah) 250
to/from Punjab & Haryana 147
to/from Rajasthan 204

to/from Tamil Nadu 393
to/from The Northeast 344
to/from Uttarakhand 177
to/from Uttar Pradesh 155
to/from West Bengal, Odisha and
Jharkhand 321
to Khajuraho (MP) 286
rail travel, scenic and heritage lines
180
Blue Mountain Railway (TN) 407
Darjeeling Himalayan Railway (WB)
325
Kalka–Simla 179
to Darjeeling (WB) 301
Raipur (Cha) 282
restaurants 285
Rajasthan 20, 201, **203**
history 204
transport 204
Rajgir (Bih) 167
Ajatasatru Fort 168
Gridhrakuta Hill 168
Jarasandha-ki-Baithak monastery
168
Jivakamhavana 168
Karanda Tank 168
Maddakuchchi 168
Manyar Math 168
Pippla Cave 168
Ratna Giri 168
Saptaparni cave 168
Venuvana 168
Vishva Shanti (World Peace) Stupa
168
Rajrappa (Jha) 334
Rama 161, 167, 396
Ramachandran, M.G. 96, 383, **391**
Ramakrishna 320
birthplace 324
Ramappa Temple (AP) 372
Ramayana **35**, 102, 161, 164, 274
Rameswaram Island (TN) 396
Ramalingesvara Temple 396
Ramanatasvami Temple 396
Rampur (HP) 181
Ramtek temple (Mah) 276
Ranakpur (Raj) 104
Ranakpur temple complex (Raj)
221
Ranchi (Jha) 334
Eastern Railway Hotel 334
Lutheran Church 334
Shiva Temple 334
St Paul's Anglican Church 334
Tribal Research Institute and
Museum 334
Ranikhet (Utt) 178, 452
Ranns of Kutch (Guj) 20, 201, **237**,
461
Ranthambore National Park (Raj)
215, 459, 486
accommodation 459
Rao Hamir (Raj) 216
Rao, P.V. Narasimha 69
Ratnagiri (Odi) 331
Ray, Satyajit 305, 307
Razaq, Abdul 378
Rekong Peo (HP) 182
religion 17, **29**, 47, 110, 169, 328
Brahmins 30, 47, 391
Buddhism **38**, 49, 154, 164, 175,
179, 186, 194
Christianity 49, 290
devotional music 93

Hinduism **31**, 33, 81, 110, 157,
161, 162, 175
in Kerala 414
in politics 80
Islam **36**, 50, 154
Jainism **39**, 49, 164
Kashmiri Pandits 189
mythology 35
Nipponzan Myohoji movement 168
religious tensions 232
Sikhism 36, **37**, 166
sun worship 332
Zoroastrian faith 254
Renuka (HP) 188
restaurants 88
Delhi 142
Goa 296
Gujarat 243
Himalayas 196
Karnataka and Andhra Pradesh 376
Kerala 426
Kolkata (WB) 316
Maharashtra, Madhya Pradesh &
Chattisgarh 284
Northeast 351
Northern Plains 170
offshore islands 437
Rajasthan 226
Tamil Nadu 410
West Bengal, Odisha and Jharkhand
335
restricted areas 431, 433, 494
Kinnaur (HP) 182
Rice, Clifford 423
rickshaws and tongas 445
Rishikesh (Utt) 177
accommodation 453
Muni-ki-Reti 177
Rizong (J & K) 195
Roerich, Nicholas 184
Roe, Sir Thomas 281
Rohtang Pass (HP) 184
Ross Island (A & N) 436
Ross, Sir Ronald 306
Roy, Arundhati 421, 421
Roy, Jamini 305
Ruantlang (Miz) 351
rugby 308
Calcutta Cup 308
Rumtek Monastery (Sik) 338
Rushikonda (AP) 374

S

Sabarimala (Ker) 416
Sagardwip (WB) 323
Kapil Muni Temple 324
Sai Baba 374, 375
Sai Baba Ashram (Kar) 362
Sajankali sanctuary (WB) 323
salt tax 62, 324
Samode (Raj) 209, 459
Sam (Raj) 225
Sanchi (MP) 101, **281**, 464
Sandakphu (WB) 327
Sanga Choelling Monastery (Sik) 338
Sanganer (Raj) 209
Sangla (HP) 182
Sanjay Gandhi National Park (Mah)
263
Sankar (J & K) 194
Sardar Sarovar dam (MP) 281
Sariska Tiger Reserve (Raj) 24, **210**,
486

Sarnath (UP) 164
  accommodation 450
  Dhamekh Stupa 164
Sasan Gir Lion Sanctuary (Guj) 240,
  461, 486
Sasaram (Bih) 167
  Sher Shah's Mausoleum 167
Saspul (J & K) 195
sati 212
Saurashtra (Guj) 232, 238
Sawai Madhopur (Raj) 215
science and technology 68, 360
Secunderabad (AP). See Hyderabad-
  Secunderabad
Sela Pass (ArP) 347
Serampore (WB) 320
  Serampore College 320
  St Olaf's Church 320
Sevagram (Mah) 276
Shah Jahan, Emperor 52, **106**, 127,
  130, 131, 154, 155
Shanta-Durga Temple (Goa) 295
Shantiniketan (WB) 324
Shatrunjaya Hill (Guj) 241
Shekhavati (Raj) 211
  accommodation 459
Sher Shah 129
Shey (J & K) 194
  Shey Gompa 194
Shillong (Meg) 345
  Bara Bazaar 345
  Botanical Garden 345
  Pinewood Hotel 345
  Raj Bhavan 345
  Ward Lake 345
Shillong Peak (Meg) 344, 345
Shiva 162, 398
Shivaji Maharaj 271
Shivpuri (MP) 279
Shoja (HP) 183
shopping 481. See also markets and
  bazaars
  crafts 130, 131, 137, 139
  designer fashions 137
  gems and jewellery 206, 371, 386,
    481
  handicrafts 255, 481
  what to buy 481
Shri Naina Devi Temple (HP) 188
Sibsagar (Assam) 343
Sidhudurg Fort (Mah) 271
Sikandra (UP) 157
Sikkim 301, **337**, 494
Silent Valley National Park (Ker) 486
Simhachalam (AP) 374
Simla (HP) 179
  accommodation 454
  Jakhu Temple 181
  restaurants 183, 197
Simlipal National Park (Odi) 332
Singh, Govind 153, 166
Singh, Maharaja Ranjit 150, 151
Singh, Manmohan 70
Singh, V.P. 69
Sinhagad Fort (Mah) 273, 275
Sinquerim (Goa) 292, 466
Sipra River (MP) 280
Sirhind (Pun) 153
Sirpur (Cha) 282
Sisters of Charity 313
Skinner, James 133
Snake Park (TN) 387
social issues 75
  child labour 77

discrimination 29, 62, 333
  literacy 76
  poverty 70, 71, 249, 261, 333
  sanitation 77
  wealth gap 76, 79, 359
society 29, 49
  caste system **29**, 154, 164, 254
  family life 31
  funerary rituals 163, 261
  marriage 30, 66
  women's status 66, 71, **83**, 414
Solang (HP) 178, 184
Somnath (Guj) 239
Somnathpur (Kar) 363, 364
  Keshava Vishnu Temple 363, 364
Sonamarg (J & K) 192
Sonepur (Bih) 167
Southern Ghats 357, 405
South, The 355
space programme 78
spas and retreats 404, 484
Spiti Valley (HP) 184
Spitok (J & K) 194
sports 308. See also by name
Sravanabelagola (Kar) 364
Sravasti (UP) 162
  Jetavana monastery 162
Sri Aurobindo 396
Sri Aurobindo Ashram (TN) 396
Sri Kalahasti (AP) 375
Sri Mangesh Temple (Goa) 295
Srinagar (J & K) 177, 190
  Chasma Shahi garden 191
  Harwan garden 191
  Hazratbal shrine 191
  Jama Masjid 191
  Nishat garden 191
  Pather Masjid 191
  Shah Hamadan Mosque 191
  Shalimar garden 191
Sri Narayana Guru 420
Sringeri (Kar) 364
Srirangam (TN) 104, 401
  Sriranganathasvami Temple 401
Srirangapatnam (Kar) 363
  Daria Daulat 363
  Gumbaz Mausoleum 363
Srisailam (AP) 373
Stagna (J & K) 194
St Alphonsa of India 422
step wells
  Adalaj Vav (Guj) 236
  Dad Hari-ni-Vav (Guj) 236
  Raniji-ki-Baori (Bundi) 218
St Francis Xavier 294, 295
Stok Palace (J & K) 194
St Thomas 49, 386
Suchindram (TN) 403
Sudhanyakali sanctuary (WB) 323
Sullivan, John 406
Sultanpur Bird Sanctuary (Har) 153
Sunderbans National Park (WB) 20,
  301, **322**, 468, 486
Sunderbans Tiger Reserve (WB)
  486
Suraj Kund (Har) 148
Surat (Guj) 242
  British cemetery 242
Surendranager (Guj) 241
Swami Vivekananda memorial (TN)
  403
synagogues
  Magen David (Kolkata) 310
  Pardesi (Kochi) 424

T

Tabo (HP) 185
Tadoba (Mah) 276
Tadpatri (AP) 375
  Ramalingesvara Temple 375
  Venkataramana Temple 375
Tagore, Rabindranath 305, 310, 319,
  324
Taj Heritage Corridor (UP) 154, 156
Tamil Nadu 21, 381
  climate 382
  transport 393
Tanjavur (TN) 104
  Art Museum 105
Tansen 278, 280
Tapti River (MP) 269
Tarakeshwar Temple (WB) 324
Tarapith (WB) 324
Tashiding Ningmapa Monastery (Sik)
  339
Tata, J.N. 255
Tata, Sir Jamshedji 334
Tawang (ArP) 347
taxis
  car with driver services 441
  Delhi 131
  prepaid taxis 442
technology. See science and
  technology
Telengana plateau 20
telephones 494
television 98, 492
temples 9, 50
  Adivaraha (Mamallapuram) 395
  Airavatesvara (Darasuram) 400
  Ajanta (Mah) 275
  Akshardham (Delhi) 101, 141
  Amba Mata (Guj) 240
  at Chamba 187
  at Jagesvar (Utt) 178
  at Kangra (HP) 186
  at Khajuraho (MP) 279
  at Sirpur (Cha) 282
  at Vrindavan (UP) 158
  Baha'i Lotus (Delhi) 139
  Bangla Sahib Gurudwara (Delhi) 131
  Bedsa (Mah) 272
  Benimadhava (Tribeni) 321
  Bhaja (Mah) 272
  Bhojpur (Bhopal) 281
  Bhutnath (Mandi) 188
  Bijli Mahadeva (HP) 182
  Birla Venkatesvara (Hyderabad) 372
  Brihadesvara
    (Gangaikondacholapuram) 400
  Brihadesvara (Thanjavur) 398
  Channekeshava (Belur) 364
  Chattarpur (Delhi) 140
  Chennakesava (Chennai) 385
  Chennammallikesvara (Chennai)
    385
  Chidambaram (TN) 398
  Chottanikkara (Ker) 424
  Dhungri (Manali) 184
  Digambara (Delhi) 132
  Dilwara Jain temples (Mount Abu)
    222
  Durga (Aihole) 366
  Durgiana (Amritsar) 152
  Dvarkadish (Dwarka) 238
  Ekambaresvara (Kanchipuram) 397
  Ellora (Mah) 275
  Ghrusnesvar (Mah) 275

Golden (Amritsar) 68, 69, 107, 147, 150
Hangsesvari (Bansberia) 321
Hanuman Chatti (Yamunotri) 177
Hanumangarhi (Ayodhya) 161
Hanuman Mandir (Delhi) 130
Hoysaleswara (Halebid) 364
ISKCON Sri Radha Krishna Mandir (Bengaluru) 361
Jagannath (Puri) 331
Jagdish (Udaipur) 220
Jain temple (Kolkata) 309
Jakhu (Simla) 181
Jor Bangla (Visnupur) 324
Kailasanatha (Kanchipuram) 397
Kalachand Sri Mandir (Visnupur) 324
Kali Bhavatarini (Dakshineswar) 320
Kali (Kolkata) 313
Kamakhya Mandir (Guwahati) 341
Kanakadurga (Vijayawada) 373
Kapelesvara Shiva (Chennai) 385
Kapil Muni (Sagardwip) 324
Karla (Mah) 272
Keshava Vishnu (Somathpur) 363, 264
Konark Sun (Odi) 301
Kotiteerth (Kolhapur) 274
Krishna (Guruvayur) 425
Krishna Paratasaraty (Chennai) 386
Lad Khen (Aihole) 366
Lakshmi Narayan (Bilaspur) 188
Lakshmi Narayan (Delhi) 131
Lingaraj (Bhubaneshwar) 329
Lord Venkatesvara (Tirupati) 375
Madan Gopal (Visnupur) 324
Madan Mohan (Visnupur) 324
Mahabaleshwar (Gokarna) 368
Mahabodhi (Bodhgaya) 169
Mahakalesvar (Ujjain) 280
Mahalakshmi (Mumbai) 261
Mahalaksmi (Kolhapur) 274
Mahavira (Mandore) 224
Mandhata (Omkaresvar) 280
Martand (J & K) 191
Minakshi Sundaresvara (Madurai) 401
Monkey (Galta) 208
monkey (Varanasi) 164
Muktesvara (Bhubaneshwar) 330
Mumba Devi (Mumbai) 259
Murugan (Madurai) 402
Nagesh (Goa) 295
Narsingh Bhagwan (Joshimath) 177
Nasiyan Jain Temple (Ajmer) 215
Navagraha Mandir (Guwahati) 341
Nikanth (Mandu) 280
Nipponzan Myohoji (Rajgir) 168
on Parasnath Hill (Jha) 334
Osian (Mandore) 224
Parasnath Mandir (Kolkata) 310
Parasuramesvar (Bhubaneshwar) 329
Parvati (Pune) 273
Patalesvar (Pune) 273
Radheshyam (Bilaspur) 188
Raghunath (Jammu town) 190
Rajarani (Bhubaneshwar) 330
Raj Madhan (Mandi) 188
Ramalingesvara (Rameswaram Island) 396
Ramalingesvara (Tadpatri) 375
Ramanatasvami (Rameswaram Island) 396

Ramappa (AP) 372
Ramtek (Mah) 276
Ranakpur (Raj) 221
Ranbireshwar (Jammu town) 190
Rani Sati (Jhunjhunu) 212
rock-cut temples (Ellora) 266
rock-cut temples (Masrur) 187
Sachiya Mata (Mandore) 224
Sas Bahu (Gwalior) 278
Shanta-Durga (Goa) 295
Shatrunjaya Hill (Guj) 241
Shinde Chatri (Pune) 273
Shiva (Ranchi) 334
Shore (Mamallapuram) 393
Shri Naina Devi (HP) 188
Shyam Rai Mandir (Visnupur) 324
Siddhesvara (Bhubaneshwar) 330
Sisiresvara (Bhubaneshwar) 329
Sispganj Gurudwara (Delhi) 132
Sri Kalahasti (AP) 375
Sri Mangesh (Goa) 295
Sri Padmanabhasvami (Thiruvananthapuram) 416
Sri Ramakrishna (Belur Math) 320
Sriranganathasvami (Srirangam) 401
Sukhlesvar Janardhan (Guwahati) 341
Sun (Konark) 332
Sun (Modhera) 236
Suraj Kund (Har) 148
Tarakeshwar (WB) 324
Teli-ka-Mandir (Gwalior) 278
temple towns (TN) 396
Thankgjing (Moirang) 351
Tiruvannamalai (TN) 397
Trimbakesvar (Trimbakesvar) 275
Tripura Sundari (Udaipur) 347
Uttaresvara (Bhubaneshwar) 329
Vadakkunnatham (Thrissur) 424
Vaital Deul (Bhubaneshwar) 329
Vasudeva (Bansberia) 321
Venkataramana (Tadpatri) 375
Virabhadra (Lepaksi) 375
Vishvanath (Varanasi) 163
Visnupada (Gaya) 168
Wat Thai Nalanda (Nalanda) 167
Yiga Cholang Gelugpa (Ghoom) 327
tennis 308, 313
Tezpur (Assam) 343
Thackeray, Bal 249
Thanjavur (Tanjore) (TN) 398
   art gallery 399
   Brihadesvara Temple 398
   palace 399
   Rajaraja Museum 399
   restaurants 411
   Saraswathi Mahal Library 399
Thar Desert National Park (Raj) 486
Thar Desert (Raj) 20, 201, 204, **225**
theatres and performance venues 477
   Cochin Cultural Centre (Kochi) 414
   India Habitat Centre (Delhi) 141
   India International Centre (Delhi) 141
   Indira Gandhi National Centre for the Arts (Delhi) 135
   Kamani Auditorium (Delhi) 141
   Kathakali Centre (Kochi) 414
   Krishna Gana Sabha (Chennai) 385
   Music Academy (Chennai) 384
   National Centre for the Performing Arts (Mumbai) 260

Rabindra Kala Sangam (Delhi) 134
   Rabindra Sadan (Kolkata) 306
   Sangeet Natak Akademi (Delhi) 141
Thiruvalluvar, image of (TN) 403
Thiruvananthapuram (Ker) 413, 416
   accommodation 475
   Margi School 417
   Napier Museum of Arts and Crafts 417
   Puttan Malika Palace 416
   restaurants 426
   shopping 483
   Shri Chitra Art Gallery 417
   Sri Padmanabhasvami Temple 416
Thrissur (Ker) 424, 475
   Archaeological Museum 425
   restaurants 427
   Vadakkunnatham Temple 424
Tibet
   border with 182
   Tibetan Government in Exile 186
Tiger Hill (WB) 326
Tikse (J & K) 194
   time zone 434, 495
Timur (Tamburlaine) 51
   tipping 495
Tipu Sultan 362
Tirathgarh Falls (Cha) 282
Tiruchirapalli (TN) 401
Tirunelveli (TN) 405
Tirupati (AP) 375, 377, 471
   Lord Venkatesvara Temple 375
Tiruvannamalai (TN) 397
Tiruvarur (TN) 400
Tod, James 219, 222
   toilets 495
tombs 105
   Ahmed Shah I (Ahmedabad) 235
   Aurangzeb (Khuldabad) 275
   Bari Dargah (Maner) 167
   Bhulbhulaiyan (Delhi) 140
   Bibi ka Maqbara (Aurangabad) 275
   Chini ka Rauza (Agra) 156
   Choti Dargah (Maner) 167
   Dargah Sharif (Ajmer) 214
   Ghaus Muhammad's mausoleum (Gwalior) 278
   Gol Gumbaz (Bijapur) 105, 366
   Gumbaz Mausoleum (Srirangapatnam) 363
   Haji Ali (Mumbai) 261
   Hauz-i-Shamsi (Delhi) 140
   Humayun (Delhi) 106, 138
   Ibrahim Rauza (Bijapur) 367
   Itimad-ud-Daula (Agra) 155
   Jamali Kamali (Delhi) 140
   Muhammad Shah (Delhi) 137
   Nila Gumbad (Delhi) 138
   Qutb Shahi tombs (Hyderabad) 372
   Safdarjang (Delhi) 138
   Saiyid Muhammad Husaini Gisu Daras (Gulbarga) 367
   Sheikh Nizamuddin Aulia 138
   Sher Shah's Mausoleum (Sasaram) 167
   Sikandra (UP) 157
   Taj Mahal (Agra) 52, 106, 107, **156**, **172**
   Tansen (Gwalior) 278
tourist information 495
tours
   camel treks 201, **213**, 224, **225**
Tranquebar (TN) 395
transport 440

trekking and hiking 480
 Himalayas 178, 182, 195
 Karnataka 364
 Kerala 418
 Madhya Pradesh 282
 Sikkim 338
 Tamil Nadu 408
 West Bengal 327
Tribeni (WB) 321
 Benimadhava Temple 321
 Darya Zafar Khan 321
Trichy (TN) 411
Trimbakesvar (Mah) 274
 Trimbakesvar Temple 275
Tripura 346
Tso Moriri (J & K) 195
Tura (Meg) 346
Tuticorin (TN) 405

U

Udagamandalam (TN)
 accommodation 473
Udaipur (Raj) 218
 accommodation 459
 Bagore-ki-Haveli 220
 City Palace 219
 Jagdish Temple 220
 Jag Mandir 220
 Jag Niwas 220
 restaurants 226
 Sajjangarh 220
 Shilpgram 220
 Tripura Sundari temple 347
Udayagiri (Odi) 330
Udaygir (MP) 281
Udhagamandalam (TN) 406
 Botanical Gardens 407
 restaurants 411
 Thread Garden 407
 Tribal Research Centre 407
Udupi (Kar) 368
Ujjain (MP) 280
 Mahakalesvar Temple 280
Unesco sites 101
 Airavatesvara Temple (Darasuram)
  400
 Ajanta (Mah) 266
 Blue Mountain Railway (TN) 407
 Brihadesvara Temple
  (Gangaikondacholapuram) 400
 Champaner (Guj) 242
 Darjeeling Himalayan Railway (WB)
  325
 Hampi (Kar) 365
 Humayun's Tomb (Delhi) 106, 138
 Khajuraho (MP) 279
 Nanda Devi National Park (Utt) 175
 Qutb Minar Complex (Delhi) 140
 Sanchi (MP) 281
 Shore Temple (Mamallapuram)
  393
 Sunderbans (WB) 322
 Taj Mahal (Agra) 52, 106, 107, **156**,
  172
 Thanjavur (Tanjore) (TN) 398

Uttarakhand 175
Uttar Pradesh 123, 145, 154

V

Vadodara (Guj) 241
 Lakshmi Vilas Palace 241
Vagator (Goa) 293, 467, 479
Vaishali (Bih) 167
Vajpayee, Atal Bihari 69
Valley of Flowers National Park (Utt)
 178, 486
Varanasi (UP) 123, 162
 accommodation 451
 monkey temple 164
 Ramnagar 164
 restaurants 171
 Sankat Mochan 164
 Vishvanath Temple 163
Varkala (Ker) 419
 accommodation 476
 restaurants 426
Varma, Raja Ravi 417
Vasai (Mah) 251
Vashisht (HP) 184
Vedanthangla (TN) 409
Velavadar National Park (Guj) 486
Vellore (TN) 397
Vembanad Lake (Ker) 421
Verinag (J & K) 191
Vidisha (MP) 281
Vijayawada (AP) 373, 471
 Kanakadurga Temple 373
 restaurants 377
Vijaydurg (Mah) 271
Viper Island (A & N) 436
visas and passports 496
Vishakapatnam (AP) 374
Vishakhapatnam (AP)
 restaurants 377
Vishnu 168, 177
Visnupur (WB) 324
 Dalmadal 324
 Jor Bangla 324
 Kalachand Sri Mandir 324
 Madan Gopal 324
 Madan Mohan 324
 Rashmancha 324
 Shyam Rai Mandir 324
Vizhinjam (Ker) 419
Vrindavan (UP) 158
Vypeen Island (Ker) 423

W

Wadhwan (Guj) 241
 Hawa Mahal 241
Waltair (AP) 374
Warangal (AP) 372
Wardha (Mah) 276
waterfalls
 Chitrakut (Cha) 283
 Dassam (Jha) 334
 Dhuandhar Falls (MP) 282
 Hirni (Jha) 334
 Hundru (Jha) 334

 Jog (Kar) 369
 Johna (Jha) 334
 Panch Ghagh (Jha) 334
 Tirathgarh (Cha) 282
Waynad (Ker) 425, 476
websites 495
weights and measures 496
West Bengal 78, 319
 transport 321
West-Central India 247
Western Ghats 20, 247, 357, 414, **422**
Wheeler, Mortimer 395
whitewater rafting 481
Wild Ass Sanctuary (Guj) 238, 486
wildlife 22. See also birdlife, national
 parks and wildlife sanctuaries
 Asiatic lions **22**, 201, 240
 bears 22
 camels 195
 conservation 27
 crocodiles 24, 27, 276, 323
 deer and antelopes 25
 elephants 20, **24**, 25, 346, 359
 game tourism 26
 Hullock gibbons 346
 Indian wild ass 238
 leopards 22, 277
 marine life 409, 433
 monkeys 181
 of Tamil Nadu 409
 of the Southern Ghats 405
 Project Elephant 27
 Project Tiger 27, 334
 rhinoceroses **23**, 27, 343
 river dolphins 25, 165
 sea turtles 24, 332
 snakes 24
 tigers 22, **23**, **24**, 201, 210, 216,
  277, 323, 346
Willingdon Island (Ker) 423
winter sports 178, 181, 184, 191
women travellers 496

Y

Yakshun (Sik) 339
Yamuna, River 162, 175
 source of 177
Yamunotri (Utt) 177
 Hanuman Chatti 177
Yercaud (TN) 408
yoga 404. See also spas and retreats

Z

Zanskar (J & K) 195
zoos
 Darjeeling (WB) 326
 Delhi Zoo 136
 Guindy Deer Park (TN) 387
 Madras Crocodile Bank (TN) 27, 387
 Nandanakanan (Odi) 332
 Nehru Zoological Park (Hyderabad)
  372
 Snake Park (TN) 387
 Zoological Gardens (Kolkata) 313

DISCARDED